STUDIES FOR DANTE

ESSAYS IN HONOR OF
DANTE DELLA TERZA

edited by
Franco Fido
Rena A. Syska-Lamparska
Pamela D. Stewart

Edizioni Cadmo

Studies for Dante : Essays in Honor of Dante Della Terza / edited by Franco Fido,
Rena A. Syska-Lamparska, Pamela D. Stewart. Fiesole (Firenze) : Cadmo, 1998.
  xxv, 512 p. ; 24 cm.
  ISBN 88-7923-177-4
  Testi in inglese, italiano, spagnolo
  1. Letteratura
809

Edizioni Cadmo
Via Benedetto da Maiano, 3
50014 Fiesole (Firenze)

Tel. (055) 5018.1
Fax (055) 5018.201
cadmo@casalini.it

Printed in Italy

Dante Della Terza

CONTENTS

FOREWORD

Dante Della Terza taught for many years in the United States: from 1959 to 1963 at the University of California at Los Angeles, then for the next thirty years at Harvard, where he chaired the Department of Romance Languages and Literatures (1970-77) and from 1983 held the title of Irving Babbitt Professor of Comparative Literature.

At UCLA and at Harvard, but also at the various universities where he was invited as Visiting Professor (Yale, Brown, Toronto, McGill, British Columbia), Della Terza played a central role in making known Italian literature, but also more generally European culture.

Having studied with Luigi Russo at Pisa, Spoerri in Zurich and Spitzer in Seattle, Della Terza adopted in his teaching an approach which combined the Italian historical tradition with the European *Stilstudien*. Thanks to his university courses, his public lectures and his scholarly publications, contemporary Italian authors gained a place on the American Academic scene alongside the Classics. A good number of Ph. D. Theses, assigned and directed by him, were subsequently published, becoming among the first and best monographs in English on Ungaretti, Montale, Gadda, to mention but a few.

The significance of Della Terza's presence in the North American academic milieu goes much beyond his role as a perceptive scholar and authoritative teacher. His exceptional talent for the exchange of ideas, interpersonal relations and cultural mediation in the best sense of this expression, allowed him to contribute, as perhaps no other, to a meeting of minds between Italian and American literary critics, and to create on this continent a community of Italianists that, prior to his lively and unflagging activity, only existed in a latent form.

His teaching years at Harvard have now come to a close. The present volume is a mark of admiration and gratitude for a career enlightened by faith in dialogue, by love of learning, and by friendship and generosity. It contains contributions by his North American students and colleagues, as well as those scholars from Italy invited by him, from time to time, to teach at Harvard.

Franco Fido,
Rena A. Syska-Lamparska, Pamela D. Stewart

ACKNOWLEDGEMENTS

The editors wish to thank Neil L. Rudenstine, President of Harvard University, and Mary Gaylord, Chair of the Department of Romance Language and Literatures (1994-1997), for their generous support and encouragement, without which the publication of this volume would not have been possibile.

They also wish to thank the editor of *Belfagor*, Carlo Ferdinando Russo, for having agreed to the publication in this volume of the portrait of Dante Della Terza by A. D'Andrea and P. D. Stewart which first appeared in a slightly different form in *Belfagor*, LII, 1997, pp. 397-413.

BIBLIOGRAFIA DEGLI SCRITTI DI DANTE DELLA TERZA
a cura di Pamela D. Stewart

Le voci di questa bibliografia sono ordinate per anno.

All'interno di ciascun anno si è seguito questo criterio di successione: libri, edizioni e traduzioni, sillogi, prefazioni, introduzioni, commenti, articoli e saggi, contributi a storie letterarie, recensioni, voci di enciclopedia, interviste. Le voci sono numerate in modo continuo dal principio alla fine.

1951

1. *Italiani a Parigi*, «Il Ponte», VII, 1951, 6, pp. 627-33.

2. Rec., in collaborazione con GIULIANO PROCACCI, a *Cinquant'anni di vita intellettuale italiana*, Scritti in onore di Benedetto Croce per il suo ottantesimo anniversario, a cura di C. Antoni & R. Mattioli, Napoli, E.S.I., 1950, «Belfagor», VI, 1951, 4, pp. 465-84.

1952

3. JEAN-PAUL SARTRE, *Ritratti critici di contemporanei*, «Belfagor», VII, 1952, 4, pp. 419-39.

1954

4. *Lettera dalla Francia*, «Il Ponte», X, 1954, 6, pp. 992-97.

1955

5. Les Mandarins *di Simone de Beauvoir*, «Il Ponte», XI, 1955, 2, pp. 210-15. [Rec. a SIMONE DE BEAUVOIR, *Les Mandarins*, Paris, Gallimard, 1954].

1956

6. *L'ultimo romanzo di Peyrefitte*, «Il Ponte», XII, 1956, 8/9, pp. 1418-23. [Rec. a ROGER PEYREFITTE, *Les clefs de Saint Pierre*, Paris, Flammarion, 1955].

7. Rec. a FRANCESCO DE SANCTIS, *Epistolario (1836-1856)*, a cura di G. Ferretti & M. Mazzocchi Alemanni, Torino, Einaudi, 1956, «Belfagor», XI, 1956, 5, pp. 592-94.

1957

8. Rec. a FRANCESCO DE SANCTIS, *Lezioni zurighesi sul Petrarca e altri scritti*, a cura di S. Romagnoli, Padova, Liviana, 1955, «Rassegna della letteratura italiana», LXI, 1957, 1, pp. 85-88.

9. Rec. a ALBERT CAMUS, *La Chute*, Paris, Gallimard, 1956, «Belfagor», XII, 1957, 3, pp. 346-50.

1958

10. *Literary Criticism in the Universities*, «Italian Quarterly», II, 1958, 2, pp. 55-63.

11. Rec. a MARIO FUBINI, *Critica e poesia*, Bari, Laterza, 1956, «Belfagor», XIII, 1958, 4, pp. 480-87.

1959

12. *Studi umanistici in America*, «Rassegna della letteratura italiana», LXIII, 1959, 3, pp. 441-51.

1960

13. *Studi danteschi in America*, «Rassegna della letteratura italiana», LXIV, 1960, 2, pp. 218-30.

14. *Postwar Poetics and Poetry*, «Italian Quarterly», IV, 1960, 13/14, pp. 39-50.

15. *Leo Spitzer (Vienna 1 February 1887 - Forte dei Marmi 16 September 1960)*, «Italian Quarterly», IV, 1960, 15, pp. 62-67.

16. *Lettere del De Meis e lettere del De Sanctis*, «Belfagor», XV, 1960, 1, pp. 93-98.

17. *Il Manierismo nella letteratura del Cinquecento*, «Belfagor», XV, 1960, 4, pp. 462-66. [Rec. a RICCARDO SCRIVANO, *Il Manierismo nella letteratura del Cinquecento*, Padova, Liviana, 1959].

1961

18. *Il realismo mimetico di P. P. Pasolini*, «Italica», XXXVIII, 1961, 4, pp. 306-13.

19. *Some Sociological Remarks on the Contemporary Italian Novel*, «Cesare Barbieri Courier», IV, 1961, 1, pp. 6-11.

1962

20. *Luigi Russo 1890-1961. An Outline of a Critical Biography*, «Italian Quarterly», VI, 1962, 6, pp. 26-50.

21. *Croce in America*, «Belfagor», XVII, 1962, 3, pp. 352-56, ora in *Da Vienna a Baltimora*, pp. 197-205, v. n. 106.

1963

22. Traduzione dal tedesco di FRIEDRICH ENGELS, *L'origine della famiglia, della proprietà privata e dello Stato*, Roma, Editori Riuniti, 1963.

23. Prefazione a ERICH AUERBACH, *Studi su Dante*, Milano, Feltrinelli, 1963, pp. VII-XIX; 6ª ediz., 1989. [*Nota ai testi* e traduzioni dall'inglese di Dante Della Terza, traduzioni dal tedesco di Maria Luisa De Pieri Bonino].

24. *Erich Auerbach, Ritratti critici di contemporanei*, «Belfagor», XVIII, 1963, 3, pp. 306-22, ora, col sottotitolo *L'esperienza di* Mimesi, in *Da Vienna a Baltimora*, pp. 73-89, v. n. 106.

25. *Tasso's experience of Petrarch*, «Studies in the Renaissance», X, 1963, pp. 175-91. Versione italiana in «Studi tassiani», XIII, 1963, 13, pp. 69-86, col titolo *L'esperienza petrarchesca del Tasso*, ora in *Forma e memoria*, pp. 177-96, v. n. 63.

1964

26. *Contemporary Italian Novelists. Language and Style in P. M. Pasinetti's* La confusione, «Italian Quarterly», VIII, 1964, 29, pp. 64-76.

27. *Italienische Literatur, Das Fischer Lexicon, Literatur* I, herausg. W. H. Friedrich & W. Killy, Frankfurt, Fischer Bucherei, 1964, pp. 142-69.

1965

28. *Galileo letterato:* Considerazioni al Tasso, «Rassegna della letteratura italiana», LXIX, 1965, 1, pp. 77-91, ora in *Forma e memoria*, pp. 197-221, v. n. 63. Versione inglese, col titolo *Galileo, Man of Letters*, in AA.VV., *Galileo reappraised*, ed. C. Golino, Berkeley, University of California Press, 1966, pp. 1-22.

29. Rec. a HUGO FRIEDRICH, *Epochen der italienischen Lyrik*, Frankfurt am Main, V. Klostermann, 1964, «Giornale storico della letteratura italiana», CXLII, 1965, 438, pp. 266-73.

1966

30. *I canti del disordinato amore. Osservazioni sulla struttura e lo stile del* Purgatorio, «Belfagor», XXI, 1966, 2, pp. 156-79, ora in *Forma e memoria*, pp. 40-70, v. n. 63.

31. *The Neorealists and the Form of the Novel*, «Italian Quarterly», X, 1966, 36/37, pp. 3-21.

1967

32. *Ernst Robert Curtius. Ritratti critici di contemporanei*, «Belfagor», XXII, 1967, 2, pp. 166-85.

33. *Two Recent Books on Dante: a Discussion*, «Dante Studies», LXXXV, 1967, pp. 85-94. [Rec. a *The World of Dante. Six Studies in Language and Thought*, ed. S. B. Chandler,

& J.A. Molinaro, Toronto, Toronto University Press, 1966; *From Time to Eternity. Essays on Dante's Divine Comedy*, ed. T.G. Bergin, New Haven & London, Yale University Press, 1967].

1969

34. *Tendenze attuali della critica americana*, «Strumenti critici», III, 1969, 2, pp. 81-97. [Numero speciale a cura di Dante Della Terza; traduzione dall'inglese del contributo di Harry Levin].

35. *Tasso's reading of Dante*, «Dante Studies», LXXXVII, 1969, pp. 103-25. Versione italiana col titolo *Tasso e Dante*, «Belfagor», XXV, 1970, 4, pp. 395-418, ora in *Forma e Memoria*, pp. 148-76, v. n. 63.

1970

36. *Auerbach e Vico*, in AA.VV., *Critica e storia letteraria. Studi offerti a Mario Fubini*, a cura di R. Ceserani, F. Giuntini & Luisa Roberti, 2 voll., Padova, Liviana, 1970, II, pp. 820-41, ora in *Forma e memoria*, pp. 296-321, v. n. 63, e anche in *Da Vienna a Baltimora*, pp. 53-72, v. n. 106.

37. *The Most Recent Image of Machiavelli: the Contribution of the Linguist and of the Historian*, «Italian Quarterly», XIV, 1970, 53, pp. 91-113, poi in *Machiavelli nel Vᵒ Centenario della nascita*, Bologna, Massimo Boni Editore, 1973, pp. 69-89; la versione italiana del saggio a pp. 203-15, ora, in *Forma e memoria*, pp. 93-114, v. n. 63.

38. *Contini, Gianfranco, Enciclopedia dantesca*, Roma, II (1970), pp. 176-77.

1971

39. *Auerbach in italiano*, «Yearbook of Italian Studies», I, 1971, pp. 334-41, ora in *Da Vienna a Baltimora*, col sottotitolo *La protostoria di* Mimesi, pp. 91-102, v. n. 106.

40. Imitatio: *Theory and Practice. The Example of Bembo the Poet*, «Yearbook of Italian Studies», I, 1971, pp. 119-41. Versione italiana, col titolo Imitatio: *teoria e pratica. L'esempio del Bembo poeta*, in *Forma e Memoria*, pp. 115-47, v. n. 63.

41. *Renato Poggioli tra «Solaria» e «Inventario» (con un'aggiunta di lettere inedite)*, «Italica», XLVIII, 1971, 1, pp. 3-33, ora in *Da Vienna a Baltimora*, pp. 123-55, con l'indicazione nel titolo: (*con alcuni inediti*), invece di: (*con un'aggiunta di lettere inedite*), v. n. 106.

1972

42. *James Laughlin, Renato Poggioli and Elio Vittorini: the Story of a Literary Friendship*, «Yearbook of Italian Studies», II, 1972, pp. 111-35. Versione italiana con revisioni e col titolo, *James Laughlin, Renato Poggioli ed Elio Vittorini: storia di un'amicizia letteraria*, in *Da Vienna a Baltimora*, pp. 157-69, v. n. 106.

43. *On Pirandello's Humorism*, in AA.VV., *Veins of Humor*, ed. H. Levin, Harvard English Studies, 3, Cambridge, Mass., Harvard University Press, 1972, pp. 17-33. Versione italiana, col titolo *Luigi Pirandello e la ricerca della distanza umoristica*, in AA.VV., *Studi in memoria di Luigi Russo*, Pisa, Nistri Lischi, 1974, pp. 405-22, ora in *Letteratura e critica*, pp. 79-93, v. n. 115.

1973

44. *The Italian Novel and the Avant-garde*, in AA.VV., *From Petrarca to Pirandello. Studies in Italian Literature in Honour of Beatrice Corrigan*, ed. J. A. Molinaro, Toronto, Toronto University Press, 1973, pp. 229-49.

45. *Innovazione e avanguardia. Riflessioni sull'VIII congresso dell'A.I.S.L.L.I. (New York 25-28 aprile 1973)*, «Lettere Italiane», XXV, 1973, 3, pp. 425-35.

46. *Mazzini's image and the Italian Risorgimento: De Amicis, De Sanctis, Ruffini*, «Yearbook of Italian Studies», III, 1973/75, pp. 107-37. Versione italiana, col titolo *L'eroe scomodo e la sua ombra. L'immagine di Mazzini e la letteratura del Risorgimento*, in *Letteratura e critica*, pp. 9-44, v. n. 115.

47. *Parodi, Ernesto Giacomo, Enciclopedia dantesca*, Roma, IV (1973), pp. 315-18.

48. *Pernicone, Vincenzo, Enciclopedia dantesca*, Roma, IV (1973), pp. 424-25.

49. *Rand, Edward Kenneth, Enciclopedia dantesca*, Roma, IV (1973), p. 850.

1975

50. *Istanze tradizionali e prospettive di aggiornamento nella critica dantesca*, «Lettere Italiane», XXVII, 1975, 3, pp. 245-62, con aggiornamenti e ritocchi ora in *Forma e memoria*, pp. 71-92, v. n. 63.

51. *Il mondo "dilatato e composto" di Carlo Emilio Gadda*, «Forum Italicum», IX, 1975, pp. 175-90, ora in *Letteratura e critica*, pp. 227-40, v. n. 115.

1976

52. *An Unbridgeable Gap? Medieval Poetics and the Contemporary Dante Reader*, «Medievalia et Humanistica», New Series 7, Cambridge, Mass., Cambridge University Press, 1976, pp. 65-76.

53. *Ricordo di Nicola Vaccaro*, «Questa Calabria», 11 sett. 1976.

54. *Schiaffini, Alfredo, Enciclopedia dantesca*, Roma, V (1976), pp. 63-64.

55. *Singleton, Charles Southward, Enciclopedia dantesca*, Roma, V (1976), pp. 264-66.

56. *Spitzer, Leo, Enciclopedia dantesca*, Roma, V (1976), pp. 393-94.

57. *Vossler, Karl, Enciclopedia dantesca*, Roma, V (1976), pp. 1148-49.

58. *Wilkins, Ernest Hatch, Enciclopedia dantesca*, Roma, V (1976), p. 1157.

1977

59. *La Fontaine lettore di Boccaccio*, in AA.VV., *Boccaccio. Secoli di vita*, Atti del Congresso Internazionale Boccaccio 1975, Università della California, Los Angeles, 17-19 ottobre 1975, a cura di Marga Cottino-Jones & E. F. Tuttle, Ravenna, Longo, 1977, pp. 239-64, ora in *Forma e memoria*, pp. 237-64, v. n. 63.

60. *Pirandello from Tale to Play: The Case of* Tutto per bene, «Modern Language Notes», XCII, 1977, pp. 63-78, cfr. n. 123.

1978

61. Introduzione a NANCY DERSOFI, *Arcadia and the Stage. An Introduction to the Dramatic Art of Angelo Beolco called Ruzante*, with an Introduction by Dante Della Terza, Madrid, Porrua Toranzas, 1978, pp. 1-10.

62. *Il canto di Brunetto Latini*, in AA.VV., *Orbis mediaevalis*, Mélanges de langue et de littérature médiévales offerts à Reto R. Bezzola à l'occasion de son quatre-vingtième anniversaire, ed. par G. Guntert, M.-R. Jung, K. Ringger, Berne, Francke, 1978, pp. 69-88, ora in *Forma e memoria*, pp. 13-39, v. n. 63.

1979

63. *Forma e memoria. Saggi e ricerche sulla tradizione letteraria da Dante a Vico*, Roma, Bulzoni, 1979.

    SOMMARIO: Avvertenza, Prefazione, *Il canto di Brunetto Latini* [n. 62], *I canti del disordinato amore. Osservazioni sulla struttura e lo stile del* Purgatorio [n. 30], *Istanze tradizionali e prospettive di aggiornamento nella critica dantesca* [n. 50], *L'immagine più recente di Machiavelli. Il contributo del linguista e dello storico della letteratura* [n. 37], Imitatio: *teoria e pratica. L'esempio del Bembo poeta* [n. 41], *Tasso e Dante* [n. 35], *L'esperienza petrarchesca del Tasso* [n. 25], Galileo letterato: *Considerazioni al Tasso* [n. 28], *Le metafore del Tesauro* [n. 70], *La Fontaine lettore di Boccaccio* [n. 59], *Misura dell'uomo e visione del mondo nelle autobiografie degli scrittori napoletani tra il Seicento e l'Ottocento* [n. 64], *Auerbach e Vico* [n. 36].

64. *Misura dell'uomo e visione del mondo nelle autobiografie degli scrittori napoletani tra il '600 e l''800*, in AA.VV., *Storia e cultura nel Mezzogiorno. Studi in memoria di Umberto Caldora*, Cosenza, Lerici, 1979, pp. 151-79, anche in *Forma e Memoria*, pp. 265-95, v. n. 63.

65. *Le Corti e il Teatro: appunti e testimonianze sul congresso di New York* (13 novembre - 18 novembre 1978), «Lettere Italiane», XXXI, 1979, 2, pp. 219-30.

1980

66. *Homage to Charles S. Singleton*, «Yearbook of Italian Studies», IV, 1980, pp. 2-4.

67. *History and the Epic Discourse: Remarks on the Narrative Structure of Tasso's* Liberata, «Quaderni d'Italianistica», I, 1980, 1, pp. 30-45. Versione italiana col titolo La Liberata *del Tasso tra storia e invenzione*, in *Tradizione ed esegesi*, pp. 87-105, v. n. 107.

68. *La corte e il teatro: il mondo del Tasso*, «Italian Quarterly», XXI, 1980, 79, pp. 21-29, anche in AA.VV., *Il teatro del Rinascimento*, a cura di Maristella de Panizza Lorch, Milano, Edizioni di Comunità, 1980, pp. 51-63, ora in *Tradizione ed esegesi*, pp. 61-70, v. n. 107.

69. *Metodologia ed esegesi nell'Italia del secondo dopoguerra*, «Yearbook of Italian Studies», IV, 1980, pp. 137-52. Versione inglese, col titolo *Methodology and Exegesis: The Italian Side*, in AA.VV., *The Analysis of Literary Texts: Current Trends in Methodology*, ed. R. D. Pope, Ypsilanti, Mich., Bilingual Press, 1980, pp. 9-20.

70. *Le metafore del Tesauro*, in AA.VV., *Simbolo, metafora, allegoria*, Atti del IV convegno italo-tedesco (Bressanone, 1976), a cura di Daniela Goldin, Premessa di Gianfranco Folena, «Quaderni del Circolo Filologico Linguistico Padovano», XI, Padova, Liviana, 1980, pp. 175-89, anche in *Forma e memoria*, pp. 222-36, v. n. 63.

71. *Pasolini critico*, «Italian Quarterly», XXI/XXII, 1980/81, 82/83, pp. 59-67, poi in *Pasolini in periferia*, Cosenza, Edizioni Periferia, 1992, pp. 5-15, ora in *Strutture poetiche*, pp. 241-52, v. n. 152.

72. *Il potere alieno e gli emergenti affetti del mondo contadino. Osservazioni sull'esperienza comica di Ruzante*, in AA.VV., *Lo Stato e il Potere nel Rinascimento*, Università di Perugia per Federico Chabod (1901-1960), Atti del seminario internazionale a cura di S. Bertelli, Prefazione di Fernand Braudel, «Annali della Facoltà di Scienze Politiche dell'Università di Perugia», 2 voll., Perugia, Grafiche Benucci, 1980/81, I, pp. 213-29, ora in *Tradizione ed esegesi*, pp. 43-59, v. n. 107.

73. *On Francesco De Sanctis (1817-1883) and Realism*, «Journal of the History of Ideas», XLI, 1980, pp. 335-41. [Rec. a AA.VV., *De Sanctis e il realismo*, 2 voll. Napoli, Giannini, 1978].

1981

74. Introduzione a ROCCO SCOTELLARO, *The Dawn is always New*, Selected poetry, translated by R. Feldman & B. Swan, Introduction by Dante Della Terza, New Haven, N.J., Princeton University Press, 1981, pp. 1-14.

75. *Eugenio Garin, critico della cultura italiana contemporanea*, «Belfagor», XXXVI, 1981, 4, pp. 381-97, ora in *Letteratura e critica*, pp. 209-26, v. n. 115.

76. Interventi sui rapporti fra l'Italia e gli Stati Uniti d'America in AA.VV., *Italia e Stati Uniti d'America: concordanze e dissonanze*, a cura di Anna Bartole & Anna Maria Dell'Omodarme, Roma, Il Veltro Editrice, 1981, pp. 23-25, 59, 265-70.

77. *Inferno V: Tradition and Exegesis*, «Dante Studies», XCIX, 1981, pp. 49-66. Versione italiana, col titolo *Inferno V: tradizione ed esegesi*, in AA.VV., *Miscellanea di studi in onore di Vittore Branca*, 5 voll., Firenze, Olschki, 1983, I, pp. 220-39, ora in *Tradizione ed esegesi*, pp. 15-28, v. n. 107.

78. *Identità e fedeltà*, «Il Domani», Periodico di S. Angelo dei Lombardi, giugno/luglio 1981.

79. *Anniversario*, «Il Domani», Periodico di S. Angelo dei Lombardi, dicembre 1981.

1982

80. *L'immagine dell'Italia nella cultura americana 1942-1952*, «Belfagor», XXXVII, 1982, 5, pp. 513-31, ora in *Da Vienna a Baltimora*, pp. 103-21, v. n. 106.

81. *Luigi Russo e l'inquieta lettura del testo crociano: bilancio e prospettive*, «Italian Quarterly», XXIII, 1982, 87, pp. 33-45, anche in AA.VV., *Lo storicismo di Luigi Russo: lezione e sviluppi*, Firenze, Vallecchi, 1983, pp. 119-31, ora in *Letteratura e critica*, pp. 157-73, v. n. 115.

82. *La recente storiografia sul Rinascimento negli Stati Uniti d'America*, in AA.VV., *Il Rinascimento. Aspetti e problemi attuali*, Atti del X Congresso dell'A.I.S.L.L.I., Belgrado, 17-21 aprile 1979, Firenze, Olschki, 1982, pp. 45-62, ora, col titolo *La recente ricerca storiografica sul Rinascimento negli Stati Uniti d'America*, in *Tradizione ed esegesi*, pp. 107-21, v. n. 107.

83. *Discorso storico e discorso letterario: gl'itinerari del primo volume della* Letteratura italiana *a cura di A. Asor Rosa*, «Gradiva», III, 1982/83, pp. 1-8. [V. nota a p. 8: «Trascrizione dell'intervento tenuto all'Istituto Italiano di Cultura di New York in occasione della presentazione della *Letteratura italiana* (Einaudi Ed.)»].

84. *Ruskin e Venezia*, «STILB», II, 1982, 11, pp. 61-62, poi in «Yearbook of Italian Studies», V, 1984, pp. 195-99. [Rec. a JEANNE CLEGG, *Ruskin and Venice*, London, Function Books, 1981].

1983

85. *Il Tasso lettore e critico del proprio poema: le ottave rifiutate dell'edizione Osanna*, «Yearbook of Italian Studies», V, 1983, pp. 49-59, ora in *Tradizione ed esegesi*, pp. 79-88, v. n. 107.

86. *Dottrina e pietà, disprezzo ed amore del secolo nei* Commentarii *di Scipione Gonzaga*, «Yearbook of Italian Studies», V, 1983, pp. 117-49, poi in SCIPIONE GONZAGA, *Autobiografia*, pp. VII-XXXIII, v. n. 108.

87. *Italianistica negli Stati Uniti*, «Bollettino d'italianistica», I, 1983, 2, pp. 195-204.

88. *Reappraising G. A. Borgese*, in AA.VV., *Giuseppe Antonio Borgese 1883-1983*, Northampton, Mass., Smith College, 1983, pp. 50-65, poi in «Gradiva», III, 1984/85, 2/3, pp. 33-40.

89. *Comico e commedia nella critica di Francesco De Sanctis*, in AA.VV., *Ambiguità del comico*, a cura di G. Ferroni, Palermo, Sellerio, 1983, pp. 135-47, ora in *Tradizione ed esegesi*, pp. 169-77, v. n. 107.

90. *Il passato come invenzione e riscontro e le categorie della ricerca letteraria tardo-rinascimentali, barocche e romantiche*, «Italian Culture», IV, 1983, pp. 171-87.

91. *Il Surrealismo italiano: ricerche e letture*, «Rivista di Studi Italiani», I, 1983, 2, pp. 86-91. [Rec. a LUIGI FONTANELLA, *Il Surrealismo italiano: ricerche e letture*, Roma, Bulzoni, 1983].

1984

92. *F. T. Marinetti e i futuristi fiorentini: l'ipotesi politico-letteraria di «Lacerba»*, «Italica», LXI, 1984, 2, pp. 147-59, ora in *Letteratura e critica*, pp. 113-28, v. n. 115.

93. *Due manifesti. Il Manifesto degli intellettuali del fascismo di Giovanni Gentile e il Manifesto degli intellettuali antifascisti di Benedetto Croce*, «Il Cavallo di Troia», V, 1984, pp. 91-97.

94. *De Sanctis e la cultura anglosassone: dalle linee programmatiche dell'apprendimento giovanile al difficile itinerario di diffusione dell'opera critica*, in AA.VV., *F. De Sanctis nella storia della cultura*, a cura di C. Muscetta, 2 voll., Bari, Laterza, 1984, II, pp. 527-45, ora in *Tradizione ed esegesi*, pp. 197-217, v. n. 107. [Il capitolo incorpora anche il contributo al volume *Francesco De Sanctis un secolo dopo*, a cura di A. Marinari, v. n. 97].

1985

95. *Il Tasso epistolografo: il culto "ostinato" della varietà e la petizione degli affetti*, in AA.VV., *La lettera famigliare*, «Quaderni di Retorica e Poetica», 1985, 1, pp. 123-30, ora in *Tradizione ed esegesi*, pp. 71-77, v. n. 107.

96. *Il fascino del quotidiano e lo spazio della letteratura: il fondamento teorico dell'esperienza diaristica di André Gide*, in AA.VV., *Le forme del diario*, «Quaderni di Retorica e Poetica», 1985, 2, pp. 107-14.

97. *De Sanctis negli Stati Uniti d'America*, in AA.VV., *Francesco De Sanctis un secolo dopo*, a cura di A. Marinari, 2 voll., Bari, Laterza, 1985, II, pp. 651-63, v. n. 94.

98. *L'esatto parlare della Maremma*, «L'Indice», II, 1985, 9, p. 11. [L'articolo riguarda il romanzo di MARIO PUCCINI, *L'odore di Maremma*].

99. *La storia di Michele* (racconto), in AA.VV., *Scrittori italiani negli USA*, «La Battana», XXII, 1985, 76, pp. 5-15, ora in *Dagli Appennini*, pp. 185-97, v. n. 160.

100. *Le storie della letteratura italiana: premesse erudite e verifiche ideologiche*, in *Letteratura italiana*, dir. da A. Asor Rosa, vol. IV, *L'Interpretazione*, Torino, Einaudi, 1985, pp. 311-29, ora in *Tradizione ed esegesi*, pp. 131-49, v. n. 107.

101. *Francesco De Sanctis: gl'itinerari della* Storia, in *Letteratura italiana*, v. n. 100, pp. 331-49, ora in *Tradizione ed esegesi*, pp. 179-96, v. n. 107.

1986

102. *Panofsky e Spitzer: la diaspora negli anni Trenta*, «Belfagor», XLI, 1986, 1, pp. 13-26, ora in *Da Vienna a Baltimora*, pp. 21-36, col titolo, *Erwin Panofsky e Leo Spitzer: la diaspora degli intellettuali tedeschi negli Stati Uniti nel corso degli anni Trenta*, v. n. 106.

103. *L'autobiografia di G. Vico: razionalità e scrittura*, in AA.VV., *L'autobiografia: il vissuto, il narrato*, «Quaderni di Retorica e Poetica», 1986, 1, pp. 97-104, ora in *Tradizione ed esegesi*, pp. 151-57, v. n. 107.

104. *La Rochefoucauld: il "tempo" della Massima*, in AA.VV., *La lingua scorciata: detto, motto, aforisma*, «Quaderni di Retorica e Poetica», 1986, 2, pp. 87-94, ora in *Tradizione ed esegesi*, pp. 123-29, v. n. 107.

105. *Charles S. Singleton: An Appraisal*, «Dante Studies», CIV, 1986, pp. 9-25.

1987

106. *Da Vienna a Baltimora. La diaspora degli intellettuali europei negli Stati Uniti d'America*, Roma, Editori Riuniti, 1987.

    SOMMARIO: Prefazione, Avvertenza, I. *Erwin Panofsky e Leo Spitzer: la diaspora degli intellettuali tedeschi negli Stati Uniti nel corso degli anni Trenta* [n. 102], II. *Auerbach e Spitzer: itinerario dell'esilio e* lecturae Dantis, III. *Auerbach e Vico* [n. 36] IV. *Erich Auerbach: l'esperienza di* Mimesi [n. 24], V. *Auerbach in italiano: la protostoria di* Mimesi [n. 39], VI. *L'immagine dell'Italia nella cultura americana, 1942-1952* [n. 80], VII. *Renato Poggioli tra «Solaria» e «Inventario» (con un'aggiunta di lettere inedite)* [n. 40], VIII. *James Laughlin, Renato Poggioli ed Elio Vittorini: storia di un'amicizia letteraria* [n. 42], IX. *Regesto di libri e riviste presenti nello studio di un intellettuale emigrato: tentativo d'interpretazione*, X. *Croce in America* [n. 21], XI. *P. M.Pasinetti: da Venezia a Los Angeles e ritorno. Una testimonianza.*

107. *Tradizione ed esegesi. Semantica dell'innovazione da Agostino a De Sanctis*, Padova, Liviana, 1987.

    SOMMARIO: [Avvertenza], *Semantica dell'innovazione e processo storico: l'esempio agostiniano* [n. 110], Inferno V: *tradizione ed esegesi* [n. 77], *La novella della marchesana di Monferrato* (Decameron I, 5), *Il potere alieno e gli emergenti affetti del mondo contadino. Osservazioni sull'esperienza comica di Ruzante* [n. 72], *La corte e il teatro: il mondo del Tasso* [n. 68], *Il Tasso epistolografo: il culto "ostinato" della verità e la petizione degli affetti* [n. 95], *Il Tasso lettore e critico del proprio poema: le ottave rifiutate dell'edizione Osanna* [n. 85], La Liberata *del Tasso tra storia ed invenzione* [n. 67], *La recente ricerca storiografica sul Rinascimento negli Stati Uniti d'America* [n. 82], *La Rochefoucauld: il "tempo" della Massima* [n. 104], *Le storie della letteratura italiana: premesse erudite e verifiche ideologiche* [n. 100], *L'autobiografia di G.B. Vico: razionalità e scrittura* [n. 103], *Francesco De Sanctis: la retorica della* Giovinezza. *Itinerario del discorso critico e spazi autobiografici, Comico e commedia nella critica di Francesco De Sanctis* [n. 88], *Francesco De Sanctis: gli itinerari della* Storia [n. 101], *De Sanctis e la cultura anglosassone: dalle linee prammatiche dell'apprendimento giovanile al difficile intinerario di diffusione dell'opera critica* [n. 93].

108. Introduzione a SCIPIONE GONZAGA, *Autobiografia* [*Scipionis Gonzagae Cardinalis Commentariorum rerum suarum Libri tres*], introduzione e traduzione di Dante Della Terza, in appendice ristampa anastatica dell'edizione latina del 1791, Modena, Edizioni Panini, 1987.

109. *A proposito dell'Autobiografia di Scipione Gonzaga: osservazioni ed aggiunte*, «Schifanoia», IV, 1987, pp. 191-98, ora in *Strutture poetiche*, v. n. 152.

110. *Tradition and Exegesis. Semantics of Innovation and the Historical Context*, «Modern Language Notes», CII, 1987, 1, pp. 1-13. Versione italiana in *Tradizione ed esegesi*,

pp. 3-14, col titolo *Semantica dell'innovazione e processo storico: l'esempio agostiniano*, v. n. 107.

111. *Mario Puccini:* Il Soldato Cola *e le tecniche della narrativa di guerra*, in AA.VV., *Mario Puccini: due giornate di studio e di testimonianze*, Atti, a cura di Ada Antonietti, di un convegno tenuto a Sinigallia, 28-29 aprile 1985, Sinigallia, Comune di Sinigallia, 1987, pp. 127-34, ora in *Letteratura e critica*, pp. 135-42, v. n. 115.

112. *Il confronto con l'ignoto*, in AA.VV., *Mal d'America. Da mito a realtà*, a cura di U. Rubeo, Roma, Editori Riuniti, 1987, pp. 38-49. [Intervista condotta a Cambridge, Mass., nel 1983, da Ugo Rubeo].

1988

113. *Le opere deleddiane all'estero: itinerario di ricezione*, «Yearbook of Italian Studies», VII, 1988, pp. 59-79, ora in *Letteratura e critica*, pp. 271-90, v. n. 115.

114. *Mario Puccini tra diario e romanzo*, «L'Indice», V, 1988, 2, p. 8. [Rec. a MARIO PUCCINI, *Caporetto. Note sulla ritirata di un fante della III Armata*, a cura di F. De Nicola, Gorizia, Goriziano, 1987, ora in *Letteratura e critica*, pp. 129-33, v. n. 115].

1989

115. *Letteratura e critica tra Otto e Novecento: itinerari di ricezione*, Cosenza, Edizioni Periferia, 1989.

SOMMARIO: Presentazione, *L'eroe scomodo e la sua ombra. L'immagine di Mazzini e la Letteratura del Risorgimento* [n. 46], *Il Verismo e la cultura meridionale. De Sanctis, Capuana, Verga* [n. 127], *Vittorio Imbriani critico: inizi desanctisiani ed itinerari polemico-eruditi* [n. 128], *Luigi Pirandello e la ricerca della distanza umoristica* [n. 43], *Pirandello dalla novella al teatro, tecniche del racconto ed itinerario della rappresentazione scenica* [n. 123], *F. T. Marinetti e i futuristi fiorentini: l'ipotesi politico-letteraria di «Lacerba»* [n. 91], *Mario Puccini tra diario e romanzo* [n. 114], *Il Soldato Cola di Mario Puccini e le tecniche della narrativa di guerra* [n. 111], *Il Frontespizio* [n. 120], *Luigi Russo e l'inquieta lettura del testo crociano: bilancio e prospettive* [n. 81], *Mario Fubini lettore di Croce* [n. 116], *Il secondo tempo della rivista «Il Baretti»: il momento napoletano* [n. 138], *Eugenio Garin, critico della cultura italiana contemporarea* [n. 75], *Il mondo "dilatato e composto" di Carlo Emilio Gadda* [n. 51], *Pasolini critico* [n. 71], *Leopardi negli Stati Uniti d'America* [n. 131], *Le opere deleddiane all'estero: itinerario di ricezione* [n. 113].

116. *Mario Fubini lettore di Croce*, «Annali della Scuola Normale Superiore di Pisa», Classe di Lettere e Filosofia, XIX, serie III, 1989, 1, pp. 65-83, ora in *Letteratura e critica*, v. n. 115.

117. *L'incontro con San Benedetto (Paradiso XXII)*, «Letture classensi», XVIII, Ravenna, Longo, 1989, pp. 49-64, ora in *Strutture poetiche*, pp. 65-81, v. n. 152.

118. *La critica dantesca in America: la lezione singletoniana*, «Letture classensi», XVIII, Ravenna, Longo, 1989, pp. 131-44, ora in *Strutture poetiche*, pp. 83-98, v. n. 152. Versione inglese, col titolo *Charles Singleton and American Dante Criticism*, in AA.VV., *Word and Drama in Dante. Essays on the Divine Comedy*, ed. J. C. Barnes & Jennifer Petrie, Dublin, Irish Academic Press, 1993, pp. 181-201.

119. *La* Gerusalemme *del Tasso: il titolo, il testo*, «Yearbook of Italian Studies», VIII, 1989, pp. 10-19; poi in AA.VV., *Il titolo e il testo*, Atti del XV Convegno interuniversitario (Bressanone), «Quaderni del Circolo Filologico Linguistico Padovano», XIV, Padova, Editoriale Programma, 1992, pp. 183-92.

120. Il Frontespizio, in AA.VV., *Il filone cattolico nella letteratura italiana del secondo dopoguerra: l'ispirazione e il contributo della cultura cattolica*, Atti del congresso internazionale, Fordham University, Bronx, N.Y., 29-31 ottobre 1987, a cura di Florinda M. Iannace, Roma, Bulzoni, 1989, pp. 151-64, ora in *Letteratura e critica*, pp. 143-56, v. n. 115.

121. *Glauco Cambon critico di poesia*, «Ipotesi 80», 25/26, 1989, pp. 11-19.

122. *I proemi del Machiavelli*, «Yearbook of Italian Studies», VIII, 1989, pp. 1-9, anche in AA.VV., *Strategie del testo: preliminari, partizioni, pause*, «Quaderni del Circolo Filologico Linguistico Padovano», XVI, Padova, Esedra, 1995, pp. 151-59.

123. *Pirandello dalla novella al teatro: tecniche del racconto ed itinerario della rappresentazione scenica*, «Rivista di Studi Pirandelliani», VII, 1989, 2, pp. 9-21, ora in *Letteratura e critica*, pp. 95-111, v. n. 115; v. nota 1, p. 110, al saggio: "L'articolo nasce dalla rielaborazione e dal ripensamento di uno scritto apparso in inglese nel 1977 nella rivista «Modern Language Notes»", v. n. 60.

124. *Il passato europeo di Felix Gilbert*, «Belfagor», XLIV, 1989, 6, pp. 689-95. [Rec. a FELIX GILBERT, *A European Past. Memoirs 1905-45*, New York-London, Norton & Co., 1988].

1990

125. Introduzione a *Edizioni dell'elefante, 1964-1990. Work of the Roman Publishers Enzo and Benedetta Crea*, An exhibition at the Houghton Library, 6 Dec. 1990 - 26 Jan. 1991, Introduction by Dante Della Terza, Cambridge, Mass., Harvard College Library, 1990.

126. *Inferno XIX*, in AA.VV., *Dante's Divine Comedy. Introductory Readings*, Vol. I, *Inferno*, Charlottesville, VA, University of Virginia, 1990, pp. 247-61. Versione italiana, col titolo *Il canto dei simoniaci: genesi teologica e gestazione poetica della protesta dantesca*, «Letture classensi», XX/XXI, Ravenna, Longo, 1992, pp. 77-94, ora in *Strutture poetiche*, pp. 27-45, v. n. 152.

127. *Il Verismo e la cultura meridionale. De Sanctis, Capuana, Verga*, in AA.VV., *Studi d'italianistica in onore di Giovanni Cecchetti*, a cura di P. Cherchi & M. Picone, Ravenna, Longo, 1990, pp. 187-203, anche in *Letteratura e critica*, pp. 45-64, v. n. 115.

128. *Vittorio Imbriani critico: inizi desanctisiani ed itinerari polemico-eruditi*, in AA.VV., *Studi su Vittorio Imbriani*, a cura di Rosa Franzese & Emma Giammattei, Napoli, Guida, 1990, pp. 119-34, anche in *Letteratura e critica*, pp. 65-78, v. n. 115.

129. *Agli studenti del Liceo «Francesco De Sanctis» di Sant'Angelo dei Lombardi*, «Periferia», XIII, 1990, 38, pp. 32-35.

male Superiore, a Zurigo, a Parigi, dove conobbe la sua futura moglie, a Toulouse, e poi, vincitore di concorso per l'insegnamento della storia e della filosofia nei Licei, ad Urbino, e infine in America, a Bellingham, vicino a Seattle, in casa dei genitori della moglie, e di lì a Los Angeles, dove ottenne un posto per l'insegnamento dell'italiano presso l'Università della California, e a Harvard, e negli ultimi anni, di ritorno in Italia, all'Università della Calabria e all'Università «Federico II» di Napoli. Rimangono in mente di questa lunga intervista soprattutto le pagine nelle quali rievoca con commozione ma anche con lucidità e con ironia gli anni dell'infanzia e dell'adolescenza, trascorsi per lo più a Sant'Angelo, il suo paese di adozione. Gli scenari di questi anni sono quelli degli angusti spazi domestici che dovevano ospitare lui, i due fratelli, il padre, operaio elettricista, la madre, donna con poca istruzione formale ma che possedeva un'innata capacità di organizzare i suoi ricordi sotto forma di gustosissimi racconti, e una zia. Una sola apertura fa eccezione, nella memoria, a questi interni poverissimi e bui: un balcone (ricordato altrove, in altri scritti autobiografici) in fondo a tre stanze buie, che si apriva sul magnifico paesaggio dell'Alta Irpinia con le sue ruvide montagne e arrampicati su di esse i piccoli paesi della zona – «...il più straordinario balcone che io abbia mai visto. Ho cominciato ad amare di lì e da allora i paesi che le limpide e trasparenti estati, gl'inverni ovattati offrivano all'orizzonte del mio sguardo».[5] Per il resto, lo sfogo era verso le strade e le piazze – la più importante, Piazza Francesco De Sanctis – dove per lo più si svolgeva la vita del paese: «Devo dire che il mio paese, Sant'Angelo, si espandeva a semicerchio dalla Cattedrale al Castello. In una *enclave* nevralgica del semicerchio s'inseriva una piazza moderna, la piazza De Sanctis, orgoglio della comunità. Essa era attraversata da eleganti marciapiedi dove la gente trascorreva lunghe ore a passeggiare specialmente durante le ore serali nei mesi d'estate».[6] Sarà soltanto quando scoprirà l'esistenza e il piacere del libro che passerà delle ore in casa, dedicandosi con passione alle sue «letture clandestine»: le *Novelle italiane*, raccolta antologica a cura di Giuseppe Lipparini, *Le mie prigioni* di Silvio Pellico, l'*Iliade* nella traduzione italiana di Vincenzo Monti. Erano libri portati in casa dal fratello maggiore, Ettore, quando cominciò a frequentare il Ginnasio. L'istituzione di un Ginnasio a Sant'Angelo, «un ginnasio 'isolato' privo cioè dei tre anni di liceo» (p. 15), rappresentò la salvezza per Dante e i suoi fratelli. L'indigenza della famiglia, infatti, rendeva estremamente difficile, se non addirittura impossibile, mandare i figli a studiare altrove. Era una scuola di indirizzo classico, «Fosse stata una scuola per ragionieri o per geometri l'avremmo frequentata senza batter ciglio e saremmo diventati ragionieri o geometri» (p. 15). C'è forse in questa affermazione una cer-

---

[5] *Anniversario*, «Il Domani», Periodico di Sant'Angelo dei Lombardi, dicembre 1981. Vedi anche il racconto, *Il "castello" di Antonio*, nel volume già citato a cura di V. Russo.
[6] *Dagli Appennini alle Montagne Rocciose (e ritorno)*, cit., p. 23.

ta *nonchalance*, tipica del suo atteggiamento e del suo stile. Ma quel che egli vuol soprattutto sottolineare non è tanto la contingenza, l'arbitrarietà dei suoi interessi intellettuali, quanto, ancora una volta, l'estrema povertà della famiglia, che precludeva ogni possibilità di scelta.

L'attaccamento alle persone, alle cose, ai luoghi, alla vita di allora, evidente nella rievocazione autobiografica, sembra direttamente proporzionale al bisogno, che egli ben presto avvertì, di sottrarsi agli angusti orizzonti di quel mondo. Vinto il concorso per l'ammissione alla Scuola Normale di Pisa e entrato in contatto con tanti compagni provenienti da tutte le parti d'Italia, si rese conto che il suo avvenire non era a Sant'Angelo, ma altrove: «Capii, discutendo con loro, che non mi era lecito tornare indietro, tornare sui miei passi, recuperando il paese che mi ero lasciato dietro le spalle, pur senza mai disamarlo» (p. 19). E vinto il concorso per l'insegnamento nei licei, fece di tutto per farsi trasferire da Sant'Angelo, dove era stato assegnato, ad Urbino, «che era sede universitaria e perciò più adatta alle sue esigenze di ricerca» (p. 30). Il desiderio di captare e di fissare, per sé e per gli altri, i ricordi di gioventù, acquista un senso di commossa urgenza quando, a seguito del terremoto del 1980, la quasi totalità di quel mondo scompare sotto le macerie. In un articolo intitolato *Identità e fedeltà*, apparso su un periodico di Sant'Angelo («Il Domani», giugno-luglio 1981), egli afferma drammaticamente il suo persistente attaccamento a quella terra, «una terra veramente nostra nel ricordo»: «Anni fa, partimmo dai monti dell'Alta Irpinia per recarci ad affrontare gli studi universitari in città che ci parevano lontane ed irraggiungibili. Ci portavamo dentro con l'umile coscienza della nostra inadeguatezza, la nostalgia delle nostre case, di volti noti ed amici, di gesti, di parole e di affetti nei quali ci riconoscevamo e ci rispecchiavamo. Quante volte abbiamo dovuto riconoscere che questa amorosa eredità che ci accompagnava fedele ed esigente non era il segno di una nostra insormontabile arretratezza, d'un nostro bisogno di rifugio in certezze ovvie, ma la nostra forza, la nostra stessa incancellabile identità?». Le interviste e gli scritti di carattere autobiografico, ai quali ci siamo riferiti, sono tutti posteriori al tragico evento, e cosi anche i due racconti aggiunti in fondo al volume curato da Vittorio Russo: *La storia di Michele* e *Il "castello" di Antonio*. Quest'ultimo si chiude con una malinconica riflessione sul caratteristico intercalare della zia Giuseppina, «su quel "niente" con cui dava inizio ad ogni suo racconto» – una figura di litote, evidentemente: «Ma, ora il suo "niente" mi si complica nella mente assorta ed attonita, diventa una prolessi, si riversa sui contenuti stessi del racconto, li erode, li distrugge, li vanifica. Castello, amici, il paese tutto mi appaiono travolti in un sogno lancinante che tutti li convoglia in uno spazio di dolorose, implacabili attese» (p. 212). Dante è ritornato più volte, per brevi visite, in quei luoghi. Ed anzi, ancora prima del terremoto, è ritornato ad insegnare in Italia, a Cosenza e più tardi a Napoli. Ma il paese delle sue lontane origini è quasi com-

caso, la revisione del Tasso va al di là delle blande obiezioni (p. 82) del Gonzaga ed arriva fino a capovolgere il contenuto della favola, come è evidente dal confronto fra la prima ottava del canto VI e la corrispondente ottava rifiutata. Mentre in questa la città assediata era descritta in preda alla fame, nel testo rivisto si insiste, invece, sulla sua prosperità. La correzione dà un rilievo del tutto diverso al personaggio dell'eroico difensore, il circasso Argante: «Una cosa è dichiarare che in Argante reagisce la coscienza militante dell'uomo d'arme che preferisce la sfida arrogante al nemico invasore, alla fame debilitante e all'avvilente inedia che soffoca ogni energia e altra cosa è dire che Argante rifiuta prosperità e l'ovattata sicurezza dell'assediato di lusso, l'inerte ordine delle cose, per chiamare a sfida l'universo mondo cristiano contro cui egli combatte una sua eterna guerra privata» (p. 84). Il Gonzaga si era limitato ad osservare che nell'ottava in questione, contrariamente a quanto era detto in precedenza, sembrava che la fame affliggesse non soltanto il popolo ma anche i soldati. Non si deve, dunque, esagerare l'importanza del ruolo del revisore. Il suo intervento è il punto di partenza di una specie di reazione a catena del tutto imprevedibile, per cui, passando da città affamata a città prospera, il Tasso riesce «con un colpo d'ala a ridare vigore e plausibilità narrativa a uno dei personaggi chiave della *Gerusalemme*» (p. 84). Ciò non toglie che il Gonzaga rappresenti «un punto di riferimento costante» nel processo revisorio del poema. Ed è opportuno ricordare a questo punto la ristampa e la traduzione, con ampia introduzione e note, a cura di Della Terza, dei *Commentarii rerum suarum*, e cioè dell'*Autobiografia* del Gonzaga, fonte preziosa di informazioni intorno all'Accademia degli Eterei, fondata dal prelato e frequentata dal Tasso durante il suo soggiorno padovano. Fu allora, appunto, che questi si legò d'amicizia col Gonzaga, con cui poi intrattenne una fitta corrispondenza.

Di alcuni anni posteriore allo studio degli echi petrarcheschi nella *Liberata* è il saggio su Tasso e Dante.[19] La proposta da parte del Tasso – in alcune lettere al Gonzaga, nell'*Allegoria* del poema e nella conclusione dell'*Apologia della Gerusalemme Liberata* – di una «trasformazione allegorizzante e strutturalmente significativa di tutta la *Gerusalemme*», e quindi di una «lettura convergente» del suo poema e della *Commedia*, si risolve in «un espediente tanto massiccio quanto ingenuo» (p. 150): «L'instabilità delle trame allegoriche escogitate dal Tasso mostra l'inconsistenza di un tentativo di avvicinarsi con intenti strutturali al concreto mondo della *Commedia*» (p. 155). Nonostante la sua «vasta erudizione dantesca» (p. 160), largamente documentata fra l'altro dalle sue annotazioni al testo della *Commedia*, il messaggio dantesco «gli sopraggiunge soltanto a frammenti» (p. 155), evocato da una memoria sconfinata, e sconfinan-

---

[19] *Tasso's reading of Dante*, «Dante Studies», LXXXVII, 1969, pp. 103-26. La versione italiana, col titolo *Tasso e Dante*, è apparsa su «Belfagor», XXV, 1970, pp. 395-418, ed è ora in *Forma e memoria*, cit., pp. 148-76.

te, che egli cerca di arginare indirizzandola verso significati plausibili (p. 170), tentando di sistemare in una nuova struttura «versi della *Commedia* disancorati e fluttuanti» (p. 163). Questa utilizzazione frammentaria, spregiudicata, insistente – a volte uno stesso episodio, per esempio quello di Ulisse, ispira episodi diversi e distanti della *Gerusalemme*, a volte «citazioni dantesche plurime» si trovano nel breve giro di una stessa ottava, come, per esempio, nell'annuncio delle future imprese di Rinaldo[20] – può risultare in una «degradazione dei significati» (p. 164), in «uno scadimento della fonte» (p. 169), in «inaspettati e involontariamente irreverenti trapianti» (p. 168), come, per dare soltanto un esempio, nel caso di Armida «suggeritrice di pensieri peccaminosi alle menti una volta austere dei guerrieri cristiani:

> Come per acqua e per cristallo intiero
> trapassa il raggio e no 'l divide o parte,
> per entro il chiuso manto osa il pensiero
> sì penetrar ne la vietata parte.
> (*G.L.* IV, 32)

Qui Tasso ricorda il Dante del secondo canto del *Paradiso*:

> Per entro sé l'etterna margarita
> ne ricevette, com'acqua recepe
> raggio di luce permanendo unita.
> (*Par.* II, 34-36)

Ma con quale differente accento! Il Tasso ha trasformato i casti accenti del linguaggio dantesco in una metafora sessuale di tipo controriformistico. *Nisi caste, saltem caute!* Il pensiero timoroso di violenza, ma ambiguamente coinvolto nell'avventura amorosa penetra e pur rimane guardingo; si spinge in avanti a spiare i segreti del corpo femmineo e pur non lascia segno» (pp. 168-69). Ma questi risultati sconcertanti, queste inevitabili "deformazioni" dell'originale dantesco, non debbono far dimenticare il significato più profondo dell'operazione assimilatoria del Tasso, della sua «estrema porosità», della sua *maniera*: «la genuina, ingegnosa ricerca di nuovi valori formali» (p. 176). Il problema della memoria poetica è esaminato da Della Terza anche in una diversa e complementare prospettiva di lettura, «tenendo conto della valenza e della funzione che essa possiede all'interno del racconto epico nel quale s'inserisce»,[21] e cioè in relazione alla trama del poema: per esempio, a proposito del racconto della nascita di Clorinda (XII, 21-25) e dell'utilizzazione di un romanzo greco del III secolo d.C., le *Etiopiche* di Eliodoro, dove la nascita di una bambina bianca da genitori neri è spiegata come effetto della contemplazione

---

[20] *Gerusalemme liberata* X, 75. Vedi *Forma e memoria*, cit., pp. 170-71, 173.
[21] *Forma e memoria*, cit., p. 4.

da parte della madre – «che bruna è sì ma il bruno il bel non toglie» – della bianca immagine di Andromeda dipinta nel soffitto. Nel soffitto della stanza in cui è stata rinchiusa dal marito geloso la madre di Clorinda, invece di Andromeda e Perseo, è raffigurato San Giorgio che libera la vergine dal drago. L'episodio è trasformato, dunque, in senso cristiano. Ma quel che più conta, per l'analisi di Della Terza, è la sua trasposizione nei termini di un accentuato manierismo, con echi di Pettarca, di Ariosto e indirettamente di Ovidio, e con un gusto marcato per l'iperbole e per un insistente cromatismo letterale e metaforico: «da ogn'uomo la nasconde, e in chiuso loco / vorria celarla ai tanti occhi del cielo»; «Vergine, bianca il bel volto e le gote / vermiglia»; «candida figlia»; «ch'egli avria dal candor che in te si vede, / argomentato in lei non bianca fede». L'argomento, accennato nell'Introduzione a *Forma e memoria* (pp. 4-6), è svolto in un saggio sulla struttura narrativa della *Liberata*.[22]

I primi saggi sulla *Commedia* sembrano seguire l'esempio dell'esegesi tassiana per il rilievo che in essi vien dato appunto al problema della memoria poetica.[23] Parole, concetti, immagini del canto V dell'*Inferno* ritornano, sul filo della tematica amorosa, nei canti X-XXVII del *Purgatorio* – i canti del «disordinato amore»[24] per adoperare l'espressione nella quale è felicemente riassunto da Della Terza il lungo ragionamento di Virgilio in *Purgatorio* XVII-XVIII. Il "ricordo interno" del canto dei lussuriosi dell'*Inferno* (*Inf.* V, 40-41, 46-47, 75, 84) è evidente in *Purgatorio* XXIV, 64-69:

> Come li augei che vernan lungo 'l Nilo,
> alcuna volta in aere fanno schiera,
> poi volan più a fretta e vanno in filo;
>   così tutta la gente che lì era,
> volgendo 'l viso, raffrettò suo passo,
> e per magrezza e per voler leggera.

E il verso «E come le grue van cantando lor lai» *(Inf.* V, 46) è «attentamente dissimilato e trasferito nella voce e gesto delle anime» dei lussuriosi del *Purgatorio* (XXVI, 43-48):

> Poi come grue ch'alle montagne Rife
> volasser parte e parte inver l'arene,
> queste del gel, quelle del sole schife,

---

[22] *History and the Epic Discourse. Remarks on the Narrative Structure of Tasso's* Liberata, «Quaderni d'italianistica», I, 1980, pp. 30-45; versione italiana, col titolo La Liberata *del Tasso tra storia e invenzione*, in *Tradizione ed esegesi*, cit., pp. 89-105.

[23] Ma vedi quel che è detto, nella Prefazione a *Forma e memoria*, a proposito dell'«uso privilegiato attribuito nel titolo al nome "memoria"», p. 2.

[24] *I canti del disordinato amore. Osservazioni sulla struttura e lo stile del Purgatorio*, «Belfagor», XXI, 1966, pp. 156-79, ora in *Forma e memoria*, cit., pp. 40-70.

> l'una gente sen va, l'altra sen vene;
> tornan, lacrimando, a' primi canti
> al gridar che più lor si convene.

Nel passare, per virtù di questi recuperi interni, dall'Inferno al *Purgatorio* e da questo al *Paradiso*, il vocabolario poetico di Dante subisce una «maturazione etica» (p. 64). Interessante è l'itinerario di "folle": dall'episodio di Ulisse nell'*Inferno* («dei remi facemmo ali al folle volo», *Inf.* XXVI, 125), a quello di Sapia senese nel Purgatorio («odi s'i' fui, com'io ti dico, folle», *Purg.* XIII, 113), alla rievocazione «velata da allusiva distanza» (p. 66) dell'episodio di Ulisse nel *Paradiso* («sì ch'io vedea di là da Gade il varco / folle d'Ulisse, e di qua presso il lito / nel qual si fece Europa dolce carco», *Par.* XXVII, 82-84): «Con lo smitizzamento paradisiaco del grande episodio infernale assistiamo alla decantazione dei sentimenti del poeta: dal racconto esaltato ed esaltante di Ulisse, passando attraverso alla disincantata e pertinente analisi che il personaggio Sapia fa della propria peccaminosa follia, raggiungiamo infine l'animo di Dante finalmente in grado di ritrovare nell'acquisita amorosa esperienza della grazia la sufficiente distanza per farsi giudice dell'umana follia» (p. 67).[25] Nel saggio sul canto di Brunetto Latini,[26] la figura del maestro riverito e umiliato emerge dai versi del canto XV dell'*Inferno* attraverso una fitta rete di reminiscenze del *Tresor* e del *Tesoretto*: una «prigione di parole» (p. 24), che garantisce l'obiettività del ritratto e ne autorizza la messa a fuoco nella duplice prospettiva di Dante pellegrino e poeta.

L'incerta cronologia delle opere di Dante e i pericoli di «ogni adesione ad uno schema diacronico con rigide coordinate di sviluppo» dovrebbero consigliare «un uso più ampio di una critica di tipo sincronico».[27] Non già che anche questa non abbia i suoi limiti e i suoi inconvenienti: Della Terza cita l'interpretazione data da Spitzer al capitolo VIII della *Vita Nuova*, per effetto della quale «il principio di costruzione, valido per la *Commedia*, si proietta a ritroso verso la *Vita Nuova* complicandone ed ampliandone oltremodo il senso» (p. 90). Ma egli ritiene che da «un'attenta lettura pragmatica degli esempi più convincenti di critica sincronica» si possa imparare ad evitare tanto «la coerenza rigida ed astratta» di un'interpretazione totalizzante, quanto «una lettura estetica che ignora il rapporto esistente tra gli episodi e la totalità del viaggio». Fra questi due estremi c'è abbastanza spazio per «molteplici modi di leggere la *Commedia*»,

---

[25] Qualcosa di simile si riscontra nell'uso del vocabolo "sterpi" in *Inf.* XIII, 7, 37, *Purg.* XIV, 95, *Par.* XII, 100 (pp. 67-68). Ma vedi anche le considerazioni a proposito di *Inf.* XV, 1-6, 10, *Purg.* XX, 43-48, XXIV, 73, *Par.* X, 94-96 (pp. 68-70).

[26] *Il canto di Brunetto Latini*, in AA.VV., *Orbis mediaevalis*, Mélanges de langue et de littérature médiévales offerts à Reto R. Bezzola, Berne, Francke, 1978, pp. 69-88, ora in *Forma e memoria*, pp. 13-39.

[27] *Istanze tradizionali e prospettive di aggiornamento nella critica dantesca*, «Lettere Italiane», XXVII, 1975, pp. 245-62, ora, con importanti modifiche, in *Forma e memoria*, pp. 71-92; p. 82.

ed è in questo spazio che egli situa il suo metodo di lettura (pp. 89-90), e cioè l'esperienza critica dei suoi primi saggi sulla *Commedia*.[28] Distanziandosi con estrema cautela (la sua adesione all'«approccio sincronico» è subordinata alla condizione ineccepibile che per esso si intenda «l'assoluta priorità data al testo e ai valori testuali del mondo dantesco», p. 84), e senza alcun accenno polemico, da Singleton e forse anche da Auerbach, che è pure uno dei critici da lui studiati con maggiore attenzione e simpatia, egli si schiera così dalla parte di Spitzer e della sua «lettura sincronica di Dante per spiegare Dante», fondata sulla «memoria dantesca operante nella trama del poema» (p. 83), e in modo meno esplicito dalla parte di Gianfranco Contini, che «ha parlato con autorità delle caratteristiche subliminali della memoria di Dante, del suo potere di associazione, dissociazione e dissimilazione» (p. 84). «Per quanto mi riguarda», egli dice, concludendo questo suo tentativo di autodefinizione, «la educazione intellettuale che ho ricevuto mi porta inevitabilmente a credere che il lettore riceverà ausilio alla comprensione della poesia di Dante se presterà la dovuta attenzione al tessuto dinamico delle immagini del poema considerandole come il campo d'individuazione di strutture culturali significative filtrate attraverso la memoria poetica dantesca» (p. 90).

I saggi sui canti del disordinato amore e su Brunetto Latini sono forse quelli di maggiore impegno fra gli scritti danteschi di Della Terza. Comunque, fatta eccezione per alcuni interventi sulla critica dantesca,[29] gli altri scritti danteschi sono tutti posteriori a questo chiarimento metodologico. Successivamente egli è tornato sui problemi della critica dantesca, con degli scritti che riguardano in modo particolare l'area nord-americana,[30] e sulla *Commedia*, con una serie di saggi che rientrano nel genere delle *Lecturae Dantis*, caratterizzate per altro da qualche ripresa del tema della memoria poetica[31] e soprattutto da un attento dialogo con la critica.[32] Nella Lettura del canto di San Benedetto *(Par.* XXII),[33] è di particolare interesse lo studio della ricostruzione dinamica, operata da Dante, della figura del santo, a partire dalle fonti da lui adoperate. A questa Lettura si ricollega il tentativo, in un saggio relativamente recente[34] – suggerito dall'invito di Singleton «ad isolare, aldilà

---

[28] Questa parte, relativa al suo metodo di lettura, è stata aggiunta per la pubblicazione del saggio nello stesso volume, *Forma e memoria*, nel quale sono inclusi anche i due saggi danteschi sopra discussi.

[29] Vedi, per es., *Studi danteschi in America*, «Rassegna della letteratura italiana», LXIV, 1960, 2, pp. 218-30, e la Prefazione a ERICH AUERBACH, *Studi su* Dante, Milano, Feltrinelli, 1963.

[30] Una continuazione dell'articolo sugli *Studi danteschi in America* è *La critica dantesca in America*, in *Letture classensi*, XVIII, Ravenna, Longo, 1989, pp. 131-44, ora, col sottotitolo *La lezione singletoniana*, in *Strutture poetiche*, cit., pp. 83-98.

[31] Vedi, per es., *Il primo canto dell'invidia (Purgatorio XIII)*, «Filologia e critica», XVII, 1992, 1, pp. 3-21, ora in *Strutture poetiche*, pp. 47-63.

[32] Vedi specialmente *Inferno V. Tradizione ed esegesi*, in AA.VV., *Studi in onore di Vittore Branca*, Firenze, Olschki, 1983, I, pp. 220-39, ora in *Tradizione ed esegesi*, cit., pp. 15-28.

[33] *L'incontro con San Benedetto (Paradiso XXII)*, in *Letture classensi*, XVIII, cit., pp. 49-64, ora in *Strutture poetiche*, cit., pp. 65-81.

[34] *Incontri nella* Commedia *lungo la verticale del viaggio*, «Le Forme e la Storia», III, 1991, 1, pp. 67-84.

degli orizzonti episodici esplorati dalle più consuete *Lecturae Dantis*, la verticale del viaggio atta a segnalarci il progresso del pellegrino verso una verità ansiosamente perseguita e finalmente raggiunta nella visione di Dio» (p. 67) di adottare il metodo promosso dallo studioso americano, «ma applicandolo alla coscienza, che Dante poeta acquisisce lungo la verticale del viaggio», delle «interne risonanze», degli «agganci episodici», e cioè dell'«unità dell'operazione poetica che egli sta svolgendo» (p. 68). «È come se Dante ritrovasse», osserva Della Terza, ritornando sulla sua Lettura di *Par.* XXII, «nell'ascesa di San Benedetto verso la cima del monte, il senso della propria ascesa»: «Si tratta d'una simpatia partecipe ed intensissima che trasforma, per così dire, Dante in un "alter Benedictus"» (p. 81).

Nel contesto di una revisione "problematica" della critica e dell'estetica crociana – di una revisione cioè intesa a mettere in luce problemi piuttosto che a proporre soluzioni –, è da collocare l'interesse di Della Terza per De Sanctis. E non sarà fuori luogo ricordare che è appunto in questi termini che egli tende a presentare l'interesse di Gramsci per De Sanctis, largamente documentato nei *Quaderni del carcere*, alla cui pubblicazione è da ricollegare, come egli dice, la rinnovata intensità dell'interesse per il grande critico negli anni '50: «Fondamentalmente Gramsci rifiuta di ridurre il compito del critico letterario alla mera definizione dell'impegno sociale o politico di un autore. Lettore esperto dell'*Estetica* di Croce, egli sa molto bene che, descrivendo l'opera d'arte soltanto in rapporto al momento storico e sociale durante il quale è stata concepita, il critico si lascia sfuggire ciò che essa ha di peculiare. E tuttavia Gramsci sottolinea la sua preferenza non per il momento egemonico dell'acquisita certezza critica – come è il caso di Croce ma per il momento della lotta quando il critico letterario e cioè De Sanctis – non separa la sua idea della forma letteraria dall'analisi della coerenza storica, logica, strutturale dell'opera d'arte».[35] Non molto diversa era, del resto, sotto questo aspetto, la posizione di Luigi Russo, citato più volte da Gramsci nei *Quaderni*.[36] La complessità della critica di De Sanctis e dei suoi presupposti teorici è il tema dell'analisi estremamente attenta e puntuale che Della Terza fa delle lezioni del 1874 su Mazzini: «Messo a confronto con una concezione dell'arte che rimanda, per delinearsi ed affermarsi, allo stabilimento d'un nuovo sistema di valori politici, il De Sanctis reagisce dapprima accettandone in qualche modo l'esigenza ed inserendo un'istanza di verità ed efficacia politica nella valutazione dell'opera d'arte, ma per negare subito dopo il diritto di cittadinanza nel mondo della letteratura ad ogni forma d'arte che si faccia ancella della politica».[37] La critica di De Sanctis, divisa fra consensi e dissensi, sia

---

[35] *On Francesco De Sanctis (1817-1883) and Realism*, «Journal of the History of Ideas», XLI, 1980, pp. 335-41, v. p. 336; cfr. A. GRAMSCI, *Letteratura e vita nazionale*, Torino, Einaudi, 1966, pp. 6-7.

[36] Vedi, per es., *Letteratura e vita nazionale*, cit., pp. 16-17.

[37] *Mazzini's Image and the Italian Risorgimento. De Amicis, De Sanctis, Ruffini*, «Yearbook of Italian Studies», III, 1973/75, pp. 107-37; versione italiana, col titolo *L'eroe scomodo e la sua ombra. L'immagine di Mazzini e la letteratura del Risorgimento*, in *Letteratura e critica tra Otto e Novecento*, Cosenza, Edizioni Periferia, 1989, pp. 9-44.

per quanto riguarda la politica, sia per quanto riguarda la letteratura, come anche naturalmente circa il rapporto dell'una con l'altra, è «ad un tempo frammentaria e complessa, mai comunque lineare e semplicistica» (p. 21). E questo non soltanto nel caso di Mazzini: «se noi trascriviamo uno dopo l'altro i giudizi del De Sanctis su un autore rispettando la diacronia della loro formulazione, ci rendiamo conto che essi s'inseriscono in modo non aforistico in circoscritti microcosmi ideologici che, malgrado la loro apparente autosufficienza, trovano il loro limite nel microcosmo contiguo del quale dobbiamo tener conto nella costruzione del quadro critico nella sua integrità» (pp. 21-22). La vocazione problematica dell'esegesi desanctisiana di Della Terza si esercita soprattutto intorno alle nozioni di ironia e di comicità e ai giudizi di De Sanctis su scrittori come Boccaccio, Ariosto, Goldoni. La denuncia del soggettivismo erosivo dell'ironia si alterna in De Sanctis ad un uso ispirato a funzionalità positiva del concetto di ironia, il riconoscimento della forza innovatrice della comicità alla diffidenza verso il valore positivo di essa: «Il riso dei grandi si chiamino essi Giovanni Boccaccio e Ludovico Ariosto viene auscultato dal critico con un misto d'interesse per la sua forza innovativa e di grave diffidenza per il vuoto che lascia dietro».[38] La difesa dell'Ariosto contro la critica moralistica del Cantù, in un saggio del '65, non impedisce a De Sanctis alcuni anni dopo, nella sua *Storia*, di deplorare nell'autore del *Furioso* la mancanza del sentimento di natura, patria, famiglia, umanità, amore, onore. E un'ambivalenza analoga si riscontra a proposito di Goldoni, ammirato per «finezza di osservazione e spirito inventivo, misura e giustezza nella concezione, calore e brio nella esecuzione», ma privo di «un mondo interiore della coscienza»[39]: «Mancò a lui quello che mancava da più secoli a tutti gl'italiani, e che renderà insanabile la loro decadenza: la sincerità e la forza delle convinzioni».[40] Un'interpretazione semplicistica di queste oscillazioni è esplicitamente scoraggiata da Della Terza, che si richiama alla loro complicata intertestualità, all'interferenza, nel pensiero di De Sanctis, della prospettiva storiografica delle *Revolutions d'Italie* di Edgar Quinet con «un referente filosofico non banale», l'*Estetica* di Hegel.[41]

Tasso, Dante, De Sanctis. Sono questi i temi più spesso ricorrenti della riflessione critica di Dante Della Terza. Ma i suoi interessi e i suoi studi si estendono agli aspetti e ai personaggi più diversi della cultura europea, soprattutto,

---

[38] *Comico e commedia nella critica di Francesco De* Sanctis, in AA.VV., *Ambiguità del comico*, a cura di Giulio Ferroni, Palermo, Sellerio, 1983, pp. 137-47, ora in *Tradizione ed esegesi*, cit., pp. 169-77; p. 173.

[39] FRANCESCO DE SANCTIS, *Storia della letteratura italiana*, a cura di Niccolò Gallo, 2 voll., Torino, Einaudi, 1958, II, p. 896; cfr. *Tradizione ed esegesi*, cit., p. 174.

[40] F. DE SANCTIS, *Storia*, cit., II, p. 905; cfr. *Tradizione ed esegesi*, cit., p. 174. Quanto a Manzoni, nelle lezioni napoletane del 1871-72, «il De Sanctis sembra incline a spostare il proprio obiettivo verso gli usi funzionali, narratologici a cui è chiamata l'ironia nel corso dei *Promessi Sposi*. Essa è mobilitata ad abbassare verso il mediocre e il consueto la tensione episodica, il livello tragico del racconto» (*Tradizione ed esegesi*, cit., p. 171).

[41] *Francesco De Sanctis: gli itinerari della* Storia, in *Letteratura italiana*, diretta da Alberto Asor Rosa, IV, Torino, Einaudi, 1985, pp. 331-49, ora in *Tradizione ed esegesi*, cit., pp. 179-96; pp. 191-94.

ma non soltanto, italiana: dall'autobiografia, al romanzo, al teatro, alla poesia, alla critica, alle riviste letterarie; da Boccaccio a Pirandello, a Pasolini, a Gadda, a Sciascia; da Machiavelli a Vico; da Leopardi a Marinetti; da Croce, a Spitzer, a Russo, a Fubini; da Panofsky a Auerbach; da Borgese a de Man; da Montaigne a La Rochefoucauld, a Gide; dalle riviste fiorentine del primo Novecento a «Belfagor». Di fronte ad un'attività così varia e molteplice si è inevitabilmente portati a cercare un elemento comune, un sia pur minimo comun denominatore, al quale sia possibile ricondurla. Vien fatto così di interrogarsi circa la natura e il significato dell'*approach* critico di Della Terza, e cioè in ultima analisi circa la natura e il significato della sua partecipazione a mezzo secolo di vita intellettuale in Europa e in America.

Storicismo, critica stilistica, revisione problematica del modello crociano, definiscono la tradizione critica alla quale Della Terza si ricollega, quella che egli chiama «la linea Croce-Russo-Fubini da me privilegiata» e alla quale egli è rimasto fedele, senza tuttavia escludere le nuove «esperienze non facilmente riportabili al consueto e al *déjà vu*»,[42] le nuove tendenze e i nuovi critici che si sono fatti avanti sulla scena italiana (l'Italia, come egli osserva, è diventata «il paese dove la polilalia è divenuta la donna più corteggiata», p. 148) o con cui egli è venuto in contatto all'estero: marxismo, strutturalismo, semiologia; attenzione filologica al testo nel suo farsi o anche «come un organismo da analizzare per determinarne le funzioni» (p. 149); interesse, non soltanto per lo «stemma codicum», ma anche «per la diffusione "orizzontale" del testo, per una caratterizzazione sociologica e storica del pubblico al quale il libro s'indirizza» (p. 149); maestri di linguistica e di studi letterari, come Contini, Branca, Binni, Segre, Corti, Avalle e altri ancora, o «appassionati di ideologia» come Lucien Goldmann. Non ci sono rinunce, non ci sono esclusioni. «L'esperienza critica», egli dice, «non si dispone mai verticalmente in una serie di superamenti, esteriorizzandosi in un finale capitolo trionfalistico di saggezza raggiunta. I critici che per noi hanno contato non cessano improvvisamente di contare per l'epifanica discesa in noi di una verità che pone tutti a tacere» (p. 152). Non ci sono schieramenti polemici, non ci sono nuove prese di posizione teoriche, nuovi pronunciamenti metodologici. Momenti e "modi" diversi della sua vita intellettuale convivono senza difficoltà nella mobile articolazione delle sue pagine critiche: ed è in questo appunto che consiste la singolarità, l'unicità, del suo stile, o, se si vuole, del suo *approach*. Egli stesso si è posto una volta il quesito, a proposito dei suoi studi di critica dantesca, se la sua partecipazione al dibattito critico non si fosse limitata ad «un atteggiamento recettivo e mimetico»[43] di fronte a tipi di critica tra loro diversi. Ma non si tratta

---

[42] *Metodologia ed esegesi nell'Italia del secondo dopoguerra*, «Yearbook of Italian Studies», IV, 1980, pp. 137-52; p. 148.

[43] *Forma e memoria*, cit., p. 89.

di mimetismo, si tratta piuttosto di disponibilità, di apertura mentale. A meno che non si intenda il rapporto mimetico come un rapporto di reciproco condizionamento fra il soggetto e l'oggetto dell'imitazione: πάντων δὲ παλίντροπός ἐστι κέλευθος. Se è vero, come egli ripete, che «si è sempre quello che si è diventati», è anche vero che la qualità dell'erba dipende dal seme, e che si diventa, dunque, quello che si è sempre stati. Ed egli è ed è sempre stato, con la sua straordinaria perspicacia, il testimone cauto e partecipe, elusivo e cordiale, di una civiltà intellettuale che diventa sempre più decisamente pluralistica.

CHRISTOPHER JONES

VERGIL AND THE LYCIANS

Like other great works of art, for example Shakespeare's *Tempest* and Verdi's *Otello* (but not its Shakespearian model), the *Aeneid* begins with a storm. The first of Aeneas' comrades to perish before his eyes is a Lycian: "unam, quae Lycios fidumque uehebat Oronten, / ipsius ante oculos ingens a vertice pontus / in puppim ferit: excutitur pronusque magister / uoluitur in caput, ast illam ter fluctus ibidem / torquet agens circum et rapidus vorat aequore uertex" (*Aen.* 1.113-117). The poet reverts to this incident twice, once in the first book where Orontes is the first of Aeneas' comrades to be remembered after the storm (1.220), and again in the sixth, where the hero sees "Orontes, the leader of the Lycian ship", among the shades of those who have perished at sea (6.334). Vergil does not mean, however, that all the Lycians perished with Orontes, since some appear among his companions in Sicily and Italy. The most conspicuous is Eurytion, brother of Pandarus, who wins the archery contest in the funeral games for Anchises (5.495-518): others include two brothers of Sarpedon, Clarus and Thaemon (10.125-126, cf. 12.516).[1]

Servius comments on the first appearance of Orontes that "the Lycians had come as allies to Troy, and after the death of Pandarus they followed Aeneas" ("hi Troiae ad auxilium uenerant, qui mortuo rege Pandaro Aeneam secuti sunt, unde et in secundo [2.796] ait 'comitum adfluxisse nouorum'"): in fact, the origin of Pandarus in Homer is a notorious problem, but in later times it was usually understood to be the historical Lycia.[2] There is nothing in Homer, however, about Pandarus' subjects joining Aeneas, and a suspicion might arise that Servius is merely combining elements of the *Iliad* and the *Aeneid*. In the earlier poem, Aeneas and Pandarus join together to fight Diomedes, with Pandarus fighting from Aeneas' chariot until he is brutally killed and Aeneas is car-

---

[1] An excellent review of Lycia and Lycians in Vergil in G. BONAMENTE, article "Licia", *Enciclopedia Virgiliana*, vol. 3, Rome, Istituto della Enciclopedia Italiana, 1987, pp. 212-213.

[2] On this difficulty see T. BRYCE, "Pandaros, A Lycian at Troy", *American Journal of Philology*, 98 (1977), pp. 213-218.

ried off by his divine mother (*Il.* 5.166-317): while in the *Aeneid* the poet emphasises the fame of Eurytion's brother, "tuus, o clarissime, frater, / Pandare, qui quondam iussus confundere foedus / in medios telum torsisti primus Achaeos" (*Aen.* 5.495-497). Nonetheless, it will be argued here that Servius has not invented this story of the Lycians following Aeneas, but is drawing on traditions much older than Vergil, which made Trojans and Lycians not merely allies but kinsmen.[3]

Perhaps the first hint of such a link is found in an obscure Lycian historian, Menecrates of Xanthus.[4] This writer is usually dated to the fifth or fourth century: the only certain evidence is that he was known to Nicander of Colophon, who is usually put in the later second.[5] His one named work is a *Lycian History* (*Lykiaka*), and this seems the likely source of a 'fragment' cited by Dionysius of Halicarnassus, who is discussing the traditions about Aeneas after the fall of Troy. Among the versions which Dionysius finds 'less persuasive' is the following:

> Menecrates of Xanthus declares that he (Aeneas) betrayed the city because of his hostility towards Alexander (Paris), and that because of this service the Achaeans allowed him to preserve his household. His account, beginning from the burial of Achilles, is as follows: 'Sorrow held the Achaeans, and they considered that the head of their army had been knocked off. Nevertheless, after according him a tomb they fought with all their power until Ilion was captured by the agency of Aeneas. For Aeneas had been dishonored by Alexander (Paris) and excluded from the spoils, and so he overturned Priam; after achieving this he became one of the Achaeans.[6]

If this is indeed from Menecrates' *Lycian History*, it follows that in some way it involved the Lycians, even if the connection is not clear from the fragment cited. Menecrates or a precedessor may have extrapolated from the alliance of Aeneas and Pandarus in Homer some joint exile of Aeneas and the Lycians after the Trojan War.

We are on surer ground with an inscription from the sanctuary of Leto at Xanthus, first published by Jeanne and Louis Robert in 1983. Dated precisely to the year 196 B.C., this honors a certain Themistocles, a citizen of Ilion (the successor of the Homeric Troy) and also a public speaker (*rhetor*). This person had "stayed no short time in our city, and proved himself unexceptionable

---

[3] I have discussed some general questions of kinship between peoples in Vergil in "*Graia pandetur ab urbe*", *Harvard Studies in Classical Philology*, 97 (1995), pp. 235-41.

[4] F. JACOBY, *Die Fragmente der griechischen Historiker*, vol. III C, Leiden, Brill, 1958, no. 769; for a full discussion, D. ASHERI, *Fra Ellenismo e Iranismo: Studi sulla società e cultura di Xanthos nella età achemenide*, Bologna, Pàtron, 1983, pp. 125-166.

[5] Menecrates in Nicander: Nicander, JACOBY, *Die Fragmente*, vol. III A, Leiden, Brill, 1954, nos. 271-272 F 23 = no. 769 F 2. On the date of Nicander, see especially JACOBY, *Die Fragmente*, vol. III A, *Kommentar*, Leiden, Brill, 1954, pp. 229-235.

[6] DIONYSIUS HALICARNASSENSIS, *Antiquitates Romanae* 1.48.3 = JACOBY, *Die Fragmente*, no. 769 F 3.

and worthy of the kinship that links us with the Ilians (τῆς ὑπαρχούσης ἡμῖν πρὸς Ἰλιεῖς συγγενείας)".[7] The Roberts inferred, surely correctly, that Themistocles had used his lectures to illustrate the hereditary links between the two cities of Ilion and Xanthus. As with Menecrates, we do not know what arguments he used. Since there is no mention of the kinship in Homer, he could have traced it to the aftermath of the Trojan War, just as in the tradition reported by Servius: in these myths of kinship between cities, which are well known from literary texts and even more from inscriptions, it is often the wanderings of the Homeric heroes, Achaean or Trojan, that create the links between cities of a later time. But ambassadors could employ a variety of myths to argue their case, as is shown by another monument from the Letoon of Xanthus, the enormous stele recording a visit by ambassadors from Cytenion in the "Dorian Metropolis" in 205. These recounted several myths to prove their kinship with the Xanthians, tracing it from the birth of Apollo and Artemis in the Letoon, and going down several generations after the end of the Trojan War.[8]

As the Roberts also observed, the inscription illuminates a passage in the historian Polybius. Recounting the visit of the Ten Commissioners sent to Asia after the defeat of Antiochus the Great in 188, the historian says that they received ambassadors from the Ilians, "requesting because of the close relations between them (διὰ τὴν πρὸς αὐτοὺς οἰκειότητα) that the Lycians be pardoned for their errors" (the Lycians had been loyal to Antiochus until his defeat, whereas the Romans had captured Ilion from Antiochus in 190).[9] Though the word οἰκειότης, often used in these contexts, need not always refer to kinship, it must surely do so here: but which people is the other party in the relationship, the Lycians or the Romans? The kinship between Troy and Rome is well known, and the Loeb translator felt confident enough to gloss the phrase, "for the sake of the friendship between Ilion and Rome".[10] But the older translation of Evelyn Shuckburgh is surely preferable, "begging, on the ground of their kindred with the Lycians, that the latter should receive pardon for their transgressions".[11] Yet again, we do not know how the link was constructed, but in this case it is likely enough that Aeneas and his alliance with Pandarus supplied part of the argument.

[7] J. and L. ROBERT, *Fouilles d'Amyzon en Carie*, Paris, de Boccard, 1983, pp. 154-163; O. CURTY, *Les Parentés légendaires entre cités grecques*, no. 76, Geneva, Droz, 1995, pp. 192-193.

[8] J. BOUSQUET, *Revue des Études Grecques*, 101 (1988), pp. 12-53; H. Pleket and R. Stroud, eds., *Supplementum Epigraphicum Graecum*, no. 1476, vol. 38, Amsterdam, Gieben, 1991; CURTY, *Parentés legendaires*, no. 75, pp. 183-191.

[9] POLYBIUS, *Historiae* 22.5.

[10] W. Paton, ed., *Polybius, The Histories*, vol. 5, London, Heinemann, New York, Putnam, 1927, p. 353; apparently followed by Frank W. WALBANK in his *Commentary on Polybius*, vol. 3, Oxford, Clarendon Press, 1979, pp. 182-183.

[11] E. SHUCKBURGH, tr., *The Histories of Polybius*, vol. 2, London, MacMillan, 1889, p. 305.

Thus the inscription of Themistocles, together with Polybius on the Ilian embassy of 188, shows that at least by the beginning of the second century there was a firmly rooted belief in the kinship between the Ilians and the Lycians. Not long after, it appears, a new variation is found whereby the Lycians and the Romans are themselves cousins. The evidence comes from a series of inscriptions which Vergil may well have seen. Since the sixteenth century, there have appeared in many parts of Rome, on the Capitol and elsewhere, fragments of a large monument on which were carved dedications made by communities and kings of Asia in honor of the Roman people.[12] The question of the date has been much debated: Mommsen opted for the aftermath of the First Mithridatic War, others for a date in 167; an attractive compromise is that the monument was first set up in 167, damaged in the fire of 83, and then reinscribed.[13] The best known of these texts, and the first to be discovered, was set up by the Lycian league in gratitude for the restoration of its "democracy". This has plausibly been referred to an event of 167, when Rome reversed a decision it had taken in 188 and deprived the Rhodians of their control of Lycia.[14] Another text is also set up by the Lycians, and here they call the Roman people "kindred, friendly, allied", *cognatum, amicum, socium.*[15] Whether or not this text too dates to 167, it shows that the Lycians, now liberated from Rhodes, claimed their own kinship with Rome. While this may be no more than an extension of their kinship with the Ilians, it surely involved the alliance of Aeneas and Pandarus, and perhaps also some later union of the two peoples like the one known to Servius.

Vergil for his part does not make the Lycians kin of the Romans, only their loyal followers. But the action of the *Aeneid*, though placed "many years" after the fall of Troy, is still within a generation: Ascanius-Iulus, who was a toddler at the time, is still not much more than a boy.[16] While the poet could hardly make the two peoples kin, his emphasis on the links between Trojans and Lycians is more than an expansion of hints in the *Iliad*: he must have known of a tradition of kinship

---

[12] The fundamental publication is by ATTILIO DEGRASSI, "Le Dediche di popoli e re asiatici al popolo Romano e a Giove Capitolino", *Bullettino della Commissione archeologica di Roma*, 74 (1951-52 [1954]), pp. 19-47; since then see especially R. MELLOR, "The Dedications on the Capitoline Hill", *Chiron* 8 (1978), pp. 319-330; A. LINTOTT, "The Capitoline Dedications to Jupiter and the Roman people", *Zeitschrift für Papyrologie und Epigraphik*, 30 (1978), pp. 137-144.

[13] This was the position of Mellor (previous note).

[14] H. DESSAU, *Inscriptiones Latinae Selectae*; no. 31, Berlin, Weidmann, 1982; E. Lommatszch, ed., *Corpus Inscriptionum Latinarum*, vol. 1, part 2, fasc. 1², no. 725, Berlin, Reimer, 1918; DEGRASSI, "Le dediche di popoli", no. 1, pp. 19-20; DEGRASSI, *Inscriptiones Latinae Liberae Rei Publicae*, no. 174, vol. 1², Florence, La Nuova Italia, 1965; L. MORETTI, *Inscriptiones Graecae Urbis Romae*, no. 5, vol. 1, Rome, Istituto Italiano per la Storia Antica, 1968.

[15] DESSAU, *Inscriptiones*, no. 32; Lommatszch, *Corpus*, no. 726; DEGRASSI, "Le dediche di popoli", pp. 20-21, no. 2; DEGRASSI, *Inscriptiones*, no. 175.

[16] For references to the length of Aeneas' wanderings, A. PEASE, *P. Vergili Maronis Aeneidos Liber Quartus*, Cambridge, Mass., Harvard University Press, 1935, p. 3, n. 3.

between the two peoples, and Servius may well be right that he considered Pandarus' subjects to have followed Aeneas to Italy.

A final thought might go to an old *crux interpretum*. In the fourth book, Aeneas tells Dido that his mission has been dictated to him by "Gryneian Apollo and Lycian responses": "Italiam magnam Gryneus Apollo,/ Italiam Lyciae iussere capessere sortes" (4.345-346). The obvious interpretation is that he had received responses (since *sortes* need mean no more than this) [17] from two well-known oracles of Apollo, Gryneion in Aeolis and Patara in Lycia: yet when narrating his own wanderings in Book Three the hero mentions only the Apollo of Delos (3.73-120, cf. 162). [18] Servius took Delos to be meant in both lines, arguing that Vergil used "Gryneian" by poetic licence for "Delian", and "Lycian" similarly for "Apolline". [19] Earlier in the fourth book, Vergil compared Aeneas to Apollo leaving Lycia and the waters of Xanthus to spend the summer in Delos, and here the ancient commentators rightly refer to Patara (4.143-145). Both in this comparison and in the enigmatic *Lyciae sortes*, Vergil seems to suggest the involvement of Lycia in the origins of Rome.

[17] P. GLARE, ed., *Oxford Latin Dictionary*, Oxford, Clarendon Press, 1982, s.v. sors 3.

[18] On Gryneion, G. D'ANNA, article "Grinio", *Enciclopedia Virgiliana*, vol. 2, Rome, Istituto della Enciclopedia Italiana, 1985, pp. 807-808; H. W. PARKE, *The Oracles of Apollo in Asia Minor*, London, Sydney, Dover, NH, Croom Helm, 1985, pp. 171-176, G. RAGONE, "Il Tempio di Apollo *Gryneios* in Eolide", in B. Virgilio, ed., *Studi ellenistici*, vol. 3, Pisa, Giardini, 1990, pp. 9-112. On Patara, PARKE, *Oracles of Apollo*, pp. 185-193.

[19] Servius on 4. 345 and 346 (A. Stocker, A. Travis, eds., *Serviani in Aeneidem III-V Commentarii*, Oxford, Oxford University Press, 1965, pp. 363-364); for a recent discussion of the problem, D'ANNA, "Grinio", p. 808. Parthenius used the phrase Γρύνειος Ἀπόλλων in his poem entitled *Delos* (H. Lloyd-Jones and P. Parsons, eds., *Supplementum Hellenisticum*, no. 620, Berlin, New York, de Gruyter, 1983), but the relevance of this to the present question is unclear.

I am grateful to Glen Bowersock for his comments.

JAN ZIOLKOWSKI

VERGIL AS SHAHRAZAD:
HOW AN EASTERN FRAME TALE WAS AUTHORIZED IN THE WEST

The text with which this essay deals is not even loosely speaking a translation of *The Thousand and One Nights*. Even so, John of Alta Silva's *Dolopathos* stands in a close relationship to the great work of Arabic literature, since the Latin prose work presents an intriguing inversion of *The Thousand and One Nights* in its chief characters and themes.[1] At the risk of advancing a conclusion where an exordium belongs, I will reveal that my main aim in this consideration of the *Dolopathos* is to highlight the changes and emphases which our author – a twelfth-century Cistercian monk writing in Latin – is likely to have implemented as he accommodated a very foreign collection of "stories within a story" to his own culture.

The oldest extant fragment of the Arabic *Thousand Nights*, which through a very modest inflation later acquired the title *The Thousand and One Nights* dates from the ninth century. The inaugural European version of *The Thousand and One Nights* began to be published in 1704, when the first of six volumes (1704-1717) by the French Orientalist Antoine Galland (1646-1715) came into print. Since that year the text has enjoyed enormous popularity, becoming famous in English under the telegraphic title of *The Arabian Nights*. However it is entitled, "no work of Arabic or even Islamic literature is as well known to the Western world".[2]

In a splendid essay entitled "The Thousand and One Nights", Jorge Luis Borges hypothesizes engagingly and convincingly that the famous Arabic book originated in innumerable episodes of oral storytelling by countless tellers and that it has changed in each retelling it has received.[3] He contends further that the book

---

[1] Latin citations will be from JOHN OF ALTA SILVA, *Dolopathos*, ed. Alfons Hilka, *Historia septem sapientum. II. Johannis de Alta Silva Dolopathos sive De Rege et Septem Sapientibus*, Sammlung mittellateinischer Texte 5, Heidelberg, Carl Winter, 1913; English from *Dolopathos, or The King and the Seven Wise Men*, translated by Brady B. Gilleland, Medieval and Renaissance Texts and Studies 2, Binghamton, Medieval & Renaissance Texts, 1981.

[2] SANDRA NADDAFF, *Arabesque. Narrative Structure and the Aesthetics of Repetition in "1001 Nights"*, Evanston, Illinois, Northwestern University Press, 1991, pp. 5-6.

[3] "The Thousand and One Nights", in *Seven Nights*, trans. Eliot Weinberger, New York, New Directions, 1984, pp. 42-57 (here: 48): "It is the work of thousands of authors, and none of them knew that he was helping to construct this illustrious book, one of the most illustrious books in all literature". See also Naddaff, p. 5: "this originally oral popular narrative".

has been transformed substantially every time it has been translated into a foreign language. Near the end of the essay Borges posits as an axiom that: "The *Nights* will have other translators and each translator will create a different version of the book".[4]

A more recent analysis of narrative technique in *The Thousand and One Nights* has added the stimulating suggestion that *The Thousand and One Nights* has been particularly prone to textual transformation in part because its narrator is a woman – whereas all of its translators have been men.[5] The essential framework of the book is the story of King Shahriyar who kills his wives successively on the morning after the consummation of their marriages, until the clever Shahrazad (whose name is also sometimes spelled Scheherazade) – the daughter of the King's vizier – contrives to save her life by relating the thousand and one stories of the book over a three-year period. She employs a strategy of interrupting each tale at an interesting juncture, so that she is kept alive to resume and complete the narration on the following night.

In its narrative structure *The Thousand and One Nights* is one of the most famous examples of a frame tale (also known as framed tale, framework-story, frame narrative, and frame story): it is a story within which other stories have been embedded as "tales within a tale".[6] Although there are a few classical texts which might qualify in this or that episode as frame tales (Ovid's *Metamorphoses* and Apuleius' *The Golden Ass* would be two), the form did not achieve full expression in Europe until the Middle Ages. The two best-known early examples in European literature are Boccaccio's *Decameron* (1353) and Chaucer's *Canterbury Tales* (ca. 1390); earlier still is the Latin *Dolopathos*.

Why the form attracted attention from the twelfth century onward and not earlier is a provocative question. Although one answer would be simply that tastes changed as complexly and mysteriously as tastes have always changed, another would be that the frame tale as a structure came into vogue under a particular cultural influence, namely, contact with Eastern and Near-Eastern traditions of storytelling. Such contact grew ever more inten-

---

[4] BORGES, p. 56.

[5] NADDAFF, pp. 5-6: "The text of the *1001 Nights* possesses no fixed boundaries beyond the limits of its frame story. Although certain story cycles recur in all recensions of the *Nights*... they alone do not constitute the sine qua non of *Alf Laylah*. To a large extent, the metamorphic value of this text is due to its original status as oral folklore, and the consequent circumstances of its performance and transmission. But I would suggest that the *1001 Nights* is particularly prone to textual transformation, that its boundaries are particularly flexible, its content, its language, particularly malleable even after it is 'fixed' in print, for two reasons. The first has to do with the essential fact that the all-important narrator of the *1001 Nights* tales themselves is a woman... Jorge Luis Borges's now classic article on the translators of the *1001 Nights* bears witness to the strong desire of any translator of this text to rewrite it in his own image (and all translators of *Alf Laylah* have up to now been men)".

[6] For a discussion of the framing techniques found in *The Thousand and One Nights*, see MIA GERHARDT, *The Art of Story-Telling: A Literary Study of "The Thousand and One Nights"*, Leiden, E. J. Brill, 1963, pp. 395-416. For a broad consideration of framing, see STEPHEN BELCHER, "Framed Tales in the Oral Tradition: An Exploration", *Fabula* 35 (1994), pp. 1-19.

sive and extensive in the twelfth century, thanks to the Crusades, to the per-
egrinations of scholars to such centers of learning as Toledo, and to the rise
of courts in regions such as southern France and Sicily where Arabic culture
was either present or nearby. The impact of written scholarly texts translated
from the Arabic in the twelfth century has long been recognized. These texts,
put into Latin mainly in Spain, altered the intellectual landscape of Latin
Christendom: without them it would be hard to imagine either universities
or scholasticism.[7] Despite the longevity of theories about the Arabic origins
of courtly love and especially of troubadour lyrics, the possible impact of oral
narrative literature from Arabic has not been probed very thoroughly yet.
Such literature could have conditioned the nature of storytelling in Western
Europe not only in the specific motifs and tale-types that are known to have
seeped into European literature from the East in the twelfth century but also
in the very structure of literature – and particularly relevant for the present
purposes would be *narrative structure*.[8] In my view the frame tale may have
been an import as significant to literature as were Arab science and technology or Arab-mediated Aristotelianism in other spheres of culture; and like all
these other importations, the frame tale required time to be absorbed and
accepted.

In scrutinizing the role of Vergil in the *Dolopathos*, I would maintain that European authors faced numerous difficulties in receiving Eastern and Near-Eastern
frame tales, one of which was the relative unfamiliarity of the literary form and
another of which was that sometimes the oriental frame tales traveled attached
to narrators who would not have been acceptable in a medieval European context.
I suggest that John of Alta Silva facilitated the reception of one frame tale by mod-
ulating it to fit the values of the medieval European educational system – for instance, by attaching it to the authority of Vergil and by linking it implicitly with
the seven liberal arts by involving seven sages.

---

[7] JOHN TOLAN, *Petrus Alfonsi and His Medieval Readers*, Gainesville, University Press of Florida, 1993, p. XIII:
"In the twelfth century a wave of Arabic texts swept north across the Pyrenees, changing the intellectual map of
Latin Europe and making possible – in the thirteenth century – the rise of the University of Paris and the birth of
Scholasticism. It was the translators who made this possible, who made these texts over into Latin and, in many
cases, physically brought them north across the Pyrenees".

[8] See MARÍA ROSA MENOCAL, *The Arabic Role in Medieval Literary History: A Forgotten Heritage*, Philadelphia, University of Pennsylvania Press, 1987, p. 60: "It requires no more than one instance of oral translation
– one singer's rendition in Provençal of the gist of a song in Arabic, one retelling in Italian or English of a story
from the *Thousand and One Nights* – to effect the transmission of a bit of literature from one language and
culture to another. It is an anachronism to assume that developments in literature were solely a scholarly enterprise". See also p. 141: "It seems wholly appropriate, for textual reasons alone, that texts such as that of
Petrus Alfonsi – and others less well known in this context but potentially just as informative, including
the *Thousand and One Nights* – should be a part of such a systematic comparative investigation of narrativity
in medieval story collections, not just adduced piecemeal for the isolated story that may have been borrowed
and recast. Given the well-documented popularity of Petrus's text and the fact that there is no possibility of
denying its accessibility, it seems surprising that the *Disciplina* is not regularly adduced in such discussions".

What little we know about John of Alta Silva we must infer from his only extant creation, which survives in six manuscripts, has been edited twice, and has been translated once into modern English. In the first sentence of the dedication, the author addresses Bishop Bertrand of Metz: "Reueren-do patri ac domino Bertrando, dei ordinatione Metensi episcopo, frater Jo-hannes, qualiscumque in Alta Silva monachus, beate uiuere et beatius uite curriculum terminare" ("To our reverend father and lord Bertrand, bishop of Metz by the grace of God, greetings. Brother Johannes, one of the monks of Alta Silva, hopes that he will live long and happily and end the course of his life in peace").[9] Since Bertrand occupied the episcopal see from 1180 to 1212, this sentence enables us to date the writing of the *Dolopathos*.[10] In the second he identifies himself as John, a monk of Alta Silva. Alta Silva (the Latin for Haute Seille) was a Cistercian monastery which had been founded in 1140 in the diocese of Toul. From this monastic affiliation we are justified in making a number of assumptions about John's religious outlook.

Although John's story is usually entitled the *Dolopathos* in modern scholar-ship, the dedication designates it as *opusculum de rege et septem sapientibus*. Apart from the dedication, the work consists of a preface and a frame tale, which contains eight inset-stories (one of which itself encloses another two stories). The frame of the tale takes place in Palermo during the reign of Cae-sar Augustus. After surviving a treacherous plot, King Dolopathos and his wife have a son. When Prince Lucinius is seven, he is sent to be tutored by Vergil. Seven years later, Lucinius is summoned home because his mother has died and his father has remarried. For unspecified reasons Lucinius is enjoined by Vergil not to speak until he and Vergil meet again. After Lucinius' muteness elicits concern at the court, the new queen undertakes to cure him of his ail-ment through allopathic treatment: since his condition was obviously provoked by sorrow, they would remedy it by inducing him to feel pleasure through a variety of means – culminating in sexual therapy. When her stepson spurns the passionate advances not only of the loveliest women in the queen's retinue – who behave more like courtisans than courtiers – but even of the queen step-mother herself, she takes offense and accuses him of rape. The death sentence decreed by his enraged father is postponed by a day every day for seven days as seven different sages materialize and tell stories. Finally Vergil appears and tells

---

[9] Ed. Hilka, p. 1.1-3; trans. Gilleland, p. 1.

[10] Gilleland and others are mistaken in the date of 1179: see WOLFGANG MAAZ, review of Gilleland's tran-slation, *Fabula*, 25 (1984), pp. 345-349 (here: p. 347), who proposes narrowing to *terminus post quem* to 1189-1190. STEPHEN BELCHER, "The Diffusion of the Book of Sindbād", *Fabula*, 29 (1987) 34-58 (here: pp. 50 and 51), writes of a dating "roughly between 1190 and 1210" although he also describes the text as having been "writ-ten between 1190 and 1205".

a story on Lucinius' behalf. Eventually Lucinius is freed, whereas the queen and her henchmen are executed.

The general outlines of the *Dolopathos* resemble two cycles of stories very popular in the late Middle Ages, a Near-Eastern one known as the *The Book of Sindebar* (also known as Sindibad or Sindbād – but *not* related to the character known as Sindbad of the Sea or Sindbad the Sailor) and a Western European one known as *The Seven Sages of Rome*.[11] "Just how *The Seven Sages* as it appeared in the East in the *Book of Sindibad* became the story as it flourished in Western Europe is a question not easy to answer".[12] And just where the *Dolopathos* should be placed in the stemma of the cycle's evolution is even more difficult to resolve. "It agrees with the former in that the prince has only one tutor, the poet Vergil".[13] It agrees "with the latter by having each sage tell only one story [whereas in the Sindibad cycle each relates two stories, one against haste and the other on the spite of women]. It disagrees with both Western and Eastern versions by suppressing the stories... [that are told by the queen or concubine each day] and showing no indication that Vergil the tutor, is acquainted with the Seven Sages... probably... the similarities between the *Book of Sindibad* and the *Dolopathos* do not show an Oriental original and that the three stories... it has in common with the *Seven Sages of Rome* indicate a closer relationship".[14]

The Western version shares too few features with any extant Eastern version to be considered a translation. If not a translation, could the Western version not have grown in part out of oral traditions – many of which may have come from the East?[15] Certainly John's version was based partly on oral sources, unless we refuse to take John at his word when he asserts that his frame story came to him orally:

[11] On the origins of the Book of Sindibad, the authoritative starting point is BEN EDWIN PERRY, "The Origin of the Book of Sindbad", *Fabula*, 3 (1959-1960), pp. 1-94 (also printed separately Berlin, 1960). For an insightful attempt to fill gaps in Perry, see BELCHER, "The Diffusion". On the relationship between the *Dolopathos* and the Seven Sages, see DETLEV FEHLING, *Amor und Psyche. Die Schöpfung des Apuleius und ihre Einwirkung auf das Märchen, eine Kritik der romantischen Märchentheorie*, Akademie der Wissenschaften und der Literatur: Abhandlungen der geistes- und sozialwissenschaften Klasse 1977, no. 9, Wiesbaden, Akademie der Wissenschaften und der Literatur, 1977, pp. 87-97.

[12] See Killis Campbell, ed., *The Seven Sages of Rome*, Boston, Ginn & Company, 1907, p. XV.

[13] Gilleland, p. 37. Compare Campbell, p. XII: "An even more salient difference is found in that, in the East, the instruction of the Prince is intrusted, not (as in the Western versions) to the seven sages, but to one man, the philosopher Sindibad. This Sindibad is the central figure of the Eastern versions; and it is for this reason that the Eastern form of *The Seven Sages* has been called the *Book of Sindibad*".

[14] Gilleland, p. 37 (with my additions in brackets).

[15] This theory is not a new one. See for instance DOMENICO COMPARETTI, *Researches Respecting the Book of Sindibad*, trans. H. C. Coote, Folklore Society 9, London, 1882, p. 2: "Only oral tradition transmutes the contents of a popular book in that manner, and it is certainly that which stands between the Eastern and the Western groups", and Campbell, p. XVI: "Such far-reaching changes establish conclusively that the parent Western version was not a translation from any Eastern version... In my judgment, they demonstrate beyond any reasonable doubt that the Western parent version grew out of oral accounts".

Hic ergo narrationi mee finem imponens lectorem rogo ne incredibilia uel impossibilia me scripsisse contendat nec me iudicet reprehensibilem, quasi eos imitatus sim quorum uitia in libri prefatiuncula carpserim, quia non ut uisa sed ut audita ad delectationem et utilitatem legentium, si qua forte ibi sint, a me scripta sunt; quamquam etiam etsi facta non sint, fieri tamen potuisse credendum.[16]

This is the end of my story. I hope the reader will not think that I have written things incredible or impossible. Nor must he accuse me of imitating those whose faults I criticized in the preface of my book. These tales, which I did not read but heard, were written by me to please and instruct the reader. I hope I have accomplished my purpose. Even if they didn't really happen, they could have happened.

If John fabricated his claim of an oral source, he would be swimming against the tide: although many medieval authors claimed as their sources texts which are unlikely ever to have existed, it is hard to find an example of one who claimed an oral source when he actually used a written one. But the information at our disposal is far too slight to enable us ever to narrow down what these oral sources were. Possibly John had one oral informant who related to him the stories in the order we have. Maybe he had more than one informant and heard variant versions of the same basic story. Perhaps he had one informant for the basic structure of the frame tale and others from whom he heard stories that he included to substitute for embedded tales that he had forgotten or that struck him as unsuitable; and nothing would have prevented him from embellishing a frame taken from oral sources with embedded tales that he drew from written sources. We cannot determine definitively even whether John heard the story as told by a storyteller who was relating what he had once heard (or read), or whether he heard it from a person who read it to him while translating simultaneously from a book in a foreign language.

Much effort has been expended in trying to discover both the immediate origins of the individual stories that John heard and their ultimate origins. For the immediate origins tempting but ultimately unverifiable hypotheses have been that the vector was a crusader, a pilgrim, or a Jewish merchant.[17] In any event, although a few of the stories were probably western European in origin, it is agreed that the essential frame of the story came from the East.[18] One controversial hy-

---

[16] Ed. Hilka, p. 107.26-32, trans. Gilleland, p. 95. For consideration of this passage, see Hilka, p. VII (quoting Latin on p. 107, line 29); Campbell, p. XX; and Morris Epstein, ed. and trans., *Tales of Sendebar*, Philadelphia, Jewish Publication Society of America, 1967, p. 334. Recently the fullest opposition to the proposition that John drew on oral sources has come from FEHLING, pp. 91-93.

[17] K. CAMPBELL, "A Study of the Romance of the Seven Sages", *Publications of the Modern Language Association of America*, 14 (1899), pp. 1-107 (here: pp. 13-19), deals with several possibilities. See also BELCHER, "The Diffusion", p. 52.

[18] PAUL GERHARD SCHMIDT, "Der Rangstreit zwischen Mann und Frau im lateinischen Mittelalter. Mit einer Edition der 'Altercatio inter virum et mulierem'," in *Dispute Poems and Dialogues in the Ancient and Mediaeval Near East. Forms and Types of Literary Debates in Semitic and Related Literatures*, ed. Gerrit Jan Reinink and Herman L. J. Vanstiphout, Orientalia Lovaniensia Analecta 42, Leuven, Departement Orientalistiek-Peeters, 1991, pp. 213-235 (here: p. 217), puts the case very clearly that the *Dolopathos* shows "many connections with the Me-

pothesis is that similarities between the Seven Sages and Hebrew versions hint at who might have mediated the tale to Europe:[19] Jews would have been ideal intermediaries of stories between the East and the West.

Whatever the source of the stories, John – for all his typically medieval protestations of inadequacy to his task – was a sufficiently experienced reader and writer to realize that he had to shape it to be instructive or edifying if he wished to offer it to a lofty ecclesiastic dedicatee and to have it succeed. The lack of a response from Bertrand to John's request for a reaction and corrections might indicate that John failed to achieve his goal of making the tale suitable and that the *Dolopathos* was deemed to be too unconventional. Yet I would argue that if John did founder, it was not for want of efforts on his part to redeem the raw material at his disposal. The *Dolopathos* burgeons with signs that its author understood the tastes, values, and interests of his prospective Latin-reading audience and that through Vergilianization and Christianization he calibrated his composition to suit their expectations.

John of Alta Silva transformed the setting of the story by locating its main action in an ancient Roman context. He realigned the frame of the story spatially and temporally by fixing it in Italy and in the reign of Augustus. The action takes place in Sicily, which John may have chosen deliberately as a halfway point between the East and the West.[20] Sicily must have seemed very remote to John, whose grasp of Italian geography was so faulty that he believed Mantua to be a Sicilian city![21]

The Sicilian location of the action takes on special significances in the light of postcolonial criticism (and I hope that the *præcolonial* Cistercian monk John is not turning in his grave at the anachronism of my introducing this topic!), which stresses the importance of paying attention to setting. In an already classic but ever controversial study of attitudes toward the East manifested in Western literature, Edward Said in *Orientalism* takes issue with what he considers "Eurocentric universalism" – an assumption that what is European or Western is superior to what is not.[22] Said reasons that although Westerners regard the Ori-

---

diterranean world, although they have not been clarified in their details". On John's use of some local materials, see JEAN-CLAUDE SCHMITT, *The Holy Greyhound: Guinefort, Healer of Children since the Thirteenth Century*, trans. Martin Thom, Cambridge, Cambridge University Press, 1983, p. 42.

[19] The chief exponents of the view that the Hebrew version was the original version of the Sindibad stories have been EPSTEIN and DETLEV FEHLING, "Die Eingesperrte ('Inclusa') und der verkleidete Jüngling ('Iuvenis femina'). Neues zur Traditionsgeschichte zweier antiker Komödienmotive nebst einem Beitrag zur Geschichte des 'Sindbad'-Zyklus", *Mittellateinisches Jahrbuch*, 21 (1986), pp. 186-207 (here: p. 192). Against this view, see NORMAN ROTH, "The 'Wiles of Women' Motif in the Medieval Hebrew Literature of Spain", *Hebrew Annual Review*, 2 (1978) 145-165 (here pp. 158-159), and BELCHER, "The Diffusion", pp. 39-40 and 51.

[20] BELCHER, "The Diffusion", p. 54, explains the setting of the tale as being "Sicily rather than Rome because no heir of Augustus' became a Christian".

[21] Ed. Hilka, p. 14.2; trans. Gilleland, pp. 13-14.

[22] EDWARD W. SAID, *Orientalism*, New York, Vintage Books, 1979.

ent as an exotic and seductive place, they make the East the repository of those traits, such as cruelty, decadence, and sensuality, which they do not wish to acknowledge in themselves. They portray Orientals as operating in accord with instinct rather than reason. Although Said's arguments were formulated in response to colonial and postcolonial literature, major elements of them can be applied fruitfully – *mutatis mutandis* – to the precolonial environment of the *Dolopathos*; for John assumes for the Latin and the Christian a superiority over the Sicilian which would later be characteristic of Europe and the West as they judged the East.

The Thousand and One Nights has been analyzed as having constituted a kind of etiquette book.[23] However tenuous the relation between it and the *Dolopathos*, it is fascinating to observe that as John of Alta Silva adapted the Seven Sages to his culture, he coordinated it in a comparable way with the mores of the Latin Cistercian culture in which he operated: the manners he had in mind were the customs of Cistercian monasticism.

One aspect of the frame story which lent itself especially well to the Cistercian way of life was the unquestioning – and unexplained – silence that Vergil enjoins upon Lucinius. Although silence is a motif attested amply in non-Cistercian literature such as the *Vita Secundi* (translated at the latest by the second half of the twelfth century) and the *Roman de Silence* (second half of the thirteenth century),[24] there can be no doubt that silence was a topic of particular interest to Cistercian monks, whose order imposed upon them rigorous speechlessness. In the *Dolopathos* silence appears in conjunction with obedience and chastity.[25]

Another feature of the book – both the frame and the inset stories – that would have been greeted approvingly by monks of many orders was its misogyny.[26] The telling of all the inset stories is precipitated by the false accusation of the lust-crazed stepmother, who first attempts to seduce Lucinius and then sets out to have him executed. This crisis in the frame narrative is resolved definitively – or authoritatively – by Vergil, who recounts a tale and produces an anti-feminist harangue as bitter as any in medieval literature. To culminate his diatribe on woman as the root of all evils, Vergil states: "Per mulierem denique totus perditus est mundus. Grande malum mulier" ("The whole world was lost through a woman. A woman is a great evil").[27]

---

[23] JAMES M. B. KEYSER, "*1001 Nights*: A Famous Etiquette Book", *Edebiyat*, 3 (1978), 11-22.

[24] On silence as a theme in medieval literature, see R. HOWARD BLOCH, "Silence and Holes: The *Roman de Silence* and the Art of the Trouvère", *Yale French Studies*, 70 (1986), pp. 81-99; VOLKER ROLOFF, *Reden und Schweigen: Zur Tradition und Gestaltung eines mittelalterlichen Themas in der französischen Literatur*, Munich, Wilhelm Fink, 1973; and UWE RUBERG, *Beredtes Schweigen in lehrhafter und erzählender deutscher Literatur des Mittelalters*, Munich, Wilhelm Fink, 1978.

[25] Trans. Gilleland, pp. 20 and 80.

[26] In accord with SCHMIDT, "Der Rangstreit", p. 218, and pace BELCHER, "The Diffusion", p. 55, who sees a "suppression of the anti-feminism in the book".

[27] Ed. Hilka, p. 88.13-15; trans. Gilleland, p. 77. On this passage, see SCHMIDT, "Rangstreit", p. 218.

The misogyny in the *Dolopathos* receives its decisive expression in the words of Vergil, which are not contested by the stepmother or any other female character. This final explosion of sentiments against women completes a process by which the female point of view has been excised or suppressed in John's work as in no other representative of the Seven Sages cycle.

The Thousand and One Nights constitutes in this respect the polar opposite of the *Dolopathos*. The impulse behind its frame is deeply misogynistic: King Shahriyar sleeps each night with a virgin and has her beheaded in the morning because he and his brother have discovered that their own wives and other women are unfaithful. But this misogyny fails to withstand both the actions and the words of Shahrazad (Scheherezade), who by telling her stories for three years both saves her own life and in the process redeems womankind as a whole.[28] If we step back and compare the *Thousand and One Nights* and *Dolopathos*, the difference between them comes into instantly sharp focus: whereas Shahrazad employs her stories to overcome the king's wanton sexuality and hostility toward women, the Seven Sages (and particularly Vergil) use their tales against the wanton sexuality and vindictiveness of the stepmother/queen.

John's attention gravitates powerfully to the male characters. Although Lucinius occupies center stage, the story is very father-centered in giving ample information about both the biological and the intellectual fathers of this character, to wit, Dolopathos and Vergil. The prominence of female characters (apart from the antagonist) – and even more so of female narrators – is correspondingly reduced. A major distinction between the *Dolopathos* and almost all other versions of the Seven Sages is that whereas the stepmother's role as an actor in the frame tale remains virtually unchanged, her role as a narrator is non-existent: the stepmother in the Latin does not tell any tales to respond to the ones that the seven wise men relate. We could devise different explanations to account for this circumstance: John of Alta Silva could have been using a version of the Seven Sages in which the stepmother told no tales; he could have heard a version in which the stepmother told tales but he could have neglected to include them in his version; and he could have known that she told tales but he could have opted to omit them anyway.[29] Of these the last-mentioned persuades me the most: unlike an oral storyteller or writer whose audience counted women among its members, a monk writing for clerical readers

---

[28] See WENDY FARIS, "1001 Words: Fiction Against Death", *Georgia Review*, 36 (1982), pp. 811-830 (here: p. 815).

[29] JESSIE CROSLAND, "*Dolopathos* and the Seven Sages of Rome", *Medium Aevum*, 25 (1956), pp. 1-12 (here: p. 3), singles out for attention an important characteristic of the *Dolopathos*. "This brings us to an important difference between the *Dolopathos* and practically all other versions of the legend, both oriental and occidental... in the *Dolopathos* the queen tells no stories. Gaston Paris suggests that the author just forgot them. This seems very unlikely if the *Dolopathos*, as has been so often supposed, had some version of the 'Seven Sages of Rome' before his eyes. Hilka merely remarks that he has completely suppressed them and offers no explanation. But the real question is – were they in the original at all?"

would have felt under no obligation to provide "equal time" or even partial time to a female character.

Finally, and more speculatively, I would propose that the closing section of the frame – in which we are told of the manner in which an early Christian converted Lucinius to his faith – emphasizes conversion preaching, which would have held special appeal among the Cistercians. In a sense John here retrojects upon the past Cistercian behavior in his own day. The White Monks were active as preachers: the Cistercian Luke of Sambucina was appointed by Pope Innocent III to preach the Fourth Crusade, and Arnold Amaury was one of numerous Cistercians to participate in the Crusade against the Albigensians. Not coincidentally, the first "art of preaching" was written by Alan of Lille, the renowned *doctor uniuersalis* of Paris who converted to Cistercianism and who preached against the Cathars (as well as in many other contexts).

Of course, not everything about the *Dolopathos* was dictated by its author's monasticism. For instance, John's choice of Vergil as the true hero of the work was not a Cistercian touch but rather a feature that would have resonated well with all readers capable of appreciating John's Latin prose, since anyone with a Latin education had learned the language in a Vergiliocentric school system. Accordingly, John brings forth Vergil in place of Sindebar/Syntipas or whoever had fulfilled the function of sage in Eastern versions. John associates Vergil not with Caesar Augustus but with King Dolopathos, who seems to hold the kingdom of Sicily as a tributary of Augustus.

On the whole John's information about Vergil is consistent with what the great nineteenth-century Italian master of the Vergilian tradition, Domenico Comparetti, designated as *literary legends*. These legends built upon Vergil's reputation as the best Roman poet to make of him a supreme wise man, an omniscient philosopher, and even a necromancer. John ascribed to his Vergil all of these qualities, even making him in his authority and wisdom all but Christian. He may not have been a Christian but at least he educated a great prince who converted to Christianity. He may not have been a Christian but at least in his poetry he foretold the coming of Christ, the Virgin, and the Crucifixion.[30]

John plays upon the powerful associations between Vergil and basic education by referring twice punningly to the conventional etymological similarity between the name *Virgilius* and the noun *virga*.[31] Education in the Classics long retained an

---

[30] Ed. Hilka, p. 104.28; trans. Gilleland, p. 93.

[31] Ed. Hilka, p. 16.10-11: "... ceterum autem sine Virgilio suo, cum fidei sue commissus esset et magisterii eius virgam supra modum pertimesceret..". (trans. Gilleland, p. 15: "... he did not dare to do anything at all without his teacher Virgil who was his guardian and whose ferule he feared very much"), and ed. Hilka, p. 18.4-5: "... paremque eum sibi in omni facultate Virgilius predicaret, nunquam tamen ei consedere voluit vel equari, sed semper sub virga eius et disciplina mansit..". (trans. Gilleland, p. 17: "Virgil proclaimed that he was equal to him in every way, nevertheless he never was willing to sit in his presence or be considered his equal. He always remained under his ferule and discipline").

association with corporal punishment, because of an assumption that a child would not learn Latin if spared the rod. Though the connection is never made explicit, John implies that the *virga* plays an indispensable role in Vergil's indoctrination of Lucinius.

Without this moral instruction that he had received from Vergil and his *virga*, Lucinius would not have been able to resist the guiles of the *virgunculae*, the houris in the queen's entourage who strive to practice "seduction therapy" on Lucinius (35.8-9). Although critics have deemed it curious that John should have assigned Vergil a misogynistic outlook,[32] the connection is understandable: Vergil exemplified grammar-teaching; grammar-teaching was an almost entirely all-male rite of passage that imparted an unfavorable view of women; and therefore Vergil must have had strong suspicions about women.

John sees fully the risk he runs in appropriating oral literature and in justifying it by associating it with the *auctor* of *auctores*, Vergil. He is well aware of the game that he plays in promoting his writing as both history and story. The paradox begins as soon as he introduces his theme, when he claims that he was propelled to write this most unclassical of accounts first from meditation on the classics and then from realization that no one would have heard of the story he sets out to relate. He knows that his narrative is not so much history (*res gestae* – or *regis gesta* in the phrase he employs on p. 3.18) as story (*narratio* p. 107.26):[33]

Ego autem dum ueterum recolo studium, dum eorum ammiror ingenia, cuiusdam regis gesta, sub quo et cui mira contigerunt, subito in memoriam deuenerunt. Que quia adhuc scriptoribus intacta uel forsitan incognita permanebant, timens ne tanta tanti regis opera paulatim successu temporis a memoria hominum omni cum tempore laberentur, presumpsi ea quamquam elinguis et ydiota, quamquam nullius discipline scienciam assecutus, saltem qualicumque stillo describere, non tam materiam phaleratis uerborum pompis cupiens colorare uel ut uerius decolorare dicam, quam materie ueritatem, prout res geste sunt, simplici pedestrique calamo satagens declarare.[34]

Once when I was deep in the study and admiration of the classics, I happened to recall the history of a certain king and the amazing things which happened to him during his reign. No writer had yet written about him, possibly because no one else had heard of his deeds, and I was worried lest the great history of this great king pass into oblivion as time went by. Although I am rather stupid and have no talent or training, I decided

---

[32] CROSLAND, p. 10: "It is not till we arrive at the last and eighth story in the *Dolopathos* that we meet with the genuine anti-feminist tale; and this, curiously enough, is put into the mouth of Virgil the Teacher".

[33] On the connection between story and history, note FRANZ-JOSEF SCHMALE, *Funktion und Formen mittelalterlicher Geschichtsschreibung: Eine Einführung*, Darmstadt, Wissenschaftliche Buchgesellschaft, 1985, for both Schmale's discussion of genres and Hans-Werner Goetz's appendix on the place of history in the system of medieval learning, and NANCY PARTNER, *Serious Entertainments: The Writing of History in Twelfth-Century England*, Chicago, University of Chicago Press, 1977, p. 195.

[34] Ed. Hilka, p. 3.16-27; trans. Gilleland, p. 4.

nevertheless to write about these things as best I could. I did not want to color (or rather discolor) the subject with an ornamental display of words but rather to write the history just as it happened in a simple prose style.

At the same time, John has little choice but to be daring; for although the links connecting his book to Vergil are farfetched, they give the story a strength that it would not have if it had dealt with an otherwise unknown sage.

The attachment of this frame tale to Vergil and a tutee of his, together with the misogyny, made sense within the ecclesiastic milieux in which John identified his readership. Nearly five hundred years would pass before female readers and writers came to represent a strong enough force for a shift of 180 degrees to take place – for a frame tale to be ascribed entirely to a woman. Shahrazad had to wait until Vergil and the rest of the Ancients had been engaged in battle by the Moderns – who included the dozens of women who took part actively in the first publishing boom of fairy tales in the late seventeenth century in France. Until then, the legendary Vergil was as close as one could come to Shahrazad in the writings of western Europe.

RON D. K. BANERJEE

THE DARKENING HEART AND THE ICON OF LIGHT: CAVALCANTI

Nearly seven centuries have passed since the death of Guido Cavalcanti in exile at Sarzana, in August 1300. Acknowledged in his lifetime as the leader of the *dolce stil novo*[1] both as its theoretician and the dominant poetic voice, young Dante's *"primo amico"*, he still remains as enigmatic a poet as he had been to his contemporaries. Aristocratic and aloof in his posture, philosopher by reputation despite the turbulence of his public life, his martial vigour and partisan passion, the unique concerns which shape the heart of his poetry seem to have been blurred by the mythic aura that surrounds him at the side of Dante. He seems merely to occupy a special niche like an isolate Gothic statue in the cathedral that is Dante's *opus*. Several factors interfere with our attempt to recover the fullness and originality of his poetic achievement on its own terms.

Literary history, of necessity, organises around the great 'touchstones' of literature, as Matthew Arnold thought. And Dante's towering genius as poet and critic, like a giant star bends our line of approach to the Italian Middle Ages. So De Sanctis, like many others, reads Cavalcanti on the way to Dante: *"E fu artefice più che artista"*.[2] Even though he allows Guido the status of *"il primo poeta italiano"*, no matter the fine Sicilian poets and Guinicelli, it is as Dante's precursor, one of those stragglers in the triumphal procession that led to the *Commedia*. Karl Vossler's comment[3] best sums up this view of Cavalcanti: "He stands like a great and nobly conceived but broken column by the road which Dante followed to the end, to completion". This assumption that there was but one Dantean way to follow insinuates itself even among more modern critics who thus find Cavalcanti's poetic vision either fragmented or phantas-

---

[1] All references to Cavalcanti's poems, their sequence indicated by Roman numerals, are to G. CONTINI, *Poeti del Dolce Stil Novo*, Milano, Mondadori, 1991.

[2] F. DE SANCTIS, *Storia della letteratura italiana*, Vol. I, Torino, Einaudi, 1958, p. 57.

[3] K. VOSSLER, *Medieval Culture: An Introduction to Dante and His Times*, Vol. II, New York, Unger, 1958, p. 148.

magoric, lacking in a capacity for transcending *"l'angoscia carnale"*.[4] The reason seems to be that the Cavalcantian 'transcendence' does not derive from the Christian scheme which both Guinicelli and Dante accept. Of course, there are others like Pound[5] who lean in the opposite direction, reading Cavalcanti as a heterodox rebel in contrast to the orthodox Dante, who allegedly had swallowed wholesale the Aquinian universe, a view that both Nardi[6] and Gilson[7] have refuted.

Other than the innate difficulty of bypassing Dante's *opus* in approaching Cavalcanti, Dante's imposition of his own figural scheme on Cavalcanti's poetry creates complications. Even young Dante, for an example, coined the *senhal* *"Primavera"/"prima verrà"* in *Vita Nuova XXIV* from Guido's *"Fresca rosa novella"*, without the slightest warranty, in keeping with his Giovanna/Giovanni analogy in relation to the analogy Beatrice/Christ. And it is a key to his own view of Cavalcanti, who prefigures him only to be superceded. As Contini pointed out, there is no sign that Cavalcanti accepted it.[8] In fact, while his response to Dante's *"A ciascun'alma presa"* engages the poem seriously (Sonnet XXXVII), he remains detached and chalks out his private space in reply to Dante's enthusiastic *"Guido, i' vorrei"*, albeit politely. His aloofness, often ironical as in some exchanges with Guido Orlandi, contrasts with Dante's attempt to draw him into his own design.

For not only is Dante's *opus* a *summa* of Medieval Italian literature as Curtius[9] said, there is that sense on Dante's part that a diapason of creative energy was moving towards him. Thus, *"Credette Cimabue nella pintura / tener lo campo, e ora ha Giotto il grido, / sì, che la fama di colui è scura: / così ha tolto l'uno all'altro Guido / la gloria della lingua; e forse è nato / chi l'uno e l'altro caccerà del nido"*. *(Purgatorio XI, 94-99)*. Even in the perspective of *vana gloria*, it is a great tribute to Cavalcanti, lifting him above Guinicelli, but Dante himself remains the implicit point of converging creative energies, the chosen one for a sacred task. So it is not fortuitous that his own poetic quest in *Inferno* X, 55-72; 110-14 shapes his ambiguous allusion to Guido, in the encounter between the pilgrim Dante and Cavalcanti's father Cavalcante dei Cavalcanti. Nor is it by chance that the oblique allusion made in the circle of the Heretics should have cast a shadow on Guido's biography.

Even ignoring the New Critics' warning against Intentional Fallacy, *intentio auc-*

---

[4] N. SAPEGNO, "Cultura e Poesia in Guido Cavalcanti", M. Fubini and E. Bonora (eds.), *Antologia della Critica Letteraria: I: Dalle Origini alla fine del Trecento*, Torino, Petrini, 1967, pp. 207ff.

[5] E. POUND, "Cavalcanti: Medievalism", *Literary Essays*, New Directions, 1968, p. 159.

[6] B. NARDI, *Dante e la cultura medievale*, Bari, Laterza, 1990.

[7] E. GILSON, *Dante and Philosophy*, New York, Evanston, London, Harper, 1963. See especially chapters III & IV.

[8] CONTINI, *Poeti, op. cit.*, p. 54, n. 2.

[9] E. R. CURTIUS, *European Literature and the Latin Middle Ages*, New York, Harper, 1963, p. 379.

toris as Eco[10] terms it, is elusive; since language seems to break out perpetually of any sort of denotative constraints. How much more so in this instance of a coded allusion circled by hesitation and a pause? So Vossler[11] thought Dante was referring to Guido's lack of interest in the Classical tradition – implausible, given the pervasive influence of the Latin classics at the time as Battaglia[12] shows, and Cavalcanti's scholarship. Again, as Contini[13] notes, grammatically the object of "*disdegno*" is Beatrice, neither Virgil nor God. Figurelli interpreted it as "*di carattere filosofico e religioso, non letterario e poetico*",[14] and dismissed Boccaccio's "*diceria*" in *Decameron* VI, IX which suggested that Cavalcanti had been a heretic, probably on the basis of his reading of *Inferno* X.

But that Boccaccio knew Dino del Garbo, the first commentator on Cavalcanti and a contemporary, has helped to keep the theory alive. As Figurelli said,[15] the myth of Guido as a romantic rebel stems from this, although neither Dino Compagni's *Cronica* nor Giovanni Villani's *Cronaca*, both contemporary Florentine sources, supports Boccaccio. So this is a case where *intentio lectoris* seems to have prevailed over both *intentio auctoris* and history. The same sort of ambiguity works in the reverse when it comes to interpreting Guido's own poems addressed to Dante. One example would suffice to show why, absent any firm chronology for Guido's poems, one is thrown on inferences in interpreting the design underlying Cavalcanti's poetry, hoping to arrive at the *intentio operis*.

Cavalcanti's *I' vegno 'l giorno a te* (Sonnet XLI) directed to Dante is obviously a "*rimprovero*" but what occasioned it has been in question. D'Ovidio and Contini[16] suggest that it was written to shake up a Dante prostrate with grief after the death of Beatrice. Pagliaro thinks it was occasioned by literary and philosophical divergence between the two friends. Montanelli feels that Dante had fallen into low life,[17] after Beatrice's death, thus Guido's harsh tone with Dante who is accused of "*l'anima invilita*" (*vil* and *vilmente* implicating Dante's life and thought appear as well). Some think it refers to Dante's desertion of the Grandi to sign on to a guild which Guido refused to do, thus disqualifying himself from holding public office according to the law. Quaglio would relate it to the break between the two which led to Cavalcanti's exile in the Spring of 1300.[18]

---

[10] U. Eco, "Overinterpreting Texts", Stepan Collini (ed.), *Interpretation and Overinterpretation*, Cambridge, New York, Port Chester, Melbourne, Sydney, 1992. Also see Collini's "Introduction: Interpretation terminable and interminable", in the same volume.

[11] Vossler, *Medieval Culture, op. cit.*, p. 147.

[12] S. Battaglia, *La coscienza letteraria del medioevo*, Napoli, Liguori, 1965.

[13] Contini, *Poeti, op. cit.*, p. 53.

[14] F. Figurelli, "Guido Cavalcanti", *Letteratura italiana: i minori*, Vol. V, Milano, Marzorati, 1969, p. 220.

[15] *Ibid.*, p. 221.

[16] Contini, *Poeti, op. cit.*, p. 53; p. 112.

[17] A. E. Quaglio, *Gli Stilnovisti*, E. Pasquini and A. E. Quaglio, *Lo stilnovo e la poesia religiosa*, Bari, Laterza, 1971, p. 57.

[18] I. Montanelli, *Dante e il suo secolo*, Milano, Rizzoli, 1965, p. 263.

Both the last two explanations are congruent with the public theme in the poem – the linkage between the threat of "*lo spirito noioso*" to Dante for keeping company with "*la noiosa gente*". If I lean towards Quaglio, it is because of the intimate pathos of the first line accented by the hyperbole in "*'nfinite volte*", which implies visits in the imagination to one dearly loved that do not take place. The breach seems complete, beyond face to face encounter. But one can only make an inference from the rhetoric, not state it as a fact.

Cavalcanti was a great lyric poet of a strong, if eclectic philosophical bent and technically superb. As commonly agreed, he expanded the horizon of Italian poetry by incorporating into it physiology, just as Guinicelli had done with astronomy. He also based on it his psychology of *l'amour-passion*, lending a more rigorous definition and sharper edge to the conventions and vocabulary of Courtly Love, mostly by subtle variations. And often his innovations show in little details, not in the explicitly stated conceptual frame. Thus, in his great canzone *Donna, mi prega*, where he turns dialectics into song, his true originality lies in that subtle shift to *Marte* as a source of the malignancy of passion, with the fine metaphor of "*diaffan da lume, – d'una scuritate*", fusing the polarities of light and darkness that spell the ambiguity of passion.

Otherwise, apart from sheer virtuosity, most of the ideas in the poem are not original, as Nardi's commentary showed. While I do not agree with Contini that it is parodistic,[19] it is a *gioco* as a response to a common *quaestio* put by Orlandi ("*è vita questo amore o vero la morte*"?), anticipated by Mostacci's *quaestio* to Piero delle Vigne. Cappellanus in *De Amore I* had already set up its parameters: "*Est igitur primo vedere, quid sit amor, et unde dicatur amor, et quis sit effectus amoris et inter quos possit esse amor...*". But Cavalcanti differs in keeping to a high intellectual level, uninterested in the practical, 'how to' approach of the pimpish Cappellanus. Nonetheless, as a key to Guido's poetry, the importance of the *canzone* can be exaggerated, although it does clarify some of his terms, relating to the role physiology plays in defining *teleios bios*.

The world of the lyric is self-enclosed, projected by the lyric voice which in its turn implies the speaker's location within its magic circle. As Langbaum said, there are no external criteria to judge lyric autenticity.[20] Yet, as it is overheard, the audience seeks verification. It is in response to that demand that paralleling the Troubadour lyrics rose the *vidas* and *razos*. Dante's *Vita Nuova* is a genial fusion of these elements into a spiritual autobiography. But Caval-

---

[19] Contini, *Poeti, op. cit.*, p. 54, writes that it verges on "*parodia e del gioco*". If *gioco* involves the interplay between *jeu* and *joy*, as analysed by CHARLES CAMPROUX, *Le Joy d'Amor des Troubadours: jeu et joie d'amour*, Montpellier, Causse & Castelnau, 1965, I agree.

[20] ROBERT LANGBAUM, *The Poetry of Experience*, New York, 1957. While Langbaum is writing about the modern lyric, his comments about the lyric enclosure, even as a poem's form may mimic 'objectivity' hold true about the lyric in general. Especially, epiphanies hinge on the unique experience projected by the lyric voice.

canti's poetry provides no such context. Yet underlying them, there is the unifying theme of a quest for *teleion agathon*, as Nardi uses the Aristotelean term, both in splendid epiphany and the desperate sense of its repeated loss. The cycle of visionary triumph and existential *angst* form a single continuum in Cavalcanti. They are polarities linked by the ebb and flow of vital energy. To read them as merely alternating instances in separate lyrics is to misread his poetry. In this brief essay, I shall touch only on a few poems to make my point. And I shall use three key terms in his dialectical design for the discussion: the Self, the Lady and the relational term Love.

It is generally agreed that Cavalcanti confines himself to the world of Nature which Averroes treated as an autonomous sphere. In visionary moments, he touches its extremes where the Unknowable is intuited. But with scrupulous rigour, he treats it as indescribable, beyond language, and presents it in the icon of the Donna. Akin to Sophia, she is the felt emblem for an ideal of demiurgic contemplation of Truth. A haunting presence, she affects the whole man, *vis animalis* to *vis sensibilis*. The dream of pure contemplation may entail sacrificing *plazer/piacimento* ("*non ha diletto ma consideranza*") but in his poetry, she remains the two-way mirror that both reflects the total self and bears intimations of the unknowable, manifesting radiant energy. And, no matter the ideal, there is no pretended *askesis* in Cavalcanti. He is no disembodied spirit. So at the opposite end of the visionary horizon is the irreducible fact of the body, with its tentacular exigencies which find their arena in the body's central organ, the heart. That is where light threatens to dwindle into darkness.

Cavalcanti, too, indulged in the Guittonean pun "*Ah, mors!*", that literary sigh (*eg.*, "*ella more*" in Sonnet VII), but the sense of personal mortality is intrinsic to his poetry. Yet, except in his last poem Ballatetta XXXV, there is hardly a reference to his own body. References to *cor, occhi*, etc., are conventional and thereby universal, as is the physiology that is the underpinning of his psychology of love.

His "*angoscia carnale*" is a reflex of the human condition, although only an *élite* (*I Fideli d'Amore*) share its awareness. But I reiterate that Cavalcanti never disowned the sexual dimension of love by way of *askesis*, notwithstanding its 'malignant' power which overthrows *mezura* and obstructs the attainment of "*buon perfetto*". His is a recurrent struggle against the contending impulses of human nature, its darker instincts which link the body to the viscosity of matter, only to rise towards transfiguring vision, even if to fall back on the self's abyss. And so his response to Orlandi's *quaestio* retains the equipoise: *amor* is not necessarily *morte*, although it can be. Sonnet XX gives us both his transformative impulse in handling the traditional love-death theme and his variation on a received convention, indicating the intertextuality that can inform his poetry.

The poem seems at first like many others, the Donna here bears Amor in her eyes, armed with three arrows, to whom the poet-lover offers his stricken soul, already wounded to "death" by two arrows, as the third impends in slow motion. The *donna-arcier* appears elsewhere. It is the variation on the Ovidian two arrows of gold and lead – symbolising love and hate – that is notable. The Provençal Giraut de Calanso had introduced the third arrow of steel (*"don fan colp de plazer"*) which Guido plays on. The third arrow not only points beyond the Ovidian *agon* of contraries, but dialectically lifts the poet-lover to a higher plane – *"perché saria dell'alma la salute"*. The final tercet thrusts up from the lower to the higher plane of being – *"la prima dà piacere e disconforta, / e la seconda disia la vertute / della gran gioia che la terza porta"*.

This tension between light and dark, joy and despair, hints at a metaphysical link between man and the cosmos. Averroes' theory of light that leaps from sphere to sphere until reaching corruptible things, is shared by both Cavalcanti and Dante but with a major difference. Dante accepts it as the manifestation of the creative energy of God; whereas Cavalcanti is silent on its source – light seems to be the mediating element between the known and the unknowable, a part of Nature and yet intangible in itself. We do not know if Guido knew Grosseteste. But what Gilson says about Grosseteste's theory seems to be relevant to Cavalcanti's treatment of light as vital energy. Gilson explains: *"La lumière est une substance incorporelle très subtile et qui se rapproche de l'incorporel. Ses propriétés caractéristiques sont de s'engendrer elle-même perpétuellement et de se diffuser... La diffusion de la lumière ne pas être contrariée que par deux raisons; ou bien elle rencontre une obscurité qui l'arrête, ou bien elle finit par atteindre la limite extrême de sa raréfaction, et la propagation de la lumière prend fin par là même"*.[21]

In Guido's poetry, the heart's half-darkness symbolises the light's exhaustion as it descends towards the materiality of the body, towards a chaotic impasse.

In his poems, light and vital energy are equivalents and both find their creative source and embodiment in the Donna; and her withholding of *merzede*, that is reciprocity, devitalises the lover-poet. To gloss, the variations of *vile*, beyond its usual connotations, should be read as contraries of *virtù*, deriving from *vis*, and its counterpart is *valor* which is the internalised sense of *virtù*. Amor, if denied, can degrade, meaning a loss of *virtù*. But Amor is not quite the *Amor-tiranno* of the Provençal and Sicilian protocol. Although it often is the irresistible force of the traditional kind – *"che solo Amor mi sforza / contra cui non val forza – né misura"* in Ballata I, at other times Amor seems to be on the lover's side, responsive to his pain: *"Amor, che lo tuo grande valor sente, / dice: 'E' mi duol che ti convien morire / per questa fiera donna, che niente / par che pie-*

---

[21] E. GILSON, *Philosophie du Moyen Age*, Paris, Payot, 1925, cited by POUND, in *Literary Essays, op. cit.*, p. 160.

tate di te voglia udire'". (Sonnet VIII). This dissociation of the Love Icon and Love makes the Donna the cruel tyrant, a figure of power and energy but a surrogate of death. On occasion, as in Sonnet XXI, she can assume, as if a transvestite, the figurative attributes of Amor, "*in guisa d'arcier*", armed with his arrows in her glance. But in the most joyous *lode*, Amor and Donna are one and the same as are vital energy and light.

In Sonnet VIII, one notes that the disjunction between the Donna and Amor is paralleled by a disjunction between the poet-lover and Amor, who becomes a third actor in an allegorical playlet. This kind of bifurcation of the self occurs repeatedly in Cavalcanti's poetry in moments of dejection, when *merzede* (without the sexual implication of Cappellanus) is withheld. And the *dédoublement* of the self may lead to prideful contempt of one part for the other in its abject surrender to passion, as if the Super Ego is judging the Id: "*L'anima mia vilment' è sbigotita*", he writes in Sonnet VII, since his unmanned heart has lost the battle. At other moments, he masks his true state in a proud protective gesture of stoicism.

To repeat, loss of reciprocity for Cavalcanti is a moment of devalorisation of the self, threatening its integrity. Then again, even in despair, Guido never shows any misogyny about the Donna. If Cappellanus' third book, an attack on the *l'amour-passion* theme of the first two and on women, is explicable by the Medieval paradox[22] – "*Eva, nomen tuum retro dici: 'fiet ave'*" – Cavalcanti has no part of it.

Guido's poetry stands on the boundary between the *Fin' Amors* tradition with its paradoxical tension between longing for the beloved and ascetic self-denial and the tradition of *l'Amour Courtois*, which allows sexual union, a distinction made by Moshe Lazar and others.[23] Guinicelli's and Dante's *dolce stil* poetry come closest to *Fin' Amors*, transforming the convention of *l'amour adultère* into a metaphor for spiritual freedom; whereas the Sicilian poets follow *l'Amour Courtois*. In Cavalcanti, it is his *lode* and *canzoni* which subscribe to the former; in the pastoral, a popular *genre*, he leans towards the latter. Ballata XLVI offers an example.

It is the only poem by Cavalcanti where one finds any detailing of the physical traits of the woman in question – the *pasturella*. Recalling similar features in Sicilian poetry,[24] she "*cavelli avea biondetti e ricciutelli*" as well as "*cera rosata*". While, in keeping with the Italian tradition, there is no class feeling in the poem that often informs the *genre*, the poem otherwise follows the protocol: the lovely shepherdess alone in the woods with the sheep, singing as the poet-swain approaches for *mer-*

---

[22] CLAUDE BURIDANT, *André Le Chapelain: Traité de l'Amour Courtois*, Paris, Klincksieck, 1974, pp. 38ff.

[23] MOSHÈ LAZAR, *Amour Courtois et Fin'Amors dans la littérature du XIIe siècle*, Paris, Klincksieck, 1964. Also, see the Introduction to PIERRE BEC, *Nouvelle Anthologie de la Lyrique Occitane du Moyen Age*, Avignon, Aubanel, 1970, pp. 15ff.

[24] DANIELE MATTALÌA, "La scuola siciliana", *Letteratura italiana: i minori*, Vol. V, Milano, Marzorati, 1969, p. 69.

zede which she accords, as if the bird's song compels love and take him for her *drudo*.

In defining her *merzede*, Cavalcanti follows the first three stages described by Cappellanus,[25] *baizar, acolar, embrassar*. But the fourth stage, which is physical consummation, he leaves to the reader's imagination as the twain disappear behind the bush. But the hint of fulfillment is unmistakable, as the speaker evokes the *otium* of the pastoral enclosure – the flowers, the fresh foliage and love's gift of "*gioia e dolzore*". A lovely song, the poem gives a sense of total harmony that accommodates the uncomplicated elective affinity of the lovers in the larger context of nature. Yet as an amusing footnote on transformative poetic imagination as it treats life, Cavalcanti had met no *pasturella* but a *valletto* on horse back, according to his brother-in-law Lapo (Lupo) Farinata degli Uberti ("*Guido, quando dicesti 'pasturella'*").[26]

The *dolce stil* poetry abjures the feudal, hierarchic ritual of Troubadour poetry, which provides a socio-political underpinning to the *distance*[27] that characterises the relation between the Madonna (often *midons* in the masculine in Provençal, to refer to her worldly authority) and the lover-poet. The *distance* here is spiritual but real as a point of reflex for the lover's longing, as well as his posture of subjection. The Madonna inevitably exists on a higher plane. Cavalcanti's poetry follows the pattern, even in this Ballad I where the planes separate slowly, as the poem rises to the *loda*.

"*Fresca rosa novella*" begins as a *proemio* which, if it looks back on Ciullo d'Alcamo's "*Fresca rosa aulente*", also evokes Guilhem de Peiteus' "*Ab la dolchor*". In fact, Cavalcanti's *cantin(n)e auselli / ciascuno in suo latino*" is a direct translation of Guilhem's "*e li aucel / chanton, chascus en lor lati*", indicative of his knowledge of the Troubadours in the original, as is true of Guittone d'Arezzo, Dante and others. The poem's use of *capofindas* stanzas, with variations of *pretz* as links, also shows Provençal influence. But Guilhem's poem is plangent with fierce physical passion for his "*Bon Vezi*", resonant with memories of love consummated and longing for its renewal. The distance between them is physical, as much as that marking the gap between memory and desire. The poem fitly ends with the phallic "*cotel*". Cavalcanti's strategy is oblique and skirts the personal and physical.

The rose is an emblem for his lady. As its redolence suffuses nature in Spring time, so her being, as a centrifugal source infuses Nature and all creatures with "*presio fino*". As the *proemio* turns into *loda*, she is identified in Guinicellian term

---

[25] BURIDANT, *André Le Chapelain, op. cit.*, pp. 59-60 (Bk.I.6A).

[26] CONTINI, *Poeti, op. cit.*, p. 119.

[27] E. KÖHLER, *Observations historiques et sociologiques sur la poésie des troubadours, Cahiers de civilisation Médiévale*, VII, n. 1, 1964, p. 36.

– *"angelicata - criatura"*. Yet as the next line shows, it is only as a vehicle of angelic essence is she a miracle of God's creation *("Oltre natura umana")*, made to be *"sovrana"*, a *"dea"* among other mortal women. She emerges from the beauty and the lifeforce of Nature in springtime, an icon that transcends the poet, his thought and language, as well as Nature. But she remains within Nature's confines, even as a perfected emblem.

The two ballads XXIX and XXX, where the distance separating the poet and the Donna is not obviously marked by the miraculous awe that the paradigmatic Donna inspires, still harken to the Cavalcantian design. The eyes of Mandetta (*"Una giovane donna di Tolosa"*) reflect the far away lady of Cavalcanti.[28] Just as in the second, the poet-lover enters the dialogue with the *"foresette nove"* by recalling Mandetta, now far away. In the *congedo*, the ballad is addressed to Mandetta in the Church of Dorata, to seek her *merzede*. Thus, in a play of mirrors, One is reflected in Many, as each love reflects an antecedent paradigm. A presence invokes an absence; an absence infuses a presence, in mutual transparency.

This is also the Cavalcantian response to the *quaestio* that Cino da Pistoia put to Dante in a *tenzone* – if it were possible to love again. Dante's reply was in the affirmative, but he meant carnal love.

If his poetry of dejection describes an introjectory phase threatening the self with chaos, Cavalcanti's *lode* describe the projective phase in which the self is integrated by the visionary act. In Sonnet II, paradisal Nature – *"li fior' e la verdura / e ciò che luce"* – is projected onto the beloved whose face, more brilliant than the sun, wears an awesome aspect of beauty that, for those who can look into it, lends *valor*. As the poem progresses, the solar icon is humanised. Her superhuman aspect is made accessible. Not in a decrescendo, but as if describing the descent of the miraculous into incarnation. She takes her place then among other ladies, merely as the best.

In Sonnet III, where a single sentence runs from the beginning to the end, all that is beautiful and admirable in the world, natural or man made, is held in balance against the beauty and worth of the lady and found wanting. In contrast to the flaring power of the last poem, here is a gentle *loda* like *"bianca neve scender senza venti"*. The world transcending icon is the same however, if presented differently. As in Ballata I, she rises against the backgound of the world but in a dreamy stasis, rather than incarnate herself by descending into it.

But the visionary horizon, the point where earth and heaven touch, seems riven by the sudden apparition of the Lady in Sonnet IV. The atmosphere is electric with her light and power – *"fa tremar di chiaritate l'äre"* – and stunned, speechless won-

---

[28] I see in it the further dimension of a variation on Jauffré Rudel's *l'amor de lonh*, but in a more complicated play between absence and presence, the Ideal and the actual.

der greets this miraculous incarnation. Cavalcanti here has deliberately invested the Lady with religious aura. The first half-line, in semiotic stretch, possibly alludes to "*Quis est iste qui venit*"? (*Isaiah, 63.1*) or to *The Song of Songs 6.9; 3.6; 8.5 – "Quae est ista quae progreditur"*? or "*Quae est ista quae ascendit*"?

The one thing in common to all three is that they describe the visionary moment. Otherwise, the closest parallel, the allusion to Isaiah, has nothing to do with love but, if anything, with an image of wrath. It seems to me that Guido's allusion is deliberately polyvalent. The very mysteriousness of the Lady is enhanced by the fluidity of the allusion surrounding her. But the Marian associations in a cultic sense are incidental, even though they lend resonance. As Eco wrote,[29] the symbol/semeion is not to be defined as "*aliquid stat pro aliquo*", but as a sign x standing for a y which is absent and the way to it is by inference. That is particularly true of the Love Icon that rises against the horizon in ambivalent splendour in Cavalcanti.

When the last darkness that is death finally gripped his throbbing heart,[30] now metaphor turned into the body's tangible fate, Cavalcanti in Ballata XXXV remained true to himself and leaned on no outside props for consolation. First and last a poet, he sent his intimations of mortality, in all their immediacy and that sense of unique isolation they confer, towards an absence, to a distant lady in his Tuscan homeland, gentle and courteous but as ever without a face and a name. In the *congedo*, he asked for no response; the only *merzede* he requested was that she takes the poem into her keeping. Perhaps, because there was neither world enough nor time.

---

[29] U. Eco, *Semiotics and the Philosophy of Language*, Bloomington, 1986, p. 2.

[30] Contini, *Poeti, op. cit.*, p. 104, dismisses the view that it was Guido's last poem of farewell before death. Indeed, as he says, there is no proof that it was. But one has to be tone deaf not to sense its existential urgency. As I mentioned elsewhere, it is the only poem where Cavalcanti refers to his body in concrete details. That the *congedo* seeks no response also carries with it its own implications.

RICARDO J. QUINONES

DANTE'S *INFERNO* IN OUR TIME

Contrary to popular expectations, and even some scholarly assumptions, the twentieth century has not been the Age of the *Inferno*. Instead, the great poetic discovery for the major literary figures – and for those of us who follow – was Dante's *Purgatorio*. Not that the *Inferno* was totally ignored; far from it – it simply was removed from the central position of concern that it had held for Romantic critics. The *Purgatorio*, with its polyphonic method, its medley of voices, its notable lack of flamboyant, dominant characters, its positive sense of directed and fervent spiritual questing in the midst of disaffection and alienation – quite simply, its sense of pilgrimage as the dominant motif of human life – became the poem of personal identification and appropriation for a host of major writers throughout our century.[1] It was the great work into which they looked to find their own interests mirrored. In fact, the *Purgatorio* became for twentieth-century Modernists what the *Inferno* had been for the Romantics.

There are two reasons for this supersession. The first, part of the counter-Romanticism of high Modernism, I can only refer to by limited, but illustrative, example. When T. S. Eliot identified the *bovaryisme* of Othello, he provided the terms of comparison by which Renato Poggioli – in his classic essay on *Inferno* V – cast Francesca as a Madame Bovary. In these readings irony prevails, as distance is introduced between the demands of the characters – the dominance of their personalities – and the perspective of the reader. But an even more telling example occurs in the air-raid section of *Little Gidding*. Eliot obviously modeled the encounter with his "familiar compound ghost" on Dante's meeting with his own mentor, Brunetto Latini in *Inferno* XV. But, while in a letter to John Hayward in 1947, Eliot makes this connection with the *Inferno* explicit, he goes on to add, "I wished the whole effect to be purgatorial, which is even more appropriate".[2]

---

[1] See my token blueprint for further study, "Dante and Modernism", *Annali d'Italianistica*, 8, 1990.
[2] In *Dante among the Moderns*, ed. Stuart McDougal, University of North Carolina Press, 1985, p. 78.

The second reason for the actual demotion of the *Inferno* derives from the oft-heard criticism, known as "the scandal of the *Inferno*". This phrase, used in a recent address to the Dante Society of America, derives from the moral concerns and developing humanitarianism of the Enlightenment, that period that gave witness to the "decline of Hell". This criticism, given renewed life by the moral fervor and activism of the 1960's, quite simply accuses Dante of being a warden filled with resentment, one who visits chastisement upon his hapless victims. This is Dante getting even, and moreover a judge who uses the sentence of eternity to inflict greater pain on the tormented souls.

The philosophical humanitarianism of the Enlightenment should not be discounted; its ultimate aim is to de-radicalize evil. Any nightmarish experience is simply that – a nightmare, which recedes at the warm light of approaching day and at first contact with the comforting reason of the normally civilized social world. Its aura is one of a sad and subdued benevolence, like the gentle yellow hues that suffuse the paintings of the eighteenth century: parents are wise and observant, friends are caring and helpful, and networking is active in this quintessential "I'm OK, you're OK" culture.

Nobody goes unredeemed, or is allowed to be banished from the human compact. Solomon Gessner, in his enormously popular *Der Tod Abels*, in essence exculpates his Cain, attributing his aberrant behavior (and it is only that) to a distressed imagination and legitimate concerns for the well-being of his own children.[3] The most telling instance of the Enlightenment's abhorrence of any radical sense of evil might well be Jean-Jacques Rousseau's horrified response to Voltaire's poem, *Sur le disastre de Lisbonne*, where the erstwhile defender of the providential order now conceives the universe to be the product of a hangman god. In his own *Lettre sur la providence* Rousseau for the first time publicly breaks with Voltaire and gives full expression to his belief in a benign universe.

There is nothing wrong with this world, except that its moralistic basis provides no true means for understanding and appreciating the nature of experience in Dante's *Inferno*. It frankly misses the point. While not denying that Dante, like other great writers, can be (even ought to be) motivated by intense personal animus, still such criticism deflects attention from the larger merits and purposes of the poem; it ignores both what the *Inferno* is and what it is not.

One can begin to gauge that poem's extraordinary qualities by registering what it is not. Surprisingly and revealingly, the *Inferno* contains nothing of the *ars moriendi*, that lugubrious meditation upon death that communicates a contempt for life, a contempt expressed in the skeletal refrain, "As I am, you

[3] See my *The Changes of Cain*, Princeton University Press, 1991, pp. 89-95.

shall be". Life is not contemptible; instead, and this is true particularly of the *Inferno* (and not of the *Purgatorio*), the high hopes and possibilities of life that have been so sadly waylaid are regarded as the necessary backdrop to the scenes of degradation that so occupy our attention. Sinners recall the "bright life", the "sweet light", the "beauty of the stars", and suicides are blamed for lamenting where they should have rejoiced.

Nor does Dante's *Inferno* provide the conventional survey of the professions, what the porter to the imaginary Hell's Gate of *Macbeth* expected: "I had thought to let in some of all the professions that go the primrose way to the everlasting bonfire". While, like the porter, we might have anticipated a line-up of the professions – the usual suspects in the satiric mode of the much later *Ship of Fools* or *Praise of Folly* – we instead witness the personal and humanized dramas of the figures of Dante's time and awareness. We meet figures who, like Macbeth, have plotted their own ways to Hell – presentations who, as in remarkable snapshots, reveal the compressed essences of their lives.

Nor do we find any of the modern sentiments about Hell, in particular the pathetic complaint that being in Hell is the condition of those unable to love. While this might describe *a* Hell, it certainly falls short as a description of the *Inferno*. Dante' s poem is a literary trope, with a philosophical disposition; with its own requirements, limitations, and dispensations; with intended emotional effects; and with its own religious, political, and moral purposes. Simply put, in every way Dante's *Inferno* transcends Hell. This might be summarized by its final episode. We recall that in the mosaic on the ceiling of the great Baptistery of Florence, Satan is also depicted with multiple serpentine heads, and each head is crammed with crowds of anonymous sinners. But in canto XXXIV of the *Inferno*, Dis himself shows the particular nature of his corrupting powers when he chomps on Cassius and Brutus and Judas. That the betrayers of universal Empire are as guilty as the betrayer of Christ, summarizes and suggests the distinctly personal reasons as well as the fuller moral, political, and religious purposes of Dante's poem.

Some of this larger design for the *Inferno* may be seen more positively in three areas: the choice of categories for placement of malefactors, the poem's linguistic arsenal, and its own philosophical limits.

Contrary to what might have been expected, the disposition of the sinners in the *Inferno* is not according to the Christian schema of the seven deadly sins. This itself is an astonishing fact, the implications of which are insufficiently remarked. The Christian schedule of offenses was reserved for the *Purgatorio*, partly because it suited the more introspective, affective mode of that poem. The *Inferno* requires a more public world; consequently Dante has recourse to the pagan classical (Aristotle *via* Cicero) arrangement of offenses: incontinence, violence, fraud, and treachery (among the incontinent, to be sure, lust, gluttony, and wrath are featured). What this permits – and what the Christian deadly sins do not allow – is a greater scope of representation, the possibility for wider casting, the vast panorama of scenes from contemporary life. Where in the Christian schema could Dante have placed the usurers, the panderers, the sycophants, divinators, simonists, barrators, thieves, false counsellors, impersonators, and many, many other figures of his world and time? None of these delinquencies might be considered as being capital, but they do contribute to and make possible a marvelous portfolio, indeed a human comedy of enormous proportions, one that conveys the issues, the people, and the language of Dante's time, the mean streets to which Dante devotes the attention of a novelist.

Moreover, this structure is also suited for a version of life unendowed with any higher purpose – in fact, one that lends itself to pejoration, a process of degradation whereby the secular gives way to the profane, which in turn produces the horrible. Neither the large canvas of scenes from public life nor the progressive deterioration of that life could have been represented under the Christian schema of sins.

Linguistically, the same prevalence of design and delimitation is apparent. While in canto XXXII, Dante expresses the wish that he had the "rhymes harsh and grating" sufficient to describe the last circle of Hell, what he claims here as being beyond his measure is, in modified form, the lexical mode of the *Inferno*, replete with those raspy, crackling, grappling words appropriate for a universe where physical and material ends predominate. This is a conscious strategy – quite different from the language of the *Purgatorio*, where a more lyrical, interiorized mode prevails – and justified by the proverb, "in church with the saints and with guzzlers in the tavern", and by the phrase from canto XXXII, where he invokes the Muse that helped build the horror city of Thebes (from Statius' *Thebaid*, the true model for the Cocytus), "so that the telling may not be diverse from the fact". And it is this aspect of the language of the *Inferno* that continues to defy all modern translators, no matter how schooled they might be in the tenets of "realism".

Philosophically, the *Inferno* also observes its own limits. Not only is the name of Christ not allowed mention, but the larger philosophical, political, and moral bases of Dante's vision are not permitted entry: they are reserved for the higher places of the pilgrim's spiritual advance. This means that any theoretical discourse is such that might be appropriate for the level of Virgil and Dante at this stage of their progress, or is otherwise restricted. The longest discourse occurs in canto VII, where Dante through Virgil registers, in another self-correction, his own expanded and altered view that Fortune is an agent of the divine will. This newly acquired wisdom will play a dramatic role in Dante's response to Brunetto Latini in canto XV, and mark his own spiritual development in accepting the insinuated but as yet unknown disaster of exile heading his way. But the fullest revelation of what this predicted event will be is as yet undeveloped, and Virgil defers an explanation until such time as Dante is ready to benefit from the better wisdom of Beatrice. Similarly, in canto XIX, where the simoniacal popes are among those being punished, Dante will dramatize his views concerning papal power (including a strong denunciation of the disastrous consequences of the so-called Donation of Constantine), but at the time of the writing (witness the reference to the death of Pope Clement V in 1314), his views had already been fully developed in the *Monarchia*, and would be made the matter of the larger discussion in cantos VI and XVI of the *Purgatorio*. The same issues, complete in Book III of the *Monarchia*, are adumbrated dramatically in canto XXVII, where Boniface VIII wrongly attributes to himself powers he does not possess. But these are shadowy matters, not yet fully explained – as they would be later – but as such perfectly suited to the *Inferno's* level of understanding.

All of this becomes even clearer when we observe that, unlike its classical model, Book VI of the *Aeneid* (and behind that Book XI of the *Odyssey*) the *Inferno* is not centrally located, but is rather only the first instalment of the great trilogy. And while it is the beginning canticle, its function is not even preparatory, but rather serves a different purpose. The *Purgatorio* after all is not a direct sequel, but rather a recommencement, another start – with better foundation and prospects – at climbing the mountain after the aborted first attempt. Consequently, and again in pointed contrast to its classical models, the task of the *Inferno* is not to communicate the essential values of a culture – those values upon which a culture is based. Its task is to exercise the arts of dissuasion, to tell what must be unlearned; in fact, the full roster, great and small, of the errors of a culture. But they are more than that; they are also the gods that have failed. From Francesca, to Farinata, to Brunetto Latini, to Ulysses, and amidst many other lesser figures along the way, Dante comes face to face with ideals that he himself had once most fervently believed in, and which now are not only of no help, but are responsible for the shipwreck that Dante has himself experienced, and the fuller crisis of his time. Superseded powers of creation, they have become obstacles preventing him in the action of the poem (as they had already been in life) from coping with the great and crushing blow heading his way (as of the poem's fictional date of 1300). Instead of guide-lines they now are like a poison in the blood, demons that must be exorcised, encumbrances that must be discarded, before Dante can know the full and expansive freedom to which he was born and called.

So powerful is Dante's capacity for identification with these gods that have failed – after all, he is able to write from within, as it were, with intimate knowledge of their appeal – that the *Inferno* continues to mystify post-Romantic critics and humanistically-inclined readers, who, expecting a Hell, find some creatures who are far from contemptible, who have some virtue, some dignity and some claim on memory. But it is this very quality that makes them all the more dangerous. In fact, in the drama of the poem, as Beatrice herself will make clear, it is Dante's own heedless commitment to these values – he was, after all, a leading poet and statesman of his time – that necessitates the radical surgery, the act of amputation that Virgil's miraculous arrival and revised itinerary impose. The people of Dante's time, and the values they represent, are false gods for which an extraordinary intervention and from which a drastic separation are necessary. This is why the *Inferno* practices the art of divestment, and its aesthetics is an anti-aesthetics of alienation and disaffection, its heroes finally anti-heroes, and its myths anti-myths.

While it is true that under the Modernist sway the *Purgatorio* has superseded the *Inferno* as a subject of personal appropriation and artistic identification, the *Inferno* has itself benefitted from this new understanding, from the need to recover the *Commedia* in all of its poetic and imaginative resources. To approach the *Purgatorio* as a special articulation of existence is to grant similar status to the *Inferno*, to regard it as a particular version of life, as one path to the river. Indeed, like the *Purgatorio* and the *Paradiso*, the *Inferno* offers a notable complex of ideas, attitudes, values, and modes of representation. A pathfinding essay suggesting this method of approach was ventured by Adolfo Jenni, in 1946, *Il "Purgatorio" nel complesso della "Commedia" e la soavità del Dante*.[4] Writing with the sensitive responsiveness of a novelist and poet, Professor Jenni calls attention to the distinguishing qualities of each canticle. "In ciascuna di esse ne sono resultati caratteri speciali, mancanti nelle altre due o, in esse, solo in germe o come in involuzione. Non son pochi né casuali quelli che conferiscono il suo aspetto specifico al *Purgatorio*". It is the very placement of the *Purgatorio* as the poem in the middle that dictates its special qualities as more humane, as more terrestrial. Consequently the *Purgatorio* has none of the super-charged extremes of the other two canticles: "Nelle anime del purgatorio non vige l'odio, come in quelle dell'inferno, né l'amore ardente, come in quelle del paradiso, ma l'affetto, sia verso i presenti che, nel ricordo, verso chi è rimasto nella vita". He does not limit himself to the simple assertion of the dominating conceptual form of the work, but rather shows by means of many particulars (such as landscape, women and love, the poetic arts) the ways that the *Purgatorio* does present a world of great imaginative consistency.

The same can be said of the *Inferno*. Much of course unfolds from its preliminary placement as the first instalment, exercising the arts of dissuasion

---

[4] Bern, Herbert Lang, 1946.

and hence requiring the second start of the *Purgatorio*. There are further characteristics of the *Inferno* – as a particular version of life – that in fact depend upon a prevailing sense of attachment to a particular locale. The recognitions of the *Inferno* take place to a remarkable extent by means of localized markers such as regional speech and dress. People are quick to identify themselves as belonging to a particular area or place. In fact, the *Commedia's* prized poetic resource, the simile, which Baretti in the eighteenth century called "the nerves and soul" of the poem, elevates this instinct into a dominant trope, as upwards of twenty-five similes, beginning intriguingly enough at the end of canto IX – that is, at the verge of the first encounter in the city of Dis – abound in references to place, as if Dante is intent on showing the earthly extent of the villainy and carnage his *Inferno* contains, but also establishing the *Inferno* as a poem where people are "sited". [5] And yet, in the *Inferno*, this is the very link that Dante must learn to sever, and in meeting after meeting in the upper Inferno, slowly but surely, his identification with his native Florence reels from successive blows, until in the flight with Geryon he is willing to commit himself to free floating, to the terrible prospect of being without a place, to a kind of no-man's land, protected only by Virgil and his as yet vague but growing faith in a guiding spiritual direction to his life. Indeed, in the deteriorating depths of the lower Inferno, this same poetry of location yields to a poetry of accumulation, as the sins of the world gather to depress him (witness the opening comparisons of canto XXVIII). This is fitting for his downward passage to the bottom of the pit, and conducive to the dominant effect as one of disgust, disaffection, and alienation. In the poem's final episode we do not need to meet up with Milton's rebellious hero, that would be discordant with the direction of the *Inferno*, rather we meet a kind of anti-climactic, even paste-board Satan, because we have already been overwhelmed by the body of wrongs he has wrought throughout human history.

This same method of individualizing the canticle is not separatist, but rather yields a highly fruitful conceptual by-play between them. If in canto XXII, Virgil's question as to whether any of the sinners is "latino" (or Italian) is duly answered, in canto XIII of the *Purgatorio*, this same query encounters a mild correction. It is Sapia, riddled with envy who responds, "O frate mio", and the term of address is significant,

> ciascuna è cittadina
> d'una vera città, ma tu vuo' dire
> che vivesse in Italia peregrina.

---

[5] This and subsequent points are amplified in my *Foundation Sacrifice in Dante's Commedia*, Pennsylvania State University Press, 1995, pp. 36-40, 56-62.

Whereas in the *Inferno* terms of recognition are based upon locale, in the *Purgatorio* a higher code prevails, that of pilgrimage. Significantly that term is used six times in the *Purgatorio* and not once in the *Inferno*.[6] Because this does not represent a change in etiquette, as much as a change in spiritual identification, the number of times is not as important as the lesson imparted. As opposed to the *Inferno's* dependence upon place, and upon identification with place, the *Purgatorio* is governed by the newly-acquired condition of spiritual pilgrimage: *homo viator*.

At this point the poem merges with the grand tripartite conceptual system of the oldest Christian philosophy. The one part – we can term it the earthly city of Cain, named after the first founder of a city and the first fratricide – is represented by the *Inferno*. The other – also a city, the city of God – is obviously contained in the *Paradiso*. And completing the ternary system contained in Sapia's remarkable response is the "middling" way of the *Purgatorio*, with the true type of the earthly Christian, that of the pilgrim, and which, if the first is that of Cain, could be called the way of Abel.

Out of the separate dispositions of each of the canticles, a genuine conceptual framework for the *Commedia* arises. And if the dominant motif of the *Purgatorio* is that of pilgrimage, the travellers on their way are all "frati" or brothers, as Sapia's address to Dante would suggest.[7] This is not a reference to any professional or ecclesiastical denomination, but to the true spiritual brotherhood of those who have separated themselves from their local conditions, and more importantly, attachments, and are enjoying the unbounded spiritual association of like-minded individuals, all attempting to direct their lives toward some reconstituted goal. These are the souls who come forward after the disaster, after the fall, as it were, and try to restore some kind of order in their own lives, if not in the community at large. And as we state this thesis, it immediately becomes apparent why the *Purgatorio* was a great rediscovery for the high modernists and their followers.

There is another way in which discussion of the individual canticles as offering separate versions of life – as indeed parts of a trilogy – has its impact on our understanding of the *Inferno*. Quite obviously, from this perspective, concern is not limited to the story of the *Commedia* (what Jenni has termed the "nota linea ascendente") but also to the stories within the *Commedia*.[8] Such an approach offers the additional advantage of transcending one of the reigning but also restrictive and limited critical approaches to the *Commedia*, the valuable and time-honored *lettura dantesca*, that is, the emphasis on highly-de-

---

[6] *Ibid.*, pp. 49-71.
[7] *Ibid.*, pp. 68-71.
[8] *Il "Purgatorio" nel complesso della "Commedia"*, p. 41

tailed readings of individual cantos. No critic of Dante is without debt to this honorable and, according to Jenni, unique to Dante's poem, method of criticism.[9] Generations of these readings, continuing now for well over a century – that is, at least four generations of critical intercalations – have provided their own archaeological markers, valuable indications of the status and condition of Dante's poem. But this very virtue of supremely-skilled presentations of individual cantos has also enjoined liabilities. It too, like the emphasis on the single line of the pilgrim's advance through the three realms of the afterlife, has by its success blocked access to the larger synoptic qualities of Dante's imagination, those qualities that moving beyond the confines of individual cantos, seek to construct other story-lines; it has detracted, inadvertently but not necessarily, from the overarching qualities of the poem. Of these qualities the *Inferno*, despite its philosophical atomism, has its fill. If for Dante and Virgil the bridges are broken, that does not mean they have to be for us.

The first of the larger story lines – "trans-cantonental" – involves the central dramatic character of the first two canticles, and perhaps of the entire poem, and that is Virgil himself. While it is in the *Purgatorio* that Virgil's rejection commands our attention, already in the *Inferno* this eventual demotion is anticipated and his limitations recorded. When Virgil is stymied at the gates of Dis and his way barred, this dramatic action simply resumes suggestions already made in cantos I and II; in fact, it returns us to these proemial cantos. The reason there are two such prologues is that Dante the pilgrim himself realizes that he will be in need of greater sponsorship if he is indeed to accomplish the journey proposed.[10] Later, in that powerhouse canto XXIII (which is, however, unjustly neglected), more specific indications of Virgil's limitations emerge. He can marvel at the punishment meted out to Caiaphas and the other high priests – they are crucified transversally – because they are being so drastically punished for the kind of rational advice that he himself endorsed in his own poem. Caiaphas counselled the Pharisees that it was fitting, or expedient, that one person should die for the many. In Book V of the *Aeneid*, in response to Venus's prayer that her favorites be spared, Neptune responds that the larger enterprise will go forward, but that one must die, a kind of symbolic votive sacrifice: *Unum pro multis dabitur caput*. Similarly, at the end of this remarkable canto Virgil is again baffled, his own rationality incapable of comprehending the "motiveless malignity" of Malacoda, who certainly had nothing to gain from deceiving the travellers into believing that a bridge was extant to the next bolgia.[11]

Following the same trains of references we can observe that in cantos III, VI,

---

[9] For several valuable insights into what could be considered unique in Dante criticism, see A. JENNI, "Paradiso XXIV" in his *Dante and Manzoni*, Bologna, Patron, 1973.

[10] See my "*Inferno 1*" supplement to *Lectura Dantis*, University of Virginia, 1990.

[11] *Foundation Sacrifice in Dante's "Commedia"*, pp. 37-41.

XIX, and XXVII Pope Boniface VIII emerges as the true *bête noire* of the *Inferno*, like Satan himself everywhere present but nowhere to be seen. Intimately related to the maneuverings of this reckless pontiff (as presented in canto XXVII, but who is also permitted a modicum of redemption in *Purgatorio* XX, when at length, at the hands of Philip IV's soldiers he endures the agony of Christ), are the events of Dante's own life, in particular the critical event of exile, preparation for which forms one of the major plot-lines of the poem. In canto VI, X, XV, and XXIV a mini-drama of spiritual readiness is played out through the series of obscure predictions alluding to Dante's pending exile (not yet known as of 1300, the fictional date of the poem). Critical to this development at the level of the *Inferno's* understanding is Virgil's discourse on Fortuna in canto VII, the only true extended theoretical discourse in the first canticle. With this in tow, Dante is able to make his frank response to Brunetto Latini in canto XV and to be congratulated by Virgil, his new mentor, in the pedagogic tenor of this section, for having mastered his studies well. In the *Commedia's* poetic strategy of progressive revelation, Dante's true justification by faith will occur in the parallel cantos XV-XVII of the *Paradiso* (corresponding with those of Brunetto Latini) where the better father Cacciaguida will clearly instruct Dante as to the bitter meaning of the obscure predictions, but at a time when he has already fully acquired the means for coping with the trauma of exile.

Clearly the very same critical forces of understanding that have led to a recovery of the *Purgatorio* have helped us to comprehend the larger poetic resources and dramatic qualities of the *Inferno*, now read as a literary trope with specific philosophical and imaginative dispositions. But this is a far cry from taking possession of the poem, from identifying with it and making it our own.

In the last fifteen years or so, all of this has changed. It is a sad and scary reflection upon our own times, upon our own world, that we have come into a better position for appropriating Dante's poem. Our own experience has led us to a reinstatement of the *Inferno* – the *Inferno* read in a far more gripping way than that represented by the Romantic dallying with doomed heroic characters, or by the moralizing condemnations of the phrase "the scandal of the *Inferno*". In our own time Hell has staged something of a comeback. With our own horrified experiences of random proliferating violence and the finality of death sentences, with our renewed acquaintance with the infra-human, we have wheeled back once again to the season of Hell.

There is a record of this change. In his own powerfully insightful collection of essays, *Admitting the Holocaust*, Lawrence Langer says similar things about our understanding of the Holocaust.[12] In fact the two, readmitting the *Inferno* and ad-

---

[12] L. LANGER, *Admitting the Holocaust*, New York, Oxford University Press, 1995.

mitting the Holocaust, can be linked because what Dante has given us in the *Inferno* is an accurate, imaginative version of what we mean by the Holocaust. The 'scandal' of the *Inferno* has been contradicted and superseded in the age of Atrocity.

While there are prodigious differences of scale between the Holocaust – its massive numbers almost defying comprehension – and individual episodes of the *Inferno* (although remember that in canto XXVIII, Dante leaves off trying to count the number of the dead from the terrible disasters of history), and while the *Inferno* contains mainly perpetrators and not their victims, still in their moral and imaginative effects the two can be compared. The essential argument of Langer's book is that the cultures of Romantic and heroic humanism, wherein we search for some redemptive action or even tragic agency in moral suffering, has ill-equipped us to understand the true dimensions of the Holocaust, whose essential purpose was to deprive human life of any such redemptive, tragic, or even sacrificial drama – indeed, to deprive death of any dignity. I quote and summarize the major points of Langer's book:

1) The Holocaust violated the principles of creation...and undermined the fundamental concepts that normally nurture human consciousness.
2) The terrible point of Auschwitz and other killing centers was that [there] the natural completion of life was violently, viciously, ruthlessly and senselessly aborted.
3) The nightmarish world was rendered real; nightmare becomes reality.
4) The Holocaust bequeaths a terrible guilt to the survivor, who has, as it were, been sentenced to life.
5) Humans are reduced to their essential animalistic instincts by this need for sheer biological survival.

All of these statements can be used to describe the overall effect of the movement from the upper to the lower Inferno, and in particular to describe the final and terrible episode of Ugolino and his children.

In the upper Inferno Dante's poem still contains remnants of what might be described as the Romantic world of heroic humanism, of fervent attachments and ideals. There still remains some partially redemptive forces of memory at work in the presentations of Francesca, Farinata, Piero della Vigne, Brunetto Latini, and the other great Florentine political leaders so dear to Dante's boyish consciousness. Dante, as pilgrim and even as poet, shares some identification with the sinners; exchanges are remarkably courteous, and the last infirmities of the noble mind – such as patriotism and the desire for fame – are memorably preserved. It was this quality of empathic identification that misled Romantic criticism, to such an extent that the dramatic and moving exchanges between

Dante and the sinners obscured the real logic of placement and the recognition that noble-seeming as they may have been their arguments and their natures are still part of the mind of Hell, and that they are flawed exemplars, holding up gods that have failed.

All of this changes in the lower Inferno, where Dante engages a new order of experience. Rather than identification the pilgrim Dante now comes to know distance and spiritual separation; there are few requests for fame or for the preservation of name. In fact, just the opposite prevails, as the damned express a bitter need for oblivion and utter silence. No remnant of anything redemptive or heroic persists in this lower realm, but rather squalor, ugliness, a piling up of bodies, and the experienced horror of what humans can do to other humans and to themselves. Rather than punishment receding into the background of dignified conversation, it comes to the fore, with bizarre contortions and ugly transformations. If Romantic criticism in the main centered on the upper Inferno, this newer reevaluation must be fixed on the lower.

This overall movement of the lower Inferno is intensified and summarized when we come to canto XXXIII, where Ugolino must contemplate and relive the desperate actions that ended his life and those of his children. And here we must remember that while Ugolino is being punished as a betrayer, still his account tells the story of a victimized father. Almost all of the statements lifted from Langer's book apply with double force to the Ugolino episode, where there is no heroism, no tragedy, nothing redemptive, and where we are left to contemplate the horrid imaginings of humans being starved to death, and what they are capable of doing in such extremities. I am one of those who have consistently argued that the cannibalism of the canto is not only required by the nature of Ugolino's punishment and by the metaphoric content of the canto, but also by the very logic of the development of Hell.[13] From the Bible to the *Inferno* to Shakespeare's *Richard III* and *Macbeth*, the massacre of the Innocents has been used to show the bankruptcy of a certain set of values, the death of history, the foreclosure of the future. In Dante's poem the actual reversion of the flesh – which epitomizes the reversals that have already taken place in the progressive degradation of history – where the father eats his children, produces so intense a revulsion that one can only reach for drastic metaphors of Hell and Satan to capture the nature of the horror. Moreover, so intense is this experience, so disgusting, that the meeting with Satan in the next canto can only be strangely brief, anti-climactic. The final experience of Hell does not produce any colorful brandishing of emotional indignation, but rather disgust, disaffection, and alienation – far more reliable emotions. Virgil's final

---

[13] More largely, see *The Changes of Cain*, pp. 63-71.

words to Dante do not have the Roman poet's usual rhetorical flourish, but are even more appropriately firm and resolved. "Let's move on: we have seen it all". *Che tutto avem veduto.*

In its overall effect, and in particular in its passage from the upper to the lower Inferno, Dante's poem amounts to a decisive step beyond culture and consciousness. It has come into an awareness of radicalized evil. In our own time we have sadly recaptured this same sense of evil that staggers but does not elude the imagination.

AMILCARE A. IANNUCCI

DANTE'S INTERTEXTUAL AND INTRATEXTUAL STRATEGIES IN THE *COMMEDIA*: THE LIMBO OF THE CHILDREN[1]

The purpose of this essay is to explore both the intertextual and intratextual strategies in the *Commedia*, that is, the strategies Dante employs in appropriating and assimilating into his text his source material and the strategies underpinning Dante's textual ordering of his poetic ideas in order to give shape to the prevalent themes of the *poema sacro*. One example will suffice to explore both strategies, the Limbo of the children, which unfolds largely in *Inferno* IV, although its main referent, the children (and their fate), will be postponed by Dante, as we shall see, until the very end of the *Paradiso*. I turn first to intertextual strategies.

Over the past two decades or so much work has been done on Dante's interaction with his sources, especially his classical sources.[2] Virgil has been the focus of this attention, although more recently Ovid has come under intense scrutiny.[3] In *Dante e la "bella scola" della poesia* (1993), edited by me, I tried to broaden the scope of inquiry to include all the poets of Dante's classical canon, i.e., the poets Dante the protagonist meets in that extraordinary encounter in Limbo, and to ground this research more rigorously, historically and philologically. There is no doubt that the most dynamic (although at times quasi-aberrant) work in this area is being done in North America where the traditional view (which still prevails in Italian and continental scholarship and

---

[1] This essay was discussed at the Department of Hispanic and Italian Studies seminar at Johns Hopkins University on Tuesday, March 4, 1997.

[2] Dante's interaction with the Bible and his vernacular sources has also received considerable attention. On the Bible, see, for example, P. RIGO, *Memoria classica e memoria biblica in Dante*, Firenze, L. S. Olschki, 1994; G. Barblan, ed., *Dante e la Bibbia*, Firenze, L. S. Olschki, 1988; C. KLEINHENZ, "Dante and the Bible: Biblical Citation in the Divine Comedy", A. Iannucci, ed., *Dante: Contemporary Perspectives*, Toronto, University of Toronto Press, 1997, pp. 74-93; on the vernacular sources, see, for example, M. PICONE, *Vita Nuova e tradizione romanza*, Padova, Liviana, 1979; T. BAROLINI, *Dante's Poets. Textuality and Truth in the Comedy*, Princeton, Princeton University Press, 1984; K. FOSTER and P. BOYDE, *Dante's Lyric Poetry*, Oxford, Clarendon Press, 1977.

[3] Cf. R. JACOFF and J. SCHNAPP, *The Poetry of Allusion*, Stanford, Stanford University Press, 1991; M. SOWELL, *Dante and Ovid. Essays in Intertextuality*, Binghampton, Center for Medieval and Early Renaissance Studies, 1991; M. PICONE, "L'Ovidio di Dante", *Dante e "la bella scola" della poesia. Autorità e sfida poetica*, A. Iannucci, ed., Ravenna, Longo, 1993, pp. 107-144.

which is best represented by Giorgio Padoan)[4] that Virgil represents for Dante supreme poetic authority (the poet, in fact, refers to Virgil's *Aeneid* as "volume" a term reserved for only that work and the Bible), and that Dante appropriates from Virgil with due reverence, has been challenged. The champion of this American position is Robert Hollander who sees Virgil's poem as a "failed text" and Virgil the character as a "failed" character,[5] a position which is articulated and is sealed for Hollander by Virgil's otherworldly plight, a life (assigned to the Roman poet by Dante) of eternal longing without hope in Limbo (cf. *Inf.* 4.42). American scholars who have followed in Hollander's footsteps and who have taken up the task have, for the most part, either attenuated Hollander's position (so, Teodolinda Barolini who argues that there is a deliberate campaign on Dante's part to lessen the authority of Virgil from the moment he enters the poem)[6] or exaggerated it (so, Anthony K. Cassell who dismisses Virgil as one who remained silent "not only in true praise of God but in his criticism of idolatry").[7] And all of this work has surprisingly taken place largely outside of Limbo and at the microtextual (rather than the macrotextual) level. My own position in this ongoing debate, as reflected in my essay in *Dante e la "bella scola" della poesia*,[8] is that for Dante Virgil is not a "failed" poet but a source of nourishment even though his text is ideologically if not stylistically incomplete and that Dante dramatizes the incompleteness of Virgil's text (and for that matter the pagan civilization he represents) in scene after scene in the *Commedia*, in the great encounter scene in Limbo (*Inf.* IV), before the City of Dis (*Inf.* VIII and IX), in the meeting with Statius (*Purg.* XXI and XXII), etc. Hence, my position is as removed from that of Hollander as it is from that of Padoan (he accepts Virgil simply as a dantean classical source and seems not to think that Dante challenges Virgil, but rather that Dante's reverence for Virgil and his text is a sign of Dante's humanism, albeit humanism of a particular sort) and Kenelm Foster (he emphasizes Virgil's limits from mainly an ideological perspective). My position, therefore, is that Dante both celebrates Virgil (without the *Aeneid* there would have been no *Commedia* just as there would have been no *Thebaid*)[9] and brings to the fore his tragic limits; ideologically his text is incomplete. This intertextual background is brought to the nar-

---

[4] Cf. "Dante di fronte all'umanesimo letterario", *Il pio Enea, l'empio Ulisse*, Ravenna, Longo, 1977, pp. 7-29.

[5] Cf. "Dante's Virgil: A Light that Failed", *Lectura Dantis,* (Spring, 1989), p. 7; see also *Il Virgilio dantesco: tragedia nella commedia*, Firenze, L. S. Olschki, 1983, p. 10.

[6] Cf. *Dante's Poets. Textuality and Truth in the Comedy*, p. 202.

[7] Cf. *Lectura Dantis Americana. Inferno 1*, Philadelphia, University of Pennsylvania Press, 1989, p. 91.

[8] A. IANNUCCI, "Dante e la 'bella scola' della poesia, (*Inf.* 4, 64-105)", *Dante e la "bella scola" della poesia*, pp. 19-37.

[9] As Statius notes in his encounter with the pilgrim and with Virgil, without Virgil's *Aeneid* which was mother and nurse to him, his "work would not weigh one ounce" ("de l'Eneïda dico, la qual mamma/fummi, e fummi nutrice, poetando: / sanz'essa non fermai peso di dramma" [*Purg.* 21.97-99]).

rative surface in the figure of Virgil, the character, the Limbo-bound shade, and is used to dramatize not only the tragic limits of pagan civilization but also to articulate the great theological themes of the *Commedia* which are the relationship between reason and revelation, the overriding necessity of grace and Baptism for salvation, free will and predestination and divine justice and human justice.

And this brings me to Dante's theological sources which during the past fifty years have received scant attention. In fact, until mid century the prevailing view, as expressed by such scholars as Busnelli,[10] Cornoldi[11] and Mandonnet,[12] was that Dante was essentially a Thomist, and that his text was made to conform with Thomistic theology. One pertinent example is G. Busnelli,[13] whose analysis of the fate of the virtuous pagans (it was due to a sin of omission on their part and opposition to God's grace) in Dante's Limbo is rigorously Thomistic (and whose logic Hollander follows although he seems hardly aware of it). This view of Dante's Thomism was subsequently swept aside by two ground-breaking texts, Bruno Nardi's *Dante e la cultura medievale*,[14] and Etienne Gilson's *Dante and Philosophy*,[15] which sought to place Dante, historically and philosophically, within the intellectual milieu of his time (a time of great ferment, of dynamic interchange of ideas and radical displacement of cherished intellectual positions as the West was now exposed to the reemergence of Greek philosophical thought through the translations and commentaries of the Arabs) and, in so doing, concluded that Dante was not, in essence, Thomistic but, above all else, eclectic in his approach to theological sources, with several often conflicting sources coming into play in Dante's work. The culmination of these researches is the best book of the last quarter of a century on this subject, Kenelm Foster's *The Two Dantes and Other Studies*,[16] in which Foster concludes that, although Dante obviously admired and even loved Saint Thomas, "Doctrinally, ...there is not much to be said for calling Dante a Thomist".[17] Rather, for Foster, as for Nardi and Gilson, Dante was an eclectic and the dantean world is "a rather uneasy synthesis of Neoplatonist and Aristote-

---

[10] G. BUSNELLI, *Cosmogonia e antropogenesi, secondo Dante Alighieri e le sue fonti*, Roma, Civiltà Cattolica, 1922.

[11] R. CORNOLDI, *La filosofia scolastica di San Tommaso e di Dante ad uso dei licei*, Roma, Civiltà Cattolica, 1931.

[12] P. MANDONNET, *Dante le théologien. Introduction à l'intelligence de la vie, des oeuvres et de l' art de Dante Alighieri*, Paris, Desclée de Brouwer, 1935.

[13] Cf. "La Colpa del 'non fare' degli infedeli negativi", *Studi Danteschi*, 23 (1938), pp. 79-97.

[14] Originally published as *Dante e la cultura medievale: nuovi saggi di filosofia dantesca*, Bari, Laterza, 1942, it immediately established itself as a classic text. It was subsequently republished in 1949 with the addition of further new studies, and again in 1984 when it was brought up to date in a new edition by Paolo Mazzantini.

[15] E. GILSON, *Dante and Philosophy*, New York, Harper Torchbooks, 1949.

[16] *The Two Dantes and Other Studies*, London, Darton, Longman and Todd, 1977.

[17] *Ibid.*, p. 61.

lian elements".[18] All of the three aforementioned works are seminal, but they are also limited, principally in their underlying approach to the relationship between poetry and theology. For it is ironic that all three, Nardi, Gilson, Foster, who are not primarily literary critics but scholars of medieval philosophy and theology, stress that Dante is first and foremost a poet and not a theologian, and yet, when it comes to practical criticism, they invariably focus on the theological aspect and reprove Dante for his lack of rigor (Foster, for example, expresses regret over Dante's theological oddities[19] and laments the fact that Dante, in his handling of the virtuous pagans, did not make greater use of the concept of 'implicit faith' to grant them salvation).[20] On the other hand, during the same period, the approach of literary scholars to Dante's use of theological sources and to the relationship between theology and poetry has also been and continues to be severely limited and is still driven by the notion of authority when dealing with theology, an approach especially evident in the commentaries where to explain certain theological notions of Dante one is simply referred to a theological source, sometimes extensively quoted. Use then of a single authority to justify one's reading of Dante (as in the case of Singleton whose reading of St. Thomas' theology of sanctifying grace to support his thesis that the pilgrim is justified atop the Mountain of Purgatory[21] has recently been called into question by Mastrobuono,[22] although, to be sure, Mastrobuono is stridently polemical and fails to see Singleton for the great scholar he was as the enabler for a new generation of readers of a well-thought out and original approach to Dante) or of several theological authorities, when one does not satisfy the particular reading of an individual scholar (cf. Anthony K. Cassell and his invocation of many theologians to justify his unflattering portrayal of Virgil),[23] has been the *modus operandi* of much of Singletonian and post-Singletonian American Dante criticism and more often than not there is little or no attempt to explore the degree of Dante's debt to his theological sources or his interaction with them. Moreover, attached to this general approximate theologizing reading of Dante is the application (often forced) by literary critics of theological allegory in the poem, a tendency best exemplified by Robert Hollander's reversal of the designation of Dante as *poeta-theologus* (he becomes *theologus-poeta*) in the name of the allegory of the theologians.[24] There can be no doubt that these twin literary approaches, the endless citing of theological authorities and the forced application to Dante's poem of the allegory of the

---

[18] *Ibid.*, p. 57.
[19] *Ibid.*, p. 166.
[20] *Ibid.*, p. 185.
[21] Cf. C. SINGLETON, *Journey to Beatrice*, Cambridge, Harvard University Press, 1958.
[22] Cf. A. MASTROBUONO, *Dante's Journey of Sanctification*, Washington, Regnery Gateway, 1990.
[23] Cf. A. K. CASSELL, *Lectura Dantis Americana. Inferno 1*, pp. 77 ff.
[24] Cf. "Dante Theologus-Poeta", *Studies in Dante*, Ravenna, Longo, 1980, pp. 39-89.

theologians, have been responsible for the recent American reaction against the theological dimension of the poem, best exemplified by Teodolinda Barolini who argues for a complete separation of theology and poetry (she wants to accept the truth claims of the poem and "move on to the consequences")[25] and proposes a "detheologized reading of the *Commedia*",[26] and Giuseppe Mazzotta who posits that theology is subsumed by poetry[27] (not a *reductio artium ad theologiam*, but the inverse) and who offers the exaggerated claim that poetry is the source of all knowledge.[28]

My own approach to Dante's use of theological sources consists of an underlying philosophy and the application of a set of rigorous methodological considerations. On the more general issue, the relationship between poetry and theology, I want to delineate the tension that exists between the two. In fact, it is impossible to separate the one from the other. To be sure, Dante is first and foremost a poet, but the ultimate truth and supreme knowledge for him lies in theology. In the *Commedia* theology does not suffocate the poetry nor does the poetry subsume the theology. Rather, they are intimately bound by Dante, theology the very source of the poetry and poetry the ultimate expression of theological truth. Nowhere can this intimate association between poetry and theology be better seen than in Limbo (although the Crocean view argues the opposite)[29] and, in what follows, it is my intention to demonstrate the dynamic interplay between theology and poetry using Limbo, especially, the Limbo of the children. These starting assumptions on the relationship between poetry and theology I hope to justify by applying to Dante's portrayal of the Limbo of the children several methodological considerations. First, I intend to lay bare the sources. Second, I want to highlight Dante's intervention with respect to his theological sources. I am not, therefore, simply interested in identifying sources and their appropriation, but also in identifying the reason behind their appropriation. In so doing, I want to determine not only by local context but also by the poet's overall strategy in the poem the manner in which the poet ferrets out and develops a particular issue, in other words, his intratextual strategy, for in that intratextual deployment is reflected the poet's intertextual strategy. In sum, I am not only interested in the what and the how but also in the why. Third, I want to root Dante's intertextual strategies

---

[25] *The Undivine Comedy. Detheologizing Dante*, Princeton, Princeton University Press, 1992, p. 13.

[26] *Ibid.*, p. 17.

[27] G. MAZZOTTA, *Dante's Vision and the Circle of Knowledge*, Princeton, Princeton University Press, 1993, p. XI.

[28] *Ibid.*, p. 3.

[29] Cf. B. CROCE, *La poesia di Dante*, Bari, Laterza, 1966, pp. 72-73; cf also G. GETTO, *Aspetti della poesia di Dante*, Firenze, Sansoni, 1966, p. 159: "la poesia [del Limbo] si risolve in una convinta liturgia della grandezza di cotesti spiriti consacrati dalla intelligenza".

in the twin realities of poetic purpose and belief for Dante's dynamic appropriation of sources is driven by poetic purpose which is, in turn driven by belief. Fourth, I wish to underscore Dante's attitude towards authority (the authority of the source being appropriated) and to stress that for Dante authority is important, but is neither paramount nor the overriding element. Thomas, for example, is Dante's main point of reference in the theological sphere just as Virgil is Dante's main point of reference in the classical sphere, but their views on a particular issue or their representation of a particular character or situation is not determining for Dante if it does not suit his poetic purpose. Moreover, what is, more often than not, determining for Dante is precisely the lack of authority on a particular issue or character and the concomitant and ongoing controversy and debate. We see this attitude played out in both the classical and theological spheres. So, for instance, Dante's unique creation of Ulysses in *Inferno* XXVI is due precisely to a lack of authority. In the absence of Homer whose works Dante did not know directly, although he was familiar with medieval paraphrases, Dante appeals to Virgil and creates a Ulysses who is pro-Trojan and anti-Greek, a critique not only of Greek epic but also of Greek speculation.[30] In a similar way, Dante clearly discerned the theological controversy which was centered on the Limbo of the children. In the absence of a clear authority, Dante chose and appropriated sources in terms not of authority (for Dante Thomas was certainly more authoritative than Bonaventure) but in terms of poetic purpose and belief – hence, a Bonaventurian Limbo of the children, although when it came to the theology of the Harrowing of Hell, Aquinas received the nod. With these methodological considerations in mind let us proceed, but one final *caveat*: in what follows, I shall refer to a number of theological texts all of which Dante did not know directly, but I would argue that he had 'interdiscorsive' knowledge of them to use Segre's useful distinction between intertextuality (points of intersection across texts) and interdiscorsivity (relationships between a given text and the surrounding culture and intellectual/theological milieu).[31] Dante could, therefore, glimpse the position of a particular theologian – St. Augustine, for instance, the *eminence grise* lurking behind the Limbo of the children – through the writings of others enjoined in the debate, Bonaventure and Aquinas, in particular.

What then of Dante's sources and their depiction of Limbo? Essentially, the theology of Limbo, especially that of the Limbo of the children, was developed

---

[30] Cf. A. IANNUCCI, "Il 'folle volo' di Ulisse: il peso della storia", *Forma ed evento nella divina Commedia*, Roma, Bulzoni, 1984, pp. 145-188.

[31] Cf. C. SEGRE, *Teatro e romanzo: due principi di comunicazione letteraria*, Torino, Einaudi, 1984, Ch. 7, pp. 103 ff. and especially, p. 111.

during the period of scholastic thought, although it reached far back into the patristic period.[32] On the general issue of Limbo scholastics were, more or less, in perfect agreement. First, there was the topography of Limbo which scholastics argued was part of the underground portion of the Christian afterlife (Limbo, Purgatory and Hell). Scholasticism's two greatest thinkers, for example, Thomas Aquinas[33] and Bonaventure,[34] portrayed the afterlife as divided into a series of *receptacula* or after-life receptacles stacked one on top of the other under the earth, two Limbos, one Purgatory, one Hell, each reserved for different categories of souls and for different types of punishment, the Limbo of the children (*limbus puerorum*), reserved for the souls of unbaptized infants who had died in a state of original sin (it is eternal and involves no physical torment), the Limbo of the Fathers (*limbus patrum*), containing the souls of the Hebrew righteous who were delivered during Christ's Harrowing of Hell (essentially a temporary abode of non-suffering and brought to an end by Christ's descent there), Purgatory, reserved for those who had died in venial sin (temporary and involving physical pain to a certain degree) and Hell, reserved for those sinners who had died apart from God's grace in a state of mortal sin (eternal and involving physical torment of the worst sort). Since the Limbo of the Fathers had come to an end with the Harrowing, scholastic speculation was devoted to the nature of the Limbo of the children. Here the debate focused on the nature of the suffering to which the children were subjected for all eternity, Aquinas arguing that unbaptized infants experience in Limbo no affliction of any kind, neither due to physical pain (*poena sensus*)

---

[32] For thorough discussions of the theology of Limbo, see, for example, J. CREEHAN, "Limbo", H. DAVIS, ed., *A Catholic Dictionary of Theology*, Vol. 3, London, Nelson, 1971, pp. 208-211; A. GAUDEL, "Limbes", A. Vacant and E. Amann, eds., *Dictionnaire de Théologie catholique*, Vol. 9, Paris, Letouzey, 1926, cols. 760-772; P. GUMPEL, "Limbo", K. Rahner, ed., *Sacramentum Mundi*, Vol. 3, New York, Herder and Herder, 1969, pp. 317-319; V. WILKIN, *From Limbo to Heaven. An Essay on the Economy of Redemption*, New York, Sheed and Ward, 1961; G. DYER, *The Denial of Limbo and the Jansenist Controversy*, Mundelein, Ill., St Mary of the Lake Seminary, 1955; G. DYER, *Limbo. Unsettled Question*, New York, Sheed and Ward, 1962; ZBIGNIEW IZYDORCZYK, *The Legend of the Harrowing of Hell in Middle English Literature*, University of Toronto, unpub. PhD Thesis, 1985, pp. 1-30; G. PHILIPS, "La Grace des Justes de l'Ancien Testament", *Ephemerides theologicae Lovanienses*, 23 (1947), pp. 521-556; J. A. MacCULLOCH, *The Harrowing of Hell*, New York, AMS Press, 1983, *passim* and especially pp. 253-287; B. GAULLIER, *L'état des enfants sans baptême d'après saint Thomas d'Aquin*, Paris, P. Lethielleux, 1962; G. DYER, "Limbo: A Theological Evaluation", *Theological Studies*, 19 (1958), pp. 32-49; M. LABOURDETTE, "Problèmes d'eschatologie", *Revue Thomiste*, 54 (1954), pp. 658-675; K. RAHNER, *On the Theology of Death*, New York, Herder and Herder, 1965; R. McBRIEN, *Catholicism*, Minneapolis, MN., Winston Press, 1989, pp. 1123 ff.; G. DYER, "The Unbaptized Infant in Eternity", *Chicago Studies*, 2 (1963), pp. 141-153; P. GUMPEL, "Unbaptized Infants: May They be Saved?", *Downside Review*, 72 (1954), pp. 342-358 and 73 (1955), pp. 317-346; W. VAN ROO, "Infants Dying Without Baptism. A Survey of Recent Literature and Determination of the State of the Question", *Gregorianum*, 35 (1954), pp. 406-473; H. DE LAVALETTE, "Les enfants morts sans baptême", *Nouvelle Revue théologique*, 82 (1960), pp. 56-69; C. JOURNET, "La volonté salvifique sur les petits enfants", *Theological Studies*, 19 (1958), pp. 32-49.

[33] *Sent.*, 4, D. 45, q. 1, as. 2 and 3.

[34] *Centoloquium*, Part 2, sect. 4.

nor due to the realization of the loss of the divine vision (*poena damni*)[35] and Bonaventure maintaining that children who die in a state of original sin live out their fate in Limbo, a fate which resembles a mid-point between grace and damnation (they share the fate of the elect, in that they have no pain, but they also share the fate of the damned, in that they are denied the vision of God and are aware that they are denied such.[36]

When one considers this scholastic treatment of Limbo and then is introduced to Dante's picture of Limbo in *Inferno* IV, one is immediately taken aback by the extraordinary newness. For in Dante's Limbo there is no compartmentalization but one continuous netherworld realm, and, more remarkably, this realm has not only children (cf. *Inf.* 4.30: "d'infanti"),[37] but also adults, and pagan adults at that (cf. *Inf.* 4.30: "di femmine e di viri") who are housed in a "nobile castello" and who are free to spend eternity pursuing the very same virtues to which they, while alive, aspired. The extraordinary newness on Dante's part was noted by the earliest commentators, especially by Dante's son, Pietro di Dante, who analyzes the canto with unusual clarity and divides it in the following manner:

"In hoc capitolo, premisso exordio ad tractatum primi circuli Inferni, quod per se satis patet, tria facit: primo tangit de Limbo Inferni in genere; secundo specialiter tangit de loco Limbi ubi sancti patres olim steterunt; tertio et ultimo tangit de quadam alia parte dicti Limbi, ubi fingit esse animas ceterorum gentilium virtuosorum".

["In this chapter, after an introduction to the treatment of the first circle of Hell, which is sufficiently clear on its own, he makes three divisions: first, he treats of Limbo in general; secondly, he provides special treatment of the Limbo where the holy fathers once were; thirdly and finally, he treats of another part of Limbo, which he creates for the souls of the other virtuous pagans"].[38]

As Pietro appreciates, Dante telescopes three Limbos into one, Limbo in general (that is, the Limbo of the children) in vv. 25-45, the Limbo of the Fathers which serves as the backdrop to Virgil's account of the Harrowing of Hell in vv. 44-63 and finally, what is a poetic invention on Dante's part, as Pietro notes by the use of the verb "fingit", namely, the Limbo of the virtuous pagans in vv. 64-147. Pietro is obviously fascinated by the *novitas* of his father's introduction of the souls of virtuous pagans into the Christian realm of Limbo, for he realizes how completely unorthodox such a poetic maneuver is. Like-

---

[35] *De Malo*, q. 5, as. 2 and 3.

[36] *Sent.*, 2, D. 33, q. 3, a. 2.

[37] The Italian text is that of G. Petrocchi, ed., *La Commedia secondo l'antica vulgata*, 4 Vols., Milan, Mondadori, 1966-1967 and the translation that of A. MANDELBAUM, *The Divine Comedy of Dante Alighieri*, 3 Vols., New York, Bantam, 1980-1982.

[38] PIETRO DI DANTE, *Il commentarium di Pietro Alighieri*, Firenze, L. S. Olschki, 1978, p. 90.

Continuo auditae voces vagitus et ingens
infantumque animae flentes, in limine primo
quos dulcis vitae exsortis et ab ubere raptos
abstulit atra dies et funere mersit acerbo.

[At once are heard voices and wailing sore
souls of infants weeping, on the very threshold
of the sweet life they shared not, torn from the breast
the black day swept off plunged in bitter death].

Aeneid 6. 426-429[47]

In careful intertextual analysis of *Inferno* IV and *Aeneid* 6, Padoan shows the close proximity that exists between Virgil and Dante on many points of detail surrounding their initial descriptions of their relative underworlds.[48] The threshold or "in limine primo" of *Aeneid* 6.427, for example, is a referent for the first circle ("primo cerchio") of *Inferno* 4.24 and in both *Inferno* IV ("d'infanti" of l. 30) and *Aeneid* 6 ("infantumque animae" of l. 427) the first souls encountered, or more properly, heard (cf. "secondo che per ascoltare" of *Inferno* 4.25 with "auditae voces" of *Aeneid* 6.426) are those of innocent children whose fate is one of distress (cf. "sospiri" of *Inferno* 4.26 with "vagitus...-flentes" of *Aeneid* 6.426-427). Moreover, the souls juxtaposed with those of the children in *Aeneid* 6.430 ("hos iuxta falso damnati crimine mortis") are those that are condemned to physical death without personal culpability and the souls juxtaposed with those of the children in *Inferno* 4.34 ("ch'ei non peccaro") are those souls who are condemned to spiritual death without personal culpability; and the very next category of souls in *Aeneid* 6.434-436 are those of suicides who are described by the medieval commentaries as having died in negligence just as the virtuous pagans are described in *Inferno* 4.34-39 as having died in negligence. And this strong influence of Virgil on Dante is not only limited to the opening description of Limbo. In fact, Padoan uses the same kind of analysis to show that echoes of Virgil's Elysian Fields resound throughout Dante's depiction of the fate of the virtuous pagans and that individual descriptive elements associated with the "nobile castello" such as its light ("la lumera" [*Inf.* 4.103]), its defensive position with its own stream ("d'un bel fiumicello" [*Inf.* 4. 108]), its verdant meadow ("di fresca verdura" [*Inf.* 4.111]) and the high vantage point within it ("in loco aperto, luminoso e alto" [*Inf.* 4.116]) are all traceable to *Aeneid* 6 as are the inclusion of heroes who are Trojan-Roman [*Inf.* 4.121 ff.], with no Greeks, in the catalogue of the great-hearted spirits, and

---

[47] The edition and translation for the *Aeneid* are those of H. Fairclough in the Loeb Classical Library, Cambridge, Harvard University Press, 1960.
[48] *Il pio Enea, l'empio Ulisse*, pp. 115 ff.

the catalogue's expansive encompassing of different types such as poets, philosophers, etc.[49]

For the present discussion two details are of the greatest significance. The first is that children constitute the first group encountered both in Avernus and in Limbo. The second is that these children exist on the very threshold of the underworld, in segregated areas that are on the far shore of the Acheron and, hence, beyond the point of no return. The closeness of these details is stark and there can be no doubt that the topography of Dante's Limbo and the inclusion in it of innocent infants have been colored by Virgil's account. Moreover, it is probable that Dante's overall and unique handling of Limbo, that is, of both the Limbo of the children and the Limbo of the virtuous pagans, was suggested to the poet by, and based on, Virgilian elements that were subsequently revamped along theologically determining lines. Be that as it may, it is clear that Limbo's topography as the first circle of Hell has been determined by a remarkable collation and fusion of theological and secular sources which result in a unique and reconstructed Limbo that is one continuous realm, a realm that is part of Hell on the far shore of the Acheron and a realm that houses both children and adults alike.

In a manner akin to his fixing of Limbo's topography, Dante again takes advantage of scholastic controversy, this time focused on the extent of Christ's Harrowing of Hell, in order to populate his Limbo. For, beginning with Peter Abelard there had been heated theological debate on exactly who was harrowed by Christ in His descent into Limbo, Abelard extending the Harrowing to include not only the Hebrew righteous, but also the souls of certain just pagans, basing that extension on his belief that it was possible for humans, quite apart from faith, to come to a belief in God by reason of their natural intellect.[50] Abelard was bitterly opposed by St. Bernard[51] (who argued that faith was the result of divine revelation)[52]

---

[49] *Ibid.*, pp. 117-118. Padoan, as a result, sees a more Virgilian shaped Limbo that is responsible for Dante's departure from the established theological tradition. And in accounting for Dante's decision to shape Limbo along Virgilian lines, Padoan believes that the answer lies in Dante's belief in the providentiality of the Roman Empire, an Empire guided by divine decree, an Empire whose people were as chosen as the Hebrew people and an Empire whose sacred book is the *Aeneid* written by a poet who had prophesied the coming of Christ in the fourth *Eclogue* (*Ibid.*, p. 120). It is this fundamental dantean belief in Rome's providentiality that constitutes Dante's real humanism: "È questa interpretazione provvidenziale dell'Impero, è questa interpretazione escatologica dell'*Eneide* che spingono Dante a violare con tanta fermezza tradizioni teologiche tanto concordi e salde. Solo partendo da questa acquisizione potremo discutere non agiograficamente dell'umanesimo dantesco. Perché di 'umanesimo', in questa grande esaltazione della civiltà antica e della virtù umana, è ben lecito parlare; è un 'umanesimo' però che sorge su un tronco dalle radici profondamente medievali, e che parte da una lettura dell'*Eneide* che sarà abbandonata dall'Umanesimo, per quella, storicamente più esatta, che vede il poema virgiliano come opera epica, di finzione poetica e di intendimento celebrativo". (*Ibid.*, pp. 120-121).

[50] Cf. *Theologia Christiana*, 1 and 2 (*PL*, 178, cols. 1140-1166 and 1172-1173).

[51] Cf. *Capitula Haeresum Petri Abelardi* (*PL*, 182, cols. 1049-1054); *Contra Quaedam Capitula Errorum Abelardi* (*PL*, 182, cols. 1053-1072).

[52] *Sermon 4, De sinu Abrahae, et altari sub quo sanctorum animas beatus Johannes audivit* (*PL*, 183, cols. 471-472).

and was eventually condemned by the Council of Sens in 1140. But that condemnation did not put the matter to rest, and many other scholastics, such as Aquinas,[53] likewise grappled with the type of faith that could secure salvation and considered the possibility that more than the Hebrew Fathers had been harrowed. Dante was aware of this debate and sure of his theological convictions. Dante places the emphasis on faith, without which, as Virgil tells Sordello (cf. *Purg.* 7.7-8: "Io son Virgilio; e per null'altro rio / lo ciel perdei che per non aver fé" ("I am Virgil, and I am deprived of Heaven / for no fault other then my lack of faith")), salvation is impossible. In this regard, Dante is thoroughly Augustinian seeing both children and adults alike, without faith as tainted by original sin, that is, the sin inherited from Adam by all humanity and the sin which could only be removed by faith and the celebration of the Sacrament of Baptism. As a result, both children and adults are conjoined (cf. Virgil to Sordello in *Purgatorio* 7.31-33: "Quivi sto io coi pargoli innocenti / dai denti morse de la morte avante / che fosser da l'umana colpa essenti" ("There I am with the infant innocents / those whom the teeth of death had seized before / they were set free from human sinfulness.") and condemned after death to a life of loss, "perduti" as Virgil explains to the pilgrim. Moreover, this faith Dante centers in divine revelation (cf. Statius' remark to Virgil in *Purgatorio* 22.76-78 that his conversion has been the result of "the true faith disseminated throughout the world by the messengers of the eternal kingdom" ("Già era 'l mondo tutto quanto pregno / de la vera credenza, seminata / per li messagi de l'etterno regno"), and not in Abelard's trust in human reason. Thus for Dante, those just pagans who died unbaptized, apart from faith, in a state of original sin could not have been harrowed.[54] And, if they were not harrowed, where would they be for all eternity? To answer, Dante drew on the long theological debate that focused on the punishment due to original sin, from Augustine's condemnation of all guilty of such sin, including children, to the fires of Hell[55] through Anselm's[56] and Abelard's[57] nuan-

---

[53] Cf. *Quaestiones Disputate, De Veritate*, q. 14, a. 11; *Summa theologiae*, 3a, q. 52, a. 4.

[54] Not all virtuous pagans, however, are condemned by Dante. In the sixth Heaven, the sphere of Jupiter, the pilgrim finds among the elect on the Eagle's brow, Trajan and Ripheus, the first saved due to the intervention of Gregory the Great and the latter an example of God's unfathomable mercy (*Par.* 20. 43 ff.). K. FOSTER, *The Two Dantes and Other Studies*, pp. 183-185, takes Dante to task for their salvation, arguing that Dante had recourse to miracles which evoked explicit faith, when, in reality, Dante could have made more of implicit faith and its role in the salvation of the virtuous pagans. I feel that Foster is missing the point. The salvation of Trajan and Ripheus, both due to the inscrutable nature of God's judgment, is a perfect example of predestination, a doctrine upon which Dante relies exclusively to justify his condemnation of the other and majority of virtuous pagans and a doctrine out of which he gives shape to his Greek tragedy of necessity.

[55] Cf. *Contra Julianum*, 6, 12, 39 (*PL*, 44, col. 843); *Opus imperfectum*, 3, 199 (*PL*, 45, col. 1333); *Serm.*, 294, 3 (*PL*, 38, col. 1337); *Enchiridion*, 93 (*PL*, 40, col. 275).

[56] Cf. *De conceptu virginali et originali peccato*, chs. 2 and 3 (*PL*, 158, col. 431) and ch. 23 (*PL*, 158, col. 456).

[57] Cf. *Expositio in Ep. ad Romanos*, 2, 5 (*PL*, 178, col. 870).

cing of the notion of original sin as something privitive and, hence, its punishment as something privitive as well, being the loss of the beatific vision, and culminating in the creation of the Limbo of the children by Saint Albert the Great as a place set aside for those unbaptizeed infants denied the vision of God due to original sin.[58] Dante thus telescopes an amazing amount of theological discussion to set up his Limbo as the eternal resting place of the virtuous pagans. For Dante's just pagans were not harrowed, but were left behind, as Virgil's eyewitness account of the Harrowing testifies (cf. *Inf.* 4.51-63), and are punished for all eternity with one reality and one reality alone, the loss of the beatific vision. And what better place for them to live out this fate than in Limbo, a Limbo that is uniquely conflated by Dante to include not only children but also adults, pagan adults who were just and had obvious merits but who did not possess faith and so died unbaptized in a state of original sin (cf. Virgil's remark to the pilgrim in *Inferno* 4.34-36: "ch'ei non peccaro; e s'elli hanno mercedi / non basta, perché non ebber battesmo, / ch'è porta de la fede che tu credi". ("they did not sin; and yet, though they have merits / that's not enough, because they lacked baptism, / the portal of the faith that you embrace".)). Dante therefore goes against all the preceding theological tradition which had maintained that there are two separate Limbos, that the Limbo of the adult Fathers had come to an end with Christ's Harrowing of Hell, and that the only remaining Limbo was the *limbus puerorum* which contained the souls of infants alone,[59] the souls of all adults existing either in Heaven, Hell or Purgatory. For Dante, there is only one sole Limbo shared by different categories of souls. Thus, Dante works from within the theological controversies of scholasticism that were centered on the Harrowing, the possible salvation of the pagan just, and the nature of faith and original sin, only to break openly with that same school of thought on the inhabitants of Limbo which, prior to Dante's depiction, had consisted of only children. Led, therefore, to a consideration that Christ's Harrowing did not include the ancient just pagans, Dante invents their being left behind, and invents in a thoroughly unorthodox manner the location of their post-Harrowing abandonment, a Limbo that joins both the *limbus puerorum* and the *limbus patrum* into one and the same place, a place shared by children and adults alike, all denied the beatific vision because of their lack of faith.

Thus, without a doubt, Dante cleverly uses theological controversy as the source for his topographic fixing and populating of Limbo. But no one issue highlights this dynamically literary appropriation of theologically differing sources better than

---

[58] *Sent.* 4, 1, 120.

[59] The sole exceptions are the souls of mentally disabled adults who are treated by the theological tradition as children.

Dante's treatment of the nature of the suffering afforded those Limbo dwellers who are denied the beatific vision. Here his theological sources were devoted entirely to the suffering of the children, since there were no adults in Limbo, the *limbus patrum* having been denuded by Christ's Harrowing of Hell. The nature of the suffering of the children was therefore front and center, being one of the most discussed theological issues in scholastic times, and on this suffering scholasticism's two greatest thinkers, Aquinas and Bonaventure, were sharply divided. A closer examination of both thinkers and an intertextual comparison with Dante will not only reveal the extent of Dante's knowledge of current theological debate but will also lead us to the poetic purpose which informs all of Dante's theological preferences in the Limbo episode.

Bonaventure deals with the fate of unbaptized infants in Book II of his *Sentences*.[60] Here the "Doctor Seraphicus" clearly breaks with earlier theological opinion which had been current from Augustine down to Anselm and which had argued that unbaptized infants would be punished by a fiery afterlife in Hell. Bonaventure will have none of this and argues that such a punishment flies in the face of a merciful God for such children through no fault of their own have been unable to avoid either the death of sin or a natural death ("qui omnino non potuerunt vitare nec mortem culpae nec mortem naturae").[61] To be sure, Bonaventure states, unbaptized children are denied the beatific vision since they have died without justice and grace, and, to be sure, they do experience this privation in a vile place ("in loco vili"), but they do not undergo physical pain since they have not longed after sin: "Non sentiunt poena ignis acerbitatem". ("They do not experience the pain of burning fire.").[62] Obviously, here Bonaventure is simply restating the distinction so often expressed by his immediate predecessors between the pain due to personal sin and that due to a sin from nature. What therefore is the pain due to the latter? Reviewing the opinions of diverse theologians, namely, that these children either suffer no afflictive pain whatsoever, or they do suffer some kind of interior pain due to the loss of Heaven, albeit a very gentle pain and one without remorse,[63] Bonaventure tries to combine the two and opines that there must exist a midway point between the election of grace and the condemnation of sin:

...videlicet quod animae parvulorum carebunt actuali dolore et afflictione, non tamen carebunt cognitione. Et illud potest satis rationabiliter intelligi per hunc modum. Decedentes enim in solo originali quasi medium tenent inter habentes gratiam, et culpam actualem: et quoniam status retributionis respondere debet statui vitae praesentis,

---

[60] *Sent.*, 2, D. 33, q. 3.
[61] *Sent.*, 2, D. 33, q. 3, a. 1.
[62] *Sent.*, 2, D. 33, q. 3, a. 1.
[63] *Sent.* 2, D. 33, q. 3, a. 2.

in tali statu debent animae parvulorum poni, ut quasi medium teneant inter beatos, et aeternis ignis cruciatos. Quoniam igitur beati carent malo poenae sensibilis, et cum hoc habent Dei visionem; damnati e contrario sunt in tenebris, et puniuntur poena sensibili: parvuli secundum rectum ordinem divinae aequitatis, debent communicare in uno cum damnatis, et in alio cum beatis: sed non possunt communicare cum beatis in habendo divinam praesentiam, quia tunc in nullo communicarent cum damnatis; praesentia enim visionis Dei non stat cum poena sensibili: ideo cum beatis communicare in hoc, quod carent omni afflictione exteriori, vel interiori, cum damnatis vero in hoc, quod privantur visione Dei et lucis corporalis. Parvuli igitur sic divino judicio justo inter beatos, et simpliciter miseros, quasi in medio constituti, hoc noverunt, ut tamen ex una parte consideratio generet desolationem, ex altera consolationem: ita aequa lance divino judicio eorum cognitio et affectio libratur et in tal statu perpetuatur, unde nec tristitia dejiciat, nec laetitia reficiat.

[And it is clear that the souls of the children will lack any pain or affliction and yet they will not lack consciousness. And this can be rationally understood in the following manner. For dying with only the stain of original sin, they hold, as it were, a mid-point between those who have grace and those who have real guilt. And since the state of retribution must correspond to the state of the present life, the souls of the children should exist in such a state that they hold, as it were, a mid-point between the blessed and those tormented by the eternal fire. Since, therefore, the blessed have the vision of God and so lack any pain, and since, on the contrary, the damned are in darkness and are punished by physical pain, it follows from the ordering of divine justice that the souls of the children share both with the damned and the blessed. They do not share with the blessed the divine Presence, since then they would share nothing with the damned for the vision of God does not co-exist with physical pain, but they do share with the blessed the absence of any exterior or interior pain. With the damned they share the privation of the vision of God and light corporeal. Therefore, by divine justice, the souls of the children are between the blessed and the damned and so they are both happy and sad. And thus by a special dispensation of divine justice their knowledge and their love are permanently fixed in state of equilibrium, in which there is not room for sadness or true joy].[64]

Therefore, for Bonaventure, children who die in a state of original sin live out their fate in Limbo, a fate which resembles a mid-point between grace and damnation. They share the fate of the elect, in that they have no pain, but they also share the fate of the damned, in that they are denied the vision of God: theirs is an eternal tension between sadness and joy.

Thomas turns to the fate of unbaptized children in Limbo, a topic which he treats in a number of texts. He begins in the *Summa* by asserting the absolute necessity of Baptism for all children.[65] Thus children who die unbaptized die in a state of original sin. What then is the fate of such children? Thomas gives his

---

[64] *Sent.*, 2, D. 33, q. 3, a. 2, conclusio.
[65] *Summa theologiae*, 3a, q. 68, a. 9.

response in question five of *De Malo*. In article 1, Thomas first maintains that the punishment due to original sin consists of the lack of the beatific vision ("conveniens poena originalis peccati est carentia visionis divinae").[66] Theologically, this position flows from Thomas' view of the state of humankind before the fall of Adam. That state had been a state of original justice, a state of both sanctifying and particular grace which allowed Adam and all of human nature to secure the beatific vision. But Adam sinned and thus was lost the right of humankind to enjoy its supernatural end. Thus original sin, like original justice, is a state, not a personal sin. An unbaptized infant, therefore, inherits original sin and, if such a child should die still unbaptized, then that child merits punishment corresponding to the fault: an absence of original justice and sanctifying grace which leads to a loss of any orientation to the supernatural and of any right to the beatific vision.

This state of privation, however, is not accompanied by any other type of punishment. Firstly, there is no physical sense pain of any kind. On this point Thomas is emphatic arguing that earlier and harsher language on the fate of unbaptized children should not be interpreted literally[67] and he employs a number of theologically insightful arguments to substantiate the denial of any physical pain for unbaptized children in Limbo.[68] Having ruled out any kind of physical pain for deceased infants in original sin, Thomas secondly turns to whether any kind of affliction accompanies the 'pain' of privation of the beatific vision. Thomas provides two responses, separated in time by some fifteen years.[69] In the *Sentences* Thomas clearly distinguishes between adults who by virtue of their free will can attain to eternal life because they are open to receive the grace that makes such a life possible and infants who are not disposed to grace in a like manner. As a result, unbaptized children in Limbo do not experience sadness of any kind and, instead, are happy in that they have received so much from God in the way of natural goods:

Unde defectus talis gratiae non magis tristitiam causat in pueris decedentibus non baptizatis quam in sapientibus hoc quod eis multae gratiae non fiunt quae aliis similibus factae sunt.

[An absence of such grace does not cause sadness in children who die unbaptized any more than the wise are saddened by not receiving many graces granted to their likes].[70]

---

[66] *De Malo*, q. 5, a. 1.

[67] *De Malo*, q. 5, a. 2, ad 1: "Ideo autem sancti tali modo loquendi usi sunt, ut detestabilem redderent errorem Pelagianorum qui asserebant in parvulis nullum peccatum esse, nec eis aliquam poenam deberi". ("Therefore, the Fathers spoke in such a way to repug the error of the Pelagians which denied the existence of any sin in children and hence of any punishment due to it").

[68] Cf. *Sent.*, 2, D. 33, q. 2; *De Malo*, q. 5, a. 2, ad 1; q. 5, a. 2, ad 2; q. 5, a. 2, ad 3.

[69] Cf. *Sent.*, 2, D. 33, q. 2, a. 2; *De Malo*, q. 5, a. 3.

[70] *Sent.*, 2, D. 33, q. 2, a. 2.

In the *De Malo*, however, Thomas goes much further theologically and argues that eternal life consists in full recognition of God, a recognition only possible through faith.[71] Since, therefore, unbaptized infants did not profess faith in this world, and did not receive the sacrament of faith, such infants cannot realize what is beyond their natural knowledge, namely that the perfect Good is the glory enjoyed by the saints. Hence, of such recognition the unbaptized child has no realization and therefore experiences no affliction of any kind in the privation of the divine vision:

> Et ideo se privari tali bono, animae puerorum non cognoscunt, et propter hoc non dolunt: sed hoc quod per naturam habent, absque dolore possident.

> [The souls of such children do not realize that they are deprived of such a great good and because of that they are not in sadness. And they enjoy their natural goods without any affliction].[72]

It is clear from a comparison of Bonaventure and Aquinas that Dante borrows heavily from the theology of the former in shaping the afterworld fate of unbaptized infants, a fate which the poet then assigns likewise to pagan adults who die without faith and Baptism. In fact, Dante's description of this fate is taken almost verbatim from Bonaventure: compare the souls of all of those in Dante's Limbo who suffer no physical pain ("non avea pianto mai che di sospiri" [*Inf.* 4.26], "sanza martiri" [*Inf.* 4.28], "sol di tanto offesi" [*Inf.* 4.41]), with Bonaventure's "carebunt actuali dolore et afflictione"; compare the loss of the beatific vision as the sole punishment in Dante's Limbo (as Virgil makes clear to Sordello in canto VII of *Purgatorio*: "...ho perduto / a veder l'altro Sol che tu desiri" ("I lost the sight that you desire, the Sun" [ll. 25-26]) with Bonaventure's "quod privantur visione Dei"; compare the consciousness of Virgil both in *Inferno* IV ("semo perduti" [*Inf.* 4.41]) and in *Purgatorio* VII: ("ho perduto") with Bonaventure's "non tamen carebunt cognitione" and Aquinas' assertion of the opposite ("animae puerorum non cognoscunt, et propter hoc non dolunt"); and, above all else, compare the depiction of the resultant and entirely ambivalent state of the souls in Limbo as described by Dante ("semo perduti, e sol di tanto offesi / che sanza speme vivemo in disio" [*Inf.* 4.41-42]) with the state described by Bonaventure ("libratur et in tal statu perpetuatur, unde nec tristitia dejiciat, nec laetitia reficiat"), a state which is far more severe than that of Aquinas ("et propter hoc non dolunt: sed hoc quod per naturam habent, absque dolore possident"). It is obvious, therefore, from the analysis above that Dante is almost totally dependent on Bonaventure[73] in develop-

---

[71] Cf. *De Veritate*, q. 14, a. 2.

[72] *De Malo*, q. 5, a. 3.

[73] For an exhaustive treatment of Dante's reliance on the theology of Bonaventure in the creation of Limbo, see T. BOTTAGISIO, *Il Limbo dantesco: studi filosofici e letterari,* Padova, Tipografia e libreria editrice antoniana, 1898.

ing his final depiction of Limbo while at the same time permitting of any other sources which can be used to advance his principal theme.

Bonaventure thus is the driving force behind Dante's depiction of the fate of his Limbo dwellers and, as a result, the thought of Aquinas recedes into the poetic background. This deliberate choice on Dante's part is a matter of no small significance. For Aquinas is a major theological source for the creation of the *Commedia* as a whole. Now to be sure, as stated earlier, Dante cannot be called a Thomist in the strict sense of that term as connoting a body of Thomistic thinking as the pioneering researches of Bruno Nardi and Etienne Gilson have shown.[74] Nor should we assume the mindset of a modern medievalist and believe that Dante had parted company completely with Aquinas simply because of his non-Thomistic depiction of Limbo.[75] But that Dante used Thomas as a leading source and that he had profound respect for him as a religious scholar and as a religious man goes without saying.[76] But in the creation of Limbo, Aquinas is, for Dante, a mere entrée to the episode and Dante's deliberate preference here for the theology of Bonaventure thus invites a consideration of why Dante would choose the harsher Bonaventurian punishment for the unbaptized children rather than Aquinas' more compassionate treatement of them. Both theologically and poetically the answer is close at hand.

It should, by now, be clear that the poetic purpose which drives Dante's unorthodox Limbo in *Inferno* IV is to describe neither the *limbus puerorum* nor the plight of infant unbaptized souls. In fact, he pays the children mere lip service, assigning them a single line ("d'infanti e di femmine e di viri" [*Inf.* 4.30]), although he will return to the fate of unbaptized children in *Paradiso* XXXII. Rather it is the tragic plight of the virtuous pagans that Dante wants to privilege poetically in *Inferno* IV and his Limbo, accordingly, is constructed around the fate of the pagan adults and the reasons for that fate. But in such an undertaking, it is clear that Dante could not rely for individual details on a preceding theological tradition of adults in Limbo, since all adults in Limbo had been liberated at Christ's Harrowing and only children remained. What better way then for Dante to shape his poetic vision of pagan adults in Limbo than to appropriate many theological details associated with the cause and fate of the children in Limbo and transfer them to the virtuous pagans? As we have already seen, both children and adults in Dante's collated Limbo are punished for one and the same wrong: they lived without faith and died without Baptism in a state of original sin. And because of their lack of

[74] See B. NARDI, *Dal 'Convivio' alla 'Commedia' (sei saggi danteschi)*, Roma, Istituto storico italiano per il medio evo, 1960 and *Saggi e note di critica dantesca*, Milano, R. Ricciardi, 1966; see also E. GILSON, *Dante and Philosophy*.

[75] Cf. E. GILSON, *Dante and Philosophy*, p. 158, n. 1: "To follow Albertus Magnus on any point undoubtedly did not signify to him parting company with St. Thomas".

[76] See K. FOSTER, "St. Thomas and Dante", in *The Two Dantes and Other Studies*, pp. 61-65.

faith and Baptism, Dante portrays both adults and children as suffering the same fate, a fate which Dante appropriates from the theological discussions on the nature of the suffering of the unbaptized children in Limbo and transfers to the virtuous pagans as well.

Transference, therefore, lies at the heart of Dante's intertextual strategy in *Inferno* IV, and, as the entire canto makes clear, Dante is preoccupied with shaping, by transference of the theological details associated with the children to the virtuous pagans, the tragic plight of the pagan just. In other words, the Limbo of the children and that of the Fathers too (but that is another story, and a long one at that) are put to the service of the virtuous pagans in order to dramatize in human terms, and in an extreme situation, – Virgil's story – the great theological themes which, as noted above, are the relationship between reason and revelation, the overriding necessity of grace and Baptism for salvation, free will and predestination and divine justice and human justice. Thus, does Dante shape the fate of the virtuous pagans in a far more interesting and compelling way and thereby creates a unique telling of their sad fate. For these pagans had lived blamelessly ("ch'ei non peccaro" [*Inf.* 4.34]), and honorably ("di molto valore" [*Inf.* 4.44]), they had merits as Virgil admits ("e s'elli hanno mercedi" [*Inf.* 4.34]) but in the afterlife they are not rewarded for their merit, and, instead, are condemned to be forever separated from God, a pitiable condition which is due exclusively to their lack of faith. Born too early or too far away, they did not have faith in Christ, nor were they baptized in Him, as Virgil tells the pilgrim explicitly in *Inferno* 4.35-36 "non ebber battesmo, / ch'è porta de la fede che tu credi" ("because they lacked baptism, / the portal of the faith that you embrace"); and Sordello in *Purgatorio* 7.7-8: "Io son Virgilio; e per null altro rio / lo ciel perdei che per non aver fé". ("I am Virgil, and I am deprived of Heaven / for no fault other than my lack of faith".). But faith follows from grace, and presupposes revelation. The ultimate fate of the virtuous pagans is therefore presented along theologically predestined lines and the drama that Dante fashions of them in *Inferno* IV resembles more a Greek drama of necessity than a Christian tragedy of possibility:[77] how tragic that the virtuous pagans were predestined to live at the wrong and graceless time, how tragic that human reason by itself could not win them God, and how tragic that, forever confined to Limbo, they are aware of their loss, but can do nothing about it. And this drama of the virtuous pagans is rooted in and receives its poignancy from the pagans' ultimate fate, a fate of conscious loss ("semo perduti" [*Inf.* 4.41]), a fate of anguished sighs ("sospiri" [*Inf.* 4.26]), a fate of eternal longing without hope ("che sanza speme vivemo in disio" [*Inf.* 4.42]). Since, therefore,

---

[77] See A. IANNUCCI's summation of Auden's distinction between a Greek and Christian tragedy in "Limbo: The Emptiness of Time", *Studi danteschi*, 52 (1981), p. 77, n. 15.

the most appropriate theological material for highlighting this tragic plight, albeit the tragic plight of infants, was to be found in Bonaventure, why not borrow, manipulate, alter and transform this material, and for that matter any supporting material, to suit a poetic end,[78] a poetic end grounded in Dante's firm belief?

Moreover, Dante, in his transference of Bonaventure's theology of the fate of unbaptized children in Limbo to the virtuous pagans, conflates and cleverly exploits a number of theological and typological links, all related to the sacrament of Baptism. First is the Harrowing of Hell and its topological link to Baptism. Theologically, as Aquinas notes,[79] the passion of Christ is the universal cause of salvation for both the living and the dead. Now the power of the passion as universal cause of salvation was applied to the dead through Christ's descent into Hell: Jesus Christ descended into the realm of Satan, the realm of death, and there He not only delivered the Hebrew just, but in rising to Heaven with them, He forever sundered Satan's and death's dominion. And the living continue to participate in the passion as universal salvation through the sacraments, especially the sacrament of Baptism. For Baptism signifies the salvific reality of Christ's passion and represents spiritual death, burial, rebirth and resurrection with Jesus Christ. In Baptism, therefore, the salvation imagery is as dramatic as in the Harrowing of Hell and the sacramental reality is the same in both cases. So does the catechumen descend into the waters of Baptism, waters that connote both death and salvation, and so does the catechumen rise with Christ, a new creature reborn with water and the Spirit, no longer under Satan's spell.[80] Thus the Harrowing has always been interpreted as a foreshadowing of Baptism and it is this link that Dante very profoundly recalls in treating the fate of the virtuous pagans. What more clever way, in fact, of underscoring the effect of non-Baptism, the effect of non-participation in the universal salvific act of Christ's passion, than to assign to those who were left behind at Christ's Harrowing, (that is, the virtuous pagans, who were excluded from the salvific activity of Christ in Hell and who are clearly aware that they have been excluded and have been left behind), the punishment that was the hallmark of Bonaventure's treat-

---

[78] If Dante had transferred Aquinas' account of the fate of the unbaptized children to the virtuous pagans, there would be no tragedy and, hence, no way to dramatize the great theological themes of the poem. Instead, there would only be a 'humanistic' celebration of their civilization. Indeed, blissfully ignorant of God, their state would resemble their condition in the Elysian Fields. In this scenario the Elysian Fields would not have been violated, ripped out of its cultural context and brutally inserted into the flow of Christian history, into Limbo.

[79] *Summa theologiae*, 3a, q. 52.

[80] Both the imagery and the reality are dramatically brought alive during the Roman liturgy of Holy Saturday when the Baptism of catechumens takes place within the celebration of the Easter Vigil, an event which focuses on Christ's death and resurrection.

ment of unbaptized children, namely, eternal loss of the beatific vision and a corresponding knowledge of that loss? Second is the very correspondence and link between non-Baptism and an eternity of conscious separation from God which is highlighted further in *Inferno* IV when the pilgrim and the poets ford the stream surrounding the noble castle "as if on hard ground" ("come terra dura" [*Inf.* 4.109]). Within the castle Virgil and the virtuous pagans enjoy a life that is markedly different from the Hell of personal sin. They, in life, were not driven by Ulysses' mad flight or "folle volo" (once again, the final immersion of Ulysses in *Inferno* XXVI recalls the Baptism motif) and, hence, they are not punished with physical torment, but their life was without faith and without Baptism and, as a result, their eternal afterlife is a life that is not fulfilled, a life of Augustine's "unquiet heart", a life that could be so much more. Finally, there is the link and contrast between reason and faith. The virtuous pagans of the noble castle represent great reason, they should have been able to come to God on their own. Yet that reason, without the illumination of grace and the faith that leads to Baptism, is insufficient, and, of itself, it cannot win them eternal life with God. Dante's pagans are acutely aware of this connection and deficiency. In fact, the very reason which the pagans possess makes them all the more susceptible to Bonaventure's described awareness of loss and the reasons for it. These links (Harrowing/Baptism, non-Baptism/conscious loss, reason/faith/Baptism) therefore buttress Dante's transference of Bonaventure's treatment of the fate of the children in Limbo to the virtuous pagans and no one episode, in short, highlights as forcefully, as does Dante's creation of Limbo, his intertextual strategies and his utterly dynamic selection and appropriation of theological sources to suit his poetic purpose and to underscore his own firm belief.

I have noted above the reluctance of the earliest commentators, based on their sensitivity to orthodoxy, to delve more deeply into Dante's bold daring in his poetic depiction of Limbo. However, I should now like to add a second reason why it was virtually impossible for them to explore the consequences of Dante's rewriting of Limbo and this reason, in turn, will serve as an introduction to Dante's intratextual strategies in his handling of the Limbo material. This reason has to do with the nature of the commentary tradition itself, a tradition which soon became fused with the *lectura dantis* founded by Boccaccio himself, the last in chronological time of the three early commentators I have cited. The tradition of the commentary – *lectura dantis* – which rules to this day Dante criticism favors a fragmentary, isolated reading of the poem. Although this kind of reading is fine for "local episodes", that is, those episodes whose significance is largely exhausted within the canto itself or within its immediate context, it is totally inadequate when it comes to dealing with those episodes which I have elsewhere defined as "structurally determining" or "textually privileged", [81] that is, those episodes extending beyond the canto of origin, episodes which continue to produce meaning throughout the poem and continue to resonate their themes and issues. These "structurally determining" episodes, located mainly in the *Inferno*, often raise an issue but do not resolve it and more often than not the nature of that issue is not clear in the core canto. It gradually becomes clearer, however, and is resolved much later in the poem in episodes located in the *Purgatorio* and especially the *Paradiso*, in structurally determining episodes whose function is not to produce meaning but rather to gather it in and bring it to completion. Canto IV of the *Inferno* constitutes the core of the Limbo episode, and the Limbo episode, driven by Virgil's story is not only a "structurally determining" episode but also one of the poem's two main frame episodes, the other being rooted in Dante's story. Moreover, the initial referent of this episode is the children and it is therefore no surprise that, although Dante bypasses the fate of these children in *Inferno* IV and treats it merely as the entrée to the greater tragedy of the plight of the pagan just, he, perfectly in line with the intratextual strategy which governs a "structurally determining episode", defers to elsewhere the fate of the children and returns there to its resolution. For the fate of the children, like the fate of the virtuous pagans, forms the core of the great theological themes of Dante's "romanzo teologico" – the relationship between reason and revelation, free will and predestination, divine and human justice, the divine will of God and its inscrutability – and, as such, must be resolved as part of God's unfolding plan to the pilgrim in the course of his miraculous journey. But in *Inferno* IV Dante the pilgrim, guided by the pagan Virgil, is still perceiving spiritual realities "through a glass darkly" and can no sooner penetrate with the help of human reason alone the eternal fate of unbaptized children any better than he can the eternal fate of negative infidels. The mystery of God's distribution of grace and the non-salvation of those without grace (and the faith it produces) cannot be resolved rationally, but must be grasped through faith. Dante thus as a pilgrim must grow in his faith: first in *Inferno* by experiencing the art of God in the sad world below in which God's power, when it allots, is just (cf. *Inf.* 19.12: "e quanto giusto tua virtù comparte"); then in Purgatory by recognizing, through Virgil's admonition, the insufficiency of human reasoning and its self-delimiting sadness in being able to describe the 'what' and not the 'why' (cf. *Purg.* 3.37-45), and by abetting his "natural thirst" to know, to know that which grace alone can offer (cf. *Purg.* 21.1-4: "La sete natural che mai non sazia / se non con l'acqua onde la femminetta / samaritana domandò la grazia" ("The natural thirst that can never be quenched / except

---

[81] Cf. A. IANNUCCI, "Paradiso XXXI", *Lectura Dantis Virginiana*, Vol. 3, *Paradiso, Lectura Dantis*, 16-17 (Spring-Fall, 1995), pp. 470-485, especially p. 471.

by water that gives grace – the draught / the simple woman of Samaria sought")); finally in Paradise by acknowledging, at the Eagle's instigation, the mysterious nature of God's justice (*Par.* 19.40 ff.) and by surrendering to its utter unfathomability (cf. *Par.* 19.97-99: "Roteando cantava, e dicea: 'Quali / son le mie note a te, che non le 'ntendi, / tal è il giudicio etterno a voi mortali'" ("Wheeling, the Eagle sang, then said: 'Even / as are my songs to you – past understanding – / such is eternal judgment to you mortals.'")). The pilgrim's full understanding of, and the poet's full treatment of, the eternal plight of the children in Limbo, therefore, cannot take place until Dante stands tried and true in his faith (cf. *Par.* 24.52 ff.), completely transformed in the Empyrean. There, towards the very end of *Paradiso* (*Par.* 32.40 ff.), it will be St. Bernard who, in his overview of the Celestial Rose, will return to the fate of the children as part of the mysterious plan of God. Moreover, even though it seems odd at first that Dante the poet should introduce children in the Rose and spend so much time on them, such a poetic strategy, in fact, is consistent with Dante's way of narrating and construction of structurally determining episodes like Limbo. For here Dante is simply bringing to completion something he had initiated in *Inferno* IV.

In *Paradiso* XXXII St. Bernard begins by explaining to the pilgrim that a major subdivision in the Celestial Rose occurs halfway down the ranks and that the places in the lower half are reserved for the souls of infants who died before reaching the age of reason, "the power of true choice" ("prima ch'avesser vere elezïoni" [*Par.* 32.45]). Sensing a doubt on the pilgrim's part St. Bernard further explains that these infants have found their places here "according to everlasting law" ("per etterna legge" [*Par.* 32.55]) and according to the grace of God which "He bestows diversely at His pleasure" ("a suo piacer di grazia dota / diversamente" [*Par.* 32.65-66]). St. Bernard then continues:

> "Dunque, sanza mercé di lor costume,
> locati son per gradi differenti,
> sol differendo nel primiero acume.
>
> Bastavasi ne' secoli recenti
> con l'innocenza, per aver salute,
> solamente la fede d'i parenti;
>
> poi che la prima etadi fuor compiute,
> convenne ai maschi a l'innocenti penne
> per circuncidere acquistar virtute;
>
> ma poi che 'l tempo de la grazia venne,
> sanza battesmo perfetto di Cristo
> tale innocenza là giù si ritenne".
>
> ["Without, then, any merit in their works,
> these infants are assigned to different ranks –
> proclivity at birth, the only difference.

> In early centuries, their parents' faith
> alone, and their own innocence, sufficed
> for the salvation of the children; when
>   those early times had reached completion, then
> each male child had to find, through circumcision,
> the power needed by his innocent
>   member; but then the age of grace arrived,
> and without perfect baptism in Christ
> such innocence was kept below in Limbo"].

Paradiso 32.73-84

It thus is clear from their position in the Rose, and from St. Bernard's explanation, that not all infants have been condemned to Limbo. In fact, St. Bernard divides the whole of salvation history, both B. C. and A. D., into a series of ages, (the "early centuries" or "early times" being the first two ages of the world – from Adam to Noah and from Noah to Abraham – and "the age of grace" being the Christian era) and stresses that, across these ages, God saw fit according to His law to save some and damn other infants. To sketch the plan of this salvation history, Dante, in yet another display of unrelenting appropriation of theological sources, turns now to the theology of Aquinas with which St. Bernard is made to conform in all details save one (see below). For St. Bernard explains that in the first period, infants merited salvation through the faith of their parents ("La fede d'i parenti"), a fact in perfect conformity with Aquinas ("Before the institution of circumcision, faith in the future Christ justified both children and adults"),[82] while, in the second, salvation came through circumcision, again a fact stressed by Aquinas who saw in circumcision a preparation for and an imperfect form of Baptism ("Circumcisio autem erat quaedam protestatio fidei... Unde manifestum est quod circumcisio fuit praeparatoria ad baptismum et praefigurativa ipsius" ["But circumcision was a protestation of faith... Consequently, it is manifest that circumcision was a preparation for baptism and a figure thereof..."]).[83] It is only with the birth of Christ and the arrival of the age of grace that infants without perfect Baptism in Christ have been condemned to Limbo, sentiments echoed almost verbatim from the writing of the Angelic Doctor ("After the Crucifixion, the unbaptized innocent children were confined below in Limbo... Baptism contains in itself the perfection of salvation ["in se continet perfectionem salutis"] to which God calls all humankind.").[84] Thus is the fate of the infants in Limbo resolved and thus stands revealed the utter 'mysterion' of God's dealings

---

[82] *Summa theologiae*, 3a, q. 70, a. 4.
[83] *Summa theologiae*, 3a, q. 70, a. 1.
[84] *Summa theologiae*, 3a, q. 70, as. 2 and 3.

with his infant creatures: God has dispensed His grace where He wills, and God, through His eternal law, has mercifully decreed that some infants, before the advent of Christ, should merit salvation, just as He has justly decreed that those infants who die without Baptism, after Christ's death and resurrection, should be condemned to Limbo. Thus is the salvation or damnation of infants predetermined according to a scheme of divine predestination, a predestination which reveals the just plan and will of God. In sum, God's predestination and God's justice are now perceived by the pilgrim for what they are, namely, realities which can be grasped only by the eyes of faith and realities which can often run counter to the speculations of theologians, no matter how authoritative they may seem. To reinforce the complete unfathomability of the divine will and to cap his treatment of God's justice and the fate of unbaptized infants, Dante includes in *Paradiso* XXXII two descriptive elements which are striking for their departure from theological conventionality and for Dante's unique vision as a *poeta/theologus*. The first of these is the fact that it is St. Bernard who utters the lines "sanza battesmo perfetto di Cristo / tale innocenza là giù si ritenne", for it was St. Bernard who, as a theologian on earth, shrank from such an apparently unjust conclusion in a treatise addressed to Hugh of St. Victor: "We must suppose that the ancient sacraments were efficacious as long as it can be shown that they were not notoriously prohibited. And after that? It is in God's hands. Not mine be it to set the limit".[85] The irony is perfectly clear: to paraphrase the Eagle, mortal vision (even the enlightened mortal vision of St. Bernard) can penetrate eternal justice no better than mortal eyes can penetrate the depth of the sea (cf. *Par.* 19.58-60). The second is the one detail in Dante's description of the children in the Rose that runs counter not only to the theology of Aquinas, but also to nearly all theologians of Dante's time. For both Aquinas[86] and others had reasoned that there could be no difference in degree of beatitude among infants in Heaven. But St. Bernard clearly states that the infants are assigned to different ranks and compares their difference in degree of beatitude to the different treatment which God extended to the twins, Jacob and Esau, the latter more favored by God (without any apparent reason) in looks and in character. Thus the difference in degree of beatitude for infants in the Rose is once again a reminder that God's ways are not the ways of humankind, that they cannot be captured by human reason and, ultimately, that we, as humans, can and must surrender in humble faith to this just truth as we can and must to the just truth of the fate of the unbaptized children and that of the virtuous pagans in Limbo.

---

[85] Both the observation and the translation are from C. SINGLETON, *The Divine Comedy. Paradiso*, Princeton, Bollingen, 1975, p. 548.

[86] Cf. *Summa theologiae*, 1a-2ae, q. 112, a.4.

With the children in the Rose we have come full circle in a calculated and daring poetic strategy. Unbaptized children and their fate began the Limbo episode in *Inferno* IV and unbaptized children and their fate are finally taken up and resolved in *Paradiso* XXXII. In between, the driving theme behind the children's fate, the theme of predestination, had been surrendered to the virtuous pagans where it was fully exploited in tragic terms in an extreme situation – sinless (as theologically unsettling as that may seem) and virtuous-meritorious adults who are excluded from salvation. This extreme example, incarnated in Virgil, stole center stage, as it were, and remained there until the children, always in the background, regained their prominence in the Celestial Rose. And the result of this deliberate interlocking of the predestined fate of the children and the virtuous pagans is a theologically exact and poetically moving formulation of the existential reality of the Limbo of the children, the fate of whom (in comparison with that of the virtuous pagans) first forces us to state and then ultimately to question our conviction of the poet's aims and priorities. For convinced in *Inferno* IV that the fate of the virtuous pagan adults is far more compelling for the poet than that of nameless children, a consideration which we use to explain away their minimal treatment, we come to appreciate in *Paradiso* XXXII that the poet's strategy is far more subtle than we had presupposed. And the result of that appreciation is that we now see that both fates, theological realities uniquely appropriated and wondrously transformed by the poet's eyes, are compelling, that both are poignant, and that both are equally powerful poetic expressions of the inscrutable nature of God's justice which can be penetrated by our mortal vision no more than mortal eye can penetrate the sea (*Par.* 19.58-60).

John Freccero

MOON SHADOWS: *PARADISO* III

The *Paradiso* has always been considered the most arduous and 'medieval' cantica of the *Divina commedia*, yet in some respects, it seems almost contemporary.
Because it claims that its subject matter is ineffable, it is, like much modern poetry,
more concerned with its own fragility than with the reality of the universe which
contains it. Even the scientific learning displayed here seems to have for its purpose
the creation of an *ad hoc* literary theme rather than the exposition of an independent cosmic order. Dante's heavens are a gossamer structure, approaching as a limit their extinction and the *page blanche*.

In this essay, I should like to read a simile in the *Paradiso* not as an historian
would, in terms of its antecedents, but rather from the standpoint of its posterity. The simile has to do with the optical phenomena of transparency and reflection, but it seems to hint at the implications of these phenomena for poetic theory. When the optics are understood figuratively, as they were by generations of
poets after Dante, they seem to stand respectively for poetry as a transparent
medium reaching out into the real world and for poetry as self-reflexive and
alone.

If the heavens are perceptible at all, it is because of shadows and the differences
introduced into the unity of the light by the otherness of creation. This cosmolo-
gical theme has its counterpart in the poetry as well: a pearl on a white forehead or
melting footprints in the snow also suggest an otherwise imperceptible difference
brought into relief by shadows. The opacity of poetry is like the otherness of creation, an imperfection which points to transcendence by its inability to make it
manifest. It is like the shadow of the Argo passing over a startled Neptune, bearing
witness to the light by eclipsing it.

The goal of the journey is the unity of vision, but that unity cannot be expressed in language, which depends upon contrast and difference for its intellig-
ibility. It is from this impossibility that the negative derives its creative power:
just as darkness makes an otherwise omnipresent light perceptible, so negation
can delineate the outlines beyond which divinity lies. Theologians and mystics

referred to this path to transcendence as the *via negativa*. We may extend this principle to the *Paradiso*, where poetry, in pursuit of formal perfection, is a form of *via negativa*, indistinguishable from theology, except that it makes no ontological claim.

Beyond the play of light and shadow there is only the blank page, an undifferentiated unity which seems like everything to the believer, yet is nothing without the leap of faith. It is that leap which distinguishes theology from poetry. Both poetry and theology have in common their pursuit of perfection, but the theologian asserts the ontological existence of the perfection he has spun from the play of light and dark, much as St. Anselm conjured up God's existence from a syllogism. The poet, on the other hand, is painfully aware of the contingent and transitory quality of the web he has woven and must remain silent when his work is over. The poignancy and the nostalgia we read in the *Paradiso* in part arises from this inadequacy.

If reference is out of reach in this journey to the absolute, then images and figures of the poem are as much about their own act as they are about their ineffable subject. The strategy of the *Inferno* was to create a fictive reality by masking the mediation of poetry – the inscription on the gates of Hell as a fictive presence rather than a representation, as if poetry were a transparent window on the damned. In the *Paradiso*, by contrast, there is only the mediation of poetry, given prominence by the absence of its subject. There is in this cantica no pretense at realistic representation; even the assignment of souls to the various heavens is based on a figure of speech. The mimetic reality of the *Paradiso* is confined to the historical and doctrinal narratives of its characters, set in contexts of increasing luminosity and abstraction.

In the heaven of the moon, we learn that moon spots are the product of the interaction of light with the specific otherness of this heavenly body. In Canto III an image of extraordinary beauty describes the play of light and shadows on a lunar surface in terms of reflection and transparency. As so often with medieval optical theory,[1] these phenomena can be readily translated into epistemological categories. Reflection may be said to stand for the self-contained, autoreflexive poetry that we usually associate with the lyric when it runs into the opacity of things, while transparency would appear to be the goal of poetry making reference to the real world. Dante merely hints at this figurative interpretation of optic phenomena. Subsequent poets, as we shall see, made it explicit.

---

[1] For the scientific importance of the experiment in Canto II of the *Paradiso* see MARK PETERSON, "Dante's Physics", *The Divine Comedy and the Encyclopedia of Arts and Sciences*, ed. G. C. Di Scipio and A. Scaglione, Philadelphia, 1988, pp. 170-171. The first line of Dante's simile in Canto III uses a technical term: "vetri tersi" renders Al-Kindi's term for a plane mirror: *corpus tersum*. See KEN'ICHI TAKAHASHI, *The Medieval Latin Traditions of Euclid's "Catoptrica"*, Kyushu, 1992, p. 56.

As Dante and Beatrice begin their ascent, the pilgrim has a vision in which many faces appear to him, eager to speak:

> Quali per vetri trasparenti e tersi,
>   o ver per acque nitide e tranquille,
>   non sì profonde che i fondi sien persi,
> tornan d'i nostri visi le postille
>   debili sì, che perla in bianca fronte
>   non vien men forte a le nostre pupille;
> tali vid'io più facce a parlar pronte;
>   per ch'io dentro a l'error contrario corsi
>   a quel ch'accese amor tra l'omo e 'l fonte.

[As through smooth and transparent glass, or through clear and still waters, not so deep that the bottom be lost to view, the outlines of our faces return to us so faint that a pearl on a white brow does not come less boldly to our eyes, so I saw many faces eager to speak, whereupon I fell into the error contrary to that which kindled love between the man and the fountain].

Narcissus mistook his reflection for reality; the contrary error is to assume these faces are merely reflections and to search beyond them for their source. Beatrice reproves Dante for turning to look elsewhere and insists that these shadowy faces, for all of their faintness, are the only reality.

In this first encounter of the *Paradiso*, Dante establishes a form of representation different from both the realism of the *Inferno* and the dream-like quality of the *Purgatorio*. At the beginning of the *Purgatorio*, the pilgrim tried to embrace Casella, only to discover that the musician's body, unlike the bodies of the damned, was as insubstantial as a shadow. The song sung by Casella for the pilgrim's consolation was in fact one of Dante's own poems from the *Convivio*. In a sense, then, their encounter was a narcissistic moment in which the poet attempted to embrace his own poetic past and, predictably, failed. As he tries this time to distinguish shadow from substance, however, he finds once more that the rules have been changed. In Paradise, it seems, there is only the reflective surface; we are not told what might lie beyond the glass or at the bottom of the pool.[2]

The pool of Narcissus and the Moon both present faces, the first by reflection as though in a mirror, the second projected there by an act of the imagination. The first was an erotic illusion, the second, perhaps less erotic but equally insubstantial,

---

[2] The point was first made by Marguerite Mills Chiarenza in "The Imageless Vision and Dante's *Paradiso*", *Dante Studies* 90 (1972), pp.77-91. I am indebted to the discussion of the poetics of the *Paradiso* in Chiarenza's article. Perhaps my own discussion differs slightly by stressing that poetry, of itself, is 'spiritual' vision and that, therefore, just as the *Inferno* is the *representation* of corporeal vision in the 'spiritual' mode, so the *Paradiso* is the *representation* of 'intellectual' vision in the 'spiritual' mode.

is the only reality in the Heaven of the Moon. To give a face to something by an act of the imagination may be rendered in Greek by the word *prosopopoiein*, from which is derived the word *prosopopoeia*, meaning a figure of speech which confers identity, gives a face, to that which is inanimate or abstract. The passage in Canto III of the *Paradiso* is *prosopopoeia* both literally and figuratively. To give a face to the moon is at the same time to invoke it as interlocutor. As in Romantic apostrophes to the Moon, de Musset's "O moribonde lune", for example, or Leopardi's "O graziosa luna", gazing at the moon is at once a theme of the lyric and a dramatization of its dominant rhetorical figure.

Prosopopoeia, according to traditional rhetoric, encompasses personification and apostrophe, and consists in portraying "absent, dead, supernatural or even inanimate beings" as if they could act, speak and answer as human beings do.[3] It might be said that the *Paradiso* is an extended *prosopopoeia*, not only because it gives voice to the dead and the divine, but because it seems to endow the transparent and silent heavenly spheres with life. Inasmuch as it animates what would otherwise remain silent or imperceptible, *prosopopoeia* is also an effective figure for the accommodation of divine things to human comprehension. According to Dante, it is the figure used in the Bible in order to describe God in human terms.

In the fourth canto of the *Paradiso* we learn that the souls of the blessed have descended from the celestial rose, where they reside, down to the planetary spheres in order to make themselves visible to the pilgrim. Dante compares this descent of the souls to the condescension of Scripture:

> Così parlar conviensi al vostro ingegno,
>   però che solo da sensato apprende
>   ciò che fa poscia d'intelletto degno.
> Per questo la Scrittura condescende
>   a vostra facultate, e piedi e mano
>   attribuisce a Dio, ed altro intende.

[Thus is it necessary to speak to your mind, since it can learn only from the senses that which later becomes worthy of intellection. For this reason Scripture condescends to your faculties and attributes hands and feet to God, when its meaning is otherwise].

The comparison suggests that the theme of the descent of the souls to the heavenly spheres is meant to be a dramatization of a figure of speech, a theological *prosopopoeia*. Moreover, the technique is said to have its origin in the rhetoric of the Bible. Not only does Dante claim to be God's scribe in inspiration, but in matters of style as well.

---

[3] Pierre Fontanier, *Les Figures du Discours*, as paraphrased by Michel Riffaterre in "Prosopopeia", *Yale French Studies*, 69 (1984), p.107.

The traditional themes associated with the Moon make it an appropriate dwelling for the souls whom Dante describes as saintly women who were forced to break their vows. In antiquity, the moon was imagined to embody feminine principles, while visual flaws in its surface – *maculae* – might be taken as an emblem of moral imperfection. The perceived irregularity of its orbit is probably responsible for its being associated with inconstancy, which is the weakness of the souls in this heaven and the traditional lover's reproach: "O, swear not by the moon, th' inconstant moon / That monthly changes in her circled orb, / Lest that thy love prove likewise variable."[4]

Water imagery is appropriate here too, since the moon was believed to control tides and to be the source of dew and other forms of moisture. Among the many theories about the nature of the spots on the moon one of the most common was the belief that they were produced by the surface motion of the moon's "seas". For all of these reasons, the association of the moon with the pool of Narcissus may have seemed less arbitrary to readers in the Middle Ages than it does to us.

The simile is perhaps more memorable for its formal qualities than for what it tells us about the moon. For one thing, its internal rhymes and alliterations are unusual for *terza rima*, since they tend to interrupt the forward movement of the verses. The phrase "non sì profonde che i fondi sien persi", for example, seems to embody the static reflection it describes, or to stand for the auditory equivalent of reflection, which is echo. The fragility of glass is perhaps alluded to with the clash of alliteration in "vetri trasparenti e tersi", and water is suggested, inevitably, by the liquid sounds in rhyme: tranquille, postille, pupille.

If there is a hint of a woman's features in the moon, it is conveyed by mention of her adornment: "perla in bianca fronte". Such an allusion is not unprecedented. In antiquity's most famous treatise on the subject of the face in the moon, Plutarch cites some verses describing the face of a maiden in the moon:

> She gleams with fire encircled, but within
> Bluer than lapis show a maiden's eye
> And dainty brow, a visage manifest.[5]

The word used to refer to this poetic depiction, *hypographein*,[6] is instructive. It

[4] *The Tragedy of Romeo and Juliet*, II, 2, 109, in *The Riverside Shakespeare*, ed. G. Blakemore Evans et al., Boston, 1974, p. 1069.

[5] PLUTARCH, "The Face on the Moon", 920E, ed., trans. and with commentary by Harold Cherniss in Plutarch's *Moralia*, Loeb Classical Library, vol. XII, London, 1957, p. 39.

[6] *Hypograph,* then *hypogram* were the words used by F. de Saussure in order to indicate "les mots sous les mots" in ancient poetry. Michel Riffaterre then borrowed the term in order to refer to the commonplace interpretant underlying the poetry he studied. See PAUL DE MAN, "Hypogram and Inscription: Michel Riffaterre's Poetics of Reading", *Diacritics* 11 (Winter, 1981), pp. 17-35.

means not only to underscore, to underline, but also to apply make-up to a woman's face. In its two acceptances, one graphic and the other cosmetic, it illustrates the poetic technique we have been describing: underlining a text that is not there, adorning a face that cannot be seen. Plutarch goes on to say that the interplay of light and shadow in the moon makes the face resemble a painting, but that its features seem impossible to discern.

The play of light and shade is all that can be perceived in Dante's Heaven of the Moon. The pearl on a white forehead is the more seductive for the absence of the beautiful face we expect, just as the hint of precious adornment in Plutarch's text – lapis lazzuli – promises a maiden's visage which cannot be seen. One is reminded of other precious surrogates for an absent lady: the two crystals reflected at the bottom of the perilous fountain at the end of the first part of the *Roman de la Rose*, the most famous medieval evocation of Narcissus,[7] or, skipping a few generations, the gold and topaz on the snow which stand for the portrait of Petrarch's beloved.[8]

The jewels, meant as ornaments, in fact replace the lady whose presence is only implied. Moreover, they do so in a timeless way, suggesting the portraiture whereby the poet is able to immortalize his absent beloved. The allusive quality adds to the seductiveness, perhaps like a Petrarchan veil, hiding the beloved, yet constituting her only reality. It is particularly appropriate in this heaven, given its subject matter, that Dante should begin with erotic *prosopopoeia* and no less characteristic that his reference should be so fleeting, as if to avoid the fetishism which is the occupational hazard of love poets.

The allusion to Narcissus, inspired perhaps by the *Roman de la Rose*, would have been recognized in the Middle Ages as condemning a complacent love of the things of this world. The word "accese", "kindled", by itself dooms Narcissus' love to failure in a watery medium. It was the word used by poets of the *dolce stil novo* and by Dante himself to denote the spontaneity and irresistibility of the passion it describes. The error of Narcissus was not that he fell in love with beauty, but rather that the beauty he loved was material and illusory, in short, a false beauty. This is the gloss given to the story by Plotinus, in a passage that urges the soul to seek spiritual beauty. His philosophical reading of the myth became the basis of moralizing interpretations of the Middle Ages.[9]

---

[7] GUILLAUME DE LORRIS, *Roman de la Rose,* ed. Lecoy, 3 vols., Paris, 1965-70, ll. 1521-40. John V. Fleming argues that the crystals must be the eyes of the lover, rather than the lady, in order to make the story conform better to its Narcissistic model, but it might be argued that the eyes of the beloved in love poetry are ultimately the eyes of the poet-lover mirrored in hers. J.V. FLEMING, *The Romance of the Rose: A Study in Allegory and Iconography,* Princeton, 1969, p. 74.

[8] *Canzoniere* XXX, "Giovene donna sotto un verde lauro" ("L'auro e i topazii al sol sopra la neve...").

[9] The source of the myth is OVID, *Metamorphoses* 3: 339-512. Plotinus' platonizing reading of the story is in *Ennead* I, 6 ("On Beauty"), trans. A.H. Armstrong, vol. I, in Loeb Classical Library, London/Cambridge, 1966, p. 257. In this passage, Plotinus also refers to the need for us to flee to our homeland, without ships or chariot, a

The error of Narcissus mentioned by Dante has its counter-part in rhetorical theory concerning the figure of *prosopopoeia*. In his discussion of that master figure of lyric poetry, Paul de Man suggests that making the dead speak, for example, results in the living being struck dumb. In other words, there would seem to be a certain *chiasmus* between subject and object in the figure of *prosopopoeia*. Michel Riffaterre paraphrases the idea: "the address calls for a reply of the addressee, the gaze that perceives animation invites gazing back from the animated object to the subject daydreaming a Narcissistic reflection of itself in things". Here too, it would appear that the animation of the faces in the moon calls Dante away from complacent reverie. [10]

We imagine the portrait of a lady in the heaven of the moon from the merest hint of her adornment. In the same way we are meant to infer the existence of the divine realm from the surface tracings and shadows of Dante's representation. In the simile we have been discussing, the contrast between surface tracings, *postille*, and a vision of the depths, the *fondi*, is represented as a contrast between transparency and reflection.

The literal point of the simile is that the faintness of the faces is comparable to the faintness of the reflections in water and glass. There is however an asymmetry in Dante's simile which might have escaped our notice were it not for the fact that modern poets have since given specific valences to "reflection" and "refraction" in poetic practice. For the moment, we note only that the first part of Dante's simile insists upon transparency as well as reflection, while the second mentions only reflection. The simile begins by describing glass that is transparent, yet reflects our faces, and waters that reflect, but also reveal their depths. These two-fold visions, reflection and transparency in the first part of the simile, are compared to only surface vision in the second part. Nothing is said of the depths. As those faces are reflected back to us, we may well wonder what were the sights upon which they were superimposed.

The logic of the figure is unassailable: reflected images are faint when they arise from transparent media. The insistence on transparency and reflection at the beginning of the figure does not require any discussion of the "fondi" at its conclusion. Yet even scientific treatises, when discussing the subject, could scarcely avoid giving examples of what one sees by "refraction" (that is, by transparency, in the uncertain terminology of the time) [11] and what by reflection. Roger Bacon, for example, contrasts sun and moon with fish and stones:

passage echoed by St. Ambrose, St. Augustine and perhaps Dante himself in the prologue scene. See JOHN FRECCERO, *Dante: The Poetics of Conversion*, Cambridge, 1985, pp. 19-20. For Narcissus in Dante, see MICHE-LANGELO PICONE, "Dante e il mito di Narciso dal *Roman de la Rose* alla *Commedia*," *Romanische Forschungen* 89 (1977), pp. 382-97.

[10] RIFFATERRE, p. 112.

[11] Up to the middle of the XIII century, the term *fractio* could indicate either reflection or refraction. See B. S. EASTWOOD, "Grosseteste's 'quantitative' law of Refraction...", *Journal of the History of Ideas*, 28 (1967), 406, cited by PIETRO ROSSI, *Grossatesta: metafisica della luce*, Milano, 1986, p. 148.

There are also certain bodies of moderate density, such as water, in which reflection and refraction occur simultaneously. For by refraction we see fish and stones in it, and by reflection we see the sun and moon, as experience teaches... Consequently, the reflection is weaker than that which would occur from a perfectly dense body and the refracted ray is weaker than if the second body were (like air) so rare that no reflection occurred.[12]

The relevance of this asymmetry, Dante's failure to make further mention of transparency, emerges when we translate these modes of vision into terms of poetic understanding. Glass and water are media, but so is the text. The mention of Narcissus has already associated reflection with that psychological drama of vision turned within, but there does not seem to be a counterpart in the *Paradiso* of poetic transparency, looking outward to the world beyond, to the fish and stones of the great sea of being.

Under the best of circumstances, glass and water are transparent, conveying light with no interruption. It is characteristic of all media, however, but particularly of poetry, to offer resistance and reflection, feedback in the transmission of information, to the point where all reference to the real world can be obscured. The first part of this simile, like all similes, refers to the real world, where transparency and reflection double our vision. In the second part, however, which is Paradise and not the real world, there is only surface, God's accommodation or, in naturalistic terms, the poet's *prosopopoeia*.

If the hint in Dante's text seems too slight to support this reading, it is one nevertheless suggested by modern texts which give these figurative meanings to the phenomena of transparency and reflection. Robert Frost, for example, may even have had Dante in mind:

For once, then, something

Others taunt me with having knelt at well-curbs
Always wrong to the light, so never seeing
Deeper down in the well than where the water
Gives me back in a shining surface picture
Me myself in the summer heaven godlike
Looking out of a wreath of fern and cloud puffs.
Once, when trying with chin against a well-curb,
I discerned, as I thought, beyond the picture,
Through the picture, a something white, uncertain,
Something more of the depths – and then I lost it.
Water came to rebuke the too clear water.
One drop fell from a fern, and lo, a ripple

---

[12] ROGER BACON, *De Multiplicatione Specierum*, II, cap. 5, trans. David C. Lindberg, in *Roger Bacon's Philosophy of Nature*, Oxford, 1983, p. 131.

> Shook whatever it was lay there at bottom,
> Blurred it, blotted it out. What was that whiteness?
> Truth? A pebble of quartz? for once, then, something.

Mirroring oneself in a well may be an emblem of the most extreme lyric self-absorption. Emily Dickinson's "What mystery pervades a well" serves as an example in the nineteenth century of placing what she calls a "glass lid" on the world. Frost is more defensive. He may even have had Dante in mind – "something white" is reminiscent of Dante's pearl – but the range from "truth" to "pebble of quartz" suggests a certain self-satisfaction with lyric solipsism. Language seems constantly to reach out toward some referent in the outside world, but is defeated by the opacity of the medium.

Early in the nineteenth century, Wordsworth gave a temporal dimension to the phenomena of transparency and reflection by staging them in a slow-moving boat. To add this fluidity to the portrait of the poet is to transform a static subjectivity into the flow of memory. A passage in *The Prelude* describes the space of memory in which past and present are confounded:

> As one who hangs down-bending from the side
> Of a slow-moving boat, upon the breast
> Of a still water, solacing himself
> With such discoveries as his eye can make
> Beneath him in the bottom of the deep,
> Sees many beauteous sights – weeds, fishes,
> Grots, pebbles, roots of trees, and fancies more,
> Yet often is perplexed and cannot part
> The shadow from the substance, rocks and sky,
> Mountains and clouds reflected in the depth
> Of the clear flood, from things which there abide
> In their true dwelling; now is crossed by gleam
> Of his own image, by a sunbeam now,
> And wavering motions sent he knows not whence,
> Impediments that make his task more sweet;
> Such pleasant office have we long pursued
> Incumbent o'er the surface of past time...
>
> (IV, 256-72)

The temporal dimension introduced here distinguishes narrative autobiography from the lyric. We are told that the flood stands for past time, but it might equally well be said that it stands for the book itself, a spatial representation of the past. Memory seems always to be spatial: mansions, caves, storehouse, perhaps because it is captured by writing, the spatial representation of time. In this spatial allegory of time, prepositions such as 'above' and 'below' take the place of 'before' and 'after', as they do in this extended simile. Moving through the water is very much like leafing through the pages of the book of memory, where impediments are made sweet by being suffused with our own continuity in time, by a confusion of the author with his persona in the past.

Because memory is so often thought of as a book, there is a certain inevitability in suggesting that the surface of the water, the intersection of the past with the present moment, is like writing. Perhaps Frost's ripples serve the same function, writing as the interference that brings together self-portraiture and the real world. There is one theme of lyric poetry, however, which explicitly gives to the intersection of reflection and refraction the significance of a written text: the poem which claims to have been written on pane of glass.

Writing about a poem of Victor Hugo ("Écrit sur une fenêtre flamande"), Michel Riffaterre mentions a story about Francois I of France having scratched a poem about the frailty of women on a pane of glass at the Chateau of Chambord. Victor Hugo adapted this anecdote for his play *Le Roi s'amuse*, the text that provided the story for Verdi's *Rigoletto*. According to this genealogy, the aria "La Donna è mobile" derives from a poem scratched on that window pane. If so, then the fickle lady in the Duke's aria also has Piccarda and the other inconstant souls as her ancestresses. [13]

In English poetry, however, John Donne probably wrote the most famous verses on a pane of glass. He locates his signature at the intersection of "through-shine" and reflection, in a poem which refers to a woman's frailty and explicitly to Dante's *Paradiso*:

A valediction: of my name in the window

My name engraved herein,
Doth contribute my firmness to this glass,
Which, ever since that charm, hath been
As hard, as that which graved it, was;
Thine eye will give it price enough to mock
The diamonds of either rock.
'Tis much that glass should be
As all confessing, and through-shine as I,
'Tis more, that it shows thee to thee,
And clear reflects thee to thine eye.
But all such rules, love's magic can undo,
Here you see me, and I am you.

The poem goes on at considerable length and in several passages echoes Dante's

---

[13] RIFFATERRE, p. 112. In the debate between Riffaterre and De Man about poetry written on window panes, what seems overlooked is that in Hugo's poem, as in that by Swift, an unspoken dimension is established by the fact that seeing *through* a window pane is often accompanied by seeing one's own reflection, with obvious consequences for poetics.

Paradiso, most notably when Donne speaks of his lady "emparadising" his soul, as Dante speaks of Beatrice as she who "imparadisa la mia mente". Both words are neologisms in their respective languages, so it would seem reasonable to assume that Donne's evocation of Dante was deliberate.[14] The fact that it is the husband's *name* which he leaves to his wife and that she is nevertheless reflected in the glass has led to speculation that the poem may refer to his wife's pregnancy, bearing the child which mirrors them both. The poem may be alluding to the theme of "nature's stylus", the sexual act as inscription. Whatever its meaning, the pane of glass serves as the ultimate emblem of the transparent, yet reflective text.

Finally, to return to the shadows on the moon, if writers and folklorists saw it in a beautiful woman, or seas, or Cain, it remained for a great scientist to see the shadows on the moon's surface as writing, at once marring the page and giving it significance. The observation was Galileo's, who compared the spots on the moon with the writing on his page. In his *Letters on the Sunspots*, he compares the spots on the sun with those on the moon, observing that the obscurity of sunspots is relative and that in fact, they are brighter than the brightest spots on the moon:

And if they yield nothing in brightness to the lightest parts of the moon, what will they be in comparison with the moon's darkest spots? [Moon spots] in comparison with the lighted portions [of the moon] are as dark as the ink with respect to this paper.[15]

To wonder about the configurations on the moon is much like puzzling out the meaning of ink-blots by free association. In this passage, Galileo hints at the analogy between the spots and linguistic signs. There is a similar hint in Dante's text. The word he uses to describe the faint outlines or tracings of our faces is "postille" which literally means "afterthoughts", inscribed as marginal notes or glosses outlining a text. The word "faccia" can also mean "page"; it has that meaning in the episode of Manfred. In the *Paradiso*, the "postille" are marginal notes outlining a face so clear that it cannot be seen. The literary implications of the image are not difficult to unfold. The text perfectly mirrors an undifferentiated reality and so is imperceptible except for the peripheral signs that designate it as text. The visual feedback, like a sign at eye-level affixed to a wall of glass, is the mark of the poet.

---

[14] Ll. 25ff: "Then, as all my souls be / Emparadised in you, (in whom alone I understand, and grow and see..." echoing *Paradiso*, XXVIII, 3: "quella che 'mparadisa la mia mente..." and *Purgatorio* XXV, 74: "...e fassi un'alma sola, / che vive e sente e sé in sé rigira...". JOHN DONNE, *The Complete English Poems*, ed. A. J. Smith, London, 1971, p. 87.

[15] GALILEO GALILEI, "Letter on the Sunspots I", in STILLMAN DRAKE, *Discoveries and Opinions of Galileo*, New York, 1957, p. 93.

One more moment in the poem brings together transparency and reflection in an emblem of divine creativity. We learn in Canto XXX that a ray of light descends from God and animates the first heaven, the *Primum Mobile*, thereby transmitting its power to the rest of the cosmos. At the same time, through the visual feed-back to which we have become accustomed in all of these texts, the light is reflected back to God, in the form of a celestial rose. The conical amphitheater of the blessed is the reflection back to God of his own light:

> E come clivo in acqua di suo imo
> si specchia, quasi per vedersi adorno,
> quando è nel verde e ne' fioretti opimo,
> sì, soprastando al lume intorno intorno,
> vidi specchiarsi in più di mille soglie
> quanto di noi là su fatto ha ritorno.

(XXX, 109-14)

It is said that mountains were objects of fear in the Middle Ages, whereas among the romantics, especially Wordsworth, they were the occasion for mystic experiences. Here, however, there would not seem to be a trace of the anxiety that is sometimes discernible in Wordsworth's text. The mountain is pleased with itself as it is reflected in its creation and the angels kindle the love that binds it to its flower.

The Dante of moon shadows is very different from the poet presented to us by Erich Auerbach and other critics who praise the poem's realism above all. Dante's mimetic power is without equal in the history of poetry, but this is true primarily of the *Inferno*. We have however already suggested that the mimetic realism of the *Inferno* begins to give way to the imaginative world of the *Purgatorio* with the meeting with Casella. It is as if Dante's prodigious imagination were directed, in the first *cantica*, to masking its own act and presenting infernal reality as though it were *there*, without the mediation of language. Purgatory, on the other hand, seems to exist in a register in which poetry is perfectly at home. The pilgrim proceeds with visions and dreams, with his own imagination as the stage on which the action unfolds. The body in Purgatory, like Casella's, is a vaporous imitation of the real body, made of the stuff of dreams. In the *Paradiso*, however, the faces in the moon are the last vestiges of human reality. Dante had already announced that the subject-matter of this last *cantica* was out of reach: "trasumanar significar *per verba* non si poria – to go beyond the human cannot be signified in words". The problem he faces in the *Paradiso* is therefore to represent the impossibility of representation, to give some hint of his subject matter by exposing the inadequacy of his medium. This negative poetics sounds very medieval, like the negative theology of the mystics, who sought to convey some idea of God by describing all that He is not. At the same time, it is the quality that gives to the *Paradiso* its distinctive modernity, a poetry dedicated to its own extinction, a play of light and shadow whose subject is its own limit.

NANCY DERSOFI

RUZANTE: TRANSLATING THE
PAROLACCE

Reviewing an English version of Ruzante's work performed at the Lyric Thea-ter, Hammersmith, Harold Hobson admonished "both the translator and the author... to buy a mouthwash, a clean typewriter and a dictionary".[1] As Hob-son's criticism focused on the monotonous repetition of offensive expressions, it is not clear whether Mike Alfred, translating a text adapted from a group of Ruzante's plays, rendered his author's ribald language faithfully, or if he misre-presented his author's coarse dialect. In its original form, Ruzante's dialect leaves wide latitude for interpretation. He speaks a stage version of *pavano*, a dialect spoken in the *Cinquecento* in the country region near Padua by farmers whose speech attaches them to the territory and its culture. Modern enthusiasm for Ru-zante is linked to the perception that his dialect-speaking characters give a true reflection of peasant life in that region in the troubled years during and after the Cambraic wars.

The belief that Ruzante's language exactly replicates a spoken regional dialect was modified in a 1970 study by Marisa Milani, who demonstrated that Ruzante and his companion rustics speak a theatrical version of *pavano*;[2] more recently, Ronnie Ferguson has argued that in Ruzante's time no one in the region actually spoke the dialect of the plays.[3] Nevertheless, Ruzante's stage language rings true to life, in part because of its *parolacce* – the obscenities and blasphemies that punctuate rustic speech. These words are stock expletives, which the playwright uses with skillful timing and keen awareness of their dramatic function, repeating words like *cancaro* with casual frequency, for example, while saving the more caustic *pota* for such emotionally taut moments as Ruzante's encounter with his estranged wife in the *Parlamento*. Translation of these terms sets the general

---

[1] H. HOBSON, "Historical tragical-pastoral," Times Literary Supplement, London, June 3, 1983, p. 5.

[2] M. MILANI, "Snaturalità e Deformazione nella Lingua Teatrale del Ruzante," L. Vanossi, M. Milani, M. Tonello, D. Battaglin, P. Spezzani, eds., *Lingua e strutture del teatro italiano del Rinascimento*, Padova, 1970, pp. 111-202.

[3] V.R. FERGUSON, "Il percorso linguistico del Ruzante fra letteratura e mimetismo," in *Angelo Beolco detto Ruzante: Atti del Convegno di studi e Programma generale 1995*, Padova, Papergraf, 1997, pp. 317-30.

tone of rustic speech and affects each scenic moment. An aggressive translation may render the rustic characters boorishly unfit for the company assembled to watch them perform; while a tempered version might characterize the rustic as merely socially inferior to his audience. In this paper, I look at cultural factors at play in Ruzante's vulgarity, and at the lessons of some recent English forays into translating the *parolacce*.

Although sixteenth-century Venetian, Paduan, and Ferrarese audiences judged Ruzante the Plautus and Roscius of his age, his contemporaries were not always tolerant of the comedian's rude words. An entry in the *Diarii* of Marin Sanudo for May 5, 1523 records that the performance offended the Signoria: "*una comedia fata per Ruzante, qual questo inverno fu fatta al Crosechieri, cosa molto discoreta da far davanti la Signoria*".[4] Another entry in Sanudo's *Diarii* reports that on February 9, 1525, a "*comedia vilanesca*" performed by Ruzante and Menato was "*tutta lasciva*" with "*parole molto sporche*";[5] audience indignation called for a substitute play for a performance on February 13 of that year. Ruzante addresses the issue directly at the end of *La Betìa* with the words "*Si ghe fosse qualche femena che diesse che la [dicesse che la commedia] fosse stà sporca, a'ghe rispondo che a'ghe dissi ananzo de dirla naturalmén, e digando naturalmén non se posséa dire con altre parole*".[6] The difference between "natural" and "dirty" was variously interpreted within Ruzante's own culture.

As standards of propriety acceptable to the *Signoria* had a political dimension, any challenge to those standards was assumed to be motivated politically. Family interests identifying the Paduan playwright with anti-Venetian factions during the Cambraic wars presumably heightened Venetian sensitivity to his rough tongue until some combination of political alliance and offensive language brought his Venetian performances to an end in 1526. In performances thereafter at Padua and Ferrara, Ruzante's rustic voice spoke to aristocrats whom the rustic community had opposed during the war, when the farmers cast their lot with Venice under the banner of San Marco. The author's close association with his patron, Alvise Cornaro, a Paduan landowner and prominent figure in Paduan cultural life, who several times petitioned, unsuccessfully, to be enrolled in the Golden Book of Venetian nobility, gives further ambivalence to Ruzante's *pavano*.

Performing during Carnival, a festival that licensed bawdiness, Ruzante translated the rustic voice into tones ranging from contentment to despair. It is uncertain whether the playwright's provocations were politically motivated or subversive; nor is it clear whether his anti-Venetian attitudes reflect peasant revolt or pa-

---

[4] M. SANUDO, *I Diarii*, vol. XXXIV, 124, cited in E. LOVARINI, *Studi sul Ruzante: la letteratura pavana*, ed. G. Folena, Padova, 1965, p. 85.

[5] *I Diarii*, vol. XXXVII, 559-560, cited in E. LOVARINI, pp. 88-89.

[6] Cited in E. LOVARINI, *Studi sul Ruzante*, p. 93.

trician anger. Moreover, with each new play he reinvented his rustic voice, responding to changing times and different audiences.

Toward the end of the sixteenth century, Ruzante's rustic speech began a stage life independent of the circumstances surrounding his political world and personal life. Galileo Galilei, a long-time resident in Padua, collected the playwright's work to read aloud to friends. In the eighteenth century, Luigi Riccoboni, arguing that comedy could withstand the use of dialects, pointed to Ruzante as the comedian who had introduced to the stage "*tutte le più barbare [lingue] dell'Italia*".[7] Obscene expletives are part of Ruzante's theatrical vocabulary from the outset. His first play, a verse *Pastoral*, begins with the lines:

> *Cancaro a i stropiegi!*
> *Pota, o'è andò gi osiegi*
> *che era chi sta doman?*
> *O pota de San...*
> (*Past., Proemio a la vilana*, 1-4)[8]

This early work, a *comedia a la villana*, introduces Ruzante as a rustic speaker accustomed to using obscenity in the mundane act of bird-trapping. Although he shares the world of the *Pastoral* with Italian-speaking shepherds and a nymph, his *parolacce* are less confrontational than expressive of his natural style. The play, not yet translated into English, offers the challenge of a text divided between *pavano* verse, based on a local poetic tradition and Italian verse modeled on works of Dante, Petrarch, Poliziano, and Sannazaro.

The expletives *cancaro* and *pota* occur throughout the plays and are the mainstay of Ruzante's *parolacce*. *Cancaro* indicates an ulcerlike sore on the body, especially the mouth; in a general sense the term signifies a sickness or rot pervading the rustic world. In Ruzante's "*personalissimo pavano*",[9] words sometimes parody their common sense: *cancaro*, meaning "canker" or "cancer" sounds enough like *cardine* meaning "hinge" or "pivot" to take its place in reference to the *cardine* (i.e. *cardinale*) on whose authority the gates of Heaven turn: "*e no cancaro che ten su l'usso, che 'l cancaro i magne igi e le so lettre, matti!*".[10] *Pota* (or *potta*), meaning female genitalia, intensifies the sexual aspect of the disease and disorder afflicting the countryside. The word functions as an obscene expletive, applied, notes Giorgio Padoan, to saints, diseases, to Ruzante's father, and even to the bad-mouthed speaker himself: "*Pota de mi!*".[11]

[7] L. RICCOBONI, *Discorso della Commedia all'Improvviso e Scenari Inediti*, ed. I Mamczarz, Milano, Edizioni Il Polifilo, 1973, p. 28.

[8] A. BEOLCO, *Il Ruzante, La Pastoral*, ed. G. Padoan, Padova, Editrice Antenore, 1978, p. 62.

[9] M. MILANI, *Snaturalità e deformazione*, p. 133.

[10] *Ibid.*, p. 186.

[11] G. Padoan, ed., *La Pastoral*, p. 60, n. 3.

After the early *Pastoral* there are a number of monolingual plays written entirely in *pavano*. Two such plays composed in the years 1529-30 are regarded as masterpieces of realistic intensity. *La Moscheta* is a five-act play structured like Plautine comedy, with a plot developed from Ruzante's attempt to test his wife's fidelity by approaching her in disguise and speaking in *lingua moscheta*. The few words he utters in this fancy Tuscan betray him, supporting the claim Ruzante makes in various prologues and monologues that the new Italian betrays the more natural, native dialect of the rustics. A shorter Dialogue of the same year, called *Il Parlamento de Ruzante che iera vegnú de campo*, conveys the misery of the rustic returning from battle; having gone to fight for Venice, Ruzante has lost his land, his wife, and his dignity. In *Bilora*, a play combining rustic speakers with Venetians and a Bergamask Zane, the rustic protagonist murders an elderly Venetian, who had become his wife's master and lover. In these plays obscenities occur frequently and to pointed dramatic effect. In English translations, the *parolacce* establish the tone and overall interpretation of the wotk.

In a recent translation of *La Moscheta*, Antonio Franceschetti and Kenneth R. Bartlett vary their translation of *cancaro*, giving "Damn it"[12] as an English equivalent in Menato's opening speech, and then, in the same speech, when Ruzante uses the term more emphatically (*"A'gh'ón el cancaro ch'a' ne magne"*[13]), they give the more literal translation: "We have this curse that eats away at us".[14] This close rendering of *cancaro* as a malevolent force consuming country life, like a cancer, serves the original text literally and effectively. Elsewhere in their translation, expletives like "damn it" and "bloody hell" are repeated without special emphasis to convey plain rustic vulgarity.

The harsher expletive, *pota*, occurs at the moment when Ruzante's wife, Betìa, all but yields to her disguised husband, asking him: *"Mo se 'l se saesse po, e che e 'l lo saesse me marìo? A' guagi mi"*, eliciting her husband's response: *"Deh, pota de chi te fe!"* (Act II, scene 4.32).[15] Franceschetti and Bartlett translate this passage as follows:

BETIA: Now, if that were to get out, and my husband found out about it? Poor me!

RUZANTE: Well, you cunt, you bloody cunt![16]

Their translation of *pota* in this instance is consistent with the denigration of

---

[12] A. BEOLCO, Il Ruzzante, La Moscheta, trans. with an Intro. and Notes by A. Franceschetti and K. R. Bartlett, Ottawa, Canada, Dovehouse Editions Inc., 1993, p. 55.

[13] RUZANTE, *Teatro*, ed. L. Zorzi, Torino, Einaudi, 1967, p. 585. This text of *La Moscheta* is cited throughout.

[14] A. Franceschetti and S. R. Bartlett, trans., *La Moscheta*, p. 55.

[15] RUZANTE, *Teatro*, p. 619.

[16] A. Franceschetti and S. R. Bartlett, *La Moscheta*, p. 72.

female sexuality that moved Ruzante to test his wife in the first place. The plot turns against the hapless rustic when his words drive his wife into the bed of a Bergamask soldier. Throughout the plays, the expletive *pota* has two aspects: one epitomizes the author's negative portrayal of women, while the other sadly regrets the failure of marriage, family, and home in the rustic world. This English translation, somewhat anacronistic for Ruzante's world, and aggressive, to my ear, for the gullible, misled protagonist of *La Moscheta*, does recognize that Ruzante's female rustic characters have little of grace or dignity.

In the *Parlamento*, Ruzante's first words upon arriving in Venice are: "*Cancaro a i campi e a la guera e a i soldè, e a i soldè e a la guera!*".[17] In his English edition of two of the one-act plays, Ronnie Ferguson translates: "The soldier's life, and war, and soldiers, and war: sod all that!".[18] Here, the sense of *cancaro* as a wasting disease yields to the perverse aspect underlying its use, although when Ruzante refers to sodomy in *L'Anconitana*, he associates the topic with upper-class, university society rather than the rustic world.

Varying his translation of *cancaro*, Ferguson produces a forceful, vigorous language. In the same opening speech: "*Cancaro a'son vegnú presto*" (scene 1.3, p. 517) becomes "Hell's bells, I got here quick!" A moment later "*Mo cancaro me magne!*" (p. 519) is translated, "Sod me for a bloody fool", followed by "No bloody way!" "Goddamit", "Jesus Christ", "Christ Almighty", "Bloody hell", and "Buggar it!" For "*Cancaro i magne igi!*" he translates "Up theirs, more like!" (p. 71). Effective in constructing a dirty-talking, character, reliant on his native tongue when all else has failed him, Ferguson's *parolacce* give Ruzante a performable vigor. The introduction of blasphemy however invites offense of a kind that the original avoids.

A 1958 translation of the *Parlamento* by Angelo Ingold and Theodore Hoffman translates Ruzante's opening line: "To hell with war, and battlefields, and soldiers!".[19] "I made good time getting here" is given where Ferguson translates "Hell's bells! I got here quick". For the most part the translators render *cancaro* with the dated but not unfamiliar expression "Pox!" which is consistent both with the sense of *cancaro* as a disease and with the work's archaism.

In the *Parlamento*, the playwright's use of *parolacce* controls the tense meeting in Venice between Ruzante and his wife, Gnua. Gnua greets her husband with the words: "*Ruzante? Situ ti? Ti è vivo, ampò? Pota!*" (scene 3.58).[20] Her expletive is a reminder of the sexuality she denies her husband, whom she has left for a

---

[17] RUZANTE, *Parlamento de Ruzante*, ed. L. Zorzi, p. 517. This text is cited throughout.

[18] A. BEOLCO, Il Ruzante, *The Veteran (Parlamento de Ruzante) and Weasel (Bilora)*, trans. with an Intro., Notes and Bibliography by R. Ferguson, New York, Peter Lang, p. 68.

[19] A. BEOLCO, "Ruzzante Returns from the Wars", in *The Classic Theatre*, ed. E. Bentley, Garden City, New York, Doubleday and Company, 1968, p. 61.

[20] RUZANTE, *Parlamento*, p. 533.

man who can feed her. Ruzante pleads in vain that he is a faithful, loving, spouse. In their brief encounter, husband and wife exchange the word *pota* eight times; then a Bravo appears, and the veteran Ruzante falls, a cowardly victim, to the blows of his wife's lover. In this scene, the term *pota*, relentlessly repeated, acquires thematic force, emphasizing that the marital relationship is at issue and driving home that the conjugal tie is broken.

Translating this scene, Ferguson turns Gnua's first speech (*"Ruzante? Situ ti? Te è vivo, ampò? Pota!"*) into the English, "Is it you? You're alive, after all? Buggar me!".[21] Later in the Dialogue, when Ruzante begins each of four speeches with *pota* and Gnua responds with *pota*, Ferguson keeps repeating "Buggar it!" This English exclamation emphasizes the failure of marriage and procreativity. Ruzante desires his wife's love and her body; but she has given him up because, in her words, *"No sètu che agno dí se magna?"* (scene 3, 66, p. 533) ("Don't you know that a body's got to eat every day?".[22] Plunder is what she expects from her veteran-husband, and her body's need for food is foremost in her thoughts. Ferguson's term expresses the frustrated sexuality their dialogue dramatizes. It is more pertinent than "Hell and damnation!" given by Ingold and Hoffman in one of the few instances when they translate *pota* at all. Their omission of the expletive results in an efficient translation that puts the message of the words into high relief, although their less explosive version of the passage does not prepare the audience for the scene's violent finale.

In addition to their thematic significance, Ruzante's *parolacce* also generate humor. In *Jokes and their Relation to the Unconscious*, Sigmund Freud says that dirty words, or smut, represent a kind of exposure of the person to whom they are directed. Naming sexual organs expresses a desire to see them, and calls on the person assailed to see them and to realize that the speaker imagines them. A joke requires the further presence of a third person, "who laughs at smut... as though he were the spectator of an act of sexual aggression".[23] Using words as if they were weapons, the rustics demean one another: "By making our enemy small, inferior, despicable, or comic, we achieve in a roundabout way the enjoyment of overcoming him – to which the third person, who has made no efforts, bears witness by his laughter".[24] From this perspective, the rustic *parolacce* give audiences both the universal pleasure of released repression and the comfort of superiority over bad-mouthed rustics, who are diminished by their dirty talk. The *parolacce* make *pavano* not simply a rustic dialect, or its thea-

---

[21] R. Ferguson, *The Veteran*, p. 79.

[22] *Ibid.*, p. 81.

[23] S. FREUD, *Jokes and their Relation to the Unconscious*, trans. and ed. by J. Strachey, New York, W. W. Norton, 1960, p. 97.

[24] *Ibid.*, p. 103.

trical representation, but a language that betrays its speakers. Often, however, when Ruzante soliliquizes passages bubbling with harsh invectives, his only listener is his audience, who is no longer his accomplice but the victim of his *brutte parole*.

The play most demeaning to the rustic world is *Bilora*, where the protagonist's desire to be reconciled with his wife drives him to murder his Venetian rival in cold blood. Violence is the keynote to his character and his language. Among his first words are the exclamation: "*Pota an l'amore!*", (scene 1)[25] followed by "*Cancaro! he bio bombe*".[26] Both expletives echo through his lines, alone and in various combinations, such as "*Pota del cancaro!*" (p. 555) Their frequency accentuates Bilora's pain and desperation at having lost his wife to the Venetian whom she prefers to her ragged, starving husband.

"Weasel" is a literal translation of the word *bilora*, and Ferguson adopts the name for his English protagonist. His translation of Bilora's invective against love ("*Pota an l'amore!*") is "Love? You can stuff it!" A translation of this play by Babette and Glenn Hughes (who keep the title *Bilora*) renders the same line: "Love-hell!".[27] Ferguson's translation of Weasel's invectives are consistent with his translation of the *parolacce* in the *Parlamento*: "*Cancaro! he bio bombe*" is "Buggar it"; "*Tamentre, al sangue del cancaro*" is "goddammit". Elsewhere he gives "Jesus Christ" for *cagasangue*, "Buggar and sod it!" for "*O pota del cancaro!*" The Hughes's translation gives "By all that's holy" in the first instance, "Damn it all!" in the second, and repeats "damned", for both *cancaro* and *pota*. "Damnation" points to the play's tragic outcome. In *Bilora*, the belittling effect of the rustic's *parolacce* is converted into action. The obscenities Bilora directs against his personal enemy, the Venetian Andronico, fall short of their mark: his wife fails to recognize him; she prefers her Venetian lover, however distasteful she finds her husband; and, finally, she hands Bilora some coins rather than taking food from the Venetian's house. Words fail Bilora, driving him to commit an action that destroys not only his Venetian antagonist but the image of a rustic figure struggling to salvage his humanity in the face of terrible adversity.

In the play that is arguably Ruzante's last work, *L'Anconitana*, the Venetian Andronico has a counterpart character in the equally decrepit Venetian Sier Tomao. Sier Tomao, lusting after a courtesan named Doralice, sends his well-fed, enterprising servant, Ruzante, to negotiate a tryst. Ruzante, meanwhile, pursues his own amours with his former rustic sweetheart, now Doralice's maid. Ruzante's role in this busy plot precludes outbursts of obstreperous rusticity, and he uses *parolacce*

---

[25] RUZANTE, *Bilora*, ed. L. Zorzi, p. 549. This text of *Bilora* is cited throughout.

[26] *Ibid.*

[27] A. BEOLCO, Il Ruzzante, *Bilora*, trans. and ed. by B. and G. Hughes, in *World Drama*, ed. by B. H. Clark, New York, Dover Publications, 1933, p. 1.

mainly to punctuate his entrances. In Act II, scene 2, for example, he comes on stage with the words: "*Cancaro a i Turchi e a i Muori, e an a i pigè preson da' Turchi!*".[28] In my translation of *L'Anconitana*, I give "Blast the Turks and the Moors and Turkish prisoners too!".[29] "Blast" has a burly sound and can express a sudden infection, and was therefore the translation I used for *cancaro* in most cases. Although there is an incantatory quality to Ruzante's repetition of the word *cancaro* as a kind of motif running through his speeches, some variations on the theme are needed; in such cases I used "pox" or "damn", as in Ruzante's ending to the speech cited above, where for "*Cancaro, l'e la bela noela!*" I gave "Damn, a fine new tale!"

More problematic is an English equivalent for *pota*. The term I adopted was "twat", a word most dictionaries omit. There is a singular instance when the Venetian Sier Tomao explodes in frustration at Ruzante's prolonged recapitulation of his progress in organizing a night of love for his master and Doralice. Sier Tomao finally exclaims: "*Va', pota de Santa Cataruza, semo intro i primi termeni!*" (Act IV, scene 3, p. 857) which I translated: "Go on! Saint Pussy-Kate, we're back to the very beginning!" (p. 131), hoping the reader would respond to a humorous, faintly archaic style, and recognize the irony in the Venetian's insulting reference to the church of Saint Catherine in Padua. There is further irony in Sier Tomao's having to resort to blasphemy in a pathetic attempt to hurry his servant's performance: in the fourth verse of his Proemio to the *Pastoral*, it is Ruzante who exclaims "*Oh, pota de San...*", or "Holy whore". From first to last, the stage is Ruzante's dominion. English-speaking audiences, with access now to five translations (three in print), will find that translations of Ruzante depend in large part on the translator's interpretation of complex and highly ambivalent texts as well as on a tacit assessment of the reader's likely reaction to the texts' dirty words. The original language holds a spectrum of tonalities, its obscenities and blasphemies representing inner helplessness, angry hostility, artful ambiguity, and commenting on discourses annulled by the ravages of war and its aftermath. Its play on words invites audiences to contemplate all aspects of a *mondo roesso* – an upsidedown, topsy turvy, ass-backwards, bottomside – upworld.

[28] RUZANTE, *L'Anconitana*, ed. L. Zorzi, p. 803.

[29] A. BEOLCO, Il Ruzzante, *L'Anconitana / The Woman from Ancona*, trans. with an Intro. by N. Dersofi, Berkeley, Univ. of Calif. Press, 1994, p. 67.

PAOLO CHERCHI

TRA SELVE E PROBLEMI NEL CINQUECENTO

La Spagna restituì al nostro Cinquecento quello che aveva preso in prestito da noi e messo a frutto nel Quattrocento. Si pensi alla *Celestina*, quell'opera «monstruosa» che affonda le sue radici nel nostro teatro umanistico e nel *De remediis utriusque fortunae* di Petrarca, e che entrò nella nostra cultura come un vortice, sia nell'originale castigliano sia nella traduzione italiana (1506) che diede il titolo poi invalso all'opera. Si pensi alla cosiddetta "novela sentimental", in particolare *La carcel de amor* di Diego de San Pedro, che si nutrì di linfe boccacciane (specialmente dell'*Elegia di Madonna Fiammetta*) e della storia *De duobus amantibus* di Alessandro Piccolomini, e che ebbe una vasta circolazione e numerosi imitatori in Italia. Non parliamo di un autore come Antonio de Guevara, imbevuto di autori italiani (da Francesco Patrizi a tanti altri umanisti), il cui *Relox de príncipes* e le *Epistolas* ebbero un successo degno di storia. Diversa è la vicenda del romanzo cavalleresco che ebbe origini autoctone spagnole, ma s'innestò sulla nostra tradizione immettendovi gli Amadigi e un'infinità di altri cavalieri erranti. Un fenomeno meno noto, ma legato alla stessa influenza spagnola in Italia è quello della *Silva de varia lección* di Pedro Mexía, che ebbe una notevole funzione nel dar vita a quel genere letterario minore che chiamiamo "selva", genere anche questo avente radici nella tradizione umanistica italiana, ma, per merito precipuo di Pedro Mexía, destinato ad affermarsi anche in lingua volgare.

La *Silva de varia lección* fu pubblicata a Siviglia nel 1540. Fu ristampata nello stesso anno con l'aggiunta di dieci capitoli, perciò nel 1543 e infine – perché fu l'ultima edizione curata dall'autore, e perciò da considerare definitiva – nel 1550 con l'aggiunta di un quarto libro. Il successo fu grandissimo non solo in castigliano (in poco meno di un secolo ebbe trentadue edizioni), ma anche in francese con una trentina di edizioni, in inglese con cinque, in tedesco con quattro, e in italiano con almeno altrettante. Perché tanto successo? La risposta è che se l'opera non scosse i lettori con la sua novità, dovette certamente sorprenderli per la sua freschezza che riuscì a rinnovare il genere e a dare impulso a tanti imitatori in volgare. La *Silva*, infatti, si rifaceva ad una tradizione classica e umanistica il cui capolavoro antico erano senz'altro le *Noctes Atticae* di Aulo Gellio. Se vediamo la prefazione gelliana troviamo una lista di molte opere al cui modello le *Noctes* si rifarebbero: sono miscellanee che vanno sotto i titoli più svariati – da *Péplon* (Il peplo) a *Kería* (Il Favo), da *Antherón* (Mazzi di fiori) a *Stromatéis* (Miscellanee), da *Storie naturali* a *Pantodapés* (Storie naturali), opere, per lo più, di difficile identificazione e molte di esse note soltanto per il titolo – che indicano lo sfondo della tradizione entro la quale Gellio compose il suo lavoro. Fra gli autori che, oltre Gellio, esercitarono un'influenza sul genere delle miscellanee umanistiche furono Solino col *Liber memorabilium*, Macrobio con i *Saturnalia*, e Clemente Alessandrino con gli *Stromata*. Quindi le opere umanistiche che potevano mediare il modello antico per Mexía erano lavori come la *Miscellaneorum centuria prima* di Poliziano, il *De honesta disciplina* di Pietro Crinito, o la *Varia historia* di Nicolò Leoniceno, o anche opere di maggior respiro come le *Antiquarum lectionum libri* di Celio Rodigino o i *Dies geniales* di Alessandro d'Alessandro. Sono tutte opere diverse, ma hanno in comune le caratteristiche della raccolta miscellanea e una matrice filologico-storica. Tale matrice si spiega col fatto che molte di queste siano nate come raccolte di *excerpta* o *scholia* dei commenti ai classici, tanto che molte delle miscellanee (anche quelle più tarde di un Pietro Vettori, o di un Girolamo Maggi) sembrerebbero raccolte di glosse o di "belle note", diremmo noi, in margine ai testi, note che potevano costituire brevi raccontini o trattatelli minimi su argomenti curiosi, che per lo più prendevano lo spunto da un dato linguistico o da un fatto storico o folklorico o anche naturale purché avesse gli attributi di "memorabile".

La *Silva* di Mexía eredita la struttura "disorganica" dei modelli, ma utilizza solo in parte minima il registro filologico-grammaticale. Il pubblico al quale si rivolge non è più quello dei filologi o dei pedanti o degli insegnanti, ma dei lettori educati ad una letteratura in volgare ormai abbastanza differenziata dalla tradizione umanistica (che in Spagna, comunque, era stata molto più debole che in Italia). A quel pubblico non interessa tanto sapere se un termine sia arcaico o no, o se un'attribuzione sia corretta o meno; interessa molto di più un dato curioso o anomalo o eccezionale, oppure una novelletta gustosa, oppure un ragguaglio sull'origine delle cose o magari di espressioni o di riti. Lo scopo dell'autore di una miscellanea in volgare, insomma, non è tanto erudire quanto incuriosire e divertire; e il suo rapporto con i testi non è quello di trovare un appiglio per una nota, bensì quello di poterne scerpare un passo da proporre ai lettori come pezzo autonomo, come brano fruibile in se stesso. Queste modificazioni rispetto ai modelli diedero alla *Silva* di Mexía quel sapore nuovo che la trasformò a sua volta in un modello su cui s'instaurò la tradizione delle selve in volgare.

Il titolo potrebbe avere origine classica. Gellio, nella *praefatio* ricordata, cita fra i tanti titoli anche quello di «silva», che secondo alcuni si riferirebbe all'opera di Stazio, ma alludendo soltanto alla varietà del contenuto,[1] o secondo altri corrisponderebbe al greco *hyle* col significato di "materia prima". È difficile credere che Mexía fosse tanto dotto da cercare un significato così arcano. Tutt'al più egli aveva in mente la definizione retorica,[2] secondo cui «silva» sarebbe uno "schizzo", la parte primigenia dell'*inventio*, ossia la materia allo stato di raccolta preliminare senza ancora alcun criterio organizzativo, il semplice cumulo di materiali anteriore alla classificazione secondo le *sedes* della *inventio*. Ma la cosa più probabile è che egli usasse il titolo proprio come l'avrebbero capito i suoi lettori, cioè come bosco, come intricato sviluppo di alberi: sembra confermarlo quanto leggiamo nel *Prohemio y prefación de la obra*: «Y como en esto, como en lo demás, los ingenios de los hombres son tan varios y cada uno va por diverso camino, siguiendo yo al mío, escogí y hame parescido escrivir este libro assí, por discursos y capítulos de diversos propósitos, sin perseverar ni guardar orden en ellos; y por esto le puse por nombre *Silva*, porque en las selvas y bosques están las plantas y árboles sin orden ni regla. Y aunque esta manera de escrivir sea nueva en nuestra lengua castellana y creo que soy el primero que en ella aya tomado esta invención, en la griega y latina muy grandes autores escrivieron assí, como fueron Ateneo, Víndice Cecilio, Aulo Gelio, Macrobio, y aun en nuestros tiempos, Petro Crinito, Ludovico Celio, Nicolao Leónico y otros algunos».[3] Non sfuggirà il fatto che, nonostante la spiegazione così dimessa, «silva» è un latinismo, come lo è «lección» che si deve intendere non nel senso di "lezione", ma di "scelta" (*lectio*), termine in parte mutuato dalla tradizione umanistica. Si tratta, in fondo, di una scelta di letture fatte dall'autore e raccomandate poi ai suoi lettori, se la selezione segna prevedibili criteri estetici, l'ordine della materia è del tutto imprevedibile.

Il risultato è a prima vista sconcertante, perché il disordine della *dispositio* consente infinite strategie di lettura: un lettore può cominciarla a partire da qualsiasi capitolo e può chiuderla a qualsiasi pagina scelta a caso; può permettersi salti da un libro all'altro senza che la lettura sia ostacolata dalla mancanza di nessi narrativi o d'altro tipo; può limitarsi alla lettura di un solo capitolo e capire la natura di tutto il libro. Tanto disordine sfida alcune norme fondamentali di poetica ispirate dalla tradizione aristotelico-oraziana, perché porta alla completa autonomia, anzi indipendenza, di ogni parte dell'opera dal tutto, contenendo in germe la poetica dell'*essay*; e non sarà questa una delle ultime ragioni per cui Montaigne ebbe in grande stima la *Silva*. Il disordine della *Silva* non riguarda solo la *dispositio* della materia, ma la varietà della stessa. La "silva", infatti, deve contenere argomenti diversi: può includere una novella ma

---

[1] Cfr. l'introd. all'ed. delle *Silvae* di Stazio a cura di J. H. Frère e H. J. Izaac, Parigi, 1961, pp. XXXII, sg.

[2] Cfr. QUINTILIANO, *Inst. orat.*, X, 3, 17: «diversum est huic eorum vitium, qui primo decurrere per materiam stilo quam velocissimo volunt et sequens calorem atque impetum ex tempore scribunt: hanc silvam vocant».

[3] P. 161 sg. del vol. I dell'edizione a cura di Antonio Castro, Madrid, Cátedra, 1989.

anche un discorso sulle età dell'uomo, un carme col commento o un trattatello sul calendario o sugli elementi naturali o sugli inventori delle campane e sull'uso delle stesse, sull'origine dei venti o sulle armi degli antichi Persiani o sugli anelli degli antichi.

Tanta libertà, naturalmente, esige un prezzo: la lettura casuale ad apertura di pagina deve garantire risultati sempre alti e uniformi (all'autore non è concesso «dormitare di tanto in tanto» come accade nelle opere d'una certa estensione), per cui ogni testo o frammento di esso deve avere in sé qualità tali da fermare l'attenzione del lettore. Gli specchietti migliori per catturare lettori ad apertura di pagina erano stati tradizionalmente le raccolte di *memorabilia* e più ancora quelle dei *mirabilia*: del primo facevano parte descrizioni del mondo o raccolte di aneddoti e apoftegmi di personaggi grandi, sulla traccia di Valerio Massimo o di Plutarco; del secondo (che si muoveva nella scia di Plinio e di Solino) facevano parte racconti di cose mostruose ed esotiche, assolutamente inverosimili (di quest'ultimo genere la Spagna ci diede un fortunatissimo esemplare nel *Jardín de flores curiosas* di Antonio de Torquemada, anch'esso tradotto in italiano). Il pubblico non sembrava mai sazio di curiosità per tutto quello che riguarda grandi personaggi o mondi esotici; Pietro Mexía usò altre forme d'incanto, anche se non eliminò del tutto elementi delle tradizioni indicate. Per lo più egli considera un dato noto a tutti i lettori, come può esserlo il segno della croce o il fatto che si portino anelli; ma poi sorprende questi suoi lettori con una domanda relativa all'origine e alla simbologia di quei dati conosciutissimi. Prendiamo, per esempio, il fatto che l'uomo fra tutti gli animali cammini ritto: non sarebbe interessante saperne il perché? E se la testa è il membro più importante dell'uomo, perché ci togliamo il capello per salutare un superiore? Nessuno si pone una domanda del genere perché la frequenza d'un tal gesto l'ha quasi banalizzato, come un rito che col tempo perde le sue valenze simboliche. Prendiamo la storia dei Guelfi e Ghibellini: la loro rivalità è proverbiale, ma proprio per questo se ne son dimenticate le cause; lo stesso dicasi di certi costumi dei Turchi o della fine dei Templari. In altre parole, il segreto di Mexía non è cercare novità mirabili o viaggiare per paesi ignoti, ma ritrovare nel mondo noto qualcosa che si è perso e che dà un senso più profondo alle cose che conosciamo. Lo stupore maggiore viene dalla scoperta archeologica non dall'esplorazione di continenti nuovi: questa può sconvolgere, mentre l'altra conforta perché riscopriamo ciò che è stato nostro. Ad avviare il viaggio basta una semplice domanda, il chiedersi il perché delle cose che sembrano più normali; e la risposta è quasi sempre sorprendente perché ciò che diventa normale e duraturo deve avere in sé qualcosa di complesso che poi il tempo ha semplificato.

La formula può esser semplice, ma la realizzazione di un progetto come la *Silva* richiedeva grande *discretio* ed immaginazione nel cogliere, come "apis Matina", da infinite specie di fiori diversi i pezzi che potevano sorprendere i lettori. Mexía evidentemente ebbe queste doti se la sua opera piacque a generazioni e generazioni di lettori. In Italia fu immediatamente tradotta da Mambrino Roseo (1547), poi da Lucio Mauro (1556), e infine da Francesco Sansovino, il quale vi aggiunse una parte su cui torneremo. Un segno sicuro del successo furono le imitazioni: per esempio quella di Gaudenzio Merula, il quale, avendo scritto un libro, *De rerum memorabilium*, lo tradusse poi col titolo di *Nuova selva di varia letione*, cioè con un titolo in concorrenza con quello di Mexía. All'opera di Merula affianca quella che Gerolamo Giglio intitola *Nuova seconda selva di varia lettione*. Vi furono perfino "selva" specializzate, come quella di Carlo Passi, *Selva di varia istoria*, ricavata dagli scritti storici di Paolo Giovio; e una fungaia di altre miscellane che sfruttavano la fortuna dell'opera spagnola, come la *Historia varia* di Ludovico Domenichi o la *Idea del giardino del mondo* di Tomaso Tomai.

La traduzione di Sansovino merita attenzione particolare perché, dopo aver tradotto i primi tre libri, abbandona l'originale nel quarto libro e produce un testo affatto nuovo rispetto all'originale. Anche Mexía aveva aggiunto un quarto libro, che però non ha niente di particolare rispetto agli altri, e continua a sceglier testi secondo la formula indicata. L'aggiunta di Sansovino, invece, si rifà a tutta un'altra tradizione, apparentemente lontanissima dalle "selve", quanto poteva esserla quella dei *problemata* pseudo-aristotelici. Per giunta Sansovino ora non traduce ma plagia. Curiosamente, però, entrambe le operazioni sono vicinissime allo spirito e alla natura della *Silva*, perché i *problemata* si interrogano su fatti che cadono sotto gli occhi di tutti, e il plagio è previsto nel concetto stesso di "lección".

I *Problemata* sono son attribuiti ad Aristotele fin dall'antichità, ma in era moderna tale paternità è stata negata; tuttavia il più recente editore, Pierre Louis,[4] si schiera in sua difesa. Se qui si accenna al problema è per notare che il dubbio non sorse nel Medioevo o nel Rinascimento, e l'opera godette del prestigio e del successo riservato a tutte le altre opere di Aristotele. Il "problema" è tecnicamente definito da Aristotele nella *Topica* quando stabilisce la differenza tra una proposizione e un problema nel modo seguente: «se io dico che "animale pedestre e bipede" è la definizione dell'uomo, non è vero? si ha una proposizione; se invece dico: forse che "animale pedestre e bipede" è o non è la definizione dell'uomo? ho un problema» (I, 4; 101b28-37). Detto in altre parole, la proposizione o la definizione afferma un fatto che si vuole che si accetti, mentre il problema considera come possibilità anche il contrario della tesi proposta e invita alla disamina degli argomenti in favore e contro la tesi proposta. Il problema è una ricerca su una questione di cui si ignora la risposta e su cui esistono vedute divergenti. Si tratta, insomma, di un procedimento dialettico che può portare alla verità.[5] Ora la natura dei *problemata*

---

[4] Per la collana Les Belles Lettres, Parigi, 1991.

[5] Cfr. ÉMILE BRÉHIER, «La notion de problème en philosophie», *Theoria*, XIV (1948), pp. 1-7; poi in *Études de philosphie antique*, Presses Universitaires de France, Parigi, 1955, pp. 10-16, particolarmente pp. 11 sg.

aristotelici è sempre molto concreta, limitata, cioè a fatti particolari e che si devono risolvere – nel senso di dare una risposta, non una soluzione che supera il problema – coi mezzi ed entro i limiti di una disciplina. Sono fatti riguardanti o la matematica o la medicina o la biologia o la morale. Un problema tipico può essere il seguente: «Perché si suda meno quando si mangia dopo aver bevuto? Sarà perché gli alimenti assorbono l'umidità come una spugna immersa nel liquido? È possibile moderare il flusso in modo non trascurabile, come nelle correnti d'acqua, con l'ingestione di nutrimento che comprime i condotti» (II, 25). Come si vede, formalmente si pongono due domande, la prima delle quali pone la questione e la seconda avanza dubitativamente una risposta ma lascia aperta la possibilità di rispondere in modo anche diverso. Se la risposta fosse ovvia non verrebbe posta in termini interrogativi, come per esempio se ci si chiede «perché (*dià tí*: è la formula che apre ogni problema) l'occhio a riposo non vede se stesso?» (*Della sensazione*, II, 437a29), è una questione che ha una risposta tanto ovvia che non viene data; oppure a volte la risposta può esser data in modo positivo: «Perché (*dià tí*) le uova non chiocciate, pur essendo vive in se stesse, l'anima nutritiva non assicura lo sviluppo dell'animale e delle sue parti?»; e la risposta è «perché (*óti*) per far ciò è necessaria l'anima sensitiva». In entrambi i casi non abbiamo dei veri "problemi".[6]

Non è difficile capire perché un tipo d'opera del genere possa diventare popolare. La traduzione di Pietro d'Abano e il relativo commento completato nel 1301 (era il momento in cui la teologia veniva invasa da "questioni" naturali che cercavano di dare spiegazioni "naturalistiche" dei miracoli), non è se non il principio di una fortuna fatta non solo di traduzioni e di commenti (per esempio quello influentissimo di Marcantonio Zimara) o dal proliferare di lavori affini (come i *Problemata* di Alessandro d'Afrodisia, tradotti da Poliziano), ma anche a tutta una serie di imitazioni. Si prenda, per esempio il libro di Girolamo Manfredi intitolato *Il perché* nella versione volgare (l'originale latino, *Liber de homine*, è del 1474), che ebbe una diffusione spentasi solo nel tardo Seicento, ed è sostanzialmente una versione dei *Problemata* pseudo-aristotelici; o si prenda l'opera di un medico come Giacchino (*Leonardi Iacchini, medici emporensis, Quaestionum naturalium libellus*, Griphius, Lione, 1540), dove si discutono tanti problemi, specialmente relativi all'amore; e che cosa sono in gran parte i *Pensieri* di Tassoni se non una cospicua collezione di *problemata*? In termini strettamente formali possono essere diversi dai problemata del Filosofo, mancando spesso la duplice domanda, ma in sostanza sono la stessa cosa; infatti che altro potrebbe essere il «perché grattando la rogna, cessa lo scadore»?[7] di Manfredi, o il «perché incanutiscono i vec-

---

[6] Cfr. P. LOUIS, l'introduzione all'ed. cit., pp. XX-XXIII.

[7] La risposta è la seguente: «La ventosità rinchiusa, ch'era cagione di scadore, grattando si viene ad essalare, et evaporare per la porosità cotanea, che si vengono ad aprire, per astersione di una certa bruttura, che teniva chiuse esse porosità, onde grattandosi toglie via quella bruttura, et si aprono, e si dilatano quelle, che di tali ventosità esce fuora» (da *Il Nuovo lume dell'arte overo Il perché - Opera copiosa di varie cognitioni*, Gattella, Padova, 1668, libro IV, p. 147).

chi» del Tassoni (*Pensieri diversi*, V, 8) se non problemi di tipo aristotelico? Bisogna aggiungere, semmai, che il modello incoraggiò la proliferazione di problemi del tutto irrilevanti e vicini alla caricatura, come si vedrà da alcuni titoli che riporteremo.

D'altra parte è anche facile vedere l'affinità tra i problemi della miglior tradizione aristotelica e i brani da *Silva* secondo il principio selettivo di Mexía. Entrambi hanno per soggetto dati che tutti conoscono, ma che nessuno studia perché la loro continua presenza li spoglia di ogni interesse; eppure basta la semplice e imprevista domanda del perché esistano e del come siano venute ad essere e, improvvisamente, quelle cose si caricano di grande interesse, e gratificante per quella freschezza dovuta alla sorpresa. L'unica differenza è che mentre i dati della *Silva* trattano quasi esclusivamente di fatti storici, gli argomenti dei *problemata* sono quasi esclusivamente di argomento naturale. Sansovino capì l'affinità fra i due generi di curiosità, e anziché tradurre la quarta parte della *Silva* di Mexía ne allestì una propria facendone una sezione di *problemata*. Per i suoi lettori non esisteva alcuna differenza perché per loro era ancora possibile aprire la *Selva* a qualsiasi pagina della prima o della quarta parte e rimanere affascinati dalle spiegazioni di fatti che sembravano non richiederne alcuna.

Per fare un lavoro più spedito, secondo le esigenze e la prassi normale dei poligrafi del secondo Cinquecento, probabilmente Sansovino copiò tutti i materiali di questa nuova parte. L'indizio non ci può ingannare: il rinvenimento della fonte di una buona parte fa sospettare che anche il resto sia copiato, per cui è prevedibile che con un po' di tempo e di pazienza o di fortuna si troverà anche questa o queste ipotetiche fonti.

I testi che Sansovino plagia sono varie sezioni dei *Problemi naturali e morali* di Girolamo Garimberto, pubblicati da Valgrisi a Venezia nel 1549. Ci limitiamo a darne qualche campione. Prendiamo per esempio il seguente problema:

Perché de cavalli e de gli asini, il maschio fiutando dove havera pisciato la femina alza la testa, e mostra i denti

Essendo il senso dell'odorato più eccellente ne gli animali irrationali, che non è nell'huomo, essi anchora saranno più pronti, e più presti nel sentir gli odori, e discerner l'uno dall'altro e più da lontano di lui. Onde veggiamo, che 'l cane cercando truova il lepre all'odore, co 'l qual trova anchora il padrone, che haverà smarrito; et semplicemente odorando lo scorge tra la moltitudine delle genti; si come scorge anchora una fiera da un'altra su la caccia: di ciò n'habbiamo l'essempio raro de cani laineri di Francia, che seguitando un cervo per piani, monti, et boschi, e per paludi, e fiumi tutto il giorno, dipoi essendogli tolto dall'oscurità della notte, la mattina seguente lo ritrovano subito all'odore; et molte volte in una folta schiera d'altri cervi, dove si cacciano i cani; ne badando a veruno degli altri, seguitano lui solo fin tanto, che vinto dalla stracchezza correndo cade lor a i piedi; tanto è grande la forza dell'odorato nel cane, et non solamente in lui, ma nel resto de gli animali, tra i quali de cavalli e de gli asini, il maschio conoscendo all'odore della natura, dove haverà pisciata la femina, subito si abbassa fiutando l'orina; i molti vapori della quale ascendendogli al cervello l'annoiano talmente, che per mandarli fuora incontinente alza la testa, et contrahe il labbro di sopra; dalla cui contrattione ne seguita, ch'ei mostra i denti, et che le narici allargandosi fanno più spedita e più libera l'uscita a quei vapori, che offendono il cervello del cavallo, e dell'asino, non per rispetto dell'odorato, conciosiache gli animali non sentono né dilettation né noia ne gli odori, ma per cagion dell'acutezza di quei vapori, che l'alterano.[8]

Il testo appare tale e quale nella *Selva* curata da Sansovino:

Perché de cavalli e de gli asini, il maschio fiutando dove havera pisciato la femina alza la testa, e mostra i denti

Essendo il senso dell'odorato più eccellente ne gli animali irrationali, che non è nell'huomo: essi anchora saranno più pronti, e più presti nel sentir gli odori, et discerner l'uno dall'altro e più da lontano di lui. Onde veggiamo, che 'l cane cercando truova la lepre all'odore, col quale truova ancora il padrone, che haverà smarrito; et semplicemente odorando lo scorge tra la moltitudine delle genti; si come scorge ancora una fiera da un'altra su la caccia, di ciò n'habbiamo l'essempio raro de cani laineri di Francia, che seguitando un cervo per piani, monti, et boschi, et per paludi, e fiumi tutto il giorno, dopo, essendogli tolto dall'oscurità della notte: la mattina seguente lo ritrovano subito all'odore; et molte volte in una folta schiera d'altri cervi, dove si cacciano i cani; nè badando a veruno de gli altri, seguitano lui solo fin tanto, che vinto dalla stracchezza correndo cade loro a' piedi: tanto è grande la forza dell'odorato nel cane: et non solamente in lui, ma nel resto de gli animali, tra i quali de' cavalli et de gli asini, il maschio conoscendo all'odore della natura, dove haverà pisciato la femina, subito si abbassa fiutando l'orina: i molti vapori della quale ascendendogli al cervello, l'annoiano talmente, che per mandarli fuora incontanente alza la testa, e contrahe il labbro di sopra; dalla cui contrattione ne seguita, ch'ei mostra i denti, et che le narici allargandosi fanno più spedita e più libera l'uscita a quei vapori, che offendono il cervello del cavallo, et dell'asino, non per rispetto dell'odorato, conciosia che gli animali non sentono né dilettatione nè noia ne gli odori: ma per cagion dell'acutezza di quei vapori, che l'alterano.[9]

Un altro problema:

La cagione perché in Vinegia siano più balbutienti, et si parli più adagio che nell'altre città d'Italia

Tra tutti gli elementi niuno ve ne ha, che manco si scompagni da noi, e che più ci alteri di quel che si faccia l'aria; percioche ne circonda sempre, et incontinente; et senza alcun mezo con la sottilità sua penetra i corpi nostri, alterando le complessioni, et rendendole più e manco humide secondo che è maggior e minor la sua humidità; perchém l'aria non solamente per natura è humido, ma sopragiunto dall'accidente è humidissimo; come dalla qualità de tempi freddi, dal sito basso e paludoso, et da venti humidi o vero freddi. Et perché Vinegia per natura, e per accidente è sottoposta a tutte queste qualità per esser settentrionale più dell'altre parti d'Italia, et situata tra le lacune, et battuta assai da venti humidi e freddi, sarà anchora più humida di tutte l'altre, onde

---

[8] Pp. 82 sg. dell'ed. citata, problema 45. Nella trascrizione di questo testo e dei seguenti si è intervenuti solo con l'aggiunta di qualche accento onde evitare ambiguità.

[9] P. 333, cap. 14, dell'ed. di G. de' Cavalli, Venezia, 1564.

gli huomini abondano di humidità soverchia, che rinchiusa nel cervello, humetta loro tanto la lingua, che essa aggravata da molto humore, non altrimenti si rende immobile alla pronuntia delle parole, che si faccia quella de fanciulli; i quali si come per la troppa lor humidità naturale sono balbutienti più de gli altri huomini; così anchora i Vinitiani, e per la natural, et per l'accidentale sono balbutienti più de gli altri italiani; et appresso di loro i Bolognesi, per l'istessa cagione, essendo Bologna città humidissima dopo Vinegia; nella quale si potrebbe dire anchora, che molti balbutiscono, perché abondano di molta flemma; il quale debilitando alcuni nervi, che vanno alla lingua, fa che ella resta impedita al pronuntiar, et tarda al muoversi, parimente per la frigidità come nemica del moto; onde i Vinitiani peccano più de gli altri Italiani, non solamente in balbutir, ma anchora nel parlar tardo, e nell'oprar tardissimo, per esser etiandio più flemmatici di loro.[10]

Ancora una volta viene copiato integralmente da Sansovino:

La cagione perché in Vinegia siano più balbutienti, et si parli più adagio che nell'altre città d'Italia
Tra tutti gli elementi niuno ve ne ha, che manco si scompagni da noi, e che più ci alteri di quel, che si faccia l'aria, percioche ne circonda sempre, et incontanente; et senza alcun mezo con la sottilità sua penetra i corpi nostri, alterando le complessioni, et rendendole più, et manco humide secondo che è maggior, e minor la sua humidità; perché l'aria non solamente per natura è humido, ma sopragiunto dall'accidente è humidissima; come dalla qualità de' tempi freddi, dal sito basso et paludoso, et da' venti humidi overo freddi. Et, perché Vinegia per natura, et per accidente è sottoposta a tutte queste qualità, per esser Settentrionale più dell'altre parti d'Italia, et situata tra le lagune, et battuta assai da' venti humidi e freddi, sarà ancora più humida di tutte l'altre, onde gli huomini abondano d'humidità soverchia, che rinchiusa nel cervello, humetta loro tanto la lingua, che essa aggravata da molto humore, non altrimenti si rende immobile alla pronuntia delle parole, che si faccia quella de fanciulli; i quali cosi come per la troppa loro humidità naturale sono balbutienti più de gli altri huomini; così ancora i Vinitiani, e per la naturale, et per l'accidentale sono balbutienti più de gli altri italiani; et appresso di loro i Bolognesi, per l'istessa cagione, essendo Bologna città humidissima dopo Vinegia; nella quale si potrebbe dire ancora, che molti balbutiscono, perché abondano di molta flemma; il quale amore [sic; ma deve essere errore per "humore"] corrompendo alcuni nervi, che vanno alla lingua, fa che ella resta impedita al pronuntiare, et tarda al muoversi, parimente per la frigidità come nemica del moto; laonde i Vinitiani peccano più de gli altri Italiani, non solamente in balbutire, ma ancora nel parlar tardo, e nell'operar tardissimo, per esser etiandio più flemmatici di loro.[11]

Infine un altro problema, non per provare la qualità del plagio, così ovvio da non richiedere commento, ma per avere un'idea migliore della natura degli argomenti:

[10] Pp. 128-129, problema 75.
[11] Pp. 328-329, cap. 8.

'D'onde viene, che quasi tutti i Genovesi hanno la testa acuta, e la maggior parte d'essi la bocca crespa.

Chi osserverà bene i costumi de gli huomini, troverà anchora, che tutti i paesi, e tutte le Città, et etiandio nelle Città istesse, tutte le gran famiglie hanno alcuna usanza tanto propria intra di loro, che mediante un lungo habito, finalmente se gli converte in natura; come quella delle donne Genovesi, le quali mosse da alcune lor vane opinioni (si come è proprio di tutte le femine), hanno per antica usanza di premere amendue le mani d'ogn'intorno, il capo de teneri fanciullini, incontinente, che sono nati, per farglielo acuto, sì come fanno; di che ne è seguito, che dove altre volte tutti i capi loro artificiosamente erano acuti, hora la maggior parte d'essi naturalmente tende alla acutezza; percioche la natura aiutata dall'arte, opera non altrimente ne gli huomini, che si faccia in una pianta, i cui frutti non solo quanto alla forma, ma anchora quanto alla spetie sono trasmutati dall'arte; la quale co'l tempo convertendosi in natura, fà che in Genova i figliuoli nascono con la testa acuta come i padri; et etiandio con la bocca crespa, per causa della pronuntia loro; la quale in Italia non altrimente è varia da una Città a un'altra, che sia nel resto del mondo da una provincia a un'altra. Imperoche i Fiorentini pronuntiano nella gorga; i Vinitiani nel palato; Napolitani ne denti; e Genovesi nella sommità delle labbra, le quali necessariamente comprimono quando vogliono formar la parola, et quelle compresse vengono ad abondar di molte grincie; che dipoi essendo impresse dall'habito nella tenerezza de fanciulli, sono cagione che gli huomini habbiano la bocca crespa per accidente, et per natura anchora: si come l'acutezza del capo, per la ragion detta inanzi; et etiandio per l'imaginatione delle donne, la quale ha forza d'imprimere ne figlioli l'imagine conforme in tutte le parti a quelle de padri; et di quegli huomini, che esse hanno sempre inanzi gli occhi: d'onde si viene in cognitione della causa, perché i Genovesi habbiano la testa acuta, e la bocca crespa. [12]

E, come sempre, tutto viene ripreso alla lettera da Sansovino:

Onde viene, che quasi tutti i Genovesi hanno la testa acuta, et la maggior parte d'essi la bocca crespa.

Chi osserverà bene i costumi de gli huomini, troverà ancora, che tutti i paesi, e tutte le città, et etiandio nelle città istesse, tutte le gran famiglie haver alcuna usanza tanto propria infra di loro, che mediante un lungo habito, finalmente se gli converte in natura; come quella delle donne Genovesi, le quali mosse da alcune lor vane opinioni, come è proprio di tutte le femine) hanno per antica usanza di premere amendua le mani d'ogni intorno, il capo de' teneri fanciullini, incontanente che sono nati, per farglielo acuto, come fanno: di che ne è seguito, che dove altre volte tutti i capi loro artificiosamente erano acuti, hora la maggior parte d'essi tende naturalmente alla acutezza; percioche la natura aiutata dall'arte, opera non altrimente ne gli huomini, che si faccia in una pianta, i cui frutti non solo, quanto alla forma, ma ancora quanto alla specie sono trasmutati dall'arte; la quale col tempo convertendosi in natura, fa, che in Genova i figliuoli nascono con la testa acuta, come i padri: et etiandio con la bocca crespa, per causa della pronuntia loro, la quale in Italia non altrimenti è varia da una città a un'altra, che sia nel resto del mondo da una provincia a un'altra. Percioche i Fiorentini pronuntiano nella gorga; i Vinitiani nel palato; Napolitani

---

[12] Pp. 129-130, problema 76.

ne' denti; et Genovesi nella sommità delle labra, le quali necessariamente comprimono quando vogliono formar la parola, et quelle compresse vengono ad abondar di molte grinze, che dopo essendo impresse dall'habito nella tenerezza de' fanciulli, sono cagione che gli huomini habbiano la bocca crespa per accidente, et per natura ancora, come l'acutezza del capo, per la ragione detta inanzi: et etiandio per l'imaginatione delle donne, la quale ha forza d'imprimere ne' figlioli l'imagine conforme in tutte le parti a quelle de' padri; et di quegli huomini, che esse hanno sempre inanzi a gli occhi: onde si viene in cognitione della causa, perché i Genovesi habbiano la testa acuta, et la bocca crespa. [13]

I capitoli che Sansovino plagia letteralmente (i nostri prelievi ne dànno una prova irrefutabile) sono in tutto venti e son concentrati nella prima metà della quarta parte, a partire dal secondo capitolo. Per stabilire un riscontro puntuale ne diamo i titoli, indicando fra parentesi i problemi corrispondenti in Garimberto:

2) *Qual è la causa, che molte città, e Provincie, che altre volte producevano gl'huomini pieni di virtù, et di valore, hora gli produchino ignoranti, et vili, e così per il contrario* (problema 69)

3) *Onde viene, che gli huomini dell'Indie Occidentali trovate a' tempi nostri habbiano havute qualche leggi, et costumi conformi a' nostri prima che essi havessero notitia alcuna di noi, et noi l'havessimo di loro* (problema 70)

4) *Qual è la causa, che i Tedeschi, et i Francesi siano più grandi, più grossi, et più bianchi de gli Italiani* (problema 71)

5) *Si cerca, perché i Tedeschi, et i Francesi essendo più grandi et più grossi de gli Italiani et de gli Spagnuoli, dopo resistano manco di loro alla fatica* (problema 72)

6) *Onde si causa, che i Francesi, et i Tedeschi siano più audaci de gli Italiani, et de gli Spagnuoli: et all'incontro siano manco forti, et manco astuti* (problema 73)

7) *Onde viene, che universalmente i Francesi, et i Tedeschi si dilettino manco della politezza, che non fanno gli Italiani, e gli Spagnuoli* (problema 74)

8) *La cagione perché in Vinegia siano più balbutienti, et si parli più adagio che nell'altre città d'Italia* (problema 75)

9) *Onde viene, che quasi tutti i Genovesi hanno la testa acuta, et la maggior parte d'essi la bocca crespa* (problema 76)

10) *Perché gli Italiani siano più differenti di complessione, et di costumi tra di loro, che non sono l'altre nationi* (problema 77)

11) *Qual è la cagione, che al Cervo cadono ogni anno le corna, et ogni anno gli rinascono* (problema 43)

12) *Onde viene, che l'asino senta manco le battiture, che non fanno gli altri animali* (problema 44)

13) *Onde viene, che i cavalli bevendo tuffino la testa nell'acqua fino a gli occhi, et gli asini lo tocchino solamente con l'estremità delle labra* (problema 45)

---

[13] P. 329, cap. 9.

14) *Perché de' cavalli et de gli asini il maschio fiutando, dove, haverà pisciato la femina, alza la testa, et mostra i denti* (problema 45)

15) *Per che causa il cane alza la gamba, quando vuol pisciare: et perché il maschio, et non la femina* (problema 47)

16) *Onde viene, che 'l cane piscia più volentieri ne gli angoli de' muri, ed'ogn'altro luogo, che non fa ne' lati* (problema 48)

17) *Perché causa, quando un cane abbaia, tutti gli altri cani del vicinato corrono ad abbaiare ancor'essi* (problema 49)

18) *Onde viene che i cani, quando vanno in colera mostrano i denti, et alzano un piede* (problema 50)

19) *Qual è la causa, che de gl'uccelli la grù, et molt'altri dormendo, si riposano su un piede solo, et con la testa sopra una spalla* (problema 52)

20) *Onde viene, che, quando un cane vuol coricarsi, il più delle volte si gira attorno due, o tre fiate* (problema 51)

Come si può vedere si tratta di un plagio di notevole estensione, anche se chi ha una certa familiarità con il fenomeno della "riscrittura" nel secondo Cinquecento non lo trova né insolito né soprendentemente ampio. Ma questa familiarità porta anche ad apprezzarlo come un episodio diverso dai tanti altri ispirati dalla necessità di far sfoggio del sapere altrui: Sansovino, infatti, opera una fusione di generi minori la cui affinità era chiara solo agli intenditori; e basterebbe soltanto un intervento del genere per elevarlo di molte spanne al di sopra dei numerosi plagiari suoi contemporanei. Egli ha anche il merito, preterintenzionale, di farci tornare sul genere dei *problemata* dal quale i lettori moderni si sono allontanati, disdegnando, forse, quel tipo di curiosità ingenua e a volte frivola, come può dedursi da alcuni dei passi e titoli riportati. Ma chi tornerà sulle raccolte dei *problemata* – magari partendo dal *De universo* di Guglielmo d'Alvernia fino al *Serraglio di tutti gli stupori del mondo* di Tomaso Garzoni – indicherà una modalità di ricerca sollecitata da quel costante sforzo di spiegare in termini "razionali" i fenomeni naturali più semplici e più complessi, proponendo un'alternativa alle interpretazioni magiche o superstiziose; e il tempo finí col dare ragione almeno alle intenzioni, se non proprio ai risultati dei nostri "problematisti".

P.S. Il sospetto che Sansovino usi un'altra fonte oltre ai *Problemi* di Garimberto era fondato: sono ora in grado di affermare che Sansovino plagia i vari capitoli non riportabili a Garimberto da Giovanni Boemo, *Gli costumi, le leggi, et l'usanza di tutte le genti,* trad. da L. Fauno *Aggiuntovi gli costumi et l'usanza dell'Indie occidentali, da P.G. Giglio,* Venezia, 1558.

Daniel Javitch

GABRIEL GIOLITO'S "PACKAGING" OF ARIOSTO, BOCCACCIO AND PETRARCH IN THE MID-CINQUECENTO

At least since the publication of Salvatore Bongi's detailed *Annali di Gabriel Giolito* (1540-1562?) it has been evident that this Venetian publisher and his editors played a pioneering role in defining and institutionalizing Italian literature in the middle decades of the Cinquecento. One of Giolito's significant contributions in this regard – but one which has only recently begun to be appreciated as more attention is given to the "phisiognomy" of sixteenth century books – was to design an editorial format for the works of the best Italian authors that identified them as master texts and that facilitated their use as such.[1] The new presentation – today it would be called "packaging" – that Giolito and his editors devised for the principal works of Boccaccio, Petrarch, and Ariosto (immediately imitated by rival Venetian publishers) did much to consolidate, and, in the case of Ariosto, to establish, the place of these writers in the Italian literary canon.[2]

Actually, although Petrarch's *Rime* and Boccaccio's *Decameron* were already considered masterworks of Italian verse and prose by the time the final version of *Orlando furioso* appeared (in 1532), it was the format and appearance of the *Furioso* that Giolito first published in 1542 that set the pattern for his modern classics. Elsewhere I have discussed the paratexts that accompanied this 1542 *Furioso* in some detail, but I must rapidly redescribe them so that the role

---

[1] See S. Bongi, *Annali di Gabriel Giolito de' Ferrari da Trino di Monferrato stampatore in Venezia*, 2 vols., Roma, Ministero della pubblica istruzione, 1890-5. For a recent overview of Giolito's publishing activities see A. Quondam, "La letteratura in tipografia", *Letteratura italiana 2: Produzione e consumo*, Torino, Einaudi, 1983, pp. 641-647.

In its original version, this essay was a lecture delivered at the Newberry Library in 1994 as part of a series on "Vernacular Literature and Printing in Renaissance Italy". Since then has appeared Brian Richardson's *Print Culture in Renaissance Italy. The Editor and the Vernacular Text 1470-1600*, Cambridge, Cambridge University Press, 1994. In the course of revising my lecture I have made some use of this valuable study, especially those parts of it that discuss Giolito and his editors. On the role of editors working for Giolito see also Paolo Trovato, *Con ogni diligenza corretto: la stampa e le revisioni editoriali dei testi letterari italiani (1470-1570)*, Bologna, Il mulino, 1991.

[2] For reasons that will be briefly considered at the end of this essay, neither Giolito's editors nor those working for his rivals made any effort to package Dante's *Commedia* as a modern classic.

of this edition as a prototype can be appreciated.[3] Most of the new features of this quarto edition in Italic were already advertised on its title page: *Orlando Furioso di M. Ludovico Ariosto novissimamente alla sua integrità ridotto & ornato di varie figure... Aggiuntovi per ciascun canto alcune allegorie et nel fine una breve espositione et tavola di tutto quello, che nell'opera si contiene*. The woodcut illustrations, the elegant layout, the *allegorie* and the *espositione'* did more than give Ariosto's poem a new look. These paratexts were included to affirm the high status of the poem. Giolito's own dedicatory letter to the Dauphin of France proclaimed from the start that the *Furioso* was not just another chivalric romance, but one of the rare poems of modern times that matched the perfection achieved by the ancient poets, and that possessed their moral range and utility. Ludovico Dolce, the actual editor of the work (and for the next twenty five years Giolito's most important editor of modern literature), revealed more specifically Ariosto's didactic intent by providing, for the first time, *allegorie* which indicated how each canto of the poem exemplified virtues to be emulated and vices to be shunned. These moralizations of the events of each canto were also an indirect way of associating the *Furioso* with Virgil's and Ovid's major poems since such allegorizations had become a traditional part of the commentary accompanying those ancient works. What established even more concretely the distinguished pedigree of the *Furioso* was the separate commentary Dolce provided on Ariosto's imitations of the ancient poets. Entitled a *"Brieve Dimostratione di Molte Comparationi et Sentenze dall'Ariosto in Diversi Autori Imitate"*, it was appended to all the Giolito editions and was also appropriated in subsequent rival editions. Dolce's commentary aimed primarily to indicate the ancient models of the poem's extended similes. Dolce was not interested in the diverse and complex sources of Ariosto's poem but primarily in its epic pedigree, and especially in its Virgilian ancestry. It was precisely because Ariosto's similes could so often be shown to have demonstrable Virgilian origins that Dolce focused on them rather than on any other imitative feature in Ariosto's poem.

Besides this commentary Dolce provided two other aids for readers in the 1542 Giolito edition: first, an *"Espositione di tutti i vocaboli... difficili"* which glossed difficult or archaic words, and names of remote places and regions, and which also elucidated mythological allusions in the poem. Second, he compiled an inventory of *"Descrittioni, ...proverbi, sentenze, & altre cose di memoria"*, intended to serve readers who quickly wanted to extract from the poem ornaments, beautiful descriptions, or pithy moral sayings with which to enrich their own rhetorical efforts. Dolce's final *florilegium* served in its own way to affirm the distinguished status of

---

[3] See my *Proclaiming a Classic. The Canonization of Orlando Furioso*, Princeton, Princeton University Press, 1991, pp. 31-36.

the *Furioso* by reminding readers that, like the canonical poems of antiquity whose rhetorical flowers and proverbial lore they were taught to collect, the Italian poem was equally a storehouse of *copia* that could be exploited to enrich their own eloquence.

These various paratexts were regularly reprinted in the numerous Giolito editions in both quarto and in octavo (the cheaper octavo edition in roman type was first published in 1543). The *"Dimostratione"* of Ariosto's borrowings and imitations enjoyed a particularly wide dissemination since, beginning with the Blado edition of the *Furioso* published in Rome in 1543, this commentary was regularly appended to numerous editions other than Giolito's for the rest of the century. That the entire format of *Orlando Furioso* conceived by Giolito and Dolce satisfied mid-century readers is attested by the fact that between 1542 and 1560 twenty-seven Giolito editions(in 4º and in 8º) were published. The success of their presentation of the poem is also attested by the efforts of rival publishers to imitate and improve upon it. Of the several rival editions of the *Furioso* that appeared in the 1550s I only want to dwell on one, for reasons that will be clarified later, namely the Valgrisi *Furioso* edited by Girolamo Ruscelli and first published in 1556.[4] Like the Giolito edition, Valgrisi's contained *allegorie*, woodcut illustrations (but now full page and more lavish), a *raccolto* of Ariosto's imitations from ancient poets, as well as glosses on difficult words, place names, historical and mythological allusions. But this edition also contained new paratexts that served to identify even more clearly the poem's canonical status.

One of these new features was the addition of G. B. Pigna's *Life of Ariosto* which was originally part of Book II of Pigna's 1554 treatise on *I Romanzi*. To appreciate the cachet proffered by this opening biography one has to recall that part of the traditional commentary on Virgil was the poet's *Life* attributed to Donatus, and that this biography regularly prefaced *quattrocento* and early *cinquecento* editions of Virgil's *Opera*. Ovid's *Opera* were similarly prefaced by his biography. Given this convention of including a biography in the works of the major ancient poets – several quarto editions of Petrarch and Boccaccio had also been prefaced by biographies – Valgrisi or Ruscelli must have deemed that the status of Ariosto as the age's poet laureate could be more strongly affirmed by beginning with Pigna's *Life*.

Except for notes he appended to each canto, and a glossary of obscure words, most of the commentary Ruscelli appended to his edition was not his own. Not that he bothered to acknowledge that the first of his *"annotationi"*, a summary

---

[4] For a description of the other competitive Venetian edition, namely that first published by G. A. Valvassori in 1553, and for a fuller account of the Valgrisi edition see D. JAVITCH, *Proclaiming a Classic*, pp. 36-43.

of resemblances between the *Furioso* and the epics of Homer and Virgil, was originally composed by Domenico Tullio Fausto da Longiano for the Bindoni and Pasini edition of the poem in 1542. From the Giolito edition Ruscelli lifted Dolce's "*Dimostratione*" of Ariosto's imitations of Virgil and other ancient poets and simply retitled it a "*Raccolto di molti luoghi, tolti, et felicemente imitati in più autori, dall'Ariosto nel Furioso*". It made a useful addition to his "*Annotationi*" given that the general aim of Ruscelli's appendix was to reveal as many resemblances as could be drawn between the *Furioso* and the epic poems of antiquity. In the notes that he appended to each canto Ruscelli also wanted to convey that, like its prestigious forebears, the *Furioso* was an encyclopedic fount of eloquence, and more than his rival Dolce, he was ready to proclaim Ariosto's poetry a linguistic as well as a rhetorical model for all aspiring writers.[5]

Even this brief description of the Giolito and Valgrisi *Furiosos* should make apparent the awareness of Venetian publishers that it did not suffice to assert the equivalence of a work of vernacular poetry to the literary achievements of the ancients: the Italian work had to be packaged as a modern classic. It acquired that "look" by being published in large illustrated editions, set in elegant italic type, prefaced by a biography, supplemented by concise commentaries, indices, and various paratextual aids that enabled readers to use it as a storehouse and model while affirming, at the same time, its status as a master text.

In my earlier study of the presentation of *Orlando Furioso* as a modern classic, I did not take into consideration the publishing fortunes of Petrarch, Dante and Boccaccio in the middle decades of the Cinquecento. Dante's *Commedia* had not enjoyed anything like the constant republication of Petrarch's *Rime* or of the *Decameron*, but I had assumed, wrongly it turns out, that editions of the major works of Petrarch and Boccaccio had already been given the look of classics before the *Furioso* acquired that phisiognomy. After all, Bembo's decisive recommendation that Italians write their literary work "con lo stile del Boccaccio e del Petrarca" had been made in the *Prose della volgar lingua* in 1525. But Bembo's canonization of the *Rime sparse* and the *Decameron* did not affect their format as published books as rapidly as I had imagined.

Consider the editorial fortunes of the *Decameron*. Bembo's call to imitate Boccaccio's prose certainly increased the demand for printed texts of the *Decameron*. As Brian Richardson has pointed out, between 1501 and 1524 only six editions had been printed, but about thirty followed in the period from 1525 to 1557.

---

[5] In his letter to Alfonso d'Este prefacing his edition, Ruscelli announces that in another work of his, still in progress, he demonstrates the capacity of the Italian language to achieve every form of stylistic or expressive excellence by citing examples from poetry. In doing so he writes "Ho proposto e nominato sempre il Petrarca, e il Furioso; e questo poi tanto più, quanto è più importante in se stesso il poema eroico, che il lirico". In other words, Ruscelli was prepared to confer on Ariosto's poetic language the authority that Petrarch's already enjoyed.

If Venetian editors did gradually realize that a master text needed more than the austere editions of the text *alone* (which had been the customary practice), it is only in the late 1530's that they begin to provide readers with aids to understand Boccaccio's text better. But it is really not until the mid 1540s, precisely when the Giolito editions of the *Furioso* first appear, that these aids for using and imitating Boccacio's prose style become standard paratextual features of the *Decamerons* published in Venice.[6]

Not suprisingly, the edition of the *Decameron* that becomes a prototype for the many that follow in the next two decades is a Giolito edition first published in 1546. This edition has an influence on the 'packaging' of the *Decameron* similar to the 1542 Giolito edition of the *Furioso* edited by Lodovico Dolce. In fact, Dolce also had a hand in shaping the format of the 1546 *Decameron*, but most of it seems to have been put together by Francesco Sansovino.[7] I will not discuss the actual text of the stories Sansovino provided because one can read Christina Roaf and Brian Richardson on Sansovino's editorial practices. Even my observations about the paratextual features of the Giolito *Decameron* repeats to a large extent what Roaf and Richardson have already said.

What were the aspects of the 1546 Giolito *Decameron* that served to identify it as a literary classic?[8] Preceding the table of contents and the text itself was a biography of Boccaccio. This was not a new feature – in fact, even though it is ampler, Sansovino's biography continues to rely on Squarzafico's rather inaccurate *Vita* composed in the Quattrocento and which last accompanied a *Decameron* twenty one years ealier. Still, a prefatory *Life* was usually reserved for the work of a master author, and the prototype, as I mentioned earlier, was Donatus' *Life of Virgil*. Although Giolito had not included a *Life of Ariosto* in the 1542 edition of the *Furioso*, it looks like he agreed with Sansovino that one of Boccaccio would add cachet to his *Decameron* four years later.

[6] See BRIAN RICHARDSON, "Editing the *Decameron* in the Cinquecento", *Italian Studies* 45 (1990), pp. 13-31.

[7] Dolce had edited a *Decameron* for Bindoni and Pasini in 1541, an edition that resembled in size, type, and lay out the 1546 edition and that already had a couple of the paratextual features that would accompany subsequent editions: brief annotations at the end of stories, and a vocabulary of nearly 300 difficult Tuscan words (which Dolce seems to have lifted from Brucioli's larger glossary in the 1538 edition). Even though it lacked several of what I would call the tell-tale trappings of a classic, this 1541 edition already reflects the transformation of the *Decameron* from a work of entertaining fiction to that of a master text. Indeed, Dolce advertises this change of status when, in the dedication to none other than Bembo, he states that the hundred stories are no longer meant simply to provide pleasure but have become the necessary means for readers to avail themselves of Boccaccio's proper Tuscan, "della proprieta e elegantia del puro e gentile sermone Thoscano".

[8] My observations about the paratextual features of the Giolito *Decameron* (1546) repeat what has already been said about it by Christina Roaf in "The presentation of the *Decameron* in the first half of the sixteenth century with special reference to the work of Francesco Sansovino", in P. Hainsworth and others. eds., *The Languages of Literature in Renaissance Italy*, Oxford, Clarendon Press, 1988, pp. 109-21. I am also indebted to B. Richardson's discussion of Sansovino's editorial interventions in "Editing the *Decameron*...", pp. 13ff. See also his *Print Culture in Renaissance Italy*, pp. 110-112.

This edition was also the first to provide alternative readings of certain passages of the texts. Aside from these variants (surely a telling marker that the text has been institutionalized as a classic) the *novelle* themselves were not accompanied by particularly telling marginal notes. Each story was prefaced, however, by a brief moral digest that served to indicate what lessons were to be derived from it. Like the *"allegorie"* that were placed at the head of each canto of the Giolito *Furiosos*, these moralizations affirmed the *Decameron*'s didactic utility. The work's usefulness as a guide for writing was more emphasized. The addition that could best help readers make easier use of the text as a linguistic model was Sansovino's *Dichiaratione di tutti i vocaboli, detti, proverbii, e luoghi difficili*...appended to the hundred stories. This *Dichiaratione*, which actually had a separate frontispiece, contained first of all a *Vocabolario* explaining about 400 Tuscan words, presumably those that would not be easily understood by non-Tuscans. This was not a new glossary in that it appropriated words already explained by Brucioli, and Dolce in earlier Venetian editions, albeit in a more convenient fashion. Sansovino provided as well a new List of nouns together with the *epithets* Boccaccio applied to them. One indication of the ongoing usefulnes of this list for writers wishing to imitate Boccaccio was its reappearance in subsequent *Decamerons* edited in the 1550s by Dolce and then by Ruscelli.

The format and paratextual aids of Sansovino's edition clearly proved very marketable: Giolito reprinted it in 1548, 1549 and 1550 and another reprint was issued by Griffio in 1549. Moreover, the 1546 edition decisively influenced the look or the contents of most of the subsequent other editions of the *Decameron* right up to 1557 when the work was condemned by the Church. For instance, the paratexts accompanying Dolce's edition for Giolito of 1552, at least in the quarto format, are virtually clones of Sansovino's edition. In fact, Dolce's text of the *Decameron* has appended to it Sansovino's *Dichiaratione*.[9] Ruscelli's rival edition for Valgrisi, also issued in 1552, appropriated Sansovino's *Life* of Boccaccio, as well as the list of epithets and notes that Sansovino had composed. Of course, Ruscelli also wanted to outdo Sansovino to make the Valgrisi edition a better buy than the Giolito. Aside from providing more variants of the text to choose from, one of the ways Ruscelli enhanced his editions was to provide occasional marginal annotations giving stylistic advice to aspiring imitators of Boccaccio's prose, sometimes even calling attention to Tuscan terms and archaisms to avoid. The Valgrisi edition was reissued at least three more times in the 1550s.

The Venetian publishing of the *Decameron* followed a pattern very similar to that of the *Furioso*. In both cases Giolito, with the help of his editors, devised a handsome and effective edition which became the prototype for virtually all the rival editions of the work for the following decade or more. And the same editors

---

[9] For more on Dolce's edition of Boccaccio's text see TROVATO, *Con ogni diligenza*, pp. 247-248.

and publishers who vied with each other to put out the most impressive *Furioso* similarly tried to capture the market with the most useful and prestigious version of Boccaccio's classic. In the case of the *Furioso* the aim of the presentation was to leave no doubt that the poem was the modern equivalent of Virgil's and Homer's epics. The packaging of the *Decameron* aimed to make easier its use as a primer for Tuscan usage and as the model for Italian literary prose. As Giolito announced to his readers in the 1552 Dolce edition, Boccaccio is nothing less than "il Cicerone della lingua volgare". Editions of the *Furioso* in the 1550s, for example Ruscelli's, also sought to facilitate the poem's use as a storehouse and guide for all would-be writers and orators,but the function of the text as a linguistic and lexical model was more pronouncedly emphasized by the paratextual aids that accompanied the *Decameron*.

One might have thought that Giolito would have encouraged his editors to package Petrarch's *Rime sparse* much like his *Decamerons*, given that, again, as a result of Bembo's canonization of Petrarch's sonnets, the sequence had become the master text to follow by anyone composing in Italian verse. But, in fact, the first Giolito editions of Petrarch's *Rime* that appear in the 1540s – I've looked at the quartos of 1544 and 1547 – are still accompanied by the Vellutello commentary which first appeared in 1525. In other words, at the time that Giolito creates his particular and influential editions of the *Furioso* and of the *Decameron* he continues to publish an edition of the *Rime* that had been on the market for about two decades. It would seem that Giolito's innovation came a little later, in 1547, when he began to issue elegant duodecimo editions of Petrarch. These pocket size *Rime* without any apparatus or commentary were reissued almost yearly into the next decade. Giolito, who often liked to advertise new features of his editions in letters to his readers, announced at the start of his Petrarchini that "essendo le rime del legiadrissimo M. Francesco Petrarca alli studiosi della lingua volgare veramente tali, quali alli studiosi della Latina le divine opere di Virgilio", he now offers them not only "emandatissime, ma in così picciola forma stampate, che ciascuno le potra haver seco in tutti i tempi & luochi senza incommodo, o fatica alcuna".[10]

It is not apparent why Giolito chose not to package his Petrarchs in the 1540s in the same way he had presented the major works of Ariosto and Boccaccio. Was it because readers who sought lexical and stylistic guidance from Petrarch's poems could turn to separately published vocabularies (e.g. Accarigi's *Vocabolario della lingua volgare,*1543) and "*rimari*" (Benedetto del Falco's *Rimario,* 1535), or even treatises on Petrarch's language (Alunno's *Osservationi sopra il Petrarca,* 1539)? But

---

[10] I quote from Giolito's letter prefacing *Il Petrarca* (in 12°) of 1550. According to Salvatore Bongi (*Annali di Gabriel Giolito,* I, p. 138), these pocket size Petrarchs were even read furtively in churches as though they were books of hours!

then the same kind of independent reference sources were available for Boccaccio's lexical and stylistic usage, and yet that did not prevent Giolito from including similar aids in his editions of the *Decameron*. Giolito did eventually publish Petrarch's poems (the *Trionfi* were also included) with such aids, but he waited until the 1550s to do so. The first of these editions to possess Giolito's typical "classic" format was published in 1554:

Il Petrarca novissimamente revisto e corretto da Messer Lodovico Dolce. Con alcuni dottiss. avertimenti di M. Giulio Camillo. et Indici del Dolce de' concetti e delle parole che nel Poeta si trovano, e in ultimo de gli epitheti; et un utile raccoglimento delle desinenze delle Rime di tutto il Canzoniere di esso Poeta.

The title omitted to mention that the book began with Vellutello's life of Petrarch, and also of Laura. There was also an edition in 12o published at the same time but which bore 1553 as its date on the title page. [11] In the 1557 and later reprints of this smaller edition Dolce provided before each sonnet a brief exposition and glosses on difficult words. Camillo's "*avvertimenti*" and Dolce's appendices were for this edition of Petrarch the equivalent of Sansovino's *Dichiaratione* appended to the Giolito Boccaccios. But because the text consisted of lyric poetry rather than prose, Dolce provided, in addition to the list of epithets and a forty page glossary (as had Sansovino), an alphabetical list of concepts, indexed lists of similes, of metaphors used by Petrarch, and a "tavola di tutte le desine". That may seem like a substantial appendix, but when Ruscelli, as was his wont, produced a rival edition published by Pietrasanta in 1554, he added an appendix of 356 pages which, in addition to the usual paratexts, included a *Rimario* compiled by Lanfranco Parmegiano, and a much ampler Vocabolario "*di tutte le voci usate dal Petrarca*". So much apparatus following the text of the poems may have proved too bulky. At any rate while the Giolito Petrarch edited by Dolce was reissued in the two sizes at least 7 times by 1560, Ruscelli's was not reprinted again for another decade.

Why does Dante's *Commedia* not figure in this discussion of Italian classics? Because the editorial presentation of Dante's poem did not conform to the development I have been describing in the cases of Ariosto, Boccaccio and Petrarch. With the exception of the one Giolito edition of the *Commedia* put together by Dolce in 1555, and the first one to have *Divina* in the title, Dante's poem did not acquire the sort of editorial format that gradually characterized the vernacular works of the other three writers. The reason for this seems quite clear: in the middle decades of the Cinquecento, outside of Florence, the *Commedia* did not possess the canonical

---

[11] The 1553 edition in 12o that I consulted actually lacked Camillo's and Dolce's appendices; according to Bongi the date 1554 is to be found at the end "dopo il registro e lo stemma". Bongi proposes (*Annali* I, p. 407), on the basis of Giolito's letter "A I Lettori" that the 8° edition of 1554 was already printed when the smaller edition appeared.

standing enjoyed by Petrarch's poetry, and even by *Orlando Furioso*. Already the publishing statistics reflect the *Commedia*'s lesser appeal. Between 1520 and the mid 1540s only three editions were published. And during the 1540s and 1550s when Italian literature was being institutionalized, when Giolito and his Venetian rivals were reprinting Petrarch, Boccaccio, and Ariosto every year, often editions in more than one size, only seven editions of the *Commedia* appeared in Italy. In this same period roughly sixty editions of Petrarch and seventy editions of the *Furioso* were published. That is to say there were ten times more editions of Ariosto's poem published in this period than of Dante's.

Already by the late 1520s Pietro Bembo seriously impaired the *Commedia*'s possible function as a linguistic and stylistic model after he found it wanting on those grounds in his *Prose della volgar lingua*. Bembo had proclaimed that Petrarch was the supreme practitioner of vernacular poetry. By contrast, he had voiced serious reservations about Dante's stylistic decorum, and, more generally, he questioned the appropriateness of writing poetry on Christian theology. Bembo's influential demotion of the *Commedia* aside, poetic theorists of the 1540s and 1550s could not classify as heroic a poem in *terze rime*, however long it was. This was not true of all rhymed verse. Despite some neoclassical opposition, *ottava rima* was claimed to have the capacity of serving as heroic verse, and Ariosto's *Furioso* was taken as proof of this capacity. But *terza rima* was not deemed fit for "la grandezza Eroica".[12] Such stylistic and prosodic considerations would have discouraged even willing publishers from packaging the *Commedia* as a modern epic, as they did the *Furioso*, or as a model of literary Tuscan. Even when, in the 1555 Giolito edition, Dolce makes the effort to present Dante's poem with the paratexts that had been accompanying editions of Ariosto and Boccaccio for a decade, he still expresses misgivings about Dante's poetic style. While he praises the *Commedia* for its wealth of "sapienza" he begins by acknowledging that "nella prima fronte si dimostri privo di quella vaghezza che contengono molti altri poemi". Dolce's rival editor, Girolamo Ruscelli, was much more critical of Dante's stylistic shortcomings even while recognizing the grandeur of his subject matter. In the preface to his 1559 treatise on composing verses in Italian, Ruscelli suggests that Dante's many transgressions ("*in*osservanza") of the rules, of the purity, and of the "leggiadria" of the language made of the *Commedia* a counter-model for those wishing to write properly. Enough *literati* shared the view that Dante had committed too many stylistic improprieties to prevent the *Commedia* from being granted full canonical status and the editorial format that came with it.

We may find it surprising that by the 1550s an editor like Ruscelli could

---

[12] See GIROLAMO RUSCELLI, *Del modo di comporre in versi nella lingua italiana...*, Venetia, G. B. et M. Sessa, 1559, p. CXVI.

confer on Ariosto, who was not Tuscan, a rank equal to Petrarch as a model of expressive and stylistic excellence while openly denying Dante such linguistic authority. But, as the astute Florentine critic Vincenzio Borghini observed, even as he defied Ruscelli, Ariosto could be deemed an arbiter of the Italian language because of the virtually unimpeachable reputation that the *Furioso* had achieved thanks to the promotion of Venetian publishers.[13] These publishers were simply not inclined nor prepared to do the same for Dante's *Commedia*. To merit the editorial trappings of a vernacular classic (if one accepts the oxymoron),the Italian work had to possess the wherewithal to be able to function as a stylistic and ethical model. Or the text had to be deemed the equivalent of an ancient counterpart which was already seen to possess such stylistic and ethical authority. Venetian publishers packaged their best Italian authors the way they did to affirm their exemplary function. This is made evident in Giolito's letter to the readers prefacing his 1554 edition of Petrarch's *Rime*. In this letter Giolito maintains that what prevents individuals from writing well is either the license some take to write as they like, or the fact that some don't understand how to follow the "concetti, l'artificio, le figure, le forme del dire, e le parole" so judiciously used by good writers. Giolito makes clear that he means good Italian writers, because it is vernacular not Latin writing that now needs to be mastered if one wants to be read. And he advertises the apparatus of notes and indexes that Dolce and Camillo provide for this edition as aids to imitate and thereby attain some of Petrarch's verbal artistry and eloquence. The paratexts are there, says Giolito, "perche a uoi prudenti e studiosi giouani non manchi uerun commodo da potere ascendere ad ogni perfettione nelle Volgar cose".[14]

Giolito's preface makes clearer than usual the propaedeutic function that Giolito wanted his editions of "good" writers to have. Save for their being described on the title pages as "utili" or "utilissimi", we are not always told what overall function the paratexts were to have. One surmises that they were provided to aid the process of imitation, but Giolito serves to confirm it. So does Girolamo Ruscelli in his epistle to the Readers prefacing his 1559 treatise on composing verses in Italian, a letter in which he provides a sort of *curriculum vitae* of his editorial activities. When describing the *Decameron* he edited for Valgrisi in 1552 he writes:

Ho dato il Boccaccio non solamente corretto con tanta cura da tanti testi antichi ...ma

---

[13] V. BORGHINI, *Ruscelleide ovvero Dante difeso dalle accuse di G. Ruscelli,* C. Arlia ed., Città di Castello, Lapi, 1898, p. 23.

[14] Giolito's letter precedes Camillo's "*Annotationi*" in the 8º edition. I wish to thank William Kennedy for kindly checking that the text in the 1554 edition in Cornell University's Petrarch collection was the same as the letter in the 1559 edition I consulted.

anchora dichiarato ne i luoghi più difficili, & illustrato d'annotationi & avvertimenti, per far fermare il pensiero e lo studio dei lettori in considerare, & conoscere per imitarle, l'infinite bellezze di quel nobilissimo scrittore.

In our times, we have tended to presume that the most telling index of a poetic work's canonicity is its adoption in a school curriculum, but school adoption cannot be used as a sign of canonization in the case of pre-modern vernacular poetry given that the curricula in grammar schools before the eighteenth century were predominantly of ancient Latin works. Texts of vernacular poetry – and Petrarch's is an excellent example – achieved canonical status centuries before they became school texts. It's not that these texts were not deemed to have educational value. Giolito's preface makes clear that Petrarch and the "good" Italian writers were becoming as important models of style and expression as the Latin ones, but for young adults, or more generally for an adult reading public of both sexes rather than for classroom students. Publishers and their editors assumed the role that schoolmasters, tied to a traditional curriculum, could not possibly undertake: they transformed the works of the best vernacular writers into Italian classics by advertising their educational value at the same time that they facilitated their function as models. Their packaging of Ariosto, Boccaccio, and Petrarch not only illustrates how these authors were first institutionalized, but that such institutionalization took place outside the classroom.

Aside from the pride both publishers and editors expressed in being able to present their best Italian writers as equals of the canonical poets of antiquity, they also took conscious pride in the handsome and impressive appearance they gave to these literary works as typographic objects. In the prefatory matter of their editions one regularly finds the sentiment that the writers in question deserve to be presented to the world as elegantly and as prestigiously as the publishers have packaged them because they are, after all, the master writers of the vernacular, the equals of Cicero and Virgil. Occasionally, one also finds the sentiment that these authors have been fortunate to have had publishers like Giolito beautify the appearance of their works as well as bring out the "bellezze" of their writing. In the preface to a Giolito Petrarch (1544), Ludovico Domenichi actually proposes that if the poets published by Giolito were alive to see how illustrious their works were made to appear they would have made an effort to write even better!

DEBORAH PARKER

IL LIBRO COME FORMA ESPRESSIVA:
LA STAMPA DELLA *COMMEDIA* NEL RINASCIMENTO

La critica recente sulla ricezione di un'opera letteraria solleva nuove questioni concernenti la storia della stampa, la storia letteraria, e la sociologia letteraria. Le ricerche di studiosi quali Christian Bec, Amedeo Quondam, e Donald McKenzie esaminano le ramificazioni teoriche della produzione materiale dei libri e il suo rapporto con la critica letteraria e sociale. Ci sono altri critici che si occupano di queste questioni ma in questa sede mi limito a riassumere brevemente gli aspetti salienti del lavoro degli studiosi soprannominati, in quanto la loro ricerca offre spunti suggestivi per lo studio della fortuna editoriale della *Commedia*. Il lavoro di Christian Bec e di Amedeo Quondam, in particolare, fornisce modelli istruttivi per la tipografia italiana. Il lavoro del bibliografo inglese Donald McKenzie, invece, indaga le ramificazioni teoriche della produzione letteraria e il suo rapporto con la critica letteraria e testuale. Anche se i campi di specializzazione di questi studiosi sono assai diversi – il lavoro dello storico francese Christian Bec si concentra sui mercanti scrittori e sui libri posseduti dai fiorentini nel Rinascimento; Amedeo Quondam si è occupato della stampa italiana rinascimentale in particolare dei programmi editoriali dei tipografi Gabriele Giolito e Francesco Marcolini; e Donald McKenzie è noto per la sua storia della Cambridge University Press oltre che per i saggi recenti sulla sociologia del testo – ci sono coincidenze notevoli fra di essi. Considerato nel suo insieme, il lavoro di questi tre studiosi offre spunti interessanti allo studio di Dante.

Nel suo *Les Livres des florentins (1413-1608)*, (1984) Christian Bec spiega il suo approccio; lo storico «tout chauvinisme mis à part», si colloca fra studiosi francesi come Lucien Febvre, Henri Jean Martin, e Robert Escarpit, che si sono occupati della «civilisation du livre».[1] Bec, accennando alla mancanza di modelli italiani per il suo studio, attribuisce la resistenza da parte dei bibliografi italiani agli studi storici del commercio librario a due tendenze: la prima deriva da una «respect traditionnel éprouvé pour le livre considéré comme une oeuvre d'art mystérieusement

---

[1] CHRISTIAN BEC, *Les livres des florentins (1413-1608)*, Firenze, Olschki, 1984, p. 7.

issue de l'inspiration géniale»; la seconda da «una tradizione di studi troppo chiusa al suo interno, quasi compiaciuta e gelosa della sua separazione istituzionale, tecnicamente risolta come bibliologia se non più come *bibliofilia*».[2] Contro una tale visione idealizzante dell'opera letteraria Bec adopera un approccio quantitativo. Attraverso lo studio del Magistrato de' pupilli – un fondo dell'Archivio di Stato di Firenze che elenca i beni di capi famiglia che non hanno lasciato testamento – Bec cerca di chiarire la cultura letteraria dei fiorentini attraverso il Quattrocento e Cinquecento.

Le osservazioni di Bec sono in parte derivate da uno studio del 1989 di Amedeo Quondam, «'Mercanzia d'onore'. 'Mercanzia d'utile'. Produzione libraria e lavoro intellettuale a Venezia nel Cinquecento». In questo articolo Quondam esamina il programma editoriale e commerciale del tipografo Gabriele Giolito che gestiva una delle stamperie veneziane più importanti del Cinquecento. Come Bec, Quondam inizia il suo articolo criticando le tradizionali procedure bibliografiche. Secondo Quondam gli studi bibliografici in Italia sono indeboliti da una mentalità territoriale che tende a produrre imprese disgiunte e singole – storie del libro cinquecentesco, storie generali del libro, storie della stampa veneziana, annali tipografici. Per Quondam tali studi contribuiscono a produrre «una mappa frammentaria e discontinua, i cui tratti costitutivi sembrano dominati in modo pressoché esclusivo dalla curiosità bibliografica e dalla passione antiquaria».[3] Inoltre, Quondam condanna l'insufficiente considerazione di elementi storici e politici in questi studi.

Non è forse riconoscibile in questo terreno comune, il segno pur camuffato ed anche degradato di una ideologia del lavoro culturale praticata (teorizzata) nel primato dello "spirito" e quindi dell'autonomia dei suoi "atti" e dei suoi attributi rispetto alle componenti materiali del lavoro intellettuale? E tutto ciò non significa pur sempre la persistenza d'una ideologia organicamente idealistico-storicistica, secondo cui il libro è l'*opera* dell'autore, autonoma in ogni caso dai meccanismi produttivi (l'editore) e dal mercato, e quindi non ha certo bisogno di interventi pubblici, di programmazione ed organizzazione della sua storia anche futura: la sua lettura pubblica, se non la sua ricezione e diffusione?[4]

Quondam propone come correzione a questa situazione un modello essenzialmente marxista, che enfatizza l'aspetto commerciale della letteratura. Come Bec, Quondam sottolinea l'importanza di considerazioni storiche per il commercio librario e i meccanismi materiali della produzione. Quondam sottolinea in partico-

---

[2] AMEDEO QUONDAM, citato nel BEC, *Les Livres*, p. 8.

[3] AMEDEO QUONDAM, «'Mercanzia d'onore.' 'Mercanzia d'utile'. Produzione libraria e lavoro intellettuale a Venezia nel Cinquecento», *Libri, editori e pubblico nell'Europa moderna*, a cura di Armando Petrucci, Bari, Laterza, 1989, p. 53.

[4] *Ibid.*, pp. 55-56.

lare la necessità di interpretare la funzione mediatrice di editori, stampatori, e correttori: gli editori "parlano" nel corpo fisico delle opere che pubblicano – nella loro scelta di formato, di caratteri, di impaginazione, e di illustrazioni. Questi elementi vanno analizzati all'interno «del sistema complessivo della comunicazione, dei suoi modi materiali di produzione».[5]

Donald McKenzie mette in pratica le raccomandazioni suggerite da Quondam. Va notato che fra gli studiosi qui considerati McKenzie è l'unico bibliografo. Perciò la posizione antagonista da lui assunta recentemente nei confronti degli studi bibliografici tradizionali rappresenta una critica all'interno della professione. McKenzie comincia il suo saggio «The Book as Expressive Form» con una critica degli scopi tradizionali delle indagini bibliografiche. In genere McKenzie mette in discussione studi che non prendono sufficientemente in considerazione le condizioni storiche. Inoltre condanna studi bibliografici che ignorano il contenuto di un testo. McKenzie perciò propone un'espansione dei parametri tradizionali della bibliografia.

The principle I wish to suggest as basic is simply this: bibliography is the discipline that studies texts as recorded forms, and the processes of their transmission, including their production and reception... It also frankly accepts that bibliographers should be concerned to show that forms affect meaning. Beyond that, it allows us to describe not only the technical but the social processes of meaning... For any history of the book which excluded study of the social, economic and political motivations of publishing, the reasons why texts were written and read as they were, why they were rewritten and redesigned, or allowed to die, would degenerate into a feebly degressive book list and never rise to a readable history.[6]

McKenzie allora vuole che la bibliografia vada intesa come studio della sociologia dei testi. McKenzie poi avanza il punto centrale della sua proposta: «whether or not the material forms of books, the non-verbal elements of the typographic notations within them, the very distribution of space itself, have an expressive function in conveying meaning». Questa sua formulazione è parallela alle osservazioni di Quondam su come gli editori "parlano" negli aspetti materiali dei libri.

Le posizioni di Bec, Quondam, e McKenzie derivano da una serie di interessi simili, fra loro intrecciati. Tutt'e tre operano sotto l'etichetta generale della sociologia della letteratura – infatti Bec e Quondam riconoscono esplicitamente il loro debito allo studio di Robert Escarpit *Sociologie de la littérature* (1958). Anche se McKenzie non è direttamente influenzato da Escarpit, lo studioso inglese

---

[5] AMEDEO QUONDAM, «Nel giardino del Marcolini, un editore veneziano tra Aretino e Doni», *Giornale storico della letteratura italiana*, CLVI, 1980, p. 75.

[6] D. F. MCKENZIE, «The Book as Expressive Form», *Bibliography and the Sociology of Texts*, London, The British Library, 1986, pp. 4-5.

condivide l'interesse di Escarpit nel chiarire il modo in cui un'opera è codificata e "commodified" dai processi materiali della sua trasmissione. Tutt'e tre gli studiosi mettono in discussione le tradizionali procedure bibliografiche e mettono in risalto l'importanza di chiarire il ruolo mediatore operato dagli editori, stampatori, e curatori, per non menzionare l'influsso esercitato da generazioni di lettori.

Vorrei ora considerare come il modo in cui la *Commedia* era stampata durante il Rinascimento influenzava la sua interpretazione e diffusione. Dato il numero delle edizioni interessate, mi limiterò a discutere le edizioni stampate fra il 1472 e il 1502.[7]

Fra gli scritti apocrifi su Dante, gli aneddoti di Franco Sacchetti raccontati nel *Trecentonovelle* sono ben noti. In una di queste novelle, Dante, durante una passeggiata, sente per caso un fabbro ferraio che batte con il martello e allo stesso tempo recita dei versi dalla *Commedia*. Il fabbro però tralascia dei versi sostituendoli con versi inventati da lui. Dante, stupefatto per questa sconsacrazione del suo poema, entra nella fucina, afferra degli arnesi, e li getta per terra. Quando il fabbro chiede a Dante di spiegare le sue azioni, il poeta risponde: «Tu canti il libro e non lo di' com'io lo feci; io non ho altr'arte, e tu me la guasti». In un altro aneddoto Dante mentre segue un asinaio, sente il contadino cantare il suo poema e gridare ogni tanto, «Arri». Irritato il poeta picchia l'asinaio urlando, «Cotesto 'arri' non vi miss'io».[8]

La semplicità di questi aneddoti contraddice l'importanza delle questioni che essi sollevano e la complessità delle soluzioni che offrono. Il motivo dominante in ciascuna storia è il pericolo che attende la diffusione del poema: cioè l'inevitabile trasformazione che accompagna ogni trasmissione. Inoltre, la violenza che accompagna il punto culminante di ciascun aneddoto testimonia l'inquietudine interpretativa che accompagna la diffusione della *Commedia*. Gli aneddoti mirano ad alleviare questa inquietudine presentando Dante stesso come garante del significato del poema. Vista così, la soluzione è chiara: dietro ad ogni lettore sta Dante che vigila affinché il suo dominio – le sue intenzioni come autore – vengano rispettate. Gli aneddoti oppongono "meaning" (quello che il poeta intendeva) alle varie "significances". Allo stesso tempo, la soluzione è una sorta di spostamento del problema dell'autorità interpretativa: poiché Dante è presente solo come una guida in questi aneddoti, la soluzione è simbolica. Le storie mirano a costruire un'ermeneutica che insiste sul discernere il significato inteso dall'autore dalle interpretazioni false; i due aneddoti perciò stigmatizzano un comportamento che è regolarmente e forse inevitabilmente

---

[7] Questo studio si concentra sulle edizioni della *Commedia* pubblicate fra 1472-1502. Per una bibliografia più ampia e un'analisi più comprensiva della fortuna editoriale del poema nel Cinquecento, vedere il mio *Commentary and Ideology: Dante in the Renaissance*, Durham, Duke University Press, 1993, pp. 124-158.

[8] FRANCO SACCHETTI, *Il Trecentonovelle*, a cura di Emilio Faccioli, Torino, Einaudi, 1970, pp. 298-302.

adottato dai lettori del poema. In effetti le intenzioni dell'autore avevano avuto poco a che fare con la diffusione susseguente della *Commedia*. Inoltre, le differenze fra le punizioni (la distruzione degli arnesi contro il battere con il martello) suggerisce che la trasgressione maggiore sta nelle aggiunte involontarie al poema, non negli emendamenti deliberati del fabbro. Gli «Arri»! dell'asinaio non sono aggiunti come emendamenti; essi sono estranei come le convenzioni tipografiche o come il modo di diffusione in generale. Quando il personaggio Dante prende il mezzo di comunicazione come il messaggio per adoperare l'espressione di Marshall McKluhan, ci ricorda l'idea di McKenzie, che un libro è una «expressive form» (una forma espressiva), e particolari come la tipografia e la storia editoriale costituiscono un codice decifrabile.

La *Commedia*, come dimostrano gli aneddoti di Sacchetti, aveva una diffusione varia e vasta. I manoscritti del poema variavano da codici splendidamente miniati a copie che presentavano, come nota Gianfranco Folena, «un testo al massimo corrotto e dialettalizzato».[9] Sia nella forma di illustrazioni sia nella forma di traduzioni in dialetto, questi interventi hanno influito sul significato del poema. I modi vari in cui i codici mediano il significato del poema – voglio dire particolari come la scrittura, la rubricazione, la fascicolazione, il numero di terzine copiate per pagina, l'inclusione del commento o meno – sono rispecchiati nelle prime edizioni stampate del poema, la disposizione della quale era basata sui codici trecenteschi.

Le edizioni del poema pubblicate fra il 1472 e il 1596 presentano una grande varietà di formati. Gli interventi di editori e tipografi sono evidenti sotto molti aspetti: se la *Commedia* è pubblicata con un commento, senza commento, con due commenti, o solo con chiose marginali; il formato; la scelta dei curatori; l'uso di illustrazioni; se l'opera ha un dedicatario; i caratteri. Come osserva Quondam, tali decisioni editoriali sono raramente neutrali» o «indifferenti»; esse mediano il testo in modo sottile e decisivo. Il processo tecnico è influenzato dal momento storico in cui l'opera è stampata e dalle condizioni del mercato. Come i gusti di diverse epoche sono riconoscibili in un'edizione, così ogni edizione costituisce una specie di interpretazione del poema.

Durante il Quattrocento e Cinquecento Dante ebbe come Petrarca e Boccaccio, lo status di un "classico" contemporaneo. Com'è ben noto lo status di Dante non era quello di *primus inter pares*. Durante il Rinascimento circolavano 167 edizioni delle opere di Petrarca, mentre furono stampate solo 49 edizioni della *Commedia* entro la fine del Cinquecento.

Nell'ultimo quarto del Quattrocento furono stampate quindici edizioni del poema, nove delle quali commentate. Le edizioni pubblicate da Vindelino da Spira

---

[9] GIANFRANCO FOLENA, «La tradizione delle opere di Dante Alighieri», *Atti del congresso internazionale di studi danteschi*, Firenze, Sansoni, 1965, pp. 3.

(1477) e da Ludovico e Alberto Piemontesi (1478) utilizzarono il commento tre-centesco di Jacopo della Lana, le altre sette, quello di Landino. Nel Cinquecento furono pubblicate 34 edizioni del poema: otto di esse senza commento; sei edizioni includevano il commento di Landino, tre edizioni avevano annotazioni marginali ricavate da Landino (quelle di 1547 de Tournes, 1572 Farri, e 1578 Farri); due edizioni avevano il commento di Alessandro Vellutello (1544), e una edizione ave-va il commento di Alessandro Vellutello (1544), e una edizione era corredata dal commento di Bernardino Daniello. Le quattro edizioni pubblicate da Guillaume Rouillè hanno annotazioni ricavate dal commento di Vellutello. Tre edizioni han-no entrambi i commenti di Landino e di Vellutello.

Le prime quattro edizioni della *Commedia* espongono molte somiglianze. Pubblicate dai primi stampatori tedeschi che introdussero la nuova tecnologia in Italia, queste edizioni sono in folio, senza commento, hanno margini ampi, e sono stampate per la maggior parte con caratteri romani. In genere ai primor-di della stampa si stampavano opere umanistiche, giuridiche, o teologiche in fo-lio. Come implica la grandezza di queste edizioni, questi volumi erano destinati ad usi scolastici, non li si poteva facilmente portare in mano. Perciò l'uso di questo formato per la *Commedia* sottolinea il suo status autorevole. L'aspetto fisico delle edizioni della *Commedia* non assomigliarono a quello di altre opere in volgare che in genere venivano stampate in quarto o in formati più piccoli. Chi comprava queste edizioni era probabilmente erudito e ricco; queste prime edizioni con i loro margini larghi assomigliavano ai codici più preziosi dell'opera dantesca. Alcuni stampatori usarono caratteri gotici per la *Commedia*; però l'uso di questo carattere è raro. In Italia, si adoperavano caratteri gotici, di solito, per stampare opere giuridiche e devozionali; si usavano caratteri romani invece per opere umanistiche e classiche. Il carattere gotico, come osserva Rudolph Hirsch, era «contrary to the spirit of humanists».[10] Finché Aldo Manuzio non adoperò il tipo corsivo, si stampava in genere la *Commedia* con caratteri romani. Si può capire qualcosa del pubblico dei lettori da tale scelta editoriale. Come il formato in folio, la scelta di caratteri romani implica un pubblico istruito, aristocratico – cortigiano e umanista. Mentre il pubblico dei manoscritti della *Commedia* era piuttosto vario, quello delle prime edizioni stampate era più ristretto. Basta dare un'occhiata ai dedicatari di queste edizioni. Nidobeato (1478), per esempio de-dicò il suo commento a Guglielmo, marchese di Monferrato.

L'aggiunta del commento trecentesco di Jacopo della Lana nelle edizioni di Vin-delino e di Nidobeato mediò più cospicuamente il poema di Dante. L'aggiunta di un commento suggerisce un uso accademico poiché si adoperavano in genere com-menti all'università. Inoltre la scelta del commento di Jacopo della Lana, noto per il suo carattere di *summa*, legò la *Commedia* allo scolasticismo.

---

[10] RUDOLF HIRSCH, *Printing, Selling and Reading 1450-1550*, Wiesbaden, Otto Harrassowitz, 1967, p. 114.

L'aspetto medievale apportato dal commento di Jacopo della Lana diminuì notevolmente con la pubblicazione del commento di Landino. Presentato alla Signoria fiorentina il 30 agosto 1481 in un'edizione sontuosa, il commento di Landino conquistò rapidamente la stima dei contemporanei. Il suo successo strepitoso fu dovuto a vari fattori: fu la prima edizione illustrata a stampa del poema, e, sintetizzando le chiose precedenti, Landino offrì la spiegazione più comprensiva fino ad allora fornita del linguaggio dantesco, e il commentatore presentò Dante come esponente delle idee neoplatoniche. Sotto molti aspetti, la fortuna straordinaria del commento di Landino rappresenta una specie di monumento al Neoplatonismo fiorentino. Il lavoro di Landino dominò il commento alla *Commedia* per quasi 120 anni. Entro la fine del Cinquecento il commento venne ristampato quindici volte.

Una delle innovazioni più notevoli – più precisamente innovazioni tentate – di questa edizione era l'aggiunta di illustrazioni. I disegni, attribuiti a Botticelli, erano incisi da Baccio Baldini. Botticelli completò solo diciannove disegni per l'*Inferno*. La stampa delle illustrazioni richiese due processi diversi di impressioni – uno per il testo, uno per le incisioni in rame. Sfortunatamente, il tipografo, Nicolò della Magna, non riuscì a unire i due processi: alcune edizioni non hanno illustrazioni affatto, altre hanno illustrazioni solo per i primi due canti, altre hanno illustrazioni per tre e più canti.

A dispetto del successo parziale di questa impresa, l'aggiunta di illustrazioni ebbe un successo notevole presso il pubblico. Tre anni dopo l'editore Ottaviano Scoto ristampò la *Commedia* con il commento di Landino. Nel 1487 il tipografo dalmata Bonino de' Bonini riuscì a stampare il poema con illustrazioni: questa famosa edizione, le cui prime 19 illustrazioni erano basate sui disegni di Botticelli, costituisce la prima edizione illustrata della *Commedia*. Bonino aveva calcolato bene il mercato dell'opera dantesca. Basta esaminare le successive cinque edizioni veneziane – tutte basate sull'edizione di Bonino. La loro somiglianza rispecchia la pratica comune di usare come esemplare di tipografia un altro testo stampato. Le edizioni in folio stampate fra 1487 e 1497 contengono xilografie derivate dall'edizione della *Commedia* di Bonino.

Come il commento di Landino sostituì velocemente le esposizioni trecentesche del poema, così l'introduzione di una serie di testi latini e volgari in ottavo da parte di Aldo Manuzio nel 1501 soppiantò le edizioni precedenti del poema. La serie dei classici antichi e moderni di Aldo introdusse cambiamenti in tre settori – formato, caratteri e la disposizione del testo. Aldo mirava a stampare edizioni accurate dei testi antichi senza l'ingombro del commento. Il ruolo sempre più ingombrante del commento si vede chiaramente nell'edizione del 1481 del poema. Lo stesso titolo sottolinea l'importanza del commentatore: *Comento di Christophoro Landino Fiorentino sopra la Comedia di Dante Alighieri Poeta Fiorentino*. Basta guardare una qualsiasi pagina delle edizioni del poema stampate fra 1481 e 1497 per vedere come il commento domina il testo. La presentazione del testo evidenziata dall'edizione di Bonino – formato grande in folio accompagnato dal commento – rispecchia le norme della stampa dei testi volgari a Venezia alla fine del Quattrocento. Così descrive l'effetto Anthony Grafton: «waves of notes printed in minute type break on all sides of a small island of text set in large Roman».[11] Non si deve sopravvalutare l'effetto prodotto dalla presentazione di autori classici in uno stato puro, senza commento. L'eliminazione del commento apparentemente permise ai lettori una fruizione immediata degli autori antichi. Gli effetti di questa presentazione nuova erano particolarmente drammatici nel caso della *Commedia*, che nell'edizione aldina vantò un titolo nuovo, *Le terze rime di Dante*. Come nota Carlo Dionisotti, il nuovo titolo mise in rilievo gli aspetti metrici del poema e svalutò il suo contenuto.

Mentre l'eliminazione del commento da parte di Aldo non significò la fine di questo apparato, essa stabilì un rapporto nuovo e diverso con la letteratura – la lettura del testo ora assumeva più importanza della sua interpretazione. Il fatto che la *Commedia* fosse spesso accompagnata da un commento ne rese più drammatica la trasformazione. Fino ad allora Dante era inseparabile dal commento di Landino. In fin dei conti, come nota Martin Lowry, l'eliminazione del commento implicò che le esposizioni non avevano importanza: «the unadorned words of the classical master, restored as nearly as possible to their original purity were what really concerned him» (lo scopo di Aldo era di presentare le parole disadorne degli antichi, restaurate quasi nella loro purezza).[12] Aldo voleva creare un pubblico per queste edizioni. Il tipografo mirava a raggiungere un pubblico di lettori piuttosto che di maestri. Da questo punto di vista le edizioni aldine in ottavo e le loro imitazioni contribuirono all'emancipazione della cultura, incoraggiando la lettura privata più che lo studio in gruppo. I ritratti di Bronzino di uomini e donne nobili che tengono in mano un libriccino esemplifica il pubblico di questi testi. Nel quadro di Andrea del Sarto *Ritratto di una giovane donna con un volume di Petrarca*, ad esempio, la donna tiene in mano un'edizione in formato piccolo di Petrarca. Sia il *Canzoniere* sia la *Commedia* furono pubblicati spesso in ottavo durante il Cinquecento.

La produzione dei testi classici in ottavo costituì un'impresa astuta e un buon affare. Questi testi emanavano un'aura esclusiva. Aldo dedicò le sue edizioni a nobili veneziani e a studiosi diplomatici, come Marin Sanudo, Antonio Morosini, e Sigismund Thurz; il corsivo di Francesco Griffo assomigliava alla scrittura elegante del calligrafo Bartolomeo Sanvito; e le edizioni vantavano una provenienza prestigiosa. Esse evocavano l'ambiente raffinato dello studioso aristocratico. Nella prefa-

---

[11] ANTHONY GRAFTON, «On the Scholarship of Politian and its Context», *Journal of the Warburg and Courtauld Institutes* XL, 1977, p. 155.

[12] MARTIN LOWRY, *The World of Aldus Manutius: Business and Scholarship in Renaissance Venice*, Ithaca, Cornell University Press, 1979, 217.

zione alla sua ristampa di Virgilio nel 1514, Aldo rivelò che il piccolo formato era ispirato dai libri dalla biblioteca di Pietro Bembo. Insomma, gli ottavi aldiniani godevano un successo strepitoso.

I tipografi successivi della *Commedia* o pubblicarono testi modellati sull'edizione aldina, o la modificarono, o si allontanarono da essa stampando invece edizioni con commento. Se seguissimo la storia editoriale della *Commedia* nel corso del Cinquecento vedremmo una serie di edizioni che soppiantano l'una l'altra. Fra le modifiche più notevoli ci sono l'aggiunta di uno spaccato dell'Inferno basato sui calcoli di Antonio Manetti nell'edizione giuntina del 1506; i nuovi caratteri corsivi creati da Alessandro Paganino; la reintegrazione del commento, ma nella forma di chiose marginali operata da Guillaume Rouillè e Jean de Tournes a Lyons; e le edizioni eleganti di Francesco Sansovino che contenevano i commenti di Landino e di Vellutello.

Nel valutare la stampa rinascimentale della *Commedia* siamo tentati inizialmente, (data la profusione di edizioni tanto diverse), di spiegare il fenomeno a seconda dei bisogni del mercato – ad attribuire la varietà di forme ad una serie di decisioni commerciali prese da tipografi, commentatori, ed editori. Però un'analisi più approfondita suggerisce, se non una continuità profonda o uno sviluppo progressivo, almeno un motivo ricorrente. Nel rintracciare le edizioni secondo quella che McKenzie ha chiamato «symbolic forms», ciò che è straordinario nel caso della *Commedia* è la malleabilità di questo simbolo. L'evidenza che da un punto di vista sembra produrre una storia molto frammentata e discontinua, vista da un'altra angolatura, suggerisce il potere produttivo della *Commedia*. La rimanipolazione continua del poema durante il Rinascimento, questa situazione flessibile e pieghevole in cui un'edizione sostituisce rapidamente l'altra dimostra con evidenza l'abilità di questo testo nell'adattarsi a momenti storici diversi. Il significato della *Commedia* è condizionato non solo da generazioni diverse di lettori ma anche dalla sua forma materiale. Tali interventi confermano l'osservazione del saggista romantico William Hazlitt: «Books are a world in themselves it is true; but they are not the only world».

LINO PERTILE

A LEZIONE DA TRIFON GABRIELE:
IL SONETTO *ANIMA, CHE DIVERSE COSE TANTE* DEL PETRARCA

Il codice miscellaneo del XVI secolo conservato presso la Biblioteca Ambrosiana di Milano con segnatura S 78 sup. contiene i testi di alcuni commenti a classici latini che la tradizione fa risalire alla libera opera didattica di Trifon Gabriele. Si tratta di commenti inediti a Cicerone (*De officiis* e *Somnium Scipionis*) e Orazio (*Odi*), scritti in un latino scolastico, interrotto di tanto in tanto da parole, frasi o talvolta interi discorsi in un volgare di spiccato colorito veneziano.[1] Tutta in volgare, ma con notevoli rinvii ai classici latini, è invece l'esposizione del sonetto CCIV del *Canzoniere* petrarchesco che si trova alle cc. 47ʳ-48ʳ dello stesso codice tra i fascicoli relativi al *Somnium* e alle *Odi*: convivenza di lingue e *auctores* tipicamente cinquecentesca e, si direbbe, distintamente trifoniana, se non fosse per l'assenza dal quadro dei nomi di Dante e Virgilio, ai quali il "Socrate veneziano" dedicò tanto assidua e organica attenzione.[2] L'esposizione è quanto ci è pervenuto di un lavoro più ampio sul *Canzoniere*, non sappiamo se completo o sistematico, naufragato, a quanto pare, nel Seicento.[3] La stampiamo qui per intero allo scopo di contribuire alla conoscenza della figura e dell'attività critica di Trifon Gabriele: personalità schiva e umbratile che godé di autorità e prestigio eccezionali al suo tempo, ed ebbe un ruolo di primo piano non solo come amico e consulente letterario di Pietro Bembo, ma anche come maestro di stile e di vita per molti giovani della genera-

---

[1] Vedi in proposito, anche per una descrizione meno sommaria dei codici trifoniani, G. BELLONI, *Laura tra Petrarca e Bembo*, Padova, Antenore, 1992, pp. 174-79. Sull'esatta paternità del commento alle *Odi* oraziane il Belloni non si esprime, ma si tratta certamente di un prodotto del circolo trifoniano, anche se forse non proprio di Trifone, vista la sorprendente mancanza di inibizioni della chiosa alla tredicesima ode del primo libro.

[2] Per Dante e Trifon Gabriele vedi ora l'ed. critica delle *Annotationi nel Dante fatte con M. Trifon Gabriele in Bassano*, a cura di L. Pertile, Bologna: Commissione per i testi di lingua, 1993; per Virgilio, tuttora inedita rimane l'esposizione al primo delle *Georgiche*, sicuramente di ascendenza trifoniana, contenuta nel codice ambrosiano Q 120 sup. Ad ogni buon conto fa testo la massiccia presenza virgiliana nel commento a Dante.

[3] Per ulteriori particolari si veda il mio *Trifone Gabriele's Commentary on Dante and Bembo's "Prose della volgar lingua"*, «Italian Studies», XL, 1985, pp. 17-30, in particolare p. 26. Nessun rinvio al nostro sonetto fra i tantissimi al *Canzoniere* presenti nelle *Annotationi nel Dante*, dove per altro si rimanda spesso a glosse di Trifone al Petrarca: v. la mia nota a *Inf.* VI 109, p. 33. Questa assenza fa pensare che l'esposizione del sonetto non fosse ancora stata fatta al tempo delle *Annotationi* (1525-27).

zione successiva che giunsero a maturità nel pieno della crisi religiosa e spirituale della Riforma.[4]

Prediletto tra i discepoli di Trifone fu il lucchese Bernardino Daniello che, nel dare alle stampe nel 1541 la sua esposizione del Petrarca, ne riconosceva il merito «per la gran parte» al maestro e, rifiutando anticipatamente le accuse di plagio, si richiamava all'esempio di Platone «il quale del suo Socrate fece quello, ch'io hora di quest'altro mio novello Socrate ho fatto, e di fare intendo per l'avvenire in tutte le cose».[5] Otto anni dopo, il Daniello pubblicava una nuova edizione del suo Petrarca, accresciuta ma priva di qualsiasi riconoscimento a Trifone che proprio in quell'anno moriva. Perciò viene da chiedersi se l'omaggio primitivo non fosse altro che una manovra pubblicitaria del letterato lucchese, resa superflua più tardi dal successo del suo commento. Per rispondere a questa domanda, bisognerebbe poter fare per il Petrarca di Trifone quel che s'è fatto per il suo Dante. Ma nella latitanza del commento petrarchesco dobbiamo accontentarci di un confronto su un solo sonetto: un campo quanto mai limitato, eppure non privo d'interesse. Ecco dunque la chiosa con tanto di nome d'autore in testa, come appare nel manoscritto.[6]

Triphon
Anima, che diverse cose tante

[1] Platone, il quale, come dice Cicerone, ha forse dato opera ad Amore più di quello che era convenevole, nelle lodi di esso amore dice che sono tre sorti d'amori, lasciato da parte quello che solo è in Dio, perfetto et singulare: l'uno divino, l'altro ferino et bestiale, il terzo humano. Il primo serà quello quando l'uomo, mosso dalla virtù, dalla bontà, dagli costumi de l'altro, è sospinto ad amarlo et li desia bene, non procedendo niente in sensi. Il secondo quando si ama solo per li sensi con desio di quelli solamente, il che propriamente è da fiera, la quale solo per li esterriori sensi si regge. Il terzo, il quale dicemo esser humano, serà mezzo [da] tra questi, come anche l'huomo è mezzo tra gli angeli et gli animali brutti, perché ha la mente vera et immortale, commune con gl'angeli, gli sensi et questo corpo corruttibile et mortale con gli brutti. [2] Fia adunque humano Amore all'horché et con la mente et con gli sensi si viene a questo desiderio ma honestamente, in modo con gli sensi che non si cada in quello che dicemo essere di fie-

---

[4] A questo proposito devo rimandare di nuovo, e me ne scuso, a un mio lavoro: *Vettore Soranzo e le "Annotationi nel Dante" di Trifon Gabriele*, «Quaderni veneti», 16, 1992, pp. 37-58, specialmente pp. 50-58.

[5] Cito dalla dedica ad Andrea Cornelio in testa a *Sonetti, Canzoni, E Triomphi di Messer Francesco Petrarcha con la Spositione di Bernardino Daniello da Lucca*, in Vinegia per Giovanni Antonio De Nicolini da Sabio, MDXLI. Sulla questione del debito del Daniello nei confronti di Trifone, ma in rapporto a Dante, cfr. D. PARKER, *Commentary and Ideology: Dante in the Renaissance*, Durham and London, Duke University Press, 1993, pp. 109-23.

[6] Nella trascrizione del testo i miei interventi sono minimi: inserisco la punteggiatura a mio avviso necessaria per leggere il testo correttamente, regolarizzo l'uso delle maiuscole e aggiungo gli accenti; sono tra parentesi quadre i segmenti biffati nel testo, tra tonde le parti di parole sciolte in trascrizione, tra uncinate gli emendamenti poi spiegati in nota.

ra, il che serà se la mente si goderà di sempre haver dinanzi la forma, parerli di udir le parole della persona amata et immaginarsi sempre di lei et pensare, et che, quanto alli sensi, si contenti del vedere et del'udire, non procedendo più oltre, ché, quando scoresse nel fatto, sarebbe l'amor di fiera.

[3] Quest'ultimo amor è quello dal quale trovaremo preso il nostro Poeta. Sempre et qui et in ogni luogho di questo parla, come nella canzone *Amor se voi ch'io torni*, ove, tutto che in tutta quella canzone non parli di altro che di questo, pure più manifestamente si vede, ove dice «rendi agl'occhi, agl'orecchi il p<roprio> oggetto», ma non dimanda la mente, perché la morte non gli haveva possuto tuor quella, come anche dice Lelio di Scipione. [4] Così anche Vergilio, volendo far Dido, castis(sim)a donna, descendere a l'amore di fiera, perché da l'estremo a l'altro estremo non si va senza mezo, piglia questo amore humano per mezo, come elli, pria che ella descenda a l'amore dishonesto, dice:

> *Multa viri virtus animo, multusque recursat*
> *Gentis honor: haerent infixi pectore voltus*
> *Verbaque...*

Così vedemo che, posta la mente, pone gli sensi liquali havemo detti, cioè il vedere et l'udire, et non va più innanzi.

[5] Così anche in questo loco parla il P(oeta) di questo amore, et dice:

> Anima che diverse cose tante
> vedi, odi et leggi et parli et scrivi et pensi;

e questi [~~sog~~] sono gli effetti de l'animo, ha posti come effetti della mente, non come sensi; et dice "anima" a la christiana, gli platonici dicono "mente", gli latini "animo", come havemo visto in Vergilio.

[6]   Occhi miei vaghi, et tu, fra gl'altri sensi,
             che scorgi al cor l'alte parole sante;

et qui mette la parte che è commune con li brutti, cioè che pertiene agli sensi, et è da notare che, havendo posto l'anima et gl'occhi per proprio nome, ha voluto porre l'orecchi per descrittione, il che molto adorna et molto bisogna avertire. Così fece anche Oratio ove disse:

> *Diffugere nives, redeunt iam gramina campis*
> *Arboribusque comae,*

che, havendo chiamato le nevi et le gramigne per proprio nome, volse le foglie de gl'arbori chiamare per circonscrittione.

[7]   Per quanto non voresti o poscia od ant<e>
             Esser giunti al camin che sì mal tiensi

Assimiglia la vita nostra ad un viaggio, come molti hanno fatto, et così dimanda a l'anima, a gl'occhi et a gl'orecchi per quanto non vorebbero esser venuti a questo viaggio prima di Laura o doppo lei, et sapemo che nel tempo è il passato, il presente, et il futuro, gli quali li buoni scrittori ogni volta che ne pongono uno pongono tutti. In questo verso ne puone il P(oeta) dui, il futuro et il passato; di sotto porrà l'altro. "che sì mal tiensi": perché come disse Paolo *omnes erraverunt in hac via*, et così dicendo mostra il viaggio esser intricato.

[8]   Per non trovar i duo bei lumi accensi
        Né l'orme impresse de l'amate piante.

Due cose si ricercano a tener un camino dritto, l'una il lume, massime nel camino oscuro, et le orme de gl'altri nell'intricato, et queste due cose aitano molto; et qui tuoglie gli occhi di Laura per il lume, et le virtuti sue per le pedate, come spesso dice lei ch'insegnò la via "de gir al cielo", come nel sonetto *Qual donna attende a gloriosa fama* et in altri mille.

[9]   Hor con sì chiara luce et con tai segni
        Errar non dessi in quel breve viaggio
        Che ne pò far di eterno albergho degni.

Nel principio di questo terzetto mette quell'altro tempo che mancava di sopra, cioè il presente, dicendo "Hor". "con luce sí chiara", risponde a "i duo lumi accensi"; "con tai segni" risponde a "l'orme impresse": non si dee errar perché havemo il lume chiariss(im)o, li segni manifesti, il viaggio breve: di sopra lo chiamò "camino". "Eterno albergo": prima mostra che di cosa breve conseguemo cosa non solo lunga ma eterna; apresso è da considerare che molto ben sta in metaphora del camino dicendo "albergo", perché proprio è desiderio d'i viatori l'agiugnere a l'albergho.

[10]   Sforzati al ciello, o mio stanco coraggio,
        Per la nebbia entro de suoi dolci sdegni
        Seguendo i passi honesti e 'l divo raggio.

Siegue pur la methaphora dicendo "sforzati" et "stanco".
"Corraggio" è parola francese, la quale molto ben compare qui, come anco in Vergilio qualche volta trovemo *gaza*, che è parola persica. "Per la nebbia de' suoi sdegni", come nel sonetto *Passa la nave mia colma d'oblio*, trovemo "pioggia di lagrimar, nebbia di sdegni", et per questo verso mostra il camino esser oscuro, come di sopra mostrò esser intricato. "Seguendo i passi honesti" risponde a "l'orme" et a "segni"; "e divo raggio" risponde ai "lumi" et a "sí chiara luce"; et raggio è proprio del sole, il qual caccia le nebbie.

Ed ecco alcune note a illustrazione di questo testo.

[1] **come dice Cicerone**: cfr. *Tusculanae disputationes*, IV 68-70. – Il Daniello rinvia qui al suo commento a *Canzoniere* LXX, «Lasso me, ch'i' non so in qual parte pieghi», dove in effetti riprende in forma ampia ed elaborata il discorso di Trifone su «questi tre amori».

[3] **Amor se voi ch'io torni**: *Canzoniere* CCLXX; il verso citato è il 41. Il ms. reca *primo*, quasi certamente scioglimento erroneo della forma abbreviata di *proprio* che ripristiniamo. – **non dimanda la mente**: «non chiede (o menziona?) il pensiero». – **come anche dice Lelio di Scipione**: probabile riferimento al finale del *Laelius de amicitia* di Cicerone dove Lelio dichiara che, anche dopo la morte improvvisa di Scipione, il pensiero di lui gli sta sempre davanti agli occhi. – **possuto**: cfr. Dante, *Purg.* III 38, «se potuto aveste veder tutto»:

la lezione corrente nel '500, citata anche nel *Vocabolario* di Alberto Acarisio (1543), era «possuto».

[4] **Multa ...Verbaque**: *Aen.* IV 3-5. Nella sua esposizione di questo sonetto anche il Daniello usa la stessa citazione per definire «l'Amor humano» (cito dall'ed. 1541, del resto identica a quella del '49 per la parte relativa a *Canzoniere* CCIV).

[5] **[sog]**: inizio di parola di non agevole lettura, forse *sog* per *sogni* (cattiva lettura del *sono* seguente?), poi biffato; al suo posto la sintassi richiederebbe un *che* relativo, che però l'uso talvolta ometteva: cfr. *Annotationi nel Dante*, p. CXXV.
– **come havemo visto in Vergilio**: Trifone si riferisce probabilmente ai vv. 724-27 di *Aen.* VI, sui quali esiste una sua esposizione inedita: vedi *Annotationi, Inf.* I 39 e nota.

[6] Osservazione stilistica tipicamente trifoniana (cfr. *Annotationi*, Indice grammaticale, voce "variatio") e il Daniello la riprende insieme al rinvio a Orazio, *Carm.* IV VII 1-2: rinvio che a sua volta ricorre in apertura al suddetto commento alle *Odi* oraziane (c. 50^r) che nel ms. ambrosiano segue l'esposizione del sonetto. – **descrittione**: non è la *descriptio* classica (per cui vedi H. LAUSBERG, *Elementi di retorica*, Bologna, Il mulino, 1969, § 169), ma quasi certamente la perifrasi (come scrive il Daniello), ovvero *circumlocutione,* voce forse "orecchiata" subito dopo in *circonscrittione,* termine molto raro, se non ignoto, nel senso di perifrasi: appare in lat. in CIC. *De oratore* III 207, e in it. nell'*Ottimo Commento* a *Par.* VI 46. Nelle *Annotationi* si trova spesso *circumlocutione* e qualche volta *perifrasi,* mai *descrittione* o *circonscrittione.*

[7] **od ant\<e\>**: il ms. reca *o d'anti* che non ha senso. – **nel tempo**: nel suo commento al primo libro delle *Georgiche* (Biblioteca Ambrosiana, ms. Q 120 sup., c. 5^v) Trifone dice che gli esseri irrazionali «ad id solum quod adest quodque presens est accomodantur, paulum admodum sententia preteritum aut futurum; rationa[bi]lia vero consequentia cernunt et causas rerum vident earumque progressus et quasi antecessiones non ignorant, similitudines comparant rebusque presentibus adiungunt atque annectunt futura. Facile totius vitae cursum vident ad eamque degendam praeparant res necessarias». – **omnes erraverunt**: cfr. Rom. 3, 12, ma San Paolo cita da Isaia 56, 11 e Ps. 13, 1. Il Daniello riprende tutto in questa forma: «Omnes erraverunt in viam suam. Non est qui faciat bonum, non est usque ad unum». – **intricato**: «impedito», «intralciato», «impacciato»; il Daniello non accoglie questa voce che, nonostante alcuni esempi d'uso nobile (vedi Acarisio), sentiva forse come troppo veneta.

[8] **nel sonetto**: CCLXI 6-8: «come è giunta honestà con leggiadria, / ivi s'impara; et qual è dritta via / di gir al ciel»; per gli «altri mille» si veda la nota a *Canzoniere* XIII 13 nell'ed. a cura di M. Santagata (Milano, Mondadori,

1996) da cui qui si cita. – **pedate:** Daniello spiega: «le vestigia impresse de l'amate piante».

[10] **la methaphora:** del viaggio, ovviamente. – **corraggio:** tipico provenzalismo, più che francesismo, col senso di "cuore", riportato anche nel *Vocabolario* dell'Acarisio. Curioso invece il parallelo con *gaza*, voce persiana che Virgilio utilizza nel senso di "tesoro", "ricchezze" a *Aen.* I 119, II 763 e V 40: forse Trifone intende giustificare il provenzalismo petrarchesco con un persianismo virgiliano. – **pioggia di lagrimar:** *Canzoniere* CLXXXIX 9. – **i passi honesti:** il Daniello riprende queste *rispondentie* alla lettera.

Possiamo fare ora qualche osservazione d'ordine generale. E anzitutto non c'è ombra di dubbio che l'esposizione del sonetto è condotta nella stessa lingua, nello stesso stile e con lo stesso metodo delle *Annotationi nel Dante*. Quanto alla lingua, dittongazioni del tipo *tuor, tuoglie, puone* o anche *siegue* sono comuni nell'opera maggiore; così si dica della desinenza in *-emo* per la prima persona plurale dell'indicativo presente dei verbi di seconda e terza coniugazione (*dicemo, havemo, conseguemo*), mentre non ha parallelo l'unico caso di prima coniugazione, *trovemo*, peraltro tipicamente veneto.[7] Lo stile è scolastico, come del resto quello delle *Annotationi*, ma con la differenza che qui non si avverte l'immediatezza del parlato; anzi, il discorso critico sembra organizzato secondo un piano semplice ma preciso. L'analisi retorica è preceduta da considerazioni morali, il sonetto inquadrato in un discorso filosofico fondato sul presupposto della continuità tra pensiero antico e cristiano, cioè tra classici del passato (Platone, Cicerone, Virgilio, Orazio, San Paolo), e Petrarca nella sua qualità di classico moderno. Trifone, da vero umanista, insegna a vivere insegnando a scrivere. Di qui anche un certo gusto per l'espressione sentenziosa, del tipo: «da l'estremo a l'altro estremo non si va senza mezo» (§ 4), o «di cosa breve – cioè la vita – conseguemo cosa non solo lunga ma eterna» (§ 9).

Secondo Trifone, argomento del sonetto è l'amore platonico che coincide essenzialmente con l'amore spirituale e cristiano (§§ 1-4). Stabilita l'area di riferimento filosofico-morale, il maestro passa all'esame del sonetto che divide in sei parti, due per ogni quartina più una ciascuna per le terzine. Questa divisione orizzontale non impedisce di mettere in rilievo l'ossatura verticale del componimento. Anzi, i fatti retorici identificati sono costituiti interamente di corrispondenze verticali: tra i due nomi «anima» e «occhi» e la perifrasi in luogo del terzo, orecchi o udito che sia (vv. 1, 3, 3-4); tra i due avverbi di tempo «poscia» e «ante» al v. 5, e il terzo, «Hor», al v. 9; infine tra le tre serie intrecciate di *rispondentie* che dal v. 6 in poi (luce-lumi-raggio, segni-orme-passi, camin-viaggio-al-

---

[7] Per la dittongazione in *-uo-* e *-ie-* cfr. *Annotationi*, rispettivamente p. CII e p. CI; per le desinenze verbali, p. CXXIX. Padano anche il futuro della prima coniugazione in *-ar-* (*trovaremo*), cfr. p. CXXX.

bergo) formano la vera nervatura del sonetto. Sono notazioni quanto mai economiche, ma sufficienti a evidenziare la ricerca strenua e sistematica di coerenza
metaforica caratteristica dell'arte di Petrarca, coerenza che in generale Trifone ritiene propria del discorso poetico e fondamentale per la sua riuscita tecnica. Vanno inoltre messi in risalto, sempre in questa parte analitica, i richiami intratestua-
li (Petrarca si spiega con Petrarca) e intertestuali (Orazio e Virgilio maestri di
stile, San Paolo maestro di pensiero). Sicché, se è vero che l'esposizione non rivela grandi interessi grammaticali, gli interessi retorici di Trifone vi appaiono ampiamente rappresentati.

Allo scopo di valutare la novità di questo approccio critico, apriamo il commento, non «di finissimo velluto» a detta di Trifone, ma che andava per la maggiore nel
secondo quarto del Cinquecento, cioè *Il Petrarcha* dell'altro lucchese, Alessandro
Vellutello.[8] Il Vellutello offre in sostanza una parafrasi del sonetto, ma una parafrasi faticosa che, anziché illuminare il testo, finisce coll'oscurarlo e appesantirlo.
Ne trascriviamo qui solo la parte relativa alle due terzine:

> Adunque dice che *con sí chiara luce*, com'è quella de la honestà che da' begli occhi
> veniva, e *con tai segni*, e con tai scorte com'essi occhi erano, bisognando a chi drittamen-
> te per la non ben conosciuta via vuol procedere e luce e buona scorta, non si debbe
> errare nel *breve viaggio* de la presente vita la dritta via del cielo, perché seguitando quei
> tai segni, da' quali la luce veniva et i quali la scorta erano, li può a la felice vita guidare e
> farli degni *d'eterno albergo*. Onde conforta il cuore a sforzarsi per mezzo la nebbia de' *dolci
> sdegni* di lei, i quali erano quelli che, quando da la dritta via torceva, lo raffrenavano a
> seguitar i suoi honesti passi, cioè ad imitar i suoi honesti costumi, i quali erano la scorta,
> e *'l divo raggio* de' begli occhi, ch'era la luce, per li cui mezi egli era scorto al cielo. (c.
> 61^r)

L'esposizione del Vellutello, tutta volta a spiegare il pensiero espresso nel sonetto, insiste pedestremente sugli equivalenti allegorico-morali delle singole immagini,
ma senza riuscire a vedere come esse si costituiscono in coerente sistema. Nella parte che non abbiamo trascritto arriva addirittura a specificare che «l'amate piante» di
Madonna Laura stanno per «pudicitia e bellezza». Nessuna attenzione invece alla
lingua, allo stile, all'arte di Petrarca.

Ma anche l'esposizione del Daniello, condotta, come lui stesso dice e noi abbiamo visto, sulla traccia di quella di Trifon Gabriele, risulta deludente. Di proprio il
Daniello mette ben poco: la spiegazione dell'aggettivo «vaghi» («cupidi e desiosi
pur di veder l'amata nostra luce») e della posizione di «entro» al v. 13 («posposto
per cagion del verso»), più una citazione oraziana accanto a quella di Virgilio al § 4.

---

[8] Tra il 1525 e il 1538 questo commento ebbe ben quattro edizioni: per i dettagli si veda BELLONI, pp. 77-80.
Qui si cita dall'ed. del '38, stampata a Venezia «per Bartolomeo Zanetti casterzagense, ad instantia di Messer Giovanni Giolito da Trino», ecc. Nel trascrivere il testo ammoderniamo la punteggiatura, aggiungiamo accenti e apo-
strofi, e utilizziamo il corsivo per distinguere il testo commentato da quello del commento.

Per il resto la sua chiosa segue, talvolta *verbatim*, quella del maestro, ma omettendone, forse perché non ne avverte l'importanza, alcune notazioni essenziali, volte a rilevare il carattere sistematico dell'arte petrarchesca. Ad esempio, il Daniello nota la perifrasi al v. 4, ma trascura di segnalarne il rapporto che la lega ai sostantivi all'inizio dei vv. 1 e 3 («anima» e «occhi»); offre sinonimi per «poscia» e «ante» al v. 5 ma non ne avverte il legame con «Hor» all'inizio del v. 9; omette, inspiegabilmente, chiose isolate quali quella sul significato e la derivazione di «corraggio» (v. 12). A conti fatti, per quanto indubbiamente più "levigata" e avvertita di quella del suo compatriota Vellutello, anche l'esposizione del Daniello risulta meno illuminante e didatticamente meno efficace di quella di Trifone. Talché noi siamo costretti ancora una volta a deplorare il destino dei libri, che ci ha conservato in moltissime copie e varie edizioni il Petrarca del Vellutello e del Daniello, ma soltanto due pagine di quello del Gabriele.

Per finire, una questione che riguarda tutti i maestri e a volte li esalta nell'esercizio delle loro funzioni, ma più spesso li sgomenta: come e dove vanno a finire le loro parole? La tradizione (e la carta su cui stanno scritte) attribuisce a Trifon Gabriele le parole che abbiamo appena reso pubbliche e annotato; ma occorre intendersi: sarà stato proprio lui a stendere o dettare l'archetipo di quel testo, o non sarà stato piuttosto un suo scolaro a comporlo sulla base di appunti presi a lezione? Il possibile equivoco per cui, come si è visto, l'estensore dell'esposizione scrive «circonscrittione» anziché «circonlocutione»,[9] farebbe propendere per un lavoro di scuola non proprio all'altezza dell'originale, o comunque abbastanza inventivo rispetto ad esso da far sorridere, se non turbare, il maestro veneziano. Anche in questo caso, dunque, come in quello del Dante trifoniano, l'originale sarebbe un evento orale irrecuperabile. Tanto più che Trifone, caso più unico che raro, non voleva saperne di pubblicare le sue parole, né reclamava diritti d'autore quando le usavano, più o meno a proposito, i suoi scolari. Queste parole, perciò, continuano e continueranno a sfuggirci, mentre tante altre ne abbiamo di cui si farebbe volentieri a meno.

---

[9] Naturalmente è possibile ipotizzare che «circonscrittione» sia cattiva lettura di copista per «circonlocutione», così come *primo* è certamente cattiva lettura per *proprio*; ma sono casi paleograficamente diversi.

LINA BOLZONI

A PROPOSITO DI *GERUSALEMME LIBERATA*, XIV, 36-38 (ACCETTANDO UNA PROVOCAZIONE DI GALILEO)

Non conosco un testo critico così umorale e eccessivo, e nello stesso tempo così ricco di suggestioni e di geniali osservazioni, come le *Considerazioni al Tasso* di Galileo.[1] Vorrei qui partire da uno dei passi più famosi – quello in cui un episodio viene considerato poco funzionale e paragonato a una rappresentazione anamorfica – per accettarne, in un certo senso, la provocazione, per vedere se è possibile trarne spunti per la lettura.

Si tratta de l canto XIV, dell'episodio in cui Carlo e Ubaldo, mandati da Goffredo alla ricerca di Rinaldo, incontrano il mago di Ascalona, il quale darà loro aiuti e suggerimenti per il compimento della missione e intanto li fa scendere nelle profondità della terra.

A che proposito, per amor di Dio, mandar questi poveri uomini da Erode a Pilato a pigliare un foglio e una bacchetta? – nota implacabile Galileo – Non gliela poteva dare il solitario Pietro, o se pure gli voleva mandare da quell'altro, ei che sapeva della lor venuta, a che effetto menargli sott'acqua e sotto terra a vedere i nascimenti de' fiumi e la generazion de' metalli e mille altre cose che non hanno che fare niente con la reparazion di Rinaldo? ...perché, pensatela pur quanto vi piace, voi non troverete che questi due cavalieri abbiano in queste sotterranee caverne veduta o intesa cosa che li serva poi punto al bisogno loro: ma gli è che avete fatto questa lunghera per servire alla vostra allegoria, ché avete voluto figurare l'una e l'altra filosofia, e questa enciclopedia delle scienze. Ma, signor Tasso, vorrei pur che voi sapessi che le favole e le finzioni poetiche devono servire in maniera al senso allegorico,

[1] Su questo testo cfr. E. PANOFSKY, *Galileo as a Critic of the Arts*, The Hague, M. Nijhoff, 1954 (tr. it. a cura di R. Micheli e L. Tongiorgi Tomasi, in «Dimensioni 2. Ideologia Scienza Giudizio Visivo», 1982, pp. 9-42); E. BIGI, "Galileo lettore," in *Saggi su Galileo Galilei*, a cura del Comitato nazionale per le Manifestazioni celebrative del IV centenario della nascita di Galileo Galilei, Firenze, Barbèra, 1967, pp. 3-24; D. DELLA TERZA, *Galileo letterato: "Considerazioni al Tasso"*, in IDEM, *Forma e memoria*, Roma, Bulzoni, 1979, pp. 197-221; T. WLASSICS, *Galileo critico letterario*, Ravenna, Longo, 1974; P. BAROCCHI, *Fortuna dell'Ariosto nella trattatistica figurativa*, in EAD., *Studi vasariani*, Torino, Einaudi, 1984, pp. 53-67; EAD., *Storiografia e collezionismo dal Vasari al Lanzi*, in *Storia dell'arte italiana*, I, 2, Torino, Einaudi, 1979, pp. 5-82 (cfr. p. 30); M. COSTANZO, *I segni del silenzio e altri studi sulle poetiche e l'iconografia letteraria del Manierismo e del Barocco*, Roma, Bulzoni, 1983, p. 31; L. BOLZONI, *La stanza della memoria. Modelli letterari e iconografici nell'età della stampa*, Torino, Einaudi, 1995, pp. 214-215; EAD., *Tra parole e immagini: per una tipologia cinquecentesca del lettore creativo*, «Lettere italiane», XLVIII, pp. 527-558 (cfr. pp. 547-555).

che in esse non apparisca una minima ombra d'obbligo, altrimenti si darà'nello stentato, nel sforzato, nello stiracchiato; e farassi una di quelle pitture, le quali perché riguardate in scorcio da un luogo determinato mostrino una figura umana, sono con tal regola di prospettiva delineate, che, vedute in faccia e come naturalmente e comunemente si guardano le altre pitture, altro non rappresentano che una confusa e inordinata mescolanza di linee e di colori, dalla quale anco si potriano malamente raccapezzare imagini di fiumi o sentier tortuosi, ignude spiagge nugoli o stranissime chimere. Ma quanto di queste sorte di pitture, che principalmente son fatte per esser rimirate di scorcio, è sconcia cosa rimirarle in faccia, non rappresentando altro che un mescuglio di stinchi di gru, di rostri di cicogne e d'altre sregolate figure, tanto nella poetica finzione è più degno di biasimo, che la favola corrente e prima direttamente veduta sia per accomodarsi all'allegoria obliquamente vista e sotto intesa, stravagantemente ingombrata di chimere e fantastiche e superflue imaginazioni.[2]

Galileo ci offre qui una straordinaria rappresentazione del rapporto ermeneutico in termini visivi. La ricezione del testo letterario viene descritta come un gioco di sguardi. Il modo infatti in cui il poema viene letto è paragonato alla collocazione da cui si guarda un quadro. È il lettore, dunque, che adotta una determinata disposizione nello spazio, che sceglie come collocarsi di fronte al testo, ma nello stesso tempo è la struttura del testo che richiede e sollecita una certa collocazione, che suggerisce dunque la prospettiva da adottare. L'allegoria interviene creando nuove profondità spaziali e quindi nuove dimensioni dell'immagine. Tutto ciò, secondo Galileo, deve essere percepibile attraverso uno sguardo centrale e diretto, attraverso cioè quella prospettiva geometrica che egli considera comune e naturale. Nella sua reazione a un artificio prospettico – l'anamorfosi – che è tipico del Manierismo, potremmo individuare, seguendo le indicazioni di Baltrušaitis,[3] anche una reazione contro qualcosa che disvela il carattere artificiale della prospettiva stessa, che rende evidente cioè come anche la prospettiva geometrica sia frutto di una scelta e di una costruzione. Il Tasso diventa colpevole, nell'ottica di Galileo, di aver subordinato le scelte narrative all'allegoria, imponendo al lettore uno sguardo "in scorcio", come fanno appunto i pittori di immagini anamorfiche. Così ad esempio la discesa dei due cavalieri nella grotta, irrilevante e quindi fastidiosa dal punto di vista dello sviluppo della narrazione, sarebbe stata inserita al solo scopo di creare un'immagine allegorica dell'enciclopedia delle scienze, del rapporto tra filosofia naturale e soprannaturale. Galileo si riferisce qui con ogni probabilità all'*Allegoria del poema*, scritta dallo stesso Tasso nel '76, in cui leggiamo:

---

[2] G. GALILEI, *Considerazioni al Tasso*, in ID., *Opere*, Firenze, Barbera, 1899, IX, p.130.

[3] J. BALTRUSAITIS, *Anamorphoses, ou magie artificielle des effects merveilleux*, Paris, Perrin, 1969[2], p. 5 (tr. it. Milano, Adelphi, 1978). Sull'anamorfosi nella cultura tra fine '500 e inizio '600, cfr. J. C. MARGOLIN, *Aspects du surréalisme au XVIe siècle: fonction allégorique et vision anamorphotique*, «Bibliothèque d'Humanisme et Renaissance», XXXIX, 1977, pp. 503-530; M. CHARLES, *Rhétorique de la lecture*, Paris, Le Seuil, 1977, p. 278 sgg.; J. PARISIER PLOTTEL, *Anamorphosis in Painting and Literature*, «Yearbook of Comparative and General Literature», XXVIII, 1979, pp. 10-19; F. HALLYN, *Anamorphose et allégorie*, «Revue de Littérature Comparée», LVI, 1982, pp. 319-330; E. G. GILMAN, *The Curious Perspective. Literary and Pictorial Wit in the Seventeenth Century*, New Haven-London, Yale University Press, 1978.

L'Eremita che per la liberatione di Rinaldo indirizza i due Messaggieri al Saggio, figura la cognitione soprannaturale, ricevuta per divina gratia, sì come il Saggio la humana sapienza. Imperoché dall'humana sapienza et dalla cognitione dell'opere della natura, et de magisteri suoi, si genera et si conferma ne gli animi nostri la giustitia, la temperanza, il disprezzo della morte et delle cose mortali, la magnanimità et ogni altra virtù morale, et grande aiuto può ricever l'huomo civile in ciascuna sua operatione dalla contemplatione.[4]

Analogo lo schema interpretativo – modellato questa volta su Dante – che il Tasso offre in una lettera a Scipione Gonzaga scritta nello stesso anno:

Ne l'altra coordinazion de l'eremita al mago naturale, io procederò come si conclude fra'l signor Flaminio e Vostra Signoria e me, quel dì che ne ragionammo: e questa invenzione sarà simile a quella di Dante. Finge Dante che Beatrice, cioè la teologia, guidi lui per mezzo di Virgilio, che vogliono alcuni che s'intenda per la scienza naturale.[5]

Se Galileo si riferisce veramente, come abbiamo ipotizzato, all'*Allegoria del poema*, dobbiamo pensare che non abbia preso in considerazione, considerandola irrilevante ai fini della sua critica, l'implicita risposta a una delle sue obiezioni («non gliela poteva dare il solitario Pietro...»?) che vi è contenuta:

Né indarno è introdotta la persona di questo Saggio [cioè il Mago di Ascalona], potendo, per consiglio solo dell'Heremita, esser trovato et ricondotto Rinaldo, perché ella s'introduce per dimostrar che la gratia del Signore Iddio non opera sempre ne gli huomini immediatamente, et per mezi estraordinarii, ma fa molte fiate sue operationi per mezi naturali [...] Questa humana sapienza adunque, indirizzata da virtù superiore, libera l'anima sensitiva dal vitio, et c'introduce la morale virtù.[6]

In ogni caso la costruzione – artificiosa e distorcente – dell'allegoria è secondo Galileo frutto della scelta consapevole del Tasso. In realtà i contorni della questione non sono così netti perché, come risulta ad esempio dalle «lettere poetiche» del '75-'76, Tasso ha nei confronti dell'allegoria un atteggiamento complesso e ambiguo, fatto di ironia, di accettazione, di sfida.[7] Basti qui ricordare il lucido distacco con

[4] T. TASSO, *Allegoria del poema*, in *La Gerusalemme liberata* cone le annotationi di Scipion Gentili et li argomenti di Oratio Ariosti, Genova, Giuseppe Pavoni, 1617, pp. 33-36 (della seconda parte): cfr. p. 34.
[5] T. TASSO, *Lettere*, a cura di C. Guasti, I, Firenze, Le Monnier, 1853, p. 125. Sul personaggio cui la lettera è indirizzata, cfr. S. GONZAGA, *Autobiografia*, a cura di D. Della Terza, Modena, Panini, 1987.
[6] T. TASSO, *Allegoria del poema*, cit., p. 35.
[7] Diverse risultano infatti, su questo punto, le posizione della critica: cfr. L. DERLA, *Sull'allegoria della "Gerusalemme liberata"*, «Italianistica», III, 1978, pp. 473-488; M. MURRIN, *Tasso's enchanted Wood*, in *The Allegorical Epic. Essays in his Rise nad Decline*, Chicago, The University of Chicago Press, 1980, cap. IV; L. OLINI, *Dalle direzioni di lettura alla revisione del testo: Tasso tra "Allegoria del poema" e "Giudizio"*, «La Rassegna della letteratura italiana», LXXXIX, 1985, pp. 53-92; L. F. RHU, *From Aristotle to Allegory: young Tasso's evolving Vision of the "Gerusaleme liberata"*, «Italica», LXV, 1988, pp. 111-130; W. STEPHENS, *Metaphor, Sacrament, and the Problem of Allegory in "Gerusalemme liberatta"*, «I Tatti Studies», IV, 1991, pp. 217-247; E. ARDISSINO, *Le allegorie della "Con-*

cui, in una lettera a Scipione Gonzaga, commenta l'*Allegoria del poema*, presentandola come uno scudo contro i censori:

> Stanco di poetare, mi son volto a filosofare, ed ho disteso minutissimamente l'allegoria non d'una parte ma di tutto il poema, di maniera che in tutto il poema non c'è né azione né persona principale che, secondo questo nuovo trovato, non contenga maravigliosi misteri. Riderete leggendo questo nuovo capriccio. [...] Farò il collo torto, e mostrerò che non ho avuto altro fine che di servire al politico; e con questo scudo cercherò di assicurare ben bene gli amori e gl'incanti.[8]

Nello stesso tempo, tuttavia, Tasso sembra conquistato dal demone dell'analogia, dal fascino delle corrispondenze. Scrive infatti subito dopo il brano che abbiamo appena citato:

> Ma certo, o l'affezione m'inganna, tutte le parte de l'allegoria son in guisa legate fra loro, ed in maniera corrispondono al senso letterale del poema, ed anco a' miei principii poetici, che nulla più; ond'io dubito talora che non sia vero, che quando cominciai il mio poema avessi questo pensiero.[9]

L'adozione del punto di vista allegorico, dunque, non solo interagisce con la revisione del poema,[10] ma tende a riscrivere anche il passato a sua immagine e somiglianza.

Fernand Hallyn, che ha dedicato un'analisi molto fine al modo in cui, fra Cinque e Seicento, si vanno costruendo delle corrispondenze fra anamorfosi e allegoria, ha sottolineato quei passi delle prose tassiane che rivelano uno scarso interesse per l'allegoria, che accennano alla pluralità di significati allegorici di cui uno stesso passo può essere investito, e che denunciano la difficoltà, o l'impossbilità, di inserire ogni componente della narrazione entro un quadro di significati 'altri' («quando anco i due cavaliere [Carlo e Ubaldo] non significassero, non crederei ch'importasse molto; pur meglio sarà che significhino; ma io non so trovar cosa che s'adatti»).[11] Da tutto ciò il critico ricava che «l'allégorie de la *Jérusalem délivrée* ne constitue pas – du moins pas dans la première moitié du texte- une anamorphose intentionnelle, mais s'apparente plûtot à la découverte d'une image que le hasard révèle lorqu'on adopte tout à coup un point de vue nouveau devant un objet connu».[12] Davanti al poeta che cerca di costruire

---

quistata" come poema dell'anima», «Filologia e critica», XVIII, 1993, pp. 45-69; EAD., «*L'aspra tragedia*». *Poesia e sacro in T. Tasso*, Firenze, Olschki, 1996.

[8] T. TASSO, *Lettere*, cit., p. 185.

[9] *Ibid.*

[10] Cfr. la lettera a Scipione Gonzaga del 5 marzo 1576: ho corretto, scrive il Tasso, il canto XIV e «migliorate molte cose che riguardavano l'allegoria, de la quale son fatto, non so come, maggior prezzatore ch'io non era; sì che non lascio passar cosa che non possa stare a martello». (*Lettere*, cit., p. 184).

[11] Cfr. la lettera a Scipione Gonzaga del 15 giugno 1576, in T. TASSO, *Lettere*, cit., pp. 195-196.

[12] F. HALLYN, *Anamorphose et allégorie*, cit., p. 328.

un significato allegorico, continua Hallyn, le parole, le invenzioni, acquistano una consistenza autonoma, diventano come delle cose dotate di proprietà strane, non prevedibili; l'apporto intenzionale del poeta «consiste dès lors à vouloir capter et orienter ces propriétés [...], à vouloir les développer de manière cohérente».[13] Il rapporto fra testo del poema e sua lettura allegorica diventa allora simile, secondo il critico, a quel rapporto fra anamorfosi presente nella natura (e scoperta per caso) e anamorfosi intenzionale, che il gesuita Athanasius Kircher descrive e teorizza nel '600, nella sua *Ars magna lucis et umbrae*, nel capitolo intitolato *De repraesentatione rerum fortuita et casuali et quomodo ea arte rebus induci possit.* C'è una somiglianza, una continuità, sostiene il gesuita, fra i due tipi di anamorfosi; in entrambi i casi «partes diversae alicuius complexi, sub certo et determinato puncto in oculum occurrentes, talem et talem figuram constituunt».[14]

L'analisi di Hallyn ha, dal nostro punto di vista, il limite di utilizzare solo parzialmente i testi tassiani sull'allegoria del poema, il che porta fra l'altro a una divisione troppo netta fra prima e seconda parte della *Gerusalemme*. I risultati cui giunge sono tuttavia molto interessanti, e non solo nell'ottica che lo interessa, e che troviamo così sintetizzata nella conclusione dell'articolo: «L'âge maniériste implique une mise en question du discours de fiction, dont le rapprochement avec l'anamorphose et son complément, l'image due au hasard, situent l'enjeu du côté de la maîtrise et de l'articulation du sens».[15] Le sue osservazioni ci stimolano infatti a riprendere il tema da cui siamo partiti, e cioè la rappresentazione che Galileo offre del rapporto ermeneutico in termini visivi. Possiamo dire che nel momento in cui l'autore guarda al proprio testo dal punto di vista allegorico, egli diventa interprete di se stesso, diventa cioè lettore, il che implica, come l'ermeneutica ci ha insegnato, anche un ruolo attivo, non di puro rispecchiamento del testo.[16] Solo che in questo caso particolarissimo la ricreazione dell'opera che la lettura comporta può avere una ricaduta sulla scrittura stessa del poema. Negli anni in cui scrive la *Gerusalemme liberata*, come già si accennava, il rapporto che Tasso ha con l'allegoria è complesso, e pesantemente condizionato dal rischio della censura. La lettura\riscrittura del testo, che cerca di garantire la possibilità di una esegesi allegorica, poteva difficilmente essere condotta – come Galileo avrebbe voluto – da una prospettiva geometrica; troppi erano gli elementi – di costrizione, oltre che di gusto – che si frap-

---

[13] Ivi, p. 329.

[14] A. Kircher, *Ars magna lucis et umbrae*, X, 2, Amsterdam, Apud Joannem Janssonium, 1671[2], pp. 710-711 (cfr. F. Hallyn, cit., p. 329).

[15] F. Hallyn, cit., p. 330.

[16] Mi limito a rinviare a E. D. Hirsch, *Teoria dell'interpretazione e critica letteraria*, tr. it. Bologna, Il mulino, 1973; W. Iser, *L'atto della lettura. Una teoria della risposta estetica*, tr. it. Bologna, Il mulino, 1987; H. R. Jauss, *Esperienza estetica ed ermeneutica letteraria*, tr. it. Bologna, Il mulino, 1987-88; *Teoria della ricezione*, a cura di R. Holub, Torino, Einaudi, 1989 e, anche per ulteriori indicazioni bibliografiche, *Il testo letterario. Istruzioni per l'uso*, a cura di M. Lavagetto, Bari, Laterza, 1996.

ponevano alla linearità dello sguardo rivolto al testo. Allegoria e anamorfosi vengono così a corrispondere, e l'esegesi allegorica si delinea come complessa contrattazione piuttosto che come lineare costruzione. [17]

Vorrei ora riprendere una delle indicazioni di lettura offerte da Galileo, quella che sottolinea, con forte connotazione negativa, il tentativo del Tasso di creare – dietro al testo, di scorcio rispetto al testo – l'immagine del sapere enciclopedico. Possiamo partire da qui per rileggere il complesso gioco intertestuale che le ottave 36-39 del canto XIV ci presentano.

Il mago si era presentato ai due guerrieri vestito di lino bianco, con una corona di faggio, e una verga in mano; aveva camminato verso di loro passando a piedi asciutti sopra le acque: un ritratto in cui le connotazioni magiche venivano smorzate, o meglio ricollocate in una luce rassicurante dal ricordo del dantesco messo celeste (*Inf.*, IX, 80) che «passava Stige con le piante asciutte»; nello stesso tempo, come ha notato Residori, resta un inquietante sapore di "romanzo", nel bel mezzo di un episodio che prepara strutturalmente il ritorno all'ordine epico. [18]

Dopo una breve allocuzione – sulla quale torneremo – il mago guida i suoi ospiti verso la sua dimora:

> Disse, e ch'a lor dia loco a l'acqua impose;
> ed ella tosto si ritira e cede,
> e quinci e quindi di montagna in guisa
> curvata pende e 'n mezzo appar divisa. (36, 5-8)

La figura che automaticamente viene evocata alla memoria del lettore, è quella di Mosè, che per salvare il suo popolo fa aprire una strada tra le acque del mar Rosso: «cumque extendisset Moyses manum super mare, ...divisa... est aqua. Et ingressi sunt filii Israel per medium sicci maris: erat enim aqua quasi murus a dextra eorum

---

[17] Ritengo di poter così continuare le riflessioni che già ho avuto modo di fare, a proposito della singolare situazione ermeneutica che le «lettere poetiche» del Tasso costituiscono, in *Tra parole e immagini*, cit.

[18] Cfr. M. RESIDORI, *Il mago d'Ascalona e gli spazi del romanzo nella "Liberata"*, «Italianistica», XXIV, 1995, pp. 453-471, e la sua discussione della interpretazione di G. BALDASSARRI, *"Inferno" e "cielo". Tipologia e funzione del meraviglioso nella "Gerusalemme liberata"*, Roma, Bulzoni, 1977. Dedica un'ampia e appassionata analisi alla figura del Mago e della sua caverna D. QUINT, *The Magus of Ascalona and the Wisdom of Job*, in ID., *Origin and Originality in Renaissance Literature. Versions of the Source*, New Haven-London, Yale University Press, 1983, pp. 92-117 (e, per la rielaborazione dell'episodio nella *Conquistata*, p. 118 sgg.). Quint individua nelle descrizione che il Mago fa delle proprie conoscenze una ripresa di alcuni versetti del libro di Giobbe e propone una lettura dell'episodio in una chiave neoplatonica, che separa nettamente il Creatore dalla creazione, la *scientia* dalla *sapientia*, la verità dei cieli dalla apparenza e illusorietà della materia. La lettura qui proposta sottolinea invece i punti di mediazione e di contatto, basati sul gioco fra unità e pluralità, e sul tema dell'ordine divino che si manifesta – agli occhi di chi sa vedere – anche nell'opacità della materia. Per altre letture della figura del mago, cfr. B. T. SOZZI, *Il magismo del Tasso*, in *Studi sul Tasso*, Pisa, Nistri Lischi, 1954, pp. 303-336; G. PETROCCHI, *Svaghi tassiani: il mago "cattolico"*, «Filologia e critica», XIII, 1988, pp. 184-191 e G. GUNTERT, *Dalla "Liberata" alla "Conquistata": racconto di nobili imprese e allegoria del "contemptus mundi"*, «Italianistica», XXV, 1995, pp. 381-394 (cfr. pp. 393-394); P. DI SACCO, *Da Ascalona alla "scalogna". Tasso, la magia e altro*, «Lettere italiane», XLVIII, 1996, pp. 602-624.

et laeva» (*Exod.*, XIV, 21-22). Possiamo pensare a un effetto analogo a quello già notato: il ricordo biblico, come prima quello dantesco, dà all'azione magica una connotazione provvidenziale. Del resto la «figura» dell'Esodo[19] funziona immediatamente da referente per un viaggio – come quello di Carlo e Ubaldo – che è teso a realizzare una missione di salvezza. L'immagine della montagna, tuttavia, («e quinci e quindi di montagna in guisa \ curvata pende») non costituisce una variante dell'immagine biblica del muro, ma è segno che un altro testo è presente, e con una forza forse maggiore, alla memoria del poeta. Si tratta dell'elegante epillio che chiude il IV libro delle *Georgiche*: Aristeo, disperato per la perdita delle api, chiede aiuto alla madre Cirene, che abita con le Ninfe nelle profondità delle sorgenti del fiume Peneo; Cirene manda allora la sorella Aretusa a fargli da guida e insieme fa aprire le acque, così che il figlio possa penetrare nella sua dimora sotterranea:

> ...simul alta iubet discedere late
> flumina, qua iuvenis gressus inferret. At illum
> *curvata in montis faciem* circumstetit unda
> accepitque sinu vasto misitque sub amnem. (IV, 359-362)

Il modello virgiliano ha del resto altri forti, importanti punti di contatto con il testo del Tasso: Cirene offre al figlio uno splendido banchetto, e gli dà le istruzioni e l'aiuto necessari per risolvere il suo problema (dovrà catturare il dio marino Proteo, tenerlo legato mentre egli assumerà diverse forme, e farsi dare il responso); penetrato nella dimora della madre, inoltre, Aristeo, può osservare l'origine di tutti i fiumi (IV, 363-373), esattamente come fanno Carlo e Ubaldo nella spelonca del mago di Ascalona (XIV, 37-38). La discesa alla sorgente primigenia delle acque è del resto – come ha notato David Quint – un topos che proprio nel Rinascimento trova una rinnovata fortuna e assume nuovi significati.[20]

Le suggestioni legate al testo virgiliano si intrecciano dunque con quelle bibliche, per prendere decisamente il sopravvento: se Mosè resta sullo sfondo, la figura di Aristeo si delinea in modo consistente sulla scena dell'episodio. E non si tratta di una presenza qualsiasi. Accanto al piacere della rievocazione di una delle parti più eleganti, e più famose delle *Georgiche*, il lettore colto cinquecentesco poteva cogliere allusioni più segrete. Già in Virgilio l'episodio di Aristeo e Proteo si collega al mito di Orfeo e si colloca entro la grande tematica della nascita, della morte, della rigenerazione. Nel Cinquecento, inoltre, veniva letto anche in chiave di sapienza riposta, con una ripresa e combinazione di antiche interpretazioni allegoriche: Pro-

---

[19] Per il significato con cui uso qui "figura", cfr. E. AUERBACH, *Figura*, in *Studi su Dante*, Milano, Feltrinelli, 1974[4], pp. 174-220.
[20] QUINT, *Origin and Originality*, cit., pp. IX-XII.

teo, il dio marino, era visto come l'immagine della materia prima, di quella dimensione unitaria e nascosta che è alla base della varietà delle forme visibili. Aristeo che lega Proteo diventava così l'immagine dell'alchimista, di colui che controlla il gioco delle metamorfosi, che diventa saggio e potente quando scopre la radice prima, unitaria del molteplice.[21] È una chiave di lettura che il Tasso dimostra di conoscere.[22]

Nella *Gerusalemme* la dottrina alchimistica sull'origine dei metalli viene ricordata subito dopo l'elenco dei fiumi (XIV, 38,5-8)[23] e la spelonca sotterranea del mago di Ascalona costituisce un osservatorio privilegiato da cui scrutare un aspetto almeno del legame fra`unità e pluralità:

> Debile e incerta luce ivi si scerne,
> qual tra' boschi di Cinzia ancor non piena;
> ma pur *gravide* d'acque ampie caverne
> veggiono, onde tra noi sorge *ogni* vena
> la qual rampilli in fonte, o in fiume vago
> discorra, o stagni o si dilati in lago. (XIV, 37)

Quel che i due guerrieri vedono è l'origine di tutte le acque; rispetto al modello virgiliano, ci si muove in un contesto esclusivamente maschile (la funzione di Cirene è svolta dal mago di Ascalona), ma una traccia almeno della componente femminile – del resto tradizionalmente legata all'acqua - resta nella connotazione delle caverne («gravide») da cui derivano tutte le forme acquatiche che si rendono visibili sulla superficie della Terra. Tutta popolata da Ninfe – con una citazione più diretta del testo virgiliano – era invece la caverna da cui nascono tutti i fiumi nella XII prosa dell'*Arcadia* del Sannazaro, così come lo sarà nella ridondante ripresa che ne farà Marino nell'*Adone*.[24]

C'è una precisa corrispondenza, nella *Gerusalemme*, tra i caratteri del viaggio che i due guerrieri dovranno compiere per portare a buon fine la loro missione e il tipo di percorso attraverso cui il mago li guida. Il giovane Rinaldo, spiega il

---

[21] Molto ricca di testimonianze è ad esempio l'opera di Giulio Camillo: su Proteo come immagine della materia prima, intesa sia in senso metafisico che retorico, cfr. G. CAMILLO, *L'idea del theatro*, a cura di L. Bolzoni, Palermo, Sellerio, 1991, p.164 e nota 6, pp. 185-186; sul significato alchimistico della legatura di Proteo, quale è raccontata da Omero e da Virgilio, cfr. pp. 114-115 e nota 54, p.195.

[22] Molto ricca di indicazioni intertestuali è la lettura che il Tasso degli ultimi anni dà del modo in cui, nella *Conquistata*, ha rielaborato l'episodio di cui ci stiamo occupando. Ricorda di aver imitato «la maravigliosa favola di Virgilio nel quarto della Georgica» e aggiunge che «queste cose si deono intendere allegoricamente... E s'io non m'inganno, in questa guisa i teologi, e i filosofi misteriosi vollero significarsi la *vicendevole trasmutazione degli elementi*, facendo l'acqua principio degli altri, secondo l'opinione di Talete Milesio» (T. TASSO, *Del giudizio sopra la Gerusalemme*, in *Opere*, a cura di G. Rosini, XII, Pisa, Niccolò Capurro, 1823, p. 284).

[23] Quint ricollega questi versi a *Job*, 28, 1-2 (QUINT, *Origin and Originality*, cit., pp. 100-101).

[24] Cfr. I. SANNAZZARO, *Arcadia*, in *Opere volgari*, a cura di A. Mauro, Bari, Laterza, 1961, pp. 111-128. La discesa nella grotta avviene in una situazione incerta fra sonno e veglia e corrisponde al ritorno di Sincero a Napoli e alla dolorosa presa di coscienza della morte della donna amata e di una tragica situazione di crisi. Cfr. G. B. MARINO, *L'Adone*, a cura di G. Pozzi, Milano, Adelphi, 1988, c. I, 89-105, pp. 71-75.

mago, «lunge è da questa \ terra in paesi incogniti ed infidi», per cui «convien che si stenda il cercar vostro \ oltre i confini ancor del mondo nostro» (XIV, 35). La discesa dei due guerrieri «ne le nascose \ spelonche» dove il mago ha la sua «secreta sede» (XIV, 36) permetterà loro di vincere intanto la sfida della conoscenza, di penetrare là dove ciò che è occulto si rivela, e ciò che è nascosto si rende visibile. La spelonca sotterranea, si diceva, è un punto di osservazione privilegiato, un luogo collocato, a sua volta, «oltre i confin ancor del mondo no-stro», che proprio per questo offre un *diverso* punto di vista sulla realtà: non solo vi si squaderna, davanti agli occhi dei due guerrieri, la radice unitaria della plu-ralità delle acque, ma anche «non asconde \ gli occulti suoi principi il Nilo quivi» (XIV, 38). Il mondo è diventato trasparente: allo sguardo ormai vittorioso dei due che si preparano per la loro missione l'enciclopedia delle acque si rivela in modo esaustivo, senza zone d'ombra. Il riferimento alle misteriose sorgenti del Nilo rin-via a un topos che torna in modo significativo in altre zone del poema. Quando Rinaldo, ad esempio, si allontana dal campo cristiano, si dice che è mosso da un desiderio di gloria, che lo spinge a progettare «magnanime imprese» e «insolite cose», come combattere, solo, tra i nemici, o

> scorre l'Egitto, e penetrar sin dove
> fuor d'incognito fonte il Nilo move. (V,52)

E nel canto III, quando Erminia indica al re Aladino il giovane Rinaldo, ne esalta il valore e dice che se altri cristiani fossero come lui, l'intero Oriente sarebbe già stato da loro conquistato,

> e forse il Nilo occultarebbe in vano
> dal giogo il capo incognito e lontano. (III, 38)

Associate dunque al giovane eroe che Carlo e Ubaldo devono ritrovare e ricon-durre al campo cristiano, le fonti del Nilo erano già comparse nel poema come l'emblema di una *quête* eroica, in cui conoscenza e dominio, esplorazione e impe-rialismo, si legano strettamente. Analoga funzione avrà poi la loro ricomparsa nel c. XVII, associata a un'eventuale crociata condotta da Alfonso II d'Este: egli potrebbe, si dice,

> ...per battesmo de le nere fronti
> del gran Nilo scoprir le ignote fonti. (XVII, 94)[25]

---

[25] Per la presenza di un analogo tema nella leggenda di Alessandro, cfr. D. S. AVALLE, *Modelli semiologici nella Commedia di Dante,* Milano, Bompiani, 1975, p. 57. Sull'imperialismo nel Tasso e nella tradizione epica cfr. D. QUINT, *Epic and Empire. Politics and Generic Form from Virgil to Milton,* Princeton, Princeton University Press, 1992; S. ZATTI, *L'ombra del Tasso. Epica e romanzo nel Cinquecento,* Milano, Bruno Mondadori, 1996.

Nel momento in cui il mago di Ascalona le rende visibili agli occhi dei due guerrieri, le fonti del Nilo diventano quasi un segno del compimento della missione, il presagio di una vittoria – morale e cognoscitiva – sull'oscurità, sull'alterità che ancora sfugge e si nasconde.

Indizi analoghi ci vengono da un altro testo che interviene nel gioco dei rinvii, e delle associazioni, creato dalla memoria letteraria, e cioè il *Fedone* di Platone. Nella parte finale Socrate espone le proprie idee cosmologiche, che rovesciano il punto di vista tradizionale: gli uomini abitano solo una piccolissima parte della Terra, entro una delle sue numerose cavità; ben lontana, e più bella e splendente è la vera superficie della Terra: là gli uomini vedono gli dei, parlano con loro, e vedono gli astri quali veramente sono (111c). Tutte le cavità della terra sono collegate fra di loro; «una delle voragini che sono nella terra è smisuratamente grande, tanto che l'immenso suo vaneggiare s'estende da un capo all'altro della terra. A questo accenna Omero quando dice: «lungi immensamente, baratro sotto la terra»: è quel baratro che in altri luoghi Omero stesso e gli altri poeti in gran numero hanno chiamato Tartaro. Il fatto è che verso questa voragine tutti i fiumi confluiscono e da questa, alla loro volta, defluiscono» (112a). [26]

La memoria del testo platonico si rivela, nella ripresa tassiana, carica di suggestioni. Siamo ben al di là della pura citazione naturalistica. La figura di Socrate viene evocata dietro quella del mago di Ascalona, e interviene a complicare il gioco di diffrazione del personaggio che abbiamo veduto finora. Come ha osservato Residori, il mago di Ascalona occupa nella topologia del poema un luogo ambiguo, ai confini tra mondo epico e mondo romanzo, fra tentazioni magiche e dimensione provvidenziale, fra passato pagano e presente cristiano, [27] e pure nello stesso tempo è il tramite della ricomposizione dell'ordine, è il personaggio aiutante che rende possibile la missione. [28] Socrate è, nel *Fedone*, in attesa di bere la cicuta, e dunque ai confini tra la vita e la morte; i suoi racconti cosmologici si legano a quelli sul destino delle anime dopo la morte (hanno infatti a che fare con i luoghi dove si compie la vicenda di purificazione e reincarnazione delle anime); fanno parte di un insegnamento che, come si diceva, vuole capovolgere i punti di vista tradizionali. Pensare la collocazione dell'uomo entro una sola delle molte caverne che si aprono sulla superficie della terra, equivale allora alla discesa di Carlo e Ubaldo nella caverna del mago di Ascalona. Possiamo pensare che la straordinaria ricchezza di pietre preziose che Carlo e Ubaldo ammirano lungo le rive di uno dei fiumi sotterranei (XIV, 39) venga a corrispondere alle splendide gemme che per Socrate si trovano sulla vera superficie della Terra, quella dove gli dei e gli astri si mostrano

---

[26] Ho usato la traduzione di Enrico Turolla (PLATONE, *I dialoghi*, Milano, Rizzoli, 1964).

[27] RESIDORI, *Il mago d'Ascalona*, cit.

[28] La funzione svolta dal mago si può infatti assimilare a una di quelle descritte da V. PROPP, *Morfologia della fiaba*, Torino, Einaudi, 1966, cap. III, pp. 31-70.

come sono, là dove risplendono gemme di cui le nostre non sono che frammenti, e «la terra è ornata oltre che dalla bellezza di queste gemme, anche dalla presenza copiosa d'oro d'argento e d'altri metalli preziosi, posti in prima vista, una quantità infinita e in tutte le parti. Stupendo spettacolo di cui godono spettatori felici!» (110e-111a).

Il mago di Ascalona è l'immagine della magia naturale, della conoscenza della natura che rinuncia programmaticamente a apporti diabolici («né in virtù fatte son d'angioli stigi \ l'opere mie meravigliose e conte \ (tolga Dio ch'usi note o suffumigi \ per sforzar Cocito e Flegetonte)», XIV, 42). Anche nel momento – quale quello su cui ci siamo soffermati – in cui egli guida i due guerrieri attraverso un percorso che rende loro visibile una parte dell'enciclopedia naturale, il gioco della memoria letteraria addensa intorno al testo suggestioni che rinviano a dimensioni più profonde e misteriose, così da creare – per riprendere la lettura galileiana – artificiosi effetti prospettici. Ma proprio l'indicazione galileiana di un'allegoria enciclopedica può offrire una nuova suggestione intertestuale che si aggiunge ai testi già presi in considerazione, e già segnalati nei commenti al poema.[29] Il modo in cui il mago rende visibile la conoscenza dell'ordine della natura ricorda alcune esperienze tardocinquecentesche in cui l'enciclopedia si intreccia con l'arte della memoria: penso in particolare alla *Tipocosmia* di Alessandro Citolini, un'opera pubblicata nel 1561 a Venezia e realizzata nello stesso ambiente veneto con cui fu in contatto il giovane Tasso.[30] L'opera descrive un processo conoscitivo che passa attraverso tutte le cose – e tutti i nomi – del mondo e culmina nella visione di un grande libro, la cui struttura – probabilmente basata su tavole diagrammatiche – permette di avere una conoscenza visiva della natura e dell'origine delle cose. Ma vediamo il passo che più ci interessa: «ne l'acque videro i fiumi, non pur di fuori, ma di dentro ne le viscere de la terra... e vi videro quanti mari, e laghi a 'l mondo si trovano...e persino ne 'l centro de la terra penetrarono, a veder le cose da 'l Conte il secondo giorno raccontate».[31]

Accanto a una ricca tradizione letteraria e filosofica, nei versi tassiani sembra dunque di riconoscere la presenza anche di suggestioni legate all'enciclopedismo contemporaneo. Ma che funzione ha tutto ciò rispetto allo svolgimento della favola? «Voi non troverete che questi due cavalieri abbiano in queste sotterranee caverne veduta o intesa cosa che li serva poi punto al bisogno loro», nota a ragio-

---

[29] Cfr. in particolare il commento di Bruno Maier.

[30] Cfr. il catologo della mostra *La ragione e l'arte. Torquato Tasso e la Repubblica veneta*, a cura di G. Da Pozzo, Venezia, Il cardo, 1995.

[31] A. CITOLINI, *La tipocosmia*, Venezia, Vincenzo Valgrisi, 1561, p. 551. Sul Citolini cfr. la voce, curata da M. FIRPO, nel *Dizionario biografico degli italiani*, XXVI, Roma, Istituto dell'Enciclopedia italiana, 1982, pp. 39-46; A. PROSPERI, *Un processo per eresia a Verona verso la metà del Cinquecento*, in «Quaderni storici», 15 (1970), pp. 773-94 e i saggi di A. ANTONINI, *La "Tipocosmia" di A. Citolini: un repertorio linguistico* e L. BOLZONI, *Memoria letteraria e iconografica nei repertori cinquecenteschi*, in *Repertori di parole e immagini. Esperienze cinquecentesche e moderni 'data bases'*, a cura di P. Barocchi e L. Bolzoni, Pisa, Scuola Normale Superiore, 1997, pp. 159-232 e pp. 13-48.

ne Galileo. O meglio: a ragione dal punto di vista strettamente narratologico. Abbiamo visto come il gioco intertestuale aiuti a cogliere la pluralità di significati, e di funzioni, che ha la conoscenza enciclopedica: il sapere che si rende visibile aiuta a entrare in contatto con l'ordine che regge l'universo; la discesa nella caverna dove il molteplice viene ricondotto all'uno diventa allora una tappa del percorso che non deve solo riportare Rinaldo a Gerusalemme, ma deve appunto restaurare un ordine che è stato troppo a lungo minacciato e incrinato.[32] Certo per cogliere questa dimensione del viaggio sotterraneo di Carlo e Ubaldo non basta adottare uno sguardo lineare, geometrico, diretto sul testo: bisogna ricorrere a quella prospettiva obliqua, "in scorcio" che è richiesta dall'anamorfosi e che a Galileo appariva come «stravagantemente ingombrata di chimere e fantastiche e superflue imaginazioni».

---

[32] Riprendo qui un tema presente in E. RAIMONDI, *Il dramma nel racconto. Topologia di un poema*, in ID., *Poesia come retorica*, Firenze, Olschki, 1980, pp. 71-202.

Rena A. Syska-Lamparska

GREGORIO CALOPRESE E IL PETRARCA

1. *Petrarca, poeta «pernicioso», ispirato da «insana concupiscenza»*

Tra le poche testimonianze biografiche su Gregorio Caloprese pervenute ai tempi nostri occupa un posto primario, sia per la mole del materiale raccolto sia per la serietà e il rigore della presentazione, lo scritto di uno degli ultimi allievi del Maestro di Scalea, intitolato *Vita e studi di Francesco Maria Spinelli scritta da lui medesimo*.[1] Lo scritto è una fonte importante per la ricostruzione del profilo intellettuale del Caloprese nonché per la conoscenza del suo metodo d'insegnamento. La *Vita* dello Spinelli ha autenticità di documento storico da cui risalta il personaggio di Caloprese, filosofo, teorico e critico letterario, educatore, uomo di sicura fede cattolica. In questa configurazione sorprende purnondimeno il fatto che in un documento di tale valore si possa trovare un brano che urta contro il tono dell'intero scritto. Il brano riguarda il *Canzoniere* del Petrarca insegnato dal Caloprese agli alunni della sua scuola.

Diamo dunque la parola allo Spinelli:

...il giovane [...] studiò [...] quasi tutto il *Canzoniere* del Petrarca; nel quale egli malamente impiegò il suo tempo, per essere un tal libro egualmente pernicioso (massimamente per la prima gioventù) di quello che sarebbe l'Aretino, perché quantunque questo oscenissimo, laddove quello per castissimo si ravvisi, nulla di meno le sporche oscenità di questo, quantunque muovano il senso, non può alla fine l'animo non nausearsene, come avviene in tutti i vizi scoperti e sfacciati; laddove nel *Canzoniere* del Petrarca esaltandovi la M. Laura ad un grado quasi di divinità, con ciò si viene a corrompere l'intelletto, avvezzandolo a dare alla creatura quel culto, che a Dio solo s'appartiene; la quale spezie d'idolatria, quantunque cattivissima, e della quale l'animo difficilmente si distacca per non ravvisarvi quella patente corruttela dell'Aretino; nulla di meno né anche in quella falsa apparente sublimità può rimanere, dovendo necessariamente quella pretesa pura venerazione dell'oggetto in appetito sensibile per esso degenerare.[2]

---

[1] Francesco Maria Spinelli, «Vita e studi di Francesco Maria Spinelli principe della Scalea scritta da lui medesimo», *Raccolta di opuscoli scientifici e filologici*, XLIX, Venezia, 1753.

[2] Riportato da Amedeo Quondam, *Cultura e ideologia di Gianvincenzo Gravina*. Milano, Mursia, 1968, p. 50.

A mo' di commento a questo brano si leggono le seguenti parole di Amedeo Quondam:

Mi sembra difficile stabilire quanto di calopresiano possa esservi nella dichiarazione dello Spinelli, davvero sconcertante, per cui Petrarca è posto accanto all'Aretino, <quantunque questo oscenissimo>, perché <egualmente pernicioso>. Certo, però, che Caloprese, nel suo *Commento* al Casa, rivela le sue preferenze e dichiara esplicitamente il suo consenso per lo stile e l'espressione poetica del Casa, da lui lodato proprio perché, <non solo non cade nel fallo dell'affettazione; ma l'unisce così bene col costume e con gli affetti, che non vi è cosa che non sia conforme alla natura>. A questo punto si dovrebbe aprire tutto un lungo discorso sulla posizione letteraria e ideologica del Caloprese, (sottolineando proprio quel <conforme alla natura>), ma mi porterebbe lontano dai miei obiettivi [...] . (Quondam, p. 51)

Certamente non sono da trascurare le obiezioni del critico, il dubbio su «quanto di calopresiano possa esservi nella dichiarazione dello Spinelli, davvero sconcertante», d'altra parte è poco probabile che le critiche riportate dallo Spinelli provengano da lui stesso. Si deve ricordare che la sua descrizione della metodologia calopresiana è priva in genere d'interventi critico-negativi e che parte ovviamente dal presupposto di una resa obiettiva del quadro d'insegnamento. D'altro lato, il parere del Caloprese sul *Canzoniere*, come testimoniano i suoi scritti, non corrisponde a quello riportato dallo Spinelli. Più precisamente, la linea petrarchesca in essi avanzata va in direzione diversa se non proprio opposta, e le obiezioni alla poetica del Petrarca, pur esistenti nei commenti critici del Caloprese, sono di natura diversa, non moralizzante ma più prettamente teorico-letteraria. In questo caso, il contesto culturale entro il quale la dichiarazione dello Spinelli potè nascere sembra più significativo dell'*authorship* stessa. Una delle componenti ideologiche del clima intellettuale del periodo, vale a dire l'influenza politica e religiosa esercitata dal potere ecclesiastico, non è infatti da trascurare nell'analisi degli scritti calopresiani, come del resto in nessun'altra analisi di testi letterari o scientifici di quel periodo. Affrontati da questo punto di vista, gli scritti dell'epoca formerebbero una specie di mappa strategica con punti di resa e attacco o un resoconto di vittorie e sconfitte. Qui vogliamo solo notare la curiosità del fatto che le precauzioni e le critiche spinelliane non siano state portate ad altri autori oggetto d'insegnamento del Caloprese, tra cui quelli messi specificamente all'*Index librorum prohibitorum* o quelli considerati indirettamente "dannosi alla fede". Il Cartesio, che aveva «il suo credito solo appresso le università Luterane»[3] e gli "eretici" del Port Royal, tutti insegnati a scuola calopresiana, formavano certamente un materiale particolarmente "pernicioso", in quanto mirante a scalzare i fondamenti filoso-

---

[3] Salvo Mastellone, *Pensiero politico e vita culturale a Napoli nella seconda metà del Seicento*, Messina, D'Anna, 1965, p. 147.

fici su cui si basava il potere secolare della Curia, un materiale dunque più suscettibile di obiezioni, critiche, e perplessità di quanto non lo fosse il *Canzoniere*. Sono tutti dunque fatti che diminuiscono il valore delle critiche riportate dallo Spinelli.[4] D'altra parte, le critiche moralizzanti mosse contro il Petrarca nel corso del Cinquecento non possono ovviamente essere legate esclusivamente all'attività controriformistica.[5] Le critiche di questo genere emerse ben prima del concilio tridentino, non di rado fornivano un momento che rinforzava più tardi quel clima postridentino in cui spesso un sano sentimento d'amore diventava oggetto di una "caccia alle streghe erotiche" intrapresa nel nome del non sempre ben inteso presupposto morale di decenza.

Ricordiamo per esempio un noto scritto di Girolamo Malipiero del 1536, *Petrarca spirituale*, una curiosa, tragicomica operazione di riscrittura dell'intero *Canzoniere*, in uno spirito edificante e moralizzante, il quale riscosse grande e larga fama (sette riedizioni nell'arco di cinquant'anni), per rientrare più tardi nell'ambito degli interessi e dell'agire dell'istituzione dell'*Index librorum prohibitorum*, come elemento originario.[6] Alla base dell'operazione di riscrittura malipieriana del *Canzoniere* sta il giudizio negativo dell'aspetto morale dei sonetti petrarcheschi in quanto ispirati a «insana concupiscenza» e non a «sana sapienza». Il Malipiero nel *Dialogo* premesso al *Canzoniere* biasima il Petrarca, il quale «come uno della invaghita schiera de' ciechi amanti, per isfogare l'occulte fiamme del [suo] cuore [descrisse] in tante rime e versi gli sconci e molto disordinati affetti e l'angosciose passioni de' miseri innamorati, insieme con le [sue] frenesie [...]».

[4] Per riportare velocemente qualche tratto dell'atmosfera in cui una descrizione come quella spinelliana potesse nascere, un'atmosfera religiosa di ripercussioni tridentine sempre vive e multiformi, in certi casi intensificate dalle crescenti idiosincrasie e invidie personali esercitate anche ad alto livello sociale o amministrativo, è sufficiente ricordare il famoso processo agli "atcisti" svoltosi in Napoli dal 1688 al 1697, concluso con la sentenza di condanna degli imputati, giuristi e scienziati di gran merito e voga, tra cui Giacinto De Cristofaro, Filippo Belli o Basilio Giannelli, discepolo, quest'ultimo, e amico di Francesco D'Andrea. Qui si veda la voce «De Cristofaro, Giacinto» di A. DE FERRARI in *Dizionario biografico degli Italiani*, Istituto della Enciclopedia italiana, 1987, vol. 33, pp. 586-589.

[5] Per esempio, il rimprovero mosso al Petrarca nella descrizione spinelliana per aver esaltato Laura «ad un grado quasi di divinità» e per «dare alla creatura quel culto, che a Dio solo s'appartiene» ha una sua storia lunga che risale al *Cantico delle Creature* come osserva il Contini in occasione di una sua analisi della nota chiusa di *Al cor gentile* di Guido Guinizelli. «Che solo al Signore appartengono le lodi – scrive il Contini – (e qui è fatta estensione a Maria, cui è infatti dedicato un largo repertorio laudistico), era stato ricordato anche dal Canto di frate Sole; e la presunzione è quella stessa che spesso Isaia rinfaccia agli idolatri: la poesia amorosa come lode (tema più tardi organicamente svolto da Dante) rivendica a una creatura, per sé empiamente, ciò che è monopolio di Dio o, se di una donna, della Vergine (il paradosso potrà poi essere coonestato dall'analogia, dalla funzione meditatoria, ecc.)». G. CONTINI, *Letteratura italiana delle origini*, Firenze, Sansoni, 1991, p. 576. Nella polemica trecentesca sulla poesia, gli oppositori come Giovanni da Vigonza o Giovannino da Mantova asserivano che il poeta, da buon cristiano, «deve cantare soltanto le lodi di Dio, della Vergine e degli Santi, la scelta di argomenti profani fuorvia il poeta stesso e i suoi lettori». Si veda M. PICCHIO SIMONELLI, *I trattati de imitatione, la questione della lingua e il petrarchismo nell'Italia del XVI secolo*, Napoli, L'Orientale, 1987, p. 1.

[6] Amedeo Quondam dedica a questo tema il saggio «Riscrittura. Citazione. Parodia del codice. *Il Petrarca spirituale* di Girolamo Malipiero», *Studi e problemi di critica testuale*, XVII, 1978, pp. 77-125. All'articolo di Quondam si riferisce anche N. LONGO in «Letteratura proibita», in *Letteratura italiana*, a cura di Alberto Asor Rosa, vol. 5. *Le questioni*. Torino, Einaudi, 1986, p. 976.

Il Malipiero si propone di "salvare" il *Canzoniere* attribuendo al Petrarca l'intenzione di «figurare la Sapienza [...] sotto velame di non so che madonna Laura». Di conseguenza tutti i sonetti del *Canzoniere* possono essere considerati "allegorici", "di sensi spirituali" e pertanto in questa ottica dovranno essere interpretati e riscritti. Un tale approccio al testo, come osserva il Quondam, è anche «la condizione necessaria per sancire l'opportunità [...] di espungere fisicamente dal testo, cosi come esso è, la presenza dominante di Amore come <insana concupiscenza>». Il Malipiero accusa Petrarca soprattutto per aver pubblicato e dato «al volgo» i suoi sonetti e canzoni, e richiede «che il potere intervenga non tanto per impedire la composizione di certe opere quanto per controllare che esse circolino solo fra pochi uomini sapienti, capaci di non farsi incantare da un testo scritto. Dunque, entro il circuito degli alfabeti è il caso di distinguere i dotti, frequentatori di <scritture oneste e sane>, dagli oziosi che traggono piacere dalla lettura di <questi vanissimi libri>, contenenti <materia conforme a tale sensualità e induttrice a' piaceri lascivi>».[7]

Tra le ammonizioni pedagogiche postridentine, merita attenzione particolare quella di Silvio Antoniano, «pedagogista: uno solo [che] ha il crisma del <classico>»:

Per tanto hanno ad esser banditi del tutto quei poeti, che a bello studio hanno scritto libri amatorii e lascivi, che corrompono i buoni costumi, si come ricorda San Basilio e come ordina il Concilio Lateranense nel decreto posto di sopra, e ultimamente il sacro Concilio di Trento nell'Indice Romano de' libri proibiti.[8]

La ben nota polemica sorta intorno al Giudizio Universale di Michelangelo è un esempio di straordinaria curiosità della difesa della moralità, condotta qui nel nome dei canoni artistici di provenienza classica. Il primo posto spetta a Lodovico Dolce il quale riferendosi ai principi del classicismo rinascimentale rimproverava Michelangelo per non aver osservato nella sua figura del Cristo le regole della fedeltà alla natura. In quel caso, rispettare la natura voleva dire imitare o aderire alla tradizione iconografica. Il Cristo di Michelangelo, senza barba, mezzo nudo, con un corpo da gladiatore, con la mano alzata e pronta a colpire, un Cristo-Uomo invincibile che si scosta drasticamente dal canone ideale, ha provocato vivissime accuse di immoralità, tra cui quella del Dolce, e il dipinto nella sua totalità veniva considerato lussurioso in quanto rappresentante «tanti ignudi che dimostrano disonestamente dritti e riversi». Di sapore unico è il fatto che nel novero degli scandalizzati si trovasse l'*enfant terrible* dell'epoca, l'autore degli scritti sull'educazione delle cortigiane e dei *Sonetti lussu-*

---

[7] NICOLA LONGO, «La letteratura proibita», *op. cit.*, p. 976.
[8] Luigi Volpicelli [a cura di], «Premessa» al suo *Pensiero pedagogico della Controriforma*, Firenze, Giuntine, Sansoni, 1960, p. IX.

riosi, Pietro Aretino (messo del resto più tardi all'Indice anche lui) il quale in una lettera indirizzata direttamente a Michelangelo rimproverò l'artista dell'arbitrarietà formale del suo *Giudizio Universale*, nel quale si manifestava sregolatezza sia morale che teologica. Benché fosse anche vero, ammetteva come per scrupolo l'Aretino, che nella sua *Nanna* si trattava della «materia lasciva e impudica», tuttavia i suoi modi espressivi rimasero sempre modesti.[9]

È proprio qui, con le critiche del Dolce e dell'Aretino che si arriva al nocciolo della questione, osserva Tibor Klaniczay, al pensiero che più tardi doveva farsi imperiosamente strada: la novità formale è per principio sospetta, in quanto nasconde all'interno del proprio contenuto una tendenza ideologica indesiderata. (Klaniczay, p. 208)

Ricordiamo infine che l'*Index librorum prohibitorum* del 1564 proibì, sotto punizione «severa» dei Vescovi, l'insegnamento dei libri «che trattano apertamente materie lascive ed oscene» in quanto corrompono la «fede» e i «costumi». Eccezione fu fatta per i libri antichi, permessi per «l'eleganza e la proprietà della lingua», in nessun caso però esse «si [dovevano] far leggere ai fanciulli».[10]

---

[9] Si veda LODOVICO DOLCE, *Dialogo della pittura intitolato l'Aretino*, in PAOLA BAROCCHI, *Trattati d'arte del Cinquecento fra Manierismo e Controriforma*, vol. 1, Bari, Laterza, 1960, p. 188: «Aretino: <Chi ardirà di affermar che stia bene che nella chiesa di San Pietro prencipe degli Apostoli, in una Roma ove concorre tutto il mondo, nella cappella del pontefice, il quale, come ben dice il Bembo, in terra ne assembra Dio, si veggano dipinti tanti ignudi che dimostrano disonestamente dritti e riversi? cosa nel vero (favellando con ogni sommessione) di quel santissimo luogo indegna>». «Per primo il Dolce, – scrive la Barocchi – in una lettera a Gasparo Ballini del 1544 manifesta predilezioni [nella polemica intorno al *Giudizio Universale*]: il disegno del Buonarroti gli appare monotono, unilaterale e persino licenzioso [...]» (PAOLA BAROCCHI, *op. cit.*, vol. 1, p. 316). «Spetta tuttavia a Pietro Aretino – continua la Barocchi – il vanto di aver tradotto tali riserve puristiche in termini controriformistici, quando scrisse nel novembre 1545 la celebre lettera diffamatoria sul *Giudizio Finale*. La licenza formale del Buonarroti implica, secondo lui, licenze morali e teologiche (<Adunque quel Michelagnolo stupendo nella fama, quel Michelagnolo ammirando ha voluto mostrare a le genti non meno impietà di irreligione che perfezzion di pittura?>); gli eccessi michelangioleschi vengono perciò contrapposti alla <grata bellezza> di Raffaello, e la stessa <divinità> e solitudine del genio buonarrotiano avvilita ad ostentazione congenere ai vizi del *Giudizio*. In sostanza l'Aretino accusa Michelangelo in nome della convenienza dell'invenzione, che a lui si configura solo come invenzione letteraria ed esige generi incontaminati». (BAROCCHI, *ibid.*, 317) Nella stessa lettera a Michelangelo l'Aretino osserva: «Se non fusse cosa nefanda lo introdurre de la similitudine, mi vanterei di bontade nel trattato della Nanna, preponendo il savio mio avedimento e la indiscreta vostra conscienza, avenga che io in materia lasciva et impudica non pure uso parole avertite e costumate, ma favello con detti irreprensibili e casti, e voi nel suggetto di s' alta istoria mostrate gli angeli e i santi, questi senza veruna terrena onestà, e quegli privi d'ogni celeste ornamento». (*ibid.*, 477) Come informa la Barocchi, la lettera dell'Aretino a Michelangelo è pubblicata in E. STEINMANN – H. POGATSCHER, «Dokumente und Forschungen zu Michelangelo», *Repert. f. Kunstwiss.*, XXIX, 1906, pp. 491 sgg. (*ibid.*, 316). Per il tema qui discusso si veda anche TIBOR KLANICZAY, *Renesans, Manieryzm, Barok*. Warszawa, P.W.N., 1986, pp. 207-210, 337 note 32 sgg. Le critiche del Dolce e dell'Aretino trovarono continuazione nel dialogo di GIOVANNI ANDREA GILIO: *Degli errori e degli abusi de' pittori circa l'istorie, con molte annotazioni fatte sopra il "Giudizio" di Michelangelo*, in *Due dialoghi* (1564).

[10] *Index librorum prohibitorum*, Roma, 1564, p. 17: «Sono proibiti del tutto i libri che trattano apertamente materie lascive ed oscene, le narrano o le insegnano, avendo cura non solo della fede ma anche dei costumi che dalla lettura di libri di questo tipo sono soliti di essere corrotti facilmente: coloro che li possiedono siano puniti severamente dai Vescovi. I libri antichi, scritti da autori gentili, siano permessi per l'eleganza e la proprietà della lingua, tuttavia per nessuna ragione si dovranno far leggere ai fanciulli». Citato da N. LONGO, *op. cit.*, p. 985.

All'interno di tale atmosfera i fini educativi non permettevano, come si è visto, nessuna discussione sulla poesia d'amore con i giovani alunni, nessuna presentazione delle passioni amorose che «muovono il senso», distolgono l'attenzione del lettore dalle cose sacre e lo rendono compiacente nella mondanità «perniciosa» alla salvezza dell'anima. Eppure nella scuola del Maestro di Scalea il fatto è accaduto: il «lascivo» *Canzoniere* fu letto e insegnato.

Intanto bisogna notare che la personalità dello stesso Giovanni Della Casa, alla cui poesia il Caloprese dedicò il lungo e faticoso lavoro della «sposizione»,[11] è particolarmente significativa per il clima religioso del suo tempo e quello del Caloprese. Sappiamo che il Casa, petrarchista di stampo nuovo, autore di uno dei numerosi indici dei libri proibiti, fu esponente di quel movimento che avvertì il clima e l'esigenza della nuova spiritualità controriformistica. Il Casa «[...] sul piano dell'ufficialità, l'uomo della Controriforma, il persecutore dell'eresia [...] l'esponente tenace degli interessi pontifici presso la Repubblica di Venezia [...]»,[12] fu il simbolo, l'epitome dei gusti e dell'ideologia controriformistica. Eppure, nonostante questo, le «passioni amorose», proprio sulla scorta del Petrarca, formano addirittura la struttura portante del ciclo delle sue *Rime*, e le lodi, che secondo il testo dello Spinelli dovrebbero appartenere solo a Dio, sono dirette in abbondanza dal Casa alla sua Donna, portata esattamente allo stesso grado di divinità al quale il Petrarca avrebbe esaltato Laura. Tra i due testi poetici ci saranno sicuramente contrasti significativi dovuti all'epoca diversa e della diversa cultura, oltre che alla diversità delle personalità poetiche dei due autori, ma le differenze presentate dal commento calopresiano si manifestano su un livello tutto diverso da quello riportato dallo Spinelli.

Possiamo aggiungere che se si dovesse comunque attribuire al Caloprese la condanna della letteratura «amorosa», tracce di tale condanna certamente si troverebbero nella sua discussione sul teatro. La polemica teatrale, iniziata in Francia con Bossuet e Nicole, tra i maggiori, sorta proprio da presupposti educativi e moralizzanti, si estese, come noto, ai vari paesi d'Europa. Ci si potrebbe quindi aspettare dal Caloprese una presa di posizione consona alle opinioni degli scrittori francesi, religiosi e moralisti, ben noti al pensatore di Scalea, contro lo spettacolo teatrale, in nome della purezza morale minacciata dalla rappresentazione delle nocive passioni amorose. Una occasione sicura per esprimere la propria posizione a questo riguardo si presentava con la lettera del Caloprese stesso indirizzata al principe di Caracciolo sulla «favola rappresentativa».[13] La lettera, concentrata sulle questioni strutturali di

---

[11] Nella mia discussione farò riferimenti alla seconda edizione delle *Spositioni: Opere di Monsignor Giovanni Della Casa. Edizione Veneta Novissima. Tomo Secondo. Contenente le Spositioni di Sertorio Quattromani sopra tutte le Rime; e quelle di M. Aurelio Severino, e di Gregorio Caloprese sopra i XXI primi Sonetti*. In Venezia. Appresso Angiolo Pasinello. In Merceria all'Insegna della Scienza. 1728.

[12] LUIGI BALDACCI, *Il petrarchismo italiano nel '500*, Padova, Liviana, 1974, p. 207.

[13] «La lettera di Gregorio Caloprese all'Illustriss. ed Eccellentiss. Sig. Niccolò Caracciolo Principe di Santobuono, ragionandogli della 'nvenzione della favola rappresentativa, del 30 maggio 1696», in *Lettere memorabili, istoriche, politiche ed erudite* scritte o raccolte da Antonio Bulifon. Raccolta quarta, Napoli, presso Antonio Bulifon, 1698, pp. 150-77.

una perfetta commedia, dedica non poca attenzione alla questione delle passioni discusse qui in funzione della problematica centrale della lettera, cioè quella formale o strutturale. La lettera affronta infatti il tema del malcostume e dei vizi come elementi portanti della struttura del componimento drammatico, puniti alla conclusione della «favola rappresentativa». Tale discussione, dimostra nella lettera calopresiana la funzione positiva del teatro, in quanto catalizzatore di un certo tipo di passioni negative. Il tema del pericolo legato alla rappresentazione scenica delle "passioni amorose" tuttavia nella lettera non appare. Il silenzio del Caloprese a questo riguardo è sicuramente eloquente.

La critica mossa al Petrarca nel resoconto dello Spinelli ha qui, per questo mio discorso, una funzione sussidiaria in quanto stimolante di un'indagine sul petrarchismo nella critica letteraria del Caloprese. L'importanza del tema fu segnalata, come si è già visto, da Amedeo Quondam, il quale ha ripreso in un'altra occasione la questione, osservando che l'edizione del 1694 delle *Rime* del Casa «costituisce il momento fondamentale di precisazione delle implicazioni teorico-ideologiche della proposta neopetrarchista avanzata dalla cultura sperimentale napoletana di fine Seicento: e sono soprattutto le < sposizioni > del Caloprese a definire con maggior rigore e più intensa problematicità il senso reale della linea petrarchistica».[14]

«Esse [*Sposizioni*] costituiscono un momento fondamentale della proposta neopetrarchista nell'ambiente napoletano di fine Seicento».[15] All'argomento si è riferito inoltre Enrico Nuzzo nella sua monografia, *Verso la "vita civile", Antropologia e politica nelle lezioni acccademiche di Gregorio Caloprese e Paolo Mattia Doria*, dove osserva che: «Il letterato di Scalea ebbe un ruolo importante, dopo il Buragna e lo Schettini, e accanto al Porcella, nella scuola petrarchista, contro le "abbominande scuole" ancora legate alle poetiche barocche».[16] Più tardi Michele Rak nel suo studio *La fine dei grammatici*[17] fa alcune osservazioni molto valide riguardanti la presenza del Petrarca nel clima intellettuale napoletano del tardo Seicento. È proposto di questa mia ricerca discutere, all'interno della poetica del Caloprese e del clima intellettuale dell'epoca, alcune «implicazioni teorico-ideologiche» della linea petrarchista avanzate nel commento calopresiano al Casa. La mia discussione non intende, ovviamente, esaurire l'intero, complesso tema, ma si limiterà a disegnare alcuni punti di partenza per uno studio ulteriore.

[14] AMEDEO QUONDAM, in *Dizionario biografico degli italiani*, cit., voce «Caloprese», p. 803.

[15] ALBERTO ASOR ROSA, dir., *Letteratura italiana, op. cit.*, vol. 1, *Dizionario: Autori - Bio-biografia*, p. 413.

[16] ENRICO NUZZO, *Verso la "vita civile": Antropologia e politica nelle lezioni accademiche di Gregorio Caloprese e Paolo Mattia Doria*, Napoli, Guida, 1984, p. 69, nota 4.

[17] MICHELE RAK, *La fine dei grammatici, teoria e critica della letteratura nella storia delle idee del tardo Seicento italiano*, Roma, Bulzoni, 1974.

2. *Il ritorno a Petrarca*

Il ritorno a Petrarca nel tardo Seicento napoletano è già per sé un fatto di un significato particolare. Il Petrarca, come abbiamo notato, diventato già nel secolo precedente un bersaglio di attacchi da parte di moralisti di diverso stampo, trovandosi poi nel Seicento al centro delle accuse dei marinisti, di quei "moderni" poeti barocchi, per i quali la linea lirica del *Canzoniere,* con l'idea del bello e dell'amore di provenienza platonica, rappresentava la tradizione ormai ripudiata, contrastante violentemente con il "nuovo". Il petrarchismo in quel secolo fu sottoposto ai violenti attacchi di Marino e dei marinisti come «espressione tipica del vecchiume restato ad ammuffire nelle menti dei letterati italiani tradizionalisti».[18] La poesia barocca «fatta di amor galante e di sensualismo erotico»[19] rappresentava un primo, massiccio ripudio dell'autorità degli "antichi" e una ricerca di strade nuove.

D'altra parte il petrarchismo continuava ad essere una componente della cultura poetica di quell'epoca: «il suo primo modo di dimostrare d'essere ancora in vita [era] quello di insinuarsi dentro i caratteri dell'esperienza barocca e di provare in una certa misura che essa non avrebbe potuto esistere senza il magistero tematico e stilistico del grande trecentista». (Asor Rosa, «Classicismo», p. 529) Il Petrarca, la sua tecnica poetica in particolare, i suoi moduli lirici fornivano un fondamentale modello poetico alla maniera marinistica. «Poteva molto bene il Secentismo reagire contro il Petrarca dopo essere in parte nato da esso. È proprio della imitazione lo esagerare snaturando [...]».[20] È sufficiente ricordare qui che la caratteristica generale del pensiero poetico del Petrarca, consistente nella tendenza a conformarsi in pluralità, spesso contrarie o in violento contrasto (pace-guerra, fuoco-gelo, luce-ombra), fu ripresa e portata all'esagerazione proprio dalla poetica barocca (e non solo italiana).[21]

Sulla mappa letteraria del tardo Seicento napoletano, estremamente complessa, riprendono forza sempre crescente le tendenze antibarocche, tutt'altro che omogenee, bensì provenienti da parti e da interessi diversi, miranti ai fini più svariati. Negli ambienti intellettuali di quel periodo si afferma infatti una crescente consapevolezza anti marinista manifestatasi dapprima sotto forma di esigenze legate all'*elocutio,* di uno stile dunque chiaro ed essenziale, in ovvia

---

[18] ALBERTO ASOR ROSA, «Classicismo e antimarinismo: poesia sacra e civile, melica e oratoria», in C. MU-SCETTA, dir., *La letteratura italiana, storia e testi,* vol. V, t. I. *Il Seicento, La nuova scienza e la crisi del Barocco.* Roma, Laterza, 1974, p. 529.

[19] RANIERO SEMENTILLI, *I problemi della letteratura italiana. Metodologia e ricerca,* Roma, Editoriale B. M. Italiana, 1988, vol. II, t. I, p. 551.

[20] ARTURO GRAF, citato da G. IZZI, voce «Petrarchismo» in VITTORE BRANCA, dir., *Dizionario critico della Letteratura italiana,* Torino, UTET, 1974, vol. 3, p. 438.

[21] DAMASO ALONSO, «La poesia del Petrarca e il Petrarchismo: Mondo estetico della pluralità», *Lettere Italiane,* 1959, v. XI, n. 3.

opposizione alla tecnica stilistica del marinismo. L'interesse rivolto alla problematica dell'elocuzione derivava in gran parte dalle esigenze espresse dal ceto forense. Il postulato dell'eleganza delle forme, unito all'esigenza di strumenti persuasivi efficaci, adatti a circoli di vario livello e varia preparazione, si realizzava nel richiamo ad una prosa scarna, essenziale ed efficace, in chiara opposizione all'oscurità e l'affettazione.[22] In questo contesto il Petrarca divenne un innegabile punto di riferimento, in quanto rappresentava l'ordine e la sobrietà stilistica, contrapposti «all'anarchico disordine, alla lussureggiante (ma un po' volgare) ricchezza del metaforeggiare barocco». (Asor Rosa, p. 530) Il ritorno a Petrarca significava la ripresa di risorse sicure, particolarmente efficaci nella lotta per il ritorno alla concreta esperienza umana, ai valori stilistici dell'espressione poetica smarriti nell'attività marinista.

Le stesse questioni linguistiche, tra cui il postulato della linearità e chiarezza espressiva del discorso, entravano anche nelle tendenze di rinnovamento culturale portate avanti dall'attività scientifica e filosofica degli Investiganti. E proprio il Petrarca fu considerato da questi ultimi «perfetto maestro di stile, di quel <culto stile>, a cui gli uomini della <rinascenza napoletana> ponevano ogni cura per impadronirsene». (Giannantonio, p. 47) «A Napoli il Di Capua ed altri imbevuti di scienza galileiana e di filosofia cartesiana, [riproponevano], in contrasto con il barocco, forme di rigido petrarchismo e di purismo per rifarsi appunto ad una matrice artistica di valore universale». (Sementilli, p. 561)

La nuova lezione petrarchesca, concentrata sull'eloquenza, risale all'opera di Carlo Buragna, di Pirro Schettini e di Camillo Colonna, e quest'ultimo, come informa Francesco D'Andrea, prima ancora che sorgesse l'Accademia degli Investiganti raccomandava lo studio del Petrarca per la «bellezza [della sua poesia] di cui era adoratore». Ciò non impedì tuttavia che lo stesso Colonna «a componere fusse più tosto imitatore di stile del Casa». (Giannantonio, p. 47) Sia il Petrarca sia il Casa infatti, furono anche se in diversa misura, al centro del discorso sul rinnovamento dello stile e della poesia in generale, che in fondo voleva dire un nuovo modo di pensare e di vedere la realtà. Petrarca assumeva qui un valore emblematico nella reazione allo stile dei manieristi, divenendo un punto focale delle tendenze di liberazione dalle forme gonfie e vuote della pratica poetica del tempo. Il Casa invece, che nelle coscienze del tardo Seicento rappresentava meglio del Petrarca il turbamento etico e intellettuale di quel clima culturale, prendeva il primo posto come modello della nuova poetica.

Il giovane Caloprese riprese la lezione petrarchesca dai suoi maestri, tra cui Giuseppe Porcella, noto petrarchista e grande ammiratore di Giovanni Della Casa

---

[22] Si veda POMPEO GIANNANTONIO, *L'Arcadia napoletana*, Napoli, Liguori, 1962, pp. 19-21.

(Quondam, *Gravina*, p. 42), e Leonardo Di Capua, uno dei promotori del ritorno a Petrarca.[23] Tuttavia, il suo debito verso gli Investiganti si articolava innanzitutto su un versante più prettamente scientifico e filosofico che gli fornì strumenti fondamentali per la sua critica letteraria, tra cui le «spositioni» alla poesia di Giovanni Della Casa. Vedremo più avanti che l'autenticità dell'esperienza vissuta ovvero i sentimenti analizzati tramite un'indagine anatomica e psicologica determinavano uno dei criteri fondamentali della critica poetica calopresiana: la "naturalezza" dell'espressione.

Nella formazione teorica/metodologica del Caloprese, sia nel campo prettamente filosofico che in quello letterario, un ruolo fondamentale spetta infatti all'esperienza degli Investiganti, al loro indirizzo scientifico-empirico-anatomico e a quello filosofico cartesiano.[24] Da questa esperienza, dal contatto con Leo-

---

[23] «[Di Capua] scrisse parimente alcune Commedie ed alquanti Discorsi, ne' quali giudicava acconciamente di molti passi de' più famosi poeti», N. AMENTA, *Vita di Lionardo di Capoa detto fra gli Arcadi Alcesto Cilleneo*, Venezia, 1710, p. 15 sgg, citato da M. RAK, in *La fine dei grammatici, op. cit.*, p. 51, n. 31. L'Amenta parla del Di Capua scrittore e critico letterario, che avrebbe lasciato «duemila sonetti amorosi in stile petrarchesco, [...] due tragedie alla maniera di G. Della Porta, [...] alcune commedie, una favola boschereccia; infine, innumerevoli scritti in prosa, tutti andati perduti a causa di un assalto di banditi, subito da Di Capua in viaggio per Napoli». (*Dizionario biografico degli Italiani, op. cit.* vol. 39, p. 712.) È una perdita irreparabile che permette solo di immaginare le dimensioni e l'indirizzo dell'impatto della teoria e critica dicapuana sulla formazione letteraria del Caloprese.

[24] Nato nel 1650 a Scalea in Provincia di Cosenza del Regno di Napoli, Gregorio Caloprese «avendo dato mostra nella sua più tenera età di quel sublime ed elevato ingegno, di cui la natura il dotò», scrive il suo biografo Giovambattista Rannucci (*Vita di Gregorio Caloprese, fra gli Arcadi Alcimedonte Cresio,* scritta dal Sig. Giovambattista Rannucci, Napoletano; e inserita nel tomo II, delle notizie istoriche degli Arcadi morti, stampate in Roma nel 1710, in 8. a cart. III. Ristampata nelle *Opere* del Casa, *op. cit.*, pp. XXII-XXIV) fu inviato all'Università di Napoli, dove sotto la guida dell'«eruditissimo» Giuseppe Porcella «letterato insigne di quei tempi», (nonché «petrarchista e grande ammiratore del Casa», QUONDAM, *Gravina*, p. 42) fece «in brevissimo tempo mirabil progresso» negli studi. «Perlochè essendo poi egli cresciuto di età e di senno, – continua Rannucci – s'inoltrò [...] nella perfetta cognizione della Filosofia, spezialmente di Renato, in cui fu celebre, e della volgar Poesia, in cui fu eccellente, e di ogni erudizion sì sacra come profana, in cui fu versatissimo, che da tutti veniva riguardato tra' primi nella letteratura de' suoi tempi. Quindi essendosi il nome del nostro Gregorio renduto cospicuo per l'Europa, si stimarono fortunate quelle Adunanze letterarie, che poterono avere in s[é] un tanto Uomo». A Napoli il giovanissimo Caloprese si avvicinò ben presto al gruppo degli Investiganti. Mancano informazioni sulla data precisa del primo incontro. Con ogni probabilità, Caloprese si trovò a Napoli ancora adolescente, appena uscito dalla «tenera età», e nel cerchio degli Investiganti entrò non appena fu «cresciuto di età e di senno», quindi poco dopo aver cominciato lo studio con il Porcella. Si può presumere dunque che l'incontro abbia avuto luogo alla metà degli anni Sessanta, Caloprese non ancora ventenne. Il Caloprese rimase in contatto diretto con Leonardo Di Capua, medico e filosofo, uno dei più insigni esponenti degli Investiganti, promotore del metodo galileiano e delle nuove dottrine scientifiche straniere, nonché promotore del ritorno a Petrarca. Stimolato da lui, Caloprese frequenta le lezioni d'anatomia, tra cui quelle di Lucantonio Porzio, studia e si laurea in medicina. (QUONDAM, *ibid.*) Pochi ma importanti fatti confermano la sua attiva partecipazione agli eventi culturali del Regno anche dopo l'allontanamento da Napoli. La lunga lista degli autori moderni forestieri insegnati alla scuola di Scalea, tra cui il Cartesio, Pascal e i portorealisti, e la corrispondenza degli studiosi napoletani (tra cui una conservata dello stesso Caloprese, ma innanzitutto quelle di Antonio Bulifon, libraio erudito ed editore napoletano, riguardanti la pubblicazione delle *Spositioni*) con Antonio Magliabechi «*trait d'union* tra gli intellettuali italiani e la cultura europea più avanzata e aggiornata» (Quondam), «personaggio eminente della Repubblica letteraria» (Mastellone, p. 101) dal Bulifon definito «capo de' letterati d'Europa» (p. 104) a cui spetta il merito di mettere in diretto contatto i «novatori napoletani» con i librai eruditi d'Europa, (p. 99) confermano la vivissima partecipazione del Caloprese a questa attività di scambio di informazioni letterarie e di commercio di libri. Caloprese

nardo Di Capua e con altri maggiori protagonisti come lo scienziato e medico Lucantonio Porzio, Caloprese assimilò largamente, come osserva il Quondam, «le proposte <moderne>, antiautoritarie e antidommatiche, sul piano sia della metodologia scientifica sia dell'elaborazione teorico-filosofica generale». (Quondam, *Dizionario*, p. 901).[25]

era certamente a conoscenza dei due più importanti periodici per le informazioni sulle pubblicazioni sul mercato europeo, seguiti con tanto interesse dai letterati napoletani (p. 95): *Nouvelles de la Republique des Lettres*, del Bayle pubblicate ad Amsterdam a partire dal 1684, che mostravano un interesse verso «le polemiche che agitavano il mondo dei letterati: la polemica contro i cartesiani, la polemica contro i giansenisti, le discussioni tra cattolici e protestanti», (p. 97) e gli *Acta eruditorum*, pubblicati a Lipsia, «vasta miscellanea enciclopedica, autentica espressione dei dotti», (p. 97) che affrontava le problematiche teologiche, giuridiche, mediche, fisiche, matematiche, storiche, geografiche, filosofiche e filologiche. Il *Giornale de' Letterati di Parma*, fondato da Benedetto Bacchini in contatto diretto con l'editoria napoletana per opera del Magliabechi, e contenente tra l'altro una recensione alla *Concione* calopresiana, è un'altra prova della presenza del Caloprese nel clima intellettuale del suo tempo. Qui va aggiunta anche la sua partecipazione alle radunanze dell'Accademia degli Infuriati, dove nel 1690 presentò la «Lettura sopra la Concione di Marfisa a Carlo Magno contenuta nel *Furioso* al canto trentesimottavo», pubblicata a Napoli nel 1691, e all'Accademia Medinacoeli, nella quale ebbe occasione di esprimere la sua posizione "civile" e filosofica. Enrico Nuzzo, nella sopraccitata monografia sulla politica nelle lezioni del Caloprese tenute a questa Accademia, ha fornito un'analisi estremamente puntuale di questo importante capitolo dell'attività filosofica e ideologica del pensatore di Scalea.

[25] Questo fu un periodo particolarmente importante e intenso per gli Investiganti, segnato dalle aspre e crescenti polemiche e scontri con gli avversari e dalle pericolose accuse dell'Inquisizione. L'Accademia, restaurata nel '62 dopo essere stata dispersa dalla peste sei anni prima, riprese la vivissima attività scientifica durata per altri sei anni consecutivi. Fin dal principio l'attività degli Investiganti incontrò vive resistenze che con gli anni crebbero notevolmente diventando sempre più minacciose. Proprio in quegli anni di maggiore fioritura delle ricerche degli Investiganti un gruppo di medici tradizionalisti formò un'altra accademia chiamata dei Discordanti. «[I]l contrasto con le ricerche degli Investiganti divenne così acuto da sfociare in aperte rotture personali e perfino in pubblici maltrattamenti» (BIAGIO DE GIOVANNI, «La vita intellettuale a Napoli fra la metà del '600 e la restaurazione del Regno», *Storia di Napoli*, vol. 8, *Cultura e letteratura*, p. 361, Napoli, Edizioni Scientifiche Italiane, 1980) la qual cosa diede al viceré occasione di «proibire le riunioni di ambedue le accademie». (*ibid.*) Il rifiuto del *nuovo* manifestato dai Discordanti esprimeva un'opinione diffusa negli ambienti della cultura tradizionale, tra i vecchi medici, scienziati, cronisti e la maggioranza dei circoli ecclesiastici. (*ibid.*) Oltre alle accuse di tipo professionale, «si insinuava qualcosa di ancora più grave: che fra i novatori si predicasse l'ateismo [...] che [...] le posizioni dei novatori menassero dritto alla negazione di Dio», notano gli storici aggiungendo che «[m]olto di meno sarebbe stato necessario, in quegli anni, per mettere in movimento la reazione ecclesiastica» (p. 362) Infatti, «nel 1671 una lettera dei cardinali inquisitori contro i novatori e contro Cartesio, il filosofo che pareva riassumere in quel momento le esigenze della nuova cultura scientifica, ha il tono di un vero documento ideologico, e la condanna dei moderni vi è pronunciata senza attenuanti» (*ibid.*) «A questa data, la breve storia dell'accademia era già conclusa». (*ibid.*) L'attività degli Investiganti, vivissima e penetrante non fu fermata però da questa formale chiusura, le discussioni continuarono. In pieno svolgimento erano le ricerche sul cartesianesimo "fisico" e "razionale", sulla nuova scienza che metteva in dubbio tutto ciò che non poteva essere accertato sperimentalmente, sulla ragione e sull'empiria contrapposte alle autorità dogmatiche. Intanto le accuse e persecuzioni si intensificarono nell'ultimo decennio del secolo. Giovan Battista de Benedictis, prefetto delle scuole gesuitiche, rappresentante della parte più attiva dei Discordanti, «non contento dell'intervento del S. Ufficio» (Mastellone, p. 146) decise per conto proprio attaccare gli intellettuali napoletani, tra cui innanzitutto, personalmente il maggior rappresentante degli Investiganti (dopo la morte di Tommaso Cornelio), Leonardo Di Capua. Negli anni Novanta escono le sue *Lettere Apologetiche*, sotto il nome finto di Benedetto Aletino, dove la *Lettera terza apologetica contro il Cartesio creduto da più di Aristotele al Sig. Leonardo di Capua* porta le accuse al Di Capua in quanto seguace della filosofia cartesiana, critica il pensiero di Cartesio partendo dal suo *cogito*, e lo considera «conforme al genio degli Eretici con cui viveva». L'osservazione conclusiva conferma l'accusa di tipo scientifico e ideologico: «Aristotele ha il suo credito appresso tutte le università Cattoliche; Renato appresso le Luterane». (Mastellone, p. 147) Apertamente nominato e criticato, Leonardo Di Capua, «avanzato negli anni, ed amareggiato per le accuse lanciate contro di lui nella *Terza lettera apologetica*, morì», ricorda il Mastellone. (p. 148)

3. Caloprese e la lezione degli Investiganti

Il presupposto generale della posizione scientifica e filosofica degli Investiganti fu la libertà di filosofare e di investigare. In chiara opposizione a una visione della vita statica, immobilizzata e gerarchica, (Mastellone, p. 86) si prospettava una visione nuova, radicalmente diversa, dinamica, ispirata da menti inquiete e penetranti, stimolata dalle letture dei «nuovi filosofi» d'oltralpe. «Il principio della libertà dell'indagare era stato adottato come criterio delle discussioni avute nell'Accademia degli Investiganti, e questo cenacolo resterà come luminoso inizio della diffusione della nuova filosofia a Napoli», osserva il Mastellone. (pp. 88/9) Il «Secondo Ragionamento» del *Parere*[26] del Di Capua porta una lista dei «moderni nostri filosofanti» tra i quali Copernico, Keplero, Bruno, Galilei, Bacone, Cartesio, Gassendi, Boyle, Hobbes, pregiati per la libertà di filosofare: «[...] quei filosofanti che alla libertà de' loro ingegni alcun freno di servitù generosamente sdegnando vogliono gir liberi a lor talento spaziando pe' vasti e smisurati campi della natura [...] liberi nello investigare i riposti e profondi misteri della natura». (Mastellone, pp. 86, 87)[27] La libertà di filosofare si estende a tutti i campi della scienza. Si propugna la libertà dell'opinione («non essendo altro le filosofie che opinazione», p. 88), la libertà di criticare la filosofia di Aristotele, di ricercare liberamente nel passato, di investigare la natura. Degli Investiganti fu

[la] fiducia in una nuova ragione critica, [la] libera capacità di *vedere* o meno la natura delle cose senza artificio, i mondi nuovi, i nuovi cieli che la scienza ritrovava sotto gli antichi miti. Non più gl'<incorruttibili> aristotelici o i <dati> fissati in strutture immobili e assolute, ma l'esperienza verificata in un fatto, in una ipotesi, in una legge da cui nascesse il verisimile rifiuto di un dogma.[28]

La libertà d'investigazione si traduceva in una critica mossa contro i dogmi, contro la scolastica, l'aristotelismo, il tomismo, la Curia, contro le istituzioni accademiche, civili, ecclesiastiche. I frequenti e crescenti attacchi, accuse e persecuzioni dell'attività scientifica degli Investiganti da parte degli ambienti ecclesiastici-gesui-

---

[26] *Parere del Signor Lionardo di Capoa divisato in otto Ragionamenti, ne' quali partitamente narrandosi l'origine e 'l progresso della medicina, chiaramente l'incertezza della medicina si fa manifesta.* In Napoli, per Antonio Bulifon, MDCLXXXI.

[27] Il primo *Progymnasma* di Tommaso Cornelio era dedicato a Caramuel il quale, in una lettera del 12 settembre 1664 spedita da Napoli e diretta a Joannes Marcus Marci ed a Godifredus Aloysius Kinner, scriveva delle riunioni degli Investiganti: «La frequentano infatti vescovi, abati, prelati, principi, duchi, marchesi, consiglieri reali, giudici, giureconsulti, teologi, oratori, medici, filosofi politici, nobili esteri, francesi, tedeschi, polacchi, ed in gran numero spagnoli. In essa non si tratta di retorica o di ritmica, come nella maggior parte delle accademie italiane, ma di filosofia, come accade in poche in Europa. Tutto ciò che vi si dice è provato da esperimenti visibili. Si procura che siano banditi i pregiudizi; l'esperienza infatti ci insegna che da essi sono sedotti anche gli ingegni grandi, o gli animi ne sono spesso turbati, ed addirittura perturbati». (N. BADALONI, *Introduzione a Giambattista Vico (1668-1700), Saggio critico*, Bari, Laterza, 1961, pp. 44-45)

[28] BIAGIO DE GIOVANNI, *op. cit.*, p. 360.

tici e dai retrivi ceti borghesi formavano un'atmosfera di continua lotta segnata da aspre polemiche tra i due campi opposti e da devastanti accuse portate ai tribunali della Curia.

Il giovane Caloprese crebbe e si formò intellettualmente in questa atmosfera militante di slanci valorosi, minacciati dal potente e pericoloso oscurantismo, un'atmosfera che lo confermò nelle proprie scelte di alleati nel campo intellettuale. Ed è proprio l'interesse per le scienze, dovuto ai contatti con gl'Investiganti, che spinse il Caloprese a rivolgersi alla filosofia cartesiana, più precisamente al suo aspetto psicofisico, e allo studio dell'anatomia da cui trasse ispirazione e spunto per la sua nuova teoria letteraria. Qui lo studio dell'*Anatomia* del Severino, l'interesse per la concezione notomista sembrano i momenti decisivi. Le passioni viste e analizzate nel loro aspetto anatomico, fisiologico, o psicofisico gli servirono da ponte per arrivare ad un nuovo modo di spiegare il fatto letterario, diverso da quello regolato da una tradizione chiusa nell'arte della persuasione e aderente invece all'esperienza umana intima e personale.

È da sottolineare che gli strumenti critici adoperati dal Caloprese, che non partono da premesse assolute e universali ma descrivono e valutano l'efficacia dell'enunciato dei singoli componenti poetici secondo la loro coerenza col sentimento del poeta o dei suoi personaggi, sono il risultato di una nuova visione del fatto artistico quale organismo vivo, in quanto vivo e in continuo movimento è l'umano sentire. La sfida dell'autorità tradizionalmente intesa come assoluto e dogma è al tempo stesso causa e risultato del mutamento nel modo di vedere la realtà, il quale non è più statico, bensì dinamico: la realtà e il mondo sono ora intesi non più come realtà data ma come realtà in divenire.

La nuova poetica calopresiana nasce quindi come *liaison* tra l'anatomia, la psicologia e la filosofia. È un assieme complesso, a cui appartengono oltre al razionalismo del Cartesio, il suo pensiero "fisico" sulle passioni (risultante soprattutto dallo studio de *Les passions de l'âme*) e oltre alle recenti scoperte in anatomia e medicina e allo sperimentalismo galileiano, anche le reminiscenze della rivolta barocca.

La critica odierna osserva che Caloprese «si qualifica sin dal suo primo apparire non su posizioni contestative e di rifiuto, ma certamente di riassorbimento e ridimensionamento di non pochi dei motivi che hanno caratterizzato il secolo che sta per finire».[29] È un'osservazione valida (non senza riserve però, come si è visto e si vedrà più avanti) tanto per i suoi studi filosofici quanto letterari. Il Caloprese seppe infatti introdurre all'interno della filosofia e delle scienze esatte di provenienza straniera e italiana, le tendenze intellettuali più progressive del Barocco, trasformandole nelle sue costruzioni teoriche. Sarà infatti l'immaginazione o fantasia, portata alla

---

[29] SILVIO SUPPA, *L'Accademia di Medinacoeli, Fra tradizione investigante e nuova scienza civile*, Napoli, Istituto [Italiano per gli Studi storici], 1971, p. 15.

ribalta proprio dai poeti e teorici del Barocco, che nelle riflessioni letterarie di Caloprese assumerà un posto particolarmente notevole. Il ruolo assegnato da Caloprese alla fantasia, proprio sulla scorta della ricca tradizione barocca e della lezione soggettivista cartesiana unitamente a quella del Bacone, è un passo notevole verso quella futura configurazione in cui la fantasia diventerà la forza contestativa del controllo della parola ovvero della mente, un controllo usurpato dai poteri civili ed ecclesiastici.[30]

Alla fantasia spetta il ruolo di regolare e moderare le passioni. Atta alla conoscenza dell'interiorità umana nelle sue commutazioni minime, la fantasia si vale della facoltà cognitiva. In tal modo, alla fantasia è attribuito il prestigio finora riservato esclusivamente alla ragione. È un ruolo importante nell'atto di produrre il testo letterario: la fantasia che desta e estingue le passioni, diventa moderatrice della loro espressione.

Leggiamo dal Caloprese:

> [...] il soggiogare le passioni non appartiene al cuore; ma è officio delle potenze dotate di conoscimento, cioè dell'intelletto e della Fantasia. Et ciò non è sanza ragione, perché come abbiamo altrove diffusamente provato, la Fantasia è quella, la quale per mezzo degli spiriti, che si spiccano dall'idee degli oggetti, desta e estingue nel cuore, et nell'altre parti il senso, et il moto delle passioni. (p. 292)

Allo stesso tempo, il Caloprese modernizza la retorica che nel suo discorso critico non ha più il carattere né della precettistica formale e dogmatica né di quella logico-razionale cartesiana, ma diventa un discorso in cui l'argomentazione biologico-scientifica e psicologica diventa argomentazione ipotetica o probabilistica, basata sulla probabilità di situazioni emotive e sul loro legame con l'espressione

4. *Presupposti della critica calopresiana*

Nell'introduzione alle *Spositioni* del Caloprese, Francesco Antonio Gravina, intellettuale e letterato, fratello di Gianvincenzo, osserva che «quantunque [il Caloprese] abbia tratto grandissima utilità dalla dottrina di Cartesio [...] il più delle volte, trapassando i termini delle cose da lui insegnate, è

---

[30] Per il ruolo del pensiero baconiano e l'eredità barocca nella formazione moderna del concetto della fantasia nell'ambito letterario, si vedano le erudite indicazioni di M. RAK nell'*op. cit.*, particolarmente pp. 219-220. Ricordiamo inoltre che in quei tempi la discussione sull'immaginazione (sul piano concettuale non distaccata ancora dalla fantasia), sulla sua essenza e funzione, è di significato sostanziale il quale supera le questioni prettamente letterarie, teoriche o critiche, entrando nell'ambito delle questioni ideologiche o addirittura politiche. La tendenza di liberare la fantasia dai nodi impostle dalla precettistica tradizionale sfida infatti in ultima analisi il sistema esistente dei poteri. Trovo qui particolarmente pertinenti le riflessioni di LUIZ COSTA LIMA nella sua monografia *Control of the Imaginary*, Minneapolis, University of Minnesota Press, 1988.

stato costretto di far da sé molte altre speculazioni». (VIII) Al Cartesio «come Filosofo, considerando l'Idee delle cose separate dalla specialità della materia, è bastato dirne i primi elementi, e le generali definizioni», mentre il Caloprese, critico letterario, rifletteva «ad ogni picciola circostanza», rivelando «molte ascose proprietà intorno alla natura degli affetti non dichiarate [...] da niun'altro». (VIII).

Ma oltre alla questione della «natura degli affetti», «altre considerazioni, non meno dotte e ingegnose» fatte da Caloprese mettono in evidenza l'eccellenza e la novità della sua critica, tra cui «l'artificio d'ingrandire gli umili e comunali concetti»; «il modo di formare le poetiche immagini, tanto con parole proprie, quanto con parole trasportate»; «l'arte di far nuove le Metafore vecchie e usitate, e di ridurle a forma d'immagini»; «i divisamenti intorno al particolareggiare i concetti generali». (*ibid.*)

Senza limitarsi al lato pragmatico di queste formulazioni calopresiane «utili e necessarie al ben poetare», Gravina sottolineava il loro valore nell'«accendere nelle menti un lume assai vivo, e molto maggiore di quello che farebbero i Retorici insegnamenti» e di mettere al centro delle «sposizioni» dei sonetti casiani la questione degli «affetti» e delle «costituzioni dell'animo».

Il senso della libertà di filosofare e d'investigare portò il Caloprese alla formulazione di nuovi criteri di critica letteraria. Nella sua già citata lettera a Caracciolo il pensatore di Scalea scriveva:

Ora venendo alla materia, non mi darò cura d'andar raccogliendo nulla di ciò che altri ce ne hanno lasciato scritto, il che tutto a voi è ben noto: ma pur quello mi sie assai disporvi, che coll'ajuto della filosofia e dell'osservazione su i buoni poeti mi c'è venuto pensato. (p. 151)

Ai presupposti filosofici della teoria letteraria del Caloprese aveva già fatto riferimento due anni prima il Gravina nella introduzione alle *Spositioni*. Il proposito del Caloprese consisteva, secondo Gravina, nel: «cavare dalla Filosofia, la quale egli stima il vivo fonte di tutte le cose, qualche metodo assai migliore di quelli che si possono cavare da' Retori». La retorica precettistica è intesa dunque solo come dottrina dell'oratoria, come modo puramente tecnico della persuasione. La filosofia invece, «il vivo fonte di tutte le cose» è il presupposto da cui si potrà «cavare» un metodo specifico, proprio all'indagine del fatto letterario.

Due momenti fondamentali specificati dal Caloprese – la filosofia intesa come teoria nel senso largo e come scienza naturale, e l'osservazione dei buoni poeti, ovvero della dotta e alta pratica poetica, sono quindi momenti base su cui si incentra la critica letteraria calopresiana e che informano il suo petrarchismo. Attraverso i frequenti riferimenti agli esempi dei «buoni poeti» tra cui al Petrarca stesso, portati nel commento al Casa, non si veniva infatti creando un nuovo criterio prescrittivo, ma si delineavano – e in questo stava la novità – varie alternative espressive e vari modi di apprensione emotiva.

Il procedere del Caloprese con la critica letteraria è riassunto dallo stesso Gravina come segue:

«[...] le più belle composizioni sono quelle, che rappresentano più al vivo le sembianze e le fattezze di cotali costituzioni [dell'animo]; e che per contrario tutte quelle, alle quali manca questa rappresentazione quantunque siano fornite di tutti i colori retorici, sono prive di ogni vigore, di ogni vivacità, non altrimenti, che se fussero corpi senza spirito; e conoscendo altresì, che la bontà dell'immagine non può consistere in altro, che in essere simile all'immaginato: si diede facilmente a credere, che la via più prossima e più spedita da conoscere le bellezze di si fatti componimenti, non fosse da ricercare in altra parte, che nella scienza degli affetti; dalla mischianza de' quali nascono queste, che costituzioni d'animo da lui si appellano; e per conseguente che intorno a ciò per ciaschedun componimento si avessero da osservare tre cose; cioè, che costituzion d'animo si cerchi in esso di esprimere; da quali accidenti, e in che maniera si sia potuto generare in colui che s'introduce a favellare; e che similitudine si trovi tra la costituzione d'animo imitata, e l'imitazione che ne forma il Poeta». (p. VIII)

La «costituzione dell'animo», termine chiave, frequente nelle *Spositioni* calopresiane, è una «mischianza degli affetti», un complesso stato psicologico del soggetto lirico composto di sentimenti di diversa natura, la cui provenienza e reciproca influenza sono oggetto della dettagliata analisi anatomica e psicologica del critico. Il criterio della «bellezza» e della «bontà» della poesia consiste nella «viva» rappresentazione della «costituzione d'animo». La «bontà» del componimento poetico, ovvero la sua «naturalezza», consiste dunque nella «similitudine» tra l'espressione poetica (intesa come «immagine»), e l'«immaginato», cioè l'oggetto rappresentato. Dalla rappresentazione si attende «vigore» e «vivacità», in quanto attributi necessari della «similitudine», possibile solo nel rapporto diretto con lo stato d'animo del poeta; impossibile invece mediante la sola precettistica retorica, persino se adornata di «tutti i colori». L'analisi critica si svolge su tre piani: il primo consiste nell'identificazione dei sentimenti del soggetto lirico, ovvero la sua costituzione d'animo, il secondo si concentra sulla verifica delle circostanze che avevano dato spunto a tale sentimento; e infine il terzo consiste nella verifica della similitudine tra «la costituzion d'animo imitata e l'imitazione che ne forma il poeta». In termini conclusivi, il nuovo criterio della critica calopresiana consisterà nella scienza degli affetti, vale a dire nella verifica della verisimilitudine e «naturalezza» degli «affetti» e della loro rappresentazione poetica, effettuata alla luce della loro motivazione e delle circostanze accompagnanti.

5. *Il paragone tra il Petrarca e il Casa nella critica cinque e secentesca*

Il dedicarsi a un incarico estremamente impegnativo quale l'analisi e interpretazione della poesia di Giovanni Della Casa, compito proposto al Caloprese da un personaggio di straordinaria esperienza del mercato intellettuale dell'epoca, il famoso editore napoletano Antonio Bulifon, è prova oltre che dell'indirizzo degl'interessi del Caloprese stesso anche della sicura attualità del Casa e del Petrarca in quello scorcio del secolo. Il Petrarca, come si è già detto, rappresentava allora l'antitesi dello stile espressivo marinista mentre il petrarchismo del Casa uno specifico clima culturale e religioso.

Era questo il clima di una crescente problematica morale, di profonde e tormentate incertezze e scelte spirituali, che segnava fortemente una nuova comprensione della poesia del Petrarca, in uno spirito ben diverso da quello di Pietro Bembo, il più ragguardevole petrarchista del primo Cinquecento. Sul finire ormai del Cinquecento, in un periodo di mutamento delle idee religiose e morali, Giovanni Della Casa si poneva al centro dell'interesse della critica alla pari del Petrarca, paragonato con lui, e addirittura prepostogli. Nel Casa si rifletteva infatti il mutarsi dell'atmosfera culturale dell'epoca, e in particolare del gusto, a pari passo con la «crisi dell'equilibrio poetico cinquecentesco verso le successive esperienze tassiane e barocche».[31] Il Casa approfondiva l'esperienza petrarchista del Bembo, «per la volontà [...] di andar oltre la pura imitazione linguistica del Petrarca e di servirsi del Petrarca per costruire una nuova poesia», in cui si rivelava una autentica forza lirica. (Izzi, p. 435) Osservava già Gianvincenzo Gravina, cugino e discepolo del Caloprese, che il Casa «tentò il nuovo stile, somigliante ad Orazio per il maestoso giro delle parole, ondeggiamento di numero e fervor d'espressione» aggiungendo tuttavia, «benché di copia, varietà, fantasia e sentimento ad Orazio ed all'istesso Petrarca inferiore».[32] Come scrive Giuseppe Izzi, la lezione dello stile del Petrarca ripresa attraverso il Bembo e filtrata dall'esperienza individuale e intima del Casa, «non tende[va] più all'*equitas*, al rasserenamento espressivo delle passioni, ma alla *gravitas*, alla sottolineatura oratoria dei sentimenti» (Izzi, p. 435).

Questa nuova linea interpretativa della poesia del Casa trovò alla fine del Cinquecento un esponente esemplare in Torquato Tasso. Nel dialogo «La Cavaletta overo de la poesia toscana»,[33] il Tasso, tramite la voce del Forestiere Napoletano, si sofferma sull'inadeguatezza della retorica precettistica per l'attività poetica e sulla necessità di «piegar[n]e» le regole all'esigenza della «materia» trattata. Nei casi in

---

[31] Giuseppe Izzi, «Petrarchismo», in *Dizionario critico della Letteratura italiana*, cit., vol. 3, p. 453.

[32] Gianvincenzo Gravina, *Della ragion poetica*, in *Scritti critici e teorici*, Bari, Laterza, 1973, p. 326.

[33] Torquato Tasso, «La cavaletta overo de la poesia toscana», in *Dialoghi*, Firenze, Sansoni, 1958, vol. 2, tomo 2.

cui, «non potendosi la materia adattare a la regola», è proprio la regola che «si piega a la materia» [...] si torc[e] e si pieg[a] secondo l'occasioni: il qual piegamento è il giudicio de l'artefice». È anche vero, aggiunge il Tasso, che le regole «rigide e dure [...] non si possano torcere in alcuna maniera», solo «le altre che sono arrendevoli e pieghevoli», (p. 655) ma la breccia nella rigidità del sistema è stata già fatta e ha portato il critico ferrarese ad un'altra osservazione: i grandi, sia oratori sia poeti, sono quelli che sanno «fingere» ostentando un «disprezzo delle regole» e delle loro «minuzie e bassezze», quantunque la «materia» lo richieda: «E quantunque Marco Tullio insegnasse [...] l'arte de l'oratore, nondimeno sprezzò tutta quella certezza, o più tosto minutezza o bassezza d'artificio, la quale da' retori s'insegnava con picciola mercede». Nei «grandi» poeti latini e in Dante stesso, «nacque il disprezzo de le regole, per lo quale non acquistarono biasimo e vergogna alcuna, ma fama e onore». Dante infatti «poco osservò alcuna di quelle regole ch'egli medesimo avea date». (p. 658)

È dunque la «grandezza» del poeta che lo conduce a superare gli ostacoli posti dalla precettistica, è quella che non gli permette di limitarsi a un mero procedimento imitativo, che lo fa invece «fingere [...] agevolmente» tramite un «artificio nascosto». Da qui risale il riconoscimento per la «grandezza» e il prestigio della lirica del Casa: «Niuno ricercò più la grandezza del Signor Giovanni de la Casa», il quale, piuttosto che non Petrarca o Bembo, diveniva esempio dello scrittore «grande», nonostante che «non conseguisse quel grado ch'era dovuto a' suoi meriti singolari». (p. 658) Il Casa veniva infatti proposto dal Tasso come nuovo modello lirico: «[...] chiunque vorrà scrivere come conviensi a' grandi, a mio parere dovrebbe proporselo [il Casa] per esempio». (p. 658)

L'indicazione del Casa e non del Petrarca come modello e come poeta di «grandezza» era stata già fatta dal Tasso in un'altra occasione. Nella «Lezione sopra il sonetto *Questa vita mortal*» del Casa presentata nell'Accademia Ferrarese,[34] il Tasso discute certi punti teorici con riferimenti precisi alla poesia degli antichi, degli stilnovisti, di Dante e Petrarca. Particolarmente privilegiato qui è il Petrarca a causa dei meriti stilistici straordinari che gli permisero di alzare la forma del sonetto ad alto livello poetico. Il Petrarca è avversario dell'opinione tradizionale che «la forma del sonetto [è] poco adatta all'altezza dello stile», e assertore invece del parere che «nel sonetto [è] convenevole la magnificenza dello stile». Altra osservazione interessante del Tasso è che, diversamente da alcuni suoi predecessori, persino i più grandi, il Petrarca seppe anche eliminare il linguaggio «scientifico» dal suo poetare sugli «effetti naturali», sul cielo e sul mondo, creando immagini altamente poetiche:

---

[34] TORQUATO TASSO, *Lezione di Torquato Tasso recitata da Lui nell'Accademia ferrarese sopra il Sonetto "Questa vita mortal di Monsignor della Casa"*, in *Discorsi di Torquato Tasso*, Pisa, N. Capurro, 1823, tomo I, pp. 42-60. Si veda a questo proposito DANTE DELLA TERZA, «L'esperienza petrarchesca del Tasso», *Forma e memoria*, Roma, Bulzoni, 1979.

[...] non si vede cosa alcuna nelle sue divinissime composizioni, che non abbia non solo del sacro, e del venerabile, ma del gentile, e delicato: dai Platonici tolse non de' più difficili e incogniti concetti, ma de' più facili, e de' divolgati piuttosto da' limitari, che dal centro della Filosofia, ma con tanta modestia e così parcamente, e così cautamente nella poesia gli trasportò, e con tanta arte gli temperò, di tali fregi gli vestì, e adornò, che pajono non forestiere, ma naturali della poesia nutriti in parnaso medesimo, non venuti dall'accademia, e dal Liceo: e quel di peregrino che in lor si vede, è per maggior vaghezza, e per maggior leggiadria. (pp. 49-50)

Eppure, non il Petrarca ma il Casa si trovava al centro del discorso tassiano. Per la seduta dell'Accademia Ferrarese il Tasso scelse il summenzionato sonetto del Casa, scrivendo: «Ed io ho eletto piuttosto di leggere composizione sua [del Casa] che d'alcun moderno o pur del Petrarca istesso [...]». L'analisi del sonetto casiano abbonda di lodi per lo stile e l'efficacia con cui il poeta esprime il sentimento drammatico: «[...] è in lui meraviglioso, la scelta delle voci, e delle sentenze, la novità delle figure, e particolarmente de' traslati, il nerbo, la grandezza, e la maestà sua [...]». (p. 44) Ma il nucleo della grandezza del Casa nell'intuizione del Tasso sembra consistere innanzitutto nella consapevolezza del mutamento del clima culturale sottostante alla lirica casiana, consapevolezza sperimentata e sofferta dal Tasso stesso.

Lo stile grave, alto e «pomposo» in cui il Casa trovò un modo espressivo aderente a quella sua drammatica esperienza interiore, si trova anche al centro di discussioni critiche posteriori, tra cui quella di Orazio Marta.[35] Il Marta, critico di voga del primissimo Seicento considerava anche lui il Casa come modello poetico. La sua è una critica che si muove tra tendenze contrastanti eppure tipiche della cultura intellettuale del tempo, con da una parte certi residui della poetica classica e dall'altra tratti che anticipano il gusto del marinismo con le lodi della piacevolezza dello stile a scapito dei valori contenutistici, e in più l'attenzione alla drammaticità e allo sgomento interiore del poeta.

Nel suo «Paralello tra Francesco Petrarca et Mons. Gio. Della Casa», il Marta offre un quadro particolarmente significativo della recezione dei due poeti nella critica contemporanea, i quali infatti «si riputano ragionevolmente i migliori di tutti i poeti c' habbiano scritto sin' hora in questa lingua», (p. 117) e che «di commune consentimento sono appellati meritamente maestri, lumi, et autori della toscana poesia». (p. 118) L'esigenza di chiarezza e di equilibrio espressivo, reminiscenza dell'eredità classica rinascimentale, si manifesta attraverso le lodi di tratti petrarcheschi come la misura e il savio uso di contrasti, creanti l'equilibrio dell'espressione. Il Petrarca, «maestro del dire», crea nel suo canzoniere «harmonia fin qui non udita» (p. 119) tendendo a «certa virtù, e

---

[35] ORAZIO MARTA, «Paralello tra Francesco Petrarca, et Mons. Gio. Della Casa», *Rime, et prose del Signor Horatio Marta. Raccolte e poste insieme fin hora da suoi scritti* [...] Napoli, appresso Lazaro Scoriggio, 1616. Ringrazio Andrea Battistini per aver portato alla mia attenzione questo prezioso documento.

forma di dire convenevole, che benchè alta, e grande non è smisurata». (p. 119) Egli «non [...] si discosta già mai dal suo grato, e chiaro stile» (p. 118), formando le nuove «voci» con «giuditio». (p. 119) Allo stesso tempo, nella critica del Marta si delinano fortemente segni dell'atmosfera in fieri della poesia marinista, accanto a presentimenti della leggerezza degli intermezzi metastasiani. Il critico si sofferma su quell'atteggiamento stilistico, abbondantemente lodato, in cui, accanto alla chiarezza dell'espressione e alla «sottile maniera del dire», (p. 118) appaiono elementi di vaghezza, fioritura, di grazia, leggiadria, dolcezza, sottigliezza, di uno stile ornato, soave, nobile, dolce. Maestro insuperabile di questo stile rimaneva il Petrarca, anche quando alla «leggiadria» e «diletto» univa la grandezza e la magnificenza. Il Petrarca era «nel trovato più d'ogni altro felice, et in ciò di gran lunga trapassa non solo i latini, ma anche i Greci scrittori», recando «tutte le sue amorose compositioni [...] piene di [...] fioretti, d'arboscelli, di colli, di ruscelli, di canti, d'augelletti, d'aure, di Dee, di Ninfe, et di Pastorelle». È difficile astenersi dal notare come in una tale rappresentazione bucolica si smarrisce tutto lo spessore ideologico della poesia petrarchesca, tutto il nodo insolubile tra attrazioni mondane e il desiderio della consolazione religiosa.

Allo stesso tempo la critica martiana testimonia quel turbamento interiore caratteristico del periodo postridentino, di quella cultura nuova più tormentata, aperta alle investigazioni dell'interiorità, la quale sul piano stilistico si esprime nella positiva valutazione di un tono grave e tormentoso. Il Casa è preferito qui al Petrarca per l'interiorità umana più profondamente sentita ed espressa. L'accento messo sull'ornamento dello stile fa infatti diminuire nel Petrarca la grandezza della sua donna, lodata «nelle altre parti», anche nel «vile», invece che nella nobiltà, mentre il Casa nella «grandezza senza freddezza» e senza «asprezza» esprime allo stesso tempo «ogni leggiadria e soavità». (p. 121) Il Casa infatti, tende «alla forma più grande del dire, e cercando in ciò d'avanzar la natura si sforza, e giunge a segno, né per ciò si conosce che dal naturale si diparta. È pieno di pompa, e per così dir fastuoso; ma non è perciò ricercato; ma torbido, e terribile, nella terribilità, e nel torbido è piacevole, et luminoso». (p. 120) Il Petrarca è sempre maestro degli ornamenti stilistici, ma l'eccessiva attenzione a tali ornamenti lo fa meno attento alla resa fedele del sentimento. Il Casa è invece considerato il poeta maggiore data la gravità e magnificenza, non priva di «soavità», con cui esprime i profondi valori della sua complessa esperienza emotiva:

[...] par che siamo costretti a preferirlo [il Casa] al Petrarca, il quale accostandosi più tosto all'ornamento, poté forse diminuire alcune fiate la grandezza della sua donna, la quale ancor nobile, viene da lui commendata con maggior copia di lodi nelle altre parti, che nella nobiltà, tanto che dà tal volta nel vile; la dove il Casa accostandosi alla grandezza, non potrai trovar luogo di trapassamento, ò di freddo né meno d'aspro, di quella asprezza, che da se parte ogni leggiadria, e soavità. Vedesi nel Casa ben dipinta la sua donna, et lo stato suo molte volte sereno, e molte amaro, congionti gli sdegni, l'ire, e gli altri accidenti insieme, benché in poche figure, per lo che si può credere, havendo occhio alla sua rara eccellenza, che rallargandosi, et distendendosi in maggior forma non meno che il Petrarca sarebbe stato atto, et valevole à mostrar così fatte cose [...]. (p. 121)

6. *Il Casa e il Petrarca nella critica del Caloprese*

Il petrarchismo calopresiano investe tutta la discussione sulle *Rime* del Casa, la quale superando le dimensioni di un discorso occasionale diventa un vero trattato teorico-letterario, sebbene non di struttura organica (il che lascia al lettore un compito non facile di trarne le coordinate). Le implicazioni teoriche della linea petrarchesco-casiana assumono un valore programmatico-teorico e formano una parte integrale di questo "trattato".

Nell'analisi calopresiana della poesia del Casa si possono individuare alcune linee cardinali tra cui: 1) l'attenzione allo stile come espressione determinata dalle passioni e dall'individuale forza lirica del poeta; 2) il valore attribuito alla problematica dell'interiorità umana e connessa ad essa l'esigenza del tono e dello stile poetico appropriato; 3) la veracità e il valore cognitivo dell'esperienza emotiva verificata dallo studio psicologico e anatomico delle «passioni»; 4) la «naturalezza» dell'espressione, ovvero la sua immediata adeguatezza all'esperienza psicologica, postulato che rispettava la diversità delle reazioni emotive a una data situazione e pertanto incoraggiava la varietà delle formulazioni espressive; 5) il valore attribuito al sottofondo etico della poesia, l'attenzione a valori come l'amore, l'amicizia e la poesia stessa, nella motivazione dei quali si incontravano il naturalismo scientifico e l'idealismo platonico rivisitato e riformato; 6) un posto preminente assegnato alla fantasia nella sua funzione creativa e cognitiva, analoga alla funzione razionale dell'intelletto in quanto regolatrice delle passioni e della loro espressione poetica.

Il petrarchismo del Caloprese si definisce all'interno della cultura intellettuale del tempo e quindi all'interno di essa va investigato e analizzato. Le specificità della cultura scientifica, filosofica, religiosa e letteraria del suo tempo, il significato del ritorno a Petrarca, la poesia del Casa come nuovo modello poetico, le esperienze poetiche di Carlo Buragna e Pirro Schettino, la critica cinque e secentesca concentrata sul paragone tra il Petrarca e il Casa, informano il petrarchismo calopresiano. Tutto il discorso critico-letterario del Caloprese sul Casa o sul Petrarca assume infatti lo spessore di una complessa problematicità che in varia misura informa diverse discipline, dalla teoria letteraria alla filosofia, dall'anatomia alla psicologia, e il merito sostanziale dell'operazione calopresiana consiste nel saper ricavare da quel materiale multiforme segni dell'epoca in arrivo e crearne un insieme teorico con cui rifiutare ciò che stava per morire e aprirsi verso ciò che doveva nascere. All'interno di questo quadro si pone in primo piano il proposito di scostarsi dalla precettistica tradizionale, proposito motivato tuttavia diversamente dai suoi predecessori, e di creare una retorica nuova di motivazione scientifica e filosofica del fatto letterario, inteso come «naturale» espressione delle «interne costituzioni dell'animo». Di qui la vecchia questione dell'*elocutio* diventerà il discorso sullo stile, con le esigenze antimariniste di chiarezza ed efficacia. Le riprese dalla lontana tradizione letteraria e filosofica tra cui il concetto platonico dell'amore, si uniranno alle proposte moderne, nuove, associate a un più progressivo pensiero scientifico e filosofico del tempo.

a) *Anatomia, psicologia, fantasia ed espressione poetica*

L'indagine letteraria del Caloprese, di matrice sperimentalista «investigante» e cartesiana, rientra nell'ambito più vasto degli interessi intellettuali del suo tempo sul rapporto tra «materia e spirito».[36] Il terreno preparato da Aurelio Severino, da Tommaso Cornelio e Leonardo Di Capua rivelava il meccanismo del corpo umano nelle sue funzioni sostanziali del trasformarsi del cibo in sangue o del pulsare del cuore (Rak, p. 95) nel loro rapporto con gli interni processi psichici. L'operazione critica del Caloprese estendeva quelle indagini al terreno teorico-letterario tramite lo studio del rapporto tra i dati anatomici e psicologici e l'espressione poetica. La straordinaria novità di questa operazione consiste nell'appoggiare la teoria e la critica letteraria sui fatti precisi delle scienze naturali. È la prima volta che la critica letteraria considera il funzionamento delle strutture anatomiche, tra cui innanzitutto quelle cerebrali e neurali, determinante per le strutture del linguaggio poetico.

Il prodotto finale, ovvero l'espressione poetica (in questo caso il linguaggio poetico del Casa o del Petrarca) viene investigato nella totalità delle componenti generative dell'organismo umano, tra cui gli impulsi sensoriali e psicologici, e le reazioni del cervello. Il tentativo di analizzare il più grande mistero del corpo umano, quello del funzionamento del cervello e della rete neurale, in stretta connessione con i fenomeni linguistici fa del Caloprese il primo studioso della neuroscienza in fieri applicata alla linguistica.

Sembra dunque opportuno, se non proprio necessario, insistere sul valore della formazione scientifica del Caloprese per la sua indagine letteraria, di quel Caloprese laureatosi in medicina, studioso dei trattati sulla «notomia» e medicina di Aurelio Severino, Lucantonio Porzio, Tommaso Cornelio, Leonardo Di Capua. Con la problematica dei sentimenti ovvero passioni, «gravi» e intensi nella poesia del Casa

---

[36] MICHELE RAK, *La fine dei grammatici*, cit., p. 9 sgg.

si apriva per il Caloprese una vasta dimensione d'indagine scientifica. L'analisi caloplesiana delle *Rime* del Casa, con frequenti riferimenti alla lirica petrarchesca, si effettua sulla scorta del procedere di base, proprio alle scienze esatte, il quale si può riassumere come proposito iniziale di dimostrare *come si spiega sperimentalmente la nascita del fatto letterario*. È un approccio che sostituisce quello tradizionale precettistico: *come esso dovrebbe essere fatto* (nonostante che quest'ultimo non sia completamente estraneo alla discussione caloplesiana, rimanendo però al margine del discorso principale).

Per darne qui l'esempio più eloquente tratto dall'indagine caloplesiana sulla lirica petrarchesca, ci si riferirà all'analisi degli «affetti» del sonetto *Io benedico il loco, il tempo e l'ora*. L'Amore del Petrarca si manifesta qui, spiega il critico, in due relativi affetti, «Allegrezza» e «Sicurtà». L'Allegrezza, «la più perfetta e compita», consiste nel «pieno compiacimento, o soddisfazione della [...] sorte». (p. 129) La Sicurtà a sua volta, «altro non è che un affetto che procede da ferma credenza, che debbiano in noi avvenire le cose, secondo il nostro desiderio», è «la felicità che spera in avvenire». (p. 129)

Il carattere del sentimento (ovvero «affetto») determina il moto del sangue, il suo tempo, ritmo e vigore. L'Allegrezza e la Sicurtà, in quanto sentimenti positivi e pacati, si valgono di movimenti «placidi e tranquilli», escludendo di conseguenza dal sangue gli «umori» e il loro impatto sul cervello. Il sangue, secondo il suo naturale movimento, sotto l'influenza di questi sentimenti pacati, passa «per le cavità del cuore, si accende, si dilata, e si assottiglia assai più agevolmente di qualunque altro umore [...] onde gli spiriti che da esso si formano, sono degli altri molto più uguali e sottili, e meno acconci a far moti impetuosi e violenti.» (p. 130) Successivamente, il sangue e gli spiriti passano al cervello, dove si distendono, si fermano a lungo, ne toccano ogni fibra esercitandovi tutta la loro forza, e stimolandola a produrre effetti secondo il suo pieno potenziale:

[...] per l'accresciuto movimento del sangue, saglione al capo in molta copia gli spiriti; i quali essendo per la loro sottigliezza, secondo le leggi del moto poco acconci a proseguire lungamente il loro corso per linea retta, non possono con molto impeto scorrere, siccome fanno altre più feroci passioni, per mezzo de' nervi ad altre parti del corpo; ma per lo più fermandosi dentro le fibre del cervello, ivi pressoché tutta la loro forza esercitano: ove tra per la lor copia, e per la molto penetrevole sottigliezza, e forse ancora, perché non potendo lungo tratto correre per un medesimo sentiero, sono costrette a riflettere in varie parti; non vi è poro s'angusto, ove lor sia disdetto il pervenire: né fibra si reposta, che non possa essere tocca e mossa da loro: sicché a qualunque parte sono dal volere sospinti, movendo ad un tratto in quel luogo ciascheduna fibra, agevolmente destano ogni qualunque specie in esse si conserva. (pp. 130-131)[37]

---

[37] È ormai fuor di dubbio che alla base del ragionamento del Caloprese si trovava il trattato cartesiano sulle passioni dell'animo, citato direttamente dal critico di Scalea, con vaste riprese testuali. Il rapporto tra il funzionamento

Tra i vari effetti che «sogliono derivare da questa passione», cioè dalla Sicurtà unita all'Allegrezza, mediati dall'impatto dei moti del sangue e dei nervi sul cervello, il critico sceglie per la sua discussione quelli che sono «più acconc[i] per iscoprire l'artificio e la bellezza» del sonetto analizzato. (p. 130) Gli effetti di questo

del corpo e dell'anima, fondamentale per il Cartesio e non meno importante nella filosofia e teoria letteraria del Caloprese, non si pone tuttavia per quest'ultimo con la stessa insistenza nella spiegazione anatomica del fatto letterario. Anche il proposito dei due approcci è diverso, quello calopresiano non ponendosi scopi didattici sotto forma di indicazioni sulla necessità di dominare razionalmente le passioni negative. La novità straordinaria del Caloprese consiste invece nell'applicare anatomia e psicologia nel tentativo di spiegare la fenomenologia del nascere del fatto poetico e il rapporto tra l'operazione cerebrale e neurale con il linguaggio. I lavori linguistici dei "Signori di Port Royal" sembrano essere qui per il Caloprese di aiuto e ispirazione.

Nel processo dell'emancipazione dell'estetica dalla precettistica retorica, propugnata tanto da Caloprese quanto dai portrealisti, il primo luogo spetta alla critica dell'autorità su cui si basava la retorica classica e alla crescente importanza dell'immaginazione (o fantasia) applicata al fatto letterario; tutto ciò in nome della crescente auto-coscienza dell'individuo. Tra i primissimi testi di importanza a questo riguardo sulla scena europea furono *La grammatica generale e ragionata* di Claude Lancelot e Antoine Arnauld e la *Logica o arte di pensare* di Antoine Arnauld e Piere Nicole, entrambi del 1660. (*Grammatica e logica di Port-Royal,* a cura di Raffaele Simone, Roma, Ubaldini, 1969.) Che a Caloprese furono noti gli scritti dei giansenisti francesi non si può aver dubbio. Il fatto trova conferma nello scritto di Spinelli. Le opere dei "Signori di Port-Royal" partono dalla critica dell'esistente sistema retorico e di quello della logica scolastico-rinascimentale, proponendone una fondamentale revisione. Tali proposte di rinnovamento si basano sul razionalismo cartesiano, sul pensiero di Pascal e sulle premesse del metodo sperimentalista. Questa è una straordinaria prova di conciliazione del razionalismo con la più severa impostazione empirica, diretta alla giustificazione delle tesi fondamentali del cristianesimo. È una interessante rivincita del pensiero di Sant'Agostino nello spirito delle tesi più moderne del razionalismo cartesiano, unita a una più spietata, in quanto ridicolizzante, critica della scolastica e retorica. È un lavoro di decisa modernità. Il razionalismo dei "Signori di Port-Royal" è una visione libera da ogni forma d'astrattismo, precettistica, inutilità e pedanteria, significa invece senso comune, evidenza, sperimento e utilità. Uno dei più interessanti colpi portati contro la retorica consiste nella negazione dell'efficacia del metodo di persuasione basato sulla certezza e convinzione, in nome della necessità di "illuminare": Il «[p]rimo difetto» [nel metodo di Geomentri] consiste nel: «Preoccuparsi più della certezza che dell'evidenza, e di convincere più che di illuminare lo spirito» (ANTOINE ARNAULD e PIERRE NICOLE, *Logica o arte di pensare,* in *Grammatica e logica di Port-Royal, op. cit.,* p. 366). «[...] Nondimeno è evidente che esse [dimostrazioni di tipo *reductio ad absurdum* e non in forza dei loro principi] possono convincere lo spirito ma non illuminarlo, mentre questo dovrebbe essere il principale frutto della scienza». (p. 368) I due trattati, tenuti rigorosamente entro il metodo adottato, non prestano un'attenzione particolare alla problematica degli affetti, passioni, immagini, dell'attività fantastica, dell'immaginazione. I pochi e marginali cenni sull'immaginazione testimoniano la noncuranza, se non proprio il dispetto degli autori per un tale tipo dell'attività mentale fuorviante dalla strada della *ratio* ed evidenza. (p. 112) Nonostante ciò, dal discorso relativo alla morfologia e l'efficacia dell'espressione, da quel discorso improntato da concretezza ed evidenza, con un palese tentativo di tenerlo entro i limiti delle esigenze di ordine e chiarezza, diventa chiara la pressante urgenza del tema degli affetti e dell'immaginazione. La discussione coerente con le premesse di evidenza e concretezza, per noi è particolarmente importante in quanto mostra un adattamento degli affetti o delle passioni (anche se piuttosto marginale all'interno dell'intero discorso) al fatto linguistico e letterario. Una delle tesi fondamentali della *Grammatica* consiste nell'opporsi alla teoria scolastica dell'unità tra il pensiero e la lingua. Esiste un'opposizione tra *oratio mentalis* e *oratio vocalis:* il che vuol dire che il significato non viene mai restituito interamente dal significante, per sua natura meno degno e più soggetto a corrompersi. La distinzione assume un carattere valutativo. Questa tesi di origine aristotelica, sviluppata da Agostino e da una lunga tradizione patristica, (Simone, XIII) diventata decisiva per l'ulteriore sviluppo (anche quello più recente) della linguistica e quindi della teoria letteraria, porta gli Autori alla discussione del rapporto tra l'icona della parola e il suo significato. In ultima analisi il significato dipende dal modo in cui l'idea viene espressa tramite la parola, ovvero dall'icona. La questione del modo espressivo è, a sua volta, in rapporto con la morfologia, con la sintassi e con lo stato emotivo del soggetto. La teoria e la critica letteraria di Caloprese partono dallo stesso sistema e dagli stessi criteri: «...l'Allegrezza da se sola fa gli uomini eloquenti...». Possiamo osservare che la critica testuale del Caloprese consiste nell'investigare il grado in cui l'*oratio vocalis,* in altre parole l'espressione poetica corrisponda all'*oratio mentalis* del poeta. Più precisamente si tratta del condizionamento del linguaggio poetico e quindi della possibilità o meno di rendere linguisticamente lo stato emotivo del poeta, condizionato a sua volta dalla situazione ambientale (si veda anche M. RAK, cit., p. 219).

processo sul piano comportamentale della mente umana e sul piano linguistico si manifestano nella ricchezza dei concetti e delle parole: «la Sicurtà per cagione dell'Allegrezza, dalla quale prende i suoi moti, [...] suol fare degli uomini le menti e le lingue assai più del solito faconde e abbondevoli di parole e di concetti». (p. 130) L'abbondanza dei concetti e delle parole è quindi determinata qui dal tranquillo e copioso moto del sangue e degli spiriti verso il cervello, tale moto preceduto e causato da un sentimento sereno e tranquillo.

Segue l'analisi dei diversi ritmi del movimento del sangue e degli spiriti, del loro impatto sul funzionamento del cervello secondo il carattere della passione. Descrizione del comportamento dell'individuo riguardo alle capacità e alle qualità espressive, delle caratteristiche dello stile e del tono dell'espressione lirica completano il quadro. Diamo ancora un esempio: «quantunque l'Allegrezza da sé sola faccia gli uomini eloquenti», la loro eloquenza può essere non «molto vigorosa», anzi «debole e snervata», in quanto relativa alla «sorte» ovvero alla qualità dell'Allegrezza stessa. Così accade con quell'allegrezza che «va dietro alla Mestizia», che muove gli «spiriti», i quali «per la lor molta sottigliezza non possono aver tanta forza che vagliano a scuoter fortemente le fibre del cervello». (pp. 134, 133) Spiegata in tal modo la catena: affetto - sangue e spiriti - nervi - cuore - cervello - linguaggio, il critico continua con l'analisi dettagliata delle «forme del dire» del poeta, e dunque dello stile, delle figure espressive, con riferimenti continui alla passione sottostante detta catena.[38]

La nascita del fatto letterario è dunque il risultato del funzionare delle più svariate componenti del microcosmo umano. Nella *poiesis* anatomico-letteraria il Caloprese cerca un ordine sperimentalmente accertato. La ricerca parte dal presupposto della presenza di una armonia delle funzioni dell'organismo umano. La scoperta di una spiegazione per la nascita del fatto poetico rivela la regolarità dei fenomeni neuromentali da cui quel fatto è determinato. Da qui il Caloprese prende le mosse per tradurre gli effetti della sua indagine anatomica in un linguaggio più propriamente filosofico e critico, di nozioni e concetti. La fenomenologia del fatto poetico non si esaurisce infatti nell'approccio naturalistico, ma si uniscono ad esso altri strumenti investigativi, più propriamente letterari, diretti verso un'ulteriore indagine. È proprio qui, all'interno dell'approccio estetico, che nella teoria calopresiana si delinea l'apertura verso l'individualità poetica, definita dalla costituzione emotiva, dall'esperienza culturale e dall'abilità espressiva del poeta. Ed è per questo che i precetti retorici diventano inefficaci. Al naturalismo oggettivo dell'investigazione di «come si spiega» il fatto letterario nella sua genesi biologica e psicologica, si unisce l'attenzione al relativismo e soggettivismo dell'ambientazione culturale del poeta, delle sue scelte individuali, abilità «inge-

---

[38] Per la questione delle passioni nella teoria di Caloprese, in particolare nel loro rapporto con il pensiero cartesiano, si vedano le erudite indicazioni di M. KAK nell'*op. cit.*, e di GIOVANNA GRONDA in *Passioni della ragione. Studi sul Settecento*, Pisa, Pacini, 1984.

gnosa» e «diversità».

Osserva il Caloprese:

Quella virtù del parlare, che riempie gli animi di tanta dolcezza e di tanta maraviglia, per comune consentimento de' Maestri del dire, non procede tanto da' primi generali concetti, quanto da' particolari divisamenti, che su di essi si fanno dall'industria degli Scrittori, e dalle leggiadre forme del favellare, colle quali i concetti s'adornano». (p. 70)

[...] Giotto Pittore [...] poté inventare tante forme di meraviglioso spavento [...] [è] da credere, che ad uno ingegnoso e attento Scrittore non manchino i modi e le vie da poter fare il medesimo con le parole. Anzi tanto più, quanto maggior sono le differenze, che possono accascare negli atteggiamenti del parlare, che nei colori, e nei movimenti del volto e del corpo. (p. 330)

Entra qui la questione del ruolo e dell'importanza della Fantasia:

A voler dunque aprir con piena contezza la natura e la forza di alcuna passione, è d'uopo por mente, e far chiaro, Prima il senso e il moto della passione, che si genere nel cuore, e per mezzo del sangue per tutto il corpo si spande. Secondo la Fantasia, dalla quale si desta e si nutrisce un tal sentimento. Terzo, le cagioni per le quali una tal fantasia s'imprime. Quarto, l'ordine col quale si muove, e avanzandosi con altri affetti si mischia. (p. 84)

Il critico continua:

[...] dico, che in formarsi l'immagine che rappresenta l'oggetto della passione, gli spiriti che da essa riflettono, parte per mezzo de' nervi vanno al cuore a dilatare o ristrignere i suoi vasi, secondo richiede la qualità di esse passioni, e parte a diverse altre viscere del corpo, o ad alterare il moto del sangue, rendendolo o più o meno veloce del solito; o a spignere dentro le vene altr' umor diverso del sangue, perchè in entrando nelle cavità del cuore, s'accenda in guisa tale, che possa somministrare per mezzo del suo girevol moto alla Fantasia spiriti che siano acconci a mantener vive l'immagini, dalle quali hanno origine i moti del cuore. (p. 84)

La fantasia è dotata di facoltà cognitiva, ovvero di conoscenza sensibile delle idee e dei sentimenti, il cui risultato è la creazione di nuove immagini. Viene in tal modo superata la visione tradizionale della fantasia depositaria delle immagini, non più aristotelicamente parte «inferiore» dell'anima, ma parte che «più» della «parte superiore dell'Intelletto [...] si accosta al materiale del corpo». (p. 83)[39] La fantasia è così considerata implicitamente parte dell'Intelletto, che partecipa al «pensiero», alla «contemplazione» delle «cose», delle passioni, del «giudicare» se esse sono «cosa» «buona o rea». (p. 83)[40] Nel conflitto tra parte

---

[39] Si veda anche E. NUZZO, *op. cit.*, p. 91.

[40] Si veda anche A. Quondam: «<Fantasia> [...] risulta nettamente definita come la parte dell'intelletto che

ragionevole e parte corporea, la fantasia, come si è detto prima, entra come regolatrice e moderatrice degli eccessi delle passioni, derivanti dalla parte corporea. (*Spositioni*, p. 292) Il conflitto si esprime tra l'intelletto e il corpo, tra la ragione e le passioni. Tuttavia, nel pensiero del Caloprese è da notare la mancanza di una netta divisione tra il corporeo e il non corporeo.

Nel suo discorso teorico possiamo distinguere infatti alcune costanti intorno alle quali vengono strutturate le tesi fondamentali della sua poetica, tra le quali quella più significativa è il ragionamento a coppie, cioè a doppie tesi parallele e allo stesso tempo opposte. Il Caloprese procede per parallelismi che si escludono e complementano a vicenda. Il numero due, individuabile nei suoi scritti, diventa numero chiave per penetrare questa dialettica *sui generis*, o meglio antidialettica, in cui l'antitesi non elimina la *raison d'être* della tesi e la mancanza di sintesi è segno della presenza di una realtà in continuo movimento, realtà soggettiva e individuale. L'aspetto fondamentale della rappresentazione dualistica all'interno di questo sistema è il concetto dell'uomo nella sua duplice qualità di mente e corpo. Come tale, l'uomo deve essere considerato nei suoi aspetti spirituale e corporeo. (Caloprese, *Lezioni sulle origini degli imperii*, p. 209). Ma tra il corporeo e il non corporeo la divisione non è né netta né rigida. La fantasia opera infatti come parte dell'intelletto nella capacità di moderare le passioni, ma è anche considerata «potenza corporea anzi che no» (*Spositioni*, p. 166). Ricordiamo qui anche il detto calopresiano sulla «continua battaglia, tra la parte ragionevole e la sensitiva», lotta nella quale «talora l'una e talora l'altra» prevale, onde si realizza un intreccio spessissimo di argomenti razionali e processi immaginativi». (Nuzzo, p. 91) Ricordiamo inoltre la constatazione che «l'anima nostra, di più di essere unita strettamente al corpo, come forma di esso, è altresì la sostanza spirituale e come tale ha le sue operazioni indipendenti dal corpo».

b) *Gli "affetti", lo stile e la "diversità"*

Alla prima lettura del commento calopresiano al Casa potrebbe sorgere l'impressione di una preferenza data dal critico alla lirica casiana rispetto alla petrarchesca. Il Caloprese-critico, col suo sovente soffermarsi sul «dir Grande» e sulla *gravitas* del Casa, sembra condividere le tendenze della critica precedente, secondo la quale il Casa è «più grande» del Petrarca ed è lui il «modello poetico». Eppure, la questione è più complessa.

La chiave interpretativa della posizione teorica e critica del Caloprese è da ritrovare in una sua breve constatazione con la quale il pensatore di Scalea fa i conti con

---

<più si accosta al materiale del corpo> e che costituisce la funzione razionale preposta alla formazione delle immagini [...]», *Dizionario biografico degli italiani, op. cit.*, p. 804.

la critica petrarchesca precedente. L'accento cade non tanto sul paragone valutativo fra i valori poetici dei due autori quanto sulla loro diversità: entrambi rappresentano i due estremi di una alternativa che vanno ugualmente rispettati. La loro è una diversità espressiva dovuta alla diversa individualità e indole poetica dei due poeti.

Osserva infatti il Caloprese:

[...] mi maraviglio non poco di alcuni, che hanno fatto paralelli tra gli stili dell'uno e dell'altro Poeta, che non abbiano avvertita sì gran diversità: e pure, se io non vo errato, la diversa imitazione degli affetti dovea essere uno de' principali fondamenti de' loro discorsi. (p. 183)

Non dunque un paragone, né una questione di modelli, ma diversi sentimenti, una «diversa imitazione degli affetti», oppure diversi modi di esprimere lo stesso sentimento.

Trattasi di una rottura con l'approccio valutativo teso a ricercare la superiorità di un poeta rispetto all'altro e a confermare la qualità del "modello" poetico. Il Caloprese si allontana quindi dal petrarchismo inteso come imitazione di un modello. Il Casa assume la qualità di poeta fondatore di una poetica propria. La sua, accanto a quella del Petrarca, è una «buona poesia»; egli entra nell'ambito dell'alta tradizione poetica come uno dei «buoni poeti». È questo un approccio che segna una nuova esegesi poetica la quale vede nel Casa e nel Petrarca poeti, non "modelli". In una tale configurazione si pone in primo piano la questione dello stile, dell'efficacia espressiva. I frequenti paragoni tra lo stile del Casa e quello del Petrarca non tendono a stabilire una priorità tra i due ma mettono a fuoco diverse alternative stilistiche.

Diamo qui la parola al Caloprese:

[...] l'eccellente Poeta dee tener cura, che ne' suoi componimenti si ravvisino quelle sembianze, e quegli atteggiamenti, che sono più proprj, e più naturali degli affetti, che egli ha tolto ad imitare. Di quegli atteggiamenti ciascheduno affetto ne ha molti: perciocché eglino non sempre conservano un' istesso volto; ma secondo la varia intelligenza, e i varj costumi e stati degli uomini compariscono, quando sotto un aspetto, e quando sotto un' altro. (p. 330)

La critica recente ha già osservato che nel Casa, all'interno della aderenza al modello formale petrarchesco il Caloprese avvertì l'universale problematica e inquietudine diventata uno dei temi fondamentali del suo discorso critico.

Scrive il Caloprese:

[...] del mio giudicio, che il Casa fu così destro e avveduto in iscegliere il più degno e il più nobile da tutte le cose di che egli si valse, in dar lume a' suoi pensieri; che in questa parte niuna delle tre lingue ha chi si possa a lui con ragione uguagliare, non che preporre. (p. 53)

E continua:

[...] Queste parole [«D'amara gioja, e bene...» del Casa] con l'ampiezza del loro significato, e per essere di suono più tosto pieno che debole; sollevando alquanto la schiet-
tezza e semplicità delle prime, rendono non men dolce, che grave e maestoso il suo dire.
Per la medesima ragione d'ingrandire lo stile, schivò a tutto suo potere tutte le particel-
le, che avessero potuto in qualche modo ristrignere l'ampiezza del dire. Non disse egli:
io mi nutriva d'un dolce tormento, o come disse Petrarca, che fu più vago della Dolcezza, *Io mi vivea contento di mia sorte.* Ma parlò in maniera più grave e più sostenuta.
(p. 66)

Il sentimento verace, unito alla fantasia creatrice di "immagini" e traslati poetici,
rende l'espressione esteticamente riuscita, senza necessità di affidarsi ad abbelli-
menti retorici:

[...] la maggior bellezza de' componimenti intorno all'esprimere i veri sembianti delle
passioni, nasce dal contenere immagini di azioni: [...] e [...] il Poeta [...] dee cercare di tenere scolpita nella Fantasia alcun' azione particolare, nella quale concorrano tutti quegli
affetti, di cui egli vuol fare immagine. Perciocchè raccogliendo da sì fatta idea i loro proprj
e veri delineamenti, può agevolmente conseguire il suo fine, senza aver bisogno d'altri ajuti.
(p. 331)

Le composizioni del Casa seguono questo "artificio" e per questo sono piene «di
spiriti [...] vivaci e ritengono l'attitudini [...] naturali [...]». (p. 331)
Nella discussione del sonetto casiano sulla morte di Marcantonio Soranzo, il critico osserva che la Mestizia la quale «contiene preparamento e disposizione a virtù
[...] togliendo dalla mente la stima de' beni frali e caduchi della terra, ne invoglia a
desiderare gli eterni e immortali». Le calamità «ci aprono gli occhi della mente a
conoscere la poca fermezza delle cose terrene, e la general miseria della vita umana». (p. 248) La lirica del Petrarca, secondo il Caloprese aperta anch'essa ai sentimenti «gravi» della caducità delle cose mondane, rappresenta un altro modo espressivo. Il poeta del *Canzoniere* è chiamato qui in causa come poeta che «di cotal dottrina si mostrò molto inteso [...] quando per la morte della sua Laura proruppe
nelle seguenti parole: < Or conosch' io, che mia fera ventura / Vuol, che vivendo
e lagrimando impari, / come nulla qua giù diletta e dura >». (*ibid.*) Il sentimento
tragico, che beninteso «non si può cagionare in ogni sorta di persona», sperimen-
tato da entrambi i poeti, è analizzato dal Caloprese in connessione alla loro individuale sensibilità e qualità espressive.
Il paragone valutativo non è però assente del tutto nelle «sposizioni» calopresiane, come del resto si è già visto in alcuni esempi sopracitati. La «naturalezza» del-
l'espressione, ovvero la corrispondenza dell'espressione con il sentimento, e la veracità o autenticità di quest'ultimo sono fondamentali criteri critici che regolano
tale procedimento. I criteri stilistici di tipo classico, come la moderazione, la bre-

vità e chiarezza dell'espressione, oltre al ripudio delle metafore vecchie e abusate sono ulteriori i criteri valutativi. In un tale paragone a nessuno dei due poeti viene assegnato il primo posto in modo assoluto, Petrarca e il Casa sono sottoposti entrambi a critiche negative o positive, secondo il caso.

Diamo qui un esempio di osservazioni critiche del Caloprese riferitesi all'espressione poetica del Petrarca:

> Questi versi [di Guido Cavalcanti] nel vero sono pieni di molta vaghezza, sì per lo concetto, come per lo numero, e per la suavità delle parole, contuttociò cedono di gran lunga alla leggiadria del Casa. Ma quello non è maraviglia in un Poeta sì antico ma che diremo se l'istesso Petrarca in tutte le tre non mai abbastanza lodate canzoni degli occhi, in più volte, che tolse a spiegar questo concetto, quantunque sempre divinamente l'ornasse, pure o cedette, o non fu superiore alla bellezza, alla quale sollevollo il nostro Poeta? (p. 63)

Le critiche negative dei modi espressivi del Petrarca sono rivolte a quei casi in cui il Caloprese non trovava la profondità di una «passione» sottostante, siccome il sentimento non vissuto interamente è incapace di produrre un linguaggio di convincente forza espressiva. In ultima analisi è lo stile che decide del valore del componimento poetico.

> Il Petrarca [...] usando quasi la medesima forma di parlare, disse: [...] Ma il Casa con farla più compressa la rese più grande. (pp. 38-39)

> [...] Petrarca, il quale in molti luoghi del Canzoniere, nel vero con poca moderatezza, le cose sacre con le profane mischiò; come fe tra gli altri in quel Sonetto, che incomincia: *Siccome eterna vita è veder Dio*, ove con assai maggior sua laude averebbe espresso l'ardore del suo vago desio; se [...] (p. 112)

Il riferimento al «mischiare» le cose «sacre» con quelle «profane» ha valenza diversa dalle critiche riportate dallo Spinelli; esso sembra piuttosto diretto alla questione dello stile; ciò che urta infatti, è il «mischiare» temi di rango diverso all'interno dello stesso stile.

Non mancano le critiche rivolte ai modi espressivi del Casa:

> Il Petrarca nel sopraccitato luogo, esprimendo, come poc'anzi ho detto, una più temperata passione, con egual giudicio, ma con dissimile artificio, cercò di fare il suo dire più piano, e non dargli cotanto impeto, quanto ne hanno i versi del Casa; per lo che fe, che in essi apparisse più chiaramente la forza dell'argomentazione. (p. 210)

Quest'ultima osservazione del Caloprese si poggia su alcuni punti fermi della critica del pensatore di Scalea: sulla «temperata passione» ovvero il «giudicio» e sulla chiarezza dell'espressione.

Procedendo con le «sposizioni» della poesia del Casa, i riferimenti alla lirica del Petrarca si fanno sempre più frequenti, l'attenzione del Caloprese alla «buona poesia» gli fa rivelare e discutere la ricchezza stilistica e sentimentale del Petrarca.

Diamo di seguito un esempio dell'analisi calopresiana della resa stilistica di una delle «costituzioni d'animo» del poeta che forse più aveva colpito il critico, se si considera il fatto che ad essa egli dedicò un'attenzione del tutto particolare, mettendola anche innanzi agli altri esempi ripresi dal *Canzoniere*. Ricordiamo che «[...] ciascheduno affetto suol dare al parlare alcun proprio e special sembiante [...]» (330) e continuiamo con le parole del Caloprese:

> [...] il vero Amor Socratico [...] altro non è che Estasi e Furore. Onde le Rime del Petrarca, il quale di un sì fatto Amore sopra ogni altro divinamente cantò, di niun'altro Affetto si veggono tanto fregiate, quanto di questi; e sopra tutto maravigliosissime sono per tal cagione le tre Canzoni degli occhi. Nel Casa, benché in varj luoghi si veggano bellissime immagini di Furore Amoroso, l'Estasi però, trattone il presente Sonetto, non saprei trovare altro componimento, ove sia stata da lui espressa [...] (pp. 182-183)

La critica calopresiana della lirica petrarchesca trova infatti la più viva espressione nell'analisi della canzone *Chiare fresche e dolci acque* esposta in occasione della lettura del sonetto XI casiano. Il critico dedica intere pagine di ammirazione ed entusiasmo alla chiarezza e scorrevolezza stilistica con cui il Petrarca ratto dall'estasi amorosa esprime il bello della natura e il fascino della donna amata. I momenti più affascinanti per il Caloprese-critico, sono quelli in cui il Petrarca «divinamente cantò» l'Estasi Amorosa con «leggiadrezza», nel senso di stile chiaro, scorrevole, cristallino, naturale e immaginativo; questi momenti sono considerati dal Caloprese imparagonabili. «[Il] Petrarca con dolcezza e leggiadria impareggiabile distinse e fe chiara la mischianza di [affetti...] nella Canzone, che incomincia: < Chiare fresche e dolci acque >», scrive il critico. La descrizione della «sua Donna [...] appoggiata ad un albero lungo la riva di un fiume» e «la natura dell'Estasi» è resa dal Petrarca «con tanto ardore, con tanta dolcezza, e con tanta energia, che non credo, che forza d'umano ingegno possa più oltre aggiungere». (p. 185) Il sentimento dell'Amore, nel suo aspetto più alto e sublime, quello dell'Estasi profondamente sentito dal Petrarca lo rende qui diverso dal Casa che nel sonetto analizzato si abbandona invece all'«Amoroso Furore».

È anche vero che questo concetto d'amore definito come «vero Amor Socratico» di «somma dignità e possanza» si fondava su presupposti prettamente neoplatonici che ormai tramontavano nella cultura del tempo e che sarebbero totalmente spariti nella successiva produzione arcadica; trattasi tuttavia di un platonismo riproposto in chiave nuova:

> [...] lasciati tutti gli altrui pareri da parte, studierommi, giusta mia possa, il mio senti-

mento far chiaro: nel quale se parrà ad alcuno, che io mi scosti dalle opinioni già calcate dagli antichi Spositori di Platone, priego il Lettore, che non sia pronto a dannare il mio parere, prima che l'abbia con attento esame considerato. (p. 183)

L'inchino alla tradizione platonica è unicamente formale e sostituito poi da riferimenti ad un pensatore che diventava il simbolo dell'età nuova. Il critico dedica intere pagine al concetto dell'Amore, che nella sua esposizione oscilla tra quello platonico e quello cartesiano. (pp. 166 sgg.) Riferimenti al trattato cartesiano sulle passioni accompagnano l'intera analisi stilistica, psicologica e anatomica: «l'Amore col suo dolce e temperato calore dilatando e assottigliando soavemente il sangue, produce e somministra a pro della maraviglia spiriti attissimi alla contemplazione», (p. 185) «[...] la maggior [...] virtù [della Meraviglia] in altro non consiste, che in raccogliere tutte le forze del pensiero alla contemplazione dell'oggetto amato; la qual cosa, siccome insegna Renato delle Carte, è solo opera della Maraviglia». (p. 187) Il platonismo ripreso e riproposto dal Caloprese si riveste qui di tratti propri dell'empirismo moderno.

Nel contesto della reazione antimarinista, il ritorno al platonismo rappresentava forse l'unica possibilità di contrapporre al concetto d'amore inteso in termini barocchi o erotici qualcosa di più sicuramente fondato su basi teoriche. Partendo dunque dal tradizionale concetto del platonismo e cercando di rinnovarlo nell'ottica della teoria moderna di *Les passions de l'âme* e delle *Epistole* cartesiane, il Caloprese modificava radicalmente il platonismo. Da qui proviene quell'attenzione tutta particolare al concetto platonico dell'«Amore Uman o Civile e Onesto» individuato nelle poesie del Casa o del Petrarca, unita a un tentativo di portarlo più vicino alla terra, al reale, e di attribuirgli le specifiche non solo dell'Amore «Celeste o Divino» ma anche di quello «Volgare o Fierino». Quest'ultimo viene in tal modo quasi nobilitato, depurato della sua connotazione negativa. Infatti, la «Cupidità», in quanto aspetto dell'«Amor Fierino», intesa nella prospettiva cartesiana, diventa in Caloprese caratteristica per se stessa naturale dell'Amore:

[Il Cartesio] conchiude, che l'Amore onesto dell'Amante verso l'amata Donna è una passione mista di molto Amore e di alquanto di Cupidità. (pp. 166-167) «Ora seguitando noi la presente dottrina, dico, che l'affetto che in questo Sonetto [del Casa] mostra portare alla sua Donna il nostro Poeta, è una passione mista di Amore e di Cupidità; e che nel primo quaternario, nel quale celebra la sua Donna per le bellezze interne, e narra gli effetti di dolcezza e di virtù, che destavano nel suo animo cotali bellezze; ne dimostra tutta la perfezione del semplice e puro Amore; il quale anco secondo la sentenza di Renato è cagione di virtù e di moral perfezione. Ove poi dice, che contuttoché stia stretto in dura prigione, e piagato di crudel colpo, pure ha cara la servitù, e dolci gli sono le piaghe; spiega quella parte di Amore, che si mischia con la Cupidità. (p. 167)

Il sentimento dell'amore così spiegato perde le connotazioni platoniche astratte e ideali, diventando più "umano" e quindi più realistico. Successivamente, rinnovato nello spirito di una sensibilità nuova, esso avrebbe trovato sviluppo e approfondimento solo nel mondo affettivo dell'Alfieri.

Franco Fido

LA SINDERESI DI GIACINTA: ANCORA SULLE *VILLEGGIATURE* DI GOLDONI

Nel quadro dei progressi compiuti dagli studi goldoniani negli ultimi quarant'anni (e precisamente a partire dal Convegno veneziano del 1957) spicca il caso della trilogia della villeggiatura (1761), che – riconosciuta finalmente per quel capolavoro che è – è stata studiata e rappresentata con crescente impegno e acume.

Oggi, grazie alle letture dei critici e alle messe in scena dei registi,[1] vari aspetti delle tre commedie (*Le smanie per la villeggiatura, Le avventure della villeggiatura, Il ritorno dalla villeggiatura*) ci appaiono evidenti, per non dire pacifici. In primo luogo, la necessità di considerarle insieme, e idealmente di vederle rappresentate di seguito, in una sequenza temporale breve, e dunque praticamente continua.

In secondo luogo, la complessa, e pur armoniosa convivenza nella trilogia di molti temi diversi:

– L'atteggiamento contraddittorio, o se vogliamo i "complessi" dei veneziani nei confronti della campagna, vagheggiata come spazio naturale ed idillico, ignorata o misconosciuta nella sua realtà demografica ed economica, luogo volta a volta di "libertà" e di "soggezione", dove bisogna "figurare" per non "scomparire", e così via.

– La discussione di ciò che può esser lecito ai grandi e illecito ai borghesi, come appunto le dispendiose villeggiature.

---

[1] Per un'accurata bibliografia dei contributi recenti sulla Trilogia si veda M. BORDIN, *Fra "negozio" e "villa". Crisi della morale borghese dal* Prodigo *alla trilogia della* Villeggiatura, in *Problemi di critica goldoniana*, a cura di G. Padoan, II, Ravenna, Longo, 1995, pp. 133-182: pp. 176-177; e soprattutto ID., *"Figurare nel mondo". La trilogia della* Villeggiatura *o la commedia del desiderio*, in *Problemi di critica goldoniana*, a cura di G. Padoan, III, Ravenna, Longo, 1996, pp. 199-281: nota 4 a p. 200. Da aggiungere la mia *Introduction* a C. G., *The Holiday Trilogy*, translated by A. Oldcorn, New York, Marsilio, 1992, pp. IX-XXXVII, e S. FERRONE, *La "Trilogia della villeggiatura": le* Smanie *di Massimo Castri*, in *Tra libro e scena Carlo Goldoni*, a cura di C. Alberti e G. Herry, Venezia, Il Cardo, 1996, pp. 149-155. Fra le regie, dopo quelle ormai canoniche di Giorgio Strehler (*Piccolo Teatro di Milano*, 1954; *Comédie Française*, Parigi, 1978) da ricordare almeno quella di Mike Alfreds (col titolo *Countrymania*, le tre commedie recitate *di seguito e integralmente nella stessa sera,* British National Theatre, Londra, 1987; quelle di Mario Missiroli e di Gabriele Vacis a ridosso del bicentenario goldoniano (1993), e infine quella di Massimo Castri (*Le smanie*, Perugia, 1995; *Le avventure* e *Il ritorno*, Prato, 1996).

– Il rapporto fra amore e matrimonio, e la possibile crisi di quest'ultimo come istituto borghese per eccellenza.

– Le relazioni fra i sessi, con l'aspirazione a una relativa emancipazione e la paura della "schiavitù" nelle donne, l'oscillazione fra paternalismo e desiderio negli uomini.

– Infine, una catena di opposizioni binarie, fra "natura" e "artificio", "sostanza" e "apparenza", "economia" e "moda", "autorità" e "trasgressione", o fra la solitudine monologante di un personaggio (Giacinta), e la vacua promiscuità della conversazione.

Da un lato, sulla presenza di questi "contenuti" nelle *Villeggiature* tutti sono, credo, d'accordo. Dall'altro, se tale ricchezza di situazioni e di problemi già conferisce alle tre commedie un forte interesse come documento di una crisi culturale e politica in atto, essa non basta ancora a darci ragione della loro straordinaria qualità e vitalità teatrale.

Non resta, per fare ulteriori progressi nella comprensione delle *Villeggiature*, che lo studio dei modi teatrali specifici attraverso i quali quei contenuti vivono sulla scena: le strutture portanti della favola; l'uso del linguaggio; la psicologia dei personaggi e le metafore ossessive (per usare una formula di Charles Mauron)[2] che scandiscono e regolano il loro destino.

Per il primo di questi elementi si pensi ad esempio all'apertura e alla conclusione della seconda commedia, con lo straordinario ricevimento mattutino dei servitori quando si alza il sipario, che è al tempo stesso leziosa e goffa imitazione e spietata parodia delle maniere e dei costumi dei padroni, eppure riesce anche a suggerire una maggiore naturalezza o naturalità dei personaggi subalterni, come Brigida, che dopo aver aiutato Giacinta a coricarsi se ne va in giardino all'alba a coglier dei gelsomini. E all'estremo opposto, prima della caduta del sipario alla fine del terzo atto, il non meno straordinario monologo di Giacinta («Signori miei gentilissimi, qui il poeta con tutto lo sforzo della fantasia aveva preparata una lunga disperazione, un combattimento di affetti, un misto d'eroismo e di tenerezza. Ho creduto bene di ometterla»), in cui da un lato per bocca della sua protagonista l'autore sottolinea la novità di *questo modo* di essere innamorati e consapevoli della propria passione, rispetto a quello più blando e compiaciuto degli eroi metastasiani, dall'altro, letteralmente, lascia la parola al personaggio, gli cede per così dire il microfono, riconoscendo il suo antagonismo nei confronti dello stesso autore, e ne registra così l'effimera ma significativa rivolta.

Per quel che riguarda il linguaggio, un'analisi puntuale del dialogo ci porterebbe troppo lontani dal discorso sintetico che sto facendo. Per fare anche in questo

---

[2] Cfr. C. MAURON, *Des métaphores obsédantes au mythe personnel. Introduction à la Psychocritique*, Paris, Corti, 1964; e anche, dello stesso, *Psychocritique du genre comique, ibid.*, 1964[2].

caso un solo esempio, si pensi all'uso dell'iperbole, che in Giacinta, almeno prima che si innamori, è sempre controllato, impressivo, finalizzato a una vittoria dialettica sui suoi interlocutori, come quando parlando col padre "prevede" i pettegolezzi che una mancata conferma dell'invito a Guglielmo in campagna non mancherebbe di provocare: «non arriva domani, che voi ed io per Livorno e per Montenero siamo in bocca di tutti: si alzano sopra di noi delle macchine, si fanno degli almanacchi [...] mi vengono i sudori freddi» (II, 10); e in bocca a Vittoria è invece sempre espressivo, segno di esasperazione e di impotenza: «Se dovessi star qui, in tempo che l'altre vanno in villeggiatura, mi ammalerei di rabbia, di disperazione» (I, 3).

Eppure (venendo ora ai personaggi), proprio la nervosa Vittoria rappresenta, con la sua ambizione di comparire e la sua gelosia per Giacinta, una relativa normalità, che fa risaltare la singolarità di altre figure attorno a lei.

Mi è capitato di osservare altrove[3] che nelle commedie scritte fra la fine degli anni Cinquanta e gli anni francesi si manifestano con maggior frequenza ed evidenza di prima dei sintomi di follia: come la mania di grandezze di Filippo zio di Eugenia negli *Innamorati*, la frenesia marziale del tenente zoppo don Cirillo nella *Guerra*, o il vivente ossimoro dell'*avare fastueux,* l'avaro fastoso della commedia omonima del 1773. Rispetto alla comica stravaganza di questi personaggi, quelli delle *Villeggiature* appaiono piuttosto dominati da una passione esclusiva che essi coltivano con una tenacia a suo modo ascetica o eroica, e che li isola in una specie di luce fredda. Così lo zio Bernardino, ideale parente e successore dei rusteghi, dello zio Cristofolo nella *Casa nova*, e di Todero, sostiene la sua parte di vecchio avaro e insensibile con un rigore, con un gusto del sarcasmo allucinanti, che retrospettivamente colpivano lo stesso Goldoni: «un carattere odioso, come quello di Bernardino, può essere sofferto e anche goduto in una Scena; ma diventerebbe noioso ed insopportabile, se una seconda volta si rivedesse» (Prefazione dell'autore al *Ritorno*).[4]

Allo stesso modo, il Ferdinando delle *Villeggiature* da un lato combina tratti del parassita famelico ma ricercatissimo dai villeggianti, già presenti per esempio nel don Ciccio della *Villeggiatura,* con quel gusto sfrenato e crudele dei pettegolezzi che ha come archetipo il Don Marzio della *Bottega del caffè;* dall'altro è molto più controllato e furbo di entrambi quei personaggi, tanto è vero che riuscirà a sposare la vecchia Sabina dopo aver ricevuto da lei una ricca donazione. E tuttavia anche un abile scroccone professionale come lui rischia di inimicarsi le famiglie in cui vorrebbe entrare perché non sa resistere al gusto d'una perfida maldicenza: si veda in particolare la scena del *Ritorno* (I, 4), in cui suscita lo sdegno di Vittoria («Oh lingua indemoniata! Si può sentire di peggio»?). Così, in un

---

[3] Cfr. F. FIDO, *La ragione in ombra e le tentazioni della follia nelle commedie degli anni francesi*, in ID., *Le inquietudini di Goldoni. Saggi e letture*, Genova, Costa & Nolan, 1995, pp. 163-185.

[4] Cfr. C. G., *Tutte le opere*, a cura di G. Ortolani, Milano, Mondadori, 1935-56, VII, p. 1148.

particolare almeno, il livore e il disprezzo con cui ripaga i suoi anfitrioni della loro ospitalità, Ferdinando anticipa il tanto più geniale, e veramente immortale Neveu de Rameau.

Ma il più inquietante di questi personaggi fissati, e certo non più comico, è Guglielmo, erede anche lui di tanti amorosi sofferenti del teatro goldoniano, che hanno come capostipite il compitissimo Florindo del *Bugiardo* , ma al tempo stesso partecipe a buon diritto del grande *revival* del seduttore nell'immaginario collettivo settecentesco, dal Lovelace di Richardson ai vari Don Giovanni Tenorio al Valmont di Laclos, senza dimenticare l'irresistibile autocandidatura di Casanova. Guglielmo sembra così deciso a conquistare l'amore di Giacinta che l'annuncio del fidanzamento di lei con Leonardo, pur sorprendendolo spiacevolmente («Questa è una novità che non m'aspettavo») lo induce a temporeggiare, non a desistere («La convenienza vuole ch'io non insista», *Smanie*, scena ultima).

Così fin quasi alla fine della seconda commedia Guglielmo persegue il suo scopo con una concentrazione e un successo che fanno pensare, come dicevo, al protagonista delle *Liaisons dangéreuses*, con la differenza che l'eroe di Laclos non amava la *Présidente*, mentre lui ama davvero Giacinta, come vediamo nelle capitali scene 2-4 del III atto delle *Avventure,* in cui al lungo soliloquio di Giacinta e poi alla sua confessione («Riflettete, signor Guglielmo, che voi ed io siamo due persone infelici», e poi *a parte* «Ah! è pur grande lo sforzo che fare mi è convenuto! Grand'affanno, gran tormento mi costa»!) corrisponde il brevissimo soliloquio di Guglielmo: «Chi ha veduto caso più stravagante e più doloroso del mio?».

La vera *stravaganza*, in questo caso, sta nella docilità con cui un consumato vagheggino come lui si lascia dettare dalla ragazza che ama il partito assurdo e crudele di sposarne un'altra. Ed è qui, forse, che possiamo meglio osservare il prodigio goldoniano per cui i casi della vita si caricano talvolta sulla scena di una speciale necessità o fatalità drammatica, senza che ciò implichi il minimo assenso a un sistema trascendente, o, appunto, fatalistico.

A un primo livello Guglielmo è chiaramente vittima di quelle *convenienze* che ha sempre in bocca, e che effettivamente sono state un'arma importante nella sua manovra di seduzione ai danni di Giacinta: ricordiamoci delle confidenze della ragazza alla sua cameriera Brigida: «quelle continue finezze, quelle parole a tempo, quel trovarsi vicini a tavola, sentirmi urtare di quando in quando (sia per accidente, o per arte), e poi chiedermi scusa, e poi accompagnare le scuse con qualche sospiro, sono occasioni fatali, insidie orribili, e non so, e non so dove voglia andare a finire» (*Avventure*, II, 1). Ma come dicevo le convenienze sono anche la trappola che si chiude su di lui: «Ah è inevitabile il precipizio. Misero me! in qual impegno mi trovo!»; e finalmente «ceda la passione al dovere» (*Avventure*, III, 4).

In tutte queste scene Goldoni non usa certo le parole a caso; dopo aver ricordato le «occasioni fatali» create da Guglielmo per farla innamorare di lui, la ragazza commenta così la capitolazione del giovane quando egli chiede finalmente la mano di Vittoria: «(Ah! la sinderesi lo ha convinto)» (*Avventure*, II, 4). A parte il *cliché* non frequentissimo, ma ancora vivo oggi «perdere la sinderesi», nel senso di non connettere più, la parola è, ed era nel Settecento, di uso rarissimo, un *apax* credo nel teatro goldoniano, e presente per quanto ne so un'altra volta soltanto in quello europeo, e non a caso in un autore noto a Goldoni, Regnard:

> Il s'élève, aussi bien, dans le fond de mon coeur
> Certain remords cuisant, certaine synderèse,
> Qui furieusement sur l'estomac me pèse
> (*Le legataire Universel*, IV, 7):

per cui, ripeto, è difficile credere a un uso casuale da parte del commediografo veneziano, e si pensa piuttosto all'accezione ascetica di *sinderesi* fino a Bossuet, come tendenza a riconoscere i primi principi morali, a provare rimorso quando non li seguiamo, o anche alla definizione scolastica, che Goldoni ex-allievo dei gesuiti a Perugia e dei domenicani a Rimini poteva forse ricordare, come «parte dell'anima non toccata dal peccato originale».[5] In altre parole, dobbiamo riconoscere nel termine la forma più vicina, nella lingua del passato, a quello che dopo Freud chiamiamo *Über-ich* o Super-ego.

A un secondo livello, il piccolo Valmont *avant la lettre* delle *Villeggiature*, caduto in una sorta di doloroso stupore, sembra obbedire anche lui a qualcosa che sta sopra le convenienze: se vogliamo, alla sinderesi di Giacinta. Ma l'imperativo morale, o come dicevo il Super-ego cui si piegano Giacinta, e financo il suo abile ma sfortunato seduttore, potrebbe anche esser fasullo, se implica (con quali compensi, quali vantaggi come contropartita? possiamo chiederci), una rinuncia alla felicità. Per tener fede alla sua immagine di fanciulla ragionevole e responsabile, e così aver ragione agli occhi di Fulgenzio, la ragazza finisce col far torto a se stessa. Ma su Giacinta si è scritto parecchio in anni

---

[5] Per qualche altra, rara testimonianza letteraria, posteriore, cfr. ANTONIO PIAZZA, *Il teatro ovvero fatti di una veneziana che lo fanno conoscere*: «Sarà meglio ch'io viva abbandonata senza rimorsi che felicitata dalla sua compagnia, col tormento della sinderesi e col sospetto d'esser creduta colpevole un giorno»: ed. moderna col titolo *L'attrice*, a cura di R. Turchi, Napoli, Guida, 1984, p. 83 (cit. da G. ANTONELLI, *Alle radici della letteratura di consumo - La lingua dei romanzi di Pietro Chiari e Antonio Piazza*, Milano, Ist. di propaganda libraria, 1996, p. 210; lo stesso ricorda anche un altro esempio sempre del Piazza: *Eugenia. Ossia il momento fatale*, Venezia, Bassaglia, 1784, p. 155: *ibid.*); e V. MONTI, *Esame critico dell'autore sopra l'*Aristodemo: «Anche nelle produzioni d'ingegno tutti abbiamo una certa coscienza, un certo rimorso che c'importuna e ci rinfaccia le nostre mancanze. Uomini che scrivete, non fate che l'amor proprio soffochi nel vostro spirito questa sinderesi letteraria. Interrogatela spesso, e ve ne troverete contenti»: in V. M., *Tragedie drammi e cantate, con Appendice di versi inediti o rari*, a cura di G. Carducci, Firenze, Barbera, 1865, pp. 208-209.

recenti, da Jacques Joly, Giovanna Gronda, Rosamaria Lavalva, Michele Bordin, e anche da me,[6] e non è il caso di ripetere cose già dette. Piuttosto, l'idea di un'assiologia fasulla, o meglio della demistificazione teatrale dei valori correnti, mi porta a un altro tema caratteristico della trilogia, quello delle nozze infelici.

Come è noto, i matrimoni d'amore – nel senso otto- e novecentesco dell'espressione – sono piuttosto rari nel teatro goldoniano, salvo che nelle commedie popolaresche o tabernarie di fine di carnevale, come *I pettegolezzi delle donne*, *Il Campiello* o *Le baruffe chiozzotte*, e con l'eccezione sottolineata dal titolo *Gl'innamorati* . Molto più frequenti i matrimoni dettati da una ragionevole convenienza, in cui basta, al massimo, che i novizzi "si piacciano", come nei *Rusteghi*. Nelle *Villeggiature* le nozze si moltiplicano: oltre ai due matrimoni, celebrati in scena, fra gli "amorosi", e quello fra i giovanissimi Rosina e Tognino contratto dietro le quinte, si annunciano quelli fra i caratteristi Sabina e Ferdinando, e quello fra Brigida cameriera di Giacinta e Paolo o Paolino servitore di Leonardo.

È Goldoni stesso a farci notare il moltiplicarsi delle conclusioni matrimoniali, non a caso per bocca del personaggio più sciocco, nell'ultima scena del *Ritorno dalla villeggiatura*:

TOGNINO (dopo il matrimonio fra Giacinta e Guglielmo, *saltando)*: Nozze, nozze, evviva; si son fatte le nozze,

e poco più avanti, dopo il matrimonio di Vittoria e Guglielmo,

saltando: Nozze, nozze, dell'altre nozze.
FILIPPO Sì nozze. E quando si faranno le vostre nozze?
TOGNINO Sono fatte, le abbiamo fatte. Sì, sì, lo voglio dire, son maritato.

Ma, tranne forse quello "plebeo" fra i due servitori, i matrimoni delle *Villeggiature* non sono certo matrimoni d'amore, e neppure matrimoni di convenienza, nel-

---

[6] Cfr. J. JOLY, *La crise du personnage et la recherche d'une structure dramatique nouvelle dans la trilogie de la Villeggiatura de Goldoni*, «Revue d'histoire du théâtre», 1972, fasc. 3, pp. 300-321; ID., *La trilogie de la* Villeggiatura, in ID., *Le désir et l'utopie. Etude sur le théâtre d'Alfieri et de Goldoni*, Clermont-Ferrand, Publications de la Faculté des Lettres, 1978, pp. 208-217; G. GRONDA, *Comparare e interpretare. Madame de Lafayette, Goldoni e la trilogia della villeggiatura*, «Intersezioni», XX, (1992), 2, pp. 247-266; EAD., *Voci della passione amorosa in Goldoni: Mirandolina, Eugenia, Giacinta*, in *Omaggio a Gianfranco Folena*, II, Padova, Editoriale Programma, 1993, pp. 1347-1358; R. LAVALVA, *Realtà dell'apparenza: forma e convenzione in Goldoni*, «Annali d'Italianistica», 11, 1993, pp. 251-263; M. BORDIN, *Fra "negozio" e "villa"*, cit.; F. FIDO, *Giacinta nel paese degli uomini: interpretazione delle* Villeggiature *e del "femminismo" goldoniano*, in ID., *Da Venezia all'Europa. Prospettive sull'ultimo Goldoni*, Roma, Bulzoni, 1984, pp. 11-58. Per un'analisi minuta ed esaustiva delle tre commedie nel quadro dell'opera goldoniana, con un'attenta discussione degli interventi critici più recenti, si veda ora soprattutto M. BORDIN, *"Figurare nel mondo". La trilogia della* Villeggiatura *o la commedia del desiderio*, cit. sopra alla n. 1.

l'usuale senso borghese di solida e pacifica istituzione domestica su cui costruire la prosperità della famiglia.

Nella trilogia, più sterile e doloroso, o assente, è l'amore, e più ci si sposa. All'entropia dei sentimenti corrisponde l'inflazione dei riti nuziali. Ma perché dunque tutta questa gente si marita? E a questo punto cos'è il matrimonio? Si potrebbe rispondere, teatralmente parlando, che nelle *Villeggiature* il matrimonio è un vuoto, uno spazio virtuale che si stende al di là dei due momenti della *scrittura* e della *partenza* , oppure che è la problematica risultante di due azioni opposte e complementari, sottoscrivere un contratto e partire, per cui si firma per poter partire e si parte per non dover firmare. Seguiamo i nostri eroi da una commedia all'altra.

Smanie, scena ultima:

FILIPPO: Signori, prima di partire si ha da fare una cosa. Il signor Leonardo ha avuto la bontà di domandarmi la mia figliuola [...] Si faranno le nozze [...] dopo la villeggiatura, e intanto s'ha da fare la scritta. Onde siete pregati ad esser voi i testimoni.
[...]
FERDINANDO: Son qui; molto volentieri. Facciamo presto quello che si ha da fare, e partiamo per la campagna.

E Giacinta nell'ultima battuta della commedia: «Sì, facciamo la scritta e subitamente partiamo».

Avventure, II atto, scena 14, dopo che Guglielmo, costretto da Giacinta, ha chiesto la mano di Vittoria:

LEONARDO: Or ora si farà la scritta; e lor signori porranno in carta la loro testimonianza.
[...]
FERDINANDO: Se volete che vi serva io della scritta, ne ho fatte delle altre...:

e non è certo senza ironia che il personaggio "specializzato" in contratti matrimoniali sia quello moralmente più risibile, inaffidabile e screditato; scena 15, dopo che Vittoria ha dichiarato di voler seguire subito il fratello a Livorno:

LEONARDO: E non volete aspettare che si sottoscriva il contratto?
VITTORIA: Ma sì, s'ha da sottoscrivere. Ehi! signor Ferdinando, ha finito?

scena ultima:

FERDINANDO: Eccomi, eccomi [...] Eccola terminata.
GUGLIELMO: Scusatemi. Non si può far a Livorno? Non è meglio farla stendere da un notaio?
FERDINANDO: Ma se è già fatta!

GUGLIELMO: S'ha da leggere, s'ha da firmare. Signor Leonardo, vi consiglio non perder tempo. È meglio assai partir subito, e si farà la scritta a Livorno [...]
LEONARDO: Non dite male. Andiamo. Si farà a Livorno.
GUGLIELMO: (Respiro un poco. Qualche cosa può nascere).

e poco più avanti Ferdinando offrendo ironicamente l'inutile scritta alla zia Sabina:

FERDINANDO: Tenga, che gliene faccio un presente.
SABINA: Cosa mi date?
FERDINANDO: Una scritta di matrimonio.
SABINA: È per me forse?
FERDINANDO: Veramente non è per lei. Perché nella sua ci ha da essere la donazione, *eccetera...*:

per cui, chiaramente, fin da qui la scritta raggiunge il *mariage* e i vari giochi d'azzardo fra le metafore ossessive della trilogia. Ma non è finita:
Ritorno, Atto I scena 1,

LEONARDO: Guglielmo tuttavia differisce a far la scritta con mia sorella.

scena 9:

LEONARDO (a Guglielmo): Ma perché intanto si differisce di sottoscrivere il nuziale contratto?

Atto terzo scena ultima:

VITTORIA (alludendo al suo fidanzamento con Guglielmo): Questa sera io spero che si sottoscriverà questa carta.
GIACINTA: A che servon le carte? A che servon le scritture? [...] Volesse il cielo ch'io avessi sposato il signor Leonardo quel giorno medesimo ch'io mi sono in carta obbligata:

battuta in cui l'eroina ribadisce involontariamente proprio l'importanza decisiva della carta nel momento stesso in cui ne dichiara con enfasi l'inutilità. Di fatto, la scrittura, già strumento capitale dell'attività mercantile, è qui un espediente per risolvere il problema legandosi le mani, legalizzando l'irreparabile, un modo di bloccare il futuro. Opposta e complementare in questo, come dicevo, alla partenza, che è un espediente per risolvere il problema rinviandolo, sottraendosi momentaneamente alla scadenza, un modo di eludere il futuro.

Rileggiamo, nell'ultima scena della terza commedia, quella specie di duetto o di antiarietta nuziale a due voci, che suggella la storia di Vittoria e Guglielmo:

VITTORIA: [...] signor Guglielmo, non forzata, come voi parete di esserlo, ma nel miglior cuore del mondo vi do la mano.

GUGLIELMO: E per mia sposa vi accetto.
VITTORIA: Abbiate compassione di me (*A Guglielmo, teneramente*).
GUGLIELMO (*a parte*): (Io merito più compassione di lei);

riascoltiamo soprattutto, dalla stessa scena, un passo del commiato di Giacinta:

Lode al cielo son maritata; parto per Genova, e parto con animo risoluto di non rammentarmi che il mio dovere.

Qui, infine, i riti della scrittura e della partenza appaiono precariamente, e a caro prezzo, riconciliati.

A questo punto, vorrei suggerire tre riflessioni, più che conclusioni. La prima riguarda la disinvoltura con cui il poeta comico e autor di commedie Goldoni sovverte radicalmente e tranquillamente, senza complessi e senza neppur più bisogno di scuse, la legge del lieto fine, offrendoci, invece che una batteria di trattati, programmi e manifesti come quelli che cominciavano a uscire in Francia sul *genre sérieux*,[7] un geniale modello *in re*, un perfetto esempio di commedia seria, o addirittura di dramma borghese.

La seconda riflessione si ricollega a quello che dicevo intorno al sacrificio di Giacinta, da un lato eroico, al limite del melodramma

(*Avventure*, III, 2: Oh cieli! cieli, aiutatemi.
Ritorno, II, 11: Si ha da penare, si ha da morire. Ma si ha da vincere, e da trionfare)

dall'altro mistificato, non tanto nella forma – la ragazza, come sappiamo, si rende conto della tentazione metastasiana sua e dell'autore, e la respinge in un famoso discorsetto agli spettatori – quanto nel suo illudersi sull'importanza della posta in gioco, nell'esagerarsi la portata esemplare, edificante, della sua sofferta vittoria. Neppure per Giacinta, tanto più sincera e appassionata di Mirandolina, tanto più intelligente e controllata di Eugenia, Goldoni prevede o sollecita una simpatia senza riserve, un'identificazione da parte del pubblico. In questo senso, oltre che la malinconia di Cechov e l'amara solitudine della Nora ibseniana, la trilogia sembra annunciare l'estraniamento, o *Verfremdung* di Brecht.

La terza e ultima riflessione viene dalla somiglianza che si può notare fra la conclusione del *Ritorno dalla villeggiatura* e uno splendido ed enigmatico affresco fra quelli dipinti da Giandomenico Tiepolo nell'ultimo decennio del secolo per la sua propria villa a Zianigo di Mirano, poi strappato, e oggi a Ca' Rezzonico a Venezia,

---

[7] Si vedano soprattutto gli scritti sul teatro di DIDEROT, *Entretiens avec Dorval* (1757, di seguito alla commedia *Le fils naturel*); *Discours sur la poésie dramatique* (1758, di seguito a *Le père de famille*); *Paradoxe sur le comédien* (composto fra il 1769 e il 1777, pubblicato nel 1830, ediz. critica di P. Vernière nel 1959), e R. MORTIER, il cap. *Diderot théoricien du drame* nel suo *Diderot en Allemagne*, Paris, P.U.F., 1954, pp. 48-138.

chiamato di solito *La passeggiata*. Vi si scorgono di spalle, come spesso nei quadri del Tiepoletto, una dama con un abito giallo a coda e una gran cuffia, fiancheggiata da un giovane col tricorno che le dà il braccio, e da un altro personaggio che la precede di un passo, coperto dall'alto cappello a staio di moda fra gli elegantoni di allora. Il terzetto, preceduto a sua volta da uno sparuto levriero, e seguito da un servo che porta in braccio un altro animale, sembra diretto verso un orizzonte di colline lontane.

È possibile che Giandomenico avesse letto le *Villeggiature*, o meglio ancora le avesse viste rappresentate a Venezia, prima di partire col padre per la Spagna nel 1762, l'anno stesso in cui Goldoni partì per la Francia, e che si fosse ricordato, mentre dipingeva tanto tempo dopo a Zianigo, di Giacinta che parte non certo per Cythère, ma semplicemente per Genova, a braccio del marito e col fantasma di Guglielmo accanto.[8] Comunque nei due capolavori, con un'operazione da storici oltre che da artisti (ma i grandi artisti sono sempre storici acuti del proprio tempo), il commediografo e il pittore hanno tradotto in forme analoghe la sospensione e la malinconia di un mondo che sta per finire, che sta andando non si sa bene dove, oppure, per riprendere una suggestiva espressione di Claudio Magris, lontano da dove: con una lucidità e un'eleganza che rimangono caratteristiche dell'arte veneziana nella sua ultima stagione.

---

[8] Cfr. il mio saggio *Goldoni e Giandomenico Tiepolo interpreti dell'antico regime*, in F. FIDO, *Le inquietudini di Goldoni*, cit., pp. 83-98.

Francisco Márquez Villanueva

PERSPECTIVA HISPANA DE DON JUAN
EN GOLDONI Y MOLIERE

El lector español que se enfrenta con las páginas de *Don Giovanni Tenorio, ossia Il dissoluto punito*, una de las obras menos conocidas de Goldoni, deberá ir prevenido para una lluvia de sorpresas. Figuran allí, puntuales, Don Giovanni Tenorio, el Comendador de Lojoa [*sic*], su hija Donna Ana, Isabella y el duque Ottavio, pero la pareja Batricio-Aminta ha sido sustituida por la de los pastores Carino-Elisa. Ha desaparecido la bella figura de Tisbea y la doctrinalmente imprescindible de Catalinón, mientras se introduce un nuevo personaje en cierto Don Alfonso, que se dice privado de un genérico rey de Castilla. Le corresponde iniciar la obra, informando a Donna Ana del alto casamiento que para ella ha decidido el monarca. Vanidosamente persuadida de que éste la elige por esposa, se apresura la dama a empear un consentimiento a ciegas. Su decepción será completa al saber que el prometido, aunque de sangre real, es sólo el duque Ottavio y la indiferencia, lindante en aborrecimiento, se vuelve mutua cuando llegan a conocerse en persona.

La reencarnación de Don Juan no aparece hasta el segundo acto. Viene de su Nápoles natal y acaba de ser despojado por unos bandidos cuando interrumpe el idilio entre el fiel Carino y la casquivana Elisa, que con harta facilidad se ablanda ante los requiebros y promesas del caballero recién llegado. Isabella, heredera de la ilustre familia ducal de Astromonte, irrumpe en escena vestida de hombre y es también atacada de forajidos, pero el duque Ottavio oportunamente la salva y le promete su auxilio tras saber que viene como «tradita amante» en busca de Don Giovanni. Es él quien la lleva ante Don Alfonso, que dice estar ya al tanto de otras aventuras de éste, por lo cual se encargará de que el rey le ajuste las cuentas. Donna Anna teme que Isabella sea una amante secreta de su todavía prometido Ottavio y ésta no consigue apartarla del todo de tal idea. Ottavio promete a la burlada desafiar al seductor y hasta se insinúa un comienzo de amor entre ambos.

Don Juan se encuentra a todo esto encantado de «la maestade Ibera», libre y olvidado de sus anteriores pasiones. Isabella le echa en cara su falso proceder, lo desafía espada en mano y hasta empiezan a batirse cuando llega el Comendador, que en ayunas de todo aquello interrumpe la pelea y se lleva a Don Giovanni de huésped a su casa, pues había sido muy amigo de su padre cuando ambos luchaban contra los moros. Es él también quien lo lleva ante Don Alfonso, que maneja la situación diplomáticamente. A solas con él le afea su conducta con Isabella, pero Don Giovanni se excusa por haber tenido que huir de Nápoles tras matar a un ministro del rey, a la vez que niega que la recién llegada sea de veras Isabella. Se presenta ésta acompañada de Ottavio, y su burlador la trata de impostora y de loca. Ella lo abruma de reproches por su abandono, Don Alfonso propone que vayan con el caso al rey e Isabella pide al duque cumpla su promesa de desafío, pero él se soslaya con alegar que es mejor dejarlo todo en manos de «i Numi». Don Alfonso se halla algo confuso y manda a Ottavio seguir a la querellante, para que no cometa algo irremediable.

Con los problemas así aplazados (acto IV), Don Giovanni cena muy amigablemente con el Comendador y su hija. Cuando el padre ha de retirarse, reclamado por graves asuntos de estado, el huésped empieza a requebrar a Donna Anna, hasta confesarle que el motivo de su presencia en Castilla no es otro que la fama de su belleza. Ella se muestra un poco más que reblandecida, pero termina por rechazarlo cuando el otro dice no querer oir nada de casamiento. Don Giovanni entonces intenta forzarla a punta de espada, pero ha de reportarse cuando el Comendador regresa inesperadamente. Es entonces cuando surge el inevitable paso de armas en que el viejo ha de perder la vida. Llega, muy oportuno, Don Alfonso y promete ser un padre para la desconsolada Donna Anna, a la vez que encarga a Ottavio que vaya a arrestar al *fellone*, lo cual tampoco hace. La desdichada termina con un encarecimiento del amor paternal por encima de las falsedades de los amantes, que sólo van en busca de sus placeres.

El acto V transcurre en cierto *Atrio con veri mausolei*, donde se halla la estatua ecuestre que de antes el rey había levantado al Comendador como premio a sus servicios. Don Giovanni soliloquia sobre su sombrío destino, pues no puede sustraerse al imperio de la belleza femenina y habrá de fenecer como víctima de la crueldad de las hembras. Incluso allí va a ser perseguido por la pastora Elisa que, aunque también quejosa, le ofrece liberarlo por unos parientes suyos si la toma por mujer. Sólo que Isabella está asimismo a la escucha y decide frustrar el intento de fuga. En un nuevo altercado se vuelven a acometer espada en mano cuando cae por allí el habitual Don Alfonso, que amonesta por sus delitos a Don Giovanni y le comunica haber sido condenado a muerte por el rey. El reo admite sus culpas, pero alega haber sido vencido de la belleza de Donna Anna, además del calor de los vinos y manjares de la mesa. Su muerte no devolverá la vida al Comendador ni la honra a su hija, con quien ahora se dice dispuesto a desposarse. Don Alonso le promete el perdón si Donna Anna acepta el trato. Llega ésta llorosa y enlutada, pero al escuchar las rendidas palabras de Don Giovanni se vienen abajo todas sus resistencias. Don Alfonso, conmovido, promete un final feliz, mientras ella reconoce su amor al homicida y pide perdón a la sombra de su padre por su mujeril flaqueza. Llega entonces un paje que entrega a Don Alfonso orden del rey de apresar a Don Giovanni por el honor de Isabella y Donna Anna da gracias al cielo de haberla salvado a tiempo, rechazando para siempre a Don Giovanni, que todavía implora su perdón. El culpable vuelve a quedar solo cuando viene por allí el pastor Carino, al que pide auxilio o al menos que le dé muerte. El ofendido pastor se limita a aconsejarle que no pida otra ayuda que la divina, pero Don Giovanni dice haber perdido hace tiempo tal costumbre y estar más dispuesto a invocar a las Furias del Averno, pues ¿acaso «i Dei» no son crueles con él? Se ofrece enloquecido a la venganza del Comendador y de los «Numi spietati», para que manifiesten su poder enviándole un rayo que lo hunda en el infierno para siempre. Cuando así ocurre puntualmente Isabella y Carino enaltecen el castigo sobrenatural, mientras que Don Alfonso celebra que éste se haya anticipado al de los hombres, en provechosa lección para éstos. Isabella y Ottavio parecen encaminados al matrimonio. Y Elisa, desaprensiva integral, se queda compuesta y sin novio, aunque no muy compungida ni, según ella cree, por mucho tiempo.

Italia ha sido claramente decisiva para la expansión extrapeninsular del magno drama teológico tirsiano. Si este *Don Giovanni Tenorio*, estrenado en Venecia para el carnaval de 1736,[1] conquista escasa gloria para Goldoni, no deja de constituir un nódulo digno de tomar en cuenta para la trayectoria mítica del Burlador. Añade además el interés de haber sido objeto de una significativa reflexión que el comediógrafo veneciano ha querido compartir con la posteridad y que constituye uno de los primeros enjuiciamientos del tema. Su introducción *A chi legge* comienza por reconocer su preeminencia en el teatro español como «commedia fortunatissima» que él cree de don Pedro Calderón de la Barca.[2] Menciona como inmediatos antecesores suyos a los

---

[1] La edición de Paperini (1754) la da como representada en el otoño de 1736, pero el testimonio de las *Mémoires* del autor es en esto irrefutable: «...on le donna, sans interruption, jusqu'au mardi gras, et fit la clôture du théâtre» (*Mémoires de M. Goldoni*, ed. Paul de Roux, París, Mercure de France, 1965, p. 164). Para historia bibliográfica y datos de interés general de la obra véase la extensa y bien informada «Nota Storica» de G. O. en *Opere Complete di Carlo Goldoni*, Venecia, Municipio di Venezia, 1926, vol. XXII, pp. 353-360. La pieza fue impresa a partir de 1754 y alcanzó al menos una docena de ediciones durante el siglo XVIII. Su bibliografía moderna puede considerarse iniciada por GEORGE GENDARME DE BÈVOTTE, *La légende de Don Juan. Son évolution dans la littérature des origines au Romantisme*, París, Hachette, 1906, pp. 312-320. Enjuiciamientos diversos de GIOVANNI MACCHIA, *Vita, avventure e morte di Don Giovanni*, Bari, Laterza, 1966, pp. 8-10, y FRANCO FUÀ, *Don Giovanni attraverso le letterature spagnuola e italiana*, Turín, S, Lattes, s.f., pp. 143-146. Ofrece después un resumen de datos literarios DIETMAR RIEGER, 'In Italia seicento e quaranta'. Goldonis Tragikomödie 'Don Giovanni Tenorio' und ihre Stellung in der Don-Juan-Stoffgeschichte», *Italianischen Studien* 11 (1988), 21-38. Comentado también por ANGELICA FORTI-LEWIS, *Maschere, libretti e libertini: il mito di Don Giovanni nel teatro europeo*, Roma, Bulzoni, 1992, pp. 117-121.

[2] *Opere Complete*, XXIII, p. 273. Aunque es más fácil que se trate de un burdo error, es curioso que una versión

que llama «traductores» de éste, el florentino Giacinto Andrea Cicognini (1606-1660) y el hoy desconocido Onofrio Giliberto.[3] Pero lo que sin duda tenía más presente era la *Opera reggia et essemplare* del primero titulada *Il convitato di Pietra,* anterior con toda probabilidad a 1632, de que se hablará más adelante.[4]

Al igual que otros compatriotas, Goldoni se hace una idea muy baja del teatro español, que al mismo tiempo saqueaban a placer.[5] La propia comedia de «Calderón» (de cuyo conocimiento no hay en su *Don Giovanni* el menor indicio) se le ofrecía «piena zeppa d'improprietà, d'inconvenienze». Rechaza, por ejemplo, la indecencia con que una doncella noble da cita a un amante en la oscuridad, así como el papel desairado que allí desempeña el rey de Nápoles. Peor aún le parece la rapidez ilógica con que Don Juan fugitivo y su criado se trasladan por las buenas a España y, tras un supuesto naufragio, llegan a sus playas perfectamente secos, con las pelucas intactas y dispuestos a intercambiar toda suerte de chocarrerías. Goldoni no quiere ocuparse de los despropósitos en que abunda cada escena, para concentrar sus iras sobre el colmo del vaso que es todo aquello de la estatua. Que el pétreo bulto hable y camine, vaya a una cena e invite a su vez a la suya, amenace por un lado y haga milagros por otro es un absurdo intolerable. El final en que todos, «passano vivi e sani in compagnia del Protagonista a casa del Diavolo» (?), mezclando la risa con el terror, entristece a las almas devotas y es objeto de irrisión para los descreídos.

Es de advertir aquí que el problema de Goldoni no proviene tanto de la causa para él perdida del teatro español, como de su perplejidad ante el uso que su maestro y siempre admirado Molière hiciera también de semejante historia. Porque esta vez, viene a decir, el gran dramaturgo se ha pasado de la raya, acentuando hasta el escándalo la impiedad del personaje y mostrándose servil hacia el original es-

---

alternativa de *El burlador de Sevilla* titulada *Tan largo me lo fiáis* aparezca atribuida a Calderón en la única «suelta» conservada. Véase Gerald O. Wade, introducción a Tirso de Molina, *El burlador de Sevilla y Convidado de piedra,* Nueva York, Scribner, 1969, p. 4.

[3] Giacinto Andrea Cicognini, Florencia, 1606-Venecia, 1660, autor de múltiples adaptaciones y refritos dramáticos, principalmente españoles, para la escena italiana. Para reseña de su obra y cronología véase Ludwig Grashey, *Giacinto Andrea Cicogninis Leben und Werke,* Leipzig, A. Deichert, 1909. En cuanto a la pieza de Onofrio Giliberto, se ha perdido por entero su rastro y Goldoni ha debido ser tal vez el último en tenerla en sus manos. Una edición hoy desconocida de 1652 es mencionada por Georges Gendarme de Bévotte, *La légende de Don Juan,* p. 97.

[4] La pieza ofrece indicios inequívocos de dicha deuda. Así, por ejemplo, su virtual irrisión de la entrada del rey de Nápoles con una vela en la mano, que Don Juan le extingue con la espada (*Qui D. Gio: con la spada gli getta la lume, e parte*), acción inexistente en Tirso de Molina. No menos orientadora es la italianización del patronímico *Ulloa* que, algo empinado para una fonética de la otra península, es en Cicognini *Oliola,* y queda visiblemente adaptado como *Lojoa* por Goldoni (es de sospechar que en cruce también con *Loyola*). Comprensiblemente, el comendador don Gonzalo se quedó por esto sin apellido en su descendencia franco-italiana.

[5] Franco Fido, «I drammi spagnoleschi di Carlo Gozzi», en *Italia e Spagna nella cultura del '700,* Roma, Accademia Nazionale dei Lincei, 1992, 63-85.

pañol al conservar el despropósito de la estatua animada. El posterior arreglo de Molière que realiza Thomas Corneille,[6] añade, tampoco ha logrado enmendar después las cosas. Él mismo no se habría atrevido a escribir aquella obra sin el ejemplo de tan ilustre precursor, pero se ha propuesto a la vez enmendarle a fondo la plana, reduciéndolo esta vez a «proprietà maggiore». Su mayor innovación será por eso desautorizar a «Calderón» para acercarse a Molière, haciendo perecer al culpable por el fenómeno natural de un rayo y no abrasado vivo por mano de la estatua de mármol. ¿No hay acaso incontables ejemplos de lo mismo en las «sacre carte»?

La trasnochada crítica de Goldoni no deja de ser valiosa por la franqueza con que sus dedos hurgan en una llaga que ha sido harto real para Molière, antes de serlo para él mismo. Derivando también de Cicognini a través de los refritos dramáticos de ambos *Festin de Pierre* de Dorimon (Nicolas Drouin) y de Villiers (Claude Deschamps),[7] como éstos a su vez de un *scenario* de Domenico Biancolelli estrenado en París en 1657,[8] su *Dom Juan* (1665) permanece hasta el día de hoy como una de las piezas más enigmáticas de su repertorio. Desconectado sin la menor duda del original español,[9] la historia italianizada del burlador sevillano le ha suscitado obvias y previsibles dificultades. Ante aquella plétora de peripecia tragicómica Molière opta por una acción abstracta, en la que tácitamente se rechaza el concepto español (Lope de Vega) de un teatro «representado» en favor del comentario retórico de lo ocurrido fuera de la escena, al modo de la tragedia académica de su tiempo. La línea dramática se ve sustituida por lo que unos llaman mera «succession de tablaux» y otros «a free collage of scenes that undermines any casual linking».[10] Es una técnica que a su vez permite, como contrapeso, la entrada de finos ornamentos episódicos, cual esa escena con el acreedor que a un español le recordaría a Lope de Rueda y sus *Aceitunas*. Molière no sospecha la trascendencia teológica del *Burlador* tirsiano. Había perecido ésta desde el pri-

---

[6] Se suprimía allí la crucial escena del Pobre y se expurgaban otras audacias para, según confiesa el autor, «adoucir certaines expressions qui avaient blessé les scrupuleux». Véase ROBERT HORVILLE, *Dom Juan de Molière. Une dramaturgie de rupture*, París, Larousse, 1972, p. 78.

[7] Editados modernamente por G. GENDARME DE BÉVOTTE, *Le Festin de Pierre avant Molière*, París, Société Nouvelle d'Édition, 1907. Y después, con amplio comentario, por ENEA BALMAS, *Il mito di Don Giovanni nel Seicento francese*, 2 vols., Milán, Cisalpino-La Goliardica, 1977. Observaciones diversas acerca de los mismos en J. W. SMEED, *Don Juan. Variations on a Theme*, Londres y Nueva York, Routledge, 1990.

[8] Estudiado por E. BALMAS, *Il mito di Don Giovanni*, II, pp. 23-45. En 1697 M. de Saint-Evremont abominaba del teatro italiano, cuyos vicios veía reunidos en esta clase de obras: «Leur *Festin de Pierre* feroit mourir de langueur un homme assez patient; et je ne l'ai jamais vû sans souhaiter que l'Auteur fût foudroyé avec son athée» (nota de *L'autore a chi legge* en *Opere Complete*, XXIII, p. 274).

[9] En 1660 una compañía española había representado con éxito en París, pero sin que sobrevivan noticias acerca de su repertorio, que no es fácil incluyera *El burlador de Sevilla*. Véase JACQUES ARNAVON, *Le 'Dom Juan' de Molière*, Copenhague, Gyldendal, 1947, p. 21.

[10] G. GENDARME DE BEVOTTE, *La légende de Don Juan*, p. 171. FRANCO TONELLI, «Molière's 'Dom Juan' and the Space of the Commedia dell'Arte», *Theatre Journal* 37 (1985), p. 441.

mer momento a manos de los refundidores extra-peninsulares, empezando por Cicognini, y es empeo fútil imaginar lo que de otro modo el tema hubiera dado de sí para el gran maestro de la escena francesa. Se sirve por eso de Don Juan como percha en que colgar (reconózcase que de un modo admirable) atrevidos discursos de época en relación tanto con el problema de los libertinos como con la mezquindad del partido o cábala devota, con que de hecho su obra se acerca a prolongar el polémico *Tartuffe*[11] que muy de cerca la precede (1664). La actitud moral de Molière hacia el protagonista es, si se va a ver, ambigua hasta el punto de no tomar ninguna actitud definida,[12] con la imprevista consecuencia de que la obra quedara abierta a ataques desde todo posible ángulo. No menos preocupada viene a ser su correlativa reserva ante los aspectos temáticos del argumento. El desasosiego de Molière se ve culminar, igual que en su discípulo dieciochesco, con el desenlace a cargo de la estatua. Se ha dado en él una intensa perplejidad en que sus instintos de dramaturgo han entrado en conflicto con lo más básico de su educación estética y el resultado es una partida irresuelta hasta el último instante. Molière atenúa incluso la pauta de sus antecesores Dorimon y Villiers para reducir al mínimo la intervención, a pesar de todo crucial, del *convidado de piedra*. Como materialización de dicha reserva ha rondado por el escenario en escenas anteriores la figura alternativa de un Espectro de mujer velada, fundida con una alegoría del Tiempo con su guadaña a cuestas. La intervención de la estatua no está, como en Tirso, planeada desde el primer momento y funciona más bien como el clásico *deus ex machina* que desanuda la acción.[13] Una «sombra» de abolengo mitológico o un *revenant* del otro mundo ha sido claramente contemplado como ejecutor de un desenlace mucho menos comprometedor, pero su papel no pasa al final de enunciar una penúltima advertencia del Cielo. Como quiera que Molière es, al fin, quien es, comprende con acierto que la historia de Don Juan deja de existir sin las escenas finales del macabro convite y la presencia «viviente» de la estatua. El encuentro de ésta es sin embargo casual, inicia ella el «diálogo» al mover la cabeza y violará un decisivo Rubicón cuando alcanza a pronunciar unas palabras, si bien sean para el caso muy pocas. La leyenda definitivamente configurada por Tirso posee una vida propia con que se sobrepone y se halla a prueba de distorsiones como las de Dorimon

---

[11] HERMAN PRINS SALOMON, *Tartuffe devant l'opinion française*, París, Presses Universitaires, 1962. El curso gemelo de ambas obras frente a censuras morales y prohibiciones diversas es reconstruido por J. ARNAVON, *Le Don Juan de Molière*. «La carrière de la pièce» en JACQUES SCHERER, *Sur le Dom Juan de Molière*, París, Société d'Enseignement Supérieur, 1967, 31-38. Y más a fondo que en ambos por R. HORVILLE, *Dom Juan de Molière*.

[12] PAUL BENICHOU, *Morales du Grand Siècle*, París, Gallimard, 1973, p. 284.

[13] «La statue du Commandeur s'explique mieux, chez Tirso, par la reconnaissance du Roi que, chez Molière, par la vanité du Commandeur lui-même», observa JACQUES SCHERER, *Sur le Dom Juan de Molière*, p. 11. Como se recordará, en Molière es el propio Comendador (no el rey) quien había gastado en vida sus caudales para labrarse, un espléndido mausoleo. En Goldoni es una estatua erigida por el rey para estimar los servicios y hazañas de alguien que no desea recompensas en dinero.

y Villiers, en quienes un ingenio como el de Molière ha podido leer muy otros alcances. Con la entrada de lo sobrenatural claudica en la pieza el patrón neoaristotélico, que ha de ceder ante un compromiso de fidelidad a la leyenda, sin la cual caería todo aquello por tierra. Lo importante no es que la estatua rehúse darse al sermoneo, como hace en Dorimon y Villiers, sino que llegue a proferir una sola palabra. Es un triunfo, limitado y hasta cierto punto deontológico (porque el público tiene tiene derecho a *su* estatua), en esa prueba que para todo ejercicio creador es el trance de habérselas con lo elemental de un arte «impuro». *Dom Juan* «est dans nos esprits une des plus impures de nos oeuvres classiques».[14]

Es, por lo mismo, en estos terrenos donde su discípulo italiano se le perfila muy distinto y netamente inferior. Ni el prestigioso ejemplo de Molière le persuadirá a dar cuartel a la estatua, eliminada en favor de un rayo del Cielo, expediente que permite cumplir con el *verisimilis* a la vez que con la ejemplaridad de un designio providencial. Siendo también de advertir que Goldoni, hijo de su siglo, no quiere tampoco penetrar en ningún terreno reconocidamente religioso, sea del color que sea. Equivaldría, claro está, a manejar una materia de algún modo séptica o comprometedora y le parece mucho más elegante desentenderse del Dios cristiano para hablar solamente de «i Dei» o «i Numi», como si todavía maniobrara en los espacios marmóreos de la antigüedad pagana. Conforme al mismo intento no de continuación sino de desguace de una materia mítica, su Don Giovanni pierde todo asomo de complejidad como figura de la transgresión para bordar la de un sujeto indeseable, nunca más fracasado y prosaico que en su desmañadísimo intento de aparecer como víctima del destino en el quinto acto. Constituyen dichas escenas un buen módulo de la completa incapacidad de Goldoni para abordar el lenguaje dramático de la catarsis trágica. Sus medios y fines son de una elemental transparencia: además de las de orden literario hay también razones de buena policia para acabar de una vez con el culpable y por ello insiste en que sepamos que el verdadero título que le envanece dar a su obra no es *Don Giovanni Tenorio*. Menos aún aquel monstruoso marbete de *Il convitato di pietra*, una vez que ha eliminado la estatua del Comendador de Lojoa, cuya vestigial efigie ecuestre es mudo testigo, pero no ejecutora de la justicia divina (o tal vez desdicha contra el cálculo de probabilidades). Su obra se pondrá desde el principio a salvo por no predicar sino la impecable admonición de *Il dissoluto punito*.

Frente a tales consideraciones, Goldoni ha de justificar todavía que tanto él como el gran Moliére cometieran semejante crimen de lesa poesía. Su respuesta no es por salomónica menos digna de atención, viniendo como viene de uno de los grandes en lo que toca al oficio del teatro en todo su esplendor y miseria. Lo que ocurre es, según él, que la historia de Don Juan posee una dinámica propia

---

[14] Jacques Guicharnaud, *Molière, une aventure théâtrale*, París, Gallimard, 1963, p. 178.

que la separa de integrar un argumento dramático como otro cualquiera. Molière se ha dado cuenta de que en aquella comedia «eravi buon capitale» y, aprovechando la experiencia de múltiples versiones francesas e italianas, decide servirse de la misma aunque claro que «variandola nella condotta». La reincidencia goldoniana consistirá por tanto en lo que él cree será radicalizar la misma fórmula, corrigiendo al francés en sus serios tropiezos con la dificultad de la tarea y de modo especial en el escándalo del inaceptable desenlace. En su obra no habrá estatua que salga de repente hablando ni se vaya después a cenar con su homicida. Al contrario que Molière, Goldoni no comprendía que el encuentro a palo seco con la estatua constituía uno de los grandes momentos dramáticos de todos los tiempos,[15] sin el cual no queda de Don Juan sino un nombre vacío.

Dicho «buon capitale» de la materia de Don Juan no es otro que «l'universale invaso dell'allettamento di questa favola», lo cual es lo mismo que decir, de primera intención, el éxito de taquilla. Goldoni ofrece con esto un testimonio inestimable al dar fe de la inaudita y para él inexplicable fidelidad de los públicos en su abrumadora respuesta al reclamo del mero nombre de Don Juan:

> Non si è veduto mai sulle Scene una continuazione d'applauso popolare per tanti anni ad una scenica Rappresentazione, come a questa, lo che faceva gli stessi Comici meravigliare, a segno che alcuni di essi, o per semplicità, o per impostura, solevano dire, che un patto tacito col Demonio manteneva il concorso a codesta sciocca Commedia. In fatti che mai di peggio poteasi vedere rappresentare, e qual altra composizione meritava più di questa negletta?[16]

Goldoni enriquece, a pesar de todo, el discurso crítico del Burlador con uno de sus puntos de sólido y permanente amarre. Para 1736 Don Juan acumulaba ya un siglo largo de presencia triunfal ante los públicos de Italia y de Francia. El *Burlador* tirsiano había sido representado en Nápoles, a poco de su nacimiento, en 1625 y 1626.[17] Su primera descendencia directa vino a cargo de *Il convitato di pietra* del florentino Giacinto Andrea Cicognini, que se representó en Pisa en 1632.[18] Adaptación directa de *El burlador de Sevilla*, falseó ya por completo su espíritu y com-

---

[15] Es aquí de tener en cuenta a Th. Gautier en un comentario de 1847: «La statue du Commandeur produit un effet d'épouvante qu'on n'a pas surpassé au théâtre... aucune tragédie n'arrive à cette intensité d'effroi» (R. HORVILLE, *Dom Juan de Molière*, p. 87).

[16] *Opere Complete*, XXIII, p. 272.

[17] ALFREDO RODRÍGUEZ LÓPEZ-VÁZQUEZ, «Sobre la argumentación en torno a la autoría sobre 'El burlador de Sevilla'», en *El mito de Don Juan*, «Cuadernos de Teatro Clásico», 2 (1988), p. 99.

[18] La dependencia de Tirso es enfocada por diversos autores, entre los cuales G. GENDARME DE BÉVOTTE, *La légende de Don Juan*, 97-103; J. W. SMEED, *Don Juan*, pp. 5-6; A. FORTI-LEWIS, *Maschere, libretti e libertini*, pp. 75-80. En especial es ahora cuidadosamente estudiada por LAURA DOLFI, «La fortuna del 'Burlador de Sevilla': sobre el 'Convitato di pietra' de Cicognini», *Revista Estudios* 189-190 (abril-septiembre, 1995), 87-106, y «Tirso e Cicognini: due Don Giovanni a confronto», en *La festa teatrale ispanica*, Nápoles, Istituto Universitario Orientale, 1995, 129-162. Su primera edicion fechada es de 1671, aunque se tiene noticia de otras anteriores perdidas. He manejado una edición seicentesca sin fecha de la Houghton Library (Universidad de Harvard).

pite respecto a anticipo cronológico con una complicada serie de *scenari* de *Commedia dell'arte* demasiado compleja para ser aquí resumida.[19] Lo importante es el dato de su vivir desde el primer momento en olor de multitudes, pues el mismo Cicognini habla de una previa representación en Florencia donde su obra «piacque fuor di modo».[20] Su logro no puede ser en sí más pobre, reducido como se halla a un apresurado *abstract* dramático, donde se entrometen de mala manera diversos personajes de *Commedia dell'Arte* y el huero sucesor de Catalinón (aquí Passarino) prodiga salidas arlequinescas, con las inevitables chuscadas y *lazzi* gastronómicos a base de macarrones.

Por encima de sus pretensiones académicas, Goldoni conocía de primera mano la sugestión avasalladora de Don Juan. De modo curioso, el duro censor se había nutrido inicialmente de relieves y platos de segunda mesa del teatro español. Es en sus *Mémoires*, donde habla con aún mayor desprecio de aquella «mauvaise pièce», confiesa también el deleite con que en su primera niñez había sido estimulado precisamente por Cicognini a realizar su primer experimento dramático: «Parmi les auteurs comiques que je lisais et relisais très souvent, Ciccognini était celui que je preferais... je l'étudiai beaucoup; et à l'age de huit ans, j'eus la témérité de crayonner une comédie».[21] Pocos años después hizo un viaje por mar con una bullanguera tropa de cómicos, cuyo director se había hecho famoso por una desgracia en el papel de Don Juan en *Le festin de Pierre*.[22] Sus recuerdos de anciano se ratifican una vez más en atestiguar el gancho poco menos que diabólico de aquellas mediocres obras:

Tout le monde connaît cette mauvaise pièce, que les Italiens appellent *Il convitato di pietra*, et les Français le *Festin de Pierre*. Je l'ai toujours regardée, à Italie, avec horreur, et je ne pouvais pas concevoir comment cette farce ayait pu se soutenir pendant si longtemps, attirer le monde en foule et faire les délices d'un pays policé.[23]

Claro que su *Dissoluto punito* y su Don Juan «riformato» por poco lo dejan en la estacada. El público veneciano, nos dice, se desconcertaba con aquel Don Juan tan atildado y de no ver aparecer por allí a Arlequín con sus habituales bufonadas. Claro que a cambio gozaba con creces con el episodio de Carino y Elisa, cuya infiel pastora, reservada a la excelente actriz Elisabetta Passalacqua, era puesta por Goldoni a representar el secreto a voces de las infidelidades en que éste, como amante, la había más de una vez sorprendido. «L'anecdote releva la pièce» y la obra quedó a

---

[19] Ahora por primera vez fácilmente asequibles gracias a MARCELLO SPAZIANI, *Don Giovanni dagli scenari dell'Arte alla 'Foire'. Qattro studi con due testi 'forains' inediti e altri testi italiani e francesi*, Roma, Edizioni di Storia e Letteratura, 1978.

[20] L. DOLFI, «Tirso e Cicognini», p. 120.

[21] *Mémoires de M. Goldoni*, p. 33.

[22] *Mémoires*, p. 47.

[23] *Mémoires*, p. 163.

salvo por el inaudito desparpajo de la cómica obligada a representarse a sí misma. «Mon Don Juan augmentait tous le jours de crédit et de concours; on le donna, sans interruption, jusquíau mardi gras, et il fit la clotûre du théatre».[24] ¿Cabe un más feliz remate de temporada?

Fueron también, como se sabe, cómicos italianos los que introdujeron a Don Juan en Francia. Lo mantuvieron siempre como una de las bases de su repertorio parisino y es de nuevo su invariable éxito de público el que levanta el rastro que conduce primero a los *Festin de Pierre* de la pareja Dorimon (1659) y Villiers (1660) y después al *Dom Juan* de Molière.[25] Se ha señalado también de siempre cómo éste ha recurrido a la habitual póliza de seguro para colmar el bache y dar trabajo a su compañía tras la prohibición de *Tartuffe* un año antes.[26] Buen conocedor además de Cicognini, a quien puso en verso su *Don García de Navarra* (1661),[27] sigue en febrero de 1665 la receta ya habitual para la temporada previa al cierre pascual de los espectáculos. Si tales consideraciones son perfectamente admisibles, no dejan de resultar a la vez reductoras frente a otras mucho más significativas porque, aparte de móviles interesados, Don Juan se había personificado en los escenarios parisinos con un vibrante desafío a la atención de un dramaturgo de primer orden. Tras la intensa granizada de Don Juanes (italianos, Dorimon, Villiers) se daba un claro estímulo o pique profesional para no permanecer silencioso. Don Juan estaba allí dando voces al frente de los públicos y, lo mismo que para Goldoni, debía perfilársele como un personaje «invasor». Por su intrínseca naturaleza de lo que hoy reconocemos como fenómeno en parte extra-literario, es sólo de imaginar la punzante incitación que aquel producto todavía marcado por los recios sabores de su cocina española debía de representar para el ingenio de Molière. Si las masas se entregaban, ingenuas, al imperio del burlador Don Juan, también los autores cedían a su tentación, deslumbrados por la promesa de un «buon capitale» que embolsillar, a costa de aquella herejía literaria, más allá también de una simple cuestión de monedas.

Con su *Dom Juan*, Molière ha cuajado una pieza ambigüamente disputada por simultáneo rechazo y fascinación cara a un problema dramático que no le ha cabido ignorar ni posponer, lo cual es ya de loar como acto de valentía. Si acepta el desafío creador de Don Juan es por hallarse en el zenith de su ca-

---

[24] *Mémoires*, p. 164.

[25] Habría éste de reencarnarse todavía en *Le nouveau Festin de Pierre ou l'Athée foudroyé* de Rosimond (1670) y la refundición de Molière con *Le Festin de Pierre* de Thomas Corneille (1677). En total, con Dorimon y Villiers y sin contar con la «prehistoria» de sus piezas italianas, cinco *Festines* en menos de veinte años de vida teatral parisina.

[26] J. ARNAVON, *Le Dom Juan de Molière*, p. 9 y ss. Enjuiciamiento más matizado de R. HORVILLE, *Dom Juan de Molière*, p. 40.

[27] Basado en *Le gelosie fortunate del prencipe Roderigo*. Véase L. GRASEY, *Giacinto Andrea Cicognini*, pp. 37-38.

rrera y por la oportunidad de iniciar con él un camino propio, auspiciado por su *Tartuffe* de 1664, que debido a circunstancias no llegó a realizarse del todo.[28] Es lógico que a la vez se le planteara, inevitable, la necesidad de podar la tradición de lo que para él parecían excesos, empezando por el de mujeres, que distan de ser en su *Dom Juan* la clase de presencia sensual que asumen en Tirso.[29] Se corría con todo esto el riesgo de ahogar en su raíz al legendario personaje, que es el escollo en que había de naufragar Goldoni. Tras lo que debe haberle costado no poca perplejidad reflexiva, Molière no va a extender tampoco un cheque en blanco a aquel advenedizo ultrapirenaico (aunque continuara la deformación material de presentarlo como siciliano). Guardando su distancia, no le abre su puerta sino después de atarlo en corto para hacerlo jugar en sus propios términos y no en los de aquellos sombríos españoles ni de los despreocupados italianos. La empresa es dificultosa, porque Don Juan no resulta fácil de domesticar: o es un huracán incontenible o no es nada y el tino de Molière ha estado en comprender dónde estaban los límites infranqueables. El personaje no es uno de tantos aristócratas libertinos, sino alguien que ha desarrollado una peculiar y única relación adversaria con lo divino y al que sólo puede hacer justicia (poética y teológica) una *eigene Todt* de orden sobrenatural. Molière deja atrás sus meandros para redescubrir la naturaleza mítica de Don Juan o, dicho en otras palabras, llegar por fin al punto de partida de Tirso. Por eso, en el momento decisivo, la estatua justiciera no va a faltar a su cita no sólo con Don Juan, sino con las multitudes de entonces y de ahora.

Los casos de Molière y Goldoni son particularmente útiles en su triangulación respecto al *Burlador* de Tirso, porque nos hallamos en ausencia casi absoluta de datos acerca de su inmediata recepción en España. No habrá dificultad, a la vista de cuanto antecede, para deducir que el personaje capaz de agitar de tal modo las aguas lejos de la península fuera a ser menos dentro de ella. La crítica reciente ha rastreado diversos aspectos relativos a trasmisión del texto, presencia posterior de reelaboraciones, etc. como prueba indirecta de un fuerte impacto sobre el público.[30] Más aún, se ha llegado a proponer una relación de causa a efecto entre el estreno de *El burlador de Sevilla* a comienzos del reinado de Felipe IV y el destierro de la corte impuesto a Tirso de Molina por la Junta de Reformación en 1625.[31] La clave se halla en la devastadora crítica del sistema de privados, tras la consolidación del Conde-duque de Olivares como ministro omnipotente. Tirso la proyecta a tra-

---

[28] Básicamente de acuerdo en esto con algunas tesis de R. HORVILLE, *Dom Juan de Molière*, 9».Une structure éclatée».

[29] Ver, entre otros estudios, el más reciente de SUSANA PENDZICK, «Female Presence in the 'Burlador de Sevilla'», *Bulletin of the Comediantes* 47 (1995), 165-182.

[30] FRANCISCO MÁRQUEZ VILLANUEVA, *Orígenes y elaboración de 'El burlador de Sevilla'*, Universidad de Salamanca, 1996, pp. 162-163.

[31] F. MÁRQUEZ VILLANUEVA, «La condena moral de la privanza», en *Orígenes y elaboración*, 153-157.

vés de Don Juan, cuya impunidad ante la justicia terrena fuerza la mano de la divina. Aparte de la preñez de cuestiones de orden religioso y moral que el personaje trae consigo, su capacidad de grabarse a fuego en los públicos revestía de especial gravedad a cualquier tipo de discurso que con él pudiera asociarse. Don Juan va por el mundo pidiendo guerra, y hasta Lorenzo da Ponte introdujo en su *Don Giovanni* un himno a la libertad de inequívoco significado en 1787. Es justo lo ocurrido también con Molière, cuyo cauteloso *Dom Juan* hubo de ser apeado por orden superior del cartel tras una quincena de representaciones[32] y desapareció de los escenarios franceses hasta 1841. La nota allí imperante terminaba por ser la problemática actitud del autor hacia su criatura, e igual que la obra de Tirso dio paso a las diluidas versiones de Antonio de Zamora (*No hay plazo que no se cumpla*) y de Alonso de Córdoba y Maldonado (*La venganza en el sepulcro*), su *Dom Juan* hubo de sobrevivir, sobre la escena, en la versión empobrecida de Thomas Corneille, que ni aun así complacía a Goldoni. Los respectivos *Don Juan* de Tirso y Molière son al menos idénticos en su calidad de obras creadas a tal altura que sus contemporáneos han de atraerlas por los pies a su propio nivel. El Burlador sevillano, como figura de la transgresión y cumbre universal de la figura primaria del *trickster*, bastaba para inducir a su alrededor un clima de molesta inquietud. En 1632 Giacopo Cicognini lamentaba que su hijo Giacinto se hubiera apresurado a representar su *Convitato di pietra* en Pisa, imprudencia que no añadiría a su reputación, pues por ella «li daranno gran tara nella sua professione».[33]

A Molière ciertamente se la dieron. Si por largo tiempo dómines y almas pacatas se mostraron suspicaces, cuando no hostiles a Molière por su escurridizo *Dom Juan*, fueron con todo menos negativos y persistentes que los del oficio de la pluma hasta vísperas del siglo XIX y aun después.[34] En 1739 Voltaire denunciaba allí el eco de lo peor de España y de Italia, verdadero catálogo de monstruosidades y dechado negativo de un teatro condenablemente «irregular»:

L'on ne se révolta point contre le monstrueux assemblage de bouffonnerie et de religion, de plaisanterie et díhorreur, ni contre des prodiges extravagants qui sont le sujet de cette Pièce, une statue qui marche et qui parle, et les flammes de l'Enfer qui engloutissent un impie sur le Théâtre díArlequin, ne souleverent point les esprits, soit qu'en effet il y ait dans cette Pièce quelqu'interêt, soit que le jeu des Comédiens l'embellit, vit plûtôt que le peuple à qui le Festin de Pierre plaît beaucoup plus qu'aux honnêtes gens, aime cette espéce de merveilleux.[35]

---

[32] Medió para su retirada lo que se ha llamado «une interdiction discrète» a raíz de muchas sordas censuras (R. HORVILLE, *Dom Juan de Molière*, p. 45).

[33] M. SPAZIANI, *Don Giovanni, dagli scenari dell'Arte alla «Foire»*, p. 16.

[34] HENRY LAGRAVE, «Don Juan au siècle des lumières», en *Mélanges offerts à Jean Fabre*, París, Klincksieck, 1974, p. 258. Igualmente el recorrido histórico de la crítica efectuado por R. HORVILLE, *Le Dom Juan de Molière*.

[35] VOLTAIRE, *Vie de Molière, avec des jugements sur ses ouvrages*, París, Prault Fils, 1739, p. 69-70. Texto reproducido por R. HORVILLE, *Le Dom Juan de Molière*, pp. 82-83.

Goldoni se ha guiado hasta la minucia por los criterios de la pleamar neoclásica de los mismos años. Fue la capacidad de la prosa para herir los oídos de los espectadores con «i sentimenti poco onesti, le massime temerarie, le pericolose proposizioni» lo que le persuadió a preferir allí el verso, contra el ejemplo en esto del maestro, pues «per dir vero non si può senza nausea leggere alcune Scene di Don giovanni nel *Festin de Pierre* di Molière medesimo». Frente a esto, Goldoni pondrá por delante la autocensura, que tan poco le ha costado, de ceñirse «all'onesto piacere degli autori discreti, ed alle Cristiane massime di questo Serenissimo pio Governo, che niuna opera lascia correre sulle scene, che riveduta prima non sia, e da ogni scandalo e da ogni disonestà rigorosamente purgata».[36] Goldoni, en efecto, no tuvo que sufrir por este lado otra consecuencia que la caída de su obra en un completo olvido por parte de los públicos.

Todo el problema aquí enfocado es reductible, más allá de una perspectiva diacrónica, al caso abstracto del choque frontal de una literatura no ya culta, sino más que nunca académica, con la realidad primigenia de una materia mítica. Se contempla una auténtica experiencia de laboratorio, un choque frontal de integrales opuestos y la idea, por ejemplo, de Voltaire tratando de hacer carrera con Don Juan basta para resultar de por sí regocijante. El incómodo personaje sale incólume de todos los exorcismos críticos y la estatua del Comendador es a la letra «piedra» de escándalo en el poder dramático de su presencia material en las tablas, ante la que nada tenían que decir los pedantes clasificadores de situaciones dramáticas.

El dato inconmovible en todo este discurso es la fidelidad y avidez de los públicos ante la figura de Don Juan, a prueba de autores buenos y malos para gritarle a la literatura que el fenómeno humano marcha a la vez por delante y a la zaga de ella. Villiers se excusa de abordar aquel tema a petición de su propia *troupe*, deseosa de medro económico, y de complacerla al amparo de que los ignorantes superan con mucho en número a los que de veras entienden el arte del teatro,[37] anticipándose a Voltaire en el superficial argumento. La gacetilla previa al estreno del *Dom Juan* recordaba el «effroyable *Festin de Pierre* si fameux par toute la terre» y la promesa de éxito de la materia «qui réussissait si bien sur le théâtre italien».[38] El autor veneciano Carlo Gozzi se maravillaba en 1773 de la capacidad de cualquier engendro donjuanesco para hacer dinero muy por encima de obras para él mucho más respetables.[39] El inalterado curso autónomo de Don Juan se perfila incomprensible para los encuadres oficiales de la época y Goldoni interesa por ser el primero en plantear con franqueza un problema que, por supuesto, no acertará a resolver.

---

[36] *Opere Complete*, XXIII, p. 276.

[37] «Mais enfin, mes Compaignons assez mediocrement soigneux de sa reputation, l'ont souhaitté de moy, dans l'opinion qu'ils ont euë que le nombre des Ignorans surpassant de beaucoup celuy de ces qui se connoissent aux Ouvrages de Theatre...». (G. DE BÉVOTTE, *Le Festin de Pierre avant Molière*, p. 153).

[38] R. HORVILLE, *Dom Juan de Molière*, p. 43.

[39] G. O., «Nota storica», *Opere complete di Carlo Goldoni*, XXIII, p. 354.

No llegaba a tanta sinceridad el mismo Voltaire, cuya excomunión de *Dom Juan* va de hecho desmentida por el simple hecho de discutirlo entre las obras señeras del maestro. No le es posible tampoco ignorar el memorable impacto de sus contadas representaciones, que pretende atribuir a virtuosismo del cuadro de actores. Claro que su olfato de viejo zorro le dice a la vez de una presencia inquietante de algo que para él no tiene claramente un nombre y que por comodidad cubrirá bajo una locución indefinida. Es ese «quelqu'intérêt» donde por supuesto yace el *quid* del problema, es decir el campo en que hoy trabajamos y en el que sus prejuicios le impedían ponerse a escarbar. El burlador Don Juan tiene un gran enemigo en la academia y un gran aliado en el pueblo.

Nótese que son condiciones opuestas a las que habían hecho posible el inicial Don Juan de Tirso. No fue éste quien, contra lo tantas veces repetido, fundiera la historia del *trickster* transgresor con la del convite sacrílego, porque ese paso había sido ya dado en el siglo XIV por una leyenda popular sevillana y de mucho antes de Tirso Don Juan tenía incluso fuera de España una reputación proverbial.[40] Los supuestos culturales del teatro español favorecían, en vez de obstaculizar, una mutua fecundación de literatura y pueblo inconcebible en Italia o Francia. La integración de lo sobrenatural en un espacio tragicómico es un grave problema para Molière,[41] pero en Tirso y en casi todo el teatro español el acercamiento de Cielo y Tierra se produce con espontánea naturalidad. Un teólogo profesional como Tirso de Molina (fray Gabriel Téllez) no hacía nada especial ni insólito al infundir en la cruda leyenda popular una tesis con aplicaciones permanentes para la eterna cuestión, no sólo religiosa, de la libertad humana. Conforme al *dictum* de Lope en su *Arte nuevo de hacer comedias* (1609) la musa cómica aceptaba como un hecho físico la soberanía inapelable del público que las mantiene económicamente a flote. Se partía en España justo de lo que estos autores francoitalianos consideraban una claudicación que había que recortar todo lo posible. Su resultado, lejos de ningún envilecimiento del arte, era una eficaz liberación de éste, como tampoco un puro fenómeno comercial, porque autores y público sabían conllevarse en un equilibrio de mutua guía educadora. Lo mismo en el terreno estético que en el moral o religioso, el corral era mucho más sabio que las academias y mucho menos gazmoño también. La rígida ortodoxia española podía reconciliarse con Don Juan, haciéndolo trabajar para ella en un plano de gran sutileza, que tanto dista de los aspavientos y largas pinzas con que se le maneja fuera de la Península. Tirso tropezó quizás con políticos (y con harto motivo) pero no con Aristarcos ni con inquisidores. El

---

[40] Sobre su pronta documentación, precisamente sobre suelo italiano, FRANCISCO MÁRQUEZ VILLANUEVA, «Nueva visión de la leyenda de Don Juan», *Aureum Saeculum Hispanum. Festschrift für Hans Flasche*, Wiesbaden, Franz Steiner Verlag, 1983, 204-216.

[41] J. GUICHARNAUD, *Molière, une aventure théâtrale*, p. 285. Se impone discrepar aquí de la contraria opinión relativa a Tirso enunciada por AMÉRICO CASTRO, «El Don Juan de Tirso y el de Molière como personajes barrocos», *Hommage à Ernest Martinenche*, París, Éditions d'Astrey, 1939, p. 97.

empaque sin engolamientos de *El burlador de Sevilla*, restallante de vigor mental y de colorido humano, vale también por un canto efectivo a la libertad creadora.

Don Juan ha sido pues una prueba, claro está que «de fuego», para la brújula interna de las respectivas literaturas. Desde el primer momento, Europa no quiso saber ya nada de su esencial vena teológica y fue algo más que casualidad el que su configuración tirsiana no tuviera ecos directos, ni se le permitiera cruzar ninguna frontera sin un previo recortarle las alas. Después de tanto hablar de Inquisición etc., resulta que Tirso servía un vino demasiado fuerte para gustos extrapeninsulares. Hasta Cicognini lo aguaba como podía al presentar a Isabella como «sforzata» y no como impúdica, lo mismo que su Don Juan debía comparecer al final para una última prédica con que remachar su caída no sólo en los infiernos, sino al nivel de mero *exemplum*. Ni Molière ni Goldoni se atrevieron a traer a escena la persona misma del príncipe, que Tirso saca en paños menores, ni a plantear en forma directa el menor problema político. Aun así, el *Dom Juan* del primero sonó en conjunto, como se sabe, a transgresivo y el haberse apartado de lo aristotélico contribuyó sin duda a la sorda reacción contra el mismo.[42] La obra, como se sabe, desapareció de la escena, no fue impresa en vida de su autor y su texto incluso estuvo a punto de perderse.[43] Parece como si la presencia material de Don Juan y su leyenda estuviera hecha de encargo para sonar como un manifiesto subversivo, lo mismo que para emanar una inefable aura liberadora. Es a su amparo como pudo surgir en el espacio dramático de Molière la compleja interacción dual entre Don Juan y Sganarelle, que algún día habrá que estudiar (*mutatis mutandis*) como un eco inteligente de la de Don Quijote-Sancho. Era preciso tomar precauciones contra aquel gran salteador literario que, más allá de un simple terreno preceptivo, determinó una avanzadilla de innovación e irregularidad, en cuanto *limes* experimental para el teatro francés. El mejor hombre de Francia, en el gran momento clásico de ésta, no puede ir más allá, con todo, de una cartesiana suspensión de juicio sobre la complejidad del Burlador. No era un acto de entrega al personaje, pero sí de respetuoso interés en la legítima esencia de éste. Cuantos venimos de Tirso de Molina tenemos de momento gran dificultad para comprender que el esquemático *Dom Juan* de Molière pueda aparecer proclamado, en el *hic et nunc* de su circunstancia ultrapirenaica, como apertura liberadora hacia un nuevo concepto de orden

---

[42] D. C. POTTS, «'Dom Juan' and Non-Aristotelian Drama», en *Molière: Stage and Study. Essays in Honour of W. G. Moore*, Oxford, Clarendon Press, 1973, p. 61. Véase el apartado «Liberté des formes» en J. SCHERER, *Sur le Dom Juan de Molière*, pp. 39-50. Sobre la lucha de Molière con las unidades en su *Dom Juan*, GIOVANNI MACCHIA, *Vita, avventure e morte di Don Giovanni*, Bari, Laterza, 1966, p. XVIII. F. Tonelli considera a la obra como el más amplio repudio de lo neoaristotélico en todo el teatro clásico francés («Molière's 'Dom Juan'», p. 441). Señala la capacidad de Don Juan para captar las proyecciones político-culturales de los medios literarios en que se gesta A. FORTI-LEWIS, *Maschere, libretti e libertini,*, p. 24. Se trata por lo demás, de un aspecto de la innata capacidad proteica de Don Juan, bien conocida de los críticos españoles (F. MÁRQUÉZ VILLANUEVA, *Génesis y elaboración*, p. 113).

[43] R. HORVILLE, *Dom Juan de Molière*, «Les avatars du texte», pp. 67-74.

extra-académico.[44] Son consideraciones todas muy básicas, pero que examinadas de cerca tienden a persuadir de la insularidad e independencia que desde principio al fin sellaron de modernidad la magna provincia de nuestro teatro. Un precoz fenómeno nacional y castizo, donde el neoaristotelismo, nominalmente acatado, reina pero no gobierna. Los españoles, por supuesto, necesitamos profundizar mucho más en nuestra propia literatura.

En Italia Don Juan continuará siendo uno de los juguetes preferidos de su *commedia dell arte*, pero ésta es una brillante esfera hueca, hipotecada a la excelencia interpretativa e impermeable para ningún concepto moderno del drama.[45] Goldoni seguía, al publicar sus *Mémoires* en 1787, en el mismo punto muerto de 1736. Su *Don Giovanni Tenorio* cuenta como un nuevo intento trivializador por la vía de una desmitificación que de hecho termina, por acercamiento de extremos, en casi la misma caricatura de los cómicos callejeros, que al menos tenían alguna gracia. Su obra no puede admitir un personaje como el Burlador y tampoco es cierto que la deliciosa Mirandolina pueda contar como un Don Juan femenino.[46] La atrevida crítica que Goldoni realiza del relativamente indeciso *Dom Juan* de Molière es por entero sintomática del atrincheramiento académico italiano contra toda apertura a la modernidad hasta el mismo advenimiento del Romanticismo. La estrafalaria ocurrencia, por ejemplo, de presentar a Isabella en duelo a espada con Don Juan no figura allí por simple desacierto, sino por gravitación de las heroínas combatientes de la épica culta ariostesca. Contra tanto especular culturalista con la idea de un Don Juan ligado al Renacimiento, una literatura por entero fundida con un manierismo humanístico realiza por mano de Goldoni un acto de sabotaje con que parar en seco el avance del mito.

Pero aunque el teatro popular italiano redujera la cena con la estatua a un mero resorte escénico, los públicos sin duda seguían viendo allí algo más,[47] porque el fenómeno mítico no debía nada a la Inquisición como tampoco a la Academia, ni era patrimonio exclusivo de tétricos españoles. Su «buon capitale» seguía mostrándose, como la bolsa del judío errante, inagotable y el periplo extra-hispano de Don Juan en el siglo XVIII es buena confirmación de hasta qué punto «myth is a stronger thing than formal literature».[48] El personaje burlador continuó su jornada italiana a través de un espeso tejido de revisiones y semiplagios, *scenari*, es-

---

[44] Véanse juicios como los de Jules Lemaître y (1886) y Coquelin (1904) en R. HORVILLE, *Dom Juan de Molière*, pp. 94-95 y 97.

[45] Como enjuicia F. TONELLI, la *Commedia dell'arte* no utilizó a Don Juan como una historia de moda, sino como «a mode of theatrical representation», con desenlace de *lazzo* infernal («Molière's 'Dom Juan'», pp. 445 y 446). Las adaptaciones del teatro español eran allí un cambio total de sistemas dramáticos (p. 451). Sobre la incapacidad de la *Commedia dell'Arte* para dar entrada a aspectos religiosos y morales, A. FORTI-LEWIS, *Maschere, libretti e libertini*, p. 70.

[46] F. FUÀ, *Don Giovanni attraverso le letterature spagnuola e italiana*, p. 144.

[47] Será preciso discrepar aquí de A. FORTI-LEWIS, *Maschere, libretti e libertini*, p. 83.

[48] C. S. LEWIS, *The Allegory of Love. A Study in Medieval Tradition*, Nueva York, Oxford UP, 1958, p. 120.

pectáculos musicales y modestas *burattinate*.[49] Salpicaduras y arrastres diversos de Goldoni llegaron hasta el mismo *Don Giovanni* de Lorenzo da Ponte,[50] inane como drama pero excelente como *libretto* (son categorías diversas), y que por lo mismo no prescindirá de la estatua ni del fuego infernal. Con él, y favorecido por el soplo divino de Mozart, el mito originalmente sevillano ascendía a una reencarnación no italiana ni española, sino inmortal y universalista.

[49] Véase DENAH LIDA, «Don Juan en Italia en el siglo XVIII,» Nueva Revista de Filología Hispánica, 40 (1992), pp. 707-17.

[50] Tales ecos son reconocibles, entre otros, en las escenas de reconciliación entre Zerlina y Masetto (I, III), claramente en repetición de las seducciones de Elisa en que triunfaba la Passalacqua (II, VII y VIII). El «mi trema il cor» (III, V) de Isabella será también después el «mi trema un poco il cor» de Zerlina (I, III). Estrictamente paralelas son también las escenas en que Don Giovanni trata de presentar las quejas de Isabella como desvaríos de una loca (III, X ante Don Alfonso y V, II ante Elisa) y «la povera ragazza / e pazza, amici miei» (I, II). Donna Anna, «un empio, un traditore» (IV, III) y Donna Elvira en Goldoni, «è un empio, è un traditore» (II, I). Admite la relación con GOLDONI G. MACCHIA, *Vita, avventure e morte di Don Giovanni*, p. 32.

CHARLES C. RUSSELL

LORENZO DA PONTE'S *DON GIOVANNI*

Mozart offered *Le nozze di Figaro* to Vienna in May 1786. Although the occasion was moderately successful, far more so was a new production in Prague towards the end of the year. When Mozart visited that city in January of 1787, he was delighted to find that people there were singing nothing but *Figaro*. Delighted, too, was Pasquale Bondini, impresario of the Prague theater where *Figaro* was playing. Bondini immediately commissioned Mozart to create a new work for the fall. When Mozart returned to Vienna, he went straight to the librettist who had prepared the *Figaro* text, Lorenzo Da Ponte, and asked him for a new text. Da Ponte suggested to Mozart the well known story of Don Juan, a topic that, Da Ponte later claimed, "infinitamente gli piacque".[1]

There were probably several reasons why Da Ponte suggested this particular story. It had been popular for more than a hundred and fifty years. For a century and a half it had proved itself easily able to draw audiences into the theater, and it was still doing so in prose versions, as ballet and, especially in the last decade or so, as opera. He had no reason to doubt its continuing appeal. Da Ponte also had a penchant for the comic genre, as a perusal of a list of his works will show, and he rightly considered the Don Juan tale as part of a long comic tradition. Thirdly, like most educated men, he would have known the story and its details well; the tale was part of his cultural baggage. Pressed as he happened to be at that moment by various other theatrical commitments, he would not have had to lose time trying to invent something entirely new. And lastly, he already had in his possession the libretto of a new Don Juan opera, *Don Giovanni o sia Il convitato di pietra*, that only a few months earlier had opened a successful run in Venice, in February of that same year, 1787. The music was by Giuseppe Gazzaniga, the libretto by Giovanni Bertati.

Da Ponte was in fact strapped for time. He had recently accepted a commission to prepare two other librettos for several composer friends: *Tarar* for Antonio Sa-

---

[1] L. DA PONTE, *Memorie e altri scritti*, Cesare Pagnini ed., Milan, Longanesi, 1971, p. 189.

lieri and *L'arbore di Diana* for Vicente Martìn y Soler. Yet he readily agreed to work with Mozart too, supremely confident in his ability to prepare three librettos simultaneously. He boasted of his undertaking to the emperor, Joseph II:

> L'informai che mia intenzione era di far queste tre opere contemporaneamente. "Non ci riuscirete"! mi rispose egli. "Forse che no", replicai; "ma mi proverò. Scriverò la notte per Mozzart [*sic*] e farò conto di legger l'*Inferno* di Dante. Scriverò la mattina per Martini e mi parrà di studiar il Petrarca. La sera per Salieri e sarà il mio Tasso". Trovò assai bello il mio parallelo; e, appena tornato a casa, mi posi a scrivere. Andai al tavolino e vi rimasi dodici ore continue. Una bottiglietta di "tockai" a destra, il calamaio nel mezzo, e una scatola di tabacco di Siviglia a sinistra. Una bella giovinetta di sedici anni (ch'io avrei voluto non amare che come figlia, ma...) stava in casa mia con sua madre, ch'aveva la cura della famiglia, e venia nella mia camera a suono di campanello, che per verità io suonava assai spesso, e singolarmente quando mi pareva che l'estro cominciasse a raffreddarsi: ella mi portava or un biscottino, or una tazza di caffè, or niente altro che il suo bel viso, sempre gaio, sempre ridente e fatto appunto per inspirare l'estro poetico e le idee spiritose. [...] La prima giornata frattanto, tra il "tockai", il tabacco di Siviglia, il caffè, il campanello e la giovine musa, ho scritte le due prime scene del *Don Giovanni*, altre due dell'*Arbore di Diana* e più di metà del primo atto del *Tarar*, titolo da me cambiato in *Assur*. Portai la mattina queste scene a' tre compositori, che appena volevan credere che fosse possibile quello che cogli occhi propri leggevano, e in sessantatrè giorni le due prime opere erano finite del tutto, e quasi due terzi dell'ultima.[2]

What Da Ponte fails to mention in this passage is that the first two scenes of *Don Giovanni*, those completed in one day only, were more or less directly copied from Bertati's libretto and that the rest of Bertati's text also served as an outline for much of the rest of Da Ponte's. In his defense, it should be kept in mind that what he did was sanctioned by tradition. If he copied from Bertati, Bertati in turn had copied at length from a play by Carlo Goldoni, *Don Giovanni o sia Il dissoluto*, first performed in 1736, and had borrowed the figure of Elvira from Molière's *Dom Juan* of 1665. Molière himself took heavily from two French contemporaries, Dorimond and Villiers. They for their part lifted the matter of their plays, both entitled *Le Festin de Pierre ou Le fils criminel*, from the Italian *commedia dell'arte*, which probably appropriated its reading of the text from an earlier Italian version by the popular Florentine playwright Giacinto Andrea Cicognini, who elaborated his version of the tale around 1630. His elaboration depended on a Spanish play by Tirso de Molina, *El burlador de Sevilla*, that dated from the second or third decade of the seventeenth century. Tirso de Molina's was the first literary version of the story; he based his work on Spanish folk tales.

Whether Da Ponte was acquainted or not with any of these versions, and there were many others as well, is hard to say. He had probably never read the Spanish

[2] *Ibid.*, pp. 189-90.

play, and it is doubtful that he was familiar with the angular and humorless French Don Juans of Dorimond or Villiers. Whether he had read Molière's great comedy in its original form or knew only the reflection of it in Bertati's libretto is perhaps still open to question. In general, he seems to have been most acquainted with the rather lighthearted Italian tradition, most versions of which bore the title *Il convitato di pietra*: those by Cicognini, by the *commedia dell'arte*, an opera libretto or two, and the popular puppet interpretations he could have seen while living in Venice.

When Da Ponte set about preparing his version, the story already had a long and successful history. Everybody knew it. It was not generally identified with any particular writer. The tale was in public domain, the narrative belonged to everyone. But precisely because it was everyone's, it was perhaps not wise for an author to change it. Audiences expected it to be told in a certain way; you don't touch the walking and talking statue. As a young man Carlo Goldoni had tried. He got rid of the statue; his version was pretty much a failure.

In brief, Italian versions of the story ran as follows: The adventure begins in Naples where Don Giovanni is caught trying to enter the apartment of Donna Isabella whom he intends to seduce. To avoid the wrath of the king of Naples, he flees the city and sets sail for Spain. On the way, he is shipwrecked but pulled from the sea by a lovely fishergirl whom he rewards with promises of marriage. After a night of love, he abandons her and proceeds to Seville where he comes across an old acquaintance, Duke Ottavio. The duke boasts of his new fiancée, Donna Anna, whom Don Giovanni then tries to seduce by slipping into her room that same night in disguise. But she resists and screams for help. Her father enters; Don Giovanni kills him and escapes. He next comes upon a country wedding and steals away the bride. Later, he meets the living statue of Donna Anna's father; to prove that he is undaunted by the statue's threats, he invites it to dinner. Unexpectedly, the statue agrees to come and appears later that evening at Don Giovanni's home. The statue in turn invites Don Giovanni to dinner. Unafraid, Don Giovanni accepts the invitation. The second meal is a ghastly affair – vipers and scorpions are usually the main course. The statue orders Don Giovanni to repent, but he obstinately refuses and is dragged down to hell. In the final scene his shrieks of pain and his cries of regret and repentance can be heard, but it is too late.

Thinking men often thought the story stupid. In England Thomas Shadwell admitted that his own version was full of "irregularities" due to the "extravagance of the subject".[3] In France Villiers apologized that for economic reasons his troupe was forced to perform such a wretched play, which he too considered irregular,

---

[3] T. SHADWELL, "Preface", *The Libertine*, vol. 3 of *The Complete Works of Thomas Shadwell*, M. Summers ed., London, Fortune Press, 1927, p. 21.

awkward and morally offensive.[4] In Italy, Goldoni, now no longer a young man, termed the legend "sciocca", "sconcia", "scorretta ed irregolare". He found it preposterous that a Don Giovanni could be washed up onto the Spanish shore after a shipwreck with his wig still properly powdered and his shoes bone dry.[5] Da Ponte had no such concerns. Nor did he care to modify the legend in any radical way, but that did not mean that he could not make significant improvements in the raw material of the story that he took as a given. In fact he prepared the best libretto ever created on the subject of Don Juan – and seven or eight librettists had already tried.[6] To a certain extent he rehabilitated a legend that, in the words of a character from Giovanni Valentini's *Il capriccio drammatico*, was frequently thought to be "una bella e stupenda porcheria" (VI).[7]

As noted, Da Ponte began his creative work on *Don Giovanni* with Giovanni Bertati's text for *Don Giovanni o sia Il convitato di pietra* close at hand. He thought little of Bertati; in his *Memorie* he called him a "ciabattino", a cobbler who stitched librettos together as best he could.[8] Yet it was with the aid of this cobbler's text that Da Ponte was able, in a single day, to complete not only half of act 1 of *Tarar* and two scenes from *L'arbore di Diana* but also the extraordinary opening scenes of *Don Giovanni*: act 1, scenes I and II – sixty verses in Bertati, fifty-nine verses in Da Ponte.[9]

But not the same verses; the ideas expressed were similar, but the expression of the idea was quite different. For Da Ponte had a far superior instinct for the word, for the right word at the right time, and he had a deeper and more assured sense of character and of drama. As he reviewed Bertati's first and second scenes, the text served him as a draft, which he rapidly analyzed, corrected and improved. He did not copy; he used Bertati as a guide, as his muse.

---

[4] VILLIERS, "A Monsieur de Corneille" and "Au Lecteur", *Le Festin de Pierre ou Le fils criminel*. The play with its two apologetic prefaces can be found in G. GENDARME DE BÉVOTTE, *Le Festin de Pierre avant Molière*, Paris, Cornély, 1907.

[5] C. GOLDONI, "L'autore a chi legge", *Don Giovanni Tenorio o sia Il dissoluto*, in vol. 9 of *Tutte le opere di Carlo Goldoni*, G. Ortolani ed., 2nd ed., Verona, Mondadori, 1960, pp. 215, 216.

[6] The following librettos on the Don Juan theme were written before Da Ponte's:

1730, Prague, *La pravità castigata*. Comp.:? Lib.: Antonio Denzio.

1776, Prague, *Il convitato di pietra o sia Il dissoluto*. Comp.: Vincenzo Righini; Lib.: Nunziato Porta.

1777, Venice, *Il convitato di pietra*. Comp.: Giuseppe Calegari; Lib.: ?

1780, Warsaw, *Il Don Giovanni*. Comp.: Gioacchino Albertini; Lib.: Nunziato Porta. Polish version by Wojciech Boguslawski, 1783.

1783, Naples, *Il convitato di pietra*. Comp.: Giacomo Tritto; Lib.: Giambattista Lorenzi.

1787, Venice, *Il nuovo convitato di pietra*. Comp.: Francesco Gardi; Lib.: Giuseppe Maria Foppa?

1787, Venice, *Don Giovanni o sia Il convitato di pietra*. Comp.: Giuseppe Gazzaniga; Lib.: Giovanni Bertati.

1787, Rome, *Il convitato di pietra*. Comp.: Vincenzo Fabrizi; Lib.: Giambattista Lorenzi.

[7] Venice, 1787. Libretto by Giovanni Bertati. Text available in C. C. RUSSELL, *The Don Juan Legend Before Mozart*, Ann Arbor, University of Michigan Press, 1993.

[8] DA PONTE, *Memorie*, p. 357.

[9] For a critical edition of Da Ponte's libretto, see L. DA PONTE, *Il Don Giovanni*, G. Gronda ed., Turin, Einaudi, 1995. Bertati's text can be found in RUSSELL, *The Don Juan Legend*.

He did not copy the June-moon rhymes that Bertati used in these two scenes –
"Un'alma nobile, no, in te non v'è. / Per dove fuggasi non so più affè" (I.I). – or
such easy rhymes as *credo, vedo; me, te; chiedete, siete; onor, ancor*. Da Ponte's
rhymes tend to be richer, a little more extensive, less predictable: *gradir, dormir,
servir, sentir; mai, saprai, guai; precipitar, perseguitar; sconsigliata, disperata;
pretendi, attendi; agonizzante, palpitante*.

Both operas open with Don Giovanni's servant standing watch outside Donna
Anna's palace. Don Giovanni is inside, on the attack. Bertati sets the action in motion with a complaint by Pasquariello: twelve *ottonari* divided into four-line stanzas. But the stanzas are without significant focus or sharpness of purpose.

> La gran bestia è il mio padrone!
> Ma il grand'asino son'io,
> che per troppa soggezione
> non lo mando a far squartar.
>   Invaghito di Donn'Anna
> là di furto si è introdotto;
> ed io gramo, chiotto chiotto,
> qui ad attenderlo ho da star.
>   Sento fame, sento noia...
> Ma che venga alcun già parmi.
> Che sia lui vo' lusingarmi,
> ma non vogliomi fidar. (I.I)

Da Ponte on the other hand begins with eleven free-flow *ottonari* sung by Leporello, each verse of which serves to further define the character of Don Giovanni,
his manservant and their ambiguous natures.

> Notte e giorno faticar
> per chi nulla sa gradir,
> piova e vento sopportar,
> mangiar male e mal dormir...
> Voglio far il gentiluomo,
> e non voglio più servir.
> Oh, che caro galantuomo!
> Voi star dentro colla bella,
> ed io far la sentinella!...
> Ma mi par che venga gente,
> non mi voglio far sentir. (I.I)

It almost seems that Bertati had a gift for lifeless verse. The Commendatore's
first words as he rushes on stage to save his daughter threatened by Don Giovanni's passions are: "Qual tradimento! Perfido! Indegno! / Sottrarti invano speri da
me" (I.II). The bluster and threats are generic. Da Ponte changed these lines to

two simple, sharp imperatives that recognize the real pain of a father whose first thought is for a daughter in danger: "Lasciala indegno, / battiti meco" (I.I). Da Ponte's verse digs deeper, often unforgettably etching out the souls of his characters. After the Commendatore's slaying, in both versions (I.II) Don Giovanni's servant turns to his master and says with irony: Good for you, two fine deeds: seducing the daughter and killing her father. The retort of Bertati's Don Giovanni is uninteresting: "Ehi, te l'ho detto ancora / che non vo' rimostranze. / Seguimi e taci. Andiamo". To which Pasquariello replies with a flat "Sì, signore". But in Da Ponte's version Don Giovanni's answer to Leporello's comment is a harsh and staccato: "L'ha voluto, suo danno". To which Leporello replies: "Ma Donn'Anna / cosa ha voluto"? From the bland verses of Bertati a hard Don Giovanni and a leering and equivocal Leporello have sprung to life.

Da Ponte had no need to limit his source of inspiration exclusively to Bertati's libretto. There were other versions available to draw upon had he so wished. Whether he actually made use of them is not important. Rather, what is worth observing is how, in almost every case, his version differs from those of others and how, in almost every case, his handling of the legend is superior. He was surely familiar with the earliest Italian reworking of the story by Giacinto Andrea Cicognini. Cicognini's play, *Il convitato di pietra*, dated from around the third decade of the seventeenth century.[10] It was then and had continued to be a very popular expression of the legend, and it frequently served as a basis for later versions as well.

Cicognini told his tale in three acts and in roughhewn prose that, while at times not unamusing, is entirely lacking in wit. He intended his version to be first a comedy, then an adventure, and, for a moment at its conclusion, a morality play. Like its Spanish source, Tirso's *Burlador*, the narrative of Cicognini's play is spread over two countries, Italy and Spain, and over an extended period of time. It is full of actions: an attempted rape, a seduction, a betrayal, an abduction, a shipwreck, a rescue, a suicide, a sword fight, a murder, disguises and narrow escapes, and triple appearances of the miraculous stone guest, two of them at dinners.

Da Ponte tightened the tale. He restricted the action to a single location and to a twenty-four-hour time period. He economized: characters were eliminated, scenes were dropped, the two dinners were reduced to one. As a result, in his libretto there is a clearer sense of intent, of a goal to be reached by the libretto's end. Da Ponte's is not a common adventure story but the tracing of a soul as it self-destructs, of its gradual descent into a spiritual hell. There is intended – even if not always perfectly achieved – a crescendo of actions which culminates in Don Giovanni's second-act betrayal of Leporello, a betrayal of the voice of his con-

---

[10] Full text in G. MACCHIA, *Vita avventure e morte di Don Giovanni*, Bari, Laterza, 1966.

science, of ordinary human reason. Upon his rejecting even that true and faithful voice, it is time for his trial and judgment, and the statue of the Commendatore speaks forth.

In Cicognini's comic adventure, characters appeared and disappeared so briefly and rapidly that they scarcely left a trace. None was developed to any significant degree. Da Ponte filled in Cicognini's outlines. In the earlier play, Donna Anna only appeared in two short scenes. In Da Ponte her presence is a dominating force from start to finish. He made of her a strong-willed young woman whose passionate nature is repressed by an iron sense of filial respect and social duty. One of the centers of the drama becomes, as it had not been earlier, a deadly contest of wills between Donna Anna, pillar of public virtue, and Don Giovanni, its scourge. It is not that Da Ponte was the first to enlarge the character of Donna Anna; Goldoni had done so too, but he clouded the matter by suggesting that she might be in love with Don Giovanni, an idea that Da Ponte rightly rejected as irrelevant to the intent of his drama. Goldoni's lovestruck Anna bore with her a slightly disturbing air of silliness. Da Ponte's drama is not a love story, but in part a tale of rectitude and responsibilities, public in the figure of Donna Anna and private in the figure of Donna Elvira. He had written a libretto that was part of a comic tradition, but he did not intend it to be silly.

Da Ponte avoided simple comic behavior for its own sake, as other tellers of the tale did not. For example, as many critics have rightly complained, his Duke Ottavio is indeed tendentious and slow to act; on the other hand, he is never foolish or ridiculous. In Cicognini he is; he is a butt of the playwright's humor, cuckolded by Don Giovanni not once but twice. In an opera by Giuseppe Calegari and an unknown librettist, *Il convitato di pietra*, written for Venice just ten years before Mozart's, Duke Ottavio is sarcastically described as one who rises early each morning because he needs to "lisciarsi, imbellettarsi e polverarsi / per esser primo in corte a far figura" (I.v).[11] Da Ponte did not make him a simple comic figure as these. He upgraded him from the merely comic so as to give him a presence and style reflecting the darker and more serious tone and intent of the libretto.

For the same reason Da Ponte avoided not clever innuendo or suggestiveness, but vulgarities. Cicognini's servant is foul-mouthed in a way that Da Ponte's sly, insinuating and witty Leporello never is. As the shipwrecked Don Giovanni and Passarino heave themselves out of the ocean onto the Spanish shore, safe at last, "Comincio a respirare", mutters Don Giovanni. "E mi me scappa da cagare", blurts out Passarino (I.xi). In the cemetery scene, Passarino turns to Don Giovanni and says, "Andem via de qui, perché mi me son fatt la triaga in t'i calzoni" (III.ii).

---

[11] Full text in RUSSELL, *The Don Juan Legend*.

Da Ponte not only modified the old, he invented the new. He created new scenes: thus, for example, the spectral presence of Donna Anna, Donna Elvira and Duke Ottavio, masked and uncertain, who with trepidation and prayer enter the house of revels of their archenemy, treading, it would seem, on unhallowed ground (I.XIX). This scene, with its tense and mysterious beauty, has no correspondence in earlier texts. And he created new characterizations: Masetto, traditionally a simple country peasant as he was in Molière, a dimwitted foil to the wiles of his country fiancée and her manipulative seducer, now a fully plumbed figure, not a dolt, but a man sadly and angrily aware that he is hopelessly in love with the wrong woman: "Bricconaccia, malandrina, / fosti ognor la mia ruina" (I.VIII). This is not the first time she has betrayed him, and it will not be the last, yet he cannot help loving her. He is bitterly aware that he cannot stop Don Giovanni's circling attack on his Zerlina. He is trapped in a social structure that he cannot escape; nonetheless, he lashes out at Don Giovanni with courage and sarcasm:

> Cavalier voi siete già,
> dubitar non posso affè:
> me lo dice la bontà
> che volete aver per me. (I.VIII)

No one before Da Ponte had defined him so clearly or so boldly.

Lastly, we need to consider the figure of Don Giovanni himself. It is here that Da Ponte made his most significant contribution. He had a variety of Don Juan types to look back upon. There had been some very nasty ones: Dorimond's cold-souled Dom Jouan who cursed and slapped his own father, or Thomas Shadwell's, whose Don John was a glutton and drunkard, rapist, arsonist, murderer and patricide. The wickedness of each was benumbing and repellent. Other writers went to an opposite extreme and created Don Juans who were downright ridiculous. That is the way he was often portrayed in *commedia dell'arte* versions, in puppet versions, and in Giambattista Lorenzi's play, *Il convitato di pietra*, in which Don Giovanni suffers the indignity from his servant of a swift kick in the pants.[12]

But many writers, particularly in Italy, created attractive, light-hearted young libertines of undeniable charm, whose presence seemed rather illuminated by sunlight. The shadows of ferocity, of corruption, of pain, evident in Shadwell or in French verse versions, were barely visible. It is true that these young men were not good persons: their actions were unlawful, their behavior deceitful, their goals despicable, but a public could not deny having been brushed by a presence which fascinated and excited.

---

[12] Scene XVI. Full text in V. MONACO, *Giambattista Lorenzi e la commedia per musica*, Naples, Berisio, 1968.

One such was created by the unknown librettist for Giuseppe Calegari. Their *Convitato di pietra* was performed during the Venetian carnival season of 1777. Calegari's protagonist is a rather agreeable fellow who enjoys having fun, even if in a somewhat irresponsible sort of manner. Nothing gets him down. Ordered out of Naples after having been caught attempting to seduce a young woman, he is immediately ready for a new Spanish adventure. He has a youthful vigor and enthusiasm, a sunlit flair for life that cannot be denied. His self-assurance, his courage, his optimism are enviable. His killing of the Commendatore is quick, clean, bloodless and devoid of nasty repartee or disrespect towards his elderly antagonist and is followed by a bold escape from two other attacking adversaries. "Sì, son buon anco per tre", he brags (I.XVIII). Seducer and murderer he may be, but these crimes seem of relative import, inserted as they are, in a lighthearted comic context where even Donna Anna is criticized for weeping too much over her father's death. This Don Giovanni loves life. As expected he is exceedingly fond of beautiful women, but he also likes to eat, likes to laugh and tell jokes, likes to sing and play the spinet. Grumbles his servant: "Un più bel matto al mondo no se trova" (II.VII).

Unlike Calegari's protagonist, Da Ponte's is hardly "un bel matto"; his desires and actions are far less lighthearted. Da Ponte makes evident the nature of his protagonist on the first page of his libretto. Under the heading *Personaggi* he writes: "Don Giovanni, giovane cavaliere estremamente licenzioso". No previous libretto had made so unequivocal a statement as that. From the very first, Da Ponte intends to give a new seriousness to his comic protagonist. The attempted violation of Donna Anna is not amusing; the murder of her father leaves a stain of real blood on the street. Da Ponte's Don Giovanni retains many of the virtues of his predecessors; he is still attractive, vigorous, masculine, but the sunlight in him has begun to fade. He attracts, but he also repels. He fascinates, but it is less the fascination of youth than of corruption, of evil. He remains a comic figure within the tradition of *opera buffa*, but there is now something more sinister about his laughter and his pranks.

Calegari offered a straightforward, smiling Don Giovanni. Da Ponte, without denying the comic tradition, began to probe beneath the surface to reveal the shadows of his mind. Da Ponte shows the downside of sexuality, a mindless pursuit of women. Leporello's catalogue of seductions is amusing – 2,065 names so far; very amusing the one thousand and three women of Spain. But less so the fact that old women are seduced merely to add to the body count. Even Bertati's Don Giovanni, "il Grande Alessandro delle femmine" (I.VII), balked at seducing old ladies. This Don Giovanni is a man who smells out women, sniffs them out with the animal instinct of a dog in heat – "Mi pare / sentir odor di femmina" (I.IV) – he says, just before Donna Elvira appears. In a scene entirely of Da Ponte's invention, Don Giovanni orders Leporello to invite all the neighborhood peasants to his home for dinner and dancing and drinking. He intends that by sunrise his list of seductions will have grown not by one or two but by ten. He is now no sunlit life force but a man obsessed. He has no time to play the spinet. The twenty-four hours of Da Ponte's libretto have become a desperate race from bed to bed, no time for a relaxed, conversational, post-coital cigarette. It is no wonder that at the end of the libretto he throws himself, perhaps heroically and tragically but perhaps also blindly and exhaustedly, into the arms of the avenging stone statue. He can rest at last.

As for Don Giovanni's difficult and perplexing relationship with the statue, it seems likely that Da Ponte more fully than others intuited the possible allegorical character of that relationship. Cicognini and Bertati were more hesitant to do so. Cicognini was clearly disturbed by the logical absurdities of a confrontation in a cemetery with a living, speaking statue, less cognizant as he was of the allegorical dimensions that such an encounter might evoke. His Don Giovanni was amusingly wicked, but he was not wickedness itself. At the very moment when Don Giovanni, angered by the vengeance-threatening words sculpted on the statue's pedestal, lifts his hand to strike the stone figure, Cicognini causes him to pause a moment and to reflect that indeed "sarebbe pazzia l'imperversare contro di un marmo" (III.II). Cicognini wants to "explain" the unexplainable. That his Don Giovanni does, then, in a kind of blind craziness, strike the statue and insultingly invite it to dinner makes no difference. That brief moment of apparently rational self-analysis is an indication that Cicognini himself is uncomfortable with the story, unwilling or unable to boost his figure into the realm of allegory. On the other hand Da Ponte, at a similar point in his version (II.XII), makes no effort to provide a realistic explanation for Don Giovanni's actions. There is no gradual transition from real life to allegory. Da Ponte moves his character immediately into a higher level of interaction. Leporello reads the threatening inscription. Instantly Don Giovanni issues his challenge: he invites the statue to dinner. With that invitation the struggle between two irreconcilable forces is joined.

There were various ways to conclude the story. At the last moment Cicognini turned his adventure story into a morality tale. In the final scene a tortured Don Giovanni cried out from hell confessing guilt and begging for pity, but all pity was denied by a chorus of upright and vengeful furies. Bertati chose a different way. As was customary, his Don Giovanni too was sent to hell, from where he was heard to cry out properly tortured and repentant. However, for the participants in a light-hearted *opera buffa*, this sort of horror was much too serious a way to end an evening's entertainment. Let's not speak another word about it, they sing in unison; let's have fun instead. And with that, Bertati's opera comes to a happy conclusion as everyone in concert begins to imitate the sound of various musical instruments, Duke Ottavio pretending to be a guitar. Da Ponte chose a more thoughtful way. As the smoke of hell clears, each character declares himself ready to return once again to normal life and to his fitting role or position in it. Then all six survivors joyfully celebrate with song a true and genuine liberation from the terrible presence of sin by which they had been nearly destroyed; they rejoice that their world has been righted, that it has returned from chaos to its natural order and harmony and balance. For theirs is a world, they sing, in which the "perfidi" are rightly punished; theirs is a world for "buona gente", for the good people there in the libretto and there on stage and there in the audience in Prague and Vienna. In this final sextet, the exuberant radiance of Mozart's music is an indication, I hope, that he too was of the same opinion; certainly there can be no doubt that this music is a final, overwhelming confirmation that the subject matter of Lorenzo Da Ponte's new libretto had indeed pleased him infinitely.

GIOVANNI DA POZZO

DUE LETTERE DEL FOSCOLO RECUPERATE

Il ritrovamento casuale di due lettere del Foscolo e la constatazione che esse non sono presenti nei volumi finora usciti dell'Edizione Nazionale delle *Opere* sono una forte e ben giustificata ragione per essere indotti a pubblicarle qui, così che almeno nel volume finale che completerà l'*Epistolario* e quindi tutta l'edizione, col recupero delle lettere sfuggite in precedenza alle ricerche dei curatori, esse possano essere incluse. La pubblicazione che qui ne viene fatta servirà all'occasione festiva a cui la presente raccolta di scritti risponde, ma contribuirà anche al completamento di un'opera scientifica che certo non si potrà dire impresa occasionale, quando si consideri che il primo volume dell'*Epistolario* (il XIV dell'intera Edizione delle *Opere*) è uscito nel 1949.

Una delle due lettere, quella del 14 aprile 1819, a John Cam Hobhouse, era già stata di fatto recuperata da Gustavo Costa, che aveva individuato la lettera in una delle sue feconde incursioni nelle biblioteche americane; e l'aveva poi pubblicata nel 1971, assieme ad altro materiale foscoliano, in un suo saggio apparso in *Modern Language Notes* (vol. 86, numero 1° di gennaio, a p. 90), di cui ho avuto una copia in estratto, inviatami dall'amico premuroso, che qui ringrazio pubblicamente. Ma nel volume VIII dell'*Epistolario* (= XXI delle *Opere* nell'Edizione nazionale), uscito ben tre anni dopo, nel 1974, quella lettera risulta ancora assente, perché presumibilmente il saggio ospitato nella rivista americana rimase sconosciuto al curatore dell'edizione, come stava per rimanere trascurato anche da me, se la pronta cortesia dell'autore non me lo avesse posto sotto gli occhi prima che io finissi la stesura di queste note.

Per evitare che la lettera possa sfuggire anche agli ultimi recuperi che troveranno posto nell'ultimo volume, sempre atteso, dell'*Epistolario*, essa si ripubblica qui come in seconda istanza, o se si vuole, per rinnovato richiamo ai fini della sua destinazione scientificamente più propria, cioè perché essa venga inserita in futuro in quel volume finale dell'*Epistolario* che sopra si è ricordato. E si confida che, comparendo in queste pagine stampate da un editore italiano, essa forse si imponga più facilmente all'attenzione di chi, gravato dalla cura dei testi epistolari foscoliani, non ha potuto probabilmente verificare la presenza di materiale utile al proprio lavoro anche nell'ambito delle varie riviste statunitensi.[1]

Anziché limitare il richiamo a un semplice rinvio bibliografico, si preferisce fornire qui una riedizione, perché essa, oltre a richiamare nuovamente l'attenzione sulla lettera con lo scopo che sopra si è indicato, offre anche l'occasione per alcune rifiniture minime alla veste grafica del testo, insieme a qualche integrazione di commento e a una considerazione complessiva sulla situazione psicologica che il Foscolo attraversava quando quella lettera venne da lui scritta. E non pare sia del tutto inutile anche qualche precisazione minore circa alcuni momenti di incertezza del Foscolo nell'atto della scrittura, palesi in alcune cassature e in qualche altro particolare grafico, da ricollegare alla varietà delle sue abitudini correttorie, le quali sembrano comunque da rispettare nel fissare in modo definitivo un testo che dovrà essere poi pubblicato in una sede così impegnata e autorevole come quella nazionale.

La seconda lettera che qui si pubblica è invece – a quanto risulta a tutt'oggi – inedita e non sembra ben conosciuta neppure nella biblioteca californiana in cui essa è conservata.

Le due lettere, che si trascrivono qui con l'accompagnamento di un essenziale commento, si collocano, dunque, l'una nella primavera del 1819, l'altra verso la fine dell'inverno 1820-21, cioè dopo il primo momento in cui, arrivato già con qualche fama in Inghilterra nella seconda settimana del settembre 1816, Foscolo si trovava impegnato ad acquisire ed allargare le proprie conoscenze, lasciando che, come in altri periodi della sua vita, i sentimenti personali, specie quello amoroso, germinassero naturalmente dai propri stessi impegni di lavoro o dal compiacimento di decantare le proprie ispirazioni di lettore di testi in una cerchia di persone amiche disposte ad ascoltarlo. E, sullo sfondo di tutto questo, aleggia, quasi come un monito non ascoltato, la sempre ritornante preoccupazione quotidiana della necessità di provvedere a se stesso.

Sono già state compiute dal Foscolo, in quella fine del secondo decennio del secolo ed inizio del terzo, le prime esperienze fondamentali che egli viene facendo dell'ambiente inglese; è già avvenuta l'utile e confortevole conoscenza della famiglia di Lord Henry Holland, il cui salotto era divenuto luogo di elezione dei *whig* del tempo; era abbastanza progredita da parte dello scrittore la penetrazione nella vita mondana dell'ambiente teatrale londinese.

La frequentazione di John Murray, l'editore che nel 1809 era riuscito a dar vita alla *Quarterly Review,* portavoce, invece, delle opinioni dell'ambiente *tory* e strumento d'informazione che intendeva bilanciare l'influenza della *Edinburgh Review,* aveva

---

[1] Occorre ricordare che G. Costa ha il merito di aver pubblicato, nello stesso suo saggio incluso nel n. 1 del 1971 di *Modern Language Notes,* anche una seconda lettera autografa inedita del Foscolo, indirizzata a Cyrus Redding e databile al 1821. Su tale lettera non mi è possibile qui fermare il discorso: ma è da confidare che anch'essa sia inclusa nel volume finale dei "recuperi" dell'*Epistolario* foscoliano, in quanto non compare nell'VIII volume di esso che avrebbe dovuto contenerla.

permesso al Foscolo di frequentare la libreria di quell'editore in Albemarle Street, dove si moltiplicavano le occasioni di incontro, di nuove conoscenze, di scambio di idee.

La cultura italiana, in quegli anni a Londra e presso il mondo inglese in generale, giocava già da tempo un ruolo di rilevante importanza grazie all'accrescersi del gusto italianizzante, che trovava opportuna occasione di risonanza anche nella fortuna dell'opera italiana nell'importante teatro di Haymarket. Il Foscolo, a quel tempo, aveva già scritto i due articoli su Dante per la *Edinburgh Review,* apparsi nel febbraio e nel settembre del 1818, smuovendo nella sua mente una massa di problemi che egli intravedeva di dover affrontare per un commento dell'intero poema dantesco. E nel 1819 stavano per uscire in pubblico l'articolo su Pio VI e quello sui *Narrative and Romantic Poems of the Italians,* nella *Quarterly Review* (vol. XXI, n. XLII, dell'aprile) oltre all'altro sulla questione di Parga, più tardi, nella *Edinburgh Review* dell'ottobre (vol. XXXII, n. LXIV).

Nel marzo-aprile Foscolo è impegnato a scrivere, tra l'altro, sui *Poemi narrativi e romanzeschi italiani,* e l'articolo relativo si leggerà nella *Quarterly Review* dell'aprile di quello stesso anno. Era già avvenuta, nel 1817, anche la frequentazione della famiglia Wilbraham e di una delle due Caroline conosciute in questo tempo, la sposa di William Lamb, per la quale il Foscolo nutrì un palese interesse, presto trasformatosi, in strategica difesa di fronte al temperamento sollecitante e volitivo di quella donna piuttosto autoritaria.

Per un'altra donna che aveva lo stesso nome di Mrs. Lamb, per un'altra Caroline, il Foscolo, verso la fine del secondo decennio del secolo, cominciò a nutrire un sentimento che divenne passione profonda, all'inizio mescolata come per gioco a un pretesto letterario. Come si sa, l'amore per Caroline Russell lasciò ben maggior segno nell'animo del Foscolo. Era questa la figlia di Henry Russell, già Presidente della Corte Suprema di Giustizia del Bengala, il quale, collocato a riposo, viveva con le figlie Caroline, Henriette, Rose Aylmer assieme alle quali era spesso presente anche Katherine, un'altra sorella, moglie dal 1816 di Henry Jones.

La residenza londinese dei Russell, in Wimpole Street, divenne anch'essa uno dei luoghi ospitali volentieri frequentati dal Foscolo. E appunto la consuetudine con i Russell assieme all'idea, maturata verso l'inizio del 1819, di scrivere un articolo sul Petrarca per la *Edinburgh Review* aveva portato il Foscolo a mettere in atto un suo proposito, quello di leggere, spiegare, commentare le liriche del Petrarca alle giovani Russell e agli altri di casa, infervorandosi sul testo ma anche lasciandosi trascinare dagli effetti che quelle parole amorose provocavano nell'animo delle presenti e di Caroline in particolare. I documenti che a questo riguardo ci rimangono[2] parlano

---

[2] Cioè le lettere scambiate reciprocamente: le lettere scritte dal Foscolo a Caroline Russell, assieme ai lacerti che di esse rimangono si trovano nel volume VIII dell'*Epistolario* (=XXI dell'Edizione nazionale) Firenze, Le Monnier, 1974, nella *Appendice* I^a (: *Reliquie delle lettere a Caroline Russell*), pp. 367-458. Le lettere di Caroline Russell al Foscolo sono nello stesso volume, a pp. 459-464. Nel *Regesto* delle pp. 484-488 si leggono alcuni biglietti delle sorelle di Caroline a Foscolo (Henriette e Rose Aylmer) e di Lady Dacre.

di una passione intensa e crescente da parte del Foscolo, ma esposta ad un perdurante equivoco.

Dalla posizione di forza di seduttore navigato il Foscolo si trovò invischiato nel ruolo di innamorato incapace di persuadere l'amata della serietà dei propri sentimenti e della giustezza di una conclusione matrimoniale, poiché la giovane Russell era portata piuttosto a un vagheggiamento sentimentale di natura contemplativa e riservata. Sicché, quando dopo alterne oscillazioni di atteggiamento nei confronti di lui, Caroline nell'estate del '19 si recò in Svizzera con la famiglia, il chiarimento dei propri sentimenti, di devozione ed amicizia, ma non di amore, almeno da parte della donna, doveva essere sostanzialmente già avvenuto. Lo confermano la lettera scritta prima del 22 novembre 1819,[3] assieme ad altri riferimenti minori che non interessa ora circoscrivere.

La storia della passione foscoliana per Caroline, nata nell'occasione e con la complicità del commento alle liriche del Petrarca, durerà poi ancora e nonostante tutto nei mesi seguenti; e non solo dopo che Caroline sarà tornata a Londra, forse intorno alla fine di ottobre del 1820. A intendere la misura del forte bisogno di comunicare con l'amata da parte del protagonista maschile in quella circostanza, sarà da ricordare che un riferimento interno alla lettera foscoliana del 9 maggio 1820[4] ci permette di dire che le lettere inviate dal Foscolo a Caroline a quella data assommavano ad oltre ventitré. Ma una pur incompleta documentazione del protrarsi dello scambio epistolare tra Foscolo e la Russell, con maggiore consistenza numerica, però, delle lettere scritte da lui, permane almeno fino al maggio 1821.[5]

A queste vicende, a questa storia di un amore che lentamente sembra costretto a finire, a spegnersi a fatica, già nei primi mesi del '19, anche se con riverberi che durano per il Foscolo certamente anche dopo quel periodo, lo svago che poteva venire a lui dalla frequentazione della famiglia di J. Cam Hobhouse, in campagna, costituisce una ben comprensibile alternativa.

Foscolo lo aveva conosciuto almeno fin dal 1818, frequentando la casa londinese di lui in Clarges Street. John Cam Hobhouse aveva percorso nella sua vita un itinerario che lo aveva portato da convinzioni radicali in gioventù a posizioni liberali e più vicine ai *whigs* negli ultimi tempi. L'intenzione di pubblicare le sue

---

[3] Cfr. lettera IIª nell'*Appendice* I del vol. VIII dell'*Epistolario* del Foscolo nell'Edizione nazionale delle *Opere*, Firenze, Le Monnier, 1974, pp. 370-374) in cui Foscolo, se da un lato afferma di non essere sicuro che «l'homme qui vous aime aie merité ce traitement de votre part» (p. 371), intendeva del resto non arrendersi («Je ne crains pas – comme l'amant à qui vous écrivez – je ne crains pas d'être *disappointed* dans mes esperances» (p. 373).

[4] Cfr. vol. VIII dell'*Epistolario*, cit., p. 385.

[5] E la vicenda della passione foscoliana per Caroline Russell sembra aver lasciato qualche segno anche nel progetto di un romanzo del Foscolo di cui rimangono solo alcuni abbozzi (si veda nel vol. XXI dell'Edizione nazionale, cioè il vol. VIII delle *Epistolario*, a pp. 499-512) nei quali, con caratteri molto simili a quelli dei personaggi della vita vissuta, compare la figura di una Miss Elton, viene rappresentata la vita inattiva in campagna e la condizione di povertà del protagonista maschile a Moulsey, viene ricordata Hampton Court; e c'è la la partenza di Helen con la sua cugina; c'è l'arrivo in Svizzera di Helen, ecc.).

Historical Illustrations to the Fourth Canto of Childe Harold (che vedranno poi la luce per l'editore J. Murray in quello stesso 1818) aveva dato l'occasione al Foscolo per una collaborazione specifica con lui in quella circostanza. Ma dalla richiesta di un aiuto di dati sulla base dei quali lo Hobhouse dichiarava che si sarebbe sentito, allora, in grado di stendere una o due pagine («to fill a sheet or two»[6]) sulla materia della attuale letteratura in Italia, si passò, nella prospettiva di ricezione del Foscolo portato come sempre alla dilatazione della scrittura, alla stesura di 4 monografie tra le quali quella dello stesso poeta: di qui dispute, fraintendimenti, contrasti verbali anche accesi, dai quali non furono disgiunte anche ragioni di ordine finanziario.

L'*Essay on the present Literature in Italy,* in sostanza del Foscolo, anche se la veste inglese del testo forse non rispettò tutte le sfumature espressive dell'originale, e anche se in qualche parte la mano dell'Hobhouse dovette essersi fatta sentire,[7] uscì comunque, incluso nel volume delle *Historical Illustrations.* E dopo l'incrinarsi dei rapporti tra i due che esso provocò, la reciproca volontà di rinverdire quel legame di stima che l'episodio aveva fortemente turbato, permise che si verificasse, intorno al 22 dicembre la svolta in senso positivo e quindi la riappacificazione.[8]

Col dicembre 1818 i buoni rapporti tra i due uomini riprendevano, dunque, assieme agli inviti rivolti a Foscolo a recarsi a Whitton Park, la residenza fuori Londra della famiglia amica.

* * *

La lettera del 14 aprile 1819 che qui si pubblica va collocata proprio in questa situazione e a questo punto, in questo clima rasserenato, nel quale erano riprese le visite alla casa di campagna degli Hobhouse, assai gradite al Foscolo, rammaricato di non poterle qualche volta accettare per contingenti ragioni di lavoro che lo trattenevano a Londra,[9] mentre ancora una speranza nell'amore di Caroline, sia pure smentita sempre più nettamente dalla fanciulla, perdurava.

È uno dei momenti, questo, che coincidono con una fase, dal vario aspetto, di una particolare inquietudine che sta trasformandosi da fervore inventivo, in mezzo

---

[6] V. lettera del 24-26 marzo 1818 (*Epistolario,* cit., vol. VII).

[7] Esso si legge, accompagnato da traduzione italiana , nel vol. XI dell'Edizione nazionale delle *Opere* del Foscolo, Parte seconda (1958), pp. 399-555.

[8] Raggiunta attraverso un gioco strategico di concessioni e di riaffermazioni della propria onestà d'intenti che si risolveva in sostanza, senza parere, in una pur attenuata sottolineatura dell'altrui ingiustizia (così ad esempio lo Hobhouse, nel momento in cui si induceva a ristabilire i loro buoni rapporti, scriveva al Foscolo di essere « delighted to see that the struggle between your reason and your anger has terminated», lettera di J. Cam Hobhouse del 22 dicembre 1818, in U. FOSCOLO, *Opere,* Ediz. naz., *Epistolario,* vol. VII, p. 458.

[9] In una lettera dell'8 aprile [1819] Foscolo si scusa con «tutte le abitatrici di Whitton Park», Ediz. naz. delle *Opere, Epistolario,* vol. VIII, p. 41. Foscolo si giustificava di non poter raggiungere gli Hobhouse nella loro casa in quanto gli stampatori londinesi non volevano lavorare che tre o quattro giorni dopo la vicina Pasqua, cosicché egli era costretto a finire il proprio lavoro che attualmente aveva in corso a Londra entro la presente settimana.

ai trascurati elementi della vita pratica, a una disposizione d'animo più complessa, in cui la maggiore consapevolezza delle difficoltà quotidiane, che il Foscolo non riusciva con efficacia a contrastare, si mescola alla convinzione di dover accettare l'avversità che in parte sembra venire dalla fortuna maligna e in parte, in maniera crescente, viene imputata agli uomini, alla ingratitudine, alla falsità, al calcolo dei molti, in un panorama che tende ad esaltarsi dal proprio interno e a farsi sempre più amara considerazione sulle disillusioni nazionali e su quelle dell'intero panorama europeo.

L'alternanza dei rientri in città, per interrompere la monotonia del soggiorno campestre, e le fughe da Londra verso quel soggiorno, quando il desiderio di aria e di luce e la presenza di persone dolci ed amiche disposte ad accoglierlo e ad ascoltarlo si rifanno sentire, contrappunta questo periodo della primavera del 1819.

Già il giorno 8 aprile [1819] (cfr. *Epistolario* VIII, p. 41) il Foscolo si scusava con John Cam Hobhouse presentando a lui la propria «apologie», e pregando di presentarla a suo padre e a «toutes *le abitatrici* de Whitton Park» (Lettera cit., p. 41), per non poter abbandonare Londra e accettare di passare lietamente qualche tempo in campagna, in visita da loro essendo impegnato nella stesura di un articolo. L'articolo (quasi certamente quello su *Narrative and Romantic Poems of the Italians*, che lo scrittore stava completando) bisognava fosse finito in tempo, dovendo egli stenderlo per la *Quarterly* entro il sabato, dato che il traduttore poteva dedicare solo le giornate di vacanza della settimana successiva a quel lavoro.

Da quanto viene detto nella prima delle due lettere foscoliane che qui si pubblicano si apprende che deve esserci stata almeno un'altra lettera dello Hobhouse in cui egli deve aver manifestato il suo dispiacere e disappunto per il fatto che il Foscolo non poteva raggiungere il gruppo di coloro che erano pronti ad accoglierlo festosamente nella loro residenza fuori Londra.

A tale più che probabile risposta dello Hobhouse, che allo stato attuale non conosciamo, e che doveva esprimere il rammarico per non aver potuto averlo come ospite, la lettera del 14 aprile, che qui di seguito si trascrive, costituisce una rassicurazione e una spiegazione della necessità di rinviare l'incontro. Sembra profilarsi anche, sullo sfondo, nel quadro nelle vicende ricordate, la suggestione che questo periodo di frequentazione della casa di campagna di John Cam Hobhouse e soprattutto delle «abitatrici di Whitton Park» doveva avere in qualche modo per il Foscolo, anche come funzione di parziale *ersatz*, di surrogato illusorio e provvisorio dei più incantevoli incontri in casa Russell, ai tempi del nascente amore per Caroline. Ma la lettera in questione ci mostra innanzi tutto un Foscolo che nella breve vacanza è un po' svagato, che aspetta per mezz'ora che il vicino di casa gli porti le chiavi della sua; che va a pranzo da Wilbraham e poi da Mansfield, che coglie l'occasione di scrivere servendosi di carta e inchiostro che trova al *post-office*, che raccomanda di non provare alcuna afflizione, che rassicura di non essere né arrabbiato né afflitto, che rimpiange, certo, la mancata partecipazione alla riunione con le «abitatrici di Whitton Park», ma che nei suoi spostamenti si compiace, comunque, di aver goduto di sole e di aria pura. Ed è un Foscolo che accenna alla necessità di tornare al lavoro, ai librai, agli stampatori e traduttori, con una punta di eleganza e compiacimento.

Il prendere però le cose come «meilleur parti», «avec indifference», come nella lettera viene detto, era affermazione destinata a rimanere solo un proposito. Non solo perché un distacco dal quotidiano sembra una possibilità lontana dalle abitudini psicologiche foscoliane, ma perché, in quei mesi, la malinconia dell'amore deluso verso Caroline perdurerà, pur attenuata, almeno fino al 1820 o '21; e Foscolo non dimenticherà in seguito di far avere alla donna che aveva amato una copia dell'edizione dei saggi sul Petrarca, quella appunto che uscirà nel '21 per gli stampatori Bentley, a spese del Foscolo stesso.

* * *

A valorizzare l'acquisizione anche della seconda lettera, quella del 22 febbraio 1821, l'altra che qui si pubblica, non servirà certo menzionare tutta la serie delle vicende di sentimenti, di lavoro, di ansie e anche di fraintendimenti, che il Foscolo attraversò nei due anni che separano i due brevi testi. Né essi possono avere, ovviamente, un vincolo organico fra di loro, in quanto appunto "lettere", brevi testi legati alla contingenza del momento. Ma non è certo inutile notare come è appunto il filo dell'interesse per Petrarca che qui non solo continua, ma si manifesta in una sua particolare fase di assestamento.

Curata la veste definitiva della *Ricciarda* presso l'editore Murray, dopo che della «più bella, la più innamorata e la più disgraziata tra le principesse»[10] lo scrittore aveva dato la sua interpretazione teatrale, superata finalmente la crisi dei rapporti con Caroline che anche in questo caso aveva avuto e stava avendo effetti e complicazioni letterarie con il trasferimento fantastico dell'esperienza vissuta alla forma di un romanzo abbozzato e non concluso, il Foscolo si dedica a completare e a rifinire il lavoro del Petrarca che assieme agli altri impegni per la *Quarterly Review* e il *New Monthly Magazine*, lo vedrà occupato fino al '23, fino al tempo dell'edizione degli *Essays on Petrarch* per l'editore John Murray.

La seconda lettera, che qui si esamina, testimonia soltanto uno dei vari momenti di rifinitura e arricchimento del testo del saggio sul Petrarca; e non si presta quindi a incorniciature ambientali e psicologiche. Ma non per questo, anche se presenta un aspetto più "tecnico", pare meno interessante. Rivolta agli stampatori Bentley,

---

[10] Cfr. lettera alla Martinetti del 14 settembre 1812, in *Epistolario*, IV, Ediz. naz. XVII, p. 148.

ma in realtà quasi certamente a Samuel che dei due era quello con cui più spesso il Foscolo trattava per motivi di lavoro, la lettera è una specie di rapido appunto del critico preoccupato di spiegare il ritardo nella restituzione delle bozze allo stampatore e sul punto quasi di restituirle. Le parole che vengono qui usate, pur nella brevità dello spazio utilizzato per comunicare, concentrano in poche righe le ragioni che scusano il ritardo dell'invio di quei fogli, non avvenuto prima, ragioni equamente ripartite tra la propria stessa persona e quella del proprio traduttore. Si potrà sospettare un poco, forse, del livello della gravità del male che aveva colpito scrittore e traduttore i quali, nelle parole del Foscolo, finiscono per apparire proprio come due segregati in casa («I am very ill, and my Translator also confined in his bed»). Ma il dettaglio che interessa, qui, è la precisazione che il Foscolo fa in merito alla disposizione della materia del secondo saggio (petrarchesco) e allo spostamento che di una sezione di esso era in procinto di compiere collocandola nel terzo di quei saggi. Questo perché, come viene in chiusa della lettera esplicitamente detto, Foscolo ha stabilito che ognuno dei tre saggi dovesse consistere di 18 sezioni.

Questa quantità, che di fatto ritorna poi anche nelle altre edizioni del saggio sul Petrarca, è dunque già chiaramente fermata dal Foscolo nella mente fino da questa stagione, diciamo fin dal febbraio 1821. Sarebbe forse di qualche interesse anche sapere non tanto come la lettera del Foscolo e l'edizione inglese del saggio sul Petrarca stampata dai Bentley nel 1821 nei pochi esemplari che sappiamo, sia arrivata nella biblioteca californiana in cui sono conservate, quanto, e più ancora, da chi esse furono poste insieme: se da un anonimo bibliotecario di certa competenza, o da un qualsiasi antiquario di lingua inglese, o (perché escluderlo?) da uno dei due Bentley stessi, più probabilmente da Samuel. Ma conviene, per materia come questa, non lasciarsi attrarre troppo facilmente in ipotesi che, come insegna l'esperienza, sono sempre avventate.

Certo è che, fosse o no molto ammalato il Foscolo, e il suo traduttore confinato nel proprio letto, il critico e lettore del Petrarca sembra ansioso (se i tempi enunciati dalla lettera riflettono la realtà) di testimoniare prontamente il proprio zelo nel giustificarsi con l'editore. La lettera è inviata la sera di giovedì 22 febbraio («Thursday Evening»); e quella scritta dall'editore, evidentemente di sollecitazione, a cui quella del Foscolo risponde, vien detta essere pervenuta la sera stessa («this evening»).

Occorreva far presto se si voleva che quella che diventerà la rara edizione Bentley del 1821, di soli 25 esemplari, potesse arrivare a compimento in tempi brevi, per mandarne una copia a qualche più caro o importante amico. Per potere mandarne una, nonostante tutto, con quel generoso egoismo di cui il Foscolo abbondava, anche a Caroline; ormai senza più speranza, solo per difendere la verità della propria parola di commentatore di un testo che dal Foscolo non era mai stato né poteva essere pensato solo come "galeotto" della propria recente esperienza amorosa.

Solo una propensione alla malignità o a una catalogazione giudiziaria dei sentimenti può portare a considerazioni sdegnose od acri circa il fatto che il Foscolo, mentre l'amore per Caroline finiva, mentre stava uscendo l'edizione del '21 degli *Essays on Petrarch,* promettesse anche a Maria Graham, interessata alle vicende del Foscolo e alla poesia del Petrarca, le bozze del primo saggio petrarchesco, quello che a suo parere era «plus interessant pour une dame; non seulement parce qu'il s'agit *d'amour,* mais parce que j'ai taché de devoiler le coeur jusq'à present mysterieux de la *Civettissima Santissima Madonna Laura*».[11] La Graham, che pubblicherà in quel 1821, presso il Murray, certi suoi *Dramas, Translations and occasional Poems,* aveva chiesto il testo dei saggi petrarcheschi del Foscolo; e con lei egli discuterà ancora, tramite lettera, dei propri scritti. Ma si tratta di capir meglio perché non solo con questa donna, ma anche con Lady Dacre, tra l'ottobre e il novembre del '21[12] il Foscolo discute della traduzione da lei fatta della canzone all'Italia e dell'altra *Chiare, fresche e dolci acque* e spartisce ancora, in qualche modo, i propri sentimenti, le proprie impressioni di lettore con queste forse più dotte , anche se meno coinvolgenti, estimatrici del cantore di Laura. È probabile che in atteggiamenti simili a questo si confermi un tratto tipico della sensibilità romantica, di quel modo personale con cui il Foscolo visse il rapporto tra singolarità, eccezionalità di una esperienza ed analogia o sollecitazioni di analogia rispetto ad essa alle quali la realtà, nella sua ricchezza può indurre. La prontezza con cui forme analogiche di rievocazione di un sentimento, di una situazione, di un referente vengono accolte, pur nella consapevolezza della impossibilità per esse di assomigliare all'unicità dell'esperienza individuale già compiuta, sembra poter legare insieme l'unicità indiscutibile, ma pur raffrontabile di questi episodi rispetto alla facoltà non solo di ricezione, ma di rilancio ed espansione vitale e, insomma, dell'impulso comunicativo dello spirito foscoliano.

Questo dinamico rapporto con il mondo, questa propensione a lasciarsene apertamente influenzare, è ben strettamente collegato per altro, come si sa, con l'altrettanto forte bisogno foscoliano di accettare la storia, di rendere conto di se stesso lungo il percorso della sua tormentata esistenza.

Quando gli *Essays on Petrarch* nell'edizione Bentley del '21, di cui la seconda lettera che qui si pubblica testimonia uno dei momenti di assestamento del testo, finalmente uscivano alla luce, una copia veniva inviata anche a Caroline Russell ed altre agli altri componenti del gentile consesso di un tempo, che ora il Foscolo, in una delle tormentate, diverse redazioni della lettera con cui accompagnava il dono a Caroline, rievocava con devozione, con più pacato affetto:

---

[11] Lettera del 3 febbraio 1821, a Maria Graham, in *Epistolario,* VIII, Ediz. naz. XXI, p. 241.

[12] Ad esempio nelle lettere alla Dacre del 1 aprile, 29 ottobre, 31 ottobre, 6 novembre, 18 novembre di quel 1821 e in quelle di lei al Foscolo del 15 agosto, 30 settembre, 9 ottobre, 29 ottobre, 3 novembre, 6 novembre, 18 novembre, tutte nel vol. VIII dell'Edizione nazionale dell'*Epistolario* (alcune con data probabile o ipotizzata).

«Soyez la dépositaire de l'exemplaire pour le petit Henry,[13] et vous le lui remet-
terez un jour, et peut-être comme un legat, en lui disant que lorsq'il pouvait à
peine prononcer mon nom, je l'amais et j'amais de jouer avec lui. M.rs H. Jones[14] m'ayant imposé le devoir de lui dire un long adieu, j'ose vous prier de lui
envoyer *de votre part* l'exemplaire qui lui appartient depuis le soir que notre
petit ouvrage a été conçu, lorsque je lisait Petrarque, et Elle était assise a coté
de moi; et s'il lui sera agréable, Elle ne devra qu'a sa soeur, tandis que je devrai
a vous, et à elle, et à votre frère, cette occasion de témoigner que je ne suis pas
un ingrat; et quoique le témoignage est inférieur à celui dont je me sens débi-
teur, il prouvera que ma reconnoissance est disinteressé, puisque je n'attende
plus de bontés pour l'avenir. Soyez hereuse; je n'oublirai pas d'avoir été votre
ami».[15]

Così, con una riaffermazione dell'impossibile mito dell'amicizia dopo la fine di
un amore, la vicenda sentimentale con Caroline poteva dirsi davvero conclusa;
mentre invece, secondo un processo che investe tanti altri scritti foscoliani, le
correzioni dell'autore al saggio sul Petrarca non si arrestavano e il testo urgeva
verso nuovi traguardi, verso l'edizione del 1822; e poi ancora verso l'altra londinese del '23,[16] chissà quanto anch'essa tormentata ancora dal Foscolo, se non
fosse stato egli sempre più stretto dall'assedio delle inquiete cure di quei suoi ultimi anni.

---

[13] Il fratello più giovane di Caroline.

[14] La sorella di Caroline, Katherine, andata sposa a Henry Jones.

[15] Abbozzo di lettera del maggio 1821 a Caroline Russell, nell'Appendice I (*Reliquie delle lettere a Caroline Russell*), in *Epistolario*, VIII, Ediz. naz. XXI, p. 431.

[16] Per le edizioni degli *Essays on Petrarch.* e al lavoro del Foscolo intorno ad esse, oltre alle pagine introduttive di CESARE FOLIGNO ai *Saggi e discorsi critici* nell'Edizione nazionale delle *Opere*, vol. X (Firenze, Le Monnier, 1953), si veda anche EUGENIA LEVI, *I saggi sul Petrarca di Ugo Foscolo*, «La Bibliofilia», XI, disp. 3-4 , a. XI, 1919; FREDERICK MAY, *The J. Deffett Francis copy of Ugo Foscolo's "Essays on Petrarch"*, «The National Library of Wales Journal», vol. XII, n. 4, Winter 1962; e la bibliografia in quel saggio riportata.

Thursday Evening
Febr. the 22.d
1821.

Sir—

I received your kind letter this evening when I intended to send back the proofs of the second Essay — *from* From my additions, and the correction will more *excessive* of the Translator you will see that those I wrote some days, the more so as I am very ill, and my Translator also confined in his bed. —

I keep the ‡ XIX section of the second Essay, having determined that each essay should consist of 18 sections; and I will put this last section in the third Essay where one is wanted — I am Sir —

Ever yours R. Foscolo.

S. Marino, California, Huntington Library, Rare book: 108739. Lettera del Foscolo del 22 febbraio 1821 a Samuel (?) Bentley. L'autografo è incollato all'interno di una copia degli *Essays on Petrarch*, London, Samuel and Richard Bentley, Dorset Street Fleet Street, XDCCCXXI, nella seconda pagina non numerata.

249

La prima lettera in questione si conserva negli Stati Uniti, alla Houghton Library dell'Università di Harvard, a Cambridge, Massachusetts, collocazione: ms. b MS Am 1631 (139).

È una lettera autografa indrizzata a John Cam Hobhouse, primo barone di Broughton.

Fu spedita da Mousley, il sobborgo di Londra dove dal 1818 il Foscolo risiedeva, nella casa trovatagli da Lady Pamela Fitzgerald e cedutagli in affitto dal falegname John Biden,[1] dove probabilmente la lettera fu scritta, luogo assai tranquillo e non molto lontano dalla villa degli Hobhouse a Whitton Park. La lettera reca solo la data del 14 aprile; ma l'anno 1819, oltre a leggersi abbastanza chiaramente nel timbro a secco dell'ufficio postale visibile sulla quarta facciata, si ricostruisce con evidenza anche dall'interno del testo per il comune accenno, presente anche nella precedente lettera dell'aprile da collocare nello stesso anno, rivolta allo stesso Hobhouse l'8 aprile di quell'anno (cfr. in Ediz. naz. delle *Opere* del Foscolo, vol. XXI [= *Epistolario*, VIII] a p. 41) alle « abitatrici di Whitton Park», alle dolci presenze femminili che allietavano in quella primavera la residenza di Hobhouse nel Middlesex, la contea vicina a Londra.

La lettera, autografa, consiste in un foglio di cm. 18.4 × 22.5, piegato in due. Il testo occupa le prime due facciate, mentre l'indirizzo si legge sulla quarta:

«John Hobhouse Esq.r
Whitton Park Middlesex[a]
   A o clock 16 Ap
     1819 E.V.»

Il timbro a secco dell'ufficio postale reca : « 12 o' clock Ap. 1819 N H». Il testo è il seguente:[*]

«Mon cher Monsieur –

Votre lettre m'a été remise à la porte de Mr. Wilbraham,[2] – mais comme il n'etait pas à diner chez lui, je n'ai pas jugé *proper*[3] d'y demeurer – j'ai mangé[b] une côte-

---

[a] « Middlesex» è leggibile a stento.

[b] «qu», cassato.

[*] Nella trascrizione del testo di entrambe le lettere si conserva il trattino, tipico della grafia foscoliana, nei punti di più o meno breve pausa del discorso. Viene rispettato anche, nella trascrizione, l'uso delle frequenti maiuscole, nonché nel francese della prima lettera l'imperfezione di qualche accento (Foscolo ad esempio scrive «repondre» anziché «répondre», «votre» anziché «vôtre», «fachons» anziché «fâchons», «indifference» per «indifférence»; e simili) secondo una incertezza d'uso attestabile, in qualche caso, nel '700 e '800 anche francese.

[1] Cfr. E. R.Vincent, *Ugo Foscolo esule fra gli Inglesi*. Edizione italiana a cura di U. Limentani, Firenze, Le Monnier, 1954, p. 82.

[2] «Mr. Wilbraham»: Roger Wilbraham (1743-1829) che aveva una villa a Twickenham , una decina di miglia fuori Londra e fu uno degli amici inglesi più devoti al Foscolo.

[3] *proper*: conveniente, opportuno. È aggettivo che dovette colpire il Foscolo per la sua ricchezza di significato e ampiezza d'uso ed è anche oggi variamente adoperato per indicare tutta l'area della opportunità, nella sua pertinenza aggettivale.

lette à Twickenham[c],[4] et je suis arrivé a Moulsey – Mon voisin qui avait *le chiavi*[5] était allé à Guilford,[6] et ce ne fut que après une[d] grosse demi heure que sa femme a reussì de les trouver – Le jour suivant j'ai fait des visites[7] dans le voisinage, et aujourd'hui je vais diner chez Wilbraham – demain chez Mr. Mansfield, un ami qui loge à Ruxley[8] – et après demain je retournerai à Londres à mon travail.

Ayant à passer tantôt par Hampton Court[9] près du post-office, je profite[e] du papier et de l'encre que je puis trouver ici – car j'ai oublié même les clefs de ma table, en ville, – pour reponde à votre note[f] d'avant hier,[10] et vous assurer que je n'en ai été aucunement ni faché, ni affligé, et l'histoire que je vous ai fait ici vous preuvera[g] que j'ai eu le desplaisir de perdre l'aimable societé delle *Abitatrici di Whitton Park*[h],[11] mais que, a cela près, j'ai passé trois jours agreables / d'autant plus que dans mes courses j'ai toujours eu pour compagnie le Soleil, et *Genitalis aura Favoni.*[12] Aussi je vous prie de ne point vous en affliger à votre tour. C'est la faute plus des choses que des hommes; et puisque[i] les choses ne nous écoutent pas lorsque nous nous fachons contr'elles, le meilleur parti est de les prendre avec indifference.

[c] la «h» è aggiunta in seguito tra la «n» e la «a».

[d] «gos», cassato.

[e] «profite», su «me servirai», cassato.

[f] «note» si legge abbastanza chiaramente. Costa, invece, trascrive: «lettre».

[g] su «prouve», cassato.

[h] Foscolo però scrive «Parck».

[i] rifatto su altra parola illeggibile.

[4] *Twickenham* : è la cittadina che si trova nella contea del Middlesex, caratterizzata dalla presenza di numerosi frutteti che fioriscono anche nelle altre zone vicine, come Brentfors e Isleworth.

[5] Così in italiano nel testo.

[6] Guilford è cittadina del Surrey, a 46 km circa a sud ovest di Londra, in amena posizione su un declivio delle montagne North Downs. Il fiume Wey, col suo percorso, la collega con il Tamigi.

[7] La lettura non è agevole, anche per una piccola lacerazione diagonale sul bordo della carta. Sembra più probabile, comunque, leggere «visites», mentre «voyages», proposto da Costa, è da escludere, per evidenza grafica e anche per ragioni semantiche.

[8] *Ruxley*: località del Kent, a sud-est di Londra.

[9] *Hampton Court* : il luogo noto per essere sede dello Hampton Court Palace, eretto nel 1514 dal cardinale Wolsey e donato poi a Enrico VIII. Arricchito in seguito di cortili e giardini, acquistò notevole rinomanza, così che il territorio ad esso circostante divenne luogo di attrazione per la costruzione di abitazioni della buona società inglese, che vi abitava nel periodo estivo o vi veniva per qualche week-end.

[10] *votre note d'avant hier* : non si ha notizia dello scritto a cui il Foscolo qui allude.

[11] *Abitatrici di Whitton Park* : l'insieme delle presenze femminili di casa Hobhouse, presenti durante le visite del Foscolo nella residenza di campagna della famiglia. La stessa espressione il Foscolo aveva usato nella lettera precedente, dell'8 aprile, con cui si scusava di non poter raggiungere entro quella settimana la famiglia amica.

[12] *Genitalis aura Favoni* : è citazione da Lucrezio; ma il testo lucreziano reca *genitabilis* non *genitalis* (: «Nam simul ac species patefactast verna dici / et reserata viget *genitabilis aura favoni...»*, *De rer. nat.*, I, 11). Si conserva, tuttavia, lo scorso di penna foscoliano, che non fu certo d'intelletto, per quanto egli voglia indubbiamente significare qui soltanto il vivificante soffio del Favonio. Costa, il precedente editore, che correda la lettera con un ottimo lavoro di annotazione, per questo punto particolare non rileva l'inesattezza foscoliana e la conserva senza commento, pur citando poi correttamente , ma fuori del testo della lettera, le parole di Lucrezio (*genitabilis aura Favoni*).

Adieu – Portez vous bien, jouissez de la campagne et du primtems, – tandis que je retournerai avec les Libraires, les imprimeurs, les traducteurs, et tous les diables – Mais il le faut – Adieu.

Moulsey, Jeudi
14 aprile.[13]   Tout à vous
                                    Hugues Foscolo».

L'altra lettera foscoliana è quella del 22 febbraio 1821, a Samuel (?) Bentley.

La lettera, autografa, è contenuta nel volume conservato alla Huntington Library di S. Marino, California, (collocazione «Rare book: 108739»), UGO FOSCOLO, *Essays on Petrarch*, London, Printed for the Author by Samuel and Richard Bentley, Dorset Street Fleet Street, MDCCC.XXI; ed è incollata nella seconda pagina non numerata di esso, dopo il frontespizio, su carta di cm 12,9 × 20,2. Fu scritta la sera del 22 febbraio, come la data specifica esplicitamente:

«Thursday Evening
Febr. the 22d. 1821.

Sir –

I received your kind letter this evening when I intended to send back the proofs of the second Essay[1] [a] From my additions, and from[b] the correction still more excessive[c] of the Translator[2] you will see that[d] I wanted some days, the more so as I am very ill, and my Translator also confined in his bed. –

---

[a]«By», cassato.
[b]«from», aggiunto sul rigo.
[c]Corretto su parola illeggibile.
[d]Su cassato «it w».

---

[13] In chiusa il Foscolo ritorna all'italiano («aprile» dunque, e non «avril»), nell'indicazione del mese della data, come a formula più consueta a cui la mano corre, quasi senza che più il pensiero la controlli.

[1] È il secondo saggio sul Petrarca, intitolato *An Essay on the Poetry of Petrarch* (cfr. Edizione nazionale delle *Opere*, vol. X, *Saggi e discorsi critici*, a cura di C. Foligno, Firenze, Le Monnier, 1953; pp. 37-78).

[2] Non sembra si possa affermare con sicurezza quale sia il traduttore del Foscolo in questo momento. Né, d'altra parte, è possibile ritenere che dicendo «the Translator» Foscolo intendesse parlare di una traduttrice, ad esempio Lady Dacre, che tradusse poi per Foscolo alcune liriche del Petrarca ad arricchimento del volume dei saggi sul Petrarca, ma solo nell'edizione del 1823; e per altro Lady Barbarina, già vedova Wilmot, che aveva poi sposato Lord Dacre, era traduttrice dall'esperienza limitata. Del resto, a escludere quella ipotesi basta il fatto che proprio in una lettera a Lady Dacre, del 30 luglio 1820, il Foscolo diceva di dover raggiungere il suo traduttore che «menace de partir pour le Devonshire, et d'y rester jusque Novembre» , precisando che colui era «eloigné douze milles de Londres» (v. Lettera a Lady Dacre cit. in *Epistolario*, VIII, Ediz. naz. delle *Opere*, XXI, p. 191). È appunto di costui che non è certa l'identità.

I keep the[e] XIX section of the second Essay, having determined that each essay should consist of *18*[f] sections : and I will put this last section in the third Essay where one is wanted[3] –

I am, Sir - Ever yours

H. Foscolo»

[e] Un'asta verticale («I») di numero romano, cassata.
[f] «18» sottolineato nell'originale.

[3] Sia il primo saggio (*An Essay on the Love of Petrarch*), che il secondo e il terzo (*An Essay on the Poetry of Petrarch* e *An Essay on the character of Petrarch*) sono ripartiti in XVIII sezioni o paragrafi. Sembra probabile, ma non è più che un'ipotesi, che sia divenuta sezione XVIII[a] dell'ultimo saggio quella che dovette essere la XIX[a] del secondo. Le espressioni dell'attuale sezione XVIII[a] dell'ultimo saggio «from *reflecting* upon the mournful events» (ed. cit., p.106) e «his restless *mind*» (*ibid.*, p. 106) potrebbero essere segni di ripresa e connettivi linguistici adattati e rioperanti nella mente dello scrittore all'atto di assestare quell'ultima sezione, ex XIX[a] dunque, staccandola dalla posizione susseguente alla XVIII[a] del secondo saggio, nella quale anche si parla della «history of *the mind* of a man of genius» (*ibid.*, p. 78) e di Petrarca che «awakens us *to reflection* upon ourselves» (*ibid.*, p. 78). Ma solo una verifica sulle bozze corrette in quel febbraio 1821 garantirebbe la certezza su questo punto.

Jonathan Culler

THE DEVIL AND MODERNITY: BAUDELAIRE'S *FLEURS DU MAL*

Paul Verlaine was perhaps the first to say it: "la profonde originalité de Charles Baudelaire est à mon avis de représenter puissamment et essentiellement l'homme moderne."[1] Whether Baudelaire embodies or portrays modern man, *Les Fleurs du Mal* is seen as exemplary of modern experience, of the possibility of experiencing or dealing with what we have come to call the modern world. T. S. Eliot writes, "Baudelaire is indeed the greatest exemplar in *modern* poetry in any language, for his verse and language is the nearest thing to a complete renovation that we have experienced. But his renovation of an attitude towards life is no less radical and no less important."[2] And outside the field of literature we find such affirmations as Harold Rosenberg's dating of "the tradition of the New" to Baudelaire, "who exactly one hundred years ago invited fugitives from the too-narrow world of memory to come aboard with him in search of the new."[3] Baudelaire, writes another critic, "did more than anyone else in the nineteenth century to make the men and women of his century aware of themselves as moderns... If we had to nominate a first modernist, Baudelaire would surely be the man."[4]

There seems a considerable consensus on this point but, surprisingly, there is great difference of opinion about what it is that makes Baudelaire modern and worthy of special attention. Is it, as Albert Thibaudet and Walter Benjamin argue, that he was the first true poet of the city, the first to take the alienated experience of life in the modern city as the norm? Or is it, as Leo Bersani claims, that Baudelaire discovered and displayed the mobility of fantasy and of the desiring imagination? Or is it that Baudelaire invents modern self-consciousness about poetry itself, producing poems which allegoricaly expose the operations of the lyric?[5]

---

[1] P. Verlaine, "Charles Baudelaire", J. Borel ed., *Oeuvres en prose complètes*, Paris, 1972, pp. 599-600.

[2] T. S. Eliot, "Baudelaire", *Selected Essays*, London, 1951, p. 426.

[3] H. Rosenberg, *The Tradition of the New*, New York, 1959, p. 11.

[4] M. Berman, *All that is Solid Melts into Air: The Experience of Modernity*, New York, 1982, pp. 132-3.

[5] For these views see, respectively, A. Thibaudet, "Baudelaire", *Intérieurs*, Paris, 1924; W. Benjamin, *Charles Baudelaire: A Lyric Poet in the Era of High Capitalism*, London, 1973; L. Bersani, *Baudelaire and Freud*, Berkeley, 1977; and P. de Man, "Anthropomorphism and Trope in the Lyric", *The Rhetoric of Romanticism*, New York, 1983.

There are many competing accounts of what is most particularly modern and important about Baudelaire, but the one thing on which contentious critics seem to agree, is that there is a side of Baudelaire which is of no interest today, which belongs to a *bas romantisme* and is the very antithesis of Baudelaire's modernity, of Baudelaire the founder of modern poetry: this is the Baudelaire who invokes demons and the Devil. Most critics today pass over this in silence, but even those who explicitly address this Baudelaire seem to find him an embarrassment. Even the author of a book entitled *The Demonic Imagination: Style and Theme in French Romantic Poetry* begins his chapter on Baudelaire: "Baudelaire has, by now, ceased to interest us for the reasons which once appeared important: his diabolical Catholicism is a familiar, historical mode of sensibility which neither shocks nor has morbid appeal...".[6] And Fredric Jameson distinguishes the modernist and the post-modernist Baudelaires – both worthy of our attention, – from what he calls the "second-rate post-Romantic Baudelaire, the Baudelaire of diabolism and of cheap *frisson*, the poet of blasphemy and of a creaking and musty religious machinery that was no more interesting in the mid-nineteenth century than it is today."[7]

But Baudelaire called his collection *Les Fleurs du Mal* and opens it with a poem which declares, "C'est le Diable qui tient le fils qui nous remuent". Can this be dismissed as an irrelevancy – something mistakenly appended to this quintessentially modern poetry? That critics of such different orientations should agree in shunting aside the Satanic Baudelaire suggests that there is something worth investigating here, something disquieting and embarrassing, which may not in fact be merely trivial – which may complicate the story of modernity that has come to depend on Baudelaire as its originator. Perhaps the Satanic Baudelaire would tell us things about modernity we don't want to know.

Certainly the idea of the Devil seems fundamentally at odds with accounts of modernity. Even Christianity itself seems to regard the Devil as outmoded mythology, irrelevant to a modern religion. The introduction to an issue of the Catholic review *Communio* devoted to "Satan, mystère d'iniquité" declares, "nous avons peine à l'évoquer. Satan nous semble d'un autre âge, classé dans les vieilles imageries térrorisantes des religions de la peur."[8] What could be less modern than Satan – a scrawny red man with horns, hooves, tail and pitchfork?

Baudelaire, however, would have laughed at the idea of progress and enlighten-

---

[6] J. P. HOUSTON, *The Demonic Imagination: Style and Theme in French Romantic Poetry*, Baton Rouge, Louisiana, 1969, p. 85.

[7] F. JAMESON, "Baudelaire as Modernist and Postmodernist: The Dissolution of the Referent and the Artificial 'Sublime'", C. Hosek and P. Parker, eds., *Lyric Poetry: Beyond New Criticism*, Ithaca, N.Y., 1985, p. 247.

[8] *Communio* IV: 3 (May-June 1979), p. 2.

ment that lies behind all these comments – which present themselves as sophisticated while continuing to rely on notions of intellectual progress he would have regarded as simplistic and deluded. His prose poem *Le Joueur généreux* reminds us, "n'oublier jamais, quand vous entendez vanter le progrès des lumières, que la plus belle des ruses du diable est de vous persuader qu'il n'existe pas!"[9] Baudelaire reserves special scorn for George Sand, who had complained in the preface to one of her novels that modern Christians shouldn't be required to believe in the Devil, that a true Christian could not believe in Hell. This just shows, Baudelaire remarks, that the Devil does not scorn "les imbéciles" but makes good use of them, to do his work for him. "Elle est *possédée*", he writes. "C'est le Diable qui lui a persuadé de se fier à *son bon coeur* et à *son bon sens*", in rejecting the idea of the Devil (I, 686-7).

Now Satan appears in few poems of *Les Fleurs du Mal*, but Baudelaire gives him a prominent place. Let me mention the most important moments before taking them up in more detail. The opening poem, *Au Lecteur*, firmly declares, "C'est le Diable qui tient les fils qui nous remuent"! The first poem of the section of *Les Fleurs du Mal* entitled *Fleurs du Mal* also features Satan. *La Déstruction* begins:

> Sans cesse à mes côtés s'agite le Démon;
> Il nage autour de moi comme un air impalpable.

And after *Les Fleurs du Mal* had been condemned for offense to public morals, Baudelaire wrote an "Épigraphe pour un livre condamné" for the second edition of the collection – though he in the end did not include it. This poem claims that readers who haven't studied with Satan, that crafty dean, should throw away this book:

> Lecteur paisible et bucolique,
> Sobre et naif homme de bien,
> Jette ce livre saturnien,
> Orgiaque et mélancolique.
>
> Si tu n'as fait ta rhétorique
> Chez Satan, le rusé doyen,
> Jette! tu n'y comprendrais rien
> Ou tu me croirais hystérique. (I, 137)

But what does it mean for him to invoke the Devil in this way? Let me say straight away that it seems likely that Baudelaire himself did not have an answer to this question – "Se livrer à Satan, qu'est-ce que c'est"? he asks in

---

[9] Ch. Baudelaire, *Oeuvres complètes*, C. Pichois ed., Paris, 1975, vol. I, p. 327. References to this edition will henceforth be given in parentheses in the text.

his *Journaux intimes* (I, 663). He would have been all too happy, one suspects, to sell himself to the Devil, if only he could discover what it entailed, for he spent his life vainly trying to sell himself to editors, publishers, even the Académie française. Indeed, one of the prose poems, *Le Joueur généreux*, represents just such a Satanic transaction, and at the end of the poem the sinner prays not for deliverance from the infernal pact but for the Devil to keep the bargain. "Mon Dieu! Seigneur, Mon Dieu! faites que le diable me tienne sa parole"! (I, 328).

But the fact that Baudelaire did not know what it would mean to give oneself to the Devil makes the question all the more important. What is the significance of the Devil in *Les Fleurs du Mal*? Is it an unimportant bit of mythological machinery or does the figure of the Devil, on the contrary, bring forward crucial problems and issues that we ignore by dismissing him? What threat does this figure pose that we need to set him aside? And if the threat is primarily to the idea of Baudelaire as the first modern or the quintessentially modern poet, why do we have such a stake in modernizing him?

Let me emphasize that I am not just asking what it meant to write poems about the Devil in mid-nineteenth-century France – a question that certainly has no simple or single answer (Baudelaire says of his contemporaries, "il est plus difficile pour les gens de ce siècle de croire au Diable que de l'aimer. Tout le monde le sent et personne n'y croit". (I, 182-3)) I am not just asking a historical question but am asking, rather, what sort of thinking can do justice to the force and distinctiveness of these poems today.

Au lecteur introduces the Devil. Here are the familiar opening stanzas.

> La sottise, l'erreur, le péché, la lésine,
> Occupent nos esprits et travaillent nos corps,
> Et nous alimentons nos aimables remords,
> Comme les mendiants nourissent leur vermine.
>
> Nos péchés sont têtus, nos repentirs sont lâches;
> Nous nous faisons payer grassement nos aveux,
> Et nous rentrons gaiement dans le chemin bourbeux,
> Croyant par de vils pleurs laver toutes nos taches.
>
> Sur l'oreiller du mal c'est Satan Trismégiste
> Qui berce longuement notre esprit enchanté,
> Et le triste métal de notre volonté
> Est tout vaporisé par ce savant chimiste.
>
> C'est le Diable qui tient les fils qui nous remuent.

The movement of *Au Lecteur* suggests that if, as the opening stanza has it, stupidity, error and sin occupy us and work us over, if we even nourish our remorse and proceed jauntily down the muddy road of sin, it is *because* our spirit is bewitched, because Satan has vaporized our will. We are his puppets. The opening line of the fourth stanza, "C'est le Diable qui tient les fils qui nous remuent"! comes with the force of an answer or explanation. The Devil holds the strings; sometimes he makes us act, sometimes prevents us from having the will to act as we would.

The next two stanzas stress not this diabolical agency presumed to cause our weakness and wickedness but our resulting complaisance or connivance with vice: it seems that the Devil pulling the strings results in our finding repugnant objects attractive, passing through stinking darkness without horror, and furtively snatching pleasures from which we try to squeeze every drop of enjoyment.

> C'est le Diable qui tient les fils qui nous remuent.
> Aux objects répugnants nous trouvons des appas;
> Chaque jour vers l'Enfer nous descendons d'un pas,
> Sans horreur, à travers des ténèbres qui puent.
>
> Ainsi qu'un débauché pauvre qui baise et mange
> Le sein martyrisé d'une antique catin,
> Nous volons au passage un plaisir clandestin
> Que nous pressons bien fort, comme une vieille orange.

But the seventh stanza reopens the question of who is responsible.

> Si le viol, le poison, le poignard, l'incendie,
> N'ont pas encore brodé de leur plaisant dessins
> Le canevas banal de nos piteux destins,
> C'est que notre âme, hélas, n'est pas assez hardie.

If the banality or triviality of our lives has not been decorated by rape, murder, arson, etc., it is because our souls are not bold enough. There is here a shift of agency in these first two lines, which makes rape and murder the agents that may or may not yet have put their designs on our fate. This shift seems to reinforce the notion that we are hapless creatures carrying out projects conceived elsewhere, but if, as the last line of this stanza sententiously declares, our lack of boldness is to blame, then what are we to think? Perhaps we are not the Devil's puppets after all – only mediocrities too timid for real sin (this is, I believe, the most common interpretation of the poem). Or is the timidity of our souls, rather, an example of what stanza three called Satan's vaporization of our will and thus an instance of his pulling the strings?

The last three stanzas shift the scene, in that strange way characteristic of Baudelaire: from an external scene where the speaker figures as a character to an allegorical space bounded by the speaker: it is as though Satan's pulling the strings of a hapless human puppet gave rise to this other space, which the poem calls "la ménagerie infâme de nos vices", where the beasts that are also demons clamor, groan, prance, or yawn.

Here is the rest of the poem:

> Mais parmi les chacals, les panthères, les lices,
> Les singes, les scorpions, les vautours, les serpents,
> Les monstres glapissants, hurlants, grognants, rampants,
> Dans la ménagerie infâme de nos vices,
>
> Il en est un plus laid, plus méchant, plus immonde!
> Quoiqu'il ne pousse ni grands gestes ni grands cris,
> Il ferait volontiers de la terre un débris
> Et dans un bâillement avalerait le monde;
>
> C'est l'Ennui! – l'oeil chargé d'un pleur involontaire,
> Il rêve d'échafauds en fumant son houka.
> Tu le connais, lecteur, ce monstre délicat,
> – Hypocrite lecteur, – mon semblable, – mon frère!

Though the Devil pulls the strings he is no longer on the scene when the poem turns to this zoo and to the ugliest, meanest, most disgusting of these monsters, *Ennui*, who dreams of executions and wouldn't mind swallowing the world in a yawn.

Is the presence of this monster in our world the work of the Devil or not? One can't be sure. The allegorical scene of yawning *Ennui* puffing his hooka like an oriental pasha seems far removed from that of Satan manipulating human puppets. Is it that, with the Devil pulling the strings and vaporizing our will, we are left vulnerable to this delicate monster? Is the very promotion of *ennui* to a fearsome monster of our inner life an example of the Devil's control?

This poem seems, in its development, to pose the problem of the Devil in a way that I would call forceful, were it not for the fact that critics succeed in ignoring it – no doubt because the poem ends not with the Devil but with *Ennui*, which becomes the focus of attention. But the poem announces, as though it were the explanation of the human predicament described in the first two stanzas, that the Devil holds the strings that move us. It then proceeds to offer further description of human complicity with vice in a scenario which reaches its climax with the worst monster, without telling us whether we know this delicate monster and lodge him in the menagerie of our vices *because* the Devil controls us or whether, on the contrary, as critics have sometimes suggested, it is the overpowering presence of *Ennui* that gives the Devil his power to seduce. What happens in the opening poem, I suggest, happens in the collection as a whole: the poems with an important framing function claim that the Devil is ubiquitous, but subsequent poems do not tell us whether the scenes or movements they narrate are examples of the Devil's work. Perhaps this is what is most worrying about the Devil – that we don't know what is his work and what is not.

The second framing poem I mentioned, *La Destruction* – the inaugural poem of the section entitled *Fleurs du Mal* – begins with another assertion of the Devil's presence:

> Sans cesse à mes côtés s'agite le Démon;
> Il nage autour de moi comme un air impalpable.
> Je l'avale et le sens qui brûle mon poumon
> Et l'emplit d'un désir éternel et coupable.

Impalpable but omnipresent, the Devil pulls the strings, seducing the speaker in the guise of a woman or proffering disgusting potions or drugs.

> Parfois il prend, sachant mon grand amour de l'Art,
> La forme de la plus séduisante des femmes,
> Et, sous de spécieux pretextes de cafard,
> Accoutume ma lèvre à des philtres infâmes.

> Il me conduit ainsi, loin du regard de Dieu
> Haletant et brisé de fatique, au milieu
> Des plaines de l'Ennui, profondes et désertes.

Here the question left open in *Au lecteur* seems to receive a definite answer. If the speaker is in the plains of *Ennui*, it is because the Devil leads him there, in this way (*ainsi*): by always stirring at his side, by filling him with culpable desires, by taking the form of the most seductive of women and by accustoming him to infamous potions. Two peculiar things are worth noting here. First, the scenario hinted at in *Au lecteur* and affirmed in *La Destruction* differs from traditional tales of Satan, where the Devil doesn't lead you _into ennui_ but out of it, by providing special powers, knowledge, or sensual opportunities (in exchange for your soul). In Baudelaire, though, *ennui* is not the condition of or point of departure for the Devil's work but its result. This is singular and distinctive. Second, the poem ends with an allegorical event considerably more enigmatical than Ennui's dreaming of scaffolds in *Au lecteur*. Here the Devil leads the speaker into the plains of *Ennui*:

> Il me conduit ainsi, loin du regard de Dieu,
> Haletant et brisé de fatique, au milieu
> Des plaines de l'Ennui, profondes et désertes.

> Et jette dans mes yeux pleins de confusion
> Des vêtements souillés, des blessures ouvertes,
> Et l'appareil sanglant de la Destruction!

The combination in these closing lines of the sonnet of strangely unresonant abstraction – "l'appareil sanglant de la destruction" – and unlocated specificity – "vêtements souillés" and "blessures ouvertes" – makes it difficult to grasp what the Devil might be throwing in his face, and this very difficulty seems to raise the possibility that any scenario elsewhere in Baudelaire's poems involving such things as wounds, destruction, blood, or soiled clothes, can be seen as the Devil's work. One might imagine that since the Devil conducts me *"ainsi"*, in the guise of a woman, what the Devil as woman throws in the speaker's face is menstruation, as sign of the monstruousness of feminine sexuality. But this interpretation may fail to live up to the curious "appareil sanglant de la destruction", which, unresonant though it be, nevertheless has a *prima facie* importance since it provides or echoes the title of the poem. The difficulty of grasping what the Devil is about here, I'm tempted to conclude – here at the point where a poem of *Les Fleurs du Mal* seems most explicitly to tell us what it is that the Devil does – heightens the question of the extent to which the Devil is at work in the adventures and obsessions of the speakers of these poems.

But there is one suggestion that needs to be pursued in the strange endings of the two poems cited so far. The puzzling "appareil sanglant de la destruction" recalls *Ennui* who "rêve d'échafauds". In one case the Devil leads the speaker into the plains of *Ennui* and throws what might well be the guillotine before his eyes. In the other the Devil leaves us threatened by *Ennui* who dreams of executions and would swallow the whole world in a yawn. Together the poems seem to carry the suggestion that Devil is behind an *ennui* linked with revolutionary executions.

Associating Satan with the French Revolution was a right-wing commonplace. Baudelaire's *maître à penser* Joseph de Maistre, had written, "Il y a dans la Révolution française un caractère satanique qui le distingue de tout ce qu'on a vu et peut-être de tout ce qu'on verra."[10] Baudelaire was certainly touched as well by the nineteenth-century tradition of revolutionary Satanism, which also identified Satan with those in revolt against authority. As Eugen Weber describes it,

Si, pour les maîtres de la Restauration, la liberté était diabolique, pourquoi les liberaux ne prendraient-ils pas parti pour le diable?... Si, pour ses ennemis, la Révolution était le fait de Satan, les partisans de la Révolution devaient lui en savoir gré. Si les ennemis de la Révolution avaient cause liée avec Dieu, si les oppresseurs des peuples... regnaient par sa grace, le liberal et le romantique (souvent une et même personne) pouvaient bien suivre Satan en son exil et rejeter un ciel trop réactionnaire et trop bourgeois, selon les régimes, pour les attirer.[11]

---

[10] J. DE MAISTRE, *Considérations sur la France* (1796), *Oeuvres complètes*, Lyon-Paris, 1884, vol. 1, p. 55.
[11] E. WEBER, *Satan, Franc Maçon*, Paris, 1964, pp. 11-12.

Baudelaire's *Abel et Caïn*, from the section of *Les Fleurs du Mal* titled "Révolte", was written during his period of revolutionary enthusiasm in 1848 and concludes with the injunction (or possibly description in the present tense),

> Race de Caïn, monte au ciel,
> Et sur la terre jette Dieu.

But in general it is striking – given Baudelaire's interest in Satan – how little he participates in the reversals of romantic Satanism that make the Devil a hero, praised for his revolt against an oppressive despot. Baudelaire's only poem that places Satan in the title, *Les Litanies de Satan,* invokes him in liturgical accents, in the form of supplication and response, and substitutes Satan for Mary in the response or refrain, "O Satan, prends pitié de ma longue misère". This poem addresses Satan as one who, responsible for evil, may have pity for humans and even offer solace to human sufferers, but solace of a kind whose value is, to say the least, ambiguous. Satan, it is said, engenders hope (which may be a further illusion and source of torture); he teaches courage in adversity (a good thing, but which does not overcome adversity); he knows where metals and precious stones are hidden underground (which inspires greed and strife); he gives men gunpowder, he inspires perversions which bring solace (such as the "culte de la plaie et des guenilles"), and so on. This Satanic poem is remarkable, I think, for the modesty of its claims for the figure it addresses structurally as a kind of God: Satan is not a heroic rebel but a figure who offers minor consolations to social outcasts.

Though Baudelaire occasionally grants Satan the beauty and grandeur of a fallen archangel – as when he calls Milton's Satan the model of virile beauty (I, 658) or speaks in *L'Irrémédiable* of "la conscience dans le Mal" as a "flambeau des graces sataniques", and "soulagement et gloire uniques", he does not seek to reverse values and rehabilitate Satan. Indeed, a passage of romantic Satanism from Balzac's *Splendeurs et misères des courtisanes,* a passage sometimes thought to contain the germ of Baudelaire's title, *Les Fleurs du mal,* will help to measure Baudelaire's distance from the conceptions of his contemporaries. In *Splendeurs et misères,* Lucien de Rubempré says to Vautrin (Carlos Herrera):

Il y a la postérité de Caïn et celle d'Abel, comme vous disiez quelquefois. Caïn, dans le grand drame de l'Humanité, c'est l'opposition. Vous descendez d'Adam par cette ligne en qui le diable a continué de souffler le feu dont la première étincelle avait été jetée sur Ève. Parmi les démons de cette filiation il s'en trouve, de temps en temps, de terribles, à organisations vastes, qui résument toutes les forces humaines, et qui ressemblent à ces fiévreux animaux du desert dont la vie exige les espaces immenses qu'ils y trouvent. Ces gens-là sont dangereux comme des lions le seraient en pleine Normandie: il leur faut une pâture, ils dévorent les hommes vulgaires et broutent les écus des niais... Quand Dieu le veut, ces êtres mystérieux sont Moïse, Atilla, Charlemagne, Mahomet, ou Na-

263

poléon; mais, quand ils laissent rouiller au fond de l'océan d'une génération ces instruments gigantesques, ils ne sont plus que Pugatcheff, Robespierre, Louvel, et l'Abbé Carlos Herrera. Doués d'un immense pouvoir sur les âmes tendres, ils les attirent et les broient. C'est la plante vénéneuse aux riches couleurs qui fascine les enfants dans les bois. C'est la poésie du mal.[12]

In romantic Satanism we have Satanic characters – either Satan himself made a character in a substantial narrative (as in Hugo and Vigny) or other characters identified as Satanic surrogates, as in Byron or here in Balzac. Baudelaire, however, does not make Satan a character in a narrative – even in *Les Litanies de Satan* he is an addressee with certain sympathies and achievements but not a figure in a story of reversal. Baudelaire, unlike many of his immediate precursors, does not participate in the rehabilitation of the Devil that structures such major efforts as Vigny's "Éloa", Lamartine's *La Chute d'un ange* and, eventually, Hugo's *La Fin de Satan*. The historian Ernest Renan wrote in 1855, two years before the publication of *Les Fleurs du Mal*, "De tous les êtres autrefois maudits que la tolérance de notre siècle a relevé de leur anathème, Satan est sans doute celui qui a le plus gagné au progrès des lumières et de l'universelle civilisation."[13] But Baudelaire was not an agent of the progress of enlightenment.

On the contrary, unrehabilitated, the Devil takes his importance in *Les Fleurs du Mal* from the way Baudelaire puts him into the poems which frame and present the book, such as *Au lecteur*, the opening poem of the book, *La Destruction*, the opening poem of the title section, and the epigraph projected for the second edition. Another poem where Satan is explicitly mentioned, *L'Irrémédiable*, from the end of the section "Spleen et l'Idéal", approaches the question of what the Devil controls in another way. (Note, incidentally, the appearance of le *diable* in the title *L'Irrémédiable*). The first seven stanzas of the poem present a series of images of human oppression and entrapment – a being fallen into "un Styx bourbeux et plombé", a "malheureux" seeking vainly to flee "un lieu plein de reptiles", and so on – images which, the poem suggests, illustrate Satan's effectiveness:

> – Emblèmes nets, tableau parfait
> D'une fortune irrémédiable,
> Qui donne à penser que le Diable
> Fait toujours bien tout ce qu'il fait!

But the phrase "donne à penser" leaves open the possibility that we may be mistaken. These images make one think that the Devil always does his work well, but perhaps the Devil isn't really responsible for these disasters and entrapments after

---

[12] H. DE BALZAC, *Splendeurs et misères des courtisanes*, A. Adam ed., Paris, 1987, pp. 473-4.
[13] E. RENAN, *L'Artiste*, 27 May 1855.

all – perhaps, for example, we are mislead by the rhyme into seeing the Devil in any fate deemed *irrémédiable*. Since *L'Irremediable* immediately proceeds in the next stanza to speak of the

> Tête-à-tête sombre et limpide
> Qu'un coeur devenu son miroir!

it is possibile that the earlier images show not the Devil's efficacy and ubiquity but rather the heart's power of projection – displaying what is generated when, as in the production of the literary works from which these images or emblems are drawn, consciousness imaginatively reflects on itself. On the other hand, it could be that this sombre self-reflection is another example of the Devil's work: he pulls the strings of self-reflexivity too, making hearts become their own mirrors, to disastrous effect. Perhaps no self-scrutiny would occur in an unfallen world or if the Devil hadn't led us into the plains of *Ennui*. Here too, the appearance in the poem of the figure of the Devil seems to give rise to this problem: is he responsible? What is most diabolical about the Devil, I am tempted to conclude, is that we can never be sure when he is at work.

The foregrounding of Satan in the framing poems, and a few others, such as *L'Irrémédiable*, poses the question of whether he is not responsible for what is described in the poems within the volume where he may make no obvious appearance. Are we observing the effects of Satanic control or his stimulation of perverse appetites, or is there some other explanation? For example, in *Les Sept Vieillards*, a poem from *Tableaux parisiens*, the speaker encounters a sinister old man with an evil glitter in his eye, who staggers along,

> Comme s'il écrasait des morts sous ses savates,
> Hostile à l'univers plutôt qu'indifférent.

This sinister figure seems to multiply himself – seven times:

> Son pareil le suivait: barbe, oeil, dos, bâton, loques,
> Nul trait ne distinguait, du même enfer venu,
> Ce jumeau centenaire, et ces spectres baroques
> Marchaient du même pas vers un but inconnu.

The speaker suspects a plot:

> A quel complot infâme étais-je donc en butte?

Is this a satanic plot? Or could be mere chance that wickedly humiliates him by making him suspect a plot?

> A quel complot infâme étais-je donc en butte,
> Ou quel méchant hasard ainsi m'humiliait?

265

> Car je comptais sept fois, de minute en minute,
> Ce sinistre viellard qui se multipliait!

This poem, like others, seems to prevent one from making a Satanic plot or Satanic influence an explanation on which one could rely.

The Devil, then, is the name of a problem. Sometimes – in Baudelaire's prose notes particularly – we may seem to be confronting a version of the traditional problem of the Devil's disguises. Writing of *Les Liaisons dangereuses*, Baudelaire speaks of "Valmont Satan" and of Mme de Merteuil as "une Ève satanique". Apparently, Satan may take the form of or work through manifest villains, such as they, but these are 18th century Satans, and in the nineteenth century, Baudelaire claims,

l'énergie du mal a baissé. – Et la niaiserie a pris la place de l'esprit... En réalité, le satanisme a gagné. Satan s'est fait ingénu [manifesting himself, for instance, in George Sand]. Le mal se connaissant était moins affreux et plus près de la guérison que le mal s'ignorant. George Sand inférieure à de Sade. (II, 68)

In the eighteenth century, he continues, "on se damnait moins bêtement".

But if the Devil can manifest himself as easily in George Sand as in Melmoth or Madame de Merteuil, or Gilles de Rais, then he has become so ubiquitous as to be a different sort of figure – one which represents above all the possibility that anything or anyone, however innocent they may appear, can work for ill. As the supreme master of ruse and deceit, the Devil incarnates the ubiquity of deception, evil – or, to put it in other terms, the speculative possibility of dialectic, in which what looks beneficial at one level may prove at another to be horrible and oppressive. One can never tell where the Devil is at work. "Il nage autour de moi comme un air impalpable", says *La Destruction,* dissolved into the very air we breathe. Sometimes he takes the form of "la plus séduisante des femmes". So there is always a question, it seems, whether a woman is a Satanic manifestation. "De Satan ou de Dieu, qu'importe"? or "Ange ou Démon, qu'importe"? exclaim Baudelaire's narrators in moments of great desperation (echoing Hugo's apostrophe to Napoleon: "Tu domines notre âge. Ange ou démon, qu'importe"?) But the fact that this "qu'importe"? comes as the climax of agonized reflection shows that usually Baudelairian speakers care very much whether they are dealing with the Devil, though they can never know for sure. If what is most diabolical about the Devil is the difficulty of deciding whether he is at work in a particular scene or situation, then the figure of the Devil poses the general question of whether there is *meaning* to the scenarios in which we are caught up or misfortunes that befall us or whether they are simply accidents. Can we escape our sense that there are malignant forces that operate independently of human intentions or that the world often works against us? "Everyone *feels* the Devil and no one believes in him", wrote Baudelaire in a projected preface to *Les Fleurs du Mal.* (I, 182-3)

But if the Devil is the name of a force that works on us against our will – if, as Baudelaire says in *Au lecteur,* "le riche metal de notre volonté / Est tout vaporisé par ce savant chimiste" – isn't he just a personification of aspects of the Unconscious or the Id, of forces that make us do what our conscious selves might reject? To make Baudelaire modern can't we just cross out *Devil* and write in *Unconscious* or, better, *Death Drive,* or *Repetition Compulsion?*

There is something to be said for this view, though one would have to work out the analogy and the substitution more precisely. Baudelaire, though, had anticipated such a possibility and in his prose poem *Le Mauvais Vitrier* he speaks of "cette humeur, hystérique selon les médecins, satanique selon ceux qui pensent un peu mieux que les médecins, qui nous pousse sans résistance vers une foule d'actions dangereuses ou inconvenantes". (I, 286) The Satanical hypothesis is clearer thinking, one surmises, because it adduces not an individual disorder but impersonal structures and forces. When Gustave Flaubert objected to Baudelaire that he insisted too much on l'*Esprit du Mal,* Baudelaire replied, "de tout temps j'ai été obsédé par l'impossibilité de me rendre compte de certaines actions ou pensées soudaines de l'homme sans l'hypothèse de l'intervention d'une force méchante extérieure à lui. – Voilà un gros aveu dont tout le 19e siècle conjuré ne me fera pas rougir."[14]

Christian theology introduces the Devil to account for the presence of evil in the world. If God is not to be held responsible for evil, there must be another creature whose free choice in deviating from good introduced evil. The Devil, thus, is not a *symbol* of evil but an agent or personification whose ability to act is essential. Just as God is not a symbol of good but, if he is anything, an agent, a creator or controllor, so the Devil is the name for evil agency – evil as a positive force, not evil as the absence of God, as modern theologians are wont to suggest. *Les Fleurs du Mal* make the Devil an actor, along with other unexpected agents, such as Prostitution, which lights up in the streets, Anguish, which plants its black flag in my skull, *Ennui,* who puffs on his houka and dreams of the gallows. To dismiss Satan as *just* a "personification" of evil, though, and thus a fiction, requires remarkable confidence about what can and what cannot act, about what forces there are at work in the universe. Behind the wish to dismiss him as personification may lie the wishful presumption that only human individuals can act, that they control the world and that there are no other agents; but the world would be a very different place if this were true. Much of its character, its difficulty, its mystery, comes from the effects produced by actions of other sorts of agents, which our grammars may or may not perso-

---

[14] CH. BAUDELAIRE, *Correspondance,* J. Bruneau ed., Paris, 1973, vol. II, p. 53 (26 June 1860).

nify: history, classes, capital, freedom, public opinion – forces not graspable at the level of the empirical actions of individuals but which seem to control the world and give events meaningful and often oppressive structures.

Baudelaire's poems, in which Anguish, Autumn, Beauty, Ennui, Hope, Hate and others do their work, pose questions about the constituents and boundaries of persons, about the forces that act in the world, and about whether this level of allegorical action does not in fact best capture the realities of body, spirit, and history. This is, finally, a question about the sort of rhetoric best suited to explore our condition, Baudelaire's practice shows a commitment to hyperbolic scenarios involving diverse and unusual actors.

In his essay on Théodore de Banville Baudelaire speaks of hyperbole and apostrophe as the forms of language not only most agreeable but also most necessary to lyric, and goes on to maintain that

l'art moderne a une tendance essentiellement démoniaque. Et il semble que cette part infernale de l'homme, que l'homme prend plaisir à s'expliquer à lui-même, augmente journellement, comme si le Diable s'amusait à la grossir par des procédés artificiels, à l'instar des engraisseurs, empâtant patiemment le genre humain dans ses basses-cours pour se préparer une nourriture plus succulente. (II,168)

This hyperbolic equation of the modern with the diabolical does not correspond at all with the critical reception of Baudelaire, which has left behind the gothic Baudelaire so splendidly encapsulated in this image of the Devil practicing a *gavage satanique*, like the producers of *foie gras*. Baudelaire here gives us, and claims as modern, an allegorical scenario with a highly original account of the forces behind a human activity that is increasingly swollen with evil. Such hyperbolic accounts may be well suited to a time when, as Baudelaire says, everyone feels the Devil but no one believes in him. Exploring and channeling this feeling without demanding belief, such allegories posit forces and meanings that might be at work in the infernal accumulations we characteristically feel but seem unable to control in what we persuade ourselves is the modern world.

MARGHERITA HEYER-CAPUT

RIFLESSIONI SU UNA METAFORA DESANCTISIANA

Per avviare queste mie considerazioni desidero soffermarmi brevemente su un brano della *Giovinezza*, di quell'opera aperta che solo per un apparente paradosso conclude la vasta produzione di Francesco De Sanctis:

Le così dette figure rettoriche, così come i tropi, non sono che l'espressione di queste relazioni [di somiglianza, di differenza e di contrasto], e hanno in esse la loro verità. [...] elle non sono solo mezzi di stile, come le avevano considerate i retori, che le veggono solo nelle parole e nelle frasi. *Le figure entrano nell'organismo stesso della composizione, e sono il modo di concepire e di guardare le cose nelle loro somiglianze, differenze e opposizioni. Esse dunque sono il processo delle cose nel loro tutto e in ciascuna parte.*[1]

È stato notato da Dante Della Terza, autore di pagine illuminanti sulla frammentaria autobiografia desanctisiana, che «'quel' frammento è come una finestra aperta sul paesaggio di un'intera vita e come tale va analizzato».[2] È proprio in tal senso che il brano citato, nel quale l'anziano professore riscrive brachilogicamente una tappa essenziale delle lezioni della sua «Prima scuola», investe di luce sincronica il microtesto che intendo analizzare in conclusione.

Dopo aver indicato il filo rosso delle lezioni sulla grammatica, sulla lingua e sullo stile nel desiderio di «capovolgere la base», ovvero di partire dalle «cose» per arrivare solo successivamente alle «forme», De Sanctis dedica il capitolo XXV ad evidenziare il punto cruciale del suo corso giovanile sulla retorica, o meglio sull'antiretorica. Come precedentemente aveva affermato in polemica con il Blair che non le regole, bensì «il ben pensare conduce al ben dire», e in polemica con il Buffon che «lo stile è la 'cosa'» e non l'uomo,[3] così sottolinea che «la retorica ha per base l'arte del ben

---

[1] F. DE SANCTIS, *La giovinezza*, a cura di G. Savarese, in *Opere di Francesco De Sanctis*, a cura di C. Muscetta, I, Torino, Einaudi, 1961, p. 172. D'ora in avanti i riferimenti a questa edizione verranno corredati in nota solo con il titolo dell'opera singola, il numero del volume ed eventualmente del tomo e il numero della pagina. Tutti i corsivi nelle citazioni sono miei.

[2] D. DELLA TERZA, *Francesco De Sanctis: la retorica della "Giovinezza". Itinerario del discorso critico e spazi autobiografici*, in ID., *Tradizione ed esegesi*, Padova, Liviana, 1987, p. 159.

[3] *La giovinezza*, I, p. 157.

pensare»[4] ovvero la logica, ma che né le regole retoriche danno «il ben dire», né le regole logiche danno «il ben pensare». Il «foco» dal quale «prendono luce sia l'una che l'altra disciplina è quell'intelletto educato alla serietà ed alla libertà nello studio delle cose, ovvero dotato delle armi complementari della sintesi e dell'analisi, che De Sanctis aveva affinato attraverso la riflessione sull'hegelismo. L'uso fine a se stesso e puramente ornamentale delle regole retoriche inaugurato dalla sofistica genera «il liscio nella forma e la superficialità nelle cose che sono i due più gravi indizi della decadenza nazionale».[5]

Per l'accordo secondo De Sanctis imprescindibile di letteratura e vita, vivificato nella sua scrittura tarda dal grandioso affresco storiografico di un itinerario verticale "capovolto" dello spirito italiano dalla trascendenza all'immanenza,[6] l'originalità artistica del singolo viene a coincidere con la dignità morale della nazione, perché basata sui medesimi strumenti intellettuali: «La storia dell'umanità si ripete negl'individui, che solo dopo le pazienti analisi salgono alle sintesi serie e reali. La sintesi è la cosa guardata non nelle sue particolarità, ma nel suo tutto e nelle relazioni con le altre cose: relazioni di somiglianza, di differenza e di contrasto».[7] Ecco allora che l'accorato appello a «studiare le cose» rivolto ai giovani riassorbe in sé anche l'uso delle figure retoriche, quando queste siano non mero ornamento bensì espressione di queste relazioni, quando esse sappiano entrare «nell'organismo stesso della composizione», diventando così «il processo delle cose nel loro tutto e in ciascuna parte».

Ciò che particolarmente colpisce in queste righe rispetto alla trattazione delle figure retoriche nelle lezioni giovanili alle quali si richiamano è l'introduzione di quella terminologia scientifica che il De Sanctis maturo aveva assorbito probabilmente in un primo momento attraverso i contatti avuti a Zurigo con il fisiologo materialista Jakob Moleschott,[8] e certamente in un secondo momento attraverso la partecipazione all'acceso dibattito culturale scoppiato a Firenze, dove l'irpino

[4] Ivi, p. 170.
[5] Ivi, p. 171.
[6] Cfr. D. DELLA TERZA, *Francesco De Sanctis: gli itinerari della "Storia"*, in *Letteratura italiana*, a cura di A. Asor Rosa, IV, Torino, Einaudi, 1985, pp. 331-349, in particolare pp. 339, 348. Si veda a questo proposito anche M. T. LANZA, *Il pianeta De Sanctis*, in *Francesco De Sanctis: recenti ricerche: Atti del convegno di studi*, Avellino 1-2 marzo 1985, Urbino, Quattroventi, 1989, p. 56.
[7] *La giovinezza*, I, p. 172.
[8] Cfr. *Epistolario (1856-1858)* II, a cura di G. Ferretti e M. Mazzocchi Alemanni, XIX, Torino, Einaudi, 1965, pp. 19, 88, 110, 255, 509; *Epistolario (1859-1860)* III, a cura di G. Ferretti e M. Mazzocchi Alemanni, XX, Torino, Einaudi, 1965, p. 6; J. MOLESCHOTT, *Für meine Freunde. Lebens-Erinnerungen*, Giessen, Emil Roth, 1894, pp. 302-305; J. MOLESCHOTT, *Francesco De Sanctis* (1884), in *La giovinezza*, I, pp. 303-305. Sulla portata di questi contatti, a mio avviso non ancora sufficientemente sottolineata dalla critica, si vedano: G. LANDUCCI, *De Sanctis, la scienza e la cultura positivistica*, in *Francesco De Sanctis nella storia della cultura*, a cura di C. Muscetta, II, Bari, Laterza, 1984, pp. 195-196; S. LANDUCCI, *Cultura e ideologia in F. De Sanctis*, Milano, Feltrinelli, 1964, pp. 159, 212; R. MARTINONI, *Gli anni zurighesi (1856-1860)*, in *F. De Sanctis nella storia della cultura*, cit., p. 97; S. ROMAGNOLI, *Studi sul De Sanctis*, Torino, Einaudi, 1962, p. 103; G. ZOPPI, *F. De Sanctis a Zurigo*, in *Studi letterari, sociali, economici della Scuola Politecnica Federale*, 5, Aarau, Sauerländer, 1932, p. 12.

allora risiedeva, in seguito alla pubblicazione nel 1864 della prima traduzione italiana del famoso saggio di Darwin *Sulla origine della specie*.[9] È stato notato da più parti che l'ambiguità terminologica che caratterizza «parole comprensive»[10] dell'estetica desanctisiana quali «forma» e «situazione», già evidenziata da Croce,[11] è riconducibile alla sfumata sovrapposizione di campi semantici filosofico-idealistici e campi semantici scientifico-positivistici. Ma è stato soprattutto Contini a evidenziare la ragione strettamente «funzionale» per cui il concetto di forma desanctisiana è stato al centro di tante «giostre lessicali». In duplice opposizione contro la nozione puristica delle forme e la nozione hegeliana del concetto o idea, la forma scientificamente connotata è funzionale «a un'unica e illustre tesi critica, secondo la quale la decadenza italiana consiste nella dissociazione della parola dalla cosa e nella sua risoluzione in musica».[12] La nozione di forma viene chiarendosi in senso organico proprio negli anni zurighesi, spettatori di una diretta esposizione desanctisiana al materialismo scientifico. La revisione alla quale il nostro autore sottopone l'hegelismo come sistema nelle lezioni e nelle conferenze tenute a Zurigo tra il 1856 e il 1860, tende così a rafforzare la inscindibile e complementare unità di contenuto e forma già presente ma non ancora centrale in Hegel:

> Per me l'essenza dell'arte è la forma, non la forma veste, velo, specchio, e che so altro, manifestazione di una generalità distinta da lei, quantunque unita a lei, ma la forma, in cui l'idea è già passata, ed a cui l'individuo si è già innalzato: qui è *la vera unità organica dell'arte*. Ora la forma non è una idea, ma una cosa; e perciò il poeta ha innanzi delle cose e non delle idee.[13]

L'opera d'arte come forma organica, proprio perché nata dall'incontro del particolare con l'universale,[14] è caratterizzata da un dinamismo intrinseco che è all'origine stessa della creazione poetica, come sottolinea la martellante anafora di «divenire» e «diventare», oltre alla esuberante presenza di verbi di moto («oltrepassare», «innalzarsi», «balzar fuori», ecc.), in un altro celebre passo sul mondo intellettuale allegorico dantesco:

[9] Cfr. S. LANDUCCI, *Cultura e ideologia in F. De Sanctis*, cit., pp. 233-256; G. LUTI, *De Sanctis e Darwin*, in *De Sanctis e il realismo*, introd. di G. Cuomo, I, Napoli, Giannini, 1978, pp. 249-270, in partic. pp. 255-259; P. MAZZAMUTO, *De Sanctis e il positivismo*, in *De Sanctis e il realismo*, cit., in particolare pp. 105-112.

[10] Si veda in particolare B. MORETTI, *La lingua di F. De Sanctis*, Firenze, Le Monnier, 1970, pp. VII-IX, 55-62.

[11] Si veda p. es. B. CROCE, *Le lezioni sulla letteratura italiana del secolo XIX* (1896), in ID., *Una famiglia di patrioti*, Bari, Laterza, 1949, p. 169.

[12] G. CONTINI, *Introduzione a De Sanctis* (1949) in ID., *Varianti e altra linguistica*, Torino, Einaudi, 1970, p. 504.

[13] *Lezioni e saggi su Dante*, a cura di S. Romagnoli, V, Torino, Einaudi, 1967 (1955), p. 610.

[14] Sul carattere prettamente romantico di questo tratto distintivo e costante della critica desanctisiana si veda in particolare W. BINNI, *Amore del concreto e la situazione nella prima critica desanctisiana* (1942), in ID., *Critici e poeti dal Cinquecento al Novecento*, Firenze, La Nuova Italia, 1969, pp. 81, 97.

Adunque l'idea in sé e il contenuto in sé non sono una base poetica, l'idea in sé, base dell'idealismo, il contenuto in sé base del realismo. Amendue sono già divenuti un'altra cosa, quando si presentano al poeta. L'idea è diventata la forma, e il contenuto è diventato la figura.

Il contenuto è figura, quando non è più il semplice materiale, ma la materia organizzata. *L'idea è forma, quando non è più il semplice pensiero, ma l'unità dell'organismo.* [15]

Il movimento che percorre «quell'unità immediata ed organica del contenuto, in cui è il segreto della vita», [16] cui corrisponde appunto la forma, è anche tratto caratterizzante della visione desanctisiana della critica letteraria, in particolare nella sua esplicitazione storiografica. Basti pensare al «principio direttivo» della *Storia* indicato dallo stesso autore nella «successiva riabilitazione della materia, un graduale avvicinarsi alla natura ed al reale». [17] Certo «il suo schema evolutivo non è però di semplice progresso o redenzione», [18] come questa autodefinizione potrebbe suggerire, ma ciò che in essa risalta è ancora una volta il tratto dinamico della *Weltanschauung* desanctisiana vista nelle sue espressioni strutturali come in quelle testuali, le quali, quand'anche si oppongano alle degenerazioni dell'hegelismo, irradiano pur sempre dal centro della filosofia hegeliana. Centro che De Sanctis avrebbe significativamente riassunto e attualizzato nell'ultima fase del suo pensiero in quei «due principi che sono la base di tutto il movimento odierno, il "divenire", base dell'evoluzione (*Entwicklung*), e l'"esistere", base del realismo». [19]

A maggior ragione significativa risulta perciò la definizione delle figure retoriche dalla quale abbiamo preso l'avvio, a tal punto dinamica da identificarle addirittura con «il processo delle cose nel loro tutto e in ciascuna parte». Ci troviamo qui di fronte a un tipico esempio di quel meccanismo tautologico che è stato spesso innescato nella storia della retorica dal tentativo di descrivere e spiegare la metafora. Per chiarire il significato dei tropi in senso antiformalistico De Sanctis si serve infatti della metafora a carattere scientifico del «processo». Tale strategia intende aggirare l'ostacolo di racchiudere in una definizione le energie semantiche della metafora intesa come «strumento di conoscenza additiva» del reale e non come ornamento, attraverso l'impiego di una metafora per analogia. [20] Isti-

[15] *Lezioni e saggi su Dante*, V, p. 613
[16] *Saggio critico sul Petrarca*, a cura di N. Gallo, VI, Torino, Einaudi, 1964 (1952), p. 19.
[17] Ivi, p. 9.
[18] R. WELLEK, *Storia della critica moderna (1750-1950). Dal realismo al simbolismo*, IV, Bologna, Il mulino, 1969, p. 136.
[19] *Zola e L'Assommoir*, in *L'arte, la scienza, la vita*, a cura di M. T. Lanza, XIV, Torino, Einaudi, 1972, p. 455. Sul carattere fondamentalmente interno all'hegelismo della critica desanctisiana al sistema idealistico hanno del resto insistito numerosi e autorevoli critici, p. es. B. CROCE, *De Sanctis e l'hegelismo* (1912), in ID., *Saggio sullo Hegel*, Bari, Laterza, 1967, p. 370; M. T. LANZA, *De Sanctis e Hegel*, in *F. De Sanctis nella storia della cultura*, cit., pp. 165, 173, 178-184; R. WELLEK, *Storia della critica moderna (1750-1950)*, cit., p. 150; R. WELLEK, *Il realismo critico di De Sanctis*, in *De Sanctis e il realismo*, cit., pp. 34-35.
[20] U. ECO, *Semiotica e filosofia del linguaggio*, Torino, Einaudi, 1984, pp. 142-143.

tuire un rapporto analogico tra la metafora ed il processo, che è il divenire della realtà nel costante mutamento delle relazioni tra il tutto e le sue parti, corrisponde esemplarmente alla famosa spiegazione aristotelica di ciò che la metafora dice: «[...] l'usare bene la metafora significa *il percepire con la mente il concetto affine*»,[21] ovvero somiglianze e dissomiglianze insospettate fra metaforizzante e metaforizzato, relazioni tra le cose che, attraverso un cortocircuito logico, animano il linguaggio e la realtà.

Cercando di ancorare nella *Giovinezza* l'uso antiformalistico dei tropi alla conoscenza scientifica dei dinamismi del reale, l'anziano autobiografo compendia metaforicamente, appunto, ciò che il giovane professore aveva esplicitamente svolto sulle orme aristoteliche nelle lezioni della prima scuola, ovvero la sostanziale identità di metafora e tropi. Al centro dell'analisi sui tropi, dopo averne precisato l'origine nella necessità arricchita dall'immaginazione, il principio nella imitazione, e le fonti nella estensione e nella comprensione, si sofferma a descrivere la catacresi, la metonimia e la metalepsi per il primo gruppo, la sineddoche, la litote e l'iperbole per il secondo gruppo. Solo a conclusione della precisa trattazione egli afferma che

[...] il principio generale, onde nasce la metonimia o sineddoche, è il paragone implicito che si fa di due oggetti; il quale dà origine alla traslazione di senso. Così: «tigre» ecc.: ora onde avviene che «tigre» è posta tra le metafore? È una confusione. Ogni metafora è o una metonimia, o una sineddoche, secondoché la simiglianza risulta dall'estensione o dalla comprensione. *Ed il termine stesso di metafora ("translatio") non è forse applicabile a tutti i tropi?*[22]

Ecco dunque che la metafora, spesso considerata nella storia della retorica il tropo fondante, viene solo fuggevolmente presentata da De Sanctis ai giovani allievi, perché ritenuta – in un senso quasi anticipatore di recenti ricerche semiotiche e linguistiche – da un lato il tropo più derivato, in quanto «presuppone altre operazioni semiotiche preliminari» quali la sineddoche e la metonimia,[23] dall'altro quello più semanticamente dinamico perché piuttosto ampiamente cognitivo che strettamente linguistico.[24]

Nelle lezioni sullo stile De Sanctis riprende e chiarifica la funzione dei tropi. Se le tre qualità principali dello stile sono la chiarezza, la forza e l'ornamento, occorre tuttavia precisare che quest'ultimo occupa una posizione ancillare rispetto alle prime due: «L'ornamento però non dee aver per fine che di fare risaltare l'idea e non di sfoggio e di pompa; che in questo caso è falso ornamento; epperò l'ornamento si

---

[21] Aristotele, *Dell'arte poetica*, a cura di C. Gallavotti, Fondazione Lorenzo Valla, Milano, Mondadori, 1974, 23, 6, 61, p. 89.

[22] *Lingua e stile (1840-41)*, in *Purismo illuminismo storicismo. Lezioni I*, a cura di A. Marinari, III, 1, Torino, Einaudi, 1975, p. 441. Cfr. *Appendice II. Proprietà e purità dell'italiano linguaggio*, ivi, p. 560.

[23] U. Eco, *Semiotica e filosofia del linguaggio*, cit., pp. 141-142.

[24] P. M. Bertinetto, *On the Inadequateness of a Purely Linguistic Approach to the Study of Metaphor*, «Italian Linguistics», IV, 1977, pp. 39, 64 ss.

confonde con la forza e l'unità; le figure, i tropi ecc. non servono che a rafforzare l'idea principale [...]».[25] Ma è nel riassunto del corso sulla lingua e sullo stile premesso alle lezioni sulla lirica dell'anno successivo (1841-1842) che la natura dinamica e cognitiva della metafora quale tropo per eccellenza si profila in rapporto alla forza dell'immaginazione:

> L'immaginazione si accende quando l'oggetto esterno fa una rapida impressione. A questo stato corrisponde la forza, la quale si procaccia con la brevità, e con la scelta degli accessori; nella lingua tutta la parte ellittica produce la forza [...]. Il primo effetto della immaginazione è di considerare le cose astratte per somiglianza delle cose fisiche, dicendosi, per es., "infiammare" per esprimere quello che la passione opera nel cuore. Da questa legge dell'immaginazione nascono nella lingua i tropi di somiglianza, detti "metafore".[26]

Nelle lezioni del 1845-1846, che testimoniano l'incontro desanctisiano con l'*Estetica* hegeliana attraverso la mediazione francese del Bénard,[27] la metafora acquista non a caso uno statuto più indipendente rispetto agli altri tropi, ed in particolare rispetto alla metonimia. Mentre i «tropi di somiglianza, o metafore» definiscono l'eleganza dello stile nata dalla fantasia, consistente nel «rendere sensibili le idee astratte», i «tropi di dipendenza, o metonimia [sic]» caratterizzano piuttosto l'eleganza della riflessione.[28] La metafora viene così a coincidere con la personificazione, in una correzione che rende in qualche modo più statica la visione desanctisiana della metafora rispetto al dinamismo insito nel primo tentativo di descrizione metaforica nelle lezioni del 1841-1842.

A questo primo effetto sistematizzante e irrigidente dell'incontro con Hegel è allora forse riconducibile la rinnovata attenzione del De Sanctis ai pericoli insiti in un uso eccessivo e ornamentale della metafora, quale è ad esempio rintracciabile nel *Saggio critico sul Petrarca*, nato sotto forma di conferenze nel 1858 a Zurigo, dunque proprio nel momento del distacco consapevole dall'hegelismo. Mostrando ai suoi uditori,[29] conoscitori più del petrarchismo che del Petrarca, come questi «con un ingombro di metafore spesso guasta i più bei sonetti», De Sanctis precisa infatti che: «La metafora è una maniera di dire, che, come nella pittura il rilievo, mette in risalto gli oggetti per via di somiglianze e di rapporti. Prender la metafora nel senso letterale, e farne un'applicazione grossolana, come se il paragone e la cosa paragonata fossero il medesimo, ti dà il concetto».[30]

---

[25] *Lingua e stile (1840-1841)*, III, 1, pp. 451-452.

[26] *Lirica (1841-1842)*, in *Purismo illuminismo storicismo. Lezioni I*, III, 1, pp. 582-583.

[27] G. W. Fr. HEGEL, *Cours d'esthétique*, analysé et traduit en partie par Ch. Bénard, 5 voll., Paris, Nancy, Aimé, Hachette, Joubert Grimblot, Ladrange, 1840-1852.

[28] *Storia della critica (1845-1846)*, in *Purismo illuminismo storicismo. Lezioni II*, III, 2, pp. 1208-1209.

[29] Tra questi sedeva come è noto anche l'hegeliano ortodosso Friedrich Th. Vischer; sui rapporti e le reciproche influenze tra De Sanctis e Vischer si veda B. CROCE, *De Sanctis e l'hegelismo*, cit., pp. 373-380.

[30] *La critica del Petrarca*, in *Saggio critico sul Petrarca*, VI, pp. 58-59.

È proprio questa "concettosità" petrarchesca che i petrarchisti hanno unilateralmente enfatizzato, concettosità che passa dunque primariamente attraverso un uso ornamentale e statico della metafora. È del resto proprio la staticità a qualificare negativamente secondo De Sanctis la poesia del Petrarca,[31] in opposizione alla dinamicità della lirica tragica del Leopardi che, insieme a Petrarca e a Dante, costituisce uno dei fili costantemente intrecciati nella riflessione desanctisiana degli anni zurighesi. Nello stesso saggio sul Petrarca Leopardi è infatti presente sia come sostegno critico con il suo commento al *Canzoniere*, sia come contrappunto tragico-eroico alla tristezza elegiaca di Petrarca.[32] Ma forse ancor più significativo è che la *Imitazione* leopardiana compaia seppur di sfuggita in quel punto centrale della lezione IV sul mondo intellettuale allegorico della *Divina Commedia* che ho precedentemente richiamato per la definizione dinamica di forma come «unità dell'organismo».

Non stupisce dunque che l'associazione tra il dramma esistenziale di Leopardi e il tropo della metafora ne metta nuovamente in rilievo gli aspetti dinamici in quel primo saggio desanctisiano sul poeta recanatese, composto nel 1849 e premesso alla ristampa dell'*Epistolario* uscita appunto in quell'anno. Riferendosi al tema della malattia, così centrale nelle lettere, De Sanctis scrive:

[...] ché a poco a poco l'infermità dell'animo e del corpo diviene un solo soffrire, con qualità comuni ed indivise, e *quella finzione che noi chiamiamo metafora, per la quale lo spirito prende faccia visibile, e i corpi son circonfusi di alcunché di etereo che ce li ruba agli sguardi*, diventa in lui una crudele realtà.[33]

Ben lontano dalla visione vichiana della metafora come prima espressione del linguaggio aurorale dell'umanità, De Sanctis attribuisce hegelianamente all'inventiva dello scrittore la metafora in quanto "finzione".[34] Ma ciò che mi preme rilevare è che qui tale finzione è caratterizzata da un duplice movimento, che va dallo spirito ai corpi e viceversa rendendo visibile l'invisibile e viceversa. La metafora diventa dunque qui, nel senso elaborato da Ricoeur, finzione capace di "ridescrivere" la realtà istituendo una "verità" nutrita della tensione che essa fa emergere tra le pieghe della realtà stessa.[35]

E proprio nel senso dinamico della «metafora viva», capace di formulare una nuova ipotesi sul reale attraverso la tensione tra il singolo lemma e l'intera propo-

---

[31] Si veda a questo proposito M. HOLLIGER, *F. De Sanctis. Sein Weltbild und seine Aesthetik*, Freiburg, Paulusdruckerei, 1949, p. 206.

[32] Cfr. C. MUSCETTA, *Introduzione*, in F. DE SANCTIS, *Leopardi*, a cura di C. Muscetta e A. Perna, XIII, Torino, Einaudi, 1960, p. XXXIII.

[33] *Epistolario di Giacomo Leopardi*, in *Leopardi*, XIII, p. 390.

[34] Cfr. G. W. FR. HEGEL, *Vorlesungen über die Aesthetik I*, Frankfurt a/M, Suhrkamp, 1986, pp. 516-523, in particolare pp. 517, 519.

[35] P. RICOEUR, *La metafora viva. Dalla retorica alla poetica: per un linguaggio di rivelazione*, trad. di G. Grampa, Milano, Jaca Book, 1981, in particolare pp. 5-6, 324-327.

sizione, che desidero leggere la metafora desanctisiana dalla quale le presenti considerazioni sono state suscitate.

Nel 1877, al centro di quei fecondi anni Settanta che vedono la pubblicazione della *Storia della letteratura italiana* e dei *Nuovi saggi critici*, la ripresa dell'attività didattica nella «Seconda scuola», ovvero l'inizio dell'interesse esplicito per il realismo con le sue tappe fondamentali – la celebre prolusione *La scienza e la vita* (1872), lo *Studio sopra Emilio Zola* (1878) e la conferenza su *Zola e l'Assommoir* (1879) -, si situa la conferenza *L'ideale*, con la quale De Sanctis inaugurava il secondo anno di attività del Circolo filologico di Napoli da lui fondato. Tutto animato dall'intento comunicativo, il breve e denso intervento desanctisiano si snoda lungo una serie di coppie oppositive che ne enfatizzano la struttura dialogica ed il dinamismo aperto della conclusione.

Mimando con un discorso diretto il monologo dialogico in cui il conferenziere vaglia con il pubblico immaginario gli argomenti a favore e a sfavore del tema scelto in un'epoca tutta votata al realismo ed al positivismo, l'autore propone dapprima di accettare l'opinione comune, l'obiezione ovvia secondo la quale «l'ideale è morto», per poi ribaltarla nel suo contrario proprio quando dichiara di voler fare una «orazione funebre»: «Non vi nascondo che ho avuto nell'animo di fare questa orazione funebre non senza un segreto desiderio che quando lo avremo accompagnato alla tomba noi ci accorgeremo che esso è sempre vivo, anzi immortale».[36] Nel momento stesso in cui sembra accettare come punto di partenza la sovrapposizione tra l'animale e l'uomo suggerita dal determinismo dell'evoluzionismo, De Sanctis capovolge l'assunto attraverso la personificazione dell'ideale, di cui intende fare l'orazione funebre come di un caro estinto. Ecco perché gli è possibile anticipare la conclusione paradossale secondo cui «l'ideale è morto, l'ideale è vivo».[37]

Nel tratteggiare un quadro diacronico di sapore vichiano dell'evoluzione umana egli indica il discrimine tra l'animale e l'uomo in quella facoltà creatrice che è la fantasia. Riprendendo così la distinzione hegeliana a lui cara tra "immaginazione" e "fantasia", egli vede quest'ultima alle prese con le idee, per esempio la gloria o la patria, nate in un'epoca anteriore dalla generalizzazione delle qualità umane attraverso l'attività intellettuale. È infatti la fantasia che «lavorando sopra» le idee

genera il sentimento e ne informa tutta la attività umana, di guisa che quella idea diviene come la colonna di fuoco che guida l'umanità.

L'ideale allora investe tutto l'uomo e prende diverse manifestazioni nell'arte nella religione nella filosofia e nella storia.[38]

---

[36] *L'ideale*, in *L'arte, la scienza, la vita*, XIV, p. 357.
[37] *Ibid.*
[38] Ivi, p. 358.

Ma parlare dell'ideale secondo quel principio del realismo come metodo di studio e rappresentazione della «vita in atto» al quale verrà dedicato anche l'ultimo intervento desanctisiano,[39] significa allora vedere l'ideale «in fieri»:

> Se è vero che l'ideale nasce insieme col sentimento della coscienza umana, come nasce? L'ideale non è cosa che sta in aria, *l'ideale è generato come il resto. Da chi è generato? Dal reale*, quel reale che voi credete suo nemico. Perché la realtà nella sua evoluzione deve giungere a un punto in cui sia capace di crearsi da se stessa l'ideale. Se l'ideale è figlio del reale, qualunque reale storico deve avere il suo ideale corrispondente.
>
> La storia dell'ideale è la storia dello spirito umano.[40]

Coerentemente con quel nucleo di riflessione costante del pensiero desanctisiano, che è la discesa dell'ideale nel reale ovvero «il limite e la misura dell'ideale»[41] sulla quale costruisce la sua interpretazione dei *Promessi sposi* nelle lezioni zurighesi e nelle successive lezioni napoletane, il conferenziere tratteggia rapidamente le tappe oppositive del percorso della civiltà umana. L'epoca a lui contemporanea rappresenta la tappa apparentemente più "riduttiva" che, tesa a rifiutare le costruzioni intellettuali dell'idealismo romantico, riconduce ogni fenomeno alle sue basi meramente materiali:

> Il pensiero diventando così l'effetto di composizioni chimiche, la moralità questione di temperamento, ci troviamo in perfetto regno animale.
>
> L'arte seguendo questo impulso, troviamo che tutte le qualità che sono proprio umane compariscono animalizzate: l'idea diviene istinto; la fantasia manifestazione meccanica; la passione appetito.[42]

Ma è proprio «quando l'umanità vede il reale immensamente lontano dall'ideale»[43] che si rinsalda l'includibile legame con quello, attraverso la protesta alla quale dà voce o l'ironia – e si pensi alle considerazioni desanctisiane sull'ironia nell'Ariosto o nel Manzoni – o il «grido di dolore» di uno Schiller o un Leopardi. Ed ecco che, a questo punto del suo intervento, il relatore compie un salto qualitativo, passando da una rievocazione del passato ad una proiezione nel futuro, dove l'orazione funebre dedicata all'ideale estinto s'interrompe improvvisamente per gettare un fascio di luce sulla funzione tutt'altro che riduttiva della scienza:

> Ed in questa credenza [che «fin che ci è sdegno e dolore, ci è la presenza dell'ideale»] mi conforta anche lo scorgere in mezzo a questo fenomeno un fatto permanente, cioè che *la*

---

[39] *Il darwinismo nell'arte*, in *L'arte, la scienza e la vita*, XIV, p. 464.

[40] *L'ideale*, XIV, p. 358.

[41] *I "Promessi sposi"*, in *Manzoni*, a cura di C. Muscetta e D. Puccini, X, Torino, Einaudi, 1955, p. 80.

[42] *L'ideale*, XIV, p. 360.

[43] Ivi, p. 361.

scienza prospera e fiorisce, che lotta colla natura e le strappa nuovi segreti e ne indaga le leggi e ne guida le forze. Questo forma *una realtà più ricca, più sicura nei metodi e nei criteri* di quella che l'ha preceduta, e *la nuova realtà debbe giungere a formarsi essa pure la sua idealità.*[44]

Questo salto verso il futuro, che accetta il dinamismo intrinseco del reale e riconosce nella "scienza" non più un sinonimo di "sapere" bensì una «entità specifica che corrisponde alle recenti acquisizioni nel campo delle scienze naturali»,[45] è forse da considerare quale ennesima espressione di quell' amore del concreto che aveva condotto De Sanctis soprattutto nelle lezioni zurighesi «alla formula della situazione come conciliazione di universale e particolare, limite vivo entro cui l'universale si fa particolare».[46]

Non stupisce quindi che questa svolta dinamica del discorso richieda l'introduzione di una metafora che mi pare esprima perfettamente il dinamismo intrinseco ad ogni «metafora viva» come finzione capace di ridescrivere la realtà:

Che cosa è infatti *questa seconda metà del secolo* se non un *laboratorio* in cui si prepara il *reale*, onde dovrà venir fuori la sua *idealità?*[47]

La complessa domanda retorica, che si articola ipotatticamente in una proposizione principale e due proposizioni relative, può essere scandita come segue:

a) Che cosa è infatti questa seconda metà del secolo se non un laboratorio
b) in cui si prepara il reale,
c) onde dovrà venir fuori la sua idealità?

Il primo segmento a) presenta una metafora *in praesentia* che pone in rilievo la relazione analogica tra la seconda metà del secolo ed il laboratorio scientifico. L'epoca storica in questione è caratterizzata dall'interesse per la realtà in divenire, dal «gusto all'osservazione, alle esplorazioni, all'esperienza»,[48] così come avviene nel laboratorio scientifico, dove ciò che interessa è il «metodo intuitivo sperimentale e genetico, cioè la cosa guardata nella sua generazione».[49] Il secondo segmento b) offre una continuazione e specificazione della metafora in a) attraverso l'ampliamento del campo metaforico che precisa l'analogia tra l'epoca e il laboratorio con il verbo «preparare». Il reale non è un semplice dato di fatto, bensì il prodotto di un'epoca in cui predomini l'attitudine sperimentale, così come l'attività sperimentale dello scienziato può scoprire aspetti sconosciuti della natura.

---

[44] *Ibid.*
[45] G. Luti, *De Sanctis e Darwin*, cit., p. 263.
[46] W. Binni, *Amore del concreto e la situazione nella prima critica desanctisiana*, cit., p. 97.
[47] *L'ideale*, xiv, p. 361.
[48] *Il darwinismo nell'arte*, xiv, p. 460.
[49] *Ibid.*

Il terzo e ultimo segmento c) è costituito da una seconda proposizione relativa di cui sia la congiunzione «onde» sia il sintagma verbale dovrà «venir fuori» sottolineano il significato dinamico. La metafora centrale tra l'epoca e il laboratorio esperisce qui un successivo ampliamento tramite l'instaurazione di una relazione metonimica di causa-effetto ovvero di interdipendenza tra contenente-contenuto. Se certamente De Sanctis non crea qui un campo metaforico del tutto nuovo, possiamo però individuarvi una sorta di "incremento" nei termini precisati da Weinrich.[50] Incremento di natura retorica ma anche e soprattutto logica, perché l'ampliamento dell'arco metaforico attraverso la relazione metonimica in c) richiama l'attenzione su una ambiguità sintattica che, a seconda della sua esplicitazione, mette in relazione due termini giudicati dall'uditorio imbevuto di positivismo e materialismo assolutamente contrapposti: l'ideale e il reale. È dunque la «determinazione contestuale», e qui in particolare la situazione comunicativa,[51] a rafforzare la contraddittorietà della predicazione metaforica, ovvero la sua forza, il suo dinamismo, il suo valore conoscitivo.

Se infatti la congiunzione «onde» si riferisce in un costrutto *ad sensum* al metaforizzante «laboratorio», la relazione metonimica indica in esso la causa dell'effetto «idealità», o al limite il contenente di cui la «idealità» è una sorta di seme in esso contenuto e che da esso si svilupperà. Ma se l' «onde» si riferisce invece al suo antecedente prossimo in b), ovvero al «reale», ecco allora unirsi in un cortocircuito gli estremi che la disputa filosofica e letteraria tra idealismo e realismo, in corso in quella seconda metà del secolo qui metaforizzata, aveva erroneamente contrapposto. Ed ecco allora scattare quel movimento reciproco tra l'invisibile e il visibile che avevamo visto caratterizzare la «metafora viva» come finzione capace di ridescrivere la realtà.

L'articolata metafora con la quale De Sanctis conclude l'orazione funebre svolge dunque proprio quella capacità di unire gli estremi nella quale Emanuele Tesauro aveva additato nel 1654 la sua principale funzione. Ed è proprio questa metafora a permettere all'oratore di riprendere la provocatoria conclusione anticipata nell'antitesi («L'ideale è morto, l'ideale è vivo») con il chiasmo finale: «Morto è l'ideale, l'ideale è risuscitato».[52] Chiasmo che non solo accentua enfaticamente la posizione dell'ideale in un'epoca caratterizzata dall'attitudine sperimentale, ma anche sottolinea (attraverso la sostituzione di «è vivo» con «è risuscitato») il dinamismo semantico, quasi soterico, della metafora che lo precede.

---

[50] H. WEINRICH, *Metafora e menzogna: la serenità dell'arte*, trad. a cura di L. Ritter Santini, Bologna, Il mulino, 1976, in particolare p. 45: «Veramente creativa è soltanto la formazione di un nuovo campo metaforico. E questo avviene ben di rado. Per lo più occupiamo solo quei posti vuoti di metafore, che vengono già dati potenzialmente dal campo metaforico esistente. Prendiamo e diamo contemporaneamente. Questa non è creazione originale, bensì opera d'autore: incremento».

[51] Cfr. ivi, pp. 76, 126; BERTINETTO, *On the Inadequateness*, cit., p. 61.

[52] *L'ideale*, XIV, p. 361.

279

Partita da un brano della *Giovinezza* dedicato alle figure retoriche che ne illuminava la natura dinamicamente conoscitiva, ho ripercorso le tappe principali della riflessione desanctisiana sulla metafora come tropo per antonomasia, rilevando la complementarità tra la concezione della metafora così intesa e la concezione della forma come unità organica di ideale e reale.

Sono così giunta ad analizzare la metafora con la quale De Sanctis concludeva la conferenza *L'ideale*, sulla quale mi ero soffermata nel corso di letture desanctisiane legate tra l'altro alla maturazione di un seme di riflessione instillato in me proprio da Dante Della Terza, mio professore harvardiano in anni lontani. Il microtesto in questione mi aveva infatti soggiogato per l'ardita ambiguità con cui intrecciava l'ideale e il reale alla metafora del laboratorio scientifico. Mettendo in evidenza la capacità di formulare una nuova ipotesi sulla realtà insita in questa «metafora viva» grazie alla tensione tra il singolo termine e l'intera frase, spero di essere riuscita ad illuminare da una angolatura metaforica il tratto dinamico e aperto dell'estetica desanctisiana, che nell'ultimo decennio si schiude agli sviluppi scientifici e letterari ad essa contemporanei, pur rimanendo fedele all'agognata sintesi di reale e ideale. Sintesi in divenire che viene quasi utopicamente prospettata nel realismo come metodo, inteso cioè

non come negazione dell'ideale, ma come limite e misura di quello, e il risultato artistico, un vero progresso, è questo, che in luogo di un ideale fantastico e retorico hai un ideale positivo e vivo, *l'ideale così come si trova nella realtà.*[53]

---

[53] *Studio sopra Émile Zola*, in *L'arte, la scienza e la vita*, XIV, p. 416.

CECILIA MATTII

REINTERPRETAZIONI DELLA STORIA ROMANA NEL NAZIONALISMO TRA OTTO E NOVECENTO

Appunti sulla ricerca di un apparato tematico-mitologico

Negli anni a cavallo tra i due secoli la storia romana acquisiva una nuova centralità presso specifici settori della prima generazione dell'Italia unita, che, dopo il fallimento della politica crispina da loro ardentemente sostenuta nei suoi esiti imperialistici ed autoritari, ricercavano uno spazio ideologico-operativo al di fuori e in opposizione all'area liberale. Si tratta di quei gruppi intellettuali che nel primo Novecento si ritroveranno a fianco di Enrico Corradini nella ventura del «Regno» e nella conseguente organizzazione concettuale e pratica del nazionalismo, costituitosi in movimento politico con il Congresso di Firenze del 1910.[1]

[1] Enrico Corradini, nato nel 1865 a Samminiatello in provincia di Firenze, segue inizialmente l'itinerario previsto per lo studente in lettere (si laurea presso l'Istituto di Studi Superiori di Firenze), di estrazione piccolo-borghese, migrato dalla provincia per uno scontato e gratificante approdo all'insegnamento presso un prestigioso liceo fiorentino, il *Galileo*. Con la fondazione nel 1891 del «Germinal», Corradini debuttava nell'editoria fiorentina e, sebbene il periodico cessasse la pubblicazione nel 1892, l'esperienza si rivelerà fruttuosa per la sua futura attività giornalistica. A collaborare al «Germinal» Corradini aveva chiamato anche Angiolo Orvieto che, con il fratello Adolfo, svolgerà un ruolo di primo piano nella organizzazione della vita culturale della Firenze di fine secolo. Agli Orvieto si devono varie imprese editoriali, alcune di breve durata come la «Vita Nuova» o «La nazione letteraria», il supplemento domenicale della «Nazione». Il fermo proposito che animava quelle riviste – sottrarre gli studi letterari all'egemonia del "metodo storico", prestigiosamente difesa dall'Istituto di Studi Superiori, dai vari Vitelli, Comparetti, Rajna, e promuovere una letteratura «viva» a spese della ricerca puramente filologica – quel proposito sarà ripreso con nuovo vigore sul «Marzocco». Del «Marzocco», fondato da Angiolo Orvieto nel 1896, con un comitato redazionale composto dai vitanuovisti Gargano e Garoglio nonché da Corradini, Edoardo Coli e Pietro Mastri, Enrico Corradini terrà la direzione nel triennio 1897-1900. Nonostante il forte impegno sul piano amministrativo, Corradini darà segni d'insofferenza sempre più marcati per la linea programmatica, fermamente sostenuta dalla redazione a cui si era aggiunto anche Angelo Conti: opposizione ad una letteratura con valenze extra-artistiche e assunzione di chiavi interpretative che esaltassero i valori intrinseci dell'opera letteraria (v. *Prologo*, ivi, I, 1896, 1). Un triennio quello di Corradini segnato da deviazioni notevoli dal tracciato operativo della rivista, tra cui la pubblicazione nel 1897 dei tre articoli di Mario Morasso contenenti un acre attacco ai letterati accusati di indifferentismo politico (*Ai nati dopo il 1870. La terza reazione letteraria*, ivi, II, 1897, 1; *La politica dei letterati: I. Il pregiudizio dell'astensione*, e II. *La teoria dei partiti politici e la lotta futura*, ivi, II, 1897, rispettivamente nei nn. 13 e 14). La stessa attività critica svolta da Corradini, e progressivamente caratterizzata dallo scoperto intento dell'autore di farsi portatore presso la rivista di istanze attivistiche, causerà aspri conflitti con il comitato redazionale. Il che confermerà a Corradini, ormai teso a rivendicare un mandato sociale per il letterato, l'impossibilità di ritenere la direzione del «Marzocco». Per pochi mesi redattore della «Gazzetta di Venezia», farà ritorno a Firenze come corrispondente del «Corriere della Sera». Con la fondazione del «Regno» nel 1903, di cui Papini fu redattore e Prezzolini collaboratore attivissimo, Corradini inserirà il nazionalismo nella vita po-

Una centralità nuova, abbiamo detto, in quanto esula da interessi storico-culturali, anche se umanistica era la formazione di quei nati dopo il '70. Si salda piuttosto ad istanze politiche germinate sul terreno della crisi di fine secolo: la cocente delusione causata dalla caduta di Crispi, l'allarme per la crisi egemonica del blocco conservatore e per l'incapacità quindi del fronte governativo di esercitare una adeguata politica di repressione nei confronti del movimento operaio e contadino.[2]

Già fissate nei loro caratteri dominanti – l'imperialismo e la rigida coesione delle classi all'interno del sistema autoritario – tali istanze costituiranno l'impianto ideologico del dramma che Corradini pubblicava nel 1902, il *Giulio Cesare*.[3] Opera esemplare ai fini del nostro discorso: in essa si attua l'aggancio tra ansie interventistiche e storia romana, secondo modalità operative che prevedono la fruizione del fatto storico ad illustrazione e promozione di scelte politiche.

Sulla funzione «animatrice» della storia romana Corradini si era già espresso in

---

litica e intellettuale italiana servendosi di un'ampia e varia griglia d'interventi, fra cui frequenti e di grande rilievo i contributi di Pareto. Il ruolo protagonistico spetta tuttavia a Corradini per i numerosi articoli che già indicavano la centralità del suo discorso all'emergere del nazionalismo dal coacervo di generiche tendenze antisocialiste ed antiriformiste ed alla collocazione del movimento al di fuori dell'area del liberalismo conservatore. Lasciata nel 1905 la direzione della rivista ad Aldemiro Campodonico, Corradini si riconfermerà come figura di primo piano nella definizione programmatica del movimento attraverso gli scritti politici e l'intensa attività giornalistica e di conferenziere. Sotto i suoi auspici avrà luogo a Firenze il primo Congresso nazionalista in cui veniva votato lo Statuto della Associazione Nazionalista. Con i successivi Congressi di Roma e di Milano, nel 1912 e nel 1914, saranno definitivamente fissate quelle componenti espansioniste-imperialiste, antidemocratiche e antiliberali che, già manifeste nel pensiero corradiniano, costituiranno i cardini del programma nazionalista.

Per gli atti conclusivi dei tre congressi cfr. P. M. ARCARI, *Le laborazioni della dottrina politica nazionale tra l'Unità e l'intervento (1870-1914)*, Firenze, Marzocco, 1939, III. Sul ruolo svolto da Corradini nello sviluppo del nazionalismo in movimento politico e sullo stesso nazionalismo, opera tuttora fondamentale si conferma F. GAETA, *Il nazionalismo italiano*, Bari, Laterza, 1981 (2). Sul carattere militante della cultura di Corradini, cfr. almeno L. STRAPPINI, *Introduzione* in *Enrico Corradini, Scritti e discorsi.1901-1914*, a cura di L. Strappini, Torino, Einaudi, 1980, pp. VII-LIX; A. ASOR ROSA, *La cultura*, in *Storia d'Italia*, a cura di R. Romano e C. Vivanti, Torino, Einaudi, 1975, IV, 2, pp. 1234-1254. Sugli scritti letterari di Corradini cfr. C. A. MADRIGNANI, *L'opera narrativa di Enrico Corradini*, in AA.VV., *La cultura italiana tra '800 e '900 e le origini del nazionalismo italiano*, presentazione di R. Vivarelli, Firenze, Olschki, 1981, pp. 235-252 e il più recente ed esauriente F. FILIPPI, *Una vita pagana. Enrico Corradini dal superomismo dannunziano a una politica di massa*, Firenze, Vallecchi, 1989; da consultarsi anche per una bibliografia degli scritti letterari e politici di Corradini. Su Corradini e «Il Marzocco», cfr. R. CONTARINO, *Corradini e «Il Marzocco»*, «Siculorum Gymnasium», XXX, 1977, 2, pp. 483-521. Quanto al «Regno», cfr., tra gli altri, D. FRIGESSI, *Introduzione*, in *La cultura italiana attraverso le riviste: «Leonardo» «Hermes» «Il Regno»*, a cura di D. Frigessi, Torino, Einaudi, 1960, I, pp. 57-85; L. MANGONI, *Le riviste del Novecento*, in *Letteratura italiana*, dir. da A. Asor Rosa, Torino, Einaudi, 1989, III, pp. 945-981. Sul «Germinal» e le riviste degli Orvieto, cfr. G. OLIVA, *I nobili spiriti.Pascoli, D'Annunzio e le riviste dell'estetismo fiorentino*, Bergamo, Minerva Italica, 1979. Per «Il Marzocco» cfr., in particolare, *Il Marzocco.Carteggi e cronache fra Ottocento e Avanguardie (1887-1913)*. *Atti del seminario di studi (12-13-14 dicembre 1983)*, premessa di M. Raicich, a cura di C. Del Vivo, Firenze, Olschki, 1985. Per i carteggi dei collaboratori, contenuti nel *Fondo Orvieto* dell'Archivio Contemporaneo del Gabinetto G. P. Vieusseux (ACGV, Or.), cfr. *Il Marzocco. Carteggi e cronache tra Ottocento e Avanguardie (1887-1913)*. *Mostra documentaria, Firenze 19 novembre 1983-14 gennaio 1984. Catalogo*, a cura di C. Del Vivo e M. Assirelli, Firenze, 1983.

[2] Cfr. G. CANDELORO, *Storia dell'Italia moderna*, Milano, Feltrinelli, 1980, VII, pp. 30-37.

[3] E. CORRADINI, *Giulio Cesare*, Edizioni Rassegna Internazionale, Roma, 1902 (poi Mondadori, Milano, 1926, da cui citeremo, con prefazione dell'autore).

due interventi pubblicati nel 1901, ed aventi come oggetto i problemi inerenti al-l'"insegnamento classico" nei licei italiani. Sotto processo il "metodo storico" a cui imputava la riduzione della storia a «un puro e semplice, freddo, obiettivo accertamento di fatti accidentali».[4]

Il prevalere, spesso esclusivo, dell'indirizzo critico ed analitico nella ricerca storica, e non solo nell'ambito della storia antica,[5] era in effetti lamentato anche dagli addetti ai lavori, ma per tutt'altro motivo. Significativo il quadro che Romano tracciava della situazione degli studi storici in Italia in quanto coglieva lucidamente i termini essenziali del dibattito in corso sui meriti e limiti dell'erudizione, e sulla necessità per lo storico di estendere gli strumenti interpretativi oltre l'area critico-filologica.[6] Più specificamente, Romano faceva il punto sul "metodo storico", sugli inestimabili servigi che aveva reso e rendeva come fase preparatoria del lavoro storiografico e sugli effetti allo stesso tempo negativi – «gran parte della nostra produzione storica presenta un carattere frammentario ed unilaterale» – che produceva per il «modo come veniva inteso e praticato dai più», non «quale poderoso strumento d'indagine ma punto di partenza e d'arrivo del lavoro storiografico». Romano rilevava pertanto la necessità impellente di procedere oltre la raccolta ed analisi dei documenti, il vaglio delle fonti, in altri termini oltre l'erudizione, per cogliere il fenomeno storico nelle sue varie complessità, e pervenire infine, tramite un'auspicabile integrazione dell'analisi con la sintesi, ad opere di largo respiro. Allo storico si richiedeva pertanto una preparazione diversificata che, estendendosi dalle scienze politiche e sociali all'economia e alle sue leggi, si servisse anche di discipline ausiliarie, quali la psicologia scientifica e l'antropologia. Strumenti con cui affrontare quel vario mondo delle passioni e degli affetti umani che lo storico non può ignorare qualora non voglia limitarsi a ricostruzioni frammentarie dell'evento.[7]

Quanto a Corradini, la sua vertenza con il "metodo storico" aveva ben poco a che fare con preoccupazioni d'ordine scientifico. L'individuazione degli strumenti con cui potenziare il processo conoscitivo, e quindi la definizione di schemi operativi in cui la verifica dei fatti si integrasse con la loro interpreta-

---

[4] E. CORRADINI, *Dell'insegnamento classico in Italia*, «Rassegna internazionale della letteratura e dell'arte contemporanea», VI, 1901, 3; *Nota sopra un'inchiesta. Ancora intorno all'insegnamento classico*, ivi, VI, 1901, 6. Entrambi ripubblicati in *La vita nazionale*, Lumachi, Siena, 1907, rispettivamente alle pp. 149-166 e 167-181, da cui v. pp.155-156 per la cit.

[5] Per un riesame critico degli studi di storia romana, tra la fine Ottocento e la prima decade del secolo, cfr. l'esauriente lavoro di F. NATALE, *Contributo alla storia della storiografia italiana sul mondo antico*, «Nuova Rivista Storica», XLII, 1958, 1-3 (con bibliografia ragionata).

[6] G. ROMANO, *Gli studi storici in Italia allo stato presente in rapporto alla natura e all'ufficio della Storiografia*, «Rivista filosofica», maggio-giugno 1900, pp. 319-339.

[7] G. ROMANO, ivi, pp. 330-335. A Romano, «uno fra i nostri storici più autorevoli», si richiamava Salvemini per condividerne le conclusioni sugli ostacoli che il frammentarismo frapponeva al progredire degli studi storici (*La storia considerata come scienza*, «Rivista italiana di sociologia», VI, 1902, p. 50).

zione e valutazione – operazioni centrali, secondo la relazione di Romano, al progredire degli studi storici – costituiranno una questione tutt'altro che prioritaria per Corradini. Associando, in modo inequivocabile, il rifiuto del metodo storico ad un dichiarato «ingenuo concetto classico della storia»,[8] l'autore finiva per attribuire alla storia criteri metodologici e valutativi corrispondenti ad immediate esigenze di persuasione retorica.[9] Quello che conta nella «visione e narrazione storica» è «l'esposizione dei fatti in tutta la loro forza», scelti innanzi tutto per il loro implicito «valore vitale», ovvero per la loro potenziale esemplarità sotto il profilo etico-politico. Altrimenti, incalzava Corradini, nelle scuole più che a «formar coscienze ricche ed energiche» si provvederà all'«inebetimento dell'italica gioventù di generazione in generazione».[10]

Da non sottovalutare come nell'equiparazione corradiniana di "insegnamento classico" e formazione del sentire nazionale, agissero, sia pure con enfasi diversa, le suggestioni che provenivano dai dibattiti dell'ultimo Ottocento sul ruolo della scuola nell'educazione del nuovo cittadino.[11] Dibattiti in cui sempre più pesantemente si faceva sentire l'evoluzione imperialistica della politica internazionale e nei quali l'insegnamento veniva progressivamente saldato alla promozione di «virtù virili», con cui preparare le generazioni post-unitarie per «una futura possibile battaglia contro un nemico esterno».[12] E parte integrante di tale formazione veniva riservata alla Roma antica, non più percepita, come per il passato, nel suo significato storico-culturale, ma indicata come *exemplum* politico nazionale. Non per nulla la questione didattica occupava una posizione di rilievo negli scritti di Pasquale Turiello, che con la sua opera maggiore, *Teoria dei governi e governati*,[13] si era imposto ai contemporanei come teorico dell'imperialismo italiano, guadagnandosi negli anni a venire la riconoscenza dei nazionalisti.[14] In un'età in cui «la storia occupa un

---

[8] E. CORRADINI, *Dell'insegnamento classico*, cit., ora in *La vita nazionale*, cit., p. 154.

[9] R. CONTARINO, *Corradini e «Il Marzocco»*, cit., p. 516.

[10] E. CORRADINI, *Dell'insegnamento classico*, cit., ora in *La vita nazionale*, cit., p. 156 e sgg.

[11] Per questo tipo di formazione educativa in cui l'insegnamento era indissolubilmente saldato alle armi, rimandiamo al noto e tuttora fondamentale lavoro di F. CHABOD, *Storia della politica estera italiana dal 1870 al 1896*, Bari, Laterza, 1976 (3), I, pp. 294-296. Chabod esamina le nuove mete a cui andava indirizzandosi la scuola sul finire del secolo in rapporto al progressivo cambiamento del clima morale e politico in Italia e in Europa. Per tali cambiamenti e per i nuovi criteri competitivi che regolavano lo scenario internazionale, cfr. cap. 1 e 2, I, pp. 23-373.

[12] Ivi, p. 293. Sul corrompersi dell'idea di Roma – dalla mazziniana Roma «maestra del vero» alla Roma «donna di province», ivi, I, pp 215-373.

[13] P. TURIELLO, *Governo e Governati. Seconda edizione rifatta*, Bologna, Zanichelli, 1889-1890, 2 voll. Sulla questione della scuola, oltre al cap. VI, II, pp. 102-182, cfr. *La virilità nazionale e le colonie*, «Atti della Reale Accademia di Scienze morali e politiche di Napoli», XXX, 1899.

[14] Federzoni, nelle sue memorie pubblicate postume, include Turiello tra i precursori del nazionalismo, tra coloro che avevano preparato nella nuova generazione, prostrata da Dogali e da Adua, «il risveglio del senso storico nazionale» in opposizione alla ripresa da parte governativa di «un regime casalingo» (*Italia di ieri per la storia di domani*, Milano, Mondadori, 1967, p. 13). Già Occhini sul «Regno», nel commemorare Turiello ad un anno dalla morte, aveva riconosciuto l'importanza del suo pensiero politico per i nazionalisti (ivi, I, 1903, 1).

campo che per la prima volta comprende tutto il mondo» e in «una scena in cui ormai... niuno Stato più si può limitare», stare a guardare è follia.[15] Rimanere spettatori, questa era la tendenza da combattere nelle nuove generazioni tramite una rieducazione delle coscienze, tesa a ricreare negli animi avviliti dalla politica del raccoglimento, sedotti dal pacifismo, l'intensità di passioni etico-civili che aveva mosso alla lotta la generazione precedente, ma con indirizzi diversi, adeguati alla posta in gioco. È ormai chiaro a Turiello, già uomo della destra storica, formatosi su un patriottismo che privilegiava l'unità e grandezza civile della patria, che «né Cavour, né Mazzini possono insegnarci più l'indirizzo de' nostri ideali politici, necessariamente oggi molto più vasti de' loro. Perché il giorno che li confinassimo tuttora tra l'Alpi e il mare, noi in questi limiti ci troveremmo in breve, tra la crescente pressura straniera».[16] Luogo deputato alla riforma di un sentire nazionale rispondente all'auspicata vastità d'indirizzi, anche in questo caso è la scuola. Da qui la proposta, non sorprendente, di un curriculum di studi finalizzato al potenziamento di abiti «ferrei e gloriosi insieme» e il frequente richiamo a Roma come modello insuperabile di disciplina e sacrificio. Su Corradini, già votato all'imperialismo e polemico nei confronti delle metodologie didattiche prevalenti, un fascino particolare doveva esercitare l'esortazione turelliana per quella correlazione, esplicita e più volte sostenuta, tra colonialismo ed «educazione virile», nella quale ciascuno dei due termini esercitava una «mutua ragione di causa e di effetto»:

L'Italia, si può dire che finché non abbia fondata una colonia sua pe' suoi figli è probabile che essa non riesca ad acquistar piena coscienza di sé; coscienza che riacquisterebbe del pari subito che fosse ravviata la sua gioventù in una educazione virile.[17]

L'esigenza di rappresentare, con il *Giulio Cesare*, un dramma dalle forti valenze politiche è da riportarsi ad una fase cruciale della biografia corradiniana, agli anni di fine secolo, in cui l'autore, dopo un lungo periodo di estraniazione dalla vita nazionale, da lui imputato alla deludente situazione dell'Italia post-unitaria,[18] ritornerà alla "patria", confrontato ormai dall'urto della storia – la disfatta di Adua. Su

---

[15] P. TURIELLO, *Il secolo XIX ed altri scritti di politica internazionale e coloniale*, a cura di C. Curcio, Bologna, Zanichelli, 1947 (1ª ed. 1902), p. 14.

[16] P. TURIELLO, *Governi e governati*, cit., I, p. 36; e II, p. 111, per la cit. seg. Sulla funzione educatrice della Roma antica, v. II, p. 110.

[17] P. TURIELLO, *La virilità nazionale e le colonie*, cit.

[18] Pier Ludovico Occhini, biografo ufficiale e compagno di cordata di Corradini, spiegava tale assenteismo come una inevitabile reazione delle nuove generazioni, dei «nati con una gran sete di larghi orizzonti, ma costretti a vivere in un ambiente di una penosa ristrettezza, in mezzo a ciarlatani e politicanti preoccupati di piccoli intrighi» (*Corradini*, Firenze, Rinascimento del Libro, 1933 (2), p. 20; prima ed. 1914). Sulla componente deprecatoria della cultura post-unitaria e sul suo ricollegarsi alla preoccupazione per l'evolversi di nuove strutture sociali ed economiche, cfr. A. ASOR ROSA, *La cultura*, cit., specie pp. 821-829. A contrasto con l'atteggiamento della cultura fortemente letteraria, Asor Rosa rileva inoltre il tentativo degli studi economici e sociali di seguire, senza pregiudizi e positivamente, il primo formarsi di strutture capitalistico-industriali (ivi, p. 828 e sgg.). Sullo sviluppo industriale nell'Italia degli anni '80-'90, cfr. V. CASTRONUOVO, *La storia economica*, in *Storia d'Italia*, cit., IV, 1, pp. 5-129.

Adua, sulla prima pagina del «Marzocco», Corradini nel 1896 pubblicava un articolo.[19] Con un susseguirsi rapido e sapiente di immagini – «bandiere sotto lontanissimo cielo», «soldati pensosi della morte ma sacri al dovere», le madri piangenti – con una costruzione tematica tesa quindi alla cattura emotiva del destinatario, l'autore coinvolgeva i giovani oppressi da «tanto tedio», in balia «di individuali aspirazioni», nelle «nobili lacrime» per la sconfitta, nella volontà di «rivincita», nell'ansia di «comunicare» con la patria. Siamo ancora lontani da quella «conversione» alla politica che Corradini, per sottolineare l'indissolubile legame tra nazionalismo e imperialismo, avrebbe in seguito anticipato al 1896, assumendo come *terminus a quo* la disfatta di Adua – un evento consacrato a tragedia nazionale da tutta una produzione letteraria che procederà ininterrotta dal *Fino a Dogali* di Alfredo Oriani alla *Guerra lontana* di Enrico Corradini.[20]

Si trattava piuttosto della necessità avvertita dall'autore nell'acuirsi della crisi politica – Crispi sarebbe caduto di lì a poco – che un nuovo tipo di rapporto doveva stabilirsi tra l'individuo e una precisa realtà storica, tra questa e l'intellettuale che la rifiuta. Un'esigenza di "comunicazione" che si risolverà, con il prevalere di un discorso politico autonomo, nella «conversione» alla politica, ma che, confinata nel futuro prossimo al recinto letterario, in quello avrebbe ricercato lo strumento d'intervento politico-ideologico. Ricerca laboriosa e che richiederà in vero tempi lunghi dal momento che in questo scorcio di secolo l'opposizione corradiniana all'Italia post-crispina si limitava alla creazione di eroi ribelli ma «accasciati».[21] Si prospettava dunque un nuovo compito per l'autore: reperire modelli tematici con cui promuovere un sentire nazionale, che non si esaurisse in un patriottismo generico,

---

[19] *Abba Carima*, «il Marzocco», I, 1896, 6, da cui le citt. sgg.

[20] «Io fui di quelli Italiani miei contemporanei che si convertirono alla fede della Patria. Come altri poi dal socialismo, io mi convertii dalla "letteratura" in cui erravo dissoluto e cieco. E la mia conversione fu per la sconfitta di Adua» (E. CORRADINI, *Prefazione* ai *Discorsi politici (1902-1923)*, Vallecchi, Firenze, 1923, p. 8).

[21] La definizione è di Occhini (cfr. *Corradini* cit., pp. 45-68). Viene riferita ai protagonisti di romanzi quali *Santamaura* del 1896, o la *Gioia* del 1897, in cui «Corradini non ha voluto mostrarci... se non delle anime in un momento di crisi». Opere in cui l'autore non avrebbe trovato ancora la sua voce, ma, preso dalla «tristezza dei tempi», si sarebbe abbandonato allo sterile pessimismo esistenziale di *Santamaura* o nella *Gioia* avrebbe creato un personaggio, Vittore Rodia, che «rammenta troppo certi personaggi dannunziani come Andrea Sperelli...». Questo sperellismo doveva essere stato notato anche da Angiolo Orvieto a cui Corradini aveva mandato in lettura la *Gioia*, e a cui scriveva: «Più che imitazione non è espressione dello stesso periodo artistico? D'Annunzio, io e quanti somigliano al primo, non siamo piuttosto figure d'uno stesso quadro più o meno debolmente disegnato? [...] Del resto per quanto mi scrivi [...] ti dico che mi hai fatto molto piacere... meno il dannunzismo s'intende» (Lettera di E. Corradini a An. Orvieto, con data del timbro postale: 25 gennaio '97, ACGV, Or.1. 635.16). Corradini riportava il suo romanzo non tanto al D'Annunzio quanto a una medesima temperie spirituale, come avrebbe poi indicato il suo amico e biografo: «Vittore Rodia rappresenta quei giovani che, in quel triste momento della vita nazionale, avevano persa ogni fede [...] vivevano senza uno scopo, scontenti e scettici» (*Corradini*, cit., p. 58). Ovviamente essere tacciato di «dannunzismo» non poteva piacere al Corradini: nel «Germinal» aveva definito D'Annunzio «il parassita e sibarita dell'arte», che nei suoi protagonisti Sperelli e Hermil rappresentava lo «stato dell'anima sua» e «lor caratteristica comune è il più profondo e raffinato egoismo» (*Elegie romane*, ivi, I, 1892, 30). Sulla stessa linea v. anche l'articolo *"L'innocente" di Gabriele D'Annunzio*, ivi, I, 1892, 20.

auto-consolatorio, confinato al «grido di dolore» per i morti di Dogali o di Adua, ma si traducesse piuttosto in una «volontà d'azione», specificata nei suoi obiettivi dall'esortazione ad una «rivincita in terra d'Affrica».[22] Si trattava infine per Corradini di adeguare i contenuti delle opere drammatico-narrative, legate per il momento a problematiche esistenziali, alle direttive che informavano il suo discorso critico.

Già preannunciato come «eminentemente pratico» nell'articolo programmatico del «Germinal»,[23] il discorso corradiniano si specificherà ulteriormente nelle note critiche pubblicate sul finire del secolo che confermano, pur nella diversità degli autori trattati – sia un Ibsen o un D'Annunzio – l'aspetto ricorrente della lettura corradiniana: investire il tema letterario di funzioni ideologiche.

Dell'interesse per il potenziale attivistico dell'opera letteraria, Corradini offre indicazioni significative in un articolo che ha per oggetto il comportamento del «pubblico a teatro».[24] Un pubblico teatrale altro non è che «il prodotto, non esso materialmente, ben s'intende, ma il suo valore psichico, la sua capacità di sentire, di pensare, di giudicare, la sua coscienza morale e estetica... di un atto di creazione dello spettacolo, né più né meno». In altri termini, i vari spettatori, appena si alza il sipario, perdono ognuno il «suo sé», la propria individualità, per entrare in uno stato di «psicologia collettiva» e diventare «folla».

Espressione in Corradini di un interesse tutt'altro che transitorio per le ricerche condotte dalle scienze sociali in materia di psicologia collettiva, la «folla» da Le Bon e Tarde in Francia, dal giovanissimo Sighele in Italia veniva studiata come unità indifferenziata di cui interessava rilevare i comportamenti irrazionali, la disponibilità alla suggestione ed in definitiva l'incapacità di opporre resistenza alla manipolazione ideologica.[25] Si trattava di autori le cui opere godevano di un'ampia circo-

---

[22] *Abba Carima*, cit.

[23] Il «"Germinal", nella sua critica letteraria sarà eminentemente pratico: la critica aprioristica, le discussioni teoriche, non viventi nel momento attuale saranno del tutto bandite dalle sue colonne» (*Programma*, ivi, I, 1891, 1). Vi collaborarono con poesie Angiolo Orvieto, Garoglio e Mastri che ebbe anche la direzione artistica. Tuttavia la loro presenza non interferì con la linea programmatica del fondatore. In polemica con gli «aristocratici del pensiero», gli artisti, «che non discendono mai dal quarto cielo della loro olimpica serenità per vedere un po'quel che si fa su la terra», Corradini proponeva una letteratura che tornasse ad occuparsi del «mondo», inserita nella realtà socio-politica (*L'Arte nel momento attuale*, ivi, I, 1892, 13, ma v. anche, tra gli altri, *Per una giovane poetessa*, ivi, I, 1892, 17). A tale proposito cfr. G. OLIVA, *I nobili spiriti*, cit., pp. 127-131.

[24] E. CORRADINI, *Il pubblico a teatro*, «Il Marzocco», I, 1896, 5.

[25] La questione della suggestionabilità della folla, in rapporto ai problemi della responsabilità penale, era stata studiata in Italia da Scipio Sighele in un lavoro pubblicato nel 1892 e di ampia circolazione tra i contemporanei, *La folla delinquente*. Sempre nel 1892 era uscito in Francia il lavoro di GABRIEL TARDE, *Les crimes des foules*, a cui appunto farà riferimento Sighele nel suo *L'intelligenza della folla* del 1903. Ma il testo probabilmente più noto tra gli scritti pubblicati alla fine dell'Ottocento sull'argomento è *La psychologie des foules* di GUSTAVE LE BON, pubblicato nel 1895. Sull'argomento cfr., tra gli altri, R. A. NYE, *The Origins of Crowd Psychology*, London, Sage Publications, 1975; L. MANGONI, *Una crisi di fine secolo. La cultura italiana e la Francia fra Otto e Novecento*, Torino, Einaudi, 1985.

lazione tra i contemporanei. [26] A proposito di Corradini, vale la pena ricordare che il suo articolo usciva ad un anno di distanza da uno scritto di Scipio Sighele del 1895, *Contro il parlamentarismo*, [27] nel quale lo studioso trentino, sempre nell'ambito dei processi coscienziali, aveva fatto specifico riferimento al pubblico teatrale quanto a suggestionabilità. Suggestione che si esercitava «in modo intenso» come «su una folla di individui insieme», per cui in una sala teatrale da spettatore a spettatore si propaga un contagio che incide sulle capacità dei medesimi di produrre giudizi obiettivi ed indipendenti. [28]

Nel suo articolo Corradini rilevava dunque l'esemplare efficacia del genere drammatico quanto a creazione di uno stato di «psicologia collettiva», saldando tuttavia il passaggio «dallo stato individuale... allo stato collettivo» alla capacità di presa emotiva dell'opera rappresentata: il pubblico è «un mostro inerte e si può rendere attivo per qualunque atto si vuole e sino al grado che si vuole» purché venga costruita una retorica adeguata, con cui scatenarne, ai fini della subordinazione, il consenso. «E se l'opera d'arte drammatica lo vuole [...] l'anima multipla e semplice, quando per lei cessa la zona della comprensione, subito entra in quella della venerazione senza comprendere». [29]

Un rapporto quindi tra teatro e «stato collettivo» che incoraggerà Corradini, quando si tratterà di cimentarsi in opere letterarie di valenze politico-esortative, a privilegiare il genere drammatico quale strumento di ampia comunicazione ed efficace persuasione. Per il momento tuttavia le modalità d'attuazione sono tutt'altro che esplicate dall'autore, anche se le premesse – generiche invero – della riduzione del pubblico a «mostro inerte» sono implicite nelle note critiche da lui dedicate alla drammaturgia nordica, ovvero nei motivi addotti a spiegazione della scarsa presa di quel teatro sugli spettatori. Esemplari, per quei sottili dilemmi coscienziali di cui erano intessute, della levatura artistica a cui poteva pervenire il «dramma psicologico», [30] le opere di Ibsen, Hauptmann, Sudermann, per quegli stessi motivi e

---

[26] Cfr. P. MELOGRANI, *Introduzione* a G. LE BON, *Psicologia delle folle*, trad. di G. Villa, Milano, Longanesi, 1980, pp. 5-17.

[27] S. SIGHELE, *Contro il parlamentarismo. Saggio di psicologia collettiva*, incluso poi nella 2ª ed. dell'*Intelligenza della folla*, Torino, Bocca, 1911, con il titolo *Il Parlamento e la psicologia collettiva*, pp. 121-165, da cui le citt. sgg. Sighele descriveva il rapporto individuo-folla in questi termini: «Il fenomeno meraviglioso che avviene nelle folle è appunto questo annientamento delle singole personalità in una personalità unica, immensa, diversa, da ognuna di quelle che lo compongono. Si direbbe che ogni individuo perde la facoltà di sentire e di pensare e diviene strumento cieco di un cervello e di un'anima ignoti. Nella folla, un uomo applaude, fischia, grida viva o morte, quasi senza saperlo. Togliete quest'uomo dalla folla, sottraetelo a quel fascino, ed egli per primo si meraviglierà di quello che ha fatto» (ivi, p. 143).

[28] Ivi, pp. 142-143. Ritornerà ad occuparsi del rapporto arte-folla nello scritto del 1903, *L'arte e la folla*, in *L'Intelligenza della folla*, cit., pp. 35-56.

[29] E. CORRADINI, *Il pubblico a teatro*, cit., da cui le citt. sgg.

[30] E. CORRADINI, *Il dramma psicologico*, «Il Marzocco», I, 1896, 1. Ai nordici, a cui aveva iniziato ad interessarsi con tre scritti su Ibsen pubblicati sul «Germinal» nel 1892 (v. nn. 31, 33, 34), dedicherà vari articoli sul «Marzocco» nel biennio 1896-97 (oltre al *Dramma psicologico*, cit., v. *La fine di Sodoma*, ivi, I, 1896, 9; e sempre del 1896, *Anime solitarie* e *A proposito delle Anime solitarie*, rispettivamente nei nn. 10 e 11, ivi, I, 1896). Corradini si allineava alle posizioni dei marzocchini, nell'assumere la drammaturgia nordica – da Ibsen a Hauptmann, a

perché «così lontane dall'indole nostra» erano confinate a gruppi selezionati di spettatori.[31] Ad un Corradini, che ricercava nel genere drammatico lo strumento di «comunicazione con la patria», quei tratti del teatro nordico, ammirati ma non ritenuti funzionali ad attivare il desiderato «stato collettivo», suggerivano, per antitesi, la necessità di individuare temi «connaturali», nelle loro linee primarie, all'indole nazionale e recepibili quindi al di là delle distinzioni socio-culturali degli spettatori.

Sul «Marzocco» del 7 febbraio 1897 – a buon punto per Corradini – Mario Morasso pubblicava un articolo[32] in cui includeva un intervento polemico contro la letteratura che non si «accordava» «simpaticamente» con l'anima della folla. Tra i grandi accusati i nordici a cui, in Italia, la folla si sentiva estranea «per solidarietà inconscia con le tradizioni etniche, con lo spirito nazionale».

A monte dello specifico interesse del sociologo genovese per l'«accordo» che, più o meno, potevasi stabilire tra arte e pubblico, si ritrovano quelle sue elaborazioni sui «nuclei psichici» o «sintesi di idee» con le quali segnalava la propria attenzione nei confronti delle modificazioni dei comportamenti coscienziali, individuali e collettivi: «Tanto nella coscienza individuale quanto in quella collettiva si formano nuclei di idee che hanno la forza di influire sulla condotta dei singoli e delle masse». Astrazioni «di una serie di impressioni forti e vive, le quali hanno agito per un tempo più o meno lungo sull'uomo», i nuclei improntano dei loro caratteri la vita di un individuo e di un popolo.[33]

L'articolo non era che il primo dei tre che il Morasso pubblicava sul periodico degli Orvieto.[34] Comune il filo conduttore: il recupero del letterato alla vita poli-

---

Sudermann a referente ideale dell'affrancamento dello scenario teatrale dai modelli francesi (grande accusato il naturalismo) e dai loro imitatori italiani, e nel proporre l'esemplarità di quel teatro per le problematiche coscienziali con cui stimolava intellettualmente gli spettatori. Nella lettura corradiniana tuttavia l'angolo visivo veniva progressivamente spostato dallo scavo psicologico al piano sociale. Il conflitto pertanto tra protagonista e realtà esterna, riportato da un Ibsen all'ansia di redenzione morale dei protagonisti, e indagato nelle varie e spesso contraddittorie forme che assumeva nelle coscienze – tale conflitto, centrale alla dinamica della drammaturgia ibseniana, finiva, nell'ottica riduttiva del Corradini, per essere confinato al piano d'interesse sociologico.

[31] Cfr. *A proposito delle Anime solitarie*, cit.: «...il dramma nordico non ha avuto presso di noi se non una debole e superficiale efficacia...». Ne dava la spiegazione là dove, nel fare un paragone tra Hauptmann ed Ibsen, di quest'ultimo affermava: «Certo la forza visiva, che scruta, profondandosi, nelle più opposte latebre della realtà umana ed elevandosi alle più alte idealità speculate, è incomparabilmente più acuta e vasta in Ibsen». L'autore «troppe ombre però avvolge intorno alla cose... in mezzo a cui egli vive, e le sue creazioni sono così lontane dall'indole nostra [...] da non sembrarci umanamente esplicabili».

[32] M. MORASSO, *Ai nati dopo il 1870*, cit. Per il retroterra ideale del Morasso fondamentale R. PERTICI, *Tardo positivismo e «vario nazionalismo»: le radici del pensiero di M. Morasso (1891-1899)*, in *Il Marzocco. Carteggi e cronache fra Ottocento e Avanguardie*, cit., pp. 119-167.

[33] M. MORASSO, *Roma*, «Idea Liberale» (I.L.) III,1894, 39.

[34] *La politica dei letterati. I. Il pregiudizio dell'astensione*, cit., e *II. La teoria dei partiti politici e la lotta futura*, cit. Sulla questione della «politica dei letterati» e Morasso cfr. R. CONTARINO, *Il primo «Marzocco» (1896-1900)*, Bologna, Patron, 1982, pp. 91-100 e *passim*; R. FEDI, *«La politica dei letterati»*, *Il Marzocco. Carteggi e cronache*, cit., pp. 97-118; e C. MATTII, *Mario Morasso: la ridefinizione del ruolo sociale del letterato*, «il Vieusseux», I, 1988,1, pp. 40-59, da cui sono tratte, con qualche cambiamento, alcune delle pagine qui incluse.

tica, da lui accusato di compiaciuto «fakirismo».[35] I toni acri, a volte violenti, che informano gli interventi morassiani, in stridente contrasto con la pacata eleganza dell'aristocratico foglio fiorentino, rilevano l'ansia nel giovane sociologo di coinvolgere gli interlocutori in un confronto aperto con l'incalzare della storia, con la temuta avanzata socialista, ampiamente confermata dalle elezioni del '95 e del '96, con le agitazioni popolari e gli scioperi (il solo 1897 ne registrava 187) e, sul fronte governativo, con la grave crisi egemonica del blocco conservatore.[36]

Le premesse politico-ideologiche degli articoli in questione risalgono a scritti degli anni '94 -'95 di forte ispirazione antisocialista ed antidemocratica. In essi Morasso richiamava gruppi intellettuali di tendenze antiliberali ad aggregarsi nel fiancheggiamento ideologico delle forze della conservazione. Solo una classe autoritaria, educata ad ideali di forza e predominio, era in grado di sbarrare la via ai socialisti e alle loro avanguardie, i democratici.[37] Sul «Marzocco» Morasso dava quindi avvio ad un'accesa campagna interventistica che assumeva la forma della «reazione letteraria».[38] Rispondente a preoccupazioni d'ordine pratico, la reazione era diretta contro le correnti letterarie contemporanee – simbolismo, misticismo, decadentismo – in quanto responsabili di un'arte avulsa dalla vita ed espressione in ultima analisi del distacco dell'artista dalla società. In altre parole l'artista era chiamato a misurarsi con i quesiti socio-politici posti dalla società di fine secolo. Urgeva ricomporre il rapporto arte-società, già operante nell'Italia risorgimentale, e ricostruirlo con una prospettiva nuova e secondo le esigenze del mutato contesto storico, o meglio secondo le interpretazioni che di tale contesto venivano date. Un rapporto quindi – date le premesse dell'articolo morassiano – ricostituito in funzione antidemocratica ed antisocialista.

La sfida veniva lanciata ai «nati dopo il 1870» sui quali un «grande fatto» – la conquista di Roma – aveva impresso «un'impronta peculiare»: «un modo di sentire e pensare» nuovo. Con l'assunzione della romanità a referente etico-politico delle nuove generazioni – una romanità reinterpretata secondo la corruzione che l'idea di Roma aveva subito nella cultura di fine secolo – si fissavano gli obiettivi contestatori della reazione: contestazione di superati ideali di marca positivista – dall'umanitarismo al pacifismo – responsabili del «rimbambimento» e viltà delle classi dirigenti e della loro inabilità ad opporre resistenza all'avanzata socialista.[39]

---

[35] *La politica dei letterati*, I, cit.

[36] Sulla notevole capacità di recupero del partito socialista, dopo le persecuzioni del '94, e sui successi riportati alle elezione del marzo 1897 (a cui faceva riferimento anche Morasso nel suo terzo articolo), cfr. G. CANDELORO, *Storia dell'Italia moderna*, VII, cit., pp. 30-37.

[37] Cfr. *Nel 1° maggio. Agli umanitari*, I.L., IV, 1895, 17 e *Nel 1° maggio. Ai lavoratori*, ivi, 29 apr. 1894, poi in *Uomini e idee del domani. L'egoarchia*, Torino, Bocca, 1898, rispettivamente a p. 190 e sgg., e alle pp. 181-184.

[38] *Ai nati dopo il 1870*, cit., da cui le citt. sgg.

[39] L'attacco alla classe politica nei suoi settori liberal-democratici si accompagna nell'intellettuale di parte reazionaria alla polemica antipositivistica ispirata, in tal caso, da preoccupazioni prevalentemente pratiche; cfr L.

Per Corradini, celebratore delle «anime solitarie» ma recettivo alle suggestioni delle teorie della «folla» e volto ad una concezione attivistica dell'opera letteraria, l'intervento del sociologo acquisiva un rilievo particolare: Morasso eleggeva il letterato a protagonista di una reazione *letteraria* nel nome ma non nella sostanza. Dal Morasso il letterato era chiamato in causa per rinnovare i contenuti dell'opera letteraria secondo esigenze praticistiche, ovvero per individuare temi con cui attivare una volontà d'opposizione alle tendenze democratiche e socialiste in atto nella vita nazionale. Nel ruolo di persuasore il letterato morassiano si trovava di fronte ad un compito ben definito: inserire nell'opera letteraria e riproporre alla coscienza collettiva «nuclei di idee» a cui affidare il messaggio politico.

La lezione morassiana, nei suoi obiettivi immediati, veniva recepita da Corradini: avviare una «reazione» letteraria rispondente a specifiche esigenze di rieducazione nazionale. Occorreva sottrarre l'anima italiana dalla «quietudine», dalla «mansuetudine» – i falsi valori predicati dalla «ciarlataneria» dell'internazionalismo socialista al solo scopo di fiaccare, a livello individuale e nazionale, la volontà di lotta e ridurre gli uomini in «pecore».[40] Tale rieducazione, lo avrebbe ripetuto negli anni successivi, non poteva certo venire dal teatro post-unitario che si era adeguato alle condizioni della vita nazionale. Un teatro in cui l'azione drammatica non faceva altro che riflettere e registrare una grave crisi spirituale e politica piuttosto che ritornare a rappresentare «l'ideale» e proporre, tramite adeguate scelte tematiche, valori alternativi.[41] Ma con l'intervista del 1898 a D'Annunzio, Morasso aveva indicato, quanto a valori ideali e a capacità comunicative, il superamento di quel teatro nella concezione drammatica dannunziana: «il dramma ritiene ottimamente Gabriele D'Annunzio, è forse la forma concessa al poeta per comunicare direttamente con la moltitudine, per rilevare all'anima innumerevole i sogni virili ed eroici che trasfigurano solitamente la vita».[42] In quell'«accordo» con la «folla intenta e muta» – accordo ri-

---

SALVATORELLI, *Storia del Novecento*, Milano, Mondadori, 1964, pp. 153-154; e N. BOBBIO, *Profilo ideologico del '900*, Milano, Garzanti, 1990, pp. 13-14 e *passim*. Al riguardo specifico, cfr. U. PISCOPO, *Mario Morasso e le ideologie antidemocratiche*, in *Letteratura italiana. Novecento*, dir. da G. Grana, Milano, Marzorati, 1982, X, pp. 60-76.

[40] E. CORRADINI, *Il sonatore di zampogna*, «Il Marzocco», III, 1898, 39.

[41] Cfr. *In morte di Giuseppe Giacosa. Dal sogno alla realtà*, in cui Corradini tirava sbrigativamente le somme di un trentennio di produzione teatrale con l'unica preoccupazione di imputarne il progressivo scadimento – «cronaca dialogata... dell'esistenza comune» – a quell'Italia che, dopo i sogni eroici del risorgimento, «passò e forse ruinò in una concezione della vita realistica senza sogni o senza illusioni e soprattutto senza eroico, anzi con la paura dell'eroico, anzi col disprezzo». Il teatro credé suo dovere diventare «fatto della realtà»: «non gli importò più affatto di essere una festa dello spirito né di essere grande, né di essere nobile; si compiacque anzi spesso di essere tutto il contrario... un tedio anche dei sensi e l'opposto della nobiltà e della grandezza, tal quale l'esistenza comune di cui volle farsi specchio» («Il Marzocco», 17 settembre 1906).

[42] Cfr. M. MORASSO, *Il futuro teatro d'Albano*, «L'illustrazione italiana», XXIV, 1897, 44, in cui l'autore, «il più fedelmente possibile», riferiva e commentava brani del colloquio da lui avuto con il poeta. Sul teatro nella sua

cercato in un rito teso a esaltarne la recettività alle suggestioni dell'irrazionale – il poeta, secondo l'interpretazione del Morasso, offriva una lezione esemplare. La trasfigurazione riscattava la folla dal grigiore ideale della società contemporanea, di cui era riflesso il teatro borghese e la coinvolgeva nel sogno evocato dalla parola poetica. Chiamata a partecipare al dramma-rito, protagonista con l'officiante di un rito agonistico, la folla si arrendeva inerme ai miti inebrianti rivelati dal poeta. Una manipolazione emotiva ed ideologica consapevole, che, nell'estendersi dell'arco scenico alla piazza pubblica, appariva finalizzata ad eccitare nelle moltitudini «le volontà virili»[43] e quindi la volontà di opposizione alla terza Roma, vile e corruttrice. E se il merito dell'apertura corradiniana all'idea teatrale del D'Annunzio va a Morasso,[44] – e non è per caso che l'articolo corradiniano[45] esca a distanza ravvicinata dall'intervista del sociologo al poeta – in quella adesione, peraltro ambigua, rientrava anche l'antico interesse dello scrittore nazionalista per la psicologia del pubblico teatrale. D'Annunzio aveva riportato al teatro «energie eroiche primordiali» dando luogo ad un «ideale spettacolo di bellezza e di forza». In altre parole, in quella generosa tensione a rappresentare la vita come aspirazione a grandi e nobili ideali, il teatro dannunziano non si era adeguato al paralizzante grigiore della realtà nazionale. Una concezione drammatica, quella dannunziana, ricca di grande «virtù» educativa che presto o tardi avrebbe dato «i suoi frutti». «Noi – concludeva Corradini – possiamo aspettare con fiducia».

Che il campo di raccolta più proficuo venisse ricercato dall'autore nell'area attivistica veniva confermato di lì a qualche mese nella recensione della *Gloria*.[46] E del resto nell'esaltazione del binomio bellezza-forza rappresentativo, nell'interpretazione corradiniana, del teatro dannunziano, l'accento batteva sul secondo termine. La bellezza – ovvero un teatro restituito alla dignità artistica – veniva assunta come strumento di comunicazione di miti di potenza e di prestigio nazionale, di espansionismo militare.[47] Nella *Gloria* quindi Corradini passava al vaglio la capacità o meno del poeta di «appressarsi alla vita» e, più specificamente, «alla forma di vita più vasta e terribile: quella po-

specifica «indole collettiva», Morasso scrive *L'origine dell'arte. L'arte primitiva*, in *Uomini*, cit., pp. 83-96. Rispondente alla necessità avvertita dalle comunità primitive di celebrare eventi di natura conflittuale, «odii», «vendette», «trionfi», la rappresentazione drammatica è percepita dal sociologo come frutto della partecipazione del gruppo al duplice livello emotivo e creativo. Le teorie nicciane sull'origine della tragedia e gli esempi wagneriani alimentavano questo interesse.

43 Cfr. G. D'Annunzio, *Proemio*, «Convito», I, genn. 1895. Interi brani saranno ripresi, e solo con qualche modifica, nel celebre «discorso della siepe», pronunciato a Pescara il 22 agosto 1897 in occasione della campagna elettorale per il collegio di Ortona, ora nel *Libro ascetico della Giovane Italia*, in *Prose di ricerca*, Milano, Mondadori, 1964 (7), I. Per le reazioni compiaciute di Morasso alla candidatura di D'Annunzio, cfr. R. Pertici, *Le radici del pensiero di Mario Morasso*, cit., p. 157.

44 A tal proposito, cfr. R. Contarino, *Corradini e «Il Marzocco»*, cit.

45 Di Corradini v. infatti, *Sogno d'un tramonto d'autunno*, «Il Marzocco», III, 1898, 41, da cui le citt. sgg.

46 E. Corradini, *La gloria*, ivi, IV, 1899, 18. Sulla recensione, v. anche Filippi, *op. cit.*, pp. 129-132.

47 Cfr. P. Alatri, *Introduzione* a *Scritti politici di Gabriele D'Annunzio*, Milano, Feltrinelli, 1980, p. 22.

litica».[48] La scelta non era casuale: la tragedia aveva «un'importanza speciale» per le sue «palesi» «mire sociali e patriottiche». L'«idea dominatrice»,[49] da cui prendeva avvio il dramma – l'eversione del potere centrale, la traslazione della conflittualità interna a «guerra sul confine e sul mare» – non poteva che incontrare l'approvazione di coloro che «invocavano per la patria un avvenire di fiere virtù e di gloria».[50] Nella resa scenica tuttavia l'intenzione civile del poeta mancava del vigore ed ardore iniziali: era affidata a personaggi la cui azione e «lusso verbale» non riflettevano una tensione patriottica. E Ruggero Flamma, l'eroe delegato alla distruzione del vecchio ordine borghese, corrotto e dilaniato da tensioni interne, incapace di venire a termine con le masse contadine e urbane in rivolta, viene in realtà meno al suo destino storico: sembra preferire la «contemplazione delle stelle» e pensare «all'erbe che odorano nell'agro lontano». «Eroe malinconico della terza Roma», Flamma si sarebbe lasciato avvincere dai lacci voluttuosi della ambiziosa e bellissima Elena Commena. Incalzato dall'eros, il presente storico retrocedeva dallo spazio scenico. L'inadempienza quindi della grande idea dominatrice, dovuta alla inettitudine di un personaggio che «Cesare o Napoleone [...] non avrebbero voluto per valletto», piuttosto che a insormontabili ostacoli politici, vanificava l'intenzione civile del dramma: comunicare alla moltitudini l'eroico politico come valore essenziale della vita individuale e nazionale.

Ancora una volta le note critiche si riconfermano come laboratorio di ricerca, e di contenuti e di direttive, con cui imprimere alla produzione letteraria valenze extra-artistiche. Una funzione pratica che già spiegava il decrescente interesse per la drammaturgia nordica e che ora rivela l'ambivalenza del rapporto instaurato da Corradini nei confronti dell'opera dannunziana. Se indubbia è l'attrazione per un apparato tematico e mitico non reperibile nella rassegnata quotidianità del teatro borghese, altrettanto netto è in Corradini il rifiuto per quello che percepiva il persistente peccato del D'Annunzio –, l'artificiosità che trattiene i personaggi dalle «azioni della vita», lo sfoggio verbale eccessivo.[51] In altri termini, nel giudizio complessivamente negativo espresso da Corradini sulla *Gloria* – D'Annunzio si era «servito male...di un grande pensiero» – nella rilevata dicotomia tra gli alti propositi e la resa scenica, erano già *in nuce*, sia pure

---

[48] E. CORRADINI, *La gloria*, cit., da cui le citt. sgg.

[49] G. D'ANNUNZIO, *La gloria*, in *Teatro*, Milano, Mondadori, 1949 (5), vol. I, p. 357: «Io e i miei compagni [...] siamo entrati nella lotta presentando l'apparizione prossima di una idea dominatrice e creatrice di cui vorremmo essere gli strumenti obbedienti e lucidi per la costruzione della Città, della Patria, della forza latina». Per la cit. sg., v. ivi, p. 369.

[50] E. CORRADINI, *La gloria*, cit., da cui le citt. sgg.

[51] A tale proposito, cfr. anche quanto Corradini scrive in *Tragedia dell'anima*: per «commuovere» il pubblico la comunicazione dei temi deve avvenire tramite un linguaggio «verbale e scenico» accessibile a tutti («Il Marzocco», IV, 1899, 1). Ad anni di distanza Corradini riprenderà lo stesso concetto nel recensire *La nave* che esemplificava ormai, nello sfoggio eccessivo di vocaboli rari, una costante del teatro dannunziano (*La nave*, «Il Marzocco», XIII, 1908, 3).

per esclusione, i criteri che dovevano presiedere alla costruzione del personaggio eletto a strumento ed espressione di un'idea «dominatrice»: azioni e tratti eroici ma a servizio della prescelta missione storica; netto rifiuto pertanto di un superomismo esercitato come auto-gratificazione, come «sovraeccitazione» egotistica;[52] e in definitiva guerra dichiarata a quello che definirà il «gesto estetico» fine a se stesso.[53]

Agli inizi del nuovo secolo, con la svolta politica inaugurata da Giolitti[54] – un grave colpo per chi, dopo la caduta di Crispi, aveva visto nel tentativo di Pelloux l'ultimo baluardo alla montante marea socialista – l'appello morassiano si era fatto più cogente. Da qui la decisione da parte di Corradini di dare forma concreta alla lezione del sociologo e di comporre un'opera letteraria dalle forti valenze politiche. Che la scelta dell'autore, dato il suo interesse per l'indole collettiva del teatro, cadesse sul genere drammatico è scontato. Quanto ai meccanismi di trasmissione, i «nuclei», Corradini si riporta alle indicazioni morassiane affidando il messaggio politico alla sintesi simbolica di maggior presa sull'anima collettiva italiana,[55] Roma, e a quella conferisce i tratti antropomorfici dell'individuo da lui considerato l'espressione massima della romanità, Giulio Cesare.[56]

Già in uno scritto[57] risalente a questi anni Corradini aveva individuato nella storia romana, in quanto ricca di figure consacrate dagli storici e dai poeti alla fama universale, la fonte privilegiata per opere teatrali in cui al protagonista si volesse conferire grande «vitalità rappresentativa». Nell'assunto metodologico dell'autore quella «vitalità rappresentativa» è conseguibile purché la figura storica, «astratta dai modi e dai segni dei tempi», venga colta e rappresentata nei suoi tratti sostanziali ed immutabili – ordine e impero nel caso di Cesare. Un'impostazione per cui quei tratti, de-contestualizzati, si prestano in effetti a reinterpretazioni di comodo, ad essere pertanto caricati di significati nuovi preordinati alla funzione assegnata dall'autore alla figura storica.

[52] E. CORRADINI, *La gloria*, cit.

[53] Cfr. E. CORRADINI, *La nave*, cit. La sovrabbondanza del «gesto estetico», non collegato con l'«atto della vita», costituiva un'altra costante del teatro dannunziano e anche quella con effetti negativi quanto a capacità dell'opera di «commuovere» il pubblico.

[54] Sull'ipotesi governativa giolittiana fondata su un riformismo per cui essenziale era l'apertura, sia pure graduale, al movimento operaio, cfr. E. GENTILE, *L'Italia giolittiana 1899-1914*, Bologna, Il mulino, 1991, p. 35 e sgg.

[55] Il massimo «accordo» era conferito dall'autore a Roma quale «sintesi di idee» con cui «ringagliardire lo spirito nazionale». Per capacità «dinamogena» Roma è infatti, nella graduatoria morassiana, il «nucleo più poderoso e colossale», «sintesi simbolica di ideali guerreschi, religiosi e politici, patriottici, tutti spinti al massimo della loro elevazione, tutti agenti con il massimo del loro fascino, incombendo sulla massa a guisa di una fatalità imprescindibile e attiva» (*Roma*, cit.).

[56] E. CORRADINI, *Prefazione* a *Giulio Cesare*, cit., p. 11.

[57] E. CORRADINI, *Fedeltà inutile*, «Il Marzocco», 13 ott. 1901, da cui le citt. sgg.; ma sulla «vitalità rappresentativa» del personaggio storico, v. anche *Nerone*, ivi, 2 giugno, 1901.

Nel 1902 usciva dunque il dramma teatrale *Giulio Cesare*, nel quale l'assunto corradiniano trovava un'applicazione esemplare. Nell'esaltazione di un Cesare *super partes*, teso alla grandezza nazionale di contro ad un'oligarchia senatoriale incapace di controllare le fazioni, il dramma costituisce in effetti un'indiscussa presa di posizione per un drastico ricambio della classe politica liberale. Nel riformismo giolittiano, percepito dall'autore come resa incondizionata agli assalti del movimento operaio, quella classe dava la prova massima della sua debolezza ed insipienza politica. Nelle pieghe del grandioso fondale romano si insinua l'inquietante alternativa politico-istituzionale proposta dal nazionalismo e che di lì ad un anno avrebbe trovato esplicita espressione nelle pagine del «Regno»: l'eversione del vecchio ordine liberale in cui, lo dimostrava il giolittismo, fruivano di ampi margini di manovra le correnti democratiche e socialiste. Responsabili della conflittualità sociale che affliggeva la vita nazionale erano, secondo Corradini, di grave ostacolo all'affermazione politico-economica dell'Italia sulla scena internazionale.[58]

Nella scelta delle modalità di trasmissione del messaggio politico, Corradini confermava la predilezione per le categorie dell'irrazionale. Eleggendo nel *Giulio Cesare* ad interlocutori i ceti medi, l'autore affidava la difesa e promulgazione della ipotesi politica alla figura storica dalle connotazioni comprensibili e quindi di maggior presa emotiva su chi della propria formazione umanistica faceva un motivo di difesa di classe.[59] Affidato ad una figura, a cui l'autore conferiva la necessaria «vitalità rappresentativa», il messaggio veniva ad acquisire risonanza e carica persuasiva. In altre parole, la plausibilità presso lo spettatore dell'ipotesi politica formulata dal testo sarebbe strettamente legata, secondo la lezione morassiana, alla capacità dell'autore di inserirla in un modello memorabile e intensamente suggestivo.

Anni dopo Pier Ludovico Occhini, il portavoce riconosciuto del futuro leader nazionalista, indicherà nella *Storia romana* di Theodor Mommsen il testo di riferimento del Cesare corradiniano.[60]

C'è invero in quell'opera giovanile del Mommsen una innegabile idealizzazione che rivelerebbe «il travaglio di uno spirito acutamente critico... non an-

---

[58] Cfr. E. CORRADINI, *Tornando sul nostro programma. III. Ancora la libertà*, «Il Regno», I, 1904, 47 e, in particolare, *Tornando sul nostro programma. II. La libertà*, ivi, I, 1904, 46, in cui per la ricomposizione del tessuto nazionale lacerato dalla lotta di classe propugna un «regime massimamente forte», «di repressione e di soppressione».

[59] Cfr. F. GAETA, *Il nazionalismo italiano*, cit., p. 48.

[60] P. L. OCCHINI, *Corradini*, cit., p. 123. Pubblicata a Berlino, presso Weidman, negli anni 1854-1856 in tre volumi, la *Romische Geschichte*, apparve in Italia nel 1867, con una traduzione basata sulla seconda edizione dell'opera (1857) a cui l'autore aveva apportato delle aggiunte. Le citt. nel presente lavoro saranno tratte da questa prima edizione italiana (*Storia Romana*, trad. di G. Sandrini, Milano, Casa Editrice Italiana M. Guigoni, 1867), come quella a cui, con ogni probabilità, doveva riferirsi Corradini. La seconda edizione italiana uscì infatti solo nel 1903.

cora affrancatosi dal mito dell' "uomo del destino"».[61] Una tensione irrisolta che si prestava tuttavia ad interpretazioni devianti da parte di un lettore, quale Corradini, interessato ad una fruizione praticistica delle fonti di riferimento.

A Cesare il giovane storico aveva conferito come tratti dominanti la risolutezza eroica e il genio militare posti al servizio di Roma, l'«assoluta indipendenza, che non consentiva influenze sul suo animo», la «sicurezza profetica» che «sapeva trovare con ogni scopo il giusto mezzo». Monarca, «non fece mai la parte di re» ed «è forse l'unico dei potenti di questa terra, che non tanto nelle cose più importanti quanto in quelle minime non abbia agito per propensione o per capriccio, ma sempre e senza eccezione seguendo il suo dovere di capo di Stato». Leader carismatico, imperava su uomini di diversa estrazione sociale con la forza del suo fascino. Dotato di una serie di virtù elevate al sommo grado – dalla «potentissima forza creatrice» e «intelligenza perspicacissima» alla «volontà assoluta» e «immensa capacità di esecuzione» – assunte per di più come «disposizioni naturali», il Cesare mommseniano si presenta con i tratti inconfondibili dell'uomo predestinato al «riscatto politico, militare e morale della nazione profondamente decaduta».[62] Tratti che ancora a decenni di distanza dalla pubblicazione della *Storia romana* continuavano ad esercitare un grande fascino presso il lettore medio attratto, in quella travagliata fine secolo, dal mito salvifico dell'uomo della provvidenza.

Quella del Mommsen si confermava quindi come un'interpretazione che prestava il fianco ad una "modernizzazione" della figura storica, ovvero alla sovrapposizione di caratteri estranei alla realtà della Roma in cui visse e operò Cesare,[63] e ri-

---

[61] Cfr. G. PUGLIESE CARRATELLI, *Introduzione* a THEODOR MOMMSEN, *Storia di Roma Antica*, Firenze, Sansoni, 1960, p. XIII. Per Pugliese un elemento importante nella valutazione di tanti «giudizi, di tante caratterizzazioni» presenti nell'opera mommseniana, e motivo di non poche perplessità, è da ricercarsi in quelle tensioni irrisolte tra «la volontà di una valutazione realistica di situazioni politiche», che si riallaccia all'«esigenza di obiettività posta allo studioso dalla sua disciplina», e un non meglio definito «sentimento poetico» che avrebbe indotto il Mommsen, fedele agli ideali dell'Europa quarantottesca, ad «ornare di più nobili tratti un atteggiamento o un disegno, come nella colorazione periclea della politica di Cesare, intesa a fondare «una repubblica libera sotto un monarca»» (*ibid.*).

[62] T. MOMMSEN, *Storia romana*, III, cit., pp. 433-436.

[63] Arnaldo Momigliano, nel suo studio, *Per un riesame della storia dell'idea di Cesarismo*, riscontra nel diciannovesimo secolo un «modernizzamento della storia romana», presente in due diversi tipi di pubblicazioni. Riscontrabile nella pubblicistica politica, che, incoraggiata dai due Napoleoni, stabiliva analogie esaltanti quanto arbitrarie con l'operato dei Bonaparte, il «modernizzamento» occorre tuttavia anche nell'ambito della storiografia classica, perfino in storici della portata del Mommsen. Un errore di prospettiva che Momigliano, studioso rigorosissimo del pensiero classico, imputa ad un «rallentamento della conversazione diretta con gli antichi», che «egli [Mommsen] poi corresse con la disciplina degli anni maturi». Caso esemplare e vistoso è dato dalla idealizzazione della figura di Cesare, dalla sua trasformazione, quasi un cedimento al presente, a «uomo del destino, super-uomo, risolutore di antinomie storiche e quindi creatore di una nuova forma politica». Ne derivava la creazione di un mito che in quanto tale aveva ben poco a che fare con la documentata figura storica di Cesare, ma rispondeva, sul piano culturale, al «culto dell'eroe come politico», uno dei retaggi della cultura romantica a cui lo stesso Mommsen non seppe sottrarsi (*Secondo contributo alla storia degli studi classici*, Roma, [s.n.], 1960, p. 273 e sgg.).

spondenti piuttosto al prepotente insorgere sullo scenario ottocentesco di un modello politico nuovo, avente un riscontro fattuale nella monarchia bonapartista. Regime dai tratti peculiari, si fonda su antinomie politico-istituzionali. Instaurato con la violazione della legalità esistente, si attua come governo autoritario centrato sul potere individuale e consolidato dalle fortune militari. Al tempo stesso attivamente ricerca una legittimazione popolare tramite lo strumento plebiscitario del tutto ignoto, è stato rilevato, ai meccanismi politici del mondo classico. [64]

L'esigenza poi di definire tale regime sul piano teorico, e farne quindi una «categoria nuova» del pensiero politico, se di per sé legittima, dà origine, allorché assume come termine di riferimento la politica dell'antica Roma, ad un concetto – il cesarismo – che per i suoi elementi costitutivi era del tutto estraneo al pensiero classico e che anzi avrebbe frapposto un filtro distorcente alla comprensione di quel pensiero e di quella realtà. [65]

Di particolare rilievo nel contesto dell'«usurpazione moderna» della cultura classica a fini immediatamente politici, l'interpretazione che in tempi più recenti Luciano Canfora ha dato del cesarismo: «un caso concreto in cui un concetto ricavato dall'esperienza del mondo antico... è stato rinnovato creativamente e usato per esprimere una realtà moderna...». [66] Un rinnovamento «politicamente produttivo» che spiegherebbe, a nostro avviso, la rinascita nella cultura politica di fine secolo dell'interesse per il cesarismo [67] quando, con il presentarsi di un quadro socio-economico strutturalmente mutato, si riproponeva con urgenza la questione dell'inserimento delle masse nella vita politica nazionale, non disgiunta dalla preoccupazione per la decadenza delle *élites* tradizionali. [68]

Nel 1857 Mommsen pubblicava la seconda edizione della *Romische Ge-*

---

[64] ARNALDO MOMIGLIANO, ivi, p. 280.

[65] Ivi, p. 281. Molto categorico Momigliano: «Il cesarismo è una nozione tipica del XIX secolo che serve eccellentemente a definire la monarchia dei due Napoleoni, ma dovrebbe essere bandito dalla storia antica» (*ibid.*). Per una prima analisi del termine in ambito politologico, del suo riproporsi nella storia moderna, delle sue varie applicazioni e rapporti con il bonapartismo e poi con il bismarckismo, cfr. C. GUARNIERI, *Cesarismo*, in *Dizionario di politica*, dir. da N. Bobbio e N. Matteucci, UTET, 1976, pp. 150-151.

[66] L. CANFORA, *Cultura classica e «usurpazione moderna»*, in *Le vie del classicismo*, Bari, Laterza, 1989, pp. 237-252. Sulla «produttività» del cesarismo, v. ivi, p. 238: «Concetto politicamente produttivo, questo di "cesarismo". Quando intorno agli anni '50 dell'Ottocento si è cercato di definire la natura del potere bonapartista, del secondo Napoleone, il concetto di "cesarismo" è servito a definire un particolare tipo di potere: un potere totalitario con un appoggio di massa, con un rapporto con le masse diverso da quello della dittatura tradizionale [...] un concetto della romanità classica, è stato rinnovato... e usato per esprimere una realtà moderna, qual è appunto il "bonapartismo"».

[67] Per la ripresa dell'idea cesarista al di là e al di qua delle Alpi, studiata nel contesto della crisi di ideali registratasi in rapporto alla grandi trasformazioni politiche e socio-economiche della fine secolo, cfr. l'esaustivo lavoro di LUISA MANGONI, *Una crisi di fine secolo. La cultura italiana e la Francia fra Otto e Novecento*, cit., pp. 178-203.

[68] Per due interpretazioni autorevoli sulla decadenza delle *élites*, cfr. la teoria della «classe politica» negli *Elementi di scienza politica* pubblicati da Gaetano Mosca nel 1896 e i concetti espressi da Vilfredo Pareto nei *Systèmes socialistes* del 1902, e in seguito perfezionati nel ponderoso *Trattato di sociologia generale* del 1916, di «classe eletta» e «circolazione delle *élites*».

schichte, nel cui terzo volume inseriva *ex novo* alcune pagine con lo scopo di sottrarre l'opera a sospetti di cedimenti nei confronti del cesarismo. Pervenire ad un distinguo netto e convincente tra il «vero Cesare», che lo storico reclamava come oggetto esclusivo della propria ricerca, e il cesarismo contemporaneo, significava innanzi tutto sottrarre l'operato di Cesare da quella dimensione dell'«imperitura esemplarità» sottesa al giudizio complessivo espresso dall'autore nei confronti del vincitore di Farsalo. Fatto di cui in questa seconda edizione Mommsen sembra essere consapevole là dove sottolinea con rinnovato vigore l'esigenza di valutare Cesare entro i limiti dell'appropriato contesto storico. Ribadiva pertanto il carattere storicamente «necessario e salutare» dell'azione politico-amministrativa avviata da Cesare, nell'ambito specifico – sottolineava – delle condizioni strutturali della società romana. In quella riaffermazione della grandezza di Cesare, correlata ora a determinate situazioni socio-politiche, e nel conseguente ridimensionamento della politica cesariana al «minor male possibile», prendeva rilievo la condanna, coerente del resto con gli ideali quarantotteschi dell'autore, del cesarismo contemporaneo – regime autocratico storicamente obsoleto e politicamente nocivo in quanto «si mostra sotto altre condizioni di sviluppo». Per non lasciare adito a dubbi, lo storico riaffermava il necessario distinguo tra la ricerca storiografica e l'«usurpazione» del fatto storico a fini politici, impartendo una lezione sulle modalità di lettura della «storia dei secoli passati»: le «narrazioni del passato» non devono usarsi come scontato terreno di ricerca delle «congiunture del presente» da cui «desumere... i sintomi e gli specifici della diagnosi e dell'arte di compor ricette per la politica». Lezione con la quale in definitiva lo storico intendeva spuntare le armi a chi volesse «trasmutare il giudizio su Cesare in un giudizio sul così detto cesarismo».[69]

Del distinguo mommseniano Corradini non tiene alcun conto, anche se la prima versione italiana della *Storia romana* si basava sulla seconda edizione della *Romische Geschichte*. La dimensione dell'«imperituro» conferita all'azione di Cesare,[70] con la quale Mommsen intendeva connotarla qualitativamente piuttosto che suggerirla come "ricetta" valida per il presente, viene usata da Corradini come avvallo, in vero prestigioso, per l'assunzione di Cesare a necessità storica proponibile nelle sue componenti essenziali – ordine e impero – oltre il contesto d'origine.

Di quel Cesare, Corradini, in rispondenza al dichiarato assunto metodologico, trascieglieva ed enfatizzava aspetti in sintonia con i presupposti praticistici che regolavano la stesura del dramma. Il criterio preposto alla scelta risponde pertanto

[69] T. MOMMSEN, *Storia Romana*, cit., III, pp. 445-447.
[70] Ivi, p. 438.

all'opposizione dell'autore nei confronti della realtà socio-politica dell'Italia giolittiana. Ne è conferma la costante tematica del dramma: la contrapposizione tra un Cesare corredato di preveggenza politica, superiore alle passioni di parte, eletto a garante di un ordine finalizzato ad una politica nazionale di ampio respiro e, dall'altra, una classe senatoriale votata alla difesa di gretti interessi di gruppo, priva di virtù egemonica ed ostaggio quindi dei «demagoghi oligarchi», organizzatori dell'«anarchia plebea».[71]

Il rilievo inoltre dato nelle varie sequenze sceniche al consenso popolare,[72] con il quale si legittimerebbe la rimozione della legalità esistente, ed in definitiva l'istituirsi di un regime a base individuale consolidato dal prestigio acquisito da Cesare nelle imprese militari, presentate come strumento di «concordia e pace entro... le mura», suggerisce da parte dell'autore una volontà specifica: promuovere, tramite la figura storica, eletta nel dramma ad interprete unica del volere collettivo, il modello di un forte potere politico, affidato, in questa fase dell'itinerario corradiniano, al leader trascinatore di folle, risolutore di antinomie, in abile equilibrio tra forza e persuasione.

Incurante del tentativo mommseniano – saldare la politica di Cesare ai problemi dalla Roma pre-augustea – Corradini consapevolmente propone in Cesare il modello di un «nuovo eroismo politico»,[73] più consono, a suo parere, ad affrontare l'assillante questione dell'entrata di nuovi soggetti sociali nella vita politica italiana. Dietro la maschera di Cesare prendeva forma il nuovo capo carismatico in grado di costituire un rapporto diretto con le masse a scapito delle discreditate istituzioni rappresentative[74] e proporsi, in apparenza, come mediatore di conflittualità sociali, allo scopo in realtà di sottrarre le masse alla paventata egemonizzazione socialista ed in definitiva consolidare il potere politico tramite la difesa degli interessi dei gruppi dominanti.

Nel 1902, contemporaneamente al *Giulio Cesare*, uscivano i primi due volumi di *Grandezza e decadenza di Roma*,[75] l'opera con cui Guglielmo Ferrero, già pro-

---

[71] *Giulio Cesare*, cit., p. 117.

[72] Ivi, pp. 22-33, e 130-131. Per la cit. sg., v. ivi, p. 132.

[73] R. CONTARINO, *Corradini e «Il Marzocco»*, cit., p. 516. Su tale interpretazione, v. anche pp. sgg.

[74] L'attacco al Parlamento come istituzione ricorre frequentemente nel «Regno» con l'immediatezza offerta dal debito strumento di comunicazione. Cfr., per es., CORRADINI, *Tornando sul nostro programma. III*, cit.; G. PREZZOLINI, *Le due Italie*, I, 1904, 26; LA RIVISTA, *Le elezioni*, I, 1904, 48.

[75] G. FERRERO, *Grandezza e decadenza di Roma*, Milano, Treves, 1902-1907. Dei cinque volumi, di cui si compone l'opera, il secondo era dedicato alla figura e all'operato di Cesare dalla guerra gallica alla morte. Sulla complessa figura dello studioso, cfr. il tuttora valido AA.VV., *Guglielmo Ferrero. Histoire et Politique au XXe siècle*, Genève, Librairie Droz, 1966, con contributi, fra gli altri, di L. Salvatorelli, A. Oltramare, E. Garin, G. Santonastaso, B. Raditsa e G. Busino; A. GAROSCI, *Pensiero politico e storiografia moderna*, Pisa, Nistri-Lischi, 1954, pp. 154-189; e il più recente *Guglielmo Ferrero tra società e politica. Atti del Convegno*, Genova 4-5 ottobre 1982, a cura di Rita Baldi, Genova, E.C.I.G, 1986. Sul Ferrero storico di Roma antica, fondamentali i lavori sgg.: C. BARBAGALLO, *L'opera storica di G. Ferrero e i suoi critici*, Milano, Treves, 1911, in cui l'autore, allievo di Ferrero, analizza, senza incorrere nell'apologia, l'opera ferreriana in rapporto alle correnti storiografiche del tardo Ottocento e primo Novecento e alle reazioni che suscitò tra i contemporanei; F.

tagonista dei dibattiti su cui si cimentava la cultura politica di fine secolo – colonialismo, militarismo, l'impreparazione della classe politica a gestire i cambiamenti strutturali in corso –[76] spostava il centro di osservazione alla Roma antica. La rappresentazione anti-eroica che dava della figura di Cesare – anti-mommseniana specificava l'autore –[77] avrebbe provocato un intervento immediato da parte di Enrico Corradini.

Dalla documentata ricerca di Ferrero emergeva un Cesare tutt'altro che lungimirante; brillante, è vero, nell'esecuzione, ma spesso «strumento inconsapevole del destino per un'opera immensa». Ne offre una prova convincente la conquista e conseguente annessione della Gallia. Un'impresa avviata e compiuta come «manovra elettorale», con la quale tuttavia la civiltà greco-latina, «senza che egli lo volesse o lo sapesse», avrebbe trovato le condizioni favorevoli per avanzare all'interno del continente europeo «preparando così una condizione essenziale della civiltà in cui viviamo».[78] Uomo tutt'altro che "fatale", anzi dubbioso di sé, lo presenta Guglielmo Ferrero. Non dominatore degli uomini e delle cose, come lo aveva proposto il Mommsen, e come lo voleva Corradini. Incalzato piuttosto dagli eventi, il Cesare ferreriano incorre spesso, nel suo operare, in ripercussioni inattese.[79] L'imprevisto – un dato rilevante nella concezione ferrariana della storia –[80] nulla toglie in ultima analisi alla sua grandezza di uomo di stato operante in una fase di gravi trasformazioni nella vita politico-istituzionale e socio-economica di Roma: la crisi di una classe «inadeguata ai nuovi compiti imposti dall'impero», l'emergere di nuove forze storiche, tra cui l'esercito e le province, che non si riconoscevano nel quadro istituzionale esistente.[81] Nulla toglie se non la «rigidezza»,

---

NATALE, *Contributo alla storia della storiografia italiana sul mondo antico*, «Nuova Rivista storica», XII, 1958, 1, pp. 257-271; e P. TREVES, *L'Idea di Roma e la cultura italiana del secolo XIX*, Milano-Napoli, Ricciardi, 1962, pp. 261-293.

[76] Tra le opere del Ferrero su tali argomenti, cfr. in particolare *Il Militarismo. Dieci Conferenze*, Milano, Treves, 1898; e *La Reazione*, Torino, C. Olivetti Editore, 1894 (le citt. alle pp. sgg. sono dalla seconda ediz. [1895?] ristampata presso lo stesso editore con il titolo *Il fenomeno Crispi e la crisi italiana*).

[77] Del Cesare mommseniano Ferrero rifiutava innanzitutto l'immutabile perfezione: «gli scrittori di storia antica hanno quasi tutti il torto gravissimo di rappresentare i grandi uomini politici dell'antichità come sempre eguali a se stessi, dal principio alla fine. Questo è il difetto principale del Cesare descritto dal Mommsen» («Rivista italiana di sociologia», VI, 1902, p. 437), cit. in P. TREVES, *L'idea di Roma*, cit., p. 277. Su questo aspetto dell'anti-mommsenismo del Ferrero, cfr. ivi, pp. 277-278.

[78] G. FERRERO, *Grandezza e decadenza di Roma*, cit., II, pp. 46-47.

[79] Sulla non «preveggenza» di Cesare, questa volta riguardo ai contraccolpi politico-militari della guerra civile, cfr. ivi, pp 353-354. Per un giudizio complessivo su Cesare, v. specialmente il cap. XVIII, pp. 513-518 e *passim*.

[80] Al riguardo cfr. il commento di Barbagallo: «poiché al di sotto del loro [politici e legislatori] operar logico, è un meccanismo, insensibile e brutale, che rivolge a sua posta la storia, l'agitarsi umano deve considerarsi come un battagliare, che non può valere, né riuscir vittorioso, quando si trovi di contro all'impulso lento, ma invincibile, di forze occulte e onnipossenti. Per questo, noi vediamo intelligentissimi ed elaborati piani di azione politica fallire...» (*op. cit.*, p. 56). Per le riflessioni di Ferrero sulle forze dell'irrazionale, cfr. L. MANGONI, *Una crisi di fine secolo*, cit., pp. 120-121.

[81] G. CLEMENTE, *Guida alla storia romana. Eventi, strutture sociali, metodi di ricerca*, Milano, Mondadori, 1990 (2), p. 212. Sulla crisi della repubblica e sulla necessità di nuovi rapporti di forza, il commento di Clemente

«l'artificiosità» di un Cesare ridotto a «uomo-idea». Il che fu poi considerato uno dei grandi meriti dell'interpretazione ferrariana di contro all'errore in cui era incorso il Mommsen.[82]

Non è qui il caso di esprimere una valutazione sulle interpretazioni ferreriane che pure suscitarono, una volta completata la pubblicazione dei cinque volumi, reazioni spesso ostili, specie da parte del mondo accademico.[83] Interessa piuttosto prendere atto della replica di Corradini, contenuta in due note critiche pubblicate sul «Marzocco»,[84] dal momento che costituisce un ulteriore strumento, questa volta offerto dall'autore, per la verifica della sua angolazione interpretativa.

Le note considerate sotto questo profilo non interessano tanto là dove l'autore, rimanendo sulla difensiva, si limita ad un'apologetica reiterazione della eccezionalità di Cesare facendo ricorso ad attributi già espressi nell'azione scenica. Rilevante è piuttosto il fatto che Corradini, nella valutazione conclusiva dell'interpretazione ferreriana, riporti la «*diminutio capitis*» operata da Ferrero al piano politico-ideologico, al «preconcetto» di «vecchio anticesarismo» di cui soffrirebbe il sociologo.[85]

Si tratta di un esplicito riferimento alla valutazione negativa che Ferrero aveva espresso sul cesarismo, da lui analizzato nell'applicazione italiana – il crispismo.[86]

---

offre un primo elemento di chiarificazione: «Le nuove forze politiche e sociali, fra le quali l'esercito ormai professionalizzato, non si riconoscevano nel meccanismo di governo senatorio fondato sulla città-stato; le province, sempre considerate un serbatoio da sfruttare, cominciavano a recuperare una loro individualità economica e politica, della quale era necessario tenere conto: l'Italia non poteva indefinitamente, da sola, costituire la struttura portante dello stato, del reclutamento dei soldati e della classe dirigente» (*ibid.*).

[82] Barbagallo, *op. cit.*, pp. 155-156. Barbagallo riporta la «riumanizzazione» della figura storica alla fruizione, da parte di Ferrero, di discipline ausiliarie – come del resto aveva raccomandato Romano (v. questo lavoro, p. 283) – quali la psicologia teorica. Il «principio della molteplicità dell'anima umana» diviene quindi per Ferrero uno dei parametri interpretativi di cui la storia deve tener conto al fine di «snodare l'anima dei personaggi, turbare e sconvolgere le categorie fisse degli eroi e dei mostri storici, riumanizzarli, curare di spiegarne ogni giorno le coerenze, le debolezze, volute o subite, le audacie, gli errori, le contraddizioni con sé e con altrui». Guglielmo Ferrero infatti «non conosce eroi, tipi, ma uomini; il suo Cesare, il suo Pompeo, il suo Cicerone, il suo Antonio, il suo Augusto non sono figure di acciaio o di fango, non i *clichés* della storia tradizionale» (ivi, p. 64).

[83] Per le reazioni da parte degli addetti ai lavori negli anni che immediatamente seguirono la pubblicazione di *Grandezza e decadenza di Roma*, e per una loro valutazione, cfr. Barbagallo, *op. cit.*, *passim* e in particolare il cap. VII, pt. II, dal titolo significativo, *Gli errori dei critici*, pp. 178-213, in cui lo storico mette in rilievo come la critica, prigioniera di pregiudizi accademici (Ferrero era un nuovo arrivato), e spesso chiusa nell'equazione ricerca storica - metodo storico, indulga in appunti particolari, sottovalutando la complessità dell'opera sia dal punto di vista tematico che metodologico – il confluire di varie linee d'indagine, tra cui quella psicologica e economico-sociale. In tempi più recenti, lontani dai dibattiti in corso ai primi del secolo, studi come quello di Natale hanno invece messo in luce i contributi dell'opera ferreriana rispetto alla problematica del trapasso dalla Repubblica all'Impero, non fosse altro come stimolo a «riproporsi il problema della fine della repubblica con aperta comprensione dei problemi economici, politici, culturali che vi si intrecciarono...» (*op. cit.*, pp. 266-267). Non diversamente, P. Treves individua nella energica ripresa della questione del «fallimentare trionfo di Cesare», lasciata irrisolta dal Mommsen, e dal Ferrero riproposta a tutto campo e secondo prospettive nuove, uno degli apporti vitali dell'opera ferreriana (*op. cit.*, pp. 277 e 282).

[84] E. Corradini, *Grandezza e decadenza di Roma*, «Il Marzocco», VII, 1902, 2; *Giulio Cesare*, ivi, 24.

[85] *Giulio Cesare*, cit.

[86] G. Ferrero, *Il fenomeno Crispi e la crisi italiana*, cit.

Messo alla prova nella difficile congiuntura di fine secolo, segnata dal presentarsi nello scenario nazionale di nuove forze sociali, dal conseguente formarsi di aggregazioni di massa, dai primi tentativi di organizzazione del nascente proletariato industriale, il crispismo non si era rivelato una forza nuova, secondo il classico assunto cesarista, di rottura con un vecchio ordine ritenuto incapace di gestire le trasformazioni in corso.

Prodotto di una classe politica – quella risorgimentale che aveva dato splendide prove di sé nel contesto delle lotte pre-unitarie – Crispi non si era preoccupato di adeguare gli strumenti critico-operativi alla nuova realtà italiana.[87] Non preparato a cogliere nei mutamenti strutturali in atto nella società italiana di fine secolo i segni di un rinnovamento che, per quanto faticoso, era necessario per liberare l'Italia dalla morsa della arretratezza socio-economica, Crispi reagiva con la repressione e al tempo stesso ne cercava una giustificazione agitando lo spauracchio ed esagerando la forza del socialismo.[88] Si proponeva come l'uomo della provvidenza, "salvatore" dell'integrità nazionale minacciata dalle forze della disgregazione, approfittando di quelle «disposizioni messianiche proprie a tutti i popoli» che si ritrovano a vivere in età di trapasso, di incertezza.[89] In effetti la sua azione "provvidenziale", favorendo «i grandi proprietari fondiari, assenteisti e oziosi; i grandi industriali bisognosi di protezioni doganali e di moltitudini passive; i grandi speculatori divoratori del denaro pubblico», si traduceva in una politica involutiva, di ostacolo alla necessaria trasformazione dell'Italia in un paese industriale, nella quale trasformazione rientrava anche la debita apertura nei confronti del nascente movimento operaio.[90]

Ovviamente la valutazione ferrariana non poteva essere condivisa dal nazionalista Corradini che contribuirà in prima persona a creare e alimentare il mito di Crispi «salvatore della patria».[91] Partendo da interpretazioni della realtà nazionale irriconciliabili con le analisi ferreriane, di fronte poi all'ulteriore rafforzarsi ai primi del secolo delle organizzazioni operaie e del partito socialista, Corradini avrebbe auspicato l'inserimento delle nuove forze produttive, ma in un sistema repressivo, in grado di garantire la conciliazione di classe e di conseguenza accelerare, tramite l'espansione coloniale, lo sviluppo politico ed

---

[87] Ivi, p. 53.
[88] Ivi, p. 24. Per lo stesso concetto, v. anche p. 30.
[89] Ivi, p. 37.
[90] Ivi, pp. 69-70.
[91] Per la celebrazione di Crispi come «l'ultimo grande uomo di Stato che l'Italia abbia avuto», cfr. l'editoriale *Crispi*, «Il Regno», I, 1904, 27: «Egli è stato l'ultimo cioè a fare della... grande politica italiana, l'ultimo a sentire in se stesso la coscienza forte della nazione, nel suo passato e nel suo futuro, al di là e al di sopra degli urli della piazza...». A queste linee s'informava la rappresentazione che di Crispi avrebbe dato Corradini nel suo romanzo, *La guerra lontana*. In esso il fallimento della politica crispina su entrambi i fronti e il conseguente ristagno della vita nazionale era imputato ai democratici e ai socialisti sobillatori della piazza (Milano, Treves, 1911).

economico della giovane nazione. Posizioni che se specificate nel «Regno»,[92] sono peraltro riscontrabili – lo abbiamo osservato – nei criteri che presiedono alle scelte tematiche del dramma, tra le quali, in posizione di rilievo, la restaurazione dell'ordine interno voluta, anzi imposta da Cesare, come premessa necessaria per il consolidamento delle conquiste romane:

> E allora prima opera nostra dev'essere comporre la discordia in casa nostra, nel focolare del mondo, perché di qui possa diffondersi per tutte le genti la maestà della pace romana. Sappiamo le fazioni! Io non sono venuto per alcuna di loro, ma per Roma [...] Le fazioni, quiriti, sono i cani che lacerano le membra della patria; bisogna uccidere questi cani, e bisogna ucciderli tutti.[93]

Ma quell'accorto riferimento al «preconcetto» anticesarista, per quanto chiamasse in causa la dichiarata opposizione del sociologo a regimi di tipo cesarista, non prelude nelle note critiche ad un'esplicita difesa del cesarismo come sistema politico-istituzionale. Riportato al contesto d'origine, in cui la polemica contro la «*diminutio capitis*» si esprime nell'esaltazione dei tratti cesaristi della figura storica, quel richiamo suggerisce piuttosto la difesa dell'angolazione interpretativa riscontrabile nel dramma stesso: la «così detta modernizzazione» della figura storica. Una questione tutt'altro che accademica per un Corradini che aveva subordinato la scelta e ricostruzione della figura storica ad esigenze d'ordine praticistico.

In altri termini la riduzione di Cesare, da parte di Ferrero, a uomo in grado solo di «reazione» e quindi «senza programma», la rimozione insomma del personaggio dal piedistallo ideale su cui Corradini, garante Mommsen, lo aveva collocato, riportata, nelle note critiche, al piano politico-ideologico, piuttosto che storiografico, costituisce un'ulteriore conferma, *ab externo*, dei presupposti extra-artistici del dramma corradiniano e del ruolo assegnato in tale ambito alla figura storica. Liberata dalla categoria del contingente, che poteva precluderne la funzione prestabilita, la figura storica, "sintesi" esemplare della romanità, viene assunta a modello forte di opposizione al presente. Se il suo fascino si può ascrivere ai panni curiali che riveste, la sua forza si esprime piuttosto in quel suo proporsi come aspettazione di una grandezza nazionale non ancora realizzata e che pertanto incombe – per riprendere la definizione morassiana – «a guisa di una fatalità attiva e imprescindibile».[94]

La lezione impartita da Morasso dalle colonne del «Marzocco» era stata recepita

---

[92] Cfr. LA RIVISTA, *A proposito di irredentismo*, «Il Regno», I, 1904, 29; G. PREZZOLINI, *A chi giova la lotta di classe?*, ivi, I, 1904, 18.

[93] *Giulio Cesare*, cit., p. 97.

[94] M. MORASSO, *Roma*, cit.

e puntualmente realizzata nel suo primo tempo. In una lettera ad Adolfo Orvieto che lo aveva sostituito alla direzione del Marzocco, Corradini annunciava l'inizio del secondo tempo: «Caro Adolfo, do ora a te per prima che ad altri una notizia [...]. La notizia è che col prossimo novembre o dicembre fondo una nuova rivista [...] più politica che letteraria».[95]

Con la fondazione del «Regno», Corradini si avviava ad attuare, a livello organizzativo, la seconda fase del «programma d'azione» morassiano: trasferire la battaglia delle idee a strumenti di comunicazione più appropriati dei consueti canali di comunicazione dei letterati, ovvero ad organi di stampa di «largo e pronto effetto», non ristretti ad aree specialistiche e che avessero la capacità di «comunicare» con un pubblico più ampio di lettori e influire sugli orientamenti etico-politici del medesimo.[96] Con il «Regno» pertanto si concretano e si definiscono i termini della "conversione": la delineazione di un programma d'azione che aveva il suo perno ideologico nell'imperialismo finalizzato all'eversione delle istituzioni liberali. Si rinnovano i quadri di riferimento culturale: sulla rivista Papini e Prezzolini, nel loro ruolo abituale di divulgatori, introducevano le teorie di Mosca e di Pareto sulla «classe politica» e «sulla circolazione delle *élites*». Teorie che avrebbero suggerito a Corradini la necessità di superare la nozione di un regime a base individualista e procedere lungo una linea più rispondente alla problematica italiana: la formazione della classe egemone quale elemento di coesione nazionale.

Invariato nondimeno permaneva l'interesse per la questione del «consentimento»[97] nella versione mediata a suo tempo, lo abbiamo notato, da quei settori del tardo positivismo in cui si tendeva a ridimensionare la portata del fattore razionale nei comportamenti collettivi.[98] Nel 1923, in un volume che costituisce una fonte primaria per la ricostruzione delle varie fasi della maturazione politico-ideologica dell'autore, Corradini sottolineava il rilievo dell'irrazionale, dei «miti» – «le forze d'essenza religiosa che operano con endemica efficacia» – nella lotta delle «teorie», condotta dai nazionalisti nei confronti dei socialisti e dei liberali per «la rigenerazione d'Italia».[99] La fisionomia del mito, del meccanismo consensuale, cambierà in

---

[95] Cfr. la lettera di Corradini ad Adolfo Orvieto [settembre-ottobre] 1903, (ACGV, Or. 1.635.183).

[96] M. MORASSO, *Contro coloro che non hanno e che non sanno*, Milano-Palermo, Sandron, 1899 pp. 12-14. In realtà il grande organo di stampa nazionalista si avrà solo con «L'idea nazionale» (redattori: Corradini, Forges-Davanzati, Maraviglia, Coppola e Federzoni), fondato dapprima come settimanale nel 1911 e poi divenuto quotidiano nel 1914, grazie ai finanziamenti di esponenti dell'industria siderurgica e meccanica. Su questo, v. F. GAETA, *Il nazionalismo italiano*, cit., pp. 163-169.

[97] Per gli anni del primo foglio nazionalista, cfr., tra gli altri, *La vita nazionale*, «Il Regno», II, 1905, 6, in cui Corradini specifica il rapporto causale tra il «consentimento» della collettività alle direttive della classe politica e la «virtù nazionale» – «lo sforzo di cui è capace un popolo a creare la sua storia».

[98] A tale proposito cfr. C. CESA, *Tardo positivismo, antipositivismo, nazionalismo*, in AA.VV., *La cultura italiana dell'800 e '900 e le origini del nazionalismo*, cit., p. 98 e *passim*.

[99] E. CORRADINI, *Discorsi politici (1902-1923)*, cit., p. 8. Nella prefazione Corradini sottolinea, ovviamento a livello ideologico, il «carattere autobiografico» dell'opera.

accordo ad un'interpretazione più articolata della realtà nazionale e delle forze sociali che la compongono.[100] La «guerra proletaria», nell'abile ricalco e manipolazione del mito sociale della «giusta violenza», proclamato e difeso a sinistra dal Sorel, conferma nelle immagini che la compongono l'esigenza, avvertita dall'autore, di dotare il nazionalismo di una idea-forza in grado di competere con le dichiarate finalità del credo socialista ed in definitiva di allargare l'area consensuale.[101] La nuova formula politica che ne derivava, la «nazione proletaria», in cui l'imperialismo, tramite un'arbitraria traslazione della lotta di classe all'arena internazionale, si saldava ad una questione di portata nazionale – l'emigrazione – acquisterà, e comprensibilmente, una posizione di tutto rilievo nel nazionalismo degli anni 1910-1914, nei quali al nuovo movimento si voleva conferire una dimensione nazionale.[102]

Nell'immaginario nazionalista tuttavia la romanità permane al di sopra e nonostante la ideazione di formule e temi di aggancio più immediato e di pronta adesione alla realtà italiana. Contrapposta alla «viltà della presente ora nazionale»,[103] Roma si impone come coscienza di un «grande passato» che, «inconsumabile», viene assunto a «morale perenne».[104] Categoria dell'irrazionale, e quindi, potremmo dire con Le Goff,[105] non rispondente ai prevedibili criteri temporali, la romanità eserciterebbe un'attrazione inesausta per valori e aspirazioni – autorità, ordine, vastità di confini– che, recepiti quale realtà di un passato esaltante, sono al presente vissuti come attesa. In altri termini, il risorgimento, «incompiuto» nell'interpretazione nazionalista per la mancata continuazione della missione imperiale di Roma,[106] e il conseguente alternarsi di fervide speranze e delusioni cocenti – dall'e-

---

[100] Cfr., su questo, C. MATTII, *Enrico Corradini alla vigilia del primo Congresso nazionalista*, «Yearbook of Italian Studies», VIII, 1989, pp. 32-43 (in particolare pp. 40 43).

[101] Sulle modalità del ricalco operato da Corradini e quindi sull'ibrido connubio di nazionalismo e sindacalismo, cfr. del medesimo: *Sindacalismo, nazionalismo, imperialismo*, conferenza letta a Trieste nel 1909, ora in, ID., *Il volere d'Italia*, Napoli, Perrella, 1911, pp. 17-47; *Nazionalismo e Sindacalismo*, «La lupa», I, 1910, 1; e tra le lettere di Corradini a Mario Viana, v. quelle scritte tra il marzo e il luglio 1909, ora in F. PERFETTI, *Sindacalismo, Nazionalismo, Imperialismo*, «La Destra», 1972, pp. 88-95. Sul concetto, in Sorel, di mito sociale che opera come «energia storica» scatenando la volontà d'azione e coinvolgendo quindi i gruppi nella lotta rigeneratrice, cfr. ID., *Considerazioni sulla violenza*, prefazione di E. Santarelli, trad. di A. Sarno, Bari, Laterza, 1970, cap. IV (la prima ediz. in italiano apparve nel 1909 presso Laterza, con la nota introduzione di Croce). Sulle ambigue componenti soreliane che offrivano l'esca ad una strumentalizzazione da parte corradiniana, e cioè sull'inserimento dell'elemento vitalistico ed irrazionale nell'ambito del pensiero socialista da parte di Sorel, cfr. E. SANTARELLI, Prefazione, cit., p. 26; e ID., *Le revisioni del marxismo in Italia. Studi di critica storica*, Milano, Feltrinelli, 1977, pp. 80-116.

[102] Per il tema della «nazione proletaria», lanciato da Corradini al Congresso di Firenze, cfr. la relazione congressuale *Classi proletarie: socialismo, nazioni proletarie, nazionalismo*, ora con il titolo *Il primo Congresso nazionalista*, in *Il nazionalismo italiano*, Milano, Treves, 1914, pp. 53-70.

[103] E. CORRADINI, *Per coloro che risorgono*, «Il Regno», I, 1903, 1.

[104] *Giulio Cesare*, Prefazione, cit., pp. 9-10.

[105] J. LE GOFF, *History and Memory*, translated by S. Rendell and E. Claman, New York, Columbia University Press, 1992, pp. 15-16.

[106] L'interpretazione nazionalista fondata sulla dicotomia tra le finalità risorgimentali e la politica del raccoglimento, si riallacciava alla mediazione oriniana della storiografia della «missione»: l'ingresso dell'Italia nella storia

sperimento crispino al fallimento della politica coloniale – il senso quindi di inadempienza che incombeva sul presente, tutto sembrava contribuire alla percezione
della recente storia nazionale come «sospensione», [107] come preparazione delle coscienze alla ripresa inevitabile di un moto storico grandioso. E qui risiedeva la capacità di presa emotiva di quel mito e la sua inesauribile «virtù dinamogena». Ad
anni di distanza e a compimento della vicenda nazionalista, Enrico Corradini non
avrebbe mancato di sottolinearlo:

[...] anche quando ebbi lasciato la letteratura per la politica, tornai di continuo sull'argomento senza mai distaccarmene: fu un tema fondamentale della mia attività interiore. [108]

---

mondiale contemporanea «si mutò in un'entrata di soppiatto», mentre «gli sforzi millenari dell'Italia, il sangue dei
suoi eroismi... non miravano che a questo giorno nel quale rientrando, attrice immortale, nella storia... velegge-
rebbe un'altra volta sui mari portatrice di nuove civiltà» (A. ORIANI, *Fino a Dogali*, prefazione di L. Federzoni,
Bologna, Cappelli, 1927 (2), pp. 337-338). Su Oriani e il nazionalismo, cfr. M. BAIONI, *Il fascismo e Alfredo
Oriani. Il mito del precursore*, saggio introduttivo di G. Santomassimo, presentazione di G. Bosi, Longo, Ravenna,
1988, pp. 75-93.

[107] Per il concetto di «sospensione» come fase intermedia, e preparatoria, tra un grande passato per quanto
remoto e la riconquista, presunta o reale, di quella grandezza nel presente, cfr. G. SANTOMASSIMO, *Saggio introduttivo*, in M. BAIONI, *Il fascismo e Alfredo Oriani*, cit. Lo studioso si riferisce ad un diverso contesto storico, al-
lorchè la sospensione era venuta meno con l'impresa etiopica: «L'affermazione del ritorno dell'Impero «sui colli
fatali di Roma», a conclusione dell'impresa etiopica, non apparve grottesca ai cittadini italiani, che erano preparati
da tempo ad una interpretazione in questa chiave. Tutta la vicenda nazionale poteva apparire una lunga *sospensione*, un'attesa preparatoria che si situava tra i due momenti di grandezza imperiale» (pp. 15-16; il corsivo è nostro).

[108] *Giulio Cesare*, Prefazione, cit., p. 9.

LUIGI FONTANELLA

LA POESIA DI MASSIMO BONTEMPELLI:*
TRA CREPUSCOLARISMO E SPERIMENTALISMO FUTURISTA

Lungo, articolato, complesso, ed estremamente fecondo, sia per originalità di esiti creativi, sia per impulsi teorici innovativi nell'àmbito della tradizione culturale italiana, appare oggi l'itinerario di Massimo Bontempelli. Un *iter* letterario che copre abbondantemente tutto il primo mezzo secolo del nostro Novecento, e che si consegna alla storia e all'intelligenza del lettore odierno ancora ricco di stimoli e fascinanti provocazioni.

Di questo itinerario la poesia occupa, nella fase iniziale, un posto decisamente previlegiato. Sarà questa, in effetti, a costituire per Bontempelli l'esercizio più assiduo e amato nei primi anni del suo apprendistato scrittorio. Si pensi che il primo libretto di versi, cui di lì a poco vari altri seguiranno, risale nientemeno che al lontano 1904, allorché Massimo è un giovane ventiseienne, da qualche anno laureato a Torino, prima in Filosofia poi in Lettere (tesi, rispettivamente, sul libero arbitrio e sulle origini dell'endecasillabo), ed è incaricato presso la Media di Cherasco.

L'attività poetica, ancorché appassionata, rimane circoscritta al primo quindicennio, e ad essa, a partire dal 1919, il nostro scrittore non ritornerà più se non, momentaneamente, nel '33 per sistemare l'edizione definitiva del *Purosangue*, ossia versi già scritti in precedenza.

Di fatto l'unico «bagaglio lirico riconosciuto», per espressa dichiarazione dello stesso Bontempelli, è oggi costituito da un singolo volume intitolato *Il Purosangue – L'Ubriaco* che, uscito appunto nel '33 presso le Edizioni La Prora di Milano, inaugurava la collana "I poeti italiani viventi", diretta da Giuseppe Villaroel. L'opera in questione racchiudeva del lavoro poetico precedentemente pubblicato in vari libriccini e libretti (si veda nella Nota a pié di pagina l'elenco completo) sol-

---

* Le uniche opere di poesia riconosciute dal Bontempelli sono *Il Purosangue – L'Ubriaco* (Milano, Facci, 1919; II edizione: Milano, La Prora, 1933). Va poi registrata, del *Purosangue*, l'edizione curata da Luigi Baldacci nel volume *Opere scelte* (Milano, Mondadori, 1978), e quella di Vanni Scheiwiller come riproposta dell'originale del '19 (Milano, Scheiwiller, 1987). Le citazioni contenute nel saggio sono tratte da quest'ultimo volume.

Le opere di poesia ripudiate dal Bontempelli sono: *Egloghe*, Torino, Streglio, 1904; *Verseggiando. Intermezzo di rime*, Palermo, Sandron, 1905; *Odi siciliane* (*ivi*, 1906); *Settenari e sonetti* (Ancona, Puccini, 1910; include le liriche di *Verseggiando*); *Odi* (Modena, Formiggini, 1910, include le *Odi siciliane*).

tanto l'ultimo titolo (appunto, *Il Purosangue – L'Ubriaco*, Milano, Facchi, 1919), parendo, al Bontempelli, le poesie precedenti, «sfacciatamente ultraclassicistiche». E anche nei confronti di quest'ultima pubblicazione del '33, da lui stesso riproposta, il Nostro aveva qualche esitazione, come si evince dall'Avvertenza da lui stesa al momento di licenziare il libro:

Rimettendo in tal modo le mani in quella mia vecchia produzione di due tempi, mi sono accorto che la prima non mi dice più niente, mentre nella seconda spuntano alcuni motivi e modi fondamentali della mia opera più tarda. Mi risolvo perciò a ripubblicare le poesie del 1916 – *Il Purosange* – e quelle del 1918 – *L'Ubriaco* – (che tutte insieme erano uscite quattordici anni or sono in una edizione di sole trecento copie, oggi introvabili) con poche omissioni e correzioni. Il volume presente è dunque tutto il mio bagaglio lirico riconosciuto. Frascati, dicembre '32-XI.

Per le poche "omissioni e correzioni", di scarsa importanza in effetti, qui basterà rilevare che Bontempelli, più che correggere, si limita a tagliare e spostare. Il cambiamento più vistoso è costituito dall'alleggerimento, nell' *Ubriaco* di quattro poesie ("Lussuria"; "Giovinezza"; "Pace"; "Vita") e nello spostamento della quarta strofe di "Giochi" in "Isola": il componimento iniziale del *Purosangue* che qui viene a costituire la seconda parte. Sicché "Giochi" che aveva originariamente quattro parti ne avrà, nell'edizione definitiva del '33, solo due perché, per l'occasione, Bontempelli provvederà a espungere anche la prima parte. Fra l'altro è proprio in "Giochi" ch'è dato ritrovare il motivo relativo alla titolazione di questo libro:

> Muori pensando: «fu bello
> galoppare sul mio purosangue
> che m'ha portato all'eternità»

> *Il Purosangue che in mezzo dondola,*
> *e nell'angolo*
> *quattro cappelli senza tony girano*
> *girano intorno su teste di niente,*
> *Felicità.*

È stato scritto che con le poesie del *Purosangue* Bontempelli opera un taglio netto verso la propria produzione poetica del passato (ripudierà tutti e cinque i libri di versi pubblicati dal 1904 al 1910) che pur aveva avuto, fra gli altri, in poeti come Francesco Pastonchi (compagno di studi), Arturo Graf (il suo maestro universitario insieme a Giuseppe Fraccaroli) e il crepuscolare Guido Gozzano (si veda la sua bella poesia "A Massimo Bontempelli" pubblicata su «Il Piemonte», 1 ottobre 1904, ispirata al primo volumetto di poesie di Massimo, poesia ora rinvenibile nel volume complessivo di G.G., *Poesie* a cura di Edoardo Sanguineti, Torino, Einaudi, 1973, pp. 290-292), tre fra i primi affettuosi lettori della sua poesia giovanile. Proprio al suo Maestro era del resto dedicata il primo libriccino, *Egloghe* (Torino, Streglio, 1904), ed è interessante notare che sùbito dopo la dedica «Al poeta Arturo Graf» seguiva «questi studi di verso», dicitura, quest'ultima, che rivelava già allora al «giovine romantico e cospiratore» (com'egli stesso si descrive sul retro di una foto del '19 inviata a Scheiwiller) ciò che la natura di quei versi doveva apparire: esercizi di stile, frequentazioni di solide letture classiche; "studi", appunto.

Misteriosamente e perversamente escluso dagli studi "ufficiali" della lirica italiana novecentesca, la poesia del Bontempelli ha trovato in singoli studiosi come Ruggero Jacobbi, Pier Vincenzo Mengaldo e Luigi Baldacci, tre solitari quanto convinti assertori.

Jacobbi, amico e sodale del Bontempelli, non ha mai mancato di esprimere il suo positivo, talora fin troppo entusiasta parere nelle molteplici occasioni che gli si sono presentate nel tempo. Basterebbe, in ogni caso, andarsi a leggere le pagine dedicate all'autore comasco nell'Introduzione a *L'avventura novecentista*, in occasione della ristampa vallecchiana, da lui curata, nel 1974.

Mengaldo ha parlato di «surrealismo secco e cerebrale» (in *Poeti italiani del Novecento*, Milano, Mondadori, 1978), che mi sembra formula felicemente riassuntiva e applicabile non soltanto alla poesia ma, a tratti, anche al teatro: un culmine emblematico potrebbe essere *Nostra Dea*.

Il Baldacci, pur mettendo in evidenza il relativo giovamento tratto dall'esperienza futurista – ancorché in lieve ritardo – ha sottolineato la novità bontempelliana consistente, essenzialmente, in «una decisa puntata verso l'informale»: all'altezza del 1916, anno in cui vengono composte le poesie parafuturiste del *Purosangue*, «né Campana né il primo Ungaretti avevano dimostrato un'altrettanta vocazione, non dico all'ermetismo, ma, ripeto, all'informale» (Baldacci 1978, p. XXVII).

E, in effetti, fin dai primi poemetti, specialmente in "Vetrate" e "Balli", il lettore assiste a una vertiginosa mobilità della scrittura che ha drasticamente accantonato le mollezze ultraclassicistiche e pastorali delle *Egloghe*. Qui i passaggi sono costituiti da "frecce-pensieri", di marinettiana memoria, tesi a promulgare un discorso poetico di notevole capacità sintetica, costituito, per lo più, da variazioni ritmiche iterative. Il tutto in un'orchestrazione cromatica, e spesso dialogica, che rimanda alle esperienze di poco precedenti di un Govoni e di un Palazzeschi. Ma qui, in Bontempelli, c'è già vivissimo il senso dissociato e alienato della vita (tanto più se casermistica), quando questa si riduce a mera esecuzione di ordini e doveri. Se in Ungaretti l'esperienza al fronte metterà a nudo la dilacerante pietà che la guerra ispira al poeta, la smorfia della bocca del compagno di trincea morto, i pidocchi, la terra; in Bontempelli, più portato a una visione riflessiva-filosofica, prevarrà il senso di frustrazione e alienazione derivante dalla libertà individualmente negata, il pensiero pesante di morte che la domina, la soffocante disciplina militaresca che tutta l'allinea e omologa:

> Avanti i primi – uno-due
> a destra a sinistra per ordine

> voltare girare
> qui.
>
> Otto pensieri di morte
> dieci doveri di vita
> sinistra poi destra per fila
> lì.
>
> (...)
> Otto cuori dieci cervelli
> su giù non uno di più
> codice articolo regola
> – uno – due – così.
> > (da "Balli")

o in "Giochi":

> Tutti gli uomini sono già morti
> di bruciore o di paura
> tutti i cani sono morti
> di fedeltà.
> Un [*sic*] scimmione su un pianoforte
> si diverte come può
> senza riuscire
> a rifabbricare l'umanità.

L'anima, così, diventa "fredda" («Non tremare, anima fredda, / danza anche tu nella luce. / Va.»), mentre stilisticamente colpisce, sempre più, il ritmico nitore della versificazione, che procede per veloci estensioni e vertiginosi rastremamenti, fin in versi improvvisi, costituiti da una singola parola (Ungaretti vi arriva in quello stesso periodo). Le parole si agglutinano in un magmatico procedere di forte suggestione evocativa ("gli originalli dei frutti"; "le violazzurre"; "i cenci-sospiri"; "la lucepolvere"; "la gocciastella"), grazie a una proliferante iterazione autogenerativa: caratteristica tipica ed essenziale della maggior parte delle poesie di questo libro. Ed è proprio questo aspetto sperimentalistico in grado di scatenare una diffusa *imagerie* visivo-visionaria non lontana, per certi versi, da quella di un Campana i cui *Canti Orfici* precedono di circa un quinquennio le poesie del *Purosangue*. Solo che Bontempelli non perde di vista il sostrato, diciamo così, filosofico che la sostiene e anima: si vedano ad esempio i due articolati poemetti centrali "Cori" e "Giochi" nei quali, fra l'altro, compaiono già figure tipicamente bontempelliane: l'automa, il burattino, la marionetta, che saranno suggestivamente frequenti sia nella successiva produzione teatrale più importante (da *Siepe a nordovest* del 1919 – la seconda edizione del '22 si avvaleva significativamente dei disegni di Giorgio De Chirico – a *Nostra Dea* del '25, a *Minnie la candida* del '28; sia in "favole metafisiche" come *La scacchiera davanti allo specchio* (1922) e ancor più, in *Eva ultima*

(1923, "favola" assai composita che originariamente Bontempelli aveva concepito come *pièce* teatrale).

Qui basterà annotare il particolare e perdurante crepuscolarismo, d'ascendenza palazzeschiana-corazziniana, in cui questi motivi bontempelliani sono circonfusi: la loro grazia aerea e surreale (si veda su tutti "Giochi") si sposa felicemente con quel tedio di fondo che Bontempelli prova dinanzi all'eterna immutabilità dei giorni in cui gli uomini rischiano di diventare «gli dei e le dee / della deforme umanità».

Il gusto fabulatorio-aereo complessivo del *Purosangue* attraversa così le frange di un futurismo ormai di maniera, sfruttando però di esso (è questo un dato originale), così com'era accaduto in Palazzeschi cui Bontempelli in questo frangente può essere parzialmente accostato, alcuni aspetti fecondi: la velocità del dettato e il libero (liberatorio) disciogliemento di una immaginazione "senza fili"; concetto felicemente intuito sul piano teorico dal Marinetti, ma di cui un Palazzeschi e un Bontempelli sapranno trarre tutto il beneficio possibile a favore d'una personale autonomia della propria poetica.

Il mazzetto di dodici poesie che compongono l'edizione definitiva dell'*Ubriaco* hanno essenzialmente, come tema, la guerra: il sottotitolo della raccolta recita per l'appunto "Poesia dalla guerra". "Ubriaco" è lo sbalestrato soldato impegnato al fronte, con il "vuoto nel cuore", ciecamente dedito a combattere e a marciare («Lo ubriaca l'odore / odore / odore del camminamento»). Gli elementi ricorrenti della guerra sono gli stessi che un altro poeta, Ungaretti, all'incirca in quello stesso torno di tempo, andava appuntando su fogli di cartone che sarebbero divenuti di lì a poco le pagine del *Porto sepolto*: il fango, gli escrementi, il "poltridume", la polvere, il compagno di trincea improvvisamente abbattuto. Ma in Bontempelli, nei confronti della guerra, è più evidente l'atteggiamento paraavanguardista (atteggiamento da cui l'Ungà del *Porto sepolto* resterà sostanzialmente estraneo): la nervosità della scrittura di fronte allo "spettacolo geometrico" delle battaglie; le continue traiettorie luminose di bombe, razzi e granate cui s'intreccia il biancore silenzioso-metafisico che incombe su tutto e su tutti nelle notti di plenilunio:

> Curva liscia del mio cannone
> sei più fredda della luna che ti diaccia.
> La luna ha sparso la terra
> d'un milione di silenzi bianchi
> fissi al suolo immobile.
>   (da "Idillio")

E ancora l'autore dell'*Allegria*, di cui il Bontempelli dell'*Ubriaco* aveva forse fatto in tempo a leggere una delle ottanta copie del *Porto sepolto* (1916) è presente con varie immagini e stilemi d'indubbia matrice ungarettiana. Eccone un paio.

BONTEMPELLI Tutto un giorno senza un colpo di cannone
(da "Pace")

UNGARETTI Un'intera nottata / buttata vicino / a un
compagno / massacrato / con la sua bocca / digrignata /
volta al plenilunio / con la congestione / delle sue
mani / penetrata / nel mio silenzio (...)
("Veglia", 23-XII-1915)

e, ancora rimandabile a questa stessa poesia ungarettiana, un'immagine bontempelliana da "Voluttà":

Quest'è un braccio. E questo un osso.
Questo non capisco cos'è.
Questa mano dura e nera
è d'un vicino o mia di me?

Linguisticamente, tuttavia, la poesia bontempelliana è più tesa, composita, ironica, spigolosa. Di fronte alla precarietà della guerra solo il *corpo*, estremo baluardo e unico patrimonio del soldato esposto ai pericoli, resta da proteggere e salvaguardare. Esso, però, in simili circostanze (anche in questo sta la novità e la modernità bontempelliana), sembra un involucro staccato da chi lo "indossa": data la situazione permanentemente a rischio esso può da un momento all'altro sbriciolarsi come un nonnulla («Il freddo mi morde la testa / in giro in giro / la testa telefona ai piedi / lontani / che cadono in pezzi / il mio corpo è un coso / enorme duro immoto che gela»; da "Grottesco").

Siamo all'altezza del 1917-1918. Questi versi dell'*Ubriaco* sono praticamente gli ultimi che Bontempelli scriverà. La forma della lirica sarà, a partire dal '18 del tutto abbandonata. Ma alcuni dei temi in essa presenti li ritroveremo più tardi nella prosa più matura, laddove – a detta dello stesso Bontempelli – «la poesia sarà raggiunta per altre vie».

ANTHONY OLDCORN

SENTIERI DI *GLORIA*

Il lettore che s'imbatte, al sessantacinquesimo posto tra i centocinquantasei componimenti dell'edizione definitiva di *Myricae* (e quarta tra le sei poesie che formano il gruppetto intitolato alle *Gioie del poeta*), nella piccola ballata *Gloria*, rischia di misconoscere l'importanza che ha rivestito nell'educazione sentimentale e poetica del Pascoli.[1] Posta *in limine* come proemio alle nove poesie pubblicate per la prima volta con il titolo di *Myricae* sul settimanale fiorentino «Vita Nuova» del 10 agosto 1890 (anniversario della morte del padre), rimase incipitaria anche in MY1891[1] e MY1892[2], per cedere il primato solo in MY1894[3] al truce *Giorno dei morti*.[2] Il vociano Arturo Onofri la considera «una della poesiole più graziose delle Myricae». E aggiunge: «Metricamente, anch'essa [come *In alto*, cioè, che nel testo definitivo la precede] simile a *Il mago*, ma si sente che *Gloria* è la vera prima, su cui sono modellate le altre».[3] Questa felice intuizione di Onofri è stata riconfermata, con argomenti filologici, da Nava (II, 396), il quale fa risalire la prima stesura al 1887, prima della pubblicazione a parte degli altri due componimenti. *Il mago* – dapprima intitolata *Il Poeta* – e *In alto* comparvero due volte insieme, senza *Gloria*,

---

[1] La presente lettura di *Gloria* comparirà, in forma più scabra ed essenziale, insieme ad altre *myricae* commentate, nell'imminente edizione delle *Poesie e prose scelte* di Giovanni Pascoli nei Meridiani Mondadori. Il progetto editoriale è di Cesare Garboli, che mi ha gentilmente invitato a collaborare e a cui devo più di un suggerimento. L'edizione critica di *Myricae* è quella a cura di Giuseppe Nava (2 voll., Firenze, Sansoni, 1974), a cui è seguita, sempre di Nava, l'impeccabile edizione commentata, ormai alla sua seconda edizione (Roma, Salerno Editrice, 1991). Le sigle MY1891[1], 1892[2], ecc. si riferiscono naturalmente alle varie edizioni che si sono susseguite vivente il Pascoli fino a MY1911[9].

[2] Le nove *myricae* pubblicate sulla «Vita Nuova» del 10 agosto 1890, con la dedica a Severino Ferrari, erano, nell'ordine: I. *Gloria*, II. *Fides*, III. *Fides* (l'attuale *Orfano*), IV. *Felicità* (poi, l'articolo che ne esalta la componente allegorica, *La felicità*), V. *Benedizione*, VI. «*Sin che parlasti il vento*» (mai accolta in volume e ora stampata, con altre tre poesie e con qualche lieve variante, nel *Primo ciclo* delle *Poesie varie*), IX. «*Noi, mentre il mondo va per la sua strada*». Alla sua prima comparsa, quest'ultima poesia (ora accolta con il titolo *Il cane* tra i madrigali dell'*Ultima passeggiata*) poteva essere letta come *explicit* e *pendant* negativo di *Gloria* che apriva il gruppo: lì, la contemplazione tra saggia e indolente e la comunione con la natura di Belacqua; qua, l'inutile indaffararsi del cane da pagliaio: tanto rumore per nulla.

[3] Le letture onofriane, uscite su «La Voce», anno VIII, nn. 1-8, dal 31 gennaio al 31 agosto 1916, si leggono ora, con prefazione di Emilio Cecchi, in ARTURO ONOFRI, *Letture poetiche del Pascoli*, Bari, Edizioni de L'Albero, 1953. La lettura di *Gloria* occupa le pp. 100-101.

sotto la rubrica di *Ballate piccole*: il 14 settembre 1889, in un opuscolo per nozze Targioni Tozzetti-Comparini Rossi, poi nel numero del 13 ottobre 1889 della «Vita Nuova», a cui il Pascoli collaborava dal gennaio di quell'anno. Come accennò già il Croce («Accade che, alcune volte, leggendo il Ferrari, par di leggere il Pascoli della prima maniera»), i conti del dare e dell'avere con l'amico del cuore di questi anni Severino Ferrari sono estremamente difficili da districare. Il primo manipolo dei *Bordatini* (14 componimenti; Ancona, Morelli, 1885) del Ferrari, dedicati al Pascoli, dopo lo pseudo-serventese paratestuale *Giovanni, come sai, questi bordati* (nello stesso metro del futuro *Giorno dei morti*), iniziava con la ballata piccola *Testina d'oro, cantano già i galli*. Una lettera di Ferrari datata da Palermo il 12 novembre 1888, quindi quasi un anno prima della iniziale comparsa delle due ballate *Il mago* e *In alto*, recita: «Le tue ballatine a me paiono *bedde*; anzi bellissime. È questione di gusti. Tu sai che elle imbroccano il mio che è poi il tuo (gusto!). E mi paiono così poetiche e verseggiate di tanta finezza che non più. Forse qualche volta un po' indeterminate: ma io penso che l'indeterminato in certi casi sia pur poesia».[4]

Punto di partenza di questo dialoghetto pascoliano, il cui tono dimesso può trarre in inganno il lettore non avvisato, è l'incontro di Dante con il negligente ed ironico Belacqua (probabile soprannome del liutaio fiorentino Duccio di Bonavia) nel c. IV del *Purgatorio*. È dell'Anonimo Fiorentino l'aneddoto secondo cui, all'invocazione da parte di Belacqua dell'apoftegma aristotelico «*Sedendo et quiescendo anima efficitur sapiens*», Dante avrebbe risposto: «Per certo, se per sedere si diventa savio, niuno fu mai più savio di te». Qui un Pascoli sorridente ma sicuro prende le distanze dalle vigenti poetiche postromantiche identificandosi in una sua reinterpretazione della figura di Belacqua. La simultanea adozione del motto bucolico virgiliano «*arbusta iuvant humilesque myricae*» (strappato al suo contesto ormai tendente al georgico) sottolinea la scelta di una poetica antitrionfalistica delle «piccole cose» (non troppo dissimile dal «Non chiederci» di Montale). Le speculazioni *ad personam* di Giovanni Cena con il loro positivismo contingente e troppo aneddotico trivializzano la parte di convinzione che presiede all'opzione pascoliana: «Questi versi che aprivano il volume [MY1892²] fanno pensare a quel che si è narrato del Pascoli, che fosse stato a ragione dal Carducci rimproverato di neghittosità».[5]

Non ci sorprende scoprire (nelle stesure antecedenti riprodotte da Nava (II, 396-397) che il nucleo originale di *Gloria* si sia presentato al Pascoli sotto la forma dei due versi rimati della ripresa: «Bello è qui porsi a star, come Belacqua. / La rana

[4] La lettera, conservata a Castelvecchio nel carteggio Ferrari-Pascoli, non è citata da Maria Pascoli nella biografia del fratello, *Lungo la vita di Giovanni Pascoli* (Milano, Mondadori, 1961). È trascritta invece dal Nava nella sua edizione critica di *Myricae* (II, 396). Il ricupero "primitivistico" della ballata due e trecentesca nella poesia dell'Ottocento è stato illustrato anche per il Pascoli da Guido Capovilla in *Occasioni arcaizzanti della forma poetica italiana fra Otto e Novecento. Il ripristino della ballata antica da Tommaseo a Saba*, «Metrica», I, 1978, pp. 95-145.

[5] *Giovanni Pascoli*, «Nuova Antologia», vol. CLVIII, serie V. 16 aprile 1912, p. 721.

del pantano chiama acqua acqua», dove anche il «porsi a star» deriva dalla clausola dantesca «a star si pone» (*Purg.*, IV, 105), in cui Belacqua, però, non è ancora protagonista ma semplice termine di paragone. Il deittico *«qui»* del primo verso dell'appunto mnemonico fa pensare ad una annotazione di taccuino buttata giù nel campo, e il fuggevole accenno ad una sosta contemplante del soggetto evoca una situazione di solitudine appartata tipica di molte altre poesie del Pascoli e che, già leopardiana, ritornerà anche nel primo Montale: basti per tutte l'attacco de *L'ora di Barga* (CC), 1-2: «Al mio cantuccio, donde non sento / se non le reste brusir del grano».

Interessanti i reperti pascoliani-danteschi addotti da Maurizio Perugi nel cappello premesso a questo testo (Giovanni Pascoli, *Opere*, 2 voll., Milano-Napoli, Ricciardi, 1980), anche se prescindono dalla trasvalutazione dell'accidia o negligenza o pigrizia implicita nell'eventuale titolo della sezione, *Le gioie del poeta*, e dallo schierarsi del poeta al fianco di Belacqua nella sua stasi – viene in mente la Mosca di Montale che «sola sapev[a] che il moto / non è diverso dalla stasi» – e contro lo stacanovismo rappresentato dalla voce fuori campo che formula la domanda retorica riportata nel primo verso. Fa parte del gioco divertito della ballata proprio l'uso di Dante contro Dante: non «leggere Dante con Dante» dunque, ma semmai «correggere Dante con Dante».

La infelice palinodia intertestuale di *Gloria* occuperà invece il primo posto tra gli *Odi ed Inni*, raccolta peraltro dal titolo carducciano pubblicata nel 1906, l'anno della morte del Carducci, con cui il Pascoli si candida (un po' troppo candidamente) al titolo di successore del Vate alzando la posta in gioco con la nuova epigrafe *«canamus»*. Si tratta dell'istrionica e («umilmente») autocelebrativa *Piccozza*, modellata sull'alcaica *Per le nozze di mia figlia* (la Bice, che nel 1880 era andata sposa non ad un Belacqua ma ad un Carlo Bevilacqua, professore di matematica e collega del Pascoli al Liceo Nicolini di Livorno), il cui dettato è interamente affidato alla voce *off* di *Gloria*. La scena, però, è cambiata: non più «dietro il sasso», siamo ormai vicini alla vetta del santo monte, al suo «puro limpido culmine», «là dove è ottimo restar». Anche la fauna con cui lo strenuo scalatore divide quel culmine è di segno diverso: non più la rana e la cicala ma le aquile. Il sangue non mente, però, e anche qui l'eroica ascesa è destinata a culminare nella morte invischiata del protagonista Giovanni Agostino Placido «placido / immerso nell'alga / vermiglia».

Diamo il testo secondo la lezione apparsa sulla «Vita Nuova» e riprodotta inalterata in MY1891[1] e MY1892[2]. Diremo a suo luogo di una significativa modifica al v. 6 introdotta in MY1897[4]; ma le altre varianti riguardano soltanto la punteggiatura. Lo schema metrico di questa ballata piccola (X ABABB X) è lo stesso de *Il mago*, *In alto*, *Il lampo*, *Il tuono*. Subisce una lieve variante in *Notte dolorosa*, dove il sesto verso non rima ma consuona (con diversa vocale tematica) con tutti gli altri versi tranne con la ripresa. Si presenta raddoppiato (con un unico verso di ripresa) in *Vespro*, *Pioggia*, *Rammarico*.

GLORIA

– Al santo monte non verrai, Belacqua? –

Io non verrò: l'andare in su che porta?
Lungi è la Gloria, e piedi e mani vuole;
e là non s'apre che al pregar la porta,
e qui star dietro il sasso a me non duole,
cantare udendo le cicale al sole,
e le rane che gracidano, acqua, acqua.

1 *santo monte*: per il sintagma, cfr. *Purg.*, XXVIII, 12. Come si vedrà, il breve testo è tra l'altro un abilissimo assemblaggio di tasselli danteschi. Anche «l'inconsueto latinismo» (Nava) «carperemo» che compariva in una variante del primo verso («– Non carperemo al monte e noi, Belacqua?») era anche e soprattutto dantismo («ch'i' mi sforzai *carpando* appresso lui» *Purg.*, IV, 50). Nel dialogo dell'Antipurgatorio il nome di Belacqua compare solo all'interno del verso (*Purg.*, IV, 123). Così, l'*agudeza* della rima «ecoica», «ecolalica» o, se si vuole, «glossolalica», «*Belacqua/acqua*», non deriva dal passo dantesco; e, con «*vuole*» (da «*volea*» però) è l'unica. Si gioca qui sull'apparente semantizzazione del nome proprio attraverso il contatto rimico con il verso delle rane, la cui riproduzione onomatopeica coincide con un elemento lessicale normalmente significante ma nel contesto desemantizzato, una delle «voci inarticolate e, però, "grammatizzate"» di cui parla Giorgio Agamben. Danno da riflettere infatti le considerazioni più generali di quest'ultimo, dove si lascia sfuggire tra l'altro un'affermazione che per quanto sibillina fa al nostro caso: «Nella poesia di Pascoli glossolalia e onomatopea parlano da un medesimo luogo». *Categorie italiane. Studi di poetica* (Venezia, Marsilio, 1996), p. 74.

2-4. *Io non verrò*: la mente corre alla reticenza del Bartleby di Melville (1856) o all'oblomovismo di Gonciarov (*Oblomov* è del 1859). – *l'andare...porta*: cfr. *Purg.*, IV, 127-129: «Ed elli: 'O frate, andar in sú che porta? / ché non mi lascerebbe ire a' martìri / l'angel di Dio che siede in su la porta», con la stessa rima equivoca «porta? / porta».

3 *e piedi e mani vuole*: cfr. *Purg.*, IV, 33: «e piedi e man volea il suol di sotto».

4 *al pregar*: cfr. *Purg.*, IV, 134: «se orazïone in prima non m'aita».

5 *dietro il sasso*: «e ivi eran persone / che si stavano a l'ombra dietro il sasso / come l'uom per negghienza a star si pone» (*Purg.*, IV, 103-105) – *a me non duole*: «Belacqua, a me non dole / di te omai; ma dimmi: perché assiso / quiritto se'? attendi tu iscorta, / o pur lo modo usato t'ha' ripriso?» (*Purg.*, IV, 123-126: nel luogo dantesco «dole» è in rima con «sole» al v. 119).

6 *cantare udendo*: il sintagma, unico momento ipotattico della stesura riportata, cederà il posto in MY1897[4] all'infinito preceduto dalla congiunzione, «ed ascoltare», che si inserisce nella sequenza tutta paratattica e polisindetica della risposta di Belacqua con notevole guadagno della sintassi poetica. Anche nei *Canti di Castel-*

vecchio la suadente voce verlainiana dell'orologio di Barga s'insinuerà nella contemplazione del poeta riluttante chiamandolo ai suoi doveri attivi, cfr. *L'ora di Barga* (CC), 7-18: «Tu dici, È l'ora; tu dici, È tardi; / voce che cadi blanda dal cielo. / Ma un poco ancora lascia che guardi / l'albero, il ragno, l'ape, lo stelo, / cose ch'han molti secoli o un anno / o un'ora, e quello nubi che vanno. // Lasciami immoto qui rimanere / fra tanto moto d'ale e di fronde; / e udire il gallo che da un podere / chiama, e da un altro l'altro risponde, / e, quando altrove l'anima è fissa, / gli strilli d'una cincia che rissa». – *le cicale al sole*: in due precedenti stesure le cicale, non nominate, erano però con i loro acuti una insistita presenza acustica («Freme dai pini un frinir trito al sole»). Il virtuosismo allitterativo è stato rintuzzato con lodevole abnegazione nella stesura più evoluta.

Lo stesso accoppiamento di suoni acuti e suoni gravi per significare la gamma non solo acustica dei fenomeni s'incontra spessissimo in Pascoli: cfr. la rana elegiaca e il grillo satirico, «il lamento eterno / della rana che rantola e del grillo / che trilla in suon di scherno» (*Astolfo*, vv. 126-128). Non dimentichiamo, però, che in quest'orchestra i componenti hanno un peso relativo e che una nuova voce dalla parte degli acuti può portare ad una rivalutazione timbrica di tutta la gamma degli strumenti: qui, nella bozza precedente, il «frinire» della cicala si distingueva nettamente dal gracidare della rana, ma in una prima stesura di un'altra *myrica*, *L'assiuolo*, i «finissimi sistri d'argento» (v. 20) delle cavallette erano «minuti così, che / pareva un gracchiare / una rana / la tarda cicala» (vv. 30-33 dell'abbozzo).

7 le rane che gracidano: cfr. *Inf.*, XXXII, 31-32: «E come a gracidar si sta la rana / col muso fuor de l'acqua». Oltre a questo luogo dantesco, l'onomatopea dell'ultimo verso chiama a raccolta una vera gamma di riferimenti intertestuali antichi e moderni. (Non è certo anticlassicismo quello del Pascoli, ma semmai un privilegiare aspetti inconsueti del patrimonio classico poco valutati prima di lui.) Si può partire dalla nota onomatopea delle *Rane* di Aristofane ricordata dal Pascoli in calce al primissimo abbozzo, oltreché nell'esemplare della strenna nuziale Bemporad-Vita (28 agosto 1887) conservato a Castelvecchio dove prima de *La rana e l'usignuolo* – l'attuale *Nozze* – (in cui però il gracidìo delle ranocchie è diversamente grammatizzato: «Quanta spocchia, quanta spocchia») sono inseriti a mano dal poeta questi due versi: «La rana, brekekek brekekek / gridava, Acqua acqua: ognuno era in bernecche». Inoltre si usa citare un verso delle *Georgiche* (1, 378): *et veterem in limo ranae cecinere querellam*. (Tutto il passo meteorologico virgiliano sarà imitato in un sonetto del secentista fiorentino Benedetto Menzini, 1646-1704, *Presagi di tempo piovoso*, antologizzato dal Pascoli in *Fior da fiore*, che inizia «Sento in quel fondo gracidar la rana, / indizio certo di futura piova, / canta il corvo importuno, e si riprova / la foliga a tuffarsi a la fontana»). Né possiamo tralasciare il verso ovidiano citato e commentato dal Pascoli nella lettera pubblica *A Giuseppe Chiarini Della metrica classica*: «Questo mi pare essenziale di riconoscere; che i Latini (mettiamo, nel tempo aureo della lor poesia) avevano due pronunzie per i versi. Eccone le prove. Se mancassero altri argomenti, basterebbe il seguente verso a provare la pronunzia energica dell'*ictus* (OV. *Met.* VI, 366): *quamvis sint sub aqua, sub aqua maledicere tentant*. Sono i ranocchi che nello stagno fanno *qua qua qua*. L'intenzione del poeta è evidente; ma vana riuscirebbe se, come sulla prima di *quamvis*, non mettessimo l'accento sull'ultima di *aqua* ripetuta a bella posta» (*Prose*, I, 929). Vedi anche Alfonso Traina, *Il latino del Pascoli*, Firenze, Le Monnier, 1971, pp. 249-251. Cfr. anche la nota a pié di pagina ai vv. 14-17 di *Nozze* nel volume *Fior da fiore*: «L'autore crede lecito pregare il giovinetto lettore di considerare i suoni gutturali o altrimenti imitativi nel parlar della rana: *qua... qua... qual... chio qua... vo... vo*». Verremo poi, nella poscritto, ai luoghi imitativi di *Colascionata Prima* (e poi di *Romagna*) riecheggiati dal Ferrari e dal Carducci.

«Notevole l'ultimo verso per le sonorità in *a*, la lunghezza delle elisioni finali e l'aggruppamento d'accenti in fondo, sulla nona e sulla decima; il tutto mirabilmente adeguato» (Onofri). Le sonorità in *a*, aggiungerei, riguardano – come era da aspettarsi tra l'altro, data la rima in comune – in minor misura anche il primo verso: «Al sAnto monte non verrAi, BelAcquA?» Questo particolare colorito timbrico spiegherà la finale opzione per il sintagma – inoltre, come abbiamo visto, più autenticamente dantesco – di «*santo monte*», contro il «*dolce monte*» con cui oscilla attraverso varie stesure. Una spigliata lettura stilistica di questa ballata da un'ottica versiliberista in Alberto Bertoni, *Dai simbolisti al Novecento. Le origini del verso libero italiano* (Bologna, Il mulino,1995), pp. 305-307.[6]

Poscritto

Fin dal loro attacco («O Severino, de' tuoi canti il nido, / il covo de' tuoi sogni io ben lo so...»), le quartine del Carducci *A Severino* premesse alla prima edizione del *Mago* (Roma, Sommaruga, 1884), e ristampate con qualche minima variante e con nuova didascalia *All'autore del Mago* nelle *Rime nuove* del 1887, sembrano rifarsi più alle quartine di *Colascionata* che a quelle del *Mago*. Giustamente dunque il Felcini: «La lirica sembra volersi inserire in quella corrispondenza in versi dei sodali Pascoli e Ferrari che aveva fruttato la prima stesura di *Romagna* col titolo *Colascionata I a Severino Ferrari Ridiverde* («Cronaca bizantina», 1 dicembre 1882, p. 92)». E dunque, più che «la più bella poesia» di Severino, del «Severino maggiore» come

---

[6] Le conclusioni provvisorie di Bertoni sono le seguenti: «Senza che si vogliano o si possano trarre da questo campione minimo conclusioni definitive, resta evidente che la dominante oratoria nel Pascoli resta imbrigliata entro ferree regole formali e si riproduce per sottili torsioni dei canoni metrici. La declamazione è qui una declamazione riflessa, di secondo grado o in sordina, che rende spesso esplicito il proprio impulso aulico all'autoannullamento in una "lingua di rane", nella negazione della grammatica».

ebbe a dire un po' crudelmente Giuseppe De Robertis (*Saggi*, Firenze, Le Monnier, 1953, p. 133), le nostalgiche quartine del Carducci sarebbero un omaggio alla maniera comune all'allievo prediletto e effusivamente devoto e all'altro allievo più chiuso e sfuggente tenuto a distanza (o che si teneva a distanza) e ai modi dei loro popolar-arcaizzanti duetti. E i versi «Allor che agosto cada, o Severino, / e chiamin l'acqua le rane canore, / noi tornerem poeti all'Alberino» (vv. 21-23), se indulgono *en passant* al "concetto" virgiliano della rana che chiama la pioggia, semplificano la partitura polifonica corale pascoliana di *Colascionata*, rifiutando implicitamente – in nome di una tradizione poetica esclusiva proprietà dei grandi ingegni umani (ci pare perfino di captare in «noi tornerem poeti» un'eco in chiave bonaria dell'ieratico «ritornerò poeta» del c. XXV del *Paradiso*) –, accanto all'assidua frequentazione degli *auctores*, la complementare immersione apprendistica in un mondo primitivo di voci poetiche prelinguistiche. Le parole di questi due testi pascoliani che abbiamo sottolineato con il corsivo implicano una continuità tra le forme poetiche e le voci della natura: «Io là dentro annidiato crogiolavo / le tue stanze, Ariosto, e le tue, Lippi; / [...] /e udìa del grillo, in mezzo al fien maggese / l'arguto *quilio* sopra i *ritornelli*, / e apprendea da' ranocchi le *riprese* / strepitanti sul fin degli *stornelli*!» (*Colascionata*, vv. 33-40), passo modificato in seguito senza però cambiare quello che è qui l'essenziale, anzi introducendo, reciprocamente, il soggetto poetante a "meditare", cioè a elaborare dentro di sé, gli spontanei componimenti poetici della natura («stormir di frondi, ecc.»): «Era il mio nido: dove, immobilmente, / io galoppava con Guidon Selvaggio / e con Astolfo; / [...] /udia tra i fieni allor allor falciati / de' grilli il *verso* che perpetuo trema, / udiva dalle rane dei fossati / un lungo interminabile *poema*. // E lunghi, e interminati, erano quelli / ch'io meditai, mirabili a sognare: / stormir di frondi, cinguettìo d'uccelli, / risa di donne, strepito di mare» (*Romagna*, vv. 33-48).

Secondo poscritto

Per una singolare coincidenza, il protagonista della prima *fiction* di Samuel Beckett (nato nello stesso anno in cui è morto il Carducci) – pubblicata sul numero 21 (marzo 1932) della rivista «Transition» – il primo archetipo dei vari Murphy, Molloy, Watt, Malone, dei ritratti d'artista esposti in quella che l'autore avrebbe chiamato la sua «*galerie de crevés*», porta anche lui il nome di Belacqua. Si tratta di una delle "avventure" – provvisoriamente intitolata, prendendo lo spunto dall'aneddoto riportato nel commento dantesco dell'Anonimo Fiorentino, *Sedendo et Quiescendo* – del protagonista del primo libro narrativo di Beckett, più una serie di episodi che un romanzo, che avrebbe poi visto la luce con il titolo *More Pricks Than Kicks* (1934). Questo bizzarro personaggio, «peccaminosamente indolente per natura, affondato nell'indolenza», studia l'italiano a Dublino con la signorina Adriana Ottolenghi, legge Dante e riflette con un distacco a cui il Pascoli poteva soltanto aspirare su alcuni scrittori italiani (ma anche su un imperatore francese) ottocenteschi: «Manzoni era una vecchietta, Napoleone era un'altra. *Napoleone di mezza calzetta fa l'amore a Giacominetta*. Perché pensava a Manzoni come a una vecchietta? Perché rendergli quell'ingiustizia? Pellico era un'altra. Erano tutti delle vecchie zitelle, delle suffragette. Doveva chiedere alla sua Signorina dove avesse potuto ricevere quell'impressione, che il diciannovesimo secolo in Italia fosse pieno di vecchie galline che cercavano di chiocciare come Pindaro. Carducci era un'altra...».

Pascoli sul sentiero che mena a Beckett? Sarebbe soltanto una *Gloria* in più.

LUCIENNE KROHA

PIRANDELLO'S POETICS OF PARADOX:
REPRESENTING THE UNREPRESENTABLE

I

In the Pirandellian universe 'unrepresentable' can be said, I believe, to have two very specific meanings. The first, closely linked to the fact that Italy was very much a traditional, Catholic nation as well as a latecomer to modernity, is something akin to 'unspeakable', as in themes and situations whose direct representation contravenes the norms of bourgeois respectability. It must be remembered that this was a society in which Luigi Capuana, the translator of Henryk Ibsen's controversial *A Doll's House*, had asked its Scandinavian author to re-write the play's ending, which he deemed too explosive for Italian audiences.[1] Pirandello wrote for these same audiences and, for a number of years, under Fascism. Though he did bring such themes as incest and conjugal violence to the stage, he did so only indirectly, by submerging them in meta-theatrical or pseudo-philosophical paradoxes which called attention away from them. For example, in the 1917 play *Così è (se vi pare)* the unrepresentable is made to coincide with the 'unknowable'. The text alludes to situations of both abuse and incest, but couches them in mystery and rhetoric about the possibility of knowing the 'truth'. Thus, while the townspeople are represented as wanting desperately to uncover the possibly unsavory details about the newcomers in their midst, the play's *raisonneur*, Lamberto Laudisi, discourages their curiosity by trying as much as possible to divert attention away from the 'facts' towards the 'metaphysics'. As a result the text's ultimate power lies in the tension between its desire to reveal on the one hand and its need to obfuscate on the other.[2]

The second meaning of 'unrepresentable' has to do with unconscious – or perhaps it would be more accurate to say pre-conscious – conflict and motivations. In

---

[1] L. CARETTI, "Capuana, Ibsen e la Duse", *L'Illusione della realtà: studi su Luigi Capuana*, M. Picone and E. Rossetti, eds., Roma, 1990, pp. 199-201.

[2] See my own "Behind the Veil: A Freudian Reading of Pirandello's *Così è (se vi pare)*," *The Yearbook of the Society for Pirandello Studies*, XII (1992), pp. 1-23.

L'umorismo Pirandello explicitly states that human beings are largely unaware of what drives them, that the past is very much alive in the present, and that some of it would be accessible to us were it not for the human proclivity for self-delusion:

> Le barriere, i limiti che noi poniamo alla nostra coscienza, sono anch'essi illusioni, sono le condizioni dell'apparir della nostra individualità relativa; ma, nella realtà, quei limiti non esistono punto. Non soltanto noi, quali ora siamo, viviamo in noi stessi, ma anche noi quali fummo in un altro tempo, viviamo tuttora e sentiamo e ragioniamo con pensieri e affetti già da un lungo oblío oscurati, cancellati, spenti nella nostra coscienza presente, ma che a un urto, a un tumulto improvviso dello spirito, possono ancora dar prova di vita, mostrando vivo in noi un altro essere insospettato. Di là da quella linea vi sono memorie, vi sono percezioni e ragionamenti. Ciò che noi conosciamo di noi stessi, non è che una parte, forse una piccolissima parte di quello che noi siamo. [...] E possono essere motivi reali di azione certe tendenze da cui ci crediamo liberati, e non aver per l'opposto efficacia pratica in noi, se non illusoria, credenze nuove che riteniamo di possedere veramente, intimamente.[3]

Pirandello's solution in the earlier stages of his career was to depict 'realistically', but with allusions to the presence of another level of reality, represented by "vicende ordinarie" and "particolari comuni" which most writers ignore, 'come se queste vicende, questi particolari non abbiano alcun valore e siano inutili e trascurabili':

> Di qui, nell'umorismo, tutta quella ricerca dei particolari più intimi e minuti, che possono anche parer volgari e triviali se si raffrontano con le sintesi idealizzatrici dell'arte in genere, e quella ricerca dei contrasti e delle contraddizioni, su cui l'opera si fonda, in opposizione alla coerenza cercata dagli altri [...].[4]

These 'particolari' often hold clues to the character's genuine motivation as Pirandello sees it, unconscious except for "certi momenti eccezionali" during which "noi sorprendiamo in noi stessi, percezioni, ragionamenti, stati di coscienza, che sono veramente oltre i limiti relativi della nostra esistenza normale e cosciente."[5] These explain the circumstances of the character's life in ways that s/he would probably deny if forced to confront them. Another way to put this is to say, as Nino Borsellino has done,[6] that Pirandello represents "false consciousness": what people say and how they narrativize and make sense of their experiences according to fixed roles or subject positions – the victim of society, the victim of chance, the cuckold, etc. Always, however, there is another layer, an alternate explanation alluded to by details of the sort that might "fall by the wayside" in a naturalistic representation

---

[3] L. PIRANDELLO, *L'umorismo*, Milano, Mondadori, 1986, pp. 157-158.

[4] *Ibid.*, p. 167.

[5] *Ibid.*, p. 158.

[6] N. BORSELLINO, "Stratigrafia dell'*Esclusa*", *Immagini di Pirandello*, Cosenza, Lerici, 1979, p. 46.

meant to carve out a trajectory in which *tout se tient*. Pirandello does believe in cause-and-effect in the lives of his characters (though they themselves often invoke 'chance') but not in the naturalistic sense:

> Ora pare all'umorista [...] che delle cause, delle cause *vere* che muovono spesso questa povera anima umana agli atti più inconsulti, assolutamente imprevedibili, l'arte in genere non tenga quel conto che secondo lui dovrebbe. Per l'umorista le cause, nella vita, non sono mai così logiche, così ordinate, come nelle nostre comuni opere d'arte [...].[7]

For example in one of his most famous novellas, *La maestrina Boccarmé*, Pirandello uses a typically naturalist character, the fallen woman ostensibly cast aside by society as a result of one youthful error, to show how circumstances can superimpose themselves on a pre-existing disposition to create the impression that it is the circumstances themselves which are being reacted to, when in fact the situation is much more complex. Mirina Boccarmé's sad but peaceful existence is shattered by a chance encounter, after many years, with a former schoolmate whose relationship to the man responsible for the maestrina's fate opens up old wounds and leads to a dramatic confrontation between the two rivals. A number of allusions throughout the text, particularly to the maestrina's predilection for solitary reverie and to the fact that, being an orphan, she was no stranger to abuse and isolation when she met Giorgio, make of this novella a very subtle and nuanced portrait of an unconscious vocation for masochism and self-exclusion:

> Perché piaceva anche, alla maestrina Boccarmé, intenerirsi così, amaramente, allo spettacolo di quelle navi che all'alba lasciavano il porto, e s'indugiava lì a sognare con gli occhi alle vele che a mano a mano si gonfiavano al vento e si portavano via quei naviganti, lontano, sempre più lontano [...]
> Quando le scuole erano chiuse per le vacanze estive, la maestrina Boccarmé non sapeva che farsene della sua libertà. Avrebbe potuto viaggiare, coi risparmi di tanti anni; le bastava sognare così, guardando le navi ormeggiate nel Molo o in partenza.[8]

That she is emotionally frozen in time is obvious, as for example when we are told that she still combs her hair the way Giorgio had taught her to twenty years ago. Less obvious, but unmistakable, is the fact that the trauma which Giorgio appears to have inflicted on her has become an alibi, and that, as an orphan, she is really still mourning a much older loss, no less powerfully experienced for having been overshadowed, and ultimately absorbed, by the transfiguration of a rape into a story of lost love:

---

[7] PIRANDELLO, *L'umorismo*, p. 165.

[8] L. PIRANDELLO, "La maestrina Boccarmé", *Novelle per un anno: Tutt'e tre, Dal naso al cielo, Donna Mimma*, E. Borzi and M. Argenziano, eds., Roma, Newton Compton, pp. 80-81.

E così, richiamato a questo prezzo dal tempo lontano che lo aveva ingiallito, ravvivato dal sangue di questa nuova ferita, ella avrebbe potuto ora riappendere alla parete il vecchio ritrattino; per sé, unicamente per sé, per sentire ancora, dentro di sé, più che mai soffuso dell'antica malinconia, il lontano azzurro della sua povera favola segreta [...].

Sì, ma se non era l'antico amore a farle da fermento dal più profondo dell'anima, perché ora quella specie d'ebrezza che le gonfiava il petto, e quello struggimento che voleva traboccarle in nuove lagrime; e non più brucianti, queste?

Per fortuna lo specchio era là nell'angolo, e la maestrina Boccarmè non vide come s'appuntiva sgraziatamente sulla sua povera bocca appassita quel vezzo che sogliono fare i bambini prima che si buttino a piangere; e il mento, come le tremava.[9]

The use of the first-person unreliable narrator in *Il fu Mattia Pascal* (1904) marks the beginning of a new phase in Pirandello's search for techniques to represent false consciousness. Real and apparent cause-and-effect are intertwined in a monologue strewn with contradiction, rationalization and fleeting moments of inadvertent 'insight' suggesting cause-and effect mechanisms very different from those being consciously cited.[10]

The theatre offered a new challenge: how to achieve in the dramatic genre the ironic distance offered in the novel or the short story by the space between author and narrator. In *Così è (se vi pare)* the solution – an unresolvable mystery – is still largely thematic, but in the plays of the meta-theatrical trilogy it becomes formal. In fact, the two 'unrepresentable' motifs from *Così è* – incest and sexual abuse – reappear, in *Sei personaggi in cerca d'autore* and in *Questa sera si recita a soggetto*, but in both cases distanced by structural or formal devices. In the first case, the incest is represented as something which was about to take place but never did, between a stepfather and stepdaughter, who moreover are assumed to be characters and not persons. In the second case the situation of abuse becomes part of a *scenario* that, supposedly, a group of actors are improvising. In the first play, the 'author' is represented by his 'absence', while in the second he is replaced, in a way, by the director Dr. Hinkfuss. In each case the two meanings of 'unrepresentable' – the real author's reluctance to take on themes which might offend the bourgeois sensibilities of his audience, and the abyss between the conventional stories that shape reality and the actual hidden, often unconscious dynamics underlying them – are collapsed into a formal structure, in which the author's 'absence' and the difficulty in arriving at the 'consensus' which would allow the plays in question to be staged or to continue functions as a metaphor for 'unrepresentability'.

In what follows I shall focus on the third of these plays, *Ciascuno a suo modo* (1924) and on the novel from which it is derived, *Quaderni di Serafino Gubbio*

[9] *Ibid.*, p. 91.
[10] See my own "Il desiderio di Mattia Pascal ovvero *Liolà*: Pirandello maschilista?", *Quaderni d'italianistica*, XV (1994) n. 1/2, pp. 75-94.

operatore (1925), originally entitled *Si gira* (1915), in order to show how the two meanings of 'unrepresentability' come together in these works, and that these works do indeed contain allusions to a decipherable 'unconscious' dynamic which have been deliberately inscribed as a sort of palimpsest, and that they occur in these texts very much like ore in nature, "frammisto alla terra" as Pirandello himself describes it in *L'umorismo*.[11] Following the analysis of the relationship between theatrical and narrative texts, I shall attempt to draw some conclusions about what exactly is – or rather is not – being represented here and its significance at a broader social and historical level in the context of the times in which Pirandello wrote.

II

Quaderni di Serafino Gubbio operatore is itself conceived as a narrative about un-representability, telling, in diary form, a mysterious story which appears impossible to reconstruct in its cause-and-effect mechanisms. It is this same 'mysterious story' which then reappears in the play.

In the novel, Giorgio Mirelli, Aldo Nuti and Varia Nestoroff are the protagonists of what appears to be the oldest story of all: the rivalry between two men for the love of the same woman. The official version of the story goes something like this: Aldo Nuti, when informed of his friend Giorgio Mirelli's engagement to Varia Nestoroff, is dismayed and alarmed. Nuti himself is engaged to Mirelli's sister Duccella, a paragon of feminine virtue and modesty. Varia, on the other hand, a Russian widow with a turbulent and somewhat mysterious past, is known for her power to reduce men to mere shadows of themselves by means of her sexual charms. In an effort to 'save' Mirelli, Nuti makes a wager with him: he will try to seduce Varia and if he succeeds Mirelli will agree to call off the marriage. Mirelli soon catches them together in a compromising situation, as planned, but instead of unleashing his anger on either one of them, he kills himself. As a result, Nuti and Nestoroff have become mortal enemies. This is the *antefatto*, the starting point for both novel and play.

In the novel, the story of Aldo Nuti, Varia Nestoroff and Giorgio Mirelli is told in fragments by an unreliable narrator with an implicit though unclarified agenda of his own. He presents the story through a series of diverging hypotheses about the real motivations of the characters and about the actual sequence of events. The opposition between past and present, self and other, is deconstructed by the inter-weaving of flashbacks, recollections, reported speech, direct discourse and first per-

---

[11] PIRANDELLO, *L'umorismo*, p. 167.

son narration in the present. Giacomo Debenedetti has called it "una vicenda in cerca d'autore."[12] The dramatization airs the same hypotheses as the novel. However the mysterious story, instead of being brought into clearer focus as one might expect, is instead obfuscated to an even greater degree. A series of meta-theatrical devices and diversionary tactics, homologous to the meta-narrative ones used in the novel, provide an even greater number of filters between epicentre and margin: the play is presented as a *dramma a chiave* based on a 'true story'. Unbeknownst to the audience, the 'real' protagonists 'happen' to be in the theatre, having come to see this play about their lives. What they find is that the play is not really about their lives at all, but about the confusion and disagreement arising among a number of otherwise uninvolved persons with clashing, inappropriately intense and highly voluble opinions a propos of their personal tragedy. At the end of the second act, the 'real' protagonists, unable to tolerate this travesty of their lives any longer, burst onto the stage in protest, interrupting the production. Paradoxically, however, instead of rejecting the theatrical representation and interpretation of their story, as is their intention, they inexplicably fall into each other's arms, imitating the scene they have just witnessed on the stage and proving once again that "love conquers all" and that "truth is stranger than fiction". At this point the 'spectators' and 'critics' planted by Pirandello in the audience, outraged, cause a brawl to take place and the director puts an end to the evening's performance prematurely: "[...] per gli spiacevoli incidenti accaduti alla fine del secondo atto, la rappresentazione del terzo non potrà più aver luogo", says the *capocomico* (Act II).

The ending of the story in the play – reconciliation – is diametrically opposed to its dénouement in the novel: Aldo Nuti assassinates Varia Nestoroff in the course of a film shoot while he himself is mauled to death by the tiger who would have been the target of his bullet had he stuck to the script. In both cases, however, Pirandello breaks the frame, collapsing the barrier between life and art. In both cases, what 'really' happened remains a mystery.

The formal convergences seem to confirm that what really matters is not the story itself, but the meta-theatrical or meta-narrative frame: Pirandello's point is about art and its relationship to life. The trite love triangle is merely a naturalistic vehicle, a topos not unlike the family dramas in *Sei personaggi* or in *Così è (se vi pare)*. In fact, the veil that shrouds Signora Ponza's face at the end of *Così è (se vi pare)*, leaving intact the mystery of what might have, but has not, been revealed, seems to be analogous to the final curtain that has fallen prematurely on Act II of *Ciascuno a suo modo*. We must remember that although the actual production ends at this point, the 'play' about the Nuti-Nestoroff story does not. It has been interrupted, truncated, it too 'rejected' by its creator.[13] Just as Pirandello turns his back

---

[12] G. DEBENEDETTI, *Il romanzo del Novecento*, Milano, Garzanti, pp. 257-258.
[13] See N. BORSELLINO, "Una poetica del rifiuto" (1976), now in *Ritratto e immagini di Pirandello*, Bari, La-

on the drama of the "six characters" by turning them into abstract symbols of the human predicament, just as he 'censors' the story of the Ponzas and Signora Frola by turning it into a parable on the relativity of truth, so he dissolves – and defuses – the tale of this equally unfortunate trio into a pseudo-philosophical meditation on the inauthenticity of opinions and on the opacity and instability of human emotions, and hence on their 'unrepresentability' through conventional artistic means.

His rejection of these characters, and of whatever is unsavory or 'too hot to handle' in their situation is attributed in the novel to Serafino who, shortly before he shoots the scene of the assassination, openly admits to his distaste for "ogni realtà che accenni a precisarsi piccola e cruda davanti agli occhi". In response to Cavalena's insistence that there is something suspicious about Nuti's calm demeanour under the circumstances (he is about to enter the tiger's cage) and that it ought to be investigated, Serafino responds thus:

– Evadere, signor Fabrizio, evadere; sfuggire al dramma! È una bella cosa, e anche di moda, le ripeto. E-va-po-rar-si in dilatazioni, diciamo così, liriche, sopra le necessità brutali della vita, a contrattempo e fuori di luogo e senza logica; sù, un gradino più sù di ogni realtà che accenni a precisarsi piccola e cruda davanti agli occhi. Imitare, insomma, gli uccellini in gabbia, signor Fabrizio, che fanno sì, qua e là, saltellando, le loro porcheriole, ma poi ci svolazzano sopra: ecco, prosa e poesia; è di moda. Appena le cose si mettono male, appena due, poniamo, vengono alle mani o ai coltelli, via, sù, guardare in sù, che tempo fa, le rondini che volano, o magari i pipistrelli, se qualche nuvola passa; in che fase è la luna e le stelle pajono d'oro o d'argento. Si passa per originali e si fa la figura di comprendere più vastamente la vita.
Cavalena mi guarda con tanto d'occhi: forse gli sembro impazzito.
– Eh, poi dice. Poterlo fare!
– Facilissimo, signor Fabrizio! Che ci vuole? Appena un dramma le si delinea davanti, appena le cose accennano di prendere un po' di consistenza e stanno per balzarle davanti solide, concrete, minacciose, cavi fuori da lei il pazzo, il poeta crucciato, armato di una pompettina aspirante; si metta a pompare dalla prosa di quella realtà meschina, volgare, un po' d'amara poesia, ed ecco fatto!
– Ma il cuore? mi domanda Cavalena.
– Che cuore?
– Perdio, il cuore! Non bisognerebbe averne!
– Ma che cuore, signor Fabrizio! Niente. Sciocchezze. Che vuole che importi al mio cuore se Tizio piange o se Cajo si sposa, se Sempronio ammazza Filano, e via dicendo? Io evado, sfuggo al dramma, mi dilato, ecco, mi dilato![14]

For someone whose stated goal in life is to observe humanity "nelle sue più ordinarie occupazioni, se mi riesca di scoprire negli altri quello che manca a me per

terza, 1991, pp. 197-202 and FRANCA ANGELINI, "Serafino Gubbio, la tigre e la vocazione teatrale di Luigi Pirandello" (1975), now in *Serafino e la tigre. Pirandello tra scrittura teatro e cinema*, Venezia, Marsilio, 1990, pp. 1-36.
[14] L. PIRANDELLO, *Quaderni di Serafino Gubbio operatore*, Milano, Mondadori (Oscar), 1986, pp. 164-165.

ogni cosa ch'io faccia: la certezza che capiscano ciò che fanno,"[15] this is strange behaviour indeed. On the other hand Serafino has also warned us that he doesn't really understand his own behaviour. Moreover, he tells us that in the course of his observations he has discovered that there is more to life than meets the eye, but that others become uncomfortable when they sense that someone has penetrated the surface of their actions: "C'è un *oltre* in tutto. Voi non volete o non sapete vederlo. Ma appena appena quest'oltre baleni negli occhi d'un ozioso come me, che si metta a osservarvi, ecco, vi smarrite, vi turbate o irritate."[16] At the very end of the novel, after the death of both Varia Nestoroff and her assassin Nuti, Serafino admits that he was well aware that Nuti was up to something that was not part of the script and that, had he acted on instinct, he could have prevented the tragedy. The irony is that he *had* penetrated the surface of Nuti's actions at that crucial moment, that he *had* caught a glimpse of the *oltre* in Nuti's demeanour and behaviour but, contrary to his claims, it was he and not Nuti who was uncomfortable and disoriented by what he sensed, and so he defended against his intuition by intellectualizing about the myriad possible interpretations of what he had just seen. When given the chance to exercise his judgment and autonomy, to come out of his passive anonimity by preventing the deaths of Varia Nestoroff and Aldo Nuti, he remains 'seraphically' detached and records the event – the 'surface' of things – for posterity instead:

[...] Mentre disponevo la macchina sul treppiedi [...] notai che il Nuti [...] si alzò e andò a scostare un po' in una parte del gabbione le fronde, come per aprirvi uno spiraglio. Io solo avrei potuto domandargli:
– Perché?
Ma la disposizione d'animo stabilitasi tra noi non ammetteva che ci scambiassimo in quel punto neppure una parola. Quell'atto poi poteva essere da me interpretato in più modi, che m'avrebbero tenuto incerto in un momento che la certezza più sicura e precisa m'era necessaria. E allora fu per me come se il Nuti non si fosse proprio mosso; non solo non pensai più a quel suo atto, ma fu proprio come se io non lo avessi affatto notato.[17]

If it is true that Pirandello is telling us something important here only about Serafino, then there must be more than meets the eye to the 'truncated' *Ciascuno a suo modo* as well. To catch a glimpse of it, one must first shift the eye away from the meta-theatrical *tre piani di realtà* as such, and focus on the so-called *dramma a chiave*. The *dramma a chiave* is not the story of the Nuti-Mirelli-Nestoroff tragedy at all: it is the story of a rivalry that takes shape around a pretext, the defence of a woman, Delia Morello, considered responsible for the suicide of a famous artist. When I say that this rivalry takes shape around a pretext, I am referring

[15] *Ibid.*, p. 3.
[16] *Ibid.*
[17] *Ibid.*, p. 173.

to the fact that neither of the two gentlemen in question, Doro Palegari and Francesco Savio, actually knows this woman. And yet one of them, Doro, seems to be as intensely involved and as highly invested in her defence as he would be if she were a sister or a close friend. Indeed, he is literally prepared to 'come to daggers' over it.

Both Savio and Palegari's mother are convinced that this impassioned defence is a sign that Doro is in love with Delia Morello: the conventional explanation for such behaviour. In the midst of the heated discussion taking place in the Palegari drawing room, a minor character designated simply as "un primo vecchio amico" points out, however, that Doro has jumped to this woman's defence "senza che abbia mai parlato con lei". Pirandello puts this remark in quotation marks in the text: "PRIMO VECCHIO AMICO. Ecco. Io ho detto: 'senza che forse abbia mai parlato con lei!'" (Act I). Doro's mother, however, ignores this 'minor detail' and continues to insist that Doro's defence of Delia is that of a man in love. Diego Cinci, the *ragionatore*, tries to convince her otherwise as well but fails because he is unwilling to offer an alternate explanation. In fact when he finds himself unable to continue the conversation, he changes the subject so abruptly that both Doro's mother and the reader are left totally disoriented:

Con estro improvviso: voce chiara, lieve, invitante:
Signora, e lei non pensa... che so, a un calessino per una strada di campagna – aperta campagna – in una bella giornata di sole?... (Act I)

There follows a long and mysterious speech about an insect that so distracted him while he was at his mother's deathbed that he saw the insect die but not his mother:

Le sembra assurdo? Lei domani riderà – gliel'assicuro io – ripensando a questo calessino che ora le ho fatto passare davanti per frastornarla. Consideri che io non posso ridere ugualmente, pensando a quell'insetto che mi cadde sotto gli occhi mentre vegliavo mia madre che moriva. (Act I)

Without attempting to offer any precise explanation of the image of the insect, it is clear that Diego did not want to watch his mother die any more than he now wants to tell Donna Livia the truth about her son (or for that matter, any more than Serafino wanted to acknowledge that there was something strange in Nuti's behavior). In fact, when Doro comes home and tries to reassure his mother that he is not in love, curiously, Diego shifts gears and insists that he is. After another long digression on his mother's death, he returns to the question of Doro's supposed love for Delia. But then an even more curious thing happens: first, Francesco Savio appears and announces that he has given some thought to Doro's defence of Delia and that he does agree with him after all, but as soon as Francesco makes this announcement, Doro declares that he, too, has changed his mind and that he now

329

feels about it the way Francesco did before! At this point pandemonium breaks out, until Delia herself arrives and introduces herself to Doro, saying that she has heard about his impassioned defence of her and has come to thank him. Delia's arrival closes Act I.

A clue as to what might be going on is offered in Act II, by another minor character in the chorus of observers, significantly and almost ominously indicated simply as "l'Altro". When Doro challenges Francesco to a duel after the latter has changed his mind, l'Altro comments on the irony of the situation: "Già! Credo non si sia mai dato il caso di due che si battono perché disposti a darsi reciprocamente ragione" (Act II). When the discussion turns again to the question of Doro's sentiments, and everyone seems to be ascribing the intensity of his emotions and his confusion to his supposed secret feelings for Delia, l'Altro interrupts repeatedly, at first tentatively, then forcefully ("con forza" say the stage directions), and insists that he has something to say. As soon as he has everyone's attention, however, he suddenly appears disoriented and refuses to speak, claiming that he has forgotten what he was about to tell them:

L'ALTRO (*con forza*). Io volevo – aspettate! – io volevo dire intanto –
    resterà in tronco, smarrito, tutti lo guarderanno, sospesi.
IL PRIMO (*dopo aver atteso un po'*). – che cosa? –
L'ALTRO – una cosa... Oh perdio! non ricordo più.
    Si presenterà a questo punto sulla soglia dell'uscio a destra Diego Cinci. (Act II)

The conflict between Doro and Francesco, which Doro insists on maintaining even when it is no longer necessary, is basically a disagreement without a real object – all the more so since, as has been pointed out, neither of them actually knows Delia Morello. In other words, what counts here is the tension and hostility between Doro and Francesco, which Doro seems determined to sustain by unabashedly doing a complete about-face when confronted with Francesco's unexpected change of heart. What I would like to suggest is that Delia Morello is neither the cause of Doro's hostility to Francesco, nor the real object of Doro's intense emotions; on the contrary, she is merely a function, inasmuch as she allows Doro's hostility to Francesco to emerge. The real object of Doro's emotions is Francesco: these emotions have merely been displaced onto Delia, and everyone jumps at the first and most conventional explanation of this: Doro must be in love with her.

So, too, in the novel, everyone thinks that Nuti is in love with Varia Nestoroff. And yet, when Nuti arrives at the Kosmograph studios to try to reconnect with her after Mirelli's suicide, he tells Serafino that before coming to Rome to seek out Varia, he had been to Sorrento, in a first desperate and futile effort to convince Duccella to take him back:

...Ho cercato finora, ho fatto di tutto per vincere Duccella; ho messo tanti amici di mezzo; ma capisco che non è possibile.... E ora io ho bisogno, bisogno d'aggrapparmi a qualcuno, di non essere più così solo.... So che non vale nulla quella donna [Varia]; ma le dà prezzo ora tutto quello che ho sofferto e soffro per lei. Non è amore, è odio, è il sangue che s'è versato per lei![18]

This is a very significant speech because it reveals that Duccella and Varia are interchangeable; they are, like Delia Morello in the play, functions of Nuti's desire to somehow remain connected to Mirelli. In fact the entire novel is strewn with evidence of the fact that the real object of Nuti's emotions, from the beginning, is Mirelli. Serafino's reconstruction of the story begins with an allusion to the fact that the first connection established was between Mirelli and Nuti; this connection was then sealed by Nuti's engagement to Mirelli's sister Duccella, thereby creating a first triangular formation. Serafino recalls Nuti's early visits to the Sorrento home of Mirelli using the naive voices and perspectives of Mirelli's sister and grand-mother, both of whom are very impressed by him. Serafino's description of Nuti as an aristocratic Neapolitan dandy with artistic pretensions come to convince Giorgio to move to the city suggests his role as a corrupting influence well before Varia Nestoroff arrived on the scene:

... È venuto già tre volte da Napoli un signorino, un bel signorino tutto profumato, col panciotto di velluto, i guanti canarini scamosciati, la caramella all'occhio destro e lo stem-ma baronale nel fazzoletto e nel portafogli. L'ha mandato il nonno, barone Nuti, amico di nonno Carlo, amico da fratello, prima che nonno Carlo, stanco del mondo, si ritirasse da Napoli, qua, nella villetta sorrentina. Voi lo sapete, nonna Rosa. Ma non sapete che il si-gnorino di Napoli incoraggia fervorosamente Giorgio a darsi all'arte e ad andarsene a Na-poli con lui. Lo sa Duccella, perché il signorino Aldo Nuti (che stranezza!), parlando con tanto fervore dell'arte, non guarda mica Giorgio, guarda lei, negli occhi, come se dovesse incoraggiare lei e non Giorgio; sì, sì, lei, a venirsene a Napoli per stare sempre accanto a lui.[19]

It is clear from this passage that the erotic dimension of Nuti's desire is being projected onto Duccella inasmuch as she is Mirelli's sister. In fact, later we learn from Serafino that Mirelli was not at all pleased about Duccella's engagement to Nuti, whom he considered "complicato".[20] In the last chapter of the novel, just before the fatal shooting, Pirandello alludes to the origin of Nuti's attraction to Mirelli, in a dialogue between Nuti and Serafino which begins as what appears to be a casual conversation about photography:

– Ho un ritratto di mio padre, morto giovanissimo, circa all'età mia; tanto che io non l'ho conosciuto. L'ho custodita con reverenza, quest'immagine, benché non mi dica nulla. S'è invecchiata anch'essa, sì, profondandosi, come lei dice, nel passato. Ma il tempo che ha

---

[18] *Ibid.*, p. 104.
[19] *Ibid.*, pp. 24-25.
[20] *Ibid.*, pp. 27-28.

invecchiato l'immagine, non ha invecchiato mio padre; mio padre non l'ha vissuto questo tempo. E si presenta a me, a vuoto, dal vuoto di tutta questa vita che per lui non è stata; si presenta a me con la sua vecchia immagine di giovane che non mi dice nulla, che non può dirmi nulla, perché non sa neppure ch'io ci sia. E difatti è un ritratto ch'egli si fece prima di sposare; ritratto, dunque, di quando non era mio padre. Io in lui, lì, non ci sono, come tutta la mia vita è stata senza di lui.[21]

Three things make it obvious that this is a very important speech: first, its placement just before his death; second, the fact that just before referring to this photograph, Nuti speaks of his horror at catching a glimpse of his own 'oltre' in the cutting room ("non mi pareva l'ora che sparisse dallo schermo"), that Serafino immediately twigs to this ("mi voltai a guardarlo"), but that as soon as Nuti senses Serafino's reaction he changes the subject immediately: ("ma mi sfuggì subito in un'ovvia considerazione"); third, that just after the speech, Nuti speaks of his 'lack' in more general terms, and then immediately again changes the subject:

"... in ogni famiglia, nei vecchi album di fotografie [...] pensi quante immagini ingiallite di gente che non dice più nulla, che non si sa più chi sia stato, che abbia fatto, come sia morta..." [...] D'improvviso cambiò discorso per domandarmi, accigliato: "Quanto può durare una pellicola?"[22]

All the evidence suggests that the drama Pirandello had in mind was this: Nuti's attraction to Mirelli is a function of the fact that he himself has remained fixated at a moment of traumatic loss in his life; Mirelli is the 'shadow' of the fantasy/photograph Nuti carries around with him, of a young, unmarried man who was to become his father. Nuti hoped to seal the connection to Mirelli through the marriage to Duccella, but when Mirelli decides to marry Varia Nestoroff, Nuti senses a threat and decides to interfere. Mirelli's unexpected suicide, provoked by Varia's supposed betrayal, for Nuti represents a repetition of the loss of his father and is more than he can bear. When Duccella and Nestoroff, his only remaining connections to Mirelli, both reject him, he resorts to murder. So, too, Mirelli's suicide is a result of his own invisible drama. In fact we are told that Mirelli lost his mother at a young age and that his relationship with Varia is a chaste one in spite of her reputation because of Mirelli's tremendous idealization of her. Once his image of her has been tarnished by his best friend he, too, cannot bear the pain.

If my reading is correct, then both Nuti and Mirelli are meant to be acting out unresolved, invisible dramas with the dead, which are chronologically in the past, but which perdure in their psyches and hence in their adult lives and loves. In Nuti's case it takes the form of unconscious homosexuality, the search for a male figure with whom to identify. To transfer this 'unrepresentable' drama to the

---

[21] *Ibid.*, p. 168.
[22] *Ibid.*

stage Pirandello resorts to what might quite literally be called a pale imitation of it, a mimetic representation of unconscious conflict. The *dramma a chiave* in *Ciascuno a suo modo*, Doro and Francesco's disagreement without a real object, is a formal repetition of the essential structure of the relationship between Aldo Nuti and Giorgio Mirelli. This is the original 'censored' or 'rejected' nucleus of this play, which Pirandello cannot represent explicitly, but which he does not want to give up. The compromise is a meta-theatrical happening which distances this nucleus, while allowing us at the same time to catch a glimpse of its structural double in the shadow of it that is projected onto the stage through Doro and Francesco. The end of the play, which comes in the second intermission when the two 'real' characters, Nuti and Moreno, fall into each other's arms in a paradoxical case of 'life' imitating 'art' is a deliberately misleading meta-theatrical device: the real repetition or imitation is elsewhere, but it takes place without anyone being aware of it.

III

With the exception of *I vecchi e i giovani*, of all of Pirandello's works, *Serafino Gubbio* is the one which makes the most explicit reference to 'history' or, at least, to the temper of the times: Serafino's fragmented reminiscences and hypotheses about what could have happened to make Mirelli commit suicide and drive Nuti mad, is accompanied by an unrelenting, self-serving tirade against machines and those 'evils' of modernity which have deprived man of his central place in the universe, the most prominent of which are technology and industrialization. Serafino actually presents himself as a disempowered male, a cameraman in the fledgling movie industry who has ostensibly become "una mano che gira una manovella,"[23] a mere cog in a wheel, the performer of a function which involves nothing but his hand, cut off from both his creativity and the end-product of his labour. In the Futurist imaginary, men are energized and revitalized by machines, in Serafino's they are reduced to mere shadows of themselves by man-eating monsters, "mostri, che dovevano rimanere strumenti e sono divenuti, invece, per forza, i nostri padroni."[24] The linotype machine is described as "una bestiaccia mostruosa , che mangia piombo e caca libri... una vera bestia, un pachiderma, che si rùguma quieto quieto il suo lungo nastro di carta traforata."[25] The darkroom at the Kosmograph is "un ventre, nel quale si sta sviluppando e formando una mostruosa gestazione

---

[23] PIRANDELLO, *Serafino Gubbio*, p. 5.
[24] *Ibid.*, p. 6.
[25] *Ibid.*, p. 16.

meccanica."[26] The technicians who work in the darkroom are also mere hands: "mani, non vedo altro che mani, in queste camere oscure; mani affaccendate su le bacinelle; mani cui il tetro lucore delle lanterne rosse dà un'apparenza spettrale. Penso che queste mani appartengono ad uomini che non sono più."[27] He himself, when he takes his camera in hand, becomes a monstrous hybrid, half-man, half-machine, or perhaps, more, possessed by the machine:

> Vado dal magazziniere a provvedermi di pellicola vergine, e preparo per il pasto la mia macchinetta.
> Assumo subito, con essa in mano, la mia maschera d'impassibilità. Anzi, ecco, non sono più. Cammina *lei*, adesso, con le mie gambe. Da capo a piedi, son cosa sua: faccio parte del suo congegno. La mia testa è qua, nella macchinetta, e me la porto in mano.[28]

At first I was puzzled by what appeared to be the lack of any readily apparent connection between the Nuti-Nestoroff-Mirelli story and its frame, the anti-technology tirade. And then it became clear – or so it seemed: Pirandello was re-creating the well-known modernist parallel between women and machines. The other 'monster' in this novel was Varia Nestoroff. She inhabits the men with whom she comes into contact to such a degree that she renders them ineffective. Her voracious animal nature – she is constantly compared to the tiger the Kosmograph keeps in a cage for its own purposes – is like that of the machines: machines eat humans and spew them out as mechanized shadows of themselves (quite literally shadows on celluloid), deprived of their hearts, their will, their humanity. Varia Nestoroff does the same to men, the proof being that Giorgio Mirelli has committed suicide and Aldo Nuti has gone mad, both supposedly consumed by the passion she inspires.

The fact that the novel is rife with figures of men who have in one way or another been deprived of their dignity either by technology or by women seemed at first to support this hypothesis. The most poignant of these figures is "l'uomo dal violino". A former typographer whose skills have been rendered superfluous by the linotype machine, he then decides to try to make his living as a violinist, only to be offered the job of accompanying an automatic piano. He now lives in a shelter for the homeless, where he eventually dies of alcoholism. When Serafino meets him for the first time, he says of him: "trasse dalla custodia il vecchio violino, un violino veramente prezioso, e lo mostrò, come un monco vergognoso può mostrare il suo moncherino."[29] Another pathetic figure is Dottor Cavalena, a medical doctor whose wife's paranoid's jealousy makes his life a living hell. Every attempt he makes to leave her is thwarted by his lack of resolve: the grotesque toupee he uses,

---

[26] *Ibid.*, p. 44.
[27] *Ibid.*
[28] *Ibid.*, p. 45.
[29] *Ibid.*, p. 15.

unsuccessfully, to camouflage his baldness, is the symbol of his status as a 'castrated' male. The other male figure who 'loses his head' so to speak, is of course Aldo Nuti, who shoots Varia Nestoroff, and then is mauled to death by the tiger he would have killed had he stuck to the script. At this point, Serafino, who has been impassibly filming the horrific scene of Nuti's death, loses his voice altogether, in yet another symbolic castration.

If it is true that the chaotic, fragmented treatment of the story is meant to mirror the chaos of an apparently random universe, it is also true that it allows Serafino to speculate at length, and from various points of view, on what might have caused Varia Nestoroff to act the way she did. At staggered points throughout the novel he airs a number of different, detailed hypotheses which serve to slowly give voice and interiority to the figure of the *belle dame sans merci*. He imagines her apparently cruel and heartless behaviour as a reaction to her own disempowerment, to years of abuse endured at the hands of men, ranging from the sexual violation of her girlhood, to the emotional neglect experienced in relationships with men who valued only her body, either sexually or, as in the case of the artist Giorgio Mirelli for whom she served as a model, esthetically. He imagines the self-hatred she has developed to be a result of the objectification she has endured, of the contempt she has suffered and internalized. When Serafino interrogates her, she confirms some of his theories and adds to them, speaking openly of her pain as a woman either abused or idealized but ultimately negated as a human being.

So, too, Signora Cavalena, who seems to be victimizing her hapless husband with her paranoid jealousy, is described as "accanita contro tutto il genere mascolino."[30] And yet when Cavalena, in conversation with Serafino, says that woman is always "la Nemica" and Serafino suggests that possibly, for example in the case of Nestoroff and Nuti, "ella non voglia essere per lui né amica né nemica, né niente", Cavalena answers quite clearly "Ma appunto per questo!.... Scusi, o che forse la donna bisogna considerarla in sé e per sé? Sempre di fronte a un uomo, signor Gubbio! Tanto più nemica, in certi casi, quanto più indifferente!"[31] The 'otherness' of women is, quite simply, unacceptable and must be erased at all cost.

The parallel Pirandello is creating in this novel is not between monstrous machines and monstrous women, but between monstrous machines and monstrous men: men have done to women – and to nature (the captive tiger) – what machines (and the tiger) are now doing to them. Just as machines are now disempowering and dehumanizing men, turning them into 'monsters' like themselves, so men have long disempowered and dehumanized women, projecting, throughout history, their own fears and fantasies into various incarnations of the *belle dame sans merci*. Now, however – and I am speaking roughly of the years 1880-1920,

---

[30] *Ibid.*, p. 118.
[31] *Ibid.*, p. 163.

which marked Italy's late and in some ways traumatic encounter with modernity – the institutionalized submission of women to men, while by no means ended, is definitely – and definitively – shaken. Whether it is through the emergence of a mass market for women writers or through the creation of jobs for women in factories, there is little doubt that industrialization and the consequent emergence of Socialism, organized feminism, and mass culture seem to be empowering women while stripping men, particularly intellectuals, of their sense of purpose, mastery and belonging. Women's desires – for civil and political rights, for sexual freedom, for cultural expression – are all exploding at a time when masculine energies are, if not depleted, certainly undergoing a period of stasis and disorientation. It is surely no coincidence that the Futurist manifesto of 1909 calls, among other things, for a glorification of the contempt for women – "il disprezzo della donna". The fantasy of engulfment by increasingly powerful women, no longer held at bay by role stability and institutional support for gender differentiation, also finds symbolic expression in images of virile women[32] or the *donna fatale* as she appears in such novels as D'Annunzio's notorious *Il piacere* and *Il trionfo della morte*.[33]

Both *Serafino Gubbio* and an earlier novel, *Suo marito* (1911) address the theme of gender relations and their changing configurations in conjunction with the theme of industrialization and its effects on cultural production. In *Suo marito* (later re-titled *Giustino Roncella nato Boggiolo)* Giustino actually exploits his wife, a successful writer, as an object of exchange, thereby becoming the functional equivalent of a pimp.[34] In *Serafino Gubbio* Giorgio Mirelli exploits Varia Nestoroff as an aesthetic object, while Aldo Nuti turns her into a sexual object. In both novels products of the Futurist and Dannunzian imaginaries are characteristically demystified and turned on their heads, giving way to images of feminized men and disempowered, objectified women. In this context, *Serafino Gubbio*'s submerged tale of unconscious homosexuality – hardly the only such tale in the Pirandellian repertoire[35] – evokes a number of possible interpretations. It is both a symbol of the distortions of sexual and social relations, fraught with lies and compromises, and a metaphor for what Pirandello sees as the infantile, narcissistic impotence of his culture, so incapable of leaving the safe, womb-like haven of its small-town provincial past that it turns even the metropolis into a claustrophobic mirror image of itself (Mattia Pascal's or Serafino Gubbio's Rome, for example). The big city,

---

[32] See B. P. F. WANROOIJ, "La crisi dei generi", *Storia del pudore. La questione sessuale in Italia 1860-1940*, Venezia, Marsilio, 1990, pp. 191-225.

[33] See L. CURRERI, "Seduzione e malattia nella narrativa italiana post-unitaria", *Otto/Novecento*, XVI (1992), n. 3-4, pp. 53-78.

[34] See my own "Scrittori, scritti e industria culturale: *Suo marito* di Pirandello", *Otto/Novecento*, XIX (1995), n. 5, pp. 167-182.

[35] On this question see L. LUGNANI, "L'infanzia felice", *L'infanzia felice e altri saggi su Pirandello*, Napoli, Liguori, 1986. Also my own "Lo scambio delle donne in Pirandello", *Rivista di studi pirandelliani*, XII (1994), n. 12/13, pp. 71-108.

the symbol of modernity, is the place where one comes face to face, daily, with real 'otherness'. Italy, in order to move into modernity, must also come out of its narcissistic isolation, but is capable only of producing self-aggrandizing (D'Annunzio, the Futurists) or ironic, self-pitying mythologies (the Crepuscolari).

One of the most powerful scenes in the novel is that in which Pirandello describes Serafino's return to Rome after his traumatic visit to Sorrento, where he had hoped to convince Duccella to come to Nuti's rescue. Here he finds that the lovely Sorrento villa of his youth is now decrepit, the lovely, pure Duccella is a bloated, homely, mustachioed old maid, and nonna Rosa, the guardian of all that had seemed innocent and decent, is a repulsive old woman. The descriptions are worth quoting, for the vengeance with which they treat these two female characters:

S'arrestò sul pianerottolo e mi guardò con gli occhi chiari, spenti nella faccia bianca, grassa, dalla bazza floscia: sul labbro, di qua e di là, agli angoli della bocca, alcuni peluzzi. Duccella.
[.....]
Per levarmela davanti le avrei dato uno spintone, anche a rischio di farle ruzzolare la scala! Che strazio molle! che cosa! Quella vecchia sorda, istolidita, senza più un dente in bocca, col mente aguzzo che le sbalzava orribilmente fin sotto il naso, biasciando a vuoto, e la lingua pallida che spuntava tra le labbra flaccide grinzose, e quegli occhiali grandi, che le ingrandivano mostruosamente gli occhi vani, operati di cateratta, tra le rade ciglia lunghe come antenne d'insetto!
– Vi siete fatta la posizione (*con la zeta dolce napoletana*) – la posi-zzi-o-ne. [36]

It is no accident that the old woman's words reproduce one of the most tired, yet most enduring clichés of the petty-bourgeois worldview, 'farsi la posizione', which once meant dignity, prestige, and respectability, and now is only an empty vessel, the rhetorical vestige of an Italy that is no longer and perhaps never was. As Serafino sits, shell-shocked, on the train speeding back to Rome, he finds himself opposite a man who has clearly been able to make a place for himself in the world as it is. He is described as a smug, self-satisfied and somewhat slimy animal (the symbol of the new, entrepreneurial Italy?) hardly less repulsive to him than Duccella and nonna Rosa:

In treno mi parve di correre verso la follia, nella notte. In che mondo ero? Quel mio compagno di viaggio, uomo di mezza età, nero, con gli occhi ovati, come di smalto, i capelli lucidi di pomata, era sì lui di questo mondo; fermo e ben posato nel sentimento della sua tranquilla e ben curata bestialità, ci capiva tutto a meraviglia, senza inquietarsi di nulla; sapeva bene tutto ciò che gli importava di sapere, dove andava, perché viaggiava, la casa ove sarebbe sceso, la cena che lo aspettava. Ma io? Dello stesso mondo? Il viaggio suo e il mio

---

[36] PIRANDELLO, *Serafino Gubbio*, pp. 148-149.

... la sua notte e la mia...No, io non avevo tempo, né mondo, né nulla. Il treno era suo; ci viaggiava lui. Come mai ci viaggiavo anch'io? com'ero anch'io nel mondo dove stava lui? Come, in che era mia quella notte, se non avevo come viverla, nulla da farci? La sua notte e tutto il tempo l'aveva lui, quell'uomo di mezza età, che ora rigirava un po' infastidito il collo nel bianchissimo solino inamidato. No, né mondo, né tempo, né nulla: io ero fuori di tutto, assente da me stesso e dalla vita; e non sapevo più dove fossi né perché ci fossi. Immagini aveva dentro di me, non mie, di cose, di persone; immagini, aspetti, figure, ricordi di persone, di cose che non erano mai state nella realtà, fuori di me, nel mondo che quel signore si vedeva attorno e toccava.[37]

What I believe Pirandello is really representing here is his own reticence as a member of a society still so wedded to its own outmoded and irrelevant categories of thought and judgment, that it continually fails to draw the most obvious conclusions about the contradictions in its own midst. Though thought of as the relentless exploder of all bourgeois myths, of the hypocrisies and small-mindedness of post-Unification Italy reflected in the term 'l'Italietta', Pirandello was well aware that he was both a critic of this society and a member of it, sharing to some degree both its sensibilities and its blind spots. Just as Nuti and Mirelli lied to themselves about the nature of their relationship to each other and to the women in their lives, so Serafino lies to himself about the past, about the present and about his role in the squalid melodrama which began in the idealized villa in Sorrento. So, too, an entire culture continues to shield itself from the truth about its most basic values, conventions and assumptions: the Futurists about their 'potence' and the future, the Crepuscolari about the idealized objects of their nostalgia and the past (represented by the villa in Sorrento[38]), men in general about their relations with women and with each other. In *L'umorismo* Pirandello talks about "il mentire psicologico" and how it inevitably gives way to "il mentire sociale."[39] *Serafino Gubbio* is about both kinds of lies, about how an entire culture creates lie upon lie until it no longer recognizes them as such, until there is no relationship at all between the forms of social life and and any sort of authenticity.

Moreover, social lies so structure our perception that arriving at our own psychological truth as individuals is practically impossible. In such a world, authors are no more reliable or trustworthy than narrators and the norms governing cultural and artistic representation, be they naturalist or modernist, can only, at best, be bared for what they are – vehicles for more lies. Pirandello spares no one, least of all himself. Through Serafino's disgust at the world around him and his refusal to 'see' and take responsibility for what he catches a glimpse of in the case of Nuti,

---

[37] *Ibid.*, pp. 149-150.
[38] "Dolce casa di campagna, *Casa dei nonni*, piena del sapore ineffabile dei più antichi ricordi familiari, ove tutti i mobili di vecchio stile, animati da questi ricordi, non erano più cose, ma quasi intime parti di coloro che v'abitavano, perché in essi toccavano e sentivano la realtà cara, tranquilla, sicura della loro esistenza". *Ibid.*, p. 20.
[39] PIRANDELLO, *L'umorismo*, p. 156.

Pirandello willfully casts a different light on his own desire to distance himself from the 'petty' naturalist dramas of daily life, and thus on his great metatheatrical inventions. By creating this homology between himself and Serafino perhaps he is warning us to be suspicious of him as well, to look beyond the meta-theatre at the substance of what is – or is not – being represented, for perhaps he, too, is 'lying' about what is really important.

Eduardo Saccone

"FEDE", "FIDUCIA", "SFIDUCIA", "SOSPETTO"
NEL *PODERE* DI FEDERIGO TOZZI

«Perché, dunque, non mi crede?» (p. 85)
«E desiderò di credere» (p. 137) [1]

All'inizio – se si può parlare d'inizio – di ogni testo narrativo tozziano c'è, o sembra esserci, un'esperienza di scollamento: l'avvertimento, non importa quanto chiaro o confuso, di una separazione, ch'è anche ciò che mette in moto per l'appunto la narrazione. Una separazione ch'è all'origine del desiderio: di colmare la differenza, di costituire, o ricostituire, l'accordo.

Si tratta, non c'è bisogno di dire, di un'esperienza dolorosa, cui segue di solito non tanto una pulsione epistemologica – e una cognizione del dolore – quanto una reazione esistenziale: di un corpo e di un'anima con gli occhi chiusi.

Ciò non vuol dire che in qualche modo lo scrittore non arrivi persino a teorizzare i termini del problema. In *Rerum fide*, un testo pubblicato nel 1919, ecco a che cosa si dichiara di dover «aprire gli occhi»: per rispondere all'attesa di «qualche vero rinnovamento». «C'è da sospettare che [tutte le nostre parole] ci costringano a un'angustia, da cui ci vogliamo liberare a tutti i costi»:[2] «si sa che tra le 'cose' e le 'parole' non c'è più quella vergine fede d'una volta».[3] Per cui, «ciò che vive attorno a noi è soltanto una rammendatura che si deve rompere tutte le volte che vogliamo adoperarla per una fatica troppo forte» (p. 278). La «domanda suprema» da «fare alla nostra realtà» è «che i nostri occhi credano a quel che vedono; trovando solo in noi stessi le spiegazioni morali che ora si confezionano con le metafore e con la rettorica» (*ibid.*); scegliendo, possibilmente, «il punto più sensibile, che forse si nasconde nel rovescio della nostra coscienza convenzionale», cauti a non «leggere troppo nel libro delle nostre abitudini», guardandoci da bontà e falsità, dalla ten-

---

[1] Le citazioni da *Il podere* si riferiscono sempre all'edizione curata per I grandi libri Garzanti da L. Baldacci, Milano, 1986. Gli altri romanzi di Tozzi sono citati dall'edizione Vallecchi delle *Opere I. I Romanzi*, a cura di G. Tozzi, Firenze, 1961.

[2] FEDERICO TOZZI, *Pagine critiche* a cura di Giancarlo Bertoncini, Pisa, Edizioni ETS, 1993, p. 276.

[3] *Ibid.*

tazione di «quella pericolosa quiete, che consiste nel farsi venire vicina la morte senza tentare mai di soffermarla con la nostra volontà» (*ibid.*). Ciò che vale insieme perdita della giovinezza («Gli uomini perdono la giovinezza soltanto quando si arrendono alle ostilità esterne ed interne» [*ibid.*]) e della speranza: di «trovare nelle cose una completa associazione con noi stessi» (p. 279).

Dall'"angustia" all'accordo, dunque, alla "completa associazione": ovvero alla "fiducia", alla "confidenza", alla "sicurezza", alla "dolcezza", invece della "sfiducia", della "diffidenza", del "sospetto", dell'"inimicizia" infine, che sembrano essere la regola del mondo di *Il podere*. Per quasi tutto il libro il giovane protagonista sembra conservare «una certa fede», prodotto o compagna della "giovinezza": «ma era troppo giovane per non avere una certa fede; sia pure indefinibile» (p. 64). Niente di stabile, di sicuro: *sine cura*, e destinato infatti a (o possibile di) tramonto o eclisse, come dovrà sperimentare tra gli altri il Giulio di *Tre croci*: il quale si accorge a un certo punto che anche la giovinezza, situata per lui in un passato remoto, creduto invulnerabile, non resiste alle infiltrazioni «di queste possibilità negative», all'invadente «disperazione».

Almeno, quand'era giovine, non gli era mai capitato di perdersi in queste possibilità negative, che ora filtravano anche nel suo passato più remoto; in quel passato che credeva invulnerabile. Invece non esisteva nessuna resistenza; e un giorno di disperazione si trovava subito a contatto con la sua giovinezza; che, con una rapidità da far paura, era doventata soltanto una verità del suo sentimento.

(*Opere I*, p. 248)

Una verità, piuttosto che una realtà, del suo sentimento. Ma è l'orizzonte che stimola il suo desiderio, e che tiene in moto la macchina narrativa. Quando esso cessa di essere in evidenza, anche questa si ferma, ovvero la storia è conclusa, finita. Ma intanto, nel *Podere*, siamo appena all'inizio: un inizio diffidente come al solito, tuttavia speranzoso. Un'apertura di orizzonte, uno squarcio che si situa significativamente tra due morti: quella inaugurale del padre e quella conclusiva del figlio. La diffidenza, e addirittura inimicizia iniziale, la mancanza di riconoscimento – in tutti i possibili sensi – tra i due,[4] si trasferisce, o per dir meglio si sposta, in quella tra il nuovo padrone della Casuccia, Remigio, e tutti gli altri. Nonostante che una volta, dopo il furto delle ciliege, parlando agli assalariati il personaggio dichiari di non poter «sospettare di nessuno, perché se sospettassi di uno di voi, lo manderei via» (p. 46), è precisamente il sospetto a regnare – a reggere, a regolare – il rapporto tra io e altri: quando, com'è giustamente implicato dalla dichiarazione di Remigio, dovrebbe essere invece la "fiducia": perché ci sia *societas*, perché la società possa darsi. E che i termini alternativi del discorso siano, come ho detto, "sospetto" da una

---

[4] «Non mi riconosci?» – chiede Remigio, appena arrivato. «Vorrei che mi riconoscesse. [...] Non mi riconosci?» – ripete il figlio (pp. 5-6). E questa è la risposta del padre, «come se avesse voluto fargli capire che non gliene importava nulla»: «Non ti devo riconoscere? Non sei Remigio?» (p. 6).

parte e dall'altra "fiducia", risulta ben evidente da questo scambio tra Remigio e la matrigna:

– Mi pare, però, che non aveva nessun motivo per *sospettare* di me! –
– Io non sospetto di te; anzi mi *fido* e ti voglio bene.

(p. 119)

Ma non è così. Se ce ne fosse bisogno, il narratore stesso ci ha precedentemente informato: «La matrigna, debole e sospettosa, gli dette un'occhiata; che gli fece capire come ne sapeva più di lui e chi sa con quali precauzioni si faceva aiutare anche dai parenti» (p. 14). Naturalmente Remigio, di cui è anche detto che «voleva comportarsi lealmente con lei», «provò una delusione cattiva. Infatti, gli dispiaceva a essere trattato con una diffidenza maliziosa» (*ibid.*). E questa «diffidenza maliziosa» – diffidenza e sospetto, che fanno male e sembrano volere il male del protagonista – si rivela generale e capillare: manifestandosi specificamente in quella che si può ben chiamare, e a volte è chiamata infatti, *invidia*, veder male, e altre volte *sfiducia*; altre ancora *inimicizia*.

Tutte e tre, in particolare la prima, si ritrovano per esempio nell'atteggiamento ostile del dottor Bianconi:

Ma quello lì ha il cervello sotto i gomiti! E finirà male. Sono contento se lei riescirà a dargli una buona lezione; perché certe indoli non si piegano altro che quando cominciano a soffrire. Ora, lui, si crederebbe di fare il padrone della Casuccia; ma non stimo che ne sia capace!

(p. 61)

E, aggiunge il narratore: «Siccome metteva da parte parecchi denari e voleva comprare un podere, per farcisi una villa, notò che Remigio lo possedeva senza esserselo guadagnato e senza doverlo pagare a nessuno» (p. 62).

E di invidia e inimicizia si può certo ancora parlare pensando al comportamento dei vari notai, sensali, avvocati e giudici che assediano Remigio con un accanimento sospetto; fino all'usciere del tribunale, «che si mise a scrutarlo; con una diffidenza ironica, che lo fece intimidire di vergogna. Gli aumentò la sfiducia; e avrebbe voluto essere in fondo alla Casuccia, a guardare la Tressa; che scorreva placida senza gorgogli, dove c'era l'erba più folta» (p. 65).

La reazione del personaggio è caratteristica. È una fuga dalla "sfiducia", ovvero la ricerca di un rifugio: dal sospetto inquietante, addirittura terrorizzante, in cui sembrano accumularsi gli attributi superegoici di un padre padrone giudicante e perseguitante. Donde anche, all'opposto, il riparo cercato in uno spazio evidentemente materno, come conferma più innanzi nel testo il passo seguente:

Andò a una specie di nascondiglio, che s'era trovato su la greppa della Tressa; come dentro un letto di erba; dove con il corpo aveva fatto ormai una buca.

(p. 131)

E, un po' prima: «Gli pareva di potersi nascondere in mezzo al podere; e di non farsi più guardare da nessuno» (p. 119).

Questa fuga ha però già anche connotati e attrazioni mortali. Ovviamente; e saranno confermati dall'attrazione del profondo, nichilistica e omicida, di Berto, l'*alter ego* di Remigio, che sarà anche il suo boia.[5] Infatti, già nell'ultimo tratto da cui citavo il sospetto della realtà – che include persone, ma anche cose e bestie (non a caso il trittico progettato dallo scrittore comprendeva *Cose e persone*, oltre a *Bestie*) – si esprimeva anche più significativamente in gesti: di rigetto o rifiuto.

> Passò accanto alle vacche, che ruminavano ferme; avevano gli occhi umidi, e la pancia della gravidanza faceva loro due buche al posto dei fianchi. Tese un braccio, per toccarne una; ma la vacca dette una scrollata e se ne andò.
>
> (p. 119)

E un po' prima:

> Remigio sentiva la sfiducia; ma non sapeva bene di che si trattava. [...] Ormai trovavasi di fronte alle cose, come una inimicizia. Anche il suo podere era un nemico; e sentiva che perfino le viti e il grano si farebbero amare soltanto se egli impedisse a qualunque altro di doventarne il proprietario. La casa stessa gli era ostile; bastava guardare gli spigoli delle cantonate. Se non aveva l'animo di distruggerla e di ricostruirla, anche la casa non ce lo voleva. Da tutto, la dolcezza era sparita.
>
> (pp. 110-111)

La constatazione della scomparsa della dolcezza significa la coscienza della crisi persino della speranza dell'accordo tra io e altro, ovvero del fallimento del progetto di possesso del podere, ch'egli si ostina tuttavia a concepire nei termini ereditati dal padre: nei termini – anziché del rispetto – del possesso per l'appunto, vale a dire dell'identificazione con esso, dunque dell'abolizione dell'alterità. Così s'era comportato anche il protagonista di *Con gli occhi chiusi* nei confronti di Ghisola: con la quale – e perciò soprattutto ella resiste – egli aveva sostanzialmente imitato l'atteggiamento paterno, anche se invertendo la direzione della manipolazione; in alto anziché in basso. Sicché: «Ma tu non ami proprio me» – aveva dichiarato con piena ragione Ghisola (*Romanzi*, p. 160). Così anche aveva cercato di sognare, continuamente disilluso – destinato a un risveglio crudele – il narratore di *Bestie*, possessore di case, di stanze, e in queste di oggetti svariati, «libri, tavoli, sedie, tagliacarte, cuscini, lampade, pareti», ovvero di poderi, di «carri verniciati di rosso», di «campi verdi», di un gallo «che la mattina fa tremare il cuore di gioia».[6] La de-

---

[5] «Mi ricordo di aver sentito dire, dal nonno, che una volta facevano grandi feste da per tutto; e, ora, invece, è silenzio da per tutto. E non si sente dire più niente. Qualche volta, vorrei entrare sotto terra; giù in fondo, più sotto dei lombrichi» (p. 87).

[6] Cfr. *Bestie* in F. Tozzi, *Cose e persone. Inediti e altre prose*, a cura di G. Tozzi, Firenze, Vallecchi, 1981, pp. 160-61.

lusione cocente sembra consistere nella constatazione della brevità del possesso («Io non avevo mai posseduto niente, che mi fosse durato molto», p. 161), che lo induce a dichiararsi «impazzito per aver pensato subito che io potevo finalmente credere: effetto del mio bisogno di credere» (*ibid.*), e a ripensare alla sua vita «quale avrebbe dovuto essere» (*ibid.*). Ma il «gallo, benché duro» che finisce mangiato (p. 163); il «paio di piccioni» comprati per lui da una madre rediviva, «a cui taglierà le ali perché non mi volino via» (*ibid.*), denunciano, più profondamente, incorporazione e possesso, assorbimento o controllo, riduzione violenta dell'alterità e asservimento al soggetto. Del resto tutti i testi di Tozzi, e *Bestie* e *Cose e persone* in particolare, sono pieni di dichiarazioni e tentativi – sempre falliti – che vanno precisamente in questa direzione: la direzione dell'"egoismo", come sarà denunciata programmaticamente sin dal titolo nel romanzo *Gli egoisti*.[7] Ecco, per un minimo promemoria, da *Cose e persone*: «Quell'umidità entra fino nella mia anima» (p. 173); «Io non vivo se non quando mi sento da me stesso» (p. 177); «Io mi accorsi, allora, che la mia anima sarebbe stata capace di fare quel che fa la primavera; e che ogni cosa che io pensassi potesse nascere da me» (p. 178); «ogni azione degli altri passava attraverso me» (*ibid.*); «Io stesso ero la primavera» (p. 183); «E pensavo d'essere io medesimo il vento» (p. 187).

Ma questo procedere nella «primavera», ovvero nella «giovinezza», «questa voglia di lasciarsi prendere dalla giocondità dell'aria» – come si legge una volta, p. 189 – è presto interrotta da un "ricordo" che l'«avverte, con la presenza soltanto, che è impossibile. Un'altra volta, dunque, ho fatto lo stesso? Un'altra volta, avevo creduto di vivere dimenticando che io sono un essere umano» (*ibid.*). Altrove, anche più icasticamente, il riferimento esplicito alla tentazione superomistica e alla mitologia della creazione artistica, e specificamente della scrittura, è incapsulato in un aneddoto fulminante:

Son così abituato a scrivere che affacciandomi alla finestra e vedendo tutto ricoperto di prati e di erba, mi pare inchiostro verde dove mi viene voglia di intingere la penna. Ma ci pensa da sé la primavera a scrivere quel che vuole [...] E vedo che ho passato tanto tempo a credermi ingiustamente da più di quel muro scalcinato che dallo spigolo della mia casa rinchiude un orto.

Io *vedo* soltanto. Ma tutto può fare a meno di me.

(p. 180)

Una volta su questa china del disincanto, i suoi occhi «cominciano a vedere gli agguati della bellezza; e perciò non credo più a niente. / E non mi fido né meno della dolce erba verde, che ha il torto di non sentire come me questo brivido che mescola la mia nascita con la mia morte. Io sono furioso di vivere, e vorrei non

---

[7] Lì leggiamo, infatti, che l'egoismo «consiste non nello sviluppare gli individui secondo i loro rapporti; ma attribuendo alle idee e ai sentimenti istintivi un'esistenza quasi indipendente. [...] Dario aveva voluto trovare dovunque i segni del proprio pensiero; credendo di potersi sostituire a tutto» (*Opere I, I romanzi*, cit., p. 508).

essere nato» (p. 201). La reazione, caratteristicamente eccessiva, la mania che si rovescia in depressione, precipita nella più straordinaria dichiarazione («Io sono morto una domenica»), in cui il soggetto di *Persone* formula il senso della sua separazione, della sua "esclusione": dagli e degli altri.

Io sono morto una domenica, quando la gente cominciava ad escire di casa ed erano già
passati per la strada della caserma i militari che andavano a suonare. E da quel giorno non
m'è importato più niente di quel che gli altri fanno. Ma ho ricevuto il senso di un silenzio,
che mi fa amare la solitudine. Anche gli altri con me hanno fatto lo stesso; e parlano di me
come se già non esistessi più. Ho sentito parecchie volte questo desiderio di escludermi per
sempre da ogni loro vita!

(pp. 233-34)

Ma al di là, e anche al di qua, della stessa altalena ignara e incapace di ogni mediazione cui sembra condannato il soggetto tozziano, ancora *Persone* contiene ora
alcune pagine, cui Glauco Tozzi diede il titolo *La morte della madre*, in cui è forse
possibile leggere una breve allegoria dell'origine – e conseguentemente della relazione sempre – traumatica dell'altro in Tozzi.

Alla morte della madre, il figlio non fa immediatamente l'esperienza della separazione. Al contrario è la relazione, l'accordo ch'è sottolineato : «Tra me e Lei c'era
qualcosa che non era tra me e gli altri. / Sentivo bene che la mia anima ci teneva
insieme» (p. 252). Ma, a guardar meglio, quest'«insieme» è in realtà un'unità: l'u-
nità della persona del figlio, in cui non solo la madre ma ogni altro è inglobato e
assorbito. È a questo punto, però, che qualcosa di nuovo – di traumatico, come
dicevo – accade.

Mi ricordo bene come io fossi continuamente esaltato, incapace di rendermi conto di
quel che avveniva intorno a me; e solo di quando in quando riuscivo a capire quel che
mi dicevano. E allora le voci mi facevano un effetto potente, quasi vellutato; e compresi
per la prima volta che *io non ero le persone che vedevo* [corsivo dell'autore].

Dopo una giornata trascorsa così, cominciai ad occuparmi della mamma; come non avevo mai fatto né meno quando era in vita. Perciò io credo che il mio affetto cominciasse
soltanto dal suo letto di morte; e di tutto ciò m'è rimasto un profondo terrore, talvolta
comprensibile e talvolta incomprensibile, che si riattacca dietro la mia fede religiosa.

Dio stette molti anni nascosto in me; ma, certo, in quei momenti egli solo disponeva
della mia anima.

(pp. 252-53)

La conoscenza che succede all'esaltazione è, come la visione del ventre di Ghisola con cui termina *Con gli occhi chiusi*, apertura degli occhi, primo riconoscimento dell'alterità dell'altro, scoperta e condizione *sine qua non* dell'amore: «Perciò io
credo che il mio affetto cominciasse soltanto dal suo letto di morte.» C'è voluta la
morte, lo stacco traumatico, perché gli individui emergessero, le identità si impo-
nessero. «E di tutto ciò m'è rimasto un profondo terrore, talvolta comprensibile e

talvolta incomprensibile». Misterioso: che s'intende e non s'intende. Comunque esso colora ogni rapporto con l'altro, con gli altri. La psicanalisi forse invocherebbe istanze superegoiche introiettate dal soggetto (l'osceno Superego, di cui parlava Lacan). Tozzi preferisce menzionare il rapporto con la "fede religiosa", evocare il Dio che «stette molti anni nascosto in me», che, «certo, [...] solo disponeva della mia anima». Dio, l'Altro assoluto, garante dell'esistenza dell'io e degli altri, garante della fiducia vincolante, del patto legante: uomo con uomo, parola con cosa. Solo che di questo Dio, è detto – s'è visto – ch'era "nascosto". E ora, sembra da intendere, non più. Dunque s'è rivelato, si rivela. Si rivela? Come? Quali sono i suoi segni? Chi li interpreta? Come si interpretano? Come devono essere interpretati?

La sera che, dopo che già un rosario di disgrazie ha duramente provato Remigio, muore anche il vitello appena nato, il giovane abbattuto e "sconvolto" si chiede: «Vorrei sapere perché tutto mi va male» (p. 130). È Berto che «a voce alta; perché fosse sentito», dice: «Io credo che queste cose non avvengano senza che Dio non le desideri» (ibid.). Ma è troppo evidente l'impossibilità di attribuire un qualsiasi privilegio autoriale o testuale all'avvenimento. Ciò che non esclude ugualmente il sospetto di Remigio.

Perché era tornato a Siena, se suo padre voleva morire senza farglielo sapere? Perché doventare il padrone della Casuccia quasi di sotterfugio? Egli aveva paura di una cosa ignota, più consistente del suo animo. Ma, benché non avesse pensato a Dio da tanti anni, non poteva credere che Dio volesse annientarlo a quel modo. Che cosa aveva fatto di male? Perché non poteva esistere anche la sua volontà? Ricordò, allora, la sorgente dell'orto, sottile come un filo, quando da ragazzo si divertiva a chiuderla con un poco di argilla: bastava che vi pigiasse sopra il pollice. Pensò anche a tutta la gente che conosceva ed era morta senza che gliene fosse importato nulla. Anch'egli, ora, poteva morire, e nessuno lo avrebbe rimpianto. Dopo qualche anno, nessuno se ne sarebbe più ricordato. Mentre la Casuccia, a ogni primavera, ridoventava verde e fresca; e i pioppi della Tressa si innalzavano sempre di più. Ora, sentiva la sua miseria!

(pp. 134-35)

La «cosa ignota, più consistente del suo animo», potrebbe ovviamente essere Dio, che – nonostante egli forse non abbia fatto nulla di male (forse, perché come può saperlo?) – potrebbe fare con lui come il ragazzo Remigio con la sorgente dell'orto. A differenza del podere, che dura e si rinnova ad ogni primavera, la fragilità, o per dir meglio la mortalità dell'uomo sembrerebbe giocare a favore dell'ancoraggio nel divino. Ma le oneste e rigorose pagine di Tozzi sembrano fermarsi sulla soglia di questo. Lo scrittore ha dunque, secondo me, rifiutato la tentazione di una conclusione ideologica che i dati in gioco nel romanzo non autorizzavano.

Il disimpegno di Remigio è rappresentato nella maniera più delicata e discreta: piena di discernimento. La mattina della domenica tutti si recano alla messa; anche Picciolo, che invita il padrone: «E lei perché non viene mai?' / Remigio si sentì prendere da un sentimento, al quale non aveva mai voluto dare retta; e desiderò di credere» (p. 137). Il testo continua: «Avrebbe voluto rispondere: 'aspettatemi'; ma, invece, sorrise impacciato, e basta» (p. 138). Alla successiva domanda: «Non crede in Dio?» Remigio risponde solo: «Non vengo!» (p. 138). Picciolo allora si scusa per l'insistenza: «Mi perdoni se mi son permesso di consigliarla così! Ma dal tetto in su nessuno sa quanto ci è» (*ibid.*). Per l'appunto: e Remigio apprezza l'intenzione: «Anzi, avete fatto bene. – E gli porse la mano» (*ibid.*).

«Desiderò di credere,» certamente. E il Giulio di *Tre croci.* impossibilitato e incapace di proseguire nell'impostura, a un tratto dichiara, anche lui: «io invidio quelli che possono credere» (*Opere I*, cit., p. 259). Si tratta ancora di Dio; di cui Niccolò non vuol sapere, sicché accusa di delirio il fratello, che finirà con scusarsi: «Ho detto... una cosa qualunque» (p. 260). Non proprio: ma neppure sembra lecito far discorso, nell'uno e nell'altro caso, di ideologia del mistero e di ideologia del sacrificio.[8] D'altra parte, dubito proprio che sia possibile formulare ideologie dell'ottativo. Quel che accade piuttosto nell'ultimo capitolo del *Podere*, come del resto nelle ultime pagine di *Tre croci*, mi sembra che vada non sorprendentemente in altra direzione, riassuntiva e epigrafica invece che conclusiva.

La condanna di Remigio da parte del tribunale non ha neanch'essa alcunché di sorprendente; e così è pure dell'odio di Berto. «Ma l'odio di Berto s'era fatto sempre più forte; e, quando vedeva Remigio nel campo gli veniva voglia di prendere l'accetta» (p. 140). La psicologia e il naturalismo naturalmente non ci hanno nulla a che fare: la necessità di tutto ciò è semplicemente strutturale. Come Caino e Abele, o Romolo e Remo, Remigio e Berto non possono non venire a conflitto, e Abele e Remo non finire massacrati dai fratelli. Ma nessuna fondazione di città seguirà alla furia del delitto: «Remigio seguitava a camminare avanti. Allora, infuriatosi, Berto gli dette l'accetta su la nuca» (p. 141). Si noti che tra l'assalariato e il giovane padrone, che gli ha ordinato di «andare con lui a buttare giù una cascia» (p. 140), non c'è fiducia, ma reciproco sospetto: un sospetto ch'è solo cresciuto con lo sviluppo del romanzo. In particolare di Remigio è detto che «voleva voltarsi per sorridergli, ma non poteva, ed aveva paura» (p. 140). Così la condizione generale di "sfiducia", di assenza di fede, di dissidio e inimicizia vigente nella realtà – che tutto il romanzo s'è incaricato di illustrare – viene ribadita e come sigillata in maniera

---

[8] Come fanno in modo diverso sia F. PETRONI che S. MAXIA (il primo in *Ideologia e logica dell'inconscio nei romanzi di Federigo Tozzi*, Firenze, Manzuoli, 1984; il secondo in *Uomini e bestie nella narrativa di Federigo Tozzi*, Padova, Liviana, 1971). Nell'eccellente, recente libro di ROMANO LUPERINI, *Federigo Tozzi. Le immagini, le idee, le opere*, Roma-Bari: Laterza, 1995, noto con interesse un distanziamento dalle posizioni di Petroni come anche di Giacomo Debenedetti (che in *Il romanzo del Novecento*, Milano, Garzanti, 1971, p. 285, parlava di «una specie di felicità pacificata, catartica» per la chiusa di *Il podere*). Non mi è molto chiaro, tuttavia, quel che Luperini dice sul «valore in sé dei sentimenti», in cui risiederebbe in conclusione «l'unica soluzione» (p. 166): «Per Tozzi la positività non sta nella morte, ma nel valore in sé dei sentimenti» (p. 167). Egualmente problematica mi pare la sua formulazione, su cui ritorna varie volte nel volume, relativa all'«insensatezza dell'esistenza» (*ibid.*), ovvero – nel caso di *Bestie* – al «mondo [che] perde il suo incanto, e diventa una congerie insensata di frammenti» (p. 119). Mi pare invece ovvio che la problematicità o l'ambiguità, o persino l'indecidibilità, dei segni non presuppongono necessariamente la loro mancanza di senso.

drammatica. La grandinata che segue, «qualche ora dopo», all'assassinio, non fa anch'essa che ribadire il dissidio: questa volta tra gli avvenimenti degli uomini e quelli della natura. Nessuna corrispondenza, e semmai estraneità. L'unica pietà sarà quella esercitata dagli umani: «Luigia, piangendo abbracciata ad Ilda, mandò Picciolo e Lorenzo a coprire Remigio con l'incerato del carro» (p. 141). Il gesto, naturalmente, corrisponde a quello delle nipoti che, nel finale di *Tre croci*, «spaccarono il salvadanaio di coccio e fecero comprare da Modesta tre croci eguali; per metterle al Laterino» (*Opere* I, p. 282). [9]

In modo non molto diverso da quello che si riscontra in *Tre croci*, dove diffidenza, inimicizia, e persino odio non risparmiano i rapporti tra i fratelli, e dove, come è detto nell'articolo dedicato da Tozzi a Pirandello, «non ci sono contrasti di vere disuguaglianze, ma lotte magari derivate dal solo bisogno di vivere e di manifestarsi» (p. 275) per una «natura umana [che] non ha mai trovato una perfezione morale» (p. 274), un mondo «concepito in una specie di gastigo, che lo costringe a ritorcersi e a limitarsi» (p. 275); anche nel *Podere* il sospetto è diffuso, endemico, capillare, e il «male e la cattiveria come una condizione naturale che non può essere abolita» (p. 273). [10] Quest'ultima nel romanzo trova una manifestazione riassuntiva, e anche la più cupa e arbitraria, nella furia distruttiva dell'umiliato e offeso Berto, personaggio – come accennavo – per molti versi simmetrico di Remigio. Se il figlio non si riconosce nel padre, non lo continua e resta estraneo all'eredità cui è pervenuto «quasi di sotterfugio» (p. 134) – erede in certo modo "illegittimo" e senza diritto ad essere ricordato («Anch'egli, ora, poteva morire, e nessuno l'avrebbe rimpianto. Dopo qualche anno, nessuno se ne sarebbe più ricordato. Mentre la Casuccia, a ogni primavera, ridoventava verde e fresca; e i pioppi della Tressa si innalzavano sempre di più» [p. 135]) – Berto ha preoccupazioni simili: «Quando sarò morto, chi si ricorderà di me? Non ho né meno un figliolo» (p. 87). Per l'uno e per l'altro manca – s'è strappato o non c'è mai stato – il tessuto di senso, sociale e culturale, che solo una legalità – un ordine superindividuale umano o divino – può fornire. Il mondo per Berto, che ormai si può «dire vecchio» (p. 87), è stato ed è un luogo confinato, oscuro e silenzioso: senza luci e suoni di feste, se mai ce ne furono («Mi ricordo di aver sentito dire, dal nonno, che una volta facevano grandi feste da per tutto; e, ora, invece, è silenzio da per tutto. E non si sente dire più niente», p. 87). Sicché fa venire desiderio di ancora più buio, ancora più silenzio: «Qualche

---

[9] E come non mi pare che il testo autorizzi in nessun modo per *Il podere* estrapolazioni come questa del Baldacci: «Dunque il sacrificio di Remigio non ha placato l'ira di Dio. La serie delle disgrazie non s'interrompe» (p. XLII dell'Introduzione al romanzo in F. Tozzi, *Il podere*, cit.), così nell'altra opera trovo molto arbitrario caricare di eccessive responsabilità ideologiche, e specificamente religiose, quelle povere croci.

[10] Questa, e le descrizioni e definizioni precedenti, sembrano applicarsi ugualmente bene ai comportamenti un po' di tutti gli antagonisti di Remigio nel romanzo, e specialmente all'accanimento, caratteristicamente eccessivo, di Giulia: di cui si dice addirittura che «era invidiosa che un altro potesse fargli del male come soltanto voleva farglielo lei! non voleva che Berto ci riescisse meglio! [...] Le pareva d'essere nata a posta per far del male a lui! Era proprio quella come ci voleva!».

volta, vorrei entrare sotto terra; giù in fondo, più sotto dei lombrichi» (*ibid.*): inducendo, dunque. a questioni più disperate e al desiderio di morte: la propria e quella di altri. «Vorrei sapere perché sono venuto al mondo e che cosa ci ho fatto. Non era lo stesso anche se non nascevo?» (*ibid.*). Desiderio di morte e di violenza, che come il temporale che s'addensa sul paesaggio, dovrà a un certo punto finire per scoppiare: «Berto alzò gli occhi verso il temporale, e si sentì pieno di cattiveria» (p. 88); «Remigio seguitava a camminare avanti. Allora, infuriatosi, Berto gli dette l'accetta su la nuca» (p. 141).

Sempre nell'articolo su Pirandello, Tozzi parla della prevalenza necessaria della negatività nelle opere dello scrittore siciliano: «Egli presuppone sempre un elemento negativo, che alla fine deve sempre prevalere; perché, dopo tutto, è il migliore e il solo che sia ragionevole» (p. 273). Inevitabile, dunque, perché logicamente deducibile dalla situazione inventata. «Non si può sostituire con niente» (*ibid.*). Ma proprio perché non si tratta fin qui di pessimismo pregiudiziale o ideologico, Tozzi può onestamente proseguire parlando di «logica implacabile, che somiglia un poco a una tragedia greca, a cui fosse tolto l'elemento divino» (p. 275). I personaggi che Pirandello ha "concepito" e fatti agire nei suoi testi – e lo stesso potrebbe ripetersi dei personaggi di Tozzi sotto questo profilo – sono «esseri che sono intelligenti fino a un certo punto e a un certo momento; poi è destino [vale a dire, è logicamente attendibile] che debbano spezzarsi» (*ibid.*). Ma – e il punto è, secondo me, capitale per una corretta interpretazione non tanto di Pirandello, quanto di Tozzi, e in particolare del *Podere*, di *Tre croci*, *Gli egoisti* e *L'incalco* – la catastrofe non ha luogo che «dopo aver capito che sarebbe necessario un cambiamento molto profondo» (*ibid.*). Questi personaggi – e il discorso mi pare valere soprattutto per quelli di Tozzi – «sono esseri che s'incontrano per intaccarsi a vicenda e per farsi quasi sempre del male. Quelli che amano, debbono restare con le loro aspirazioni sospese, al di fuori della loro vita quotidiana e immaginata. Debbono convincersi che, a un dato segno della via percorsa, non c'è altro da fare; e si riversano l'uno contro l'altro, perché non bastano a se stessi; ma né meno gli altri bastano, per quanto facciano assaggi magari senza scrupoli. Tutti devono perire nel momento che hanno finito di capire quanto sono inutili e vani i loro sentimenti» (*ibid.*).

Nessuno basta a se stesso, e per questo ognuno si riversa contro l'altro, "intacca" l'altro con cui viene in relazione: inevitabilmente. Finché l'esigenza, per l'appunto da questa condizione imprescindibilmente sollevata, non sarà soddisfatta: «di un cambiamento molto profondo». Che dovrebbe sovvertire i termini della questione, e permettere ai soggetti di rinunciare al sospetto, di ritrovare la fiducia, di credere nuovamente: «che i nostri occhi credano a quel che vedono»,[11] «per trovare nelle cose che ci stanno attorno una completa associazione con noi stessi».[12]

[11] *Pagine critiche*, cit., p. 278 .
[12] *Ivi*, p. 279.

GIOVANNI CECCHETTI

SULL'ALTRO MONTALE*

Anni fa mi trovai a passare alcuni giorni con Sergio Campailla, lo studioso del
Leopardi, del Verga e di tanta letteratura del Novecento; critico letterario finissimo, ma soprattutto romanziere di vaglia, meno apprezzato di quanto veramente
si meriti (quello di non esser riconosciuti in vita fu del resto il destino di tanti; basti
pensare appunto al Leopardi e, per il nostro secolo, al Landolfi). Era da poco uscito
Il Paradiso terrestre, un titolo antifrastico, per una Sicilia che muore di sete e vuole
acqua; ma poi, quando arriva, l'acqua porta la morte anziché la vita; una Sicilia
dominata da un destino avverso, dalla Moira greca, che dopo aver fatto esperimen-
tare al protagonista tutte le spinte vitali, lo trascina nell'Averno. Si tratta d'un romanzo di grande vastità e di grande ricchezza, che fa pensare a un De Roberto di
cent'anni dopo, affascinato dalle tradizioni greche e dalla Mafia, con in mezzo la
nobiltà in tranquilla, e quindi definitiva, decadenza, e con al lato il sesso senz'amore e la violenza vendicativa del nostro tempo.

Ma allora con Campailla parlavo d'altre cose. Soprattutto di quel che stava ac-
cadendo all'università – un ambiente a cui ambedue appartenevamo – e nelle riviste, dove di solito si pubblicava per ragioni d'una carriera fatta o da fare. A un certo
momento mi disse che voleva ritornare sulla Via Appia Antica; che mi toccò una
corda quanto mai sensibile; per cui non osai nemmeno chiedergliene il perché.
Eravamo in uno dei punti più fascinosi della Roma residenziale, dove il Campailla
ha una magnifica casa. Entrammo in macchina, per andare ad azzuffarci con la colluvie smaniante immobile del traffico cittadino, sperando di riuscire a espugnarla.
Alla fine arrivammo e, stanchi d'automobile, ci si mise a camminare sotto i pini.
Più tardi seppi perché il Campailla c'era voluto andare: proprio allora stava scrivendo *Domani domani*, parte del quale ha luogo in una villa in quei paraggi. Per me
invece, totalmente privo di motivi precorritori, quella visita risultò in qualcosa d'altrettanto imprevisto.

Si sa che lungo l'Appia Antica ci s'eran fatta la tomba i Romani più in vista,

* Questo saggio rappresenta il ripensamento d'una nota, per necessità di cose assai più breve, dallo stesso titolo,
uscita in «Campi immaginabili» I/II, la rivista diretta da Rocco Mario Morano.

351

quelli che si credevano illustri, e tanto importanti da decidere il destino degli altri; e più erano gli "altri" e più si sentivano importanti. Ora, di ciascuna di quelle tombe rimane qualche mattone sbrecciato e qualche pezzo di travertino, che non si sa nemmeno a chi sia appartenuto. Ci sono pochissimi nomi, e pressoché indecifrabili. Davanti a quei rottami mi sentii pervaso da un gran senso di tristezza, non solo per quegli antichi gonfi e tronfi, ma per chiunque si costruisce la vita come un castello di superciliose vacuità. E le ceneri? Ci cominciai a pensare intensamente, quasi le volessi vedere. Dove sono le ceneri? E vidi che nei campi limitrofi, tra l'erba che pareva grano, c'erano delle pecore belanti, in cerca d'un agnello, o di qualcuno che le andasse a salutare. Saranno finite lì le ceneri, mille o duemila anni fa? I fumidi, tracotanti Romani trasformati in belati di pecore?

Me ne stavo lì immobile, come abbacinato dai belati, quando mi scosse la voce amica di Sergio Campailla, che, dopo avere accennato a varie cose, si soffermò su certe dicerie che proprio in quei giorni circolavano nei salotti romani, e che dai salotti erano sfociate nei giornali. Lì per lì mi fecero l'impressione di altri belati provenienti da pecore d'altra natura, cioè non visibili nell'erba alta dei campi circostanti. Poi, siccome la cosa cominciò a interessarmi, decisi di occuparmene un po', se non altro per curiosità. Dopo tutto, anche un grande poeta, se perseguitato dal bisogno, può momentaneamente finire su un binario sbagliato, senza però minimamente manomettere o deformare le sue grandi opere. L'*humani* di *humani nihil a me alienum puto* implica anche le possibili cadute dei grandi poeti, altrimenti non sarebbero umani essi stessi, come sicuramente Terenzio ci potrebbe dire anche oggi. Che i tracotanti Romani questo non lo capissero vien dimostrato dal fatto che ci fu bisogno che lo dicesse proprio un poeta.

Era verso la fine di novembre del 1989. I giornali e le riviste accusarono Montale d'essersi fatto scrivere le recensioni dei libri inglesi e americani da Henry Furst, uno studioso notevole, che aveva anche collaborato alla «New York Review of Books». Dicevano che Montale gliele chiedeva con ansiosa insistenza, poi le rimaneggiava in uno stile che fosse veramente suo e le passava al «Corriere della Sera». Doveva aver cominciato verso la fine degli anni Trenta e continuato sino ai Sessanta (Furst morì nel 1967). Questa notizia andava provocando discussioni d'ogni genere, fino a tradursi in un quasi scandalo. Come? Un grande poeta, colui che aveva parlato per tutti nel Novecento italiano, era anche capace di frode?

Chi aveva dato il via era stato, senza volerlo, Mario Soldati, per lunghi decenni amico di Furst, in un libretto di ricordi, *Rami secchi*, uscito in quei giorni. Soldati aveva anche trascritto una specie di poemetto in prosa che, composto da Montale per Furst nel 1943, sarebbe stato stampato solo nel 1969, sul «Corriere della Sera», del 18 maggio 1969. «Per cui», commenta Soldati, «l'amarezza mia e di tutti gli amici di Furst corrisponde in ragione inversa allo splendore del piccolo poema poiché Furst non ebbe mai la gioia di leggerlo».[1] A parte il fatto che il testo uscito sul «Corriere» era in realtà lo stesso (seppure con qualche variante) che Montale aveva già pubblicato molti anni prima, in quelle pagine narrava una visita fatta al Furst e, siccome aveva la mania dei nomi trasformati, di Enrico (Henry) aveva conservato la prima e l'ultima lettera, facendolo diventare Erasmo: un complimento tutt'altro che trascurabile. Il Soldati accennava brevemente a come il Furst aveva collaborato con Montale, eppoi aggiungeva: «Racconto queste cose perché non ci vedo nulla di male».[2] Però non era così per la stampa e per i salotti romani. Si sa: andare in cerca di notizie scandalose, o addirittura inventarle, è una malattia diffusa; i mediocri credono di diventare importanti sparlando di chi non è come loro.

Ma le lettere che Montale scriveva a Furst per chiedergli recensioni urgenti indicano che poi gli passava il compenso pagatogli dal giornale. C'era quindi un accordo, una specie di contratto, che cancella ogni sospetto di sfruttamento da parte di Montale. Non c'è dubbio che gran parte dello scalpore nascesse, come succede, da un senso di delusione, accentuato a sua volta dal fatto che non molto tempo prima s'era diffusa la notizia secondo cui Luisa Rodacanachi aveva fatto da traduttrice-ombra dei capolavori stranieri per conto di Elio Vittorini.

Avvenne anche che, siccome in Italia si giustifica subito tutto con pretesti politici, un allora autorevole esponente del PCI, in un articolo apparso su «Manifesto», si mettesse a dichiarare che Montale aveva fatto benissimo a frodare il «Corriere»; anzi ne aveva tutto il diritto, quel diritto che hanno i poveri (il poeta) di rubare ai ricchi (l'organo ufficiale della borghesia). Aggiungeva che l'Italia doveva sentirsi addirittura in debito verso Montale, per aver avuto questo coraggio, e metteva sullo stesso piano altre frodi civili, considerandole perfettamente legittime, come il rifiuto di pagare le tasse allo Stato. Al che altri obiettarono: perché allora non assolvere anche la Mafia e la Camorra, che a loro modo agiscono contro lo Stato? Pare che quel personaggio del PCI non si rendesse conto che, parlando di azioni frodolente,

---

[1] MARIO SOLDATI, *Rami Secchi*, Milano, Rizzoli, 1989, pp. 123-124. Tutto il capitolo intitolato *Due amici* è dedicato al rapporto di Montale con Furst. *Rami secchi* uscì alla fine d'ottobre. Quanto ai giornali, e specialmente ai settimanali, basta scorrere quelli del tempo per trovarvi commenti e accuse a Montale (non, naturalmente, a Furst). Quando venni a conoscenza di questa vicenda, rimasi turbato. Varie di quelle recensioni eran passate nel volume montaliano *Sulla poesia*, curato da Giorgio Zampa (Milano, Mondadori, 1976), che molti, incluso me, avevan letto, e magari citato, quando andavano alla ricerca di concetti critici, se non estetici, che aiutassero in qualche modo a capir meglio il poeta. A volte m'era accaduto di meravigliarmi che Montale fosse così bene informato su poeti americani e inglesi, come Emily Dickinson, della quale conosceva tutte le raccolte postume e specialmente l'importantissima edizione critica di T. J. Johnson, o come T. S. Eliot ed Ezra Pound – di cui m'ero saltuariamente, seppur modestamente, occupato anch'io.

Il piccolo poema in prosa, che il Soldati dà per inedito sino al 1969, era stato stampato, quasi subito dopo essere stato composto, in «Lettere d'Oggi», n. 3-4 (marzo-aprile 1943), e quindi il Furst aveva avuto ampia possibilità di leggerlo. Il testo uscito sul «Corriere della Sera» del 18 maggio 1969 contiene alcune varianti, poi collazionate per l'edizione critica einaudiana del 1980: E. MONTALE, *L'opera in versi*, a cura di Rosanna Bettarini e Gianfranco Contini, pp. 973-976.

[2] *Op. cit.*, p. 146.

sia pure per giustificarle, non faceva che accusare Montale. Ma questo era parte della logomachia bizantina dei discorsi politici.

Ancor più interessante è che in quei medesimi giorni un dispaccio dell'ANSA dichiarò che Montale non chiedeva recensioni soltanto al Furst, ma anche a Maria Luisa Spaziani, la poetessa torinese che, appena ventiquattrenne, s'era innamorata di lui. Personalmente, la lettura di questa notizia mi riportò al Congresso montaliano tenutosi a Genova sette anni prima, e al quale avevo partecipato su invito appunto di Sergio Campailla. Fra i tanti interventi che avevo ascoltati ce n'era stato uno proprio della Spaziani, che aveva parlato d'una ragazza torinese (cioè di se stessa in terza persona) in possesso di ben ottocento lettere d'amore del poeta, nelle quali non mancavano poesie inedite. S'era espressa con vigoroso ardore, insistendo fra l'altro che Montale aveva dato ordine categorico di non pubblicare quelle lettere prima che fossero trascorsi almeno cinque anni dalla sua morte. Siccome alcune delle sue poesie erano in inglese, aveva chiesto a Glauco Cambon di leggergliele.

Disse anche che la ragazza a cui eran dirette quelle lettere era la Volpe di tante poesie note. E citò una scherzosa imitazione d'Ungaretti da parte di Montale, con questa sua risposta:

> La volpe
> si sconta
> vivendo.

Nonostante il senso d'affettuosa giocosità, pensai che almeno in apparenza Montale, chiamandola Volpe, non l'aveva glorificata; non mi pareva l'appellativo da darsi alla donna che si ama. Eppure la risposta ungarettiana che lei aveva data conteneva qualcosa di spontaneo, quasi un invito tutt'altro che superficiale.[3]

Una decina di giorni dopo vidi Gianfranco Contini, da tempo immemorabile amico e confidente di Montale, e gli raccontai del Congresso di Genova e della Spaziani. Mi disse d'aver sempre saputo che l'ormai celebre Volpe non era altro che lei; ma nelle sue parole c'era un filo di profonda tristezza.

Io avevo conosciuto Montale quand'ero studente universitario e frequentavo il caffè delle «Giubbe Rosse», dove si riuniva il gruppo di poeti e scrittori fiorentini. Poi l'avevo rivisto negli anni Settanta, quando gli diedero la cittadinanza onoraria di Firenze. Non gli ero mai stato amico, anche perché non sapevo di che cosa parlare, fuorché della sua poesia, che m'illudevo di poter benissimo leggere da me; come potevo leggere gli articoli che andava pubblicando. Ero invece rimasto amico di altri, fra cui Mario Luzi, e soprattutto Piero Bigongiari; anche, naturalmente Gianfranco Contini, che però alle «Giubbe Rosse» ci capitava di rado, perché viveva in

---

[3] L'intervento di Maria Luisa Spaziani fu stampato negli «Atti del Convegno Internazionale tenuto a Genova dal 25 al 28 novembre 1982, *La poesia di Eugenio Montale*», a cura di Sergio Campailla e Cesare Federico Goffis, Firenze, Le Monnier, 1984, pp. 322-324. Tutte le citazioni dalla Spaziani derivano da questa versione stampata.

Isvizzera. Tutti e tre li potei poi accogliere in California. Maria Luisa Spaziani invece la conobbi fuggevolmente solo in quel memorabile Congresso genovese, attraverso Glauco Cambon. Avevo letto un paio dei suoi libri, che m'eran sembrati frutto d'una penna diversa da quella di Montale. Quando le fui di fronte, rimasi colpito dalla sua persona, davanti a cui gli uomini potevano anche sentirsi piuttosto piccoli. Non so come si sentisse Montale; che pure era pieno di succhi vitali, nonostante la ritrosia che lo premeva con coloro con cui non era troppo familiare. È probabile che nella Spaziani trovasse non solo calore, ma anche una gracilità e delicatezza interna che andava oltre il fisico. Incontratala nel 1949 a Torino, le era rimasto affezionato per molti anni (l'ultimo contatto fu una cartolina che le spedì da Stoccolma nel 1975, in occasione del premio Nobel).

Pare che ne subisse profondamente il fascino soprattutto nel periodo iniziale. Le tante poesie che allora scrisse per lei le raccolse ne *La bufera*, che uscì a Venezia nel 1956. Fra di esse hanno notevole peso i *Madrigali privati*, in uno dei quali si legge: «Come Pafnuzio nel deserto, troppo / volli vincerti, io vinto». Che Montale stesso commentò così: «Di fronte alla 'volpe' mi sono paragonato a Pafnuzio, il frate che va per convertire Thais ma ne è conquistato. Vicino a lei mi sono sentito un uomo astratto vicino a una donna concreta: lei viveva con tutti i pori della pelle. Ma anch'io ne ricevevo un senso di freschezza, il senso soprattutto d'essere ancora vivo».[4] In un'intervista concessa ad Annalisa Cima, mise la Volpe a confronto con Clizia: «Clizia e la Volpe... una salvifica... l'altra terrena».[5] La Volpe dà quindi il colpo di grazia a Clizia, o almeno vien da sospettarlo; ma presto anche quell'amica volpina sparisce dalla poesia; rimane, a quanto pare, una sostanza epistolografica, e non solo per noi lettori.

Quando l'incontrò, la Volpe aveva quasi trent'anni meno di lui; per lui fu dunque una ventata di giovinezza. Questo l'ha detto anche la Spaziani: nelle lettere del poeta il tono fondamentale è «la gioiosa scoperta d'una condizione sentimentale nuova, il ritrovamento delle emozioni della prima giovinezza e perfino una scintillante allegria». Ha anche aggiunto che «è probabile che la verità di Montale sia in queste lettere, libere dall'ipoteca di quel pudore o ritegno o fastidio che lui sovente dimostrava con le persone che conosceva poco». Tutte frasi in cui si sente la compiacenza e l'orgoglio della donna, non solo d'essersi impadronita dell'uomo (e in questo caso d'un uomo illustre), ma d'avergli dato una vita intensa. Insomma, a differenza delle donne angelicate, come Clizia, la Volpe è tutta forza carnale («lei viveva con tutti i pori della pelle»). Di qui il senso di quel travaso ungarettiano: «La Volpe / si sconta / vivendo». Eppure il poeta l'aveva chiamata «volpe», cioè colei che lo circuiva e l'avvolgeva con la sua sensualità. Credo che la Spaziani abbia capito benissimo tutto il significato di questo nomignolo, e se ne sia sentita fiera, perché conteneva la sua irresistibile femminilità.

---

[4] In GIULIO NASCIMBENI, *Eugenio Montale*, Milano, Longanesi, 1969, p. 156.
[5] In *Eugenio Montale. Profilo di un autore*, a cura di Annalisa Cima e Cesare Segre, Milano, Rizzoli, 1977, p. 194.

Quando la Spaziani entrò nella sua vita, Montale viveva da anni con Drusilla Tanzi, che per lui aveva abbandonato il marito. La chiamava «Mosca», insetto svolazzante e prevedibile, incapace d'astuzia e di trappole. Ben diverso da «volpe». Se la Spaziani ci dice che varie volte le parlò di matrimonio, non credo che questo andasse oltre la normale chiosa offerta a una donna innamorata in momenti felici. Infatti finì con lo sposare la Mosca; cosa che non aveva fatto prima, ma che ora fece allo scopo indubbio di ritrovare se stesso, libero da una passione che sapeva di non poter mantenere accesa. E le circa cinquecento lettere d'amore della Volpe? Le distrusse. Lo fece per proteggere se stesso? Per proteggere lei? O per proteggere le lettere, che avrebbero potuto anche sembrare ripetitive e deludenti, com'è quasi sempre il caso delle lettere d'amore; mentre, rimanendo ignote, avrebbero acquistato il fascino prestato loro dalla fantasia dei non lettori? Ora poteva sentirsi in pace. La Mosca morì nel 1963, e per lei scrisse i bellissimi *Xenia*. Non ritornò alla Volpe.

La notizia dell'ANSA, secondo cui Montale sollecitava recensioni anche dalla Spaziani, è sorprendente. La Volpe ha rivelato con chiarezza che il suo sodalizio col poeta «implicava collaborazioni di vario genere, traduzioni fatte in comune, sporadici interventi nelle rispettive opere, poesie, articoli...». Insomma, non più di quel che fanno due molto vicini, che commentano quel che scrivono. Non pare si tratti d'un Montale che si rivolgeva a lei per recensioni da pubblicare a suo nome sul «Corriere».

Questa volta non posso interrogare il vecchio amico Gianfranco Contini, che purtroppo se n'è andato da qualche anno anche lui. Ma lo vedo sorridere sardonicamente per conto suo. Se la sapeva lunga da vivo, non la deve saper meno lunga da morto. E forse con lui sorride sotto sotto anche Montale, pensando alla sua vecchia Volpe. Per lei scrisse una serie di poesie d'amore, fra le più belle del secolo e forse di tutta la letteratura italiana; tutte in un linguaggio personalissimo quasi completamente fuori della tradizione, in versi davvero memorabili, anche quando ci lampeggian dentro i momenti intimi, o forse proprio allora; fino a quell'*Anniversario*, momento stupefatto, che segna la fine della poesia d'amore di Montale (non è poesia d'amore quell'*Annetta* del *Diario del '71 e del '72*, ma solo di rimpianto della «stagione più ridicola / della vita»), e insieme ci dice che il periodo vissuto con la Volpe è stato di grande importanza per lui; forse è stato proprio allora che ha capito il significato delle apparizioni dentro quei fili di lampeggiamenti che rendono possibile la vita.

* * *

Ma ora debbo passare a una storia che preferirei non fosse mai esistita. Si tratta di un Montale che per un po' si trova su un binario sbagliato e non riesce a scendere. Questa volta c'è una documentazione ben diversa da quella delle recensioni scritte in collaborazione con Furst, col quale, dopo tutto c'era, come s'è visto, un accordo non solo d'amicizia, ma di compenso. Non ultimo quello d'avere scritto per lui un piccolo poema in prosa. Qui c'è davvero l'*humani* di Terenzio; che non bisogna dimenticare, anche se si vorrebbe che non ce ne fosse bisogno.

Nel 1941 una certa Bice Chiappelli presentò a Nicola Spano, direttore delle Edizioni Universitarie di Roma, la traduzione di *The Strange Interlude* di Eugene O' Neill. Lo Spano le scrisse che questa traduzione doveva ormai considerarsi acquisita dalle Edizioni Universitarie e che l'avrebbe fatta esaminare da un «professore competentissimo perché la rivedesse in qualche parte»; aggiungeva poi che la Chiappelli non se ne doveva dolere, perché si trattava di piccolezze. Quindici giorni dopo lo Spano le riscriveva per dirle che il Comitato non aveva riconosciuto la sua traduzione all'altezza delle esigenze letterarie della casa editrice. Non molto dopo quest'altra lettera, il «Giornale della libreria» annunziò che nella collezione diretta proprio da Nicola Spano stava per essere pubblicata una traduzione di *The Strange interlude*, eseguita da Eugenio Montale, il quale poi risultò essere quel «professore competentissimo», a cui era stato dato l'incarico di revisione della traduzione della Chiappelli. La quale, ritenendo che si trattasse d'un plagio, diffidò Montale dal pubblicarla, e contemporaneamente depositò la propria presso la società degli autori.

Nonostante la diffida, Montale non si oppose alla pubblicazione. Ne furono stampate due edizioni, di cui solo la seconda, con poche correzioni che avevano forse lo scopo di cancellare qualche somiglianza col testo della Chiappelli, venne messa in vendita. La prima però era stata depositata presso il Ministero della cultura popolare, dove la Chiappelli la potè esaminare; col risultato che decise di far causa a Montale per plagio aggravato. Nell'inchiesta fu stabilito che il professor Vittorio Amadasi, amministratore della Società Edizioni Italiane, che pubblicava la serie Teatro dell'Università di Roma, aveva suggerito a Montale d'intraprendere la traduzione del dramma di O' Neill, ma poi l'aveva pregato di sospendere il lavoro e di procedere invece alla revisione di quella della Chiappelli. Molti personaggi entrarono nella vertenza, fra cui anche Sergio Baldi, allora professore di letteratura inglese all'università di Pisa. In conclusione, le due versioni furono giudicate molto simili, sino al punto di contenere perfino gli stessi errori. Il processo finì con la condanna di Montale a pagare centomila lire di risarcimento. L'accusa era stata sporta nel settembre del 1947 e la sentenza fu pronunciata nel luglio del 1950.

Montale ricorse in Appello. Deve essersi servito d'un avvocato alquanto ingenuo e sprovveduto, che non solo cercò di provare che il suo cliente non aveva plagiato, ma accusò la Chiappelli d'essere stata lei responsabile di plagio nei confronti di Montale, un fatto che la cronologia più elementare dimostrava impossibile. Montale perse anche l'appello, e fu condannato a pagare le spese processuali nella somma di L. 229.259, più tre quarti delle spese del giudizio d'appello «prenotato a debito». La sentenza fu emessa il 4 maggio 1953. Ma nelle bibliografie montaliane la traduzione del *The Strage Interlude* di O'Neill appare regolarmente come opera sua.

Per quanto io sappia, tutta la storia di questo caso giudiziario fu depositata in qualche sottoscala, dal quale sembra sia uscita solo per venirmi a far visita in California.[6] Nel 1975, appena ricevuto il Nobel, a un giornalista americano che gli chiedeva quale effetto gli facessero i tanti milioni che quel premio comportava, Montale rispose: «Ora mi sento meno infelice». Vien da domandarsi se la (per quel tempo) grossa somma, che il tribunale fiorentino l'aveva condannato a versare nel 1953, non gli fosse pesata per anni.

Va anche aggiunto – sia pure per semplice associazione cronologica – che quel periodo di tensioni e delusioni giudiziarie, concluso nel 1950, ma per subito riaprirsi, fu anche quello dei più intensi rapporti con la Volpe, che certamente dovette fare da contrappeso alle sue sventure.

* * *

Così sulla Via Appia Antica mi trovai a rovistare in tutta una storia d'imprevisti risvolti montaliani, mentre il Campailla si lasciava trascinare dalle sue fantasie romanzesche. Eravamo rimasti in silenzio per quasi un'ora; anche le pecore avevano smesso di belare e s'erano eclissate. Per noi ormai era come se non fossero mai esistite. A un certo momento il Campailla, come uscendo da una specie di *trance*, disse:

«Non credi sia l'ora di tornare a casa?»

Ci si rimise in macchina un po' di malavoglia, forse anche per via della colluvie marasmatica con cui ci si doveva azzuffare un'altra volta. A un certo momento cominciai a parlare di quel che s'andava dicendo di Montale e delle sue recensioni. Avevo esitato un po' a cominciare, probabilmente a causa di tutto ciò che mi s'assiepava dentro. Ben presto arrivai a una conclusione:

«Ne sono un po' turbato. Però non mi sento di dar troppo peso a cose del genere. Nella vita si sbaglia tutti. Quel che rimane, e quindi quel che conta, è quel che si fa. Montale ha scritto alcune delle maggiori poesie del secolo. Questo è ciò che davvero importa».

Campailla annuiva in silenzio. Allora mi misi a recitare quattro esametri dalla chiusa delle *Metamorfosi*, di quell'Ovidio che di sbagli ne aveva fatti di assai più gravi, ma aveva anche regalato a tutti manipoli di grande poesia. Tanto che poteva orgogliosamente cantare:

> Iamque opus exegi, quod nec Iovis ira nec ignis
> nec poterit ferrum nec edax abolere vetustas...

---

[6] Va da sé che né gli Atti del processo del luglio 1950, né quelli del ricorso in Appello del maggio 1953 sono stati mai pubblicati. In mio possesso c'è la copia dei secondi, dai quali si ricavano anche i dati riguardanti il primo processo. Quando, per la prima volta, lessi di questa traversia in cui era caduto Montale, e della quale era stata deuteragonista Bice Chiappelli, siccome in questo caso si trattava d'un cognome pistoiese poco diffuso, domandai a Fredi Chiappelli – un collega del cui trasferimento in California ero stato almeno in parte responsabile – se la conosceva. Mi rispose che non ne sapeva nulla.

parte tamen meliore mei super alta perennis
astra ferar, nomenque erit indelebile nostrum.

(Ho compiuto un'opera che né l'ira di Giove né il fuoco
né il ferro né il tempo divoratore potran mai annullare...
Il meglio di me volerà immortale oltre le stelle
sublimi, ed il mio nome rimarrà indelebile).

LUCIANO REBAY

MONTALE TESTIMONE DEL NOVECENTO[1]

Il Novecento è stato marcato dalla presenza di Montale quasi da un capo all'altro, fino a questo tardo 1996 che giusto nel primo centenario della sua nascita è venuto ad arricchirsi di una sua postrema silloge di versi, le ottantasei poesie di *Diario postumo* pubblicato da Mondadori lo scorso febbraio. Vi fa spicco un componimento intitolato *Secondo testamento*, datato «1976», allorché il testante aveva dunque ottant'anni:

> Non so se un testamento in bilico
> tra prosa e poesia vincerà il niente
> di ciò che sopravvive.
> L'oracolare tono della versificazione
> non cadrà nell'indifferenza
> e un brandello, una parte della mia
> impotenza farà vendetta del prima
> e dell'ignoto. Non scelsi mai la strada
> più battuta, ma accettai il fato
> nel suo inganno di sempre.
> Ed ora che s'approssima la fine getto
> la mia bottiglia che forse darà luogo
> a un vero parapiglia.
> Non vi è mai stato un nulla in cui sparire
> già altri grazie al ricordo son risorti,
> lasciate in pace i vivi per rinvivire
> i morti: nell'aldilà mi voglio divertire.

Se da una parte, mentre «s'approssima la fine», Montale estendeva a proprio beneficio non senza festosa malizia il palazzeschiano «E lasciatemi divertire!», dall'altra ovviamente intendeva affiancare questo *secondo* testamento al precedente, integrandolo cioè con il *Piccolo testamento* stilato nel '53 e unitamente al «Sogno del

---

[1] Intervento al Convegno Internazionale *Roma per Montale nel centenario della nascita 1896-1996*, Roma, Sala dell'Ercole (Campidoglio), 31 maggio 1996.

prigioniero» posto a conclusione "provvisoria" della *Bufera e altro*, nel quale si dichiarava che l'«eredità» affidabile in quel momento all'avvenire non poteva essere se non la «testimonianza / d'una fede che fu combattuta / d'una speranza che bruciò più lenta / di un duro ceppo nel focolare». Seguiva la lucida riflessione che «una storia non dura che nella cenere / e persistenza è solo l'estinzione», in cui veniva posto l'accento non solo sull'ineluttabilità del perire, ma anche su un "durare" e "persistere", cioè sull'idea che, nel mondo, qualcosa dell'uomo può in qualche modo sopravvivere alla sua morte. Infine nel componimento che chiudeva il libro, «Il sogno del prigioniero», in effetti si affermava che ciò che conta è il coraggio di ripudiare quanti sostengano che solo «chi abiura e sottoscrive / può salvarsi». Cosicché ora, un ventennio dopo, *Secondo testamento* può implicitamente concludere che tirate le somme è stato giusto non seguire «la strada / più battuta», giusto accettare il proprio destino di isolato e persino di «impotente» rifiutando di consentire a ideologie o fedi qualsivoglia solo perché abbracciate da una maggioranza. Della bottiglia gettata in mare con gesto reminiscente di un altro componimento della *Bufera*, rimontante al 1940, «Su una lettera non scritta», è oggi fiduciosamente prevedibile l'approdo anche se il messaggio in essa contenuto potrà poi suscitare controversie e dissensi.

A quindici anni dalla sua scomparsa la "testimonianza" di Montale rimane quella non solo di un grande poeta e scrittore, insuperato fra i moderni, ma di un uomo esemplare del nostro tempo. Un uomo che dagli anni giovanili del «meriggiare pallido e assorto» fra gli orti dei limoni e il mare delle liguri Cinque Terre, fino a quelli dell'età avanzata che lo videro successivamente Doctor Honoris Causa dell'Università di Cambridge, senatore a vita della Repubblica del suo paese, e infine Premio Nobel, non ha mai cessato di impartire una lezione di coerenza e di misura, nonché di quella speciale qualità che in una sua celebre pagina viene chiamata «decenza quotidiana (la più difficile delle virtù)» – il tutto rifuggendo da atteggiamenti o intonazioni *ex catedra* ma anzi alzando la voce il meno possibile. Di modo che l'autore il quale aveva composto non ancora trentenne «Non chiederci la parola» mentre l'Italia soccombeva al fascismo, e che anni dopo, in «Primavera hitleriana», concludeva che di quel nefasto capitolo di storia «nessuno» – cioè nessun Italiano – poteva considersi «incolpevole»; più tardi ancora, mentre nuove generazioni s'apprestavano ad approdare sulla luna, insisteva in una rappresentazione di se stesso e della condizione umana secondo una sua concezione del mondo tipicamente riduttrice e demitizzante:

> Ho contemplato dalla luna, o quasi,
> il modesto pianeta che contiene
> filosofia, teologia, politica,
> pornografia, letteratura, scienze
> palesi o arcane. Dentro c'è anche l'uomo,
> ed io tra questi. E tutto è molto strano.

Tra poche ore sarà notte e l'anno
finirà tra esplosioni di spumanti
e di petardi. Forse di bombe o peggio,
ma non qui dove sto. Se uno muore
non importa a nessuno purché sia
sconosciuto e lontano.

Intitolato «Fine del '68» e composto al tempo della guerra americana nel Vietnam che agli occhi dello scrivente vanificava qualsiasi eventuale motivo di vanto per conquiste extraterrestri, questo testo fu incluso in *Satura*, pubblicato a quindici anni di distanza dalla *Bufera*, nel 1971. A cominciare da quella raccolta, e continuando poi con le altre che dovevano farvi seguito in rapida successione, frutto di un getto ispirativo di impeto e tenacia senza precedenti nella sua carriera, Montale in un certo senso compie un passo indietro: lo chiamerà lui stesso nel corso della tenzone con Pier Paolo Pasolini (*Diario del '71*) «un rispettabile / prendere le distanze». Ciò gli consente fra l'altro di rivisitare i fondali di quelle pietre miliari della sua opera che sono *Ossi di seppia*, *Le occasioni* e *La bufera*, di riassimilarne toni e motivi alla luce di una diversa prospettiva che il trascorrere degli anni rendeva ora possibile, e infine di riorchestrare il discorso su un nuovo registro in cui lo stile alto mantenuto fino agli anni Cinquanta viene volontariamente abbassato di tono anche allo scopo di sottolineare un impegno di partecipazione alle più vive istanze del suo tempo sotto il segno di una caparbia indipendenza di pensiero e di un sistematico *understatement*. Impegno, in particolare, a prendere posizione contro il pregiudizio, l'intolleranza e la chiusura dogmatica, in nome della libertà di giudicare, di dubitare, di accettare il diverso e di affermare il contrario. Onde per esempio, poniamo sul piano teologico-religioso, o delle scelte in campo politico, quella sorta di bibbia laica o antibibbia – commenti, riflessioni, aforismi – in cui frequentemente s'imbatte il lettore, tipo: «Tutte le religioni del Dio unico / sono una sola; variano i cuochi e le cotture». Oppure: «È neonato anche Dio. A noi di farlo / vivere o farne senza». O anche: «Ora / vivo dentro due chiese che si spappolano, / dissacrate da sempre, mercuriali, / dove i pesci che a gara vi boccheggiano / sono del tutto uguali». O in sede che potremmo chiamare di "teoria della letteratura", rasentando il *nonsense* con l'occhio rivolto a presumibili addetti ai lavori: «L'angosciante questione / se sia a freddo o a caldo l'ispirazione / non appartiene alla scienza termica. / Il raptus non produce, il vuoto non conduce, / non c'è poesia al sorbetto o al girarrosto. / [...] Il fatto non è importante». E si potrebbe continuare.

Ma resta da aggiungere almeno questo. Nel perseguire il disegno minimizzante caratteristico della sua seconda maniera, Montale non esita a dirigere la satira, l'ironia, e fin l'irrisione contro sé medesimo; ed è qui che la sua opera si distingue recisamente da quella di quasi ogni altro fra i "maggiori" non solo del Novecento, ma dell'intera tradizione letteraria italiana, nella quale gli autori capaci di ridere di se stessi e all'occorrenza di autoumiliarsi si contano tutt'al più sulle dita di una sola mano. Oltre che nel genere comico gli italiani possono infatti eccellere nell'impiego dell'ironia e del sarcasmo, oppure – ma questo solo pochissimi – nella dissacrazione di alto livello formale. Si pensi a quella che riesce a compiere, di Dante, un eccezionale poeta qual è Carlo Porta, il quale magistralmente rovescia dall'interno e fa esplodere in riso non solo alcuni brani canonici dell'*Inferno*, ma l'altrettanto sacro e quasi per tacita convenzione inviolabile «Tanto gentile e tanto onesta pare», cui il poeta milanese oppone il mirabile «Sura Caterinin», sonetto cui il Belli darà poi due repliche in romanesco. Si tratta però sempre di ricorrenze in cui la satira, il sarcasmo, la parodia, anche se di superiore fattura, operano esclusivamente a scapito di qualcun altro, cioè appunto del parodiato. Sulla scia di una linea autoironizzante che nella poesia moderna ha radici in un Laforgue, e, in Italia, in un Gozzano o in un Palazzeschi, Montale ha invece lasciato anche in questo campo una sua impronta inconfondibile. Inevitabile il confronto con il maggior vate degli inizi del secolo, il «maestro di tutti noi» come lo chiamava Ungaretti ancora negli anni Venti, D'Annunzio, il quale per esempio grandiosamente battezzava la sua villa-mausoleo sul Garda «Il Vittoriale degli Italiani». Mette conto ricordare questo particolare per rilevare che alla sua propria "vittoria" nell'ambito della storia letteraria del Novecento Montale giunge non già adducendo trionfi, ma al contrario annoverandosi per così dire fra i perdenti. In un mondo di aquile e di topi non si periterà di identificarsi con i secondi, con i limiti e le tare che tale libera ammissione comporta, ma così facendo distaccandosi aristocraticamente dai molti che, veri topi, vanamente vorrebbero passare per aquile. È quanto viene implicitamente affermato nell'austero, amaro finale di «Botta e Risposta-I», il componimento del 1961 che apre *Satura*:

> (Penso
> che forse non mi leggi più. Ma ora
> tu sai tutto di me,
> della mia prigionia e del mio dopo;
> ora sai che non può nascere l'aquila
> dal topo).

E non è tutto. Dieci anni più tardi, nel *Diario del '71*, oserà rincarare audacemente l'autoirrisione in un piccolo capolavoro di volontario *self-punishment* nato da uno spunto di vita vissuta, come sempre nella sua opera, nella fattispecie una frase dialettale rivoltagli in punto di morte dalla milanesissima "Mosca", la quale, vedendo il marito muto e accasciato, gli avrebbe lanciato contro a bruciapelo, si può immaginare per scuoterlo dal suo malinconico torpore, un epiteto volgare corrente nella parlata di Milano. Recepito in extremis esso "agì" non diversamente dal nome «Buffalo» nell'omonimo componimento delle *Occasioni*, e ne risultò una poesia così meravigliosamente autodenigratoria, «Il pirla», che forse non ha l'uguale nella storia della lirica europea:

> Prima di chiudere gli occhi mi hai detto pirla,
> una parola gergale non traducibile.
> Da allora me la porto addosso come un marchio
> che resiste alla pomice. Ci sono anche altri
> pirla nel mondo ma come riconoscerli?
> I pirla non sanno di esserlo. Se pure
> ne fossero informati tenterebbero
> di scollarsi con le unghie quello stimma.

Fermo rimane, si capisce, che in ultima analisi anche un poeta del rango di Montale non può che porre il lettore di fronte a uno specchio. La saggezza di guardarvi dentro e il coraggio di riconoscervi tratti magari imbarazzanti – quella saggezza e quel coraggio ognuno dovrà trovarli in se stesso.

PIER MASSIMO FORNI

IL PANE DI NOVENTA

Quasi ogni discorso sulla poesia di Giacomo Noventa riconduce a bene attestati nodi critici che coinvolgono strumento linguistico, ambiti di predicabilità poetica e livelli di stile.[1] Di rigore, in particolare, il riferimento al saggio fondativo di Giacomo Debenedetti, nel quale decisamente caratteristiche sono affermazioni di questo tipo: «Ma il dialetto può parlare enfaticamente, senza le stonature e il ridicolo dell'enfasi. Nel dialetto anche le cose più grandi, più monumentali paiono bonarie, come in un vecchio proverbio. Il dialetto restituisce confidenzialità anche alle affermazioni più solenni. [...] Il dialetto di Noventa è come una citazione latina rovesciata: invece che la sublimità di un parlare classico ed aulico, l'umiltà di un'apparente bonomia, di un parlare che smorza la grandezza del tono» (Debenedetti, pp. 193-194).

Passe-partouts accettabili, quando si abbia l'accortezza di passare poi a distinguere in fase di analisi testuale. Non direi per esempio, che il registro stilistico del verso «E me continuo vardando nel çiel» nella lirica *El saòr del pan...* coincida con quello dei tre che lo seguono: «Ancùo so che Dio no' pol esser / Lontan da mi: / E ch'el xé dapartuto». Si potrà dire di questi ultimi che il dialetto restituisce confidenzialità

[1] Per questa lettura ho consultato, assieme ad altri, i seguenti contributi. F. MANFRIANI, *Prefazione* a G. NOVENTA, *Versi e poesie*, a cura di F. Manfriani, Venezia, Marsilio, 1986, pp. XI-LXV (dall'edizione Manfriani ho tratto i testi di Noventa qui utilizzati); G. DEBENEDETTI, *Noventa*, in ID., *Poesia italiana del Novecento. Quaderni inediti*, Milano, Garzanti, 1974, pp. 185-209; G. PAMPALONI, *Giacomo Noventa. L'"appello al valore" nell'ideologia "cattolica liberale": il dialetto veneto e la rimozione della lingua aulica italiana*, in *Novecento. I contemporanei. Gli scrittori e la cultura letteraria nella società italiana*, a cura di G. Grana, IV, Milano, Marzorati, 1979, pp. 3762-3775; F. FORTINI, *Noventa e la poesia*, in ID., *Saggi italiani*, Milano, Garzanti, 1987, pp. 76-92; R. LUPERINI, *Il Novecento. Apparati ideologici ceto intellettuale sistemi formali nella letteratura italiana contemporanea*, Torino, Loescher, 1981; E. GIOANOLA, *Giacomo Noventa: dialetto e poesia*, in *Giacomo Noventa*, a cura di F. Manfriani, Firenze, Olschki, 1988, pp. 50-62; F. BREVINI, *Giacomo Noventa*, in *Poeti dialettali del Novecento*, a cura di F. Brevini, Torino, Einaudi, 1987, pp. 155-166; G. DE ROBERTIS, *Versi e poesie*, in ID., *Altro Novecento*, Firenze, Le Monnier, 1962, pp. 340-43; M. PRALORAN, *Il "cantar" allusivo. Metrica e stile in Noventa*, «Rivista di Letteratura Italiana», IX, 1991, 3, pp. 521-564; F. FIDO, *Introduzione alla lirica veneta del Novecento*, in ID., *Il paradiso dei buoni compagni. Capitoli di storia letteraria veneta (Ruzante, Calmo, Giancarli, Parabosco; Baretti, Chiari, Casanova, Goldoni; Noventa, Marin, Giotti, Pasolini)*, Padova, Antenore, 1988, pp. 194-229; S. FISH, *Literature in the Reader: Affective Stylistics*, in ID., *Is There a Text in This Class? The Authority of Interpretive Communities*, Cambridge, Massachusetts, 1980, pp. 21-67.

ad un'affermazione solenne, o perlomeno che smorza la grandezza del tono. Nel caso del primo, invece, il dialetto sembra operare meno efficacemente in senso riduttivo. Una vibrazione di sublime s'impone a dispetto dello strumento linguistico (o forse in parte grazie ad esso). Il fatto è che Noventa bara al gioco del dialetto, se è barare il ricorrere a soluzioni non strettamente dialettali, utilizzare una lingua mista, che si libera dalle pastoie vernacolari. Come afferma con evidenza incipitaria in un altro testo lo stesso poeta: «Mi me son fato 'na lengua mia / Del venezian, de l'italian».

Rimane tutto sommato condivisibile che solo grazie al dialetto Noventa «ha potuto rinominare cose, fatti, persone, affetti riconsiderandoli patriarcalmente, in un rapporto quotidiano e tradizionale di cui la poesia contemporanea non sa né può più tener conto: i figli, la moglie, la madre riappaiono qui con esplicita immediatezza, coi nomi che si usano anche in prosa; ma questi nomi, figlio, moglie, madre possono figurare poeticamente in una poesia solo perché sono divenuti dialettalmente: "fioi, mugèr, mare". Così ridimensionati in dialetto, questi nomi cantano con tutta la loro forza di propagazione sentimentale ed emotiva: mentre nella poesia in lingua la citazione nuda di questi nomi sembrerebbe dare al discorso una piega di banale sentimentalismo, parrebbe subito una di quelle cose che in poesia non si fanno più» (Debenedetti, p. 198).

Doveroso insistere sulle nozioni di "esplicita immediatezza", di "citazione nuda": osservare cioè che in gioco non è soltanto il repertorio ma anche lo stile. Se è vero che il dialetto consente di parlare di cose interdette alla poesia in lingua, grazie al dialetto è possibile parlare *in un certo modo*, di cose ammissibili anche nella poesia in lingua: un certo modo che consiste spesso nell'eliminare le stilizzazioni e rarefazioni che rendono predicabili quelle cose nella poesia in lingua. Di nuovo: non si tratta della sola sfera del *cosa*, ma anche di quella del *come*.

Come abbiamo cominciato a vedere, tuttavia, bisognerà far uso assai cauto delle categorie della semplicità e dell'immediatezza (nozionali ed artistiche) nel dare ragione critica di questi testi indubbiamente segnati da una certa qual minorità linguistico-stilistica. La poesia di Noventa «è, consapevolmente, al tempo stesso aristocratica e popolare. Popolare per la vena del canto, l'abbandono a immagini semplici, di aperta passionalità, e per la stessa violenza dei sarcasmi e della carica politica. Aristocratica per la elegantissima strumentazione letteraria della vena popolaresca, per l'intervento sempre pungente dell'intelligenza e dell'ironia, per la raffinata sapienza metrica, per il modo con cui si pone come erede della grande tradizione letteraria. E la "lingua" del poeta è esattamente aristocratica e popolare, con il sigillo di continue variazioni inventive sul fondo memoriale e materno del "dialetto" di cui s'impossessa» (Pampaloni, p. 3773).[2]

---

[2] «Per Noventa il dialetto è appena un velo della pronuncia, un modo di tenere a distanza l'impossibile lingua della tradizione letteraria nazionale». Così Fortini (p. 81), che poi specifica: «Sono pochissime le locuzioni propriamente dialettali. In una sola poesia, probabilmente una delle prime, *garanghèlo, ciacolàr, schèi, stracarse*. Nelle

Tra i testi più frequentemente usati a riprova di consolidate opinioni critiche sulla poetica di Noventa è la poesia cui abbiamo accennato, *El saòr del pan....* In realtà si tratta soprattutto di un utilizzo sommario del primo verso, che colpisce per immediatezza, per nuda menzione degli oggetti. Noventa, ci ricorda Debenedetti, elabora una critica radicale della modernità: avendo la cultura moderna scelto una strada sbagliata «bisogna intanto mettersi a parlare diversamente da lei, in un linguaggio che torni a chiamare pane il pane. Perché gli inganni di quella cultura sono probabilmente così sofistici, aberranti ed enormi, che il pane non si chiama più pane, e non vi si distingue né si gode più di quello che Noventa ritrova al principio di [una] sua poesia: "el saòr del pan e la luze del çiel"» (Debenedetti, p. 199). Nella scia di Debenedetti si colloca, tra altri, Luperini, affermando che il poeta eleva la propria lingua-dialetto «a dignità e valore, a luogo di una vagheggiata unificazione di aristocrazia e di popolo, a linguaggio privilegiato capace di restituire verginità alle cose e al discorso che le nomina, di rendere "el saòr del pan e la luse del çiel"» (Luperini, p. 658).

Non mi risulta che alla fortuna critica del verso sia corrisposta finora una puntuale disamina della poesia cui esso appartiene. Di qui il progetto di chiosa concretatosi in queste pagine. Anziché utilizzare il testo, o parti di esso, per sostenere proposte critiche di carattere generale, ho inteso mettere in luce lo specifico interesse poetico del testo stesso, un interesse che ritengo tutt'altro che secondario. Sarà il lettore a decidere se e in che misura i risultati del lavoro siano utilizzabili al di là dell'oggetto d'immediato interesse. Mentre possiamo contare su un buon numero di saggi di ricognizione complessiva, la fase della lettura esercitata con pazienza critico-filologica su singoli testi si trova tuttora, se non sbaglio, alle battute iniziali. Il mio lavoro vuol essere principalmente e semplicemente un contributo a questa nuova pagina nella fortuna critica del poeta di Noventa di Piave.

* * *

El saòr del pan...

(a Franca)

El saòr del pan, e la luse del çiel
Gèra inçerti prima de tì.
Ancùo me par una grazia el me pan,
E me continuo, vardando nel çiel.
Ancùo so che Dio no' pol esser
Lontan da mi:

altre, *cofà, tosi, putela, zigarò, massa, sgorlar, ancùo, mone, sconti, sbrissada, bonorive, sentarse, destraviarme, un fià, a remengo, foghèr...* Mentre la sintassi è tutta di origine colta e di tradizione classica, non senza arcaismi, criptocitazioni, ecc.». (p. 81, n. 2).

E ch'el xé dapartuto.
Mi te strenzo: e cô i brassi te perde,
Mi te çerco e te trovo partùto.

Il primo distico è una sorta di prologo all'Inferno, o al Limbo, l'impressionistica resa di un'epoca non ancora benedetta dall'epifania femminile, evocazione dell'universo del *tunc* dal quale viene liberandosi quello del *nunc*. Tutta la poesia si coordina su una spartizione temporale, o meglio su una contrapposizione epocale. L'irredento mondo del *tunc* è tutto confinato in questi versi di apertura. Fortissimo l'effetto di soglia: il verso 2 sigillato nel marcato accento di «prima de tì», il 3 avviato con la inequivocabile determinazione temporale «Ancùo». Il discorso lirico è, appunto, reso possibile dallo snodo eventivo tra il mondo del "prima" e quello dell'"ancùo" in cui si attua la *conversio* del soggetto lirico. La demarcazione temporale è poi rinforzata a breve distanza: «Ancùo so che Dio no' pol esser / lontan da mi».

Su un totale di nove versi, i primi sette instaurano, sia pure non esclusivamente, ritmi fratti. Si osservi la varianza del conto sillabico, la marcata non corrispondenza di unità metrica e unità logica («Ancùo so che Dio no' pol esser / Lontan da mi»), l'impuntarsi di piú d'un verso su un accento di ultima sillaba. Il distico conclusivo porta una facilmente percepibile correzione. Rimangono cosí individuate due compagini ritmiche in cui prevale rispettivamente il parlato e il cantato. La divisione ritmica corrisponde alla divisione tematico-temporale. Lo scioglimento dei nodi del parlato lirico in afflato melico («Mi te strenzo, e cô i brassi te perde, / Mi te çerco e te trovo partùto») avviene in corrispondenza del dissolvimento della distinzione epocale. Con gli ultimi due versi un eterno presente si afferma in modo definitivo sulla coscienza delle frazioni di tempo grazie alle quali la voce poetica era affiorata all'esistenza («prima de tì [...] Ancùo [...] Ancùo»).

La ripetizione di "ancùo" in posizione incipitaria fa parte di un sistema di echi o legature:

del pan – el me pan
del çiel – nel çiel
prima de tì – lontan da mi
dapartuto – partuto
Mi te strenzo e – Mi te çerco e
te perde – te trovo

Questa legatura è, in parte, risposta alla libertà del parlato, correzione dei ritmi prosastici che contribuisce a stabilire il tono poetico medio del testo. Ammessa almeno un'escursione nel sublime:

E me continuo, vardando nel çiel.

Il verso è la punta lirica, l'anelante vibrazione di maggior frequenza, l'acuto poetico di tutto il componimento. Vale forse la pena di precisare (non sono mancate le sviste) che si fonda su di una forma verbale non attiva ma riflessiva. «Me continuo» non significa "io continuo" ma "mi continuo", "continuo me stesso". Non si predica qui un banale continuare a vivere guardando nel cielo, ma una continuazione dell'essere nell'infinito celestiale. L'io poetante si protende con abbandono verso il cielo, si stempera nel cielo, va a sostanziarsi di cielo. Dantescamente: s'inciela. La distinzione è importante anche perché consente di rendere puntuale giustizia alla componente religiosa dell'esperienza configurata. Il cielo sta per diventare, infatti, il cielo di Dio.[3] L'essere supremo, presente in modo implicito nei primi quattro versi (il "çiel" di 1 e 4 e la "grazia" di 3), viene esplicitamente nominato nel verso 5: «Ancùo so che Dio».

La presenza divina nel componimento appare strettamente connessa con quella del "tu" cui il discorso è rivolto. Si osservi intanto, a proposito di questo "tu", che non affiora in alcun punto un'indicazione di genere grammaticale. Non un participio passato, non un pronome, nulla che possa indicare se il "tu" lirico sia da intendere al maschile o al femminile. Si vedano, per contrasto, le quartine del sonetto *Colpa d'amor...* (un testo ravvicinabile al nostro per lo schema della divisione epocale instaurata dall'avvento della donna) dove l'identificazione è inequivocabile:

> Colpa d'amor, e no' mancanza d'arte,
> Fa che i poeti moderni sragiona:
> I se contenta de qualunque dona,
> E po' i la vol beata su le carte.

> A sta busía mi gò concesso in parte
> Movendo i primi passi in Elicona;
> Ma tì ti-ssi vignùa, e in tì no' stona
> El nostro vero amor co' 'l me inventarte.

Per consolidare un'identità femminile nel *Saòr del pan...* bisogna invece affidarsi alla periferia del testo, dove compare una dedica "a Franca". Ricognizioni extratestuali portano a Franca Reynaud, sposata da Noventa poco dopo la composizione di questi versi, collocabile nel Febbraio del 1933. La dedica a Franca, ovviamente,

---

[3] Per il nesso cielo-luce-Dio in Noventa si vedano i luoghi seguenti: «Cô no' ghe sarà più stele nel çiel, / E anca el sol sparirà / Ne la luse de Dio» [*Cô no' ghe sarà più stele... (Il giudizio universale)*]; «In alto, in alto, nel çiel, / Dove una volta ai me veci, / E anca ai tui, Franco Lattes!, / Se mostrava el Signor, / Vola una cagna» [*In alto, in alto, nel çiel (Dopo il primo Sputnik russo)*]; «"Cossa ghe xé, pare mio, / Al de là de 'sto çiel?" / "Çiel, fio." / "E al de là?" / "Çiel ancora." / "E al de là?" / "In malora: al de là ghe xè Dio."» [*Cossa ghe xè, pare mio... (Teologie)*]. «Società puramente razionale è per Noventa la casta degli intellettuali e dei politici, che proprio per questo non hanno più nulla da dire, del tutto disertati ormai dalla poesia e dall'ispirazione avendo fatto deserto dei valori. Per questo il linguaggio della casta, l'italiano nato dalla letteratura assieme con l'epoca moderna, è vuoto e sterile, luogo del Detto e non del Dire, dei concetti e non del desiderio, lingua incatenata e morta perché non può più dire Dio» (Gioanola, p. 57).

orienterebbe la nostra lettura anche se non sapessimo nulla di Franca Reynaud: poesia per una donna, lode della donna amata, nel solco della tradizione lirica di tutti i tempi e di tutti i paesi.

Ma immaginiamo di non essere orientati dalla dedica: i primi quattro versi possono portarci in una diversa direzione, grazie agli accenti di preghiera e di resa di grazie (forse anche eucaristica) che li pervadono. Del tutto normale intendere il "tu" di quella compagine come Dio: Dio che entra nella vita di un uomo dando ad essa un marchio di verità e una sostanza di grazia che prima non aveva. Ecco però che con il verso 5 ci troviamo costretti a rivedere la nostra presupposizione: il testo c'induce infatti a considerare Dio entità diversa rispetto a quella del "tu" lirico.[4] La nostra "errata" lettura della prima parte della poesia segna, tuttavia, la percezione della seconda. Non è possibile, cioè, un approccio vergine ai versi dove affiora nuovamente un "tu" («Mi te strenzo: e cô i brassi te perde, / Mi te çerco e te trovo partùto») dato il "tu" divino che ci accompagna. La nostra immagine mentale di Dio si trasforma in quella di una persona amata, e la metamorfosi diventa parte del significato poetico-nozionale del testo.[5]

Un effetto simile può essere tuttavia prodotto anche da una lettura orientata, in cui il "tu" venga inizialmente inteso come rivolto alla Franca della dedica. Il poeta si rivolge alla donna riconoscendo i benefici effetti prodotti dall'avvento di questa nella sua vita. Nozioni di storia letteraria permettono d'inserire il componimento nella tradizione lirica della esaltazione e venerazione della donna che ha alle proprie origini nel volgare italiano i Siciliani, gli Stilnovisti, il giovane Dante. Questo bagaglio culturale ci predispone a modellare i contenuti su schemi poetico-spirituali in cui la donna è vista come agente di salute morale e salvezza e, infine, a intravvedere un elemento di complessità che risulta arricchimento decisivo della signifi-

---

[4] A meno di non pensare a questo improbabile schema: 1) i primi quattro versi si rivolgono a Dio; 2) i versi 5-7 rappresentano un intermezzo (riflessione interna o rivolta a un altro interlocutore o a un pubblico); 3) l'ultimo distico riprende il colloquio con Dio. Ovviamente, in questa lettura arzigogolata l'intermezzo potrebbe anche iniziare al verso 3.

[5] Riscopriamo cosí l'importanza della componente temporale (il *temporal flow* di cui parla Stanley Fish) ovvero della sequenzialità nella fruizione dei testi letterari. «The basis of the method is a consideration of the *temporal flow* of the reading experience, and it is assumed that the reader responds in terms of that flow and not to the whole utterance. That is, in an utterance of any length, there is a point at which the reader has taken in only the first word, and then the second, and then the third, and so on, and the report of what happens to the reader is always a report of what has happened *to that point*. (The report includes the reader's set toward future experiences, but not those experiences)» (Fish, p. 27). Le esperienze future risultano poi colorate dalle aspettative sequenzialmente prodottesi. «What I am suggesting is that there is no direct relationship between the meaning of a sentence (paragraph, novel, poem) and what its words mean. Or, to put the matter less provocatively, the information an utterance gives, its message, is a constituent of, but certainly not to be identified with, its meaning. It is the experience of an utterance – *all* of it and not anything that could be said about it, including anything I could say – that is its meaning» (*ivi*, p. 32). Ovviamente questo modo di vedere la produzione di significato privilegia la prima lettura. Bisognerà poi tener conto degli aggiustamenti portati da letture successive in cui l'approccio temporale (sequenziale) venga sostituito da uno essenzialmente spaziale (strutturale). Rischio del lettore professionista è di ancorare troppo saldamente il proprio discorso critico all'oggetto finito, all'oggetto come struttura data, come configurazione spaziale, finendo col non rendere giustizia alla complessità eventiva della fruizione testuale.

cazione poetica complessiva.[6] Mentre inscena esplicitamente una contrapposizione epocale in scala minore (la storia di un uomo e di una donna), il testo infatti evoca una contrapposizione epocale di vastissimo interesse (la storia dell'intera umanità).

«Ancùo so che Dio no' pol esser / Lontan da mi: / E ch'el xé dapartuto». "El xé dapartuto": sembrano le disadorne parole di un catechista di campagna che illustri le piú elementari verità di fede a un pubblico semplicissimo. Magia del dialetto, cui, come già si disse, è consentito accedere ad ambiti nozionali e immediatezze espressive interdetti alla lingua. Il "dapartuto" del terzultimo verso risuona con riduzione sillabica nell'ultimo: "partùto", cosicché risulta possibile percepire la presenza divina nel distico finale:

> Mi te strenzo e cô i brassi te perde,
> Mi te çerco e te te trovo partùto.

Dunque: dapprima Dio viene predicato come presente dappertutto, poi qualcuno viene cercato e trovato dappertutto. Questo qualcuno finisce con l'essere Dio, *anche Dio*, anche se una fredda logica punta l'indice, ovviamente, sull'interlocutrice. Ecco allora questo "tu-Dio" informare di sé il "tu" del distico iniziale:

> El saòr del pan, e la luse del çiel
> Gèra inçerti prima de tì.

Quel "tu" lirico può con buona ragione essere percepito come Dio, o magari come il Cristo. Ritornando a quanto si accennava, vediamo cosí che la spartizione epocale acquista in significato. Non si tratta piú soltanto di un *tunc* ed un *nunc* separati dall'avvento decisivo di una donna nella vita di un uomo, ma anche del *tunc* e *nunc* della storia dell'umanità segnata dall'avvento redentivo del Cristo. Per una verifica ci si potrà rivolgere a versi (*Do grandi date...*) rimasti inediti fino alla comparsa dell'edizione Manfriani:

> Do grandi date storiche
> Val par mi:
> Cô Gesù Cristo xé sta messo in crose,
> E mì da tì.

Documento di notevole interesse non solo per il chiaramente esplicitato collegamento tra grande e piccola epocalità, ma anche perché vi si trova volto in negativo lo spirito di *El saòr del pan...*. Percepito il rapporto perlomeno analogico tra interlocutrice umana e interlocutore supremo, percepito che la macrostoria della reden-

---

[6] Opportuno, intanto, tornare a *Colpa d'amor...*, di cui trascrivo le terzine: «La verità xé anzi un fià piú bela / De quel che vogio dir parché ogni amante / Credendo invidii la mia bona stela. / Manco làgreme al mondo saría piante, / Se gavesse mi pur più fede in ela, / Come lesendo in Beatrice e in Dante».

zione di tutti si trova inscritta nella microstoria individuale, risulta quasi inevitabile scoprire, o riscoprire come più persuasiva, una risemantizzazione del pane nel primo e soprattutto nel terzo verso («me par una grazia el me pan»). Quel pane che si trasforma sotto i nostri occhi in cibo eucaristico conferisce sigillo sacramentale all'esperienza d'amore configurata dal testo.

Robert S. Dombroski

GADDA'S CREATIVE BODIES:
ON THE THEORY AND PRACTICE OF THE GROTESQUE

Italian prose fiction in the early twentieth century, like the modernist currents in the rest of Europe, was characterized by its belief in the novel as an ideal vehicle for the exploration of individual subjectivity. The conception of the Self that informed the works of all the major writers of the period, however different its modes of identification and transmission, placed the human subject (the protagonist as embodiment of the consciousness of the author) at center stage, where it was made to command constant attention. There it bore the burden of being represented as a subject 'in crisis' in order to reconstitute itself in and through the very experience that challenged its integrity. Though the representation of an afflicted or disquieted subjectivity, the fulfillment denied to the subject at the level of theme was achieved at the formal level, its status decided by a language and a style that belonged to it alone and that qualified it as the central agent of the narrative act. To put it differently, the individual subject in the principal narrative texts of Italian modernism, from D'Annunzio to Pirandello and Svevo, was always the subject of representation, which, to use Heidegger's phrasing, is the place where the truth of the world speaks itself. And it was by narrating itself that the subject 'in crisis' gained the reassuring certainty of myth.

The main lines of Gadda's development that converge in his baroque manner all intersect at one principal (aesthetic and ethical) concern: to extract the Self from representation by making its existence as a narrative structure problematic. This will entail the work of 'petrification', a virtual 'killing' of the Self, making it thing-like by reducing it to a grotesque surface reality. The theoretical basis for such a procedure is to a notable degree already present in *Meditazione milanese*, the work in which Gadda establishes his philosophical interest in the interrelation of the self, consciousness, and the object world of perception.

Meditazione milanese begins with a disclaimer: that the philosopher's terrain is unstable ("Il terreno del filosofo è la mobile duna o la savana deglutitrice"[1])

---

[1] CARLO EMILIO GADDA, *Meditazione milanese*, in *Scritti vari e postumi*, Dante Isella ed., Milano, Garzanti, 1993. Henceforth in the text as *M.M.*

and, moreover, that the author's particular journey of knowledge has no star to guide it. At the same time, his faith in the mind's ability to disentangle reality gives him confidence to venture on. Gadda, who had studied Kantian philosophy with Piero Martinetti in Milan,[2] maintained that order in the universe was possible because the conscious mind was capable of perceiving it. However, this starting point did not presuppose for Gadda (as it did for Kant) that consciousness was an unalterable, *a-priori* given.[3] Instead, he believed that states of consciousness were variable and thus capable of changing with every new perception. Gadda's approach to knowledge is, in Gian Carlo Roscioni's words, "constructivist,"[4] which means that every moment or phase in the acquisition of knowledge is perceived as a system in itself. So even if Gadda remained confident in the mind's capacity to order the world, he sensed early on that human expression was not always governed by the conscious mind. And while it is right to maintain, as Roscioni does, that everything in Gadda's philosophical repertoire seems to be under the control of his pragmatic spirit, common sense, and preference for exact, concrete analyses, it cannot be ignored that his fundamental notions about reality run counter to his stated belief that the multiple data of the universe can be ordered into ready-made concepts.

In any case, however problematic Gadda's relationship with philosophy might have been, it was a lasting relationship that helped sharpen his interest in psychoanalysis and that extended to the heart of his fiction. It is no coincidence that *L'egoista*, a dialogue on self love written in 1953 echoes notions from *Meditazione* on multiplicity and dialectical causality that are part and parcel of detective Ingravallo's oft-cited philosophical wisdom: "Sosteneva, fra l'altro, che le inopinate catastrofi non sono mai la conseguenza o l'effetto che dir si voglia d'un unico motivo, d'una causa al singolare: ma sono come un vortice, un punto di depressione ciclonica nella coscienza del mondo, verso cui hanno cospirato tutta una molteplicità di causali convergenti."[5] Ingravallo's 'philosophy' no doubt regulates the universe of Gaddian narrative, which, like a 'vortex', or 'cyclonic point of depression' is made

---

[2] Piero Martinetti (1872-1934) taught theoretical philosophy at the University of Milan until 1931, when he was forced to leave his Chair for not having sworn allegiance to Fascism. In opposition to Croce and Gentile, Martinetti's idealism, which incorporated the findings of science, was a sort of "empirical metaphysics" aimed at establishing the unity of all empirical knowledge. The influence of Martinetti on Gadda is mostly limited to the role played by metaphysics in the cognitive process. "Nessun pensiero è possibile se non in quanto si inquadra in una concezione metafisica" (P. MARTINETTI, *Introduzione alla metafisica*, Torino, Einaudi, 1904, 8) is echoed in Gadda's reflection on his own poetic: "Quando scriverò la Poetica, dovrà ognuno che si proponga di intenderla, rifarsi dal leggere l'Etica: e anzi la Poetica sarà poco più che un capitolo dell'Etica: e questa deriverà dalla Metafisica" (C. E. Gadda, "Meditazione breve circa il dire e il fare", in *Saggi Giornale Favole I*, Dante Isella ed., Milano, Garzanti, 1991, p. 444).

[3] On this point, see Gian Carlo Roscioni's Introduction to the first published edition of *Meditazione milanese*, G. C. Roscioni ed., Torino, Einaudi, 1974, pp. XXV-XXVII.

[4] *Ibid.*, p. XI.

[5] *Quer pasticciaccio brutto de via Merulana*, in C. E. GADDA, *Romanzi e racconti II*, Dante Isella ed., Milano, Garzanti, p. 16. Henceforth in the text as *QP*.

up of constant alteration (deformation), disturbances, and changes of tension and energy.[6]

There are two sides to this vision present in *Meditazione*. One is characteristically Leibnizian, rooted in the conviction that the universe is correlated to the extent that an event occurring in any of its parts has a recoiling or rebounding effect in all of the others. As Gadda has Teofilo state at the beginning of *L'egoista*: "Se una libellula vola a Tokyo, innesta una serie di reazioni che raggiungono me."[7] Gadda also takes from Leibniz his idea of the monad: multiple, self-enclosed, autonomous centers of force of which the universe is made. And it would not be exaggerated to say that the multilingualism and polyphony so characteristic of Gadda's writings finds one of their many lines of support in Leibniz's notion of 'possible worlds' which are not far in kind from the 'plurality of worlds' described in modern physics. But Gadda's Leibniz has been filtered through rather extensive readings of Bergson. And it is this side of Gadda's intellectual formation that is decisive.

Meditazione milanese is a philosophical reflection on knowledge. Its principal argument may be summarized as follows. If it is true that knowledge presupposes the organization of a particular datum in a system, it is also true that the configuration of that system depends on the predisposition of the knowing subject: "La nostra analisi [riceve] inizio da un nostro dato psicologico e storico, cioè personale ed ambientale, che si devolve in un flusso, che è in una velocità; che è labile, mobile" (*MM*, p. 628). Here the adjectives 'storico', 'personale', and 'ambientale' collapse into 'psicologico.' Knowledge is a psychological experience of the subject who changes (alters or deforms) the datum by inserting his perception of it into it. Knowledge for Gadda is thus a *becoming* in the Bergsonian sense of *duration*, that is, a continuous enlarging of experience; simply stated, a process. As the object of knowledge, the datum itself exists in a flux; we intuit it as a system, but it is a system existing in relation to other systems. The datum, however, does not exist in a state of pure becoming. While our perception of it deforms its previous composition, something remains or 'persists': a trace of what was. Here too Gadda seems to have drawn from Bergson's ideas on change and substance, maintaining, as he does, the continuation in existence of some sort of substrate. For it would be impossible to make sense of a universe in which change is not the change of something: "Se tutto fosse movibile e mosso, nessuna forma o figura sarebbe pensata" (p. 631). But the substratum cannot escape having been affected by the change it experiences. Therefore what continues continues in an imperfect state, influenced

---

[6] With particular reference to the *Pasticciaccio*, it has been argued that the novel "si presta a essere letto come la messa in opera sperimentale delle ipotesi teoriche definite negli anni tra il *Racconto italiano di ignoto del Novecento* (1924) e la *Meditazione milanese* (1928), F. AMIGONI, *La più semplice macchina. Lettura freudiana del* Pasticciaccio, Bologna, Il mulino, 1995, p. 26.

[7] *SGF I*, p. 654.

by the change in its surrounding components. Gadda takes as an example the game of chess.[8] The configuration of the pieces on the chessboard constitutes a system. The movement of any one piece in the original configuration introduces a change into the system which deforms it in the sense that it bears upon all subsequent moves. The deforming element is one single piece that, in its having been moved, acts on the remaining elements of the system. While they continue to exist as a system, their existènce, on account of the original deformation, is flawed. ("L'elemento deformatore sembra a noi essere il solo pezzo attualmente mosso, mentre la restante massa dei pezzi ci appare il 'persistere attuale' del sistema: è peraltro un persistere sui generis, un persistere che risente della mossa eseguita, un gramo e imperfetto persistere altro" [p. 631]). Knowledge then for Gadda is not the re-production in the mind of a reality external to the knower; it is instead a transformative action that consists not in the apprehension but in the construction of meaning:

> Data una realtà (sia pure concepita come esterna) l'attribuirle successivamente con penetrante intuito significati integranti, e cioè passare dal significato n-1 ad n, n+1, n+2, è *costruire* perciocché è inserire quella realtà in una cerchia sempre più vasta di relazioni, è un crearla e ricrearla, un formarla e riformarla (p. 753).

The construction of meaning by 'knowing' the data of the world is the principal concept of Gaddian epistemology, and it is the idea on which the notion of plurality rests. For when we know, we modify, thus we disturb, realigning, albeit momentarily, the components of a system, changing the tensions and deployment of energy within that system, creating new rhythms in an endless field of becoming. When Gadda attributes to Ingravallo the conviction that cause and effect are never to be considered in the singular and that entanglement is infinite, he is drawing from the center of Bergson's philosophy of the real as *élan vital*. The *groviglio* is the essence of life; infinite differentiation and dissociation. Things within the tangle are alienated from their own material form at the very moment they are known, that is, given to the consciousness of others, which initiates the flow of differentiation: "Nel mondo delle relazioni non esistono monete tesaurizzate nell'arca e dimenticate dalla pulsazione vitale, ma tutte si muovono e rappresentano soltanto rapporti" (p. 649). Thus Gadda makes no attempt to mend the rift he sees between being and meaning. The world is knowable only through the pulsations of the human subject who can make no claim to centrality. And, while Gadda would maintain that the world is to be grasped in relation to the knowing subject as a correlate of its consciousness, unlike the phenomenologists, he does not uphold the transcendental nature of that consciousness and, therefore, of subjectivity. The subject is just a part of the world; it has no central position from which it can claim cognitive authority.

---

[8] See Roscioni's discussion of Gadda and Saussure, *Gadda*, 1974, VII-XI.

The difficulties Gadda encounters in his first attempt at narrating in the classical manner stem directly from his belief that the world of data to which the subject belongs is unstable and that it therefore cannot be re-assembled in its actual parts, for those parts are not separate substances existing in relation to one another and signifying the reality of the whole. But rather, in their *duration*, the parts contract and expand, going beyond their own material limits to constitute a kind of perpetual otherness. In one of the more important 'compositional notes' of *Racconto italiano di ignoto del Novecento*, Gadda remarks that his greatest difficulty in narrating is plot construction; it is crucial that the plot of his novel be not a mere winding out of a series of events, but that it respond to *"l'istinto delle combinazioni"*, that is, *"al profondo ed oscuro dissociarsi della realtà in elementi"*.[9] In contrast to the 'vecchi romanzi,' the whole in Gadda 's view is never given, because plots are actual life, and in 'life' there are as many worlds as there are living beings (*"quale ingarbugliato intreccio"*!).

Another difficulty for the young Gadda consists in selecting a point of view: *"il punto di vista 'organizzatore' della rappresentazione complessa"*. On this issue, Gadda's notes make a good case for reading him in the light provided by the experimentalists of the Gruppo 63 and which now goes under the sign of textuality or post-modernism. This fundamental narrative category (i.e., "point of view") grew out of the need in the late nineteenth century to institutionalize the fiction of the individual (bourgeois) subject which was suffering the effects of disintegration and reification in a market economy. It is the instrument that restores form to a consciousness shattered into numerous fragments.[10] While Gadda is aware that representation has as its object the radical plurality of the world that defies systemization or closure, he is concerned with finding a theoretical justification for style. Expression, he states, must be commensurate to point of view and point of view depends on subjective disposition: *"lo stile mi è imposto dalla passione (intuizione) del momento e ...lo scrivere con uno stile pre-voluto è uno sforzo bestiale, se questo non è uno stile corrispondente al 'mio momento conoscitivo'"* (*RI*, 461). The problem, Gadda goes on to acknowledge, is that if he were to write according to the passion of the moment, and therefore employ different points of view and, as a result, different styles, according to subjective disposition, he would be accused of *"variabilità, eterogeneità, mancanza di fusione, mancanza di armonia, et similia"*, that is, of those very traits that distinguish his work and give it the character of random narration, free association, and unlimited textuality.

In *Meditazione*, Gadda includes the Self in the *"flusso deformatore dell'universo"* (*MM*, p. 760) and makes it clear that his metaphysics prevents him from conceiving of the individual as a unity:

---

[9] C. E. GADDA, *Racconto italiano di un ignoto del Novecento*, in *Scritti vari e postumi*, p. 460; henceforth in text as *RI*.

[10] See F. JAMESON, *The Political Unconscious: Narrative as a Politically Symbolic Act*, Ithaca, New York, Cornell University Press, 1981, pp. 219-222.

Ogni pausa espressiva è un io e ogni io è una pausa espressiva. Ogni limitazione o allontanamento di relazioni menoma l'io, ogni convergere conferisce all'io, al sistema. E il sistema è una deformazione perenne, che mai non è identico a sé stesso, se non nella grossa apparenza... (*Ibid*).

Hence the Self defies individuation and, like the multiplicities that form the world, obeys a logic of its own. Such a position will no doubt affect Gadda's approach to psychoanalysis, as Guido Lucchini has argued, for it is not limited to the areas of metaphysics and poetic but extends also to the sphere of ethics: individuation is not only an illusive process, it is an intrinsically evil one.[11] We shall return to this point later; now it will be useful to consider further the implications that Gadda's anti-substantialist, largely Bergson-inspired, views have for narration.

In Italy, the fiction of the individual subject had already been illustrated by Pirandello who created an entire aesthetic around the notions of psychic fragmentation and depersonalization. But while Pirandello's narratives and plays disclose all the negative effects of reification, the vision they convey is one in which one's many individual selves coexist, either adapting to the reality they claim to repudiate or exiting from it into myth or madness; the result being that, in defending against fragmentation, Pirandello, like other genuine modernists, forges a powerful ideological instrument: a conception of the world centered on the Self. The center-staging of the Self is a means of reinforcing and perpetuating the myth of a world that because of modern science and democracy has disintegrated into self-sufficient fragments. It involves the acceptance of individuation and individual autonomy at the very same time it underscores the relativity of being. It is in this sense that the Pirandellian point of view can be seen as an *a priori* philosophical construct, expressed in a variety of tones but in essentially the same voice. The voice is that of the author to whom the market economy has given a secondary role to play and whom Pirandello harks back to with nostalgia. It is the subject of narrative, the perspective from which the art work is organized and expressed, that his work in the last analysis safeguards.

It becomes clear from the *Racconto* that Gadda's narrative difficulties lie in his inability to find a center, a stable point of view from which the real can be represented. From his very first entry, we sense Gadda's need to order the chaos within himself; it is from there that the characters and events of his novel must emerge: "Dal caos dello sfondo devono coagulare e formarsi alcune figure a cui sarà affidata la gestione della favola" (*RI*, p. 395). The subject's internal chaos will not lead him to seek order in art regardless of his desire to work out a theoretical dimension in which it is possible to do so. The Self in its chaos cannot be internally stabilized, nor can it be fixed in its relation to set boundaries and objects. In other words, its

---

[11] G. LUCCHINI, *L'istinto della combinazione. Le origini del romanzo in Carlo Emilio Gadda*, Pisa, EPT, 1988, p. 109.

space cannot be circumscribed because it, like the object worlds of its mimetic desires, is trapped in the flux of existence. Therefore, right from the start, Gadda's vision precludes conceiving the novel as the organic reconstruction of character and the social order; it rules out all sorts of historical narratives that depend on history as a repository of truth; and is wary about the liabilities involved in safeguarding the contents of consciousness.

But one must be careful in attributing too much Bergsonism to Gadda. True that his lyric register facilitates the plunge into 'the stream of life' and emotional identification; but the immersion is always temporary and has all the earmarks of a sudden impulse rather than a total vision. The Gaddian Self is never lost in fluidity or spontaneity because it is watched over by an intelligence which checks the compensatory impulse by moving the focus from the private depths of the pure present to the grotesque surface of public reality. Put differently, in Gadda, the pain of existence leads not to self-indulgence, but rather to satirical excess. That part of the Gaddian psyche which continually seeks fulfillment in the romantic language of the soul takes on the status of a mere 'text' or 'discourse' subject to revision, commentary, and interpretation. This process is well illustrated in *Approdo alle Zàttere*, one of the sketches of *Crociera mediterranea*, contained in *Il Castello di Udine*. Cruising along the coast of Corfu, the traveler (Gadda) reflects on the beauty of the island's capital, pointing to the familiarity of its architecture:

> E, in città, case che paiono nostre, come d'un Veneto ottocentesco e pedrocchiano, con presagio di acquate, pieno di estrema poesia: al limite d'un disperato abbandono. Il Foscolo. Poi, se non fosse stata la luce, a una scogliera coronata di cipressi, l'Isola dei Morti, di Böcklin. Ma, poi, il romantico mi parve troppo zelante, m'ero troppo incantato alla sua isola, ai suoi cipressi, alla sua morte. Allora, nel grottesco de'miei dispiaceri vani, dopo la deformazione, il suo significato: l'Isola dei Morti, di De Chirico.[12]

This commentary on a lived memory describes to a large extent the cognitive process of Gadda's aesthetic. The traveler's gaze falls first on the neo-classical architecture of the city's houses: his response is emotional and driven by an initial impulse toward harmony, but at the same time laced with dread and poetic surrender. Foscolo comes to Gadda's mind: his *I Sepolcri* and *Le Grazie* record the striving of the poet's soul to find an eternal language of 'death' and 'beauty' as compensation for an existence fragmented by history. Gadda's attention then turns to the cliff, surrounded by cypresses, from which the Swiss painter Arnold Böcklin took inspiration for his "Island of the Dead". The traveler re-visualizes the beauty of Böcklin's dark, melancholic canvas, but immediately realizes the liability of such an escape into a metaphysics of death. The painter's excessive zeal unsettles Gadda's intellect, as he remembers De Chirico's parodic deforma-

---

[12] C. E. GADDA, *Il castello di Udine*, in *Romanzi e racconti I*, Dante Isella ed., Milano, Garzanti, 1988, p. 207.

tion of Böcklin's romantic, supernatural mood. [13] Deformation, he states, generates meaning.

Equally important is the footnote Gadda appends to this passage, which connects Böcklin's work to the doleful, but heroic, mood of 'l'isola de'poeti' in Carducci's poem *Presso l'urna di P. B. Shelley*. But crucial to a thorough understanding of the narrator's memory and reflection on it is his gloss of the phrase "Nel grotesco de' miei dispiaceri vani": "il suo [the traveler/narrator's] stato d'animo non è da crociera: e risulta di un pasticcio psichico", where "risulta di" indicates not consequence but rather causality: his state of mind refracts into a psychological tangle: "Nievo-Ortis-Bandiera bianca-Dalmazia-Corfù" (*CU*, p. 217). Gadda's position in the cited passage is one of scepticism before the discursive truth of romanticism: De Chirico, in parodying the painting of his former mentor, interrogates its truth claims. But for Gadda the basis of the interrogation lies in an ultimately unrepresentable (because themselves subject to parody) "dispiaceri vani": not 'worthless pleasures', it should be noted, but 'worthless sufferings', ("dispiaceri") which, on account of Gadda's intellectual surveillance, cannot be transformed romantically into art, no matter how tempting the desire. The lyrical-romantic impulse therefore becomes of necessity a register of citations, one among the many elements of pastiche.

The mention of De Chirico, moreover, helps us understand better the function of Gadda's own particular kind of grotesque. The sharp lines and smooth geometrical surfaces that the painter imposes on organic life, his mixing of historically incompatible objects (ancient sculptures and common modern tools, Renaissance buildings and factory smokestacks) pose, as do Gadda's own grotesques, an enormous challenge to the Western cultural heritage. A simple example of how Gadda achieves alienation through distortion, reproducing in writing the merciless light that bathes De Chirico's elongated shadows, is his description, in *La cognizione del dolore*, of Battistina, one of the Pirobuttiro's domestics, who, descending the path from the villa, runs into the doctor on his way to visit Gonzalo. Like many of Gadda's descriptions, this grotesque portrait of the washerwoman contains a distinct meta-literary directive:

La donna aveva un piccolo incarto sotto il braccio diritto, e con le due mani reggeva un piatto fondo, coperto da un piatto rovesciato: la faccia si rivolgeva a sinistra, che pare si fossero sbagliati a inchiodargliela sul busto, quasi di un pupazzo dignitoso verso occidente: in realtà per far luogo al gozzo, tre o quattro ettogrammi. Aveva l'aria un poco sospettosa e intimidita, con quel desinare che le impegnava le mani, come un animale a cui possano contendere il cibo; e il gozzo pareva un animale per conto suo che, dopo averla azzannata nella trachea, le bevesse fuori metà del respiro, nascondendosi però sotto la pelle di lei come il fotografo sotto la tela. [14]

---

[13] For a complete discussion of Gadda and De Chirico, see M. LIPPARINI, *Le metafore del vero. Percezione e deformazione figurativa in Carlo Emilio Gadda*, Pisa, Pacini, 1984, pp. 109-126.

[14] C. E. GADDA, *La cognizione del dolore*, in *Romanzi e racconti I*, p. 609; henceforth *in text as CD*.

But Gaddian satire in its most developed form possesses a distinct feature that sets it apart from both ancient satire and from the modern kind propounded and practiced by Lewis. While it carries out all the destructive and denunciatory functions of the genre in exposing the folly of human life, and while it does so, as Lewis preached, in a moral but not moralistic way, it does not constitute itself (as satire) according to any one point of view or any one particular style. What distinguishes Gadda from the satirists and macaronics of old, from Swift or Sterne, from Joyce and from the variants of plurilingualism and humorous writing he could look to in his own native Italian tradition (Dossi, Faldella, etc.) is his practice of dispersing the narrative voice along a varied trajectory of different linguistic registers. By this I mean that Gadda's fiction texts are wholly decentered, deprived of an overriding consciousness that frames the narrative, which conveys the story's message either thematically or by means of the style it employs.

Criticism, beginning with Contini, has been keen on describing the 'fragmentary' and 'unfinished' quality of Gadda's work, particularly of *Quer pasticciaccio* which, on account of its being conceived as a detective story, is all the more strange. On this matter, I agree with Stefano Agosti who remarks on the problematic nature of such a description.[19] I shall return later to Agosti's reading of the *Pasticciaccio*, but first I would like to bring into this discussion two examples from Gadda's vast satiric holdings that focus on the human body. I have chosen this perspective because the body is the main vehicle for the Gaddian grotesque and because, given the distinctly autobiographical character of Gadda's writing, the body can be seen as an allegory of the narrative and, in turn, of the authorial voice. The human body provides Gadda with an avenue to the root of existence, to life as object-reality, beyond meaning and discursive closure. In the cold objectification of life, the subject as an individuating force fades or disappears altogether.

My first example is a short narrative entitled *Anastomòsi*,[20] in which Gadda describes a surgical operation, a resection of the duodenum. The scene is set in a university clinic. The narrator, admitted into the operating theater as spectator (it is assumed that he is a medical student), is in a position to survey from above the work of a master surgeon. The narration unfolds as a commentary on the event, written in the margin of the patient's text: namely his human body, anesthetized on the operating table. The whole narration takes place in a suspension ("un breve tumulto del mio sentire" [p. 329]). No referents are provided as to who the patient is, except a chart hanging from his bed indicating ("quasi incidentalmente" [*Ibid.*]) his profession which, however, is not disclosed. Hence, from the reader's standpoint, the patient is only a body subject to the surgeon's art and the narrator's probing gaze. The description is circular in that it mimics the circular process

---

[19] S. AGOSTI, "Quando il linguaggio non va in vacanza: una lettura del Pasticciaccio", in *Le lingue di Gadda*, M. A. Terzoli ed., Roma, Salerno Editrice, 1996, pp. 249-250.

[20] In *SGF I*, pp. 329-339.

of the surgery. The patient is cut, opened up, his entrails displayed, examined, the suspected diseased parts removed, then sutured, his body restored to its original volume. The narration ends precisely with the final stitch which secures the contents of the body in their casing. What is striking in this piece is that its subject (anastomosis) informs the writing at every level: like the operation, the narrative voice severs and reconnects the subject's parts in an attempt to locate and identify a reality beyond closure, a kind of de-ideologized pure matter, mysterious and sacred in its unfathomable materiality. The surgeon's cut, much like the writer's, desecrates the mystery, the spirit (soul) of the person to reveal the evidence of its physical composition, to understand nature's design.[21] Like the painters of old who dissected human corpses to penetrate the secret of their form, the surgeon/ writer makes his subject emerge through the disruption of its form, thus, the undermining of its metaphysics: its sacrifice which leads to its resuscitation:

> Profanando il buio segreto e l'intrinseco della persona, ecco il risanatore ne ha evidenziato lo schema fisico: ha letto l'idea di natura nel mucchio delle viscide parvenze. Sul corpo disteso, disumanato, insiste con gli atti farciti della sua bianchezza: che mi appare quasi alta e muta madre o matrice della resurrezione. Ripenso, delle nostre antiche pitture, sant'Anna, sopra la Figlia, e Lei sopra il corpo illividito del figliolo (p. 338).

By 'subject' I am referring at once to the 'subject matter', or focus, of the narration conveyed through the narrator's living consciousness of the event ("E l'ago avanza, avanza....Gli esseri del silenzio bianco, ora vedo....Carpiani, ecco, entra nella sala....etc. [p. 330]), not recollection but simultaneity, and to the heuristic process embodied in the narrative voice. The question is one of how the subject represents itself and how it relates to the process of disruption and alienation it describes. The human figure lying on the operating table is, metaphorically, a text subject to transgression ("eviscerazione", "spaventosa effrazione", "nefando pasticcio" are the terms used to describe the event). Before it is cut, it suggests an unqualified, formal nakedness and the potential vulnerability of an unprotected surface. Therefore, it has all the earmarks of a symbolic presence, governed by some moral law. The operation could be viewed, mistakenly on my view, as an attempt by Gadda to depict dramatically the precariousness of the (ideal) human and, by extension, social body, rendered infirm by industrialization, democracy, etc. In spite of Gadda's conservative politics and anti-democratic impulses, there is here, as far I can see, no such instance of symbolic representation. Material or factual data do not enclose a meaning or truth that transcends them, hence Gadda's stated aversion to neo-realism and to other then-current varieties of realism, and his oft-stated fondness of what he regarded as the Manzonian 'grotesque'. Rather the body lying before the surgeon is (for the surgeon and his operating team) nothing but a

---

[21] For an excellent discussion of Gadda as surgeon, see Gian-Paolo Biasin's reading of *Anastomòsi* in *Literary Diseases: Theme and Metaphor in the Italian Novel*, Austin, Texas, University of Texas Press, 1975.

body; it belongs to no symbolic or conceptual order; it is not regarded as a moral or ideological being and, since it does not speak, it is beyond language. The narrator, in fact, in a subtle disclosure of the author's viewpoint, states with regard to the surgeon's preparatory ritual: "È strano: il gesto della indifferenza morale vien compiuto con la sollecitudine serena di chi ha preso conoscenza dei fini e dei mezzi, con la pacata insistenza della ragione" (p. 331). Moral indifference, total knowledge of the process, guided by reason, which will lead to expulsion of the evil that prevents the body from functioning ("il modo proprio di chi ben sa e benignamente provvede, ed escluderà il male dalla tenebra corporea e dopo gli esatti minuti vi ricomporrà le ragioni della vita" (*Ibid*). The cut body will then disclose its own order of reality, one that is 'undecidable' in terms of meaning, while at the same time being the source of enchantment: the repository of nature's secrets and mysteries, of an obscure, *material* profundity. We are at the beginning of the subject's eclipse as a signifying entity or discursive force and its re-making as an alienated object. But, as I shall illustrate, we are not dealing with the substitution of one element with another, with dichotomy and division, but rather with tension and contradiction.

Thematically, the body is a paradox. It emerges as the subject of the narrative at the very moment it begins its decline as the body of an individual, that is, as an epistemological and psychological center of attraction; in other words, as a character. More importantly, its potential centeredness is lost because the narrative voice has deprived it of a style consonant to its being. While Gadda maintains the point of view relatively fixed within the narrative frame of the voice as spectator and scribe, he destabilizes it through the deployment of different stylistic registers. Scientific and philosophical prose intersects with sublime and lyrical sequences, which in turn are interrupted by the comic and the grotesque. These multiple components of Gadda's language or stylistic codes are not employed with the purpose of creating a new unity of tone. Rather, in their movement between 'high' and 'low' styles, they highlight their incompatibility and strangeness with respect to any overriding stylistic norm. The sentence contains the alienation it is intent on describing:

I visceri venivano presi ed estratti come una sequenza informe di molli enigmi (per me), che i colori rosati, e rossi, e biancastri, e giallicci, mi dicevano appartenere all'attività prima e centrale della natura vivente. E questa non geometrica espressione dell'io vivo, già plasma, e negli anni organato da una 'idea' differenziatrice (tale sembrò nella immagine), l'operatore lo solleva d'una sua mano sopra le garze e la raggiera delle pinze, lo 'esteriorizza' nella chiarità dell'elettrico, frugandovi, frugandovi, come a volervi scoprire qualche ostinata reticenza, una simulazione pervicace, antica. Rigattiere dal bavaglio che cerca una moneta dimenticata in una vecchia veste frusta. Le dita ironiche sembravano palpare la frode. Ma non una goccia ne ricadeva, della calda porpora. Palese, a lui e ai suoi, nella celere veggenza degli atti in una lunga scuola ammaestrati, l'intimo e insostituibile dispositivo della organicità; che si rivela invece così sconvolto, informe, superfluità rossa ed inane, o anzi miseria d'un pupazzo sbuzzato senza battesimo, alla mia cognitiva d'ignaro d'ogni antropologio e groviglio, smemorata di lontani studi, scarsa, incerta (p. 335).

The function of this stylistic practice is quite the opposite of what it seems. The narrative voice, intent on capturing the Real and reproducing it by combining its multiple elements, is, like the surgeon, faced with its ultimate inaccessibility. In coming face to face with the viscera of the human condition, the narrator can opt either to represent them in detail, knowing that in so doing he would fall victim to the illusion of their reality, their inauthenticity ("Le dita ironiche sembrano palpare la frode."), or to contaminate the object by deforming its appearances which are nothing other than the grotesque substitutes of phenomena, the external cover of some archaic essence, a plenitude beyond the realm of his discursive power. In the last analysis, the operation orders the patient's spiritual death, his depersonalization into a kind of canvas for the author's satiric collage.

In this light, we see how Gadda brings the once dissipated subject back to center stage and how its monadic isolation is ultimately defeated in comedy. The effect of such a re-positioning, however, is that the subject disappears as a locus of meaning to become a locus of creation. As it gets lost in the text of satire, and as its parts are distilled in language, it loses its capacity to symbolize realities beyond its material form. This can be also viewed in those episodes in the novels where the narrator focuses on the human body as the scene of some inexplicable outrage. Where the body is made vulnerable to the narrator's gaze, it is not only objectified, but becomes something more than an object : the site of the creative play of language, the intersection of desire and reference, analogous to the operating table where the surgeon exhibits his creative energy in his search for some divine, magical essence. Among the many possible examples, two in particular are instructive: Gadda's description of the doctor's examination of Gonzalo that begins the third segment of *La cognizione* and the dead body of Liliana Balducci in *Quer pasticciaccio brutto de via Merulana*.

The son is stretched out on his bed on a white blanket:

Su quel candore conventuale il lungo corpo e la eminenza del ventre diedero una figurazione di ingegnere-capo decentemente defunto, non fossero stati il colorito del volto, e anche lo sguardo e il respiro, a prevalere sulla immobilità greve della testa; che affondò un poco nel cuscino, bianco e rigonfio, tutto svoli. Subito la linda frescura di quello nobilitò la fronte, i capegli, il naso: si sarebbe pensato ad una maschera, da dover consegnare alle gipsoteche della posterità. Era invece la faccia dell'unico Pirobutirro maschio vivente che guardava alle travi del soffitto. Orizzontale sul bianco.

Le due scarpe a punta, lucide, nerissime, parvero due peperoni neri, per quanto capovolti, puntiti. Movendo nelle àsole e nelle bretelle mani bianche, lunghe, il morto si preparava all'auscultazione. Dalla parete di fronte, tra le finestre, da una cornice di noce, la guardata corusca del generale Pastrufacio, in dagherotipo. Vigeva a mezzo busto nella penombra, con il poncho, e due cocche alla spalla manca d'un fazzoletto sudamericano: e in capo quel suo berretto, tra familiare e dogale, cilindrico; torno esornato d'alcuni fregi di fil d'oro, in disegno di cirri, rare ghiande, viticchi. La bionda capellatura dell'eroe, schiaritasi molti anni avanti nel bagno di fissaggio, scendevagli armoniosa alle spalle e quivi giunta si ripigliava dolcemente in una rotolatura nobilissima, da parer fatto d'Andrea Mantegna o Giovanbellino: come d' un paggio degli Este o dei Montefeltro venuto alle pampe, e agli anni di bandiera e di schioppo. Trascesa la cinquantina, tutte le gote e il disotto dei labbri s'infoltivano d'una generosità maschia del pelo, d'un vigore popolano ed antico: incrudito alla vastità delle guerre e superfluente dalle cornici dei ritratti.

La visita fu "coscienziosa". Il dottore palpò l'ingegnere a lungo, e anche a due mani, come a strizzarne fuori le budella: pareva una lavandaia inferocita sui panni, alla riva d'un goriello; poi, mollate le trippe, l'ascoltò un po' per tutto, saltellando in qua e in là, con il capo e cioè con l'orecchio, pungendo e vellicandolo con la barba. Poi gli mise lo stetoscopio sul cuore e sugli apici: per gli apici, sia davanti che dietro. Alternò l'auscultazione con la percussione digitale e digito-digitale, tanto i bronchi e i polmoni che, di nuovo, il ventre. Gli diceva: "si volti": e di nuovo: "si rivolti". Nell'ascoltarlo dalla schiena quando era seduto sul letto e tutto inchinato in avanti, con il gonfio e le pieghe del ventre in mezzo ai femori, a crepapancia, e tra i ginocchi la faccia, la camicia arrovesciata al di sopra il capo come da un colpo di vento, oppure sdraiato bocconi, mezzo di sbieco, mutande e pantaloni senza più nesso, allora il dottore aveva l'aria di comunicargli per telefono i suoi desiderata: gli fece dire parecchie volte trentatré, trentatré; ancora trentatré. All'enunciare il qual numero l'ingegnere si prestò di buona grazia, col viso tra i ginocchi (*CD*, pp. 620-621).

Here the crisis of the subject takes on one of many personal articulations found throughout the novel. As in the description of Battistina, we are dealing with the deformation of a naturalist aesthetic technique in such a way that the human object described, the son, becomes marginal to itself, as some kind of reified otherness. This focus allows the narrative to express the collapse of the individual subject on three distinct levels.

First, on the narrative level, in terms of point of view, it destabilizes the literary character by combining the reality of the individual with its surroundings so that, through caricatural insistence, it is transformed into something else. The body dissolves into the blanket and pillow, its face becomes a mask of itself, as the narrator constructs its degraded existence with comic reference to its shoes ("le due scarpe a punta, lucide, nerissime, parvero due peperoni neri, per quanto capovolti, puntiti") that at once stand out as signs of the protagonist's concern for his appearance amid the filth of his surroundings and as items of some phallic significance.[22] Such an association is meant to divert attention from the "deep structure" of Gonzalo the patient, from his "male invisibile", his misanthropy, or his obsession with the memory of his dead brother. Its purpose is to show that the (thematically highlighted) isolated subject has lost its formal consistency because it has become the subject of a wandering, observing eye constantly distracted by objects that tempt its gaze. In fact, once Gonzalo is portrayed as corpse-like, the narrator's attention is drawn to another gaze, "la guardata corusca del generale Pastrufacio, in dagherotipo".

---

[22] Manzotti, in his annotated edition of the novel (Torino, Einaudi, 1987), reminds us of similar shoes worn by Don Lorenzo Corpi in *Quer pasticciaccio*: "le lunghe scarpe ... nere e stralucide .. in riposo, lustre... [che] priapavano fuori dalla vesta che pareveno du affari proibbiti" (p. 140).

Thus between the reader and the spiritual categories of the protagonist is placed one more deviation, itself composed of numerous folds of historical and literary materials.[23] Then, in the actual medical examination, the subject is displaced at the literal level of the text as he becomes a virtual puppet whose degraded existence is caught somewhere between the laundry of the washerwoman and the ignominy of the doctor's scrupulous exploration; hence its caricature, a sign of its vulnerability, whether seated "la camicia arrovesciata al di sopra il capo come da un colpo di vento"or stretched out "mezzo di sbieco, mutande e pantaloni senza più nesso". While the examination concludes that Gonzalo has nothing to worry about, it exhibits his degraded existence both as an object of knowledge and as the focal point of the narrator's gaze. The doctor's manipulation of the body becomes, in this respect, one with the author's semantic and formal manipulation, the effects of which lead to the text's structural 'indecidability.' The simple question of what is the narrator's point of view in regard to his subject cannot be easily answered.

The second level of dispersion is both psychological and psychoanalytical. The narrative voice in *La cognizione* wavers between identification with Gonzalo, as here in the pathos conveyed in mentioning the "letto più interno, il suo" or in the closing comment on the examination scene "il malato si ricomponeva da un oltraggio non motivato nelle cose" and impersonal detachment, signaled by the medical inspection. Its description of the patient may be viewed as a way of defending against the power and intrusion of authorial emotion, an attempt to take possession and control of the Self through satire. The authorial personality, as refracted in the character of Gonzalo, exists in deep, self-imposed isolation; to protect that refuge and the psychological horrors it holds it must divert attention from itself (the real, but hidden, subject of narration) by satiric depersonalization. The deadly force of writing, which ranges from playful to violent onslaught, is, in other words, an antidote to the "male invisibile" (the hidden cause of the protagonist's malaise).[24] On the thematic level, the struggle between mother and son in the novel may be read in a particularly Freudian vein as a means of overcoming the Oedipus complex and thus as that point of entanglement at which the subject is produced and constituted and when it begins to accept reality, forsaking the pleasure principle and incest in behalf of culture. If there is anything that Gonzalo opposes it is the patriarchal law and if there is anything he is deprived of it is the voice of conscience. Finally, Gonzalo has no specific gender role to play; he accepts no

---

[23] The visual reference is to the official portrait of Giuseppe Garibaldi, which Gadda conveys parodically through echoes of Carducci's *Ode al Piemonte* ("La bionda capellatura dell'eroe"...) On Gadda and Carducci, see A. ARBASINO, *Certi romanzi*, Torino, Einaudi, 1977, pp. 366-367.

[24] A recent exploration of the biographical terrain of Gadda's works has uncovered a repressed fratricidal fantasy that could easily account for the displacement of aggression from the Other to the Self. See F. PEDRIALI, "The Mark of Cain: Morning and Dissimulation in the Works of Carlo Emilio Gadda, in *Contemporary Perspectives on Carlo Emilio Gadda*, M. Bertone and R. S. Dombroski eds., Toronto & London, University of Toronto Press, 1997.

authority, nor has any desire to reproduce family and society, while, at the same time, he delays no satisfaction (his proverbial gluttony).[25]

The third level, which incorporates both the narrative and psychological, is social. Gadda has repeatedly given his family's *déclassment* as the cause of his unhappiness.[26] On account of his father's imprudent investments his family allegedly lost the bourgeois status it previously enjoyed. A recurring theme in Gadda's biography, this sense of having fallen down the social ladder is also crucial to the rendering of Gonzalo in *La cognizione*, particularly to an explanation of his contempt for the paternal villa. The anxiety generated by the loss of place is not, however, a class anxiety articulated in class terms (as is the case with Naturalism), "the terror of falling into a social space that is radically Other,"[27] but rather an "obscure sense that [his] own social space is contracting all around [him], that soon [he] will have no structural or institutional space of [his] own"... (*Ibid.*) In this respect, what may be justifiably read as a symptom of the author's pathology projected on to his alterego, Gonzalo, takes on a socially symbolic value. The crisis of the individual subject results from its being pushed out of the social space it had once commanded. Such a loss of place, the definitive loss of social status, is commensurate to the loss of the subject's textual space; its being made thing-like to be moved around by a narrator who, however, has no true voice of his own that would give some guarantee of representation. Other voices intrude to cloud the story's meaning. Hence, the loss/absence can be seen in the continual variation of point of view, in the lack of a wholly referential linguistic framework, and in the novel's ending that, while centering on the murder of the mother, gives the reader not the slightest clue as to who the killer might be. On the authorial level, the loss of social status, while no doubt explaining Gadda's anti-Socialism – which would be seen by him as the institutionalization of his loss – also explains his aversion toward the populist strains in the then ruling Fascism.

Let us now consider our last example of Gaddian satire which takes the human body as its focus:

Il corpo della povera signora giaceva in una posizione infame, supino, con la gonna di lana grigia e una sottogonna bianca buttate all'indietro, fin quasi al petto: come se qualcuno avesse voluto scoprire il candore affascinante di quel dessous, o indagarne lo stato di nettezza. Aveva mutande bianche, di maglia a punto gentile, sottilissimo, che terminavano a metà coscia in una delicata orlatura. Tra l'orlatura e le calze, ch'erano in una lieve luce di

---

[25] For a discussion of the conflict between Oedipus and Narcissus in Gadda, see R. S. Dombroski, "Overcoming Oedipus: Self and Society in *La cognizione del dolore*", *MLN*, 1984, pp. 80-100.

[26] "L'infelicità maggiore proveniva dalla povertà della mia famiglia. Per quanto nei primi anni abbiamo avuto delle condizioni abbastanza buone, poi le cose si sono aggravate per errori economici di mio padre. Spendeva più di quanto potesse poi recuperare. Non era un bravo uomo d'affari, sia detto con rispetto. Era un maniaco della terra, della campagna, della gente brianzola" (C. E. GADDA, *"Per favore, mi lasci nell'ombra". Interviste 1950-1972*, C. Vela ed., Milano, Adelphi, 1993, p. 156).

[27] See F. JAMESON, *op. cit.*, p. 114.

seta, denudò se stessa la bianchezza estrema della carne, d'un palore da clorosi: quelle due cosce un po' aperte, che i due elastici – in un tono di lilla – parevano distinguere in grado, avevano perduto il loro tiepido senso, già si adeguavano al gelo: al gelo del sarcofago, e delle taciturne dimore. L'esatto officiare del punto a maglia, per lo sguardo di quei frequentatori di domestiche, modellò inutilmente le stanche proposte d'una voluttà il cui ardore, il cui fremito, pareva essersi appena esalato dalla dolce mollezza del monte, da quella riga, il segno carnale del mistero...quella che Michelangelo (don Ciccio ne rivide la fatica, a San Lorenzo) aveva creduto opportuno di dover omettere. Pignolerie! Lassa perde!

Le giarrettiere tese, ondulate appena agli orli, d'una ondulazione chiara a lattuga: l'elastico di seta lilla, in quel tono che pareva dare un profumo, significava a momenti la frale gentilezza e della donna e del ceto, l'eleganza spenta degli indumenti, degli atti, il secreto modo della sommissione, tramutata ora nella immobilità di un oggetto, o come d'uno sfigurato manichino. Tese, le calze, in una eleganza bionda quasi una nuova pelle, dàtale (sopra il tepore creato) dalla fiaba degli anni nuovi, delle magliatrici blasfeme: le calze incorticavano di quel velo di lor luce il modellato delle gambe, dei meravigliosi ginocchi: delle gambe un po'divaricate, come ad un invito orribile. Oh, gli occhi! Dove, chi guardavano? Il volto!...Oh, era sgraffiata, poverina! Fin sotto un occhio, sur naso!... Oh, quel viso! Come era stanco, stanco, povera Liliana, quel capo, nel nimbo, che l'avvolgeva, dei capelli, fili tuttavia operosi della carità. Affilato nel pallore, il volto: sfinito, emaciato dalla suzione atroce della Morte.

Un profondo, un terribile taglio rosso le apriva la gola, ferocemente. Aveva preso metà il collo, dal davanti verso destra, cioè verso sinistra per lei, destra per loro che guardavano: sfrangiato ai due margini come da un reiterarsi dei colpi, lama o punta: un orrore! Da nun potesse vede. Palesava come delle filacce rosse, all'interno, tra quella spumiccia nera der sangue, già raggrumato, a momenti; un pasticcio! Con delle bollicine rimaste a mezzo. Curiose forme, agli agenti: parevano buchi, al novizio, come dei maccheroncini color rosso, o rosa. "La trachea", mormorò Ingravallo chinandosi, "La carotide! La iugulare... Dio!".

Er sangue aveva impiastrato tutto er collo, er davanti de la camicetta, una manica: la mano: una spaventevole colatura d'un rosso nero, da Faiti o da Cengio (don Ciccio rammemorò subito, con un lontano pianto nell'anima, povera mamma!). S'era accagliato sul pavimento, sulla camicetta tra i due seni: n'era tinto anche l'orlo della gonna, il lembo rovescio de quela vesta di lana buttata su, e l'altra spalla: pareva si dovesse arggrinzare da un momento all'altro: doveva de certo risultarne un coagulato tutto appiccicoso come un sanguinaccio.

Il naso e la faccia, così abbandonata, e un po'rigirata da una parte, come de chi nun ce la fa più a combatte, la faccia! rassegnata alla volontà della morte, apparivano offesi da sgraffiature, da unghiate: come ciavesse preso gusto, quer boia, a volerla fregiare a quel modo. Assassino!

Gli occhi s'erano affisati orrendamente: a guardà che, poi? Guardaveno, guardaveno, in direzione nun se capiva de che, verso la credenza granne, in cima in cima, o ar soffitto. Le mutandine un ereno insanguinate: lasciaveno scoperti li du tratti de le cosce, come du anelli de pelle: fino a le calze, d'un biondo lucido. La solcatura del sesso... pareva d'esse a Ostia d'estate, o ar Forte de marmo de Viareggio, quanno so'sdriate su la rena a cocese, che te fanno vede tutto quello che vonno. Co quele maje tirate d'oggiggiorno (pp. 58-60).

In a recent essay, Stefano Agosti cites this passage in support of his reading of Gadda, particularly *Quer pasticciaccio*, in the light of Lacanian psychoanalysis. Few readers would doubt that the question of the subject in Gadda, its place in society and its relationship to language are not suitable topics for such an approach. Agosti's argument, roughly stated, is that the act of enunciating in Gadda does not disclose from what position or with what end in mind something is said. As we have seen above, the position from which Gadda's styles are generated cannot be clearly determined and that such an 'undecidability', according to Agosti, ("la barra della mancanza di verità imposta da Gadda sulla forma dell'espressione, vale a dire sullo stile e, per ciò stesso, sull'ordine simbolico"[28]) gives Gadda entry into what Lacan calls the "Real", i.e., that inaccessible realm beyond the reach of signification and therefore beyond representation and ideology: "La descrizione del cadavere di Liliana Balducci costituisce il cuore di questa operazione, che si estende senza una falla, senza una fessura ("Le réel est sans fissure"... avverte Lacan), in una infallibile omogeneità, per tutto lo spazio del testo" (Agosti 1996, p. 258).

According to Agosti, Gadda's *Pasticciaccio* presents a simulacrum of the structure of the Real, that is, a structure devoid of both a foundation and orientation whose internal logic is metonimically constituted. This would explain the dispersion of the narrative, the magnification of detail and the deployment of elements that have no function whatsoever with regard to the novel's proposed focus. To buttress such a suggestive argument, Agosti cites Lacan's comment on the description of Irma's throat in Freud's dream: "Il y a donc apparition angoissante d'une image qui résume ce que nous pouvons appeler la révélation du réel dans ce qu'il a de moins pénétrable, du réel sans aucune médiation possible, du réel dernier, de l'objet essentiel qui n'est plus un objet, mais ce quelque chose devant quoi tous les mots s'arrêtent et toutes les catégories échouent" (cited in Agosti, p. 261). By analogy, Liliana's cut-open throat is a similar revelation of the Real, thus the suspension of meaning; the Real that for Lacan exists in strict conjunction with death. Liliana's throat so horribly slaughtered is then, according to Agosti, the reverse image of her unfulfilled desire for maternity. One could also, as a parallel Lacanian reading, consider the description of Liliana's corpse as the figuration of a precious object (meaning) that is hunted for in vain. The narrative voice can never attain or possess it simply because it exists in the form of a metaphor, that is, as language. Its meaning can never be truly established because it is regulated by the pulsations of the unconscious. The dead Liliana thus could be seen as a reflex of the human subject which is always dispersed in the discourses of which it is constituted. Keeping in mind these readings, let us now approach the description from the standpoint of its two most characteristic aspects: its abundance of sexual markers and its humor.

The position of the body on the floor demands that the narrator's cold, yet libidinous eye, return continually, as in a refrain, to Liliana's parted thighs, her un-

---

[28] S. AGOSTI, "Quando il linguaggio non va in vacanza: una lettura del Pasticciaccio", cit., p. 258.

derpants, the white flesh between her garters and stockings, the *mons veneris* and the mysterious line or furrow, "la solcatura del sesso".[29] The reader's attention is thus drawn to what for the philosopher-detective Ingravallo could be most disturbing: the sexual attractiveness of the murdered woman, her cold voluptuousness, an appeal which the narrative voice humorously deflects on to a register of detailed description, common to the purpose of any homicide report. The form the deflection actually takes, however, is in itself unstable. As soon as one descriptive norm or point of view is established, it gives way to another, leaving open once more the question of who is speaking or better what consciousness, or form of consciousness, is the narrative voice speaking through. It is reasonable to expect, given the work's conception as a 'giallo', that the perspective is that of the detective, his investigative eye which, like the narrator in *Anastomòsi*, surveys the scene in its every detail from above. The assumption in itself is sound because of the numerous points of contact and identification that exist between Gadda and Ingravallo. But if Gadda is the detective, he has transferred to him the same cognitive dynamics, the same pulsations, the same play of unconscious drives and their relative forms of censorship, that characterize his writing in general. In other words, we could say that the enunciating subject (the narrator) attempts to imprint a specific law (a language) on an object that resists becoming he subject of the narrative and thus "objectified" in one perspective. The constituted form becomes the object of verbal play from which the horrible outrage becomes comic spectacle. The formal play consists of various descriptive codes, from simple reportage of the kind to be found in a newspaper story ("Il corpo della povera signora giaceva....") to a host of different points of view): polite curiosity ("il candore affascinante di quel *dessous*"), obsession with cleanliness ("lo stato di nettezza") and with refinement ("mutande... di maglia a punto gentile"), mixed together with libidinous attraction ("le cosce un po' aperte"), scientific ("palore da clorosi") and poetic ("il gelo del sarcofago e delle taciture dimore") reflection on death, and, of course, dialect. In Lacanian terms, one could say that Desire has dispersed the subject, made it swerve outward toward the desire of the Other into an impersonal frame or scene wherein the subject as a speaking consciousness is dissolved. But it is possible that the narrating subject has something else in mind. As it literally 'deconstructs' any pretense of centeredness, as it displays its omissions and contradictions, as it produces divergent meanings, it does so with the manifest purpose of diverting the reader's attention from the object-ideal, Liliana, to its grotesque caricature, and thus of masking his obsession for the object by negating in humor its profound psychological appeal. The canceling of one register for another can be seen as a form of negation, in the Freudian sense of *Verneinung*, that while pointing to the re-

---

[29] For a study of sexual imagery in Gadda, see M. DE BENEDICTIS, *La piega nera. Groviglio stilistico ed enigma della femminilità in C. E. Gadda*, Anzio, De Rubeis, 1991.

pressed, signals the process of repression.[30] The recurring movement from Italian to dialect (from norm to transgression), needless to say, is the major source of humor in *Quer pasticciaccio*.

But within the polyphonic description of Liliana's corpse, there is an abrupt, and rather unexpected, swerve in the narration that brings the reader in contact with another stream of blood and another body: "la mano: una spaventevole colatura d' un rosso nero, da Faiti o da Cengio (don Ciccio rammemorò' subito, con lontano pianto nell' anima, povera mamma!)". Here it would seem that Gadda has given to Ingravallo his own experience of loss, which may be summed up in William Weaver's gloss of the reference: "Faiti and Cengio are mountains where the Italian army fought bitterly and suffered severe losses in the First World War, and where Gadda's brother was killed. For a moment, here, Gadda identifies himself openly with Ingravallo and attributes his own bereavement to the fictional character."[31] This intervention is crucial because it involves another of the author's texts in which the detective is absent, namely *La cognizione*, where mother and dead brother are principal reference points and which concludes with the murder of La Signora. The trace of the other text is, as every student of Gadda knows, the trace of another trace and so on as we move backwards in time from one work to the next. And although the trace may be seen to go beyond Gadda's writings (into, say, texts of writers such as Dostoevski and Céline whose works Gadda knew well), there can be no doubt that the private sphere of the author's concrete experience is decisive here in the *Pasticciaccio* as elsewhere. But the point I want to stress is that Liliana's body, which we have viewed so far as an object deflected into different perceptions, may now be seen as the point at which meaning converges and is disseminated. In his interpretation of Leibniz, Deleuze makes the apparently cryptic statement that "Il n'y a pas de l'obscur en nous parce que nous avons un corps, mais nous devons avoir un corps parce qu'il y a de l'obscur en nous" (p. 113). "The obscure object in us" is another way of decribing the subject of the *Pasticciaccio*. Liliana (in her absence) is that subject, a subject of its very nature dispersed because, as Deleuze goes on to say, in every monad there is "une infinité de petits plis (inflexions) qui ne cessent de se faire et de se défaire en toutes directions" (p. 115). The fetishization and desecration of the body that produces the grotesque is the means Gadda uses to transform his deepest anxieties and desires into a surface reality, a soul-less piece of written matter devoid of affect, that is, into a negation-repression of the obscure. At the same time, the techniques that work the fetishization and desecration remain in full view as reminders of the obscurity the reader will never be able to decipher (e.g., Gadda's sexuality) for the

---

[30] On Freudian negation, see FRANCESCO ORLANDO, *Lettura freudiana della "Phedre"*, Torino, Einaudi, 1971, pp. 14-17.

[31] C. E. GADDA, *That Awful Mess on Via Merulana*, translated by William Weaver, London, Quartet Books, 1985, p. 69.

simple fact that it comes without a local code, and that master codes, like those provided by Freud or Lacan, will in the final analysis not suffice. Liliana, therefore, in all her fragmentation and figural excess, "is" nothing but allegorical writing: [32] the more she is defiled by the gaze of the Other, the more suggestive (seductive) she becomes; the more she escapes the grasp of the dissipated subject, the more humorous her tragedy becomes; just as, while we are instructed by generic convention to look for a fictional killer, the text keeps telling us that the "real" criminal is Gadda himself and that the scene of the crime is, like every other scene in the novel, the scene of satire. Sexuality and humor therefore take us to the heart of the masquerade; to a style that (like the criminal) escapes apprehension.

To conclude, the samples of satire discussed above could be taken as proof of how Gadda abandons history and representation in favor of what Barthes has called the "pleasure of the text". Although in certain respects this may be true, it should not lead one to hold that there is no determinate meaning in Gadda's writings. 'Undecidability' is a strategy, rather than a cognitive principle by which Gadda abides. He does not move from the premise that the identity of the subject is ruptured and diffused by the free play of language, rather, inversely, that the relative free play of language is a highly suitable means of restoring an identity to a subject inhibited and terrorized by history. It is a surrogate identity, a mask to hide behind, but one that allows him to destroy the logic of narrative systems in which are embedded the social institutions deemed responsible for his malaise. This false Self which does not lie, and which knows no identity except that of the Other, is the baroque subject of Gaddian narration.

---

[32] On the perverse and hysterical nature of allegorical writing, see C. BUCI-GLUCKSMANN, *La raison baroque*, Paris, Éditions Galilée, 1984: "Par son excès figural et sa brisure permanente, l'écriture allégorique s'avéreait à la fois 'perverse' et 'hystérique'. Perverse, car le surcodage rhétorique et poétique répond bien à la 'mentalisation' de la pulsion propre à la perversion selon Freud: le mot et la création de langue se substituent au désir et le Jeu poétique n'est là que comme le spectateur, le témoin d'un théâtre où toutes les actions sont *vues* et toujours le fait de l'autre. Hystérique, car 'culte des images' doit donner sa matérialité propre au corps, une proximité tout imaginaire, un non-renoncement à ce corps maternel premier et archaïque." (pp. 215-216)

Manuela Bertone

IL CURIOSO CASO GADDA-CONRAD

Poco si sa del legame che ha unito Carlo Emilio Gadda a uno dei massimi scrittori di lingua inglese a cavallo fra Otto e Novecento, Joseph Conrad. Va da sé che intendiamo fare riferimento a un legame letterario, libresco, ideale, e non a un rapporto di natura personale, poiché è certo che le loro strade non si sono, nella realtà, mai incrociate. È forse superfluo rammentare che quando Conrad soggiorna in Italia con la famiglia, nel 1905, Gadda è appena un ragazzo dodicenne e che, proprio nell'anno in cui Gadda, poco dopo il ritorno dall'Argentina, dà inizio a Milano al suo primo tentativo di romanzo, *Racconto italiano di ignoto del Novecento*, – nel 1924, dunque – Conrad muore sessantasettenne nel Kent.

Sappiamo però che nel 1953 Gadda firma per Bompiani la traduzione dall'inglese di *The Secret Agent* di Conrad, anche se, come è noto, quella traduzione è stata dallo scrittore milanese soltanto riveduta. Si tratta probabilmente di una delle numerose traduzioni di classici stranieri prodotte ma non firmate da Lucia Rodocanachi, alla quale esse venivano sub-appaltate da artisti affermati (Gadda e Vittorini erano nel numero) in cerca di rapidi e facili guadagni, ma carenti di conoscenze sufficienti per svolgere in proprio le versioni che la «gentile signora»[1] era invece in grado di sfornare a getto continuo. A dire il vero, per questo Conrad, né – se di lei si tratta – Lucia Rodocanachi, che sapeva l'inglese, né Gadda, del cui inglese è lecito dubitare,[2]

---

[1] Cfr. in proposito, C. E. GADDA, *Lettere a una gentile signora*, Milano, Adelphi, 1983. Nel volume, che raccoglie i testi di lettere, cartoline, biglietti, inviati da Gadda all'amica traduttrice fra il 1935 e il 1964, non compaiono riferimenti espliciti alla traduzione dell'*Agente segreto*, mentre abbondano gli accenni a svariate altre traduzioni dall'inglese che Gadda vorrebbe "proporre" agli editori, soprattutto per far fronte alle proprie ristrettezze economiche. Ma Gadda non è in grado di cavarsela da solo nemmeno a livello semplicemente propositivo; e allora sollecita la competente Lucia Rodocanachi: «Insomma proponga, proponga, proponga: biografie, autobiogr., carteggio, storia» (lettera del 31 agosto 1938, p. 86). E a lei chiede sempre un parere quando dall'editore è già giunta una proposta: «stamane mi *telefona* Bompiani se voglio tradurre un libro (credo romanzo) dello Steinbek (si scrive così?) – pagine 360 tempo 3 mesi e 1/2. Posso nuovamente ricorrere a Lei? Prima *di dir di sì* vorrei conoscere la sua opinione» (lettera del 28 agosto 1939, pp. 105-106, corsivi dell'autore); «ho anche ricevuto l'incarico di leggere, per un responso, il libro di Samuel Butler: The way of all flesh [...] Devo dare responso. Lei lo ha letto? Che ne dice?» (lettera del 27 gennaio 1939, p. 95); poi, sempre a proposito del Butler: «Come devo comportarmi? Che devo lasciargli presagire?» (lettera del 24 aprile 1939, p. 100).

[2] Fra i libri e opuscoli posseduti da Gadda, ora conservati alla Biblioteca del Burcardo in Roma, spiccano sì un

sembrano aver speso tesori di accuratezza e di inventività, poiché la versione cosiddetta "gaddiana" dell'*Agente segreto*, «ben lungi dal mostrare le caratteristiche invenzioni linguistiche tipiche del Gran Lombardo o dall'offrire soluzioni stilistiche originali, sorprende per la dimostrazione che fornisce della scarsa conoscenza dell'inglese da parte del traduttore».[3]

Andrebbe appurato, tuttavia, quando Gadda avesse avuto occasione di leggere per la prima volta il romanzo di Conrad, uscito in rivista fra il 1906 e il 1907, apparso in volume nel 1907 e poi, sotto forma di dramma in quattro atti, rappresentato nel 1922 e dato alle stampe nel 1923. E questo perché sono numerosi gli spunti tematici e addirittura gli stilemi che possono indurre a credere che una parentela diretta leghi *The Secret Agent* a diversi scritti di Gadda e, di conseguenza, a ritenere che Gadda abbia accettato di effettuare (ovvero di rivedere) la traduzione del romanzo in ragione del fatto che già conosceva piuttosto bene il testo di Conrad.

Si paragonino, a titolo di esempio, le considerazioni conradiane, contenute nella *Author's Note* del 1920, a proposito dei personaggi della sua storia, «both law-abiding and lawless», a quelle depositate da Gadda nel 1924 nel *Racconto italiano-Cahier d'études* in merito all'*in lege* ed *ex lege*. Anche a voler credere nel caso suddetto ad una pura coincidenza, ovvero ad una riflessione sulla società figlia delle letture paretiane del giovane Gadda più che di una condivisione dello sguardo portato sui protagonisti del racconto dal maturo Conrad, che dire di altre, più sorprendenti somiglianze fra il testo del *Secret Agent* e quelli dell'*Adalgisa* e del *Pasticciaccio*? Intendiamo fare riferimento, innanzitutto, al brano incipitale del "disegno milanese" intitolato *Al parco, in una sera di maggio*, che vede come protagonista donna Eleonora, milanese «dama incocchiata», condotta a spasso sulla propria carrozza da una macchietta di conducente: «il cocchiere [con] una puntuta coccarda [che], a ritta,

certo numero di testi utili per l'apprendimento della lingua inglese, ma si tratta di manuali di conversazione, di grammatiche, di corsi confezionati ad uso e consumo del turista ovvero del principiante. Si tratta, per esempio, del *Manual of Conversation English-Italian with the Italian figured pronounciation for English tourists in Italy* (Milano, Bietti, s.d.), della *Grammatica razionale della lingua inglese ad uso delle scuole superiori e medie* (a cura di C. Formichi, Milano, Vallardi, 1925²), del *Corso elementare di lingua inglese* (Giordano-Orsini, Firenze, La Nuova Italia, 1939). Anche a supporre che Gadda fosse perfettamente familiarizzato con le strutture basilari della lingua, è indubbio che per tradurre una prosa della complessità di quella di Conrad gli ci sarebbe voluta una preparazione da specialista dell'idioma anglosassone. D'altronde, proprio all'amica traduttrice, egli confida: «vorrei finalmente arrivare a conoscere l'inglese e lo studio un po'» (C. E. GADDA, *Lettere a una gentile signora, op. cit.*, lettera del 26 febbraio 1941, p. 128); «studio l'inglese con il fratello di Joyce [Stanislaus, allora residente a Firenze, n.d.r.]» (lettera del 12 novembre 1941, p. 134), ma non compaiono segnalazioni di superamento di questa fase di apprendistato.
[3] M. CURRELI, *Nota alle traduzioni*, in J. CONRAD, *Opere. Romanzi e racconti 1904-1924*, a cura di Mario Curreli, Milano, Bompiani, 1995, p. CVII. Sulla versione gaddiana, «non proprio bella e neppure fedele» (*ibid.*), si vedano le pp. CVII-CX della *Nota* di Curreli in cui vengono accuratamente repertoriati svarioni, imperfezioni, travisamenti, garbugli traduttivi e refusi.
Siamo grati a Mario Curreli dell'Università di Pisa, direttore del Centro Studi Conradiani "Ugo Mursia", per averci messo a disposizione materiali e documenti conradiani altrimenti irreperibili. Senza la sua competente e cortese disponibilità, la redazione di questo testo sarebbe stata impossibile.

gli sopravanzava sul tetto del cilindro». Gadda sembra recuperare la descrizione del passeggio in carrozza sul Row presso Hyde Park su cui esordisce il capitolo II del romanzo di Conrad; analoghe le circostanze, dunque, ma addirittura identica la scelta di dedicare un accenno al cocchiere attraverso la sottolineatura del medesimo dettaglio vestimentario: anche a Londra, come a Milano, nella più sobria epifania approntata da Conrad, spicca un «groom with a cockade to his hat» (un «palafreniere con la coccarda sul cappello», come si legge nella versione Gadda). [4]

Diverso e più complesso il caso del *Pasticciaccio*, latore di somiglianze macroscopiche con il *Secret Agent*, ma anche di svariate sottigliezze disseminate qua e là, che sembrano essere rimbalzate dalle pagine di Conrad a quelle di Gadda. Entrambi i romanzi, costruiti sul canovaccio del giallo, si aprono sulla presentazione della "coppia" degli interpreti principali: una figura di protagonista-pensatore le cui azioni-ruminazioni reggono le sorti dell'intreccio e una figura di donna-angelo del focolare lanciata verso un destino sciagurato. Al silenzioso e misterioso Mr. Verloc, agente segreto-filosofo, talvolta scettico, talvolta pessimista, sembra corrispondere il taciturno e tenebroso Ciccio Ingràvola (poi Ingravallo), [5] commissario-filosofo e teorico delle concause; Liliana Balducci, dal canto suo, spartisce con Winnie Verloc un numero tale di caratteristiche – elencate nello stesso ordine e in termini pressoché identici – da rendere poco plausibile l'ipotesi della casualità. Può non sorprendere il tratto di riservata cordialità che le accomuna, ma colpisce invece la selezione di identiche caratteristiche: la pelle, l'acconciatura. Per Winnie, «her clear complexion», l'«extremely neat and artistic arrangement of her glossy hair»; per Liliana, «una pelle stupenda», «un viluppo di bei capelli castani». [6] Di Winnie viene sottolineata «the air of unfathomable indifference» e, poco dopo, «the provocation of her unfathomable reserve», con la reiterazione significativa dell'aggettivo, "unfathomable". Gadda lo traduce entrambe le volte con "impenetrabile": e dell'impenetrabilità di Winnie dota anche Liliana, anche se per giocare, con humor e sarcasmo, sul risultato di quell'impenetrabilità – l'infertilità, la maternità mancata: «si sarebbe detto [...] ch'egli, il Balducci, non avesse valutato, non avesse penetrato tutta la bellezza di lei: quanto vi era in lei di nobile e di recondito: e allora... i figli non erano arrivati». Conrad non instaura davvero il rapporto causa-effetto fra l'impenetrabilità della protagonista e la sua sterilità, come Gadda decide

---

[4] Tutte le citazioni riferite alla traduzione di Gadda sono tratte dal volume VII delle *Opere complete di Joseph Conrad*, Milano, Bompiani, 1953. *L'agente segreto* è preceduto da un saggio introduttivo di Thomas Mann (nella traduzione di Gabriella Bemporad).

[5] Ingràvola, lo ricordiamo, è il cognome di don Ciccio all'altezza della prima redazione del romanzo, quella uscita in rivista nel 1946-'47. In questa sede, non rimandiamo alla versione Garzanti 1957, poiché vogliamo insistere sul fatto che, nel 1946, la prima lettura di Conrad era, a nostro avviso, già avvenuta.

[6] Le nostre citazioni da *The Secret Agent* si riferiscono alla *Collected Edition of the Works of Joseph Conrad*, 21 voll., London, Dent, 1946-1955. Quelle tratte dagli scritti di Gadda, all'edizione delle opere curata da Dante Isella: *Racconto italiano di ignoto del Novecento*, in *Scritti vari e postumi*, Milano, Garzanti, 1993; *L'Adalgisa*, in *Romanzi e racconti* I, Milano, Garzanti, 1988; *Quer pasticciaccio brutto de via Merulana*, redazione di «Letteratura», in *Romanzi e racconti* II, Milano, Garzanti, 1989.

di fare; eppure, guarda caso, anche nel romanzo inglese, come in quello italiano, la maternità è negata alla protagonista. Se parliamo di «maternità negata» (laddove, giova sottolinearlo, entrambi i romanzi esordiscono con un bilancio di sterilità che riguarda entrambi i coniugi – «the Verlocs had no children»; «non hanno figli»), è perché i due racconti propongono e sviluppano fino in fondo il tema della maternità inadempiuta della protagonista, fino a farne il motivo dinamico scatenante di tutta la vicenda, mentre la paternità mancata è trattata dai due scrittori come ovvia e pura conseguenza del fatto che le mogli dei non-padri non sono madri. *The Secret Agent* e *Quer pasticciaccio brutto de via Merulana* potrebbero definirsi romanzi della maternità traslata e tragica. Traslata, poiché sia Winnie che Liliana vengono munite, dai rispettivi autori, di succedanei dei figlioli mai avuti. Per Winnie, *ersatz* eccellente è il fratello semi-deficiente, Stevie: «Winnie found an object of quasi-maternal affection in her brother», «Winnie, his sister, glanced at him from time to time with maternal vigilance». Per Liliana, fanno da rimpiazzo le servette-nipoti che si avvicendano nell'appartamento di via Merulana: «La signora Liliana, non potendo scodellare del proprio... così ogni anno... Il cambio della nipote doveva di certo valere nel suo inconscio come un simbolo, in sostituzione del mancato scodellamento...». Entrambe si estasiano alla vista dei loro oggetti d'amore materno: «That ardour of protecting compassion exalted morbidly in her childhood by the misery of another child tinged her sallow cheeks with a faint dusky blush, made her big eyes gleam under her dark lids»; «La signora Liliana allora la guardava compiaciuta, quasi con tenerezza: come vedesse un fiore ancor chiuso e un po' raggelato dall'aurora dischiudersi e risplendere sotto i suoi occhi nei prodigi del giorno». Ed è precisamente per aver guardato tutt'e due da madri quegli individui che figli non sono che, entrambe, acciecate dal sentimento materno, vengono trascinate verso la tragedia. Infatti, se abbiamo parlato di romanzi della maternità tragica oltre che traslata, è perché nei due romanzi i figli/non-figli occupano il centro della scena sulla quale si svolge il fatto di sangue che decide del destino delle due madri/non-madri.

Non si può terminare questa prima campionatura delle *corrispondenze* più macroscopiche senza richiamare almeno l'inserimento nelle prime battute di ambedue i racconti dell'adagio "vieto" (la parola è di Gadda), ma non certo obbligato (viene voglia di suggerirgli), «cherchez la femme», lasciato ovviamente tale e quale nella versione gaddiana dell'*Agente segreto*, ripreso alla lettera nel *Pasticciaccio*, ma anche riproposto (e quindi ribadito con sottolineatura) nella «tarda riedizione italica» del commissario Ingràvola: «'i femmene se retroveno addò n'i vuò truvà».

Vogliamo poi segnalare che, nel suo romanzo, Gadda utilizza alcuni degli ingredienti che già comparivano nella ricetta narrativa di Conrad, pur facendone uso in fasi e in modi diversi della preparazione del proprio impasto romanzesco. Così innesta una biforcazione geografica importante, quella fra Roma e le borgate, spaziando via via negli appartamenti della Roma-bene di via Merulana, nei locali della questura, nelle baracche della periferia; in modo analogo, la vicenda conradiana si snoda fra il centro della capitale e le sue zone estreme, ma anche fra i bassifondi e i salotti, fra strade fangose e commissariati, fra osterie infrequentabili e ambasciate. Proprio nel salotto di una dama dell'alta società vengono ricevuti contemporanea-mente il Vicesovrintendente Heat, che indaga sulle trame dei cospiratori anarchici, e l'anarchico Michaelis, colui che fabbrica la bomba che esploderà a Greenwich Park, uccidendo Stevie e stroncando l'esistenza di Winnie Verloc; così in casa di Liliana Balducci si trovano temporaneamente riuniti la figliastra-servetta ladra e complice del suo assassinio e l'invitato-commissario Ingravòla che svolgerà le inda-gini sulla sua morte. Andrà infine ricordato che nemmeno la *trovata* più felice e originale del *Pasticciaccio* gaddiano, quella del *pastiche* linguistico fatto di multipli registri e diverse parlate, è totalmente estranea alla vicenda narrata da Conrad. Be-ninteso, Conrad scrive, come suo solito, un inglese straordinariamente nitido, oltre che innegabilmente ricco; ma proprio nel *Secret Agent* compaiono numerose sotto-lineature riguardanti l'accento, la coloritura, l'intonazione e la pronuncia dei diver-si parlanti, quasi che la tessitura plurilinguistica dell'espressione, anche se non for-malizzata, andasse almeno denotata[7] nel testo quale elemento veramente notevole ai fini della comprensione della vicenda. La paternità di queste sottolineature è per lo più attribuita al poliglotta Verloc, agente segreto dall'orecchio fine, somigliante quindi, anche per questa sua abilità nel maneggiare e distinguere diversi idiomi e linguaggi, al commissario Ingravòla.

∗ ∗ ∗

Nel commentare la traduzione gaddiana del romanzo di Conrad, Mario Curreli non dimentica di segnalare che Gadda traduce, sbagliando, "Assistant Commissio-ner" con "Vice Commissario" (anziché con "Vicesovrintendente"), e precisa: «può fare poca differenza che l'Assistant Commissioner venga reso con il "Vice Commis-sario", il quale tuttavia si troverebbe più a suo agio in Via Merulana che sulla scena del delitto a Brett Street».[8] Quella che dalla penna di Curreli esce anzitutto come arguta *boutade*, è in realtà un'osservazione da raccogliere per ricordare che, nell'a-genda del lavoro gaddiano, la traduzione-revisione del *Secret Agent* e la ripresa della stesura del *Pasticciaccio* per la pubblicazione in volume presso Garzanti hanno luo-go a ridosso l'una dell'altra. Il cantiere del giallo, a seguito delle numerose insisten-ze di Livio Garzanti (peraltro precedute da proposte di Giulio Einaudi risalenti al

---

[7] Si vedano gli esempi seguenti: «Mr. Vladimir began, with an amazing guttural intonation not only utterly un-English, but absolutely un-European, and startling even to Mr. Verloc's experience of cosmopolitan slums»; «his interlocutor [...] switched the conversation into French»; «some of your revolutionary friends' effusions are written in a *charabia* every bit as incomprehensible as Chinese»; «his enunciation would have been almost totally unintelligible to a stranger».

[8] M. CURRELI, *Nota alle traduzioni*, in *op. cit.*, p. CIX.

'52)[9] si riapre in quello stesso 1953 che vede la pubblicazione della traduzione da Conrad. Non è impossibile, insomma, che il Gadda già autore di un *Pasticciaccio*, quello in rivista, abbia tradotto o abbia accettato la traduzione erronea di un termine semplicemente perché lo rimanda all'universo del giallo che a lui allora più sta a cuore, quello di via Merulana, la cui redazione-rifacimento è continuamente d'attualità fra il 1946 e il 1953. D'altro canto, è probabile che proprio l'incontro con il giallo di Conrad abbia contribuito (almeno quanto le richieste dell'editore) a far rinascere in un Gadda provato dal lavoro presso la RAI, il desiderio di metter mano al manoscritto del romanzo. Ma queste osservazioni a proposito dell'incrociarsi delle strade dei due gialli negli anni '50 non cancellano e non esauriscono il quesito sollevato in apertura, al quale ora, a esemplificazione avvenuta delle somiglianze salienti fra testi gaddiani – soprattutto quelli degli anni '40 – e testo conradiano, diventa urgente tentare di trovare una risposta: quello cioè dell'epoca del primo incontro fra Gadda e Conrad, particolarmente il Conrad del *Secret Agent*.

Secondo quanto risulta dal catalogo del "Fondo Gadda alla Biblioteca e Raccolta Teatrale del Burcardo", Gadda possedeva soltanto tre volumi delle *Opere* di Conrad edite da Bompiani negli anni '50, due nelle traduzioni di Jahier (*Appunti di vita e letteratura* e *Lo specchio del mare*), nonché uno di quella stessa edizione tradotto da Pellizzi (*L'avventuriero*). Ma vale per Gadda ciò che vale per chiunque: non possedere un libro non significa affatto non averlo letto; nel caso di Gadda, poi, il fatto che un libro non faccia parte del novero di quelli suoi conservati al Burcardo, non vuol dire che egli non lo abbia posseduto (e prestato, o perduto durante uno dei frequenti spostamenti).

Gadda potrebbe davvero avere incontrato per la prima volta l'opera di Conrad negli anni '20. È infatti alquanto improbabile che, reduce dal soggiorno argentino, aspirante romanziere, egli sia rimasto sordo alla creazione, nel centro della sua Milano (in via Montenapoleone), di *Bottega di Poesia*,

luogo d'incontro sofisticato, con scaffali e arredi disegnati dall'arch. De Finetti. [...] Per i suoi libri più preziosi *Bottega di Poesia* usò l'arte tipografica di Modiano, le invenzioni protosurrealiste di Alberto Martini, e testi di Lucini, Bacchelli, D'Annunzio, Conrad (ma stampò anche le *Lettere d'amore alle sartine d'Italia* di Guido da Verona); scoprì il *Sentir Messa* di Manzoni, ospitò molti di quegli artisti che nel 1923 alla Galleria Pesaro daranno il via al Novecentismo sotto tutela della Sarfatti. Nel marzo '24 Marinetti vi presenterà la prima rassegna antologica postuma di Boccioni.[10]

Nel dicembre del 1924 proprio le edizioni Bottega di Poesia danno alle stampe la versione italiana (di A. C. Rossi) di un capolavoro conradiano, *Heart of Darkness*

---

[9] Per ulteriori ragguagli sull'iter compositivo del *Pasticciaccio* (uno e due), cfr. la nota di G. PINOTTI in *Romanzi e racconti* II, *op. cit.*, particolarmente le pp. 1137-1155.

[10] G. LOPEZ, *La città e il suo sfidante. Milano e Marinetti 1909-1924*, in AA.VV., *Marinetti e il futurismo a Milano* (catalogo della mostra omonima, Milano, Biblioteca Nazionale Braidense, 10 ottobre-18 novembre 1995), Milano, De Luca, 1995, (pp. 13-29), p. 27.

(*Cuore di tenebra*), sorta di omaggio-celebrazione in onore dello scrittore recentemente scomparso. Ma – e lo ricordano gli editori milanesi nella loro introduzione *in memoriam* – se Conrad approda tardi agli italici lidi, più di un decennio prima, in Francia, era incominciata la traduzione delle sue opere: ai primi anni '10 risale la traduzione gidiana di *Typhoon*, al 1912 la traduzione del *Secret Agent* (*L'Agent secret*) firmata da Henry Davray per le edizioni Mercure de France. È più che verosimile che Gadda, alla ricerca di maestri e di modelli di scrittura, abbia cercato di avvicinarsi a Conrad in francese, se non prima di leggere *Cuore di tenebra* e la nota editoriale che l'accompagna, almeno a lettura ultimata e del capolavoro e della nota da cui apprende che la traduzione delle opere complete di Conrad è già disponibile oltralpe. D'altronde, attraverso la Francia e la sua lingua passano numerose, significative letture di Gadda fra gli anni '20 e '30: ricordiamone almeno una delle più importanti ai fini della comprensione del suo lavoro di scrittore, quella delle opere di Freud.[11]

Un altro illustre suggerimento potrebbe aver raccolto Gadda per avviare o approfondire la propria conoscenza dell'opera conradiana: quello di Emilio Cecchi. Infatti, poco prima della pubblicazione milanese di *Cuore di tenebra*, nell'agosto del 1924, esce sulle pagine di «Il Convegno» un saggio biografico-critico di Cecchi dedicato a Conrad, morto il giorno 3 di quello stesso mese. Si tratta di una lunga nota commemorativa in cui vengono riassunti gli scritti e illustrati gli intenti del romanziere inglese.[12] È assai poco probabile che a Gadda, impegnato com'era nell'organizzazione della sua prima storia tenebrosa e, come si è già accennato, nella riflessione sulla propria scrittura e su quella di illustri predecessori, siano sfuggite le parole di Cecchi a proposito del *Secret Agent*, presentato come prima «apparente diversione verso il romanzo poliziesco» attraverso la quale Conrad «portava i suoi disperati dall'oriente nei bassifondi europei».

Ci si può legittimamente accontentare di abbracciare una tesi minimalista, ed escludere che le pagine del *Racconto italiano* debbano alcunché a quelle del *Secret Agent*. Viceversa, si dovrà almeno credere che Gadda non ha dovuto attendere di essere diventato egli stesso traduttore (o revisore di una traduzione) di Conrad per conoscere l'*Agente segreto*. Escludere, poi, che l'abbia conosciuto attraverso le due versioni pubblicate nel 1928 da Alpes (nella traduzione di Lula Jahn) e da Sonzogno (nella traduzione di Gastone Rossi) significa rigettare un fatto lampante per insufficienza di prove.

---

[11] Gadda possiede (annota e sottilinea) le versioni francesi delle seguenti opere di S. FREUD: *Essais de psychanalyse*, Payot, 1929, *Essais de psychanalyse appliquée*, Gallimard, 1933, *Introduction à la psychanalyse*, Payot, 1929, *La psychopathologie de la vie quotidienne*, Payot, 1926.

[12] Il saggio di Cecchi, *Joseph Conrad*, viene ristampato nel 1925 in «Almanacco letterario», poi è incluso, con altri testi dedicati a Conrad, in E. CECCHI, *Scrittori inglesi e americani*, Lanciano, Carabba, 1935, e in tutte le successive edizioni (Il Saggiatore, Mondadori, Garzanti) del volume comparse negli anni.

ERNESTO G. CASERTA

MOTIVI DOMINANTI E PERSONAGGI
IN *UNA SPINA NEL CUORE* DI CHIARA

Il motivo più appariscente del romanzo è un sentimento di rimorso e di pietà, "la spina nel cuore", che si vorrebbe estrarre, ma continua a pungere, a causare dolore, sebbene tale motivo non sia il nucleo ispiratore, né la coordinata principale. Anzitutto va chiarito che il romanzo giallo non è pura opera di fantasia né autobiografica, per quanto intimamente intessuta di ricordi personali, di sentimenti provati dall'A. in un periodo della sua giovinezza, che nel romanzo si vorrebbe rimettere in luce al fine di trovare una spiegazione ed un'espiazione.*

I motivi che dominano l'azione del romanzo sono essenzialmente quelli della sessualità nelle sue varie forme e gradi (lussuria, erotismo), del male (oppressori contro vittime disarmate), del mistero e dell'imprevisto, che creano un'atmosfera ambigua, tesa e sospesa fino all'ultima pagina del romanzo. Predominano aspetti tragici, a cui s'intrecciano altri avventureschi, picareschi in uno sfondo storico stagnante, fascista, ma potrebbe essere anche medievale o secentesco: il signorotto locale che tiranneggia la provincia e sceglie fra le povere contadine quelle che più eccitano la sua libidine; il piccolo impiegatuccio, che corre di qua e di là per lavorare, per sopravvivere e difendere i suoi diritti, come ai tempi di don Rodrigo e di Renzo. La cittadina di Luino, il Metropole, covo di fannulloni e di giocatori d'azzardo, non rappresentano una vita cittadina sana, completa, evoluta, ma piuttosto una vasta tela fissa, che si apre e si chiude secondo la scena o si sposta in diversi angoli. Regna in questo ambiente socio-politico il materialismo, l'opportunismo e il machiavellismo. La morale, cattolica o d'altra origine, non agisce nella coscienza dei personaggi.

Fra i motivi dominanti, infine, va sottolineato quello dell'evasione del narratore che, intrappolato nel suo paese e irretito nella storia di Caterina, aspira ad evadere a

---

* P. Chiara, *Una spina nel cuore,* ed. Oscar narrativa, Milano, Mondadori, 1988. La prima edizione, pubblicata da Mondadori, è del 1979. Per un'analisi puntuale del contenuto e della struttura del romanzo, si veda il mio articolo, «Una spina nel cuore di Piero Chiara», *Canadian Journal of Italian Studies*, XVI, 1993, 47, pp. 169-181. Per un generale orientamento critico su Chiara, cfr. G. Tesio, *Piero Chiara*, «Il Castoro, 192», Firenze, La Nuova Italia, 1983, e E. Ghidetti, *Invito alla lettura di Chiara*, Milano, Mursia, 1977. Dal romanzo è stato tratto il film omonimo diretto da A. Lattuada, 1985.

quell'isola di Caso che gli avrebbe dato ricchezza e felicità. Esaminiamo da vicino alcuni di questi motivi nel contesto dell'azione del romanzo. Gli oppressori, i malvagi, i furbi egoisti, prevalgono nello svolgimento del racconto, e fra di essi ha un posto privilegiato lo stesso narratore, il quale ha rimorso d'aver contribuito alla tragedia e alla morte di Caterina. Teme di aver appena intuito la spiritualità di Caterina, di non aver intuito il mistero del suo animo, d'aver fatto parte della lega degli oppressori malvagi che riuscirono a ucciderla. Questo motivo, sebbene non sufficientemente sviluppato, della colpa e del rimorso, costituisce l'aspetto lirico del romanzo, che esteriormente si presenta come una rievocazione storica e una sterile espiazione. Il narratore regge nelle sue mani i fili dell'azione anche se non li controlla tutti (Dionisotti aveva rovinato Caterina prima che l'A. la conoscesse e il dr. Trigona continuerà ad abusare di lei prima e dopo le nozze), ma non fa nulla per salvare la sua Caterina; al contrario contribuisce da parte sua a umiliarla, a degradarla. Rimorso e desiderio d'espiazione che nascono dallo stesso stato d'animo del narratore, che guarda e racconta la storia da angolazioni diverse, ma senza cambiare atteggiamento: raggiungere una dinamica tragica nemmeno davanti alla tomba di Caterina.

È noto che il fascismo esaltava la potenza virile, e Dionisotti, da bravo fascista, voleva che la sua collezione della selvaggina femminile non fosse inferiore a quella di nessuno; faceva pertanto strage di donne di ogni età e forma tanto da guadagnarsi l'appellativo di papà della valle. Caterina per un capriccio del destino cadde anche lei nella grande retata e vi rimase prigioniera per più di tre anni. La stessa Adelaide Biotti cadde nel vischio e rimase scottata a lungo, e non se la salvarono nemmeno quei due mostri delle figlie del dr. Trigona, due rospi di difficile digestione. Il mito di Casanova, autore studiato ed amato da Chiara, il donnaiolo di professione e persino il pappagallo di strada (cfr. Orlando) hanno sempre goduto in Italia un grande prestigio. L'ozio, il gioco, le donne facevano parte della vita normale e dilettevole durante gli anni del regime fascista.

Il motivo della sessualità, dell'erotismo, è il tema dominante del romanzo e traspare in misura diversa un po' ovunque, ravvivando scene e l'azione quando la narrazione cala di tono o s'intorbida. Sul retro della copertina del romanzo, Chiara dichiara che «il contenuto di questo romanzo è il tentativo di penetrare il mistero dell'animo femminile, delle scelte che una donna forse ritiene opportuno fare, delle esperienze che istintivamente è portata a fare, con una motivazione che sfugge a chi cade in questo sortilegio femminile». In verità, quest'aspirato studio dell'animo femminile resta solo una promessa, in quanto l'A. non indaga la psiche di Caterina (il cui animo rimane indecifrabile al lettore), ma descrive l'azione, gli eventi, gli oppressori erotomani. L'amore che domina l'azione e i personaggi si esprime al livello di lussuria, di libidine, quello della Venere terrestre e carnale, non già quello della Venere celeste, spirituale, fatta eccezione dell'idillio romantico dei due giovani amanti, il narratore e Caterina, durante i primi mesi del loro innamoramento.

Caterina, sappiamo, era già stata violentata dall'inferocito satiro Dionisotti, allorché conobbe il giovane idealista, poco esperto di donne e propenso a innamorarsi della bella campagnola conterranea. Questo primo amore, sincero, appassionato, costituisce l'aspetto più genuino ed ideale del romanzo. Ma l'amore del narratore, dopo il suo ritorno al paese nel 1933, e di conseguenza persino quello di Caterina, cadono al livello sessuale, carnale, a una forma d'oppressione e d'abuso in maniera non diversa da quella degli altri luridi seduttori. Basta pensare ai vari incontri notturni al Metropole: un altro signorotto prepotente come Dionisotti, che voleva umiliare Caterina, trattarla da prostituta. Quel primo amore non c'è più ed è stato sostituito dalla libidine: da sentimenti d'oppressione e di vendetta. Nell'ultimo incontro fra il narratore e Caterina, avvenuto a casa di Adelaide, invece di sentire pietà per quella povera ragazza, orfana, abusata da tutti, risoluta infine a sposare quel mostro di Tibiletti, con il suo brillante di fidanzamento al dito, vestita elegantemente come una signora di classe, la fa salire in camera da letto per non perdere quell'occasione d'oro, riducendosi cosí al livello di Sberzi e di Orlando: ladruncoli, approfittatori della debolezza altrui. Il tormento principale del narratore qui è il possesso assoluto della donna, senza curarsi dei suoi sentimenti, di assicurarsi della sua preda sbarazzandosi dei rivali: cani affamati che continuavano ad attaccare da ogni canto per strappargli di bocca Caterina.

L'amore si riduce a un oggetto, che si usa e possiede a proprio piacere. Caterina non conta, deve giacere e abbracciare il mostro Tibiletti per scomparire insieme dalla terra, dal branco dei lupi. Il narratore è diventato uno di questi, pur cercando di capire, di rendersi conto, di uscire dal mondo della lussuria. La sua condotta non è molto diversa da quella del tiranno Dionisotti e del maligno dottor Trigona; tutti volevano possedere e controllare il corpo di Caterina. L'amore spirituale, il voler bene a qualcuno disinteressatamente, sembra che scompaia del tutto nella relazione fra il narratore e Caterina e si cade nel cerchio degli altri lussuriosi.

Inoltre, quella proposta di matrimonio mandata all'improvviso a Caterina, la visita al parroco Galiberti per parlare del suo matrimonio con Caterina, sembrano delle vere allucinazioni; segni evidenti d'una mente febbricitante o un puntiglio d'onore (anche Dionisotti aveva chiesto la mano di Caterina), perché non sembra chiaro perché, a questo punto, il narratore volesse sposare Caterina, dopo aver sentito da lei e da altri tutta la sua torbida e tragica vita.

L'amore di Caterina per il narratore è di una tempra diversa. Per lei è l'unico vero amore, che l'avrebbe liberata dalla schiavitù e fatta felice in un altro paese, come l'isola di Caso faceva sognare il nostro giovane narratore. Sfortunatamente il giovane innamorato non sembra consapevole di ciò, non ha la serietà dell'amore di Caterina, mentre il suo non va al di là dell'infatuazione, della passione e della libidine. Quando ritornò dal suo lavoro, infatti, non andò a cercare subito Caterina, non le chiese perché non aveva più scritto, ma la costrinse a venire più notti al Metropole, umiliandola in pubblico, e esponendola ad altri cani affamati (p. es.

Sberzi, a cui il narratore non fa obiezione). Certo le sue speciali prestazioni sessuali a casa dell'amica Teresita non sembrano forzate e nemmeno quelle con il furbo stregone Trigona, tanto meno quelle con Orlando e altri, che potrebbero apparire non tanto dei maligni oppressori quanto dei don Giovanni alla caccia di ragazze disponibili.

Caterina, secondo una tale prospettiva, può sembrarci una ragazza di facili costumi, che non sa dire di no, estinguendo la sete degli ingordi quasi per amore del prossimo, offrendosi come ostia sacra. L'amore di Caterina non è difatti passionale, erotico, ma soffocato, represso: un servizio e un atto di sottomissione per appagare la libidine altrui. Non si avverte in lei il senso della colpa nei suoi incontri amorosi. L'amore di Tibiletti è egualmente puro, spirituale: quello della vittima generosa che s'immola per il bene degli altri. Unito a Caterina, quasi dalla forza del destino, la sposa per inforcare insieme sulla moto la strada della morte: due sventurati annientati contro il muro di una curva, cacciati dal mondo dalla congiura dei malvagi e degli oppressori. L'amore di Caterina per il narratore, finito in quel cimitero di Sant'Anna, resta uno dei fili conduttori più saldi: si chiudeva per lui un lungo periodo della sua vita: confuso, tormentato, doloroso, e se ne apriva un altro.

Il motivo dell'amore, che pervade tutta la tessitura del romanzo, negli altri personaggi è monocorde e unidimensionale: è l'amore sessuale, carnale, l'atto fisico, soddisfatto il quale, si pensa ad altro. Lussuriosi sono il prepotente Dionisotti e il furbo dottor siciliano Trigona; una carogna libidinosa era Sberzi, e altrettanto cagnetta in calore era Teresita, che si faceva vedere le parti intime per invitare i timidi clienti. Sullo stesso piano si muove l'amore di Adelaide, passata per le zampe di quel rubicondo satiro di Dionisotti, e poi rattrappita come una lumaca in convivenza con Trigona, pur mostrando un'avversione a tutti gli uomini. L'amore di Tibiletti, invece, è eroico, puro, di una generosità illimitata, che sopporta tutto, soprusi e corna, pur di sposare Caterina, anche se per poco, e morto insieme come un antico cavaliere. L'amore spirituale, ideale, è solo delle vittime, di Tibiletti e di Caterina, rimasta ingenua e pura pur essendo stata pasto di belve feroci o volpine.

Bisogna osservare che non tutti questi lussuriosi sono degli spietati oppressori e non tutti dello stesso tipo. Teresita e Adelaide, indubbiamente, ebbero un ruolo nella graduale corruzione e degradazione di Caterina. La loro condotta era guidata da interessi personali; dal piacere sadico di vedere ridotta alla loro medesima condizione una ragazza semplice e innocente. Certo non furono amiche anche se entrambe aiuteranno il narratore a dargli informazioni sulla povera vittima; quindi non c'era un legame d'affetto, ma una situazione di sudditanza, di tenutaria verso la cliente bisognosa. Tuttavia, in una scala immaginaria d'oppressione, le due signorine civette occupano il gradino più basso: avrebbero potuto soccorrere, guidare la povera ragazza smarrita, invece finiscono di rovinarla. A capo della lista degli oppressori malvagi, alla don Rodrigo, va messo il milanese Guerrino Dionisotti, il quale violenta le donne della sua provincia a suo piacere, trattandole come oggetti di diletto. Era chiamato il papà della valle. Caterina fu una delle sue vittime, di cui abusò fisicamente e psicologicamente nel suo palazzotto. La figura risulta esternamente alquanto vaga e imprecisa, la sua condotta arrogante e piratesca ricorda il signorotto spagnolo don Rodrigo del Seicento, a cui le donne si prostravano e s'immolavano come per onore. Senza i suoi atti di violenza, che risuonano nella valle come fulmini e tuoni spaventevoli, il personaggio manca di una vita interiore, d'una personalità distinta.

Al secondo posto nella scala dei reprobi e degli oppressori va collocato il dottor Trigona, la cui arte più che di leone, fu volpina, di sornione maligno mascherato. Aveva conosciuto Caterina dalla nascita, come aveva conosciuto e ricomposto Tibiletti; con moglie e due figlie, a sessant'anni, aveva attirato Caterina alla sua rete, alla camera di Adelaide e se la godeva a suo piacere. Caterina, vittimizzata dallo sporco stregone, avrebbe potuto ribellarsi, denunciare il fatto, dirlo semmai al narratore appena tornato, ma lei è la vittima silenziosa e rinunziataria, che s'immola non vedendo altra via di scampo. Il piano di ricoverarla in un sanatorio, suo stratagemma, per godersi di nascosto la ragazza, portarla a Roma, e accettare la sua morte senza nessuna lacrima in seguito al fatale incidente stradale, – fanno di questo personaggio il più abietto e detestabile, più ancora di Dionisotti: un Gerione dantesco. Sberzi e Orlando sono anche loro fra i lussuriosi approfittatori; più maligno e lurido il primo, avventuriero, pappagallo di strada, spiritoso e spigliato il secondo.

La tecnica del romanzo poliziesco, che si fonda sul mistero e l'imprevisto, non manca d'una visione etica, che condiziona sia l'azione che il tessuto connettivo delle altre storie annodate a quella principale (quella di Caterina e del narratore-personaggio). Il racconto si sviluppa secondo le coordinate etiche del bene e del male, degli oppressori contro i buoni. Due mondi opposti, che a volte si confondono (p. es. il narratore che spesso cade fra i maligni lussuriosi che sfruttano l'ingenuità, la debolezza di Caterina). Una lotta feroce e d'astuzia in cui gli oppressori e i malvagi trionfano, mentre le vittime, i vinti, sono schiacciati, sono costretti a lasciare questo mondo.

A questo gruppo, fra gli oppressi, sta Caterina, che non è né Lucia, né Beatrice, che salvò il suo devoto amante. La religione, la fede è quasi del tutto assente in questo mondo materialistico e pansessualistico. Caterina era una ragazza semplice, buona, sincera, ma debole, inerme senza artigli; cedeva facilmente alle insidie dei suoi corteggiatori. Uno dei difetti principali del suo carattere è un'eccessiva passività, una poca stima di sé. Ella non si difende, non lotta. Nel romanzo si rimane al di fuori dell'analisi del mistero dell'animo di Caterina, delle scelte che ella fa di fronte alle varie circonstanze, davanti all'ingordigia maschile che premeva da ogni lato. Caterina resta avvolta in un cupo, ostinato silenzio: passiva e misteriosa, simile a tante altre vittime che l'avevano preceduta nella storia, dai tempi barbarici a quelli più recenti. Caterina lascia sul lettore un vivo senso di dolore e di pietà. Era una povera contadina, orfana, indifesa, bestialmente strupata da Dionisotti e da una serie di uomini lussuriosi, egoisti ed incoscienti. Ricorda la schiava antica e dei nostri giorni: abusata, oppressa nella parte più intima dell'animo. Nella relazione con il narratore, fin dall'inizio s'avverte un che di misterioso nella sua condotta, una sorta di male oscuro che impedisce l'intimità. Mantiene sigillato il suo segreto, e solo al ritorno del narratore, gli rivela in parte la sua tragedia; ma ormai nelle notti passate al Metropole, lei e il sornione giocatore avevano sostituito la libidine all'amore sincero e romantico dell'anno prima. Caterina era una persona distrutta, un'odalisca docile ed ubbidiente, disposta a fare la serva al narratore, se rifiutasse di sposarla. Si potrebbe chiedere perché si comporta cosí? Perché si riduce cosí male, come una comune prostituta, dandosi persino a quel maiale di Sberzi, a quel mafioso di Trigona e a quel frivolo donnaiolo di Orlando? Infine, come possiamo spiegare quelle numerose prestazioni speciali fatte a casa della sua amica Teresita per certi clienti più distinti ed esigenti? Questo comportamento misterioso e assurdo di Caterina ci promette di svelare Chiara, ma ci lascia purtroppo nella perplessità e nell'oscurità.

Dalle varie esperienze sessuali non risulta che Caterina avesse una libidine eccessiva, fosse ninfomane, né durante l'amplesso amoroso lei provasse un gran piacere; resta al contrario passiva, gelida come una statua marmorea. Le sue scelte o decisioni sono dunque dovute alla confusione del suo animo, alla sua incapacità di superare il suo trauma giovanile, causato soprattutto dal feroce Dionisotti, di crearsi una propria vita e destino. Le sue relazioni amorose non sono certo cercate e volute dalla povera contadina, che è colta dagli uomini come un frutto maturo e odoroso. Certo il parroco, la chiesa le avevano dato dei principi morali, un ordine spirituale, ma non bastavano. Il mistero dell'animo di Caterina si spiega nel contesto del racconto, nel passato della ragazza e nel branco dei lupi affamati da cui lei non sapeva difendersi.

Il narratore, che regge le fila della storia, fa lui le scelte per Caterina, stabilendo il fine della sua vita. Fino al suo ritorno, l'amore di Caterina per il giovane impiegato è intenso e senza riserve. Secondo questa direzione, il segreto di Caterina si sarebbe sciolto; lei avrebbe scelto di passare la sua vita accanto a lui; ma la reazione dispotica e vendicativa del narratore, che si transforma in uno Sberzi qualunque, distrugge l'amore e questa prospettiva di felicità. A che serve essere sincera ed onesta? Tanto vale distribuire l'ostia benedetta a chi la vuole. Questo è uno dei misteri dell'animo di Caterina. Nel delirio della febbre e nel rimorso della coscienza, dopo aver appreso l'intera storia di Caterina, il narratore vorrebbe redimersi, e come un eroe melodrammatico afferma di voler sposare Caterina, di voler fissare la data dello sposalizio con il parroco; ma Caterina comprende la teatralità del gesto e rifiuta, perché già promessa a Tibiletti, il suo vero compagno di martirio, vittima anche lui della malvagità umana.

Caterina ha tagliato tutti i ponti con il passato. Sposandosi con il buon Tibiletti

sarebbe stato come sposarsi con un mostro infernale, che l'avrebbe rapita alla morte. Prima però della partenza definitiva, concede quel suo corpo, abusato da tanti, a quell'orco bavoso del dottor Trigona, che la inizia al rito funebre con le sue arti magiche. Il narratore, d'altra parte, si ritira dalla scena inorridito, e vedrà, dopo un paio d'anni, al suo ritorno in paese, su una piccola lapide di marmo i nomi dei due sventurati, mentre lo stregone, più curvo e bieco di prima, s'aggira ancora con la sua nuova macchina intorno a quelle misere ceneri.

Se il personaggio di Caterina è avvolto in una nube di mistero, quello del narratore non è meno ambiguo e incoerente. Pur collocandosi essenzialmente fra i buoni e i perseguitati (le vittime), il personaggio non è né un eroe né un martire. Sa che Caterina, sposando il mostruoso Tibiletti, si sottopone a un martirio, ma il giovane galante ed erotomane non fa nulla per salvarla; resta tranquillamente in paese a giocare a carte al Metropole. Manda lo sciocco Penella a raccogliere le notizie sulle nozze, che dovevano essere una farsa: una macabra rappresentazione teatrale, un rito funebre anticipato con i vestiti da cerimonia.

Il personaggio del narratore, da principio e nel corso dell'azione, ha quindi facce mutevoli, contraddittorie. Al principio si comporta da amante sincero e appassionato, romantico, che suscita teneri affetti in Caterina, la quale durante i mesi di lontananza gli scrive giornalmente. Al suo ritorno al paese, invece, egli assume la veste del signorotto arrogante, fannullone, che passa le giornate a giocare a carte al Metropole con tipi come Sberzi, uno dei porci della mandra di Epicuro, capaci di portare in camera una ragazza con una bottiglia d'acqua minerale. Questo strano avventuriero non risiede a casa, in famiglia, di cui parla pochissimo, ma al Metropole, un vecchio albergo che somiglia a un covo di dissoluti birbanti.

Nelle sue ricerche su Caterina, il narratore non è tanto interessato a conoscere il passato di Caterina (chi è? che cosa di traumatico le è accaduto?), quanto ad assicurarsi il controllo assoluto del suo corpo. Caterina intuisce questo totale cambiamento nell'animo del narratore, perciò rifiuta la sua ridicola proposta di matrimonio preferendo sposare Tibiletti, che le voleva veramente bene. Le allettanti proposte dell'amico Bogni attiravano il nostro giovane narratore molto di più: si va in Sud America, Africa o nell'isola di Caso? Egli è ossessionato dal desiderio di evasione, ma ad un tempo esita a lasciare il suo paese, «origine...d'ogni bene, e d'ogni male». (p. 157) Caterina rappresenta appunto questo mondo familiare e locale; il paese e il lago, e gli abitanti, che pur lasciandoli per breve tempo, bisogna rivederli, fare ritorno.

Il personaggio di Arturo Tibiletti è forse il più tragico e grottesco del romanzo, e con Caterina è la vittima più oppressa e infelice, e come una liberazione dal mondo, va con la sua sventurata compagna alla morte. Tibiletti aveva sposato Caterina nella chiesetta di Sant'Anna dinanzi al parroco e gli invitati. Caterina apparteneva di diritto a lui, anche se molti furbi e maligni avevano posseduto il suo corpo. Da generoso amante, a lui ciò non importava molto, era disposto a condividere Caterina con i suoi amici rivali. Chi voleva bene a Caterina, voleva bene a lui. Non poteva essere più generoso di questo. Provò la gioia indescrivibile del viaggio di nozze a Roma, e a colmare la felicità gli arrivò infine la lieta inaspettata notizia di diventare padre. Come Caterina, Tibiletti è un vinto, schiacciato da una società brutale e spietata, che opprime i deboli e gli ingenui. Il personaggio di Tibiletti viene descritto nei suoi minuti particolari somatici, ma non è analizzato in profondità dall'A. Durante lo svolgimento della storia il personaggio è ridotto a uno stato servile, a un non-uomo, a una figura mostruosa di uomo; uno stato fra l'umano e il ferino che muove a pietà e compassione. Le corna che gli adornano il capo, sono invisibili a lui; gli basta stare accanto a Caterina. Sposando Caterina, tuttavia, Tibiletti firma anche il patto con il diavolo. Alla guida della sua Galloni, dopo pochi mesi dallo sposalizio, scompare da questo mondo con la sua Caterina.

La dolorosa storia di Caterina richiama alla memoria tante altre storie simili, p.es. quella di Caterina Medici, che innocente fu bruciata sul rogo nel Seicento, falsamente accusata di stregoneria (cfr.P.Verri, Manzoni e ultimamente il romanzo di L. Sciascia). Un'accusa, fondata su pregiudizi e la malignità umana, bastò a mettere su tutta Milano contro quella povera innocente; durante quello stesso periodo Renzo fuggiva da Milano, e Lucia era rapita dall'Innominato.

La Caterina moderna, questa descritta da Chiara in questo romanzo, non è una strega, né è bruciata viva, né è religiosa e casta come la Lucia di Manzoni; nondimeno, al pari di Lucia e di milioni di altre donne oppresse, Caterina è una vittima tragica, una martire della società feroce; è una vittima dell'ingordigia sessuale dell'uomo, abusata e ridotta ad uno stato di schiavitù, costretta a servire i suoi sadici signori. Una vittima, tuttavia, che a differenza delle altre, non si ribella, non si difende, non prega né implora misericordia, ma si lascia abusare dai suoi carnefici, dai sozzi cani che se la divorano. Somiglia ad un agnello sperduto, inseguito costantemente da un branco di cani affamati, con i denti aguzzi e latranti, finché non afferrano nei loro artigli la preda stanca, che si lascia sbranare.

Insomma, quella dolorosa spina nel cuore, descritta dall'A. nella sua storia, è sentita anche dal lettore, che prova turbamento e pietà per Caterina. L' A., d'altra parte, in retrospettiva, sente rimorso della sua parte tenuta nella tragedia di Caterina, e sente anche lui compassione davanti alla sua vittima. Dal punto di vista artistico, il romanzo ci sembra uno dei migliori dell'ultimo Chiara. Gli elementi autobiografici, segnalati nel corso dell'analisi, vanno giudicati non a sé e identificati alla lettera con la vita dell'autore, né bisogna imputare l'autore di egoismo, di vigliaccheria, d'immoralità; ovviamente ci troviamo nel mondo della finzione e dell'arte, non già del documento storico e della biografia, che nell'arte sono trasformati, superati e riplasmati secondo criteri estetici e artistici, generando da quella materia grezza vita nuova.

Remo Ceserani

OSSERVAZIONI SPARSE SUL ROBINSON DI TOURNIER

Mi è capitato di dire, in varie occasioni, che Michel Tournier, con il suo romanzo *Vendredi, ou le lymbe du Pacifique* (1957),[1] ha dimostrato di essere uno dei pochi, fra gli scrittori e gli uomini di cultura del nostro tempo, ad avvertire, con una sensibilità precisa e quasi esasperata, il cambiamento che ha investito, nel corso degli anni Cinquanta, le nostre strutture sociali e culturali.

Il cambiamento, come si sa, è stato forte e profondo. Esso è avvenuto non su tutta la terra, ma solo nel cosiddetto primo mondo, con esclusione netta del terzo mondo, mentre il secondo mondo è rimasto a lungo blindato contro i cambiamenti, salvo poi, d'improvviso e affannosamente, cercare di annullarsi e di omologarsi al primo mondo. È stato una specie di grande terremoto, di quelli che hanno origine nelle viscere recondite della terra e che sul momento possono ingannare gli osservatori e gli strumenti di misurazione e apparire non particolarmente potenti e sconvolgenti, ma che sulla distanza risultano aver trasformato totalmente un intero paesaggio naturale e sociale.[2]

Mi pare di poter sostenere che Tournier, riscrivendo in quel libro la storia di Robinson Crusoe e di Venerdì, avesse dato, con mezzi romanzeschi e immaginari (gli unici disponibili in quel momento), una grande e perfetta rappresentazione metaforica del cambiamento, mettendo addirittura in scena, a metà della vicenda, un vero e proprio terremoto, insieme con una eruzione vulcanica e uno scoppio disastroso delle polveri accumulate dal naufrago in fondo a una grotta: da quel momento il Robinson di Tournier ha cessato definitivamente di essere, anche solo parzialmente, il Robinson di Defoe, paradigma simbolico del borghese moderno,

---

[1] Il romanzo è divenuto nel tempo un piccolo classico, corredato di innumerevoli interpretazioni critiche, commenti, apparati, ecc. Non entro qui nelle questioni genetiche e variantistiche e neppure mi misuro con la folta interpretazione critica. Il testo a cui mi riferisco (indicando le pagine fra parentesi) è quello, rivisto e integrato, che si legge in *Vendredi ou les limbes du Pacifique*, con una postfazione di G. Deleuze, Paris, Gallimard, folio, 1972. In italiano è stato fatto tradurre quasi subito da Italo Calvino presso Einaudi. Ho presente l'edizione italiana, anch'essa integrata, di *Venerdì o il limbo del Pacifico*, trad. di C. Lusignoli, Torino, Einaudi, 1994.

[2] Cfr. R. Ceserani, *Raccontare il postmoderno*, Torino, Bollati-Boringhieri, 1997. In questo libro sostengo, in via di ipotesi, che di cambiamenti simili ne sono avvenuti pochi altri nella storia e, con lo stesso peso e portata, solo all'inizio della modernità, nel passaggio fra Sette e Ottocento.

colonizzatore e pioniere, coltivatore e imprenditore, fondatore di un piccolo stato con una sua costituzione e organizzatore del lavoro proprio e di Venerdì, e si è trovato di nuovo nudo e crudo, spiazzato e disorientato, costretto a ripartire da zero, a ripensarsi, a ripensare lo stesso suo rapporto con l'altro, l'improvvisamente libero e leggero Venerdì.

Raccolgo qui, in ordine sparso, alcune osservazioni di lettura del romanzo, che riguardano strategie narrative, procedimenti della rappresentazione e nuclei tematici della storia raccontata da Tournier e da lui esemplata sulla storia raccontata da Defoe. Alcune di queste osservazioni confermano, a me pare, la straordinaria capacità, da parte di Tournier, di avvertire i motivi profondi del mutamento e le conseguenze della nuova condizione postmoderna.

La trama: semplificazioni, complicazioni, spiazzamenti, scambi di ruolo, rovesciamenti

Riprendendo la classica trama della storia di naufragio e sopravvivenza, Tournier era perfettamente consapevole del carattere fondante per l'immaginario della modernità della storia di Robinson, divenuta "mito" attraverso le tante e quasi ossessive rivisitazioni, i tanti *remakes* (Karl Marx li chiamava *Robinsonaden*).[3] Egli riconosceva il valore esemplare, quasi allegorico, di quella vicenda e sapeva che essa, come tutti i grandi miti, ha degli elementi costitutivi estremamente semplici: l'isola, il mare, la nave che affonda, gli strumenti del lavoro e della vita che Robinson recupera dalla nave e sono fondamentali, insieme con la sua cultura, il suo *know-how* e la costante lettura della Bibbia, per compiere l'opera a cui, come personaggio, è narrativamente destinato. Probabilmente Tournier era anche consapevole della possibile interferenza di altri testi e sottotesti (quelli, per esempio, che raccontano la storia di Ulisse, o di Sindbad il marinaio, o di Landolfo Rufolo), così come avvertiva, istintivamente, che al tema del naufragio poteva sovrapporsi il sentimento moderno, e anche postmoderno, della catastrofe.

Rispetto al modello, o ai modelli, Tournier ha operato, per quel che riguarda la trama del racconto, interventi di spiazzamento (come la modificazione dello sfondo geografico e storico della vicenda), di semplificazione (lo sfrondamento degli episodi inutili, l'approfondimento degli elementi principali, la concentrazione sui punti di svolta della vicenda), di complicazione (l'introduzione premonitoria con

---

[3] Cfr., oltre al classico libro di HANS BLUMENBERG, *Naufragio con spettatore. Paradigma di una metafora dell'esistenza*, Bologna, Il mulino, 1985, Laura Sanna Nowé e Maurizio Virdis (a cura di), *Naufragi. Atti del Convegno di Studi Cagliari 8-9-10 aprile 1992*, Roma, Bulzoni, 1993, nel quale è raccolto anche il bel saggio di MARIELLA DI MAIO, *Tre volte Robinson (Verne, Giraudoux, Tournier)*, pp. 515-526; e Mariella Di Maio (a cura di), *Naufragi. Storia di un'avventurosa metafora*, Milano, Guerini, 1994.

il linguaggio arcano dei tarocchi, la reduplicazione del naufragio, che la seconda volta prende la forma di una catastrofe, il diverso sviluppo dei personaggi e dei loro rapporti, il rovesciamento dell'esito finale).

Gli spiazzamenti hanno la funzione di dare una sistemazione e una contestualizzazione nuova a gran parte degli elementi costitutivi del mito. L'aver spostato, per esempio, l'isola del naufrago dall'oceano Atlantico al Pacifico e il periodo storico di sfondo dal Seicento al Settecento ha l'effetto di avvicinare più direttamente l'avventura di Robinson al grande momento illuministico della scoperta scientifica e antropologica dei popoli primitivi e delle isole felici della zona tropicale. È come se su quell'isola, che pure viene rappresentata come un pezzo di mondo inesplorato e mai toccato da essere umano, fossero già arrivati (prima di Robinson, prima di Tournier, prima degli stessi selvaggi araucani che ci arrivano da lontano per celebrare sulla spiaggia i loro riti feroci) i grandi antropologi del Novecento, da Margaret Mead a Malinowski. Su quell'isola, la cui mappa immaginaria è stata a lungo sul tavolo di lavoro di Tournier, accanto agli atlanti geografici e geologici, alle enciclopedie, ai trattati di zoologia e botanica delle isole del Pacifico meridionale, accanto alle relazioni dei viaggiatori del Settecento e agli esploratori successivi, è come se fossero già approdati in tanti. Per questo il narratore può descriverla con precisione scientifica e Robinson goderne tutte le straordinarie e generose bellezze e ricchezze. Per questo i suoi sforzi e programmi di sopravvivenza e addomesticamento possono apparire molto più facili di quelli del Robinson di Defoe e superati con euforico senso di trionfo, dopo i momenti iniziali di angoscia e infelicità esistenziale. Tanto più riuscirà sorprendente e radicale l'improvviso rivolgimento catastrofico della natura, che ha evidentemente lo scopo di mettere in crisi gli ingenui programmi e i facili trionfi della ragione illuministica, così come mise in crisi quelli dei *philosophes* il terremoto di Lisbona del 1755.

Uno degli spostamenti più rilevanti, o più sorprendenti, rispetto alla trama di base, riguarda lo sfondo sociale e familiare del personaggio di Robinson, il mondo da cui proviene. Il padre del Robinson di Defoe era stato un piccolo commerciante, immigrato in Inghilterra da Brema, si era ritirato dagli affari e faceva il *rentier*. A seguito della morte dei fratelli Robinson era divenuto figlio unico. Il padre lo voleva avvocato, voleva che facesse il salto dalla vita rischiosa dei commerci a quella socialmente più solida e prestigiosa delle libere professioni. Ammalato, severo, saggio, egli aveva accolto con molto dispiacere i propositi di avventura sul mare del figlio e aveva cercato di dissuaderlo, insegnandogli la virtù del non correre rischi, dell'accontentarsi, dello scegliere una vita di giusta misura. Tutto questo, in Defoe, serviva ancor più a far spiccare le caratteristiche psicologiche del suo personaggio, il suo spirito avventuroso, la sua vocazione imprenditoriale.

Il Robinson di Tournier viene da una famiglia di livello sociale più basso e ha lasciato dietro di sé addirittura una sua famigliola, con una moglie e un figlio. Il padre era un commerciante di tessuti, era afflitto non dalla gotta ma da un eterno raffreddore, viveva in una bottega piena di stoffe, morbida e felpata, era un vecchietto minuto, timido e freddoloso, e al figlio aveva proposto, come modello, una filosofia della vita mediocre e rinunciataria. Molto più forte era stata la madre, donna di polso, con la quale Robinson aveva avuto un rapporto più intenso. A lei è tuttora legato da ricordi che lo assillano in modo angoscioso, fra cui quello di una sorellina piccola, dal nome wordsworthiano di Lucy, morta nell'infanzia. Il triangolo freudiano che lo incatena a ricordi dolorosi non lo aiuta certo a sopravvivere nella solitudine acuta dell'isola, lo trascina in momenti di rinuncia e depressione, lo spinge a cercare (nel pantano, nella grotta) occasioni di ritorno alla vita informe prenatale, rifugi nell'utero materno, o per converso disperati e frenetici tentativi di fuga.

Il libro di Tournier è diviso chiaramente in tre parti (precedute da un'introduzione) e in ciascuna delle tre parti la vicenda prende un nuovo sviluppo. Nella prima parte (capitoli 1-4) Robinson, approdato sull'isola, reagisce cercando di costruirsi un mezzo di fuga e facendo un clamoroso errore di programmazione e di calcolo, quando costruisce una barca che non può con le sue sole forze trascinare fino al mare. Si rifiuta di esplorare l'isola e cerca solo, disperatamente, di rivolgersi al mare, facendo segnali e aspettando l'arrivo di qualche salvatore. In questa fase egli conosce esperienze di abbattimento e di regressione, ma poi, attraverso un lento esame di sé, del suo passato, delle sue pulsioni e allucinazioni, attraverso gli incontri con gli animali che popolano l'isola, il graduale controllo dello spazio e del tempo, l'amicizia con il cane Tenn, l'addomesticamento delle capre, il successo delle coltivazioni, la creazione simbolica di istituzioni, leggi, riti, fortificazioni, pesi e misure, egli comincia a far sua l'isola, rivolge tutta la sua attenzione alla terra, le impone la sua organizzazione e il suo dominio. Un giorno assiste per la prima volta a un rito sulla spiaggia degli indigeni araucani, venuti con le loro piroghe da un'altra isola.

Nella seconda parte (capitoli 5-8), il rapporto fra Robinson e l'isola si approfondisce e si complica. Con la discesa nella grotta egli giunge a recuperare strati ancora più profondi del suo passato e a conoscere i limiti estremi della solitudine, della sospensione del tempo, della fragilità creaturale, dell'esaltazione quasi mistica per la luce, dell'attrazione rischiosa per le viscere della terra. L'isola, non più solo oggetto di un'opera di coltivazione e assoggettamento, diviene anche l'oggetto del suo amore. Tornano gli araucani e accanto a lui fa la sua comparsa un nuovo compagno, Venerdì, sul quale si concentra, quasi in modo ossessivo, il suo esercizio di potere e assoggettamento. La presenza di Venerdì complica, rendendolo triangolare, il suo rapporto con Tenn e anche quello con l'isola. Un'agitazione sempre più inquietante si impossessa di lui, finché la deflagrazione provocata dalle polveri e il terremoto non distruggono d'un colpo tutto il suo lavoro di anni.

Nella terza parte (capitoli 9-12), dopo la deflagrazione, il romanzo cambia direzione, è come un film fatto girare all'indietro, è come se Robinson facesse di nuovo naufragio. Il mondo, attorno a lui, è fatto solo di relitti (*épaves*):

Robinson regardait autour de lui d'un air hébété, et machinalement il se mit à ramasser les objets que la grotte avait vomis avant de se refermer. Il y avait des hardes déchirées, un mousquet au canon tordu, des fragments de poterie, des sacs troués, des couffins crevés. Il examinait chacune de ces épaves et allait la placer délicatement au pied du cèdre géant. Vendredi l'imitait plus qu'il ne l'aidait, car répugnant naturellement à réparer et à conserver, il achevait généralement de détruire les objets endommagés. (pp. 186-187)

Gli strumenti che erano sfuggiti al primo naufragio e avevano consentito l'operazione di sopravvivenza e conquista dell'isola sono andati tutti in frantumi: è rimasto, significativamente, solo il cannocchiale, che servirà in futuro per contemplare l'isola, senza più violarla, per scrutare il cielo e il sole, e per avvistare la nave liberatrice. L'eruzione del vulcano e il terremoto hanno scosso la terra che lui ha amato e che d'improvviso gli si è ribellata contro. Venerdì ha vinto e Robinson può solo far propri i valori di Venerdì, divenendo lui, con un rovesciamento dei ruoli, il soggetto da educare. Egli si libera di tutti gli apparati che si è dato: i vestiti, i riti, il modo di suddividere e occupare il tempo. Si rende conto che l'isola, e Venerdì, avevano una forza che non si poteva controllare. Guidato da Venerdì impara ad apprezzare l'aria, la leggerezza delle creature che volano in cielo, il calore e la luce del sole e questo diviene la sua nuova divinità.

Il nuovo sviluppo della vicenda comporta un diverso rapporto dei personaggi con se stessi e con le proprie concezioni di vita e dei personaggi fra loro. Il sistema molto semplice dei personaggi su cui era costruito il romanzo viene radicalmente sconvolto. C'era stata all'inizio, nell'introduzione, la coppia costituita dal capitano Van Deyssel e da Robinson, poi, in seguito al naufragio, la lunga solitudine di Robinson, poi la coppia Robinson-Venerdì, per molto tempo disuguale, costruita sul rapporto padrone-schiavo, con totale dipendenza del secondo dal primo. Dopo il cataclisma, il rapporto tra Robinson e Venerdì si trasforma in un rapporto fra eguali, che comunicano alla pari e possono anche scambiarsi i ruoli. Con l'arrivo della nave, e con la piccola società umana che porta con sé, i rapporti si complicano, i personaggi si costituiscono in relazione con gli altri personaggi. Il nuovo capitano è l'esatto opposto di Van Deyssel: l'altro aveva rinunciato a governare la nave, questo è in pieno controllo della piccola società cui è preposto. L'altro aveva cercato di predire il destino futuro di Robinson, questo sembra non provare nessun interesse né per l'avventura passata di Robinson né per il suo presente. Le reazioni di Robinson e Venerdì si divaricano. Venerdì non prova nessuno stupore di fronte alla prima nave che vede in vita sua (e che si colloca sulla stessa linea dei suoi aquiloni, dei suoi essere alati), Robinson è solo un poco stupito di vedere che la nave, nel modo come è costruita, dimostra un miglioramento tecnico rispetto alle navi che conosceva lui (le guerre, i commerci, la tratta degli schiavi hanno stimolato l'inventività ingegneristica dell'uomo); Venerdì si adatta con grande facilità al mondo umano della nave, Robinson si sente ormai estraneo a quella società, dopo averla tanto rimpianta.

La vicenda si conclude con un improvviso rovesciamento delle previsioni e dei destini dei personaggi: Venerdì parte salendo sulla nave, Robinson rimane sull'isola. Ma non ci rimane, con un'ultima sorpresa, da solo. La nave, che ha portato via Venerdì, ha lasciato dietro di sé un nuovo personaggio, che verrà a costituire una nuova coppia con Robinson: il bambino che, imbarcato come mozzo, si era rivelato ribelle e refrattario all'educazione impostagli dal cuoco e dai marinai, era divenuto vittima delle loro violenze e, con la sua aria infelice e malinconica, aveva suscitato un moto di simpatia in Robinson. È come se, nel momento estremo, Robinson e l'isola avessero prodotto un figlio. È come se a fare di nuovo visita all'isola venissero chiamati l'*Émile* di Rousseau o l'*enfant sauvage* di Truffaut. Alla coppia padrone-schiavo può ora sostituirsi la coppia, molto illuministica, maestro-allievo o padre-figlio. Il sole, nascendo sull'isola, illumina di sé e accende di colori trionfali i capelli del piccolo estone albino dagli occhi verdi. Robinson, che già ha compiuto più volte il rito della *nominatio*, dando il nome all'isola (due volte), alla barca, a Venerdì, e con ciò segnando il suo dominio su di essi, ora compie un ultimo gesto, dando un nome al piccolo Jaan:

– Comment t'appelles-tu? lui demanda Robinson.
– Je m'appelle Jaan Neljapäev. Je suis né en Estonie, ajouta-t-il comme pour excuser ce nom difficile.
– Désormais, lui dit Robinson, tu t'appelleras Jeudi. C'est le jour de Jupiter, dieu du Ciel. C'est aussi le dimanche des enfants. (p. 254)

Il libro si chiude, come *Le Roi des aulnes*, con l'immagine di un bambino, salvato e forse salvifico. Difficile dire se si tratta davvero dell'inizio di una nuova storia, in direzione utopistica e decisamente illuministica. Il gesto di speranza verso il futuro, rappresentato da un nuovo rapporto affettivo e da un nuovo progetto di educazione, è reso debole e precario da alcuni elementi che hanno ormai segnato in profondo la scena dell'isola e la vita di Robinson: il terremoto, che ha incrinato irrimediabilmente ogni immagine di natura intrinsecamente buona, il confronto deludente con la società umana portata lì dalla nave (e reduce da guerre imperialistiche), che ha incrinato ogni fede in una comunità civile ideale e suggerito a Robinson di preferire piuttosto quella sua isola solitaria, chiusa nella sua rude e primitiva arcaicità.

Esplorazioni della soggettività e procedimenti narrativi

La voce narrante del romanzo di Tournier, nettamente diversa da quella della prima persona autobiografica di Defoe, non può che essere la voce di un narratore anonimo, abbastanza vicino ai suoi due personaggi, ma anche sufficientemente distanziato da essi per poterne rappresentare anche le duplicità e complicatezze interne, soprattutto di Robinson, al quale peraltro viene ogni tanto ceduta la parola tramite l'artificio, ripreso da Defoe, del giornale di bordo (il *log-book*). Rispetto al Robinson di Defoe, uomo pratico e puritano, che è rappresentato quasi solo nelle sue azioni e comportamenti, nei suoi calcoli e inventari, nei "consigli" che tiene con se stesso, nella capacità di affrontare le "situazioni" e risolvere i problemi, di usare la scrittura come forma di ordinamento e controllo del tempo e del disordine caotico della realtà, e sembra non avere una dimensione interiore (se non quella di alcuni sentimenti che di volta in volta lo riempiono: l'esaltazione, l'orgoglio di sé, la gioia, il terrore, l'angoscia che, quando c'è, lo fa correre su e giù per la spiaggia), il Robinson di Tournier ha una notevole stratificazione interiore, una vita ricca di percezioni ed emozioni, di reazioni fisiche e psicologiche (il rovello della mente, la depressione, la nausea, il disgusto, la vertigine, l'eccitazione, il gesto nevrotico). Egli ha, come è giusto per un personaggio post-freudiano, un inconscio, una memoria da scavare, una capacità di sognare, di provare allucinazioni, e anche, naturalmente, una sessualità (e ciò lo differenzia nettamente dal Robinson di Defoe, che è invece asessuato, al tempo stesso quintessenza dell'*homo oeconomicus* e dell'inglese puritano).

Nel Robinson di Defoe la vita interiore sembra affiorare soltanto, con prepotenza, in una celebre pagina, che ha avuto un ruolo di fondazione geniale per il romanzo moderno: la pagina in cui viene descritta, con perturbante inquietudine, l'angoscia non troppo esplicita, ma fortissima, che prende Robinson quando scorge sulla sabbia, per la prima volta, l'orma lasciata da un altro essere umano.

Il Robinson di Tournier è poco economico anche nei suoi gesti, conosce il disorientamento totale, la perdita del senso del tempo, il vuoto esistenziale enorme, ontologico, che può prendere la creatura nella sua solitudine e nei suoi tentativi frenetici di sfuggire alla disperazione. Oltre che postfreudiano egli è anche postheideggeriano e sperimenta la vertigine assoluta del rapporto fra essere e tempo:

> Combien de jours, de semaines, de mois, d'années s'étaient-ils écoulés depuis le naufrage de la *Virginie*? Robinson était pris de vertige quand il se posait cette question. Il lui semblait alors jeter une pierre dans un puits et attendre vainement que retentisse le bruit de sa chute sur le fond. Il se jura de marquer désormais sur un arbre de l'île une encoche chaque jour, et un croix tous les trente jours. Puis il oublia son propos. (pp. 32-33)

Osservando Robinson da una posizione un po' distanziata, il narratore di Tournier può rivelare anche le motivazioni inconfessate delle azioni del personaggio:

> La sagesse aurait été de procéder sans plus tarder aux opérations de débarquement qui présenteraient d'immenses difficultés pour un homme seul. Pourtant il n'en fit rien, se donnant comme raison que vider la *Virginie*, c'était la rendre plus vulnérable à un coup de vent et compromettre sa meilleure chance de sauvetage. En vérité il éprouvait une in-

surmontable répugnance pour tout ce qui pouvait ressembler à des travaux d'installation dans l'île. (p. 21)

Egli inoltre può, con lo svolgersi della trama, sostituire al punto di vista di un personaggio quello dell'altro, al punto di vista di Robinson, e ai suoi valori, alla sua concezione del mondo, quelli di Venerdì. È un passaggio fondamentale per poter dare non solo una parità di trattamento ai due personaggi, ma anche per poter conferire una vera e propria coscienza al personaggio di Venerdì.

Il tema del corpo. L'incontro con se stesso. Lo sprofondamento nell'infanzia

Il tema del corpo umano, della nudità del naufrago solitario, della necessità o meno di ricoprirlo con i vestiti era già presente nel libro di Defoe, dove un Robinson puritano e asessuato si mostrava molto sensibile a questo aspetto della natura umana e subito dopo la necessità di procurarsi il cibo aveva preso in esame quella di ricoprirsi e anche quando aveva dovuto spogliarsi per raggiungere a nuoto il relitto, era stato bene attento a non togliersi i pantaloni.

In Tournier il tema diviene, con sensibilità moderna, centrale nel libro e si arricchisce di sviluppi e sfaccettature, collegandosi con l'orgoglio e i turbamenti del sentirsi vivere dentro un corpo caldo e pulsante, con la necessità di controllare la forza prorompente degli impulsi sessuali, con le esperienze esistenziali della nudità creaturale, con le forme culturali della rappresentazione e della autorappresentazione del corpo.

I due momenti in cui il tema viene impostato e riceve una iniziale elaborazione sono quelli del primo denudamento di Robinson, nell'episodio dell'acquazzone, e delle prime descrizioni degli effetti della vita solitaria sulle forme e i lineamenti stessi del suo corpo. Nella scena dell'acquazzone l'atto del denudarsi, e poi quelli dell'orinare sotto la pioggia, del paragonarsi a una foca, dell'accennare passi festosi di danza danno al tema una connotazione di gioco bambinesco, di autoironia sottile, di compiaciuto ritorno al mondo infantile e a quello dei popoli primitivi. Lo slancio di allegria puerile viene poi pagato con un mutamento di umore improvviso e serotino, con un rapido passaggio ai temi della fragilità creaturale:

Les premières gouttes mitraillèrent la coque de l'*Évasion*. Robinson voulut d'abord ignorer ce contretemps imprévu, mais il dut bientôt retirer ses vêtements dont la pesanteur trempée gênait ses mouvements. Il les rangea à l'abri dans la partie achevée de la coque. Il s'attarda un moment à regarder l'eau tiède ruisseler sur son corps couvert de croûtes de terre et de crasse qui fondaient en petites rigoles boueuses. Ses toisons rousses, collées en plaques luisantes, s'orientaient selon des lignes de forces qui accentuaient leur animalité. "Un phoque d'or", pensa-t-il avec un vague sourire. Puis il urina, trouvant plaisant d'ajou-

ter sa modeste part au déluge qui noyait tout autour de lui. Il se sentait soudain en vacan-
ces, et un accès de gaieté lui fit esquisser un pas de danse lorsqu'il courut, aveuglé par les
gouttes et cinglé par les rafales, se réfugier sous le couvert des arbres. [...]

L'élan de gaieté puérile qui avait emporté Robinson était tombé en même temps que se
dissipait l'espèce d'ébriété où l'entretenait son travail forcené. Il se sentait sombrer dans un
abîme de déréliction, nu et seul, dans se paysage d'Apocalypse, avec pour toute société
deux cadavres pourrissant sur le pont d'une épave. Il ne devait comprendre que plus tard
la portée de cette expérience de la nudité qu'il faisait pour la première fois. Certes, ni la
température ni un sentiment de quelconque pudeur ne l'obligeaient à porter des vêtements
de civilisé. Mais si c'était par routine qu'il les avait conservés jusqu'alors, il éprouvait par
son désespoir la valeur de cette armure de laine et de lin dont la société humaine l'enve-
loppait encore un moment auparavant. La nudité est un luxe que seul l'homme chaude-
ment entouré par la multitude de ses semblables peut s'offrir sans danger. Pour Robinson,
aussi longtemps qu'il n'aurait pas changé d'âme, c'était une épreuve d'une meurtrière témérité. Dépouillée de ces pauvres hardes – usées, lacérées, maculées, mais issues de plu-
sieurs millénaires de civilisation et imprégnées d'humanité –, sa chair était offerte vulné-
rable et blanche au rayonnement des éléments bruts. (pp. 29-30)

Al termine della costruzione della barca destinata alla fuga, e che gli è costata
fatiche immani, il corpo di Robinson porta inciso sulla pelle e nella carne la storia
del lungo lavoro. Il suo corpo, come in certe invenzioni di romanzi di fantascienza
postmoderni, "racconta" e "parla", in un modo diretto e inquietante e senza le *dif-
férences* derridiane dell'*écriture*, con una immediatezza che non potrà avere il giornale di bordo (a quel punto non ancora iniziato):

L'*Évasion* était terminée, mais la longue histoire de sa construction demeurait écrite à
jamais dans la chair de Robinson. Coupures, brûlures, estafilades, callosités, tavelures in-
délébiles et bourrelets cicatriciels racontaient la lutte opiniâtre qu'il avait menée si longtemps pour en arriver à ce petit bâtiment trapu et ailé. A défaut de journal de bord, il re-
garderait son corps quand il voudrait se souvenir. (p. 35)

La parte del suo corpo che è destinata a esprimersi e significare, il viso, vista allo
specchio recuperato dalla *Virginia*, racconta in modo eloquente cosa succede a chi
si trova d'improvviso senza interlocutori, senza possibilità di comunicazione:

Aucun changement notable n'avait altéré ses traits, et pourtant il se reconnut à peine.
Un seul mot se présenta à son esprit: *défiguré*. "Je suis défiguré", prononça-t-il à haute
voix, tandis que le désespoir lui serrait le coeur. [...] On aurait dit qu'un hiver d'une ri-
gueur impitoyable fût passé sur cette figure familière, effaçant toutes ses nuances, pétrifiant
tous ses frémissements, simplifiant son expression jusqu'à la grossièreté. Ah, certes, cette
barbe carrée qui l'encadrait d'une oreille à l'autre n'avait rien de la douceur floue et soyeuse
de celle du Nazaréen! C'était bien à l'Ancien Testament et à sa justice sommaire qu'elle
ressortissait, ainsi d'ailleurs que ce regard trop franc dont la violence mosaïque effrayait.

Narcisse d'un genre nouveau, abîmé de tristesse, recru de dégoût de soi, il médita longue-
ment en tête à tête avec lui-même. Il comprit que notre visage est cette partie de notre chair que
modèle et remodèle, réchauffe et anime sans cesse la présence de nos semblables. (p. 89-90)

Dopo l'arrivo di Venerdì e soprattutto dopo la deflagrazione le cose cambiano. Quel corpo, che ancora nel corso dell'esperienza nella grotta era risultato estraneo, sfigurato, sempre sul punto di ricadere in una nudità primitiva e colpevole, si libera finalmente di vergogna e vestiti, diviene oggetto di compiacimento di sé e autocostruzione, diviene strumento e scopo di esercizi ginnici arditi, si modella sul corpo vigoroso, flessibile e decisamente "bello", di Venerdì. "Eccolo!", dice Robinson quando vede avvicinarsi Venerdì:

> Saurai-je jamais marcher avec une aussi naturel majesté? Puis-je écrire sans ridicule qu'il semble drapé dans sa nudité? Il va, portant sa chair avec une ostentation souveraine, se portant en avant comme un ostensoir de chair. Beauté évidente, brutale, qui paraît faire le néant autour d'elle. (p. 221)

I temi del rapporto con l'altro, dello sdoppiamento, del travestimento, dello straniamento

Nel libro di Tournier l'incontro di Robinson con Venerdì è preceduto da una serie di incontri con animali. In questo la differenza con il *Robinson* di Defoe è abbastanza rilevante. Nel romanzo dello scrittore inglese c'è, a questo proposito, quasi un elemento di distrazione narrativa. In un primo tempo, mentre vengono narrate meticolosamente le spedizioni di Robinson sul relitto per recuperare tutte le cose che potranno riuscirgli necessarie, non si fa menzione di animali; poi, come in un ripensamento o un'aggiunta, salta fuori che fra le cose recuperate ci sono anche i preziossimi cane Tenn e i gatti, che vanno a creare con Robinson, dopo l'incontro con il gatto selvatico, una piccola società domestica.

Nel libro di Tournier arriverà a un certo punto anche il cane Tenn, prelevato dal bastimento precedente di Defoe, ma arriverà in modo dapprima inquietante, come un animale del tutto inselvatichito e spaventato, che rinuncia alla sua natura di cane, digrigna i denti e va a inselvarsi nella foresta. Poi, quando il Robinson di Defoe deciderà di rinunciare alla fuga e di dedicarsi all'addomesticamento dell'isola, tornerà a farsi vivo anche Tenn, e verrà a offrirgli la sua compagnia e amicizia, quasi a suggerirgli, con la sua domesticità ritrovata, di costruirsi una casa.

Ma prima di quello con Tenn, che avviene in un momento di crisi nella fabbricazione della barca *Evasione*, ci sono altri incontri di Robinson con animali, e molti ne seguiranno, e saranno quasi tutti all'insegna dell'estraneità, dell'indifferenza e della non comunicabilità. Comincia il caprone, che gli taglia stolidamente la strada, seguono gli avvoltoi goffi e maligni (il "consiglio di amministrazione", li chiama) che stanno là in alto sospesi in attesa della sua carogna, e poi i granchi, che con il rumore ossessionante delle chele provocano in lui uno stato di allucinazione e di inganno, poi i porci del pantano, poi la piccola razza che scatena in lui un sogno d'infanzia, poi i topi, le capre selvatiche, gli aguti, le tartarughe marine, gli insetti, tanti altri ancora.

Quando arriva Venerdì, egli si sottomette a Robinson con una vera e propria cerimonia rituale, ponendo il piede dell'uomo bianco sulla propria testa nera, e comunicandogli (nel linguaggio del suo codice culturale) che, a seguito della scissione da lui sperimentata fra anima e corpo, egli è ormai tutto suo:

> Vendredi est d'une docilité parfaite. En vérité il est mort depuis que la sorcière a dardé son index noueux sur lui. Ce qui a fui, c'était un corps sans âme, un corps aveugle, comme ces canards qui se sauvent en battant des ailes après qu'on leur a tranché la tête. Mais ce corps inanimé n'a pas fui au hasard. Il a couru rejoindre son âme, et son âme se trouvait entre les mains de l'homme blanc. Depuis, Vendredi appartient corps et âme à l'homme blanc. Tout ce que son maître lui ordonne est bien, tout ce qu'il défend est mal. Il est bien de travailler nuit et jour au fonctionnement d'une organisation délicate et dépourvue de sens. Il est mal de manger plus que la portion mesurée par le maître. Il est bien d'être soldat quand le maître est général, enfant de choeur quand il prie, maçon quand il construit, valet de ferme quand il se consacre à ses terres, berger quand il se préoccupe de ses troupeaux, rabatteur quand il chasse, pagayeur quand il vogue, porteur quand il voyage, guérisseur quand il souffre, et d'actionner pour lui l'éventail et le chasse-mouches. Il est mal de fumer la pipe, de se promener tout nu et de se cacher pour dormir quand il y a à faire. Mais si la bonne volonté de Vendredi est totale, il est encore très jeune, et sa jeunesse fuse parfois malgré lui. Alors il rit, il éclate d'un rire redoutable, un rire qui démasque et confond le sérieux menteur dont se parent le gouverneur et son île administrée. (pp. 148-149)

Dopo la deflagrazione e il cambiamento dei rapporti, c'è un'esplosione anche fra i due, uno scoppio dei sentimenti che arriva all'orlo dello scontro fisico. A questo punto è Venerdì che prende in mano la situazione, ricorre alla sua cultura per risolvere il conflitto dei sentimenti senza scontro fisico, attraverso un gioco teatrale di rappresentazioni e travestimenti. Venerdì crea un manichino che rappresenta Robinson e sfoga su di lui la sua aggressività e le pulsioni distruttive, Robinson risponde creando una statua di sabbia che rappresenta Venerdì e la prende a frustate. Ciascuno dei due impara a travestirsi in modo da assomigliare all'altro. Da quel momento i personaggi che vivono sull'isola sono quattro: Robinson, Venerdì e le rappresentazioni dell'uno e dell'altro. Per mezzo di questo piccolo teatro privato le tensioni si stemperano nella comicità e nel riso liberatorio, la storia passata viene rivissuta e rielaborata, i ricordi e i rimorsi esorcizzati.

> Un après-midi, [Vendredi] réveilla assez rudement Robinson qui faisait la sieste sous un eucalyptus. Il s'était fabriqué un déguisement dont Robinson ne compris pas tout de suite le sens. Il avait enfermé ses jambes dans des guenilles nouées en pantalon. Une courte veste couvrait ses épaules. Il portait un chapeau de paille, ce qui ne l'empêchait pas de s'abriter sous une ombrelle de palmes. Mais surtout il s'était fait une fausse barbe en se collant des touffes de poils roux de cocotier sur les joues.
> – Sais-tu qui je suis? demanda-t-il à Robinson en déambulant majestueusement devant lui.

– Non.

– Je suis Robinson Crusoé, de la ville d'York en Angleterre, le maître du sauvage Vendredi!

– Et moi alors, qui suis-je? demanda Robinson stupéfait.

– Devine!

Robinson connaissait trop bien maintenant son compagnon pour ne pas comprendre à demi-mot ce qu'il voulait. Il se leva et disparut dans la forêt.

Si Vendredi était Robinson, le Robinson de jadis, maître de l'esclave Vendredi, il ne restait à Robinson qu'à devenir Vendredi, le Vendredi esclave d'autrefois. [..] Il se contenta de se frotter le visage et le corps avec du jus de noix pour se brunir, et d'attacher autour de ses reins le pagne de cuir des Araucans que portait Vendredi le jour où il débarqua dans l'île. Puis il se présenta à Vendredi et lui dit:

– Voilà, je suis Vendredi!

Alor Vendredi s'efforça de faire de longues phrases dans son meilleur anglais, et Robinson lui répondit avec les quelques mots d'araucan qu'il avait appris du temps que Vendredi ne parlait pas du tout l'anglais.

– Je t'ai sauvé de tes congénères qui voulaient te sacrifier pour neutraliser ton pouvoir maléfique, dit Vendredi.

Et Robinson s'agenouilla par terre, il inclina sa tête jusqu'au sol en grommelant des remerciements éperdus. Enfin prenant le pied de Vendredi, il le posa sur sa nuque. (pp. 211-212)

La scoperta liberatoria del riso procede di pari passo con la costituzione di una coppia di eguali e con la ripetuta celebrazione allegorica della liberazione degli schiavi. Robinson si appropria lentamente dei valori di Venerdì: il gioco, la leggerezza, il valore dello straniamento e del riso, la relativizzazione dei punti di vista, la funzione delle rappresentazioni, la sublimazione delle pulsioni istintuali, la rinuncia a ogni essenzialismo nei ruoli sessuali. Egli si apre così, forse inconsapevolmente, verso alcuni dei valori, fra quelli sicuramente positivi, del mondo a noi contemporaneo.

Il tema dell'oro

C'è un episodio curioso nel *Robinson* di Defoe. Quando egli, risalito sulla nave, trova gli strumenti e i materiali preziosi che gli permetteranno di organizzare la sopravvivenza sull'isola, trova anche delle monete d'oro. Di fronte a questo elemento fondamentale della società mercantile e all'antico simbolo dell'umana avidità di ricchezza, il cui potere si riduce a nulla in un'isola deserta, egli assume d'improvviso un tono molto eloquente e pronuncia una vera e propria invettiva contro il denaro: «Oh roba inutile... a cosa mi servi?»

L'invettiva ha precise fonti letterarie, fra cui, in posizione preminente, un episodio del *Timone d'Atene* di Shakespeare (IV, 3), là dove si racconta di quando Timone, maledetti gli ateniesi governati solo dall'avidità del denaro e ritiratosi a vivere solitario in una grotta, mentre scava la terra alla ricerca di radici da mangiare, trova un mucchio di denaro, per lui ormai privo di significato, e pronuncia una condanna solenne del potere malefico dell'oro:

> [....] What is here?
> Gold? Yellow, glittering, precious gold?
> No, god [...]
> Thus much of this will make
> Black white, foul fair, wrong right,
> Base noble, old young, coward valiant.
> Ha, you gods! [...]
> This yellow slave,
> Will knit and break religions, bless th'accursed [...]

Il fatto curioso è che il personaggio di Robinson, in questo momento, dimostra di avere idee diametralmente diverse da quelle che aveva il suo creatore Daniel Defoe, il quale, appartenendo pienamente alla società mercantile del suo tempo e ai valori di un'Inghilterra che stava costruendo la sua potenza proprio sui commerci, aveva addirittura scritto, sulla *Review* di cui era il direttore, un articolo contenente un grande elogio del denaro «grazie al quale sono compiute tutte le grandi cose del mondo», "male" quindi "necessario" sul quale è basato ogni potere e ogni atto politico. [4]

Il fatto ancora più curioso, e rivelatore del valore di pura variazione letteraria dell'invettiva di Robinson, suggerita dalla situazione contingente, da quel suo trovarsi ormai solo su un'isola come un eremita costretto a nutrirsi di radici, e non dalla logica del personaggio e dell'azione, è che il Robinson di Defoe, dopo aver detto tutto il male possibile del denaro, decide di tenerselo. Questa decisione, che può apparire contraddittoria e quasi incomprensibile, in realtà è rivelatrice della logica vera del personaggio. Essa è al tempo stesso un riconoscimento dei valori della società di origine e appartenenza e al tempo stesso un atto magico e un po' fiabesco, una specie di pegno per il futuro. La mano invisibile che l'ha salvato dal naufragio forse gli indica che nel futuro ci sarà una possibilità non solo di salvezza, ma di arricchimento. Ed è quello che effettivamente avverrà al termine della sua avventura. Nonostante l'eccezionalità dell'esperienza del Robinson di Defoe, anzi proprio da quella eccezionalità viene confermata la straordinaria importanza della moneta, dell'oro, per la società e l'economia mercantile dominanti nel tempo in cui fu scritto.

Nettamente diversa è la vicenda raccontata da Tournier, il quale ha ambientato la sua storia in un'epoca successiva, nella quale la moneta era una protagonista non solo dei commerci, non solo delle ossessioni psicologiche degli uomini, ma anche

---

[4] D. DEFOE, *Denaro, denaro!*, in *Opere*, a cura di C. Izzo, Firenze, Sansoni, 1958, vol. III, pp. 844-846.

delle discussioni degli economisti e delle teorizzazioni dei *philosophes*. Il Robinson di Tournier trova sulla nave il cofanetto con le monete d'oro e senza stare troppo a pensarci lo porta con sé e lo deposita nella grotta, tenendolo lì più o meno come una moderna banca centrale tiene nel *caveau* la sua riserva aurea.

Quando, più tardi, Robinson è nella fase culminante della sua attività imprenditoriale di coltivatore e dominatore dell'isola, egli scopre le leggi fondamentali dell'economia moderna, l'importanza del controllo e della monetarizzazione del tempo, la virtù dello scambio e del mercato, l'utilità straordinaria dell'oro e della moneta. La sua celebrazione delle virtù della moneta potrebbe essere stata scritta, più che dal Defoe della *Review*, da un economista scozzese del Settecento; è, da parte di Tournier, un pezzo di bravura parodico, che fissa questa precisa fase dell'evoluzione del suo personaggio, ma al tempo stesso fa il verso alle tante invettive contro il dio giallo dell'oro:

> J'obéirai désormais à la règle suivante: toute production est création, et donc bonne. Toute consommation est destruction, et donc mauvaise. En vérité ma situation ici est assez semblable à celle de mes compatriotes qui débarquent chaque jour par navires entiers sur les côtes du Nouveaux Monde. Eux aussi doivent se plier à une morale de l'accumulation. Pour eux aussi perdre son temps est un crime, thésauriser du temps est la vertu cardinale. Thésauriser! Voici qu'à nouveau la misère de ma solitude m'est rappelée! Pour moi semer est bien, récolter est bien. Mais le mal commence lorsque je mouds le grain et cuis la pâte, car alors je travaille pour moi seul. Le colon américain peut sans remords poursuivre jusqu'à son terme le processus de la panification, car il *vendra* son pain, et l'argent qu'il entassera dans son coffre sera du temps et du travail thésaurisés. Quant à moi, hélas, ma misérable solitude me prive des bienfaits de l'argent dont je ne manque pourtant pas!
>
> Je mesure aujourd'hui la folie et la méchanceté de ceux qui calomnient cette institution divine: l'argent! L'argent spiritualise tout ce qu'il touche en lui apportant une dimension à la fois rationnelle – mesurable – et universelle – puisqu'un bien monnayé devient virtuellement accessible à tous les hommes. La vénalité est une vertu cardinale. L'homme vénal sait faire taire ses instincts meurtriers et asociaux – sentiment de l'honneur, amour-propre, patriotisme, ambition politique, fanatisme religieux, racisme – pour ne laisser parler que sa propension à la coopération, son goût des échanges fructueux, son sens de la solidarité humaine. Il faut prendre à la lettre l'expression *l'âge d'or*, et je vois bien que l'humanité y parviendrait vite si elle n'était menée que par des hommes vénaux. (pp. 61-62)

Quando però poi scoppia la polvere da sparo e cade tutta la costruzione che Robinson ha faticosamente sovrapposto all'isola, le monete d'oro vengono investite dalla deflagrazione e vengono sparse all'intorno, e però ormai nessuno, né Robinson né Venerdì, prova un minimo interesse per loro. Le cose cambiano quando arriva la nave del comandante Hunter e dei suoi marinai. Questi uomini vengono dall'antico mondo di Robinson, dominato da quegli stessi valori che Robinson, al momento della celebrazione delle virtù del denaro, aveva esaltato. Quando i nuovi visitatori incontrano il vecchio naufrago non c'è in essi, dominati solo da passioni e cupidigie, nessuno stupore. Non gliene importa niente di Robinson e non vogliono conoscere la sua storia. L'interesse di Robinson è tutto rivolto all'isola, al sole, alla natura; il loro interesse è, egoisticamente, tutto rivolto ai guadagni e alle ricchezze. Per Robinson l'oro ha perso da tempo ogni significato, l'idea dello scambio ha perso ogni valore. La deflagrazione ha strappato le monete dal loro deposito nella grotta e le ha sparse tutt'intorno. I marinai, quando cominciano a trovarne qualcuna, si scatenano. Per loro l'isola è, al pari di tutto il resto del mondo dove sono arrivati con la loro nave, un luogo di preda. La reazione di Robinson è di totale indifferenza; si sente di appartenere ormai a un'altra dimensione. Non si addolora, né si arrabbia.

Il tema dell'arpa eolia

È certamente un fatto abbastanza curioso, e credo molto significativo, che d'improvviso, nel libro di Tournier, non solo compaia, ma abbia un posto centrale nella mitologia di Venerdì, il grande tema romantico dell'arpa eolia. Il Venerdì di Tournier, uomo naturale, ma anche uomo flessibile e adattabile, uomo dell'aria, del vento e del canto che nell'aria si diffonde, personificazione calviniana della leggerezza, dopo l'epica lotta contro il caprone Andoar, ne utilizza il corpo per realizzare due progetti, che permettano al pesante caprone, morto volando nell'aria, di trasformarsi: in uno strumento per volare come l'aquilone, e in uno strumento per cantare come l'arpa eolia. Questi strumenti sono gli elementi costitutivi e funzionali dell'universo di Venerdì. Accanto a essi ci sono anche l'arco che scaglia frecce che vanno a perdersi in cielo e la bella nave che, leggera come un aquilone e sonora come un'arpa, lo porterà alla fine con sé, verso nuovi paesi, ignoti eppure non temibili, perché Venerdì non paventa nessun trabocchetto e nessuna sorpresa.

L'arpa eolia, invenzione ingegnosa di quel Settecento illuministico che nel libro di Tournier si pone in rapporto dialettico con il mondo primitivo delle creature selvagge e roussoiane che popolavano lontane isole e continenti, ha riempito di sé, come è noto, l'immaginario preromantico e romantico, facendo la sua comparsa nella poesia di Goethe, nei romanzi di Jean Paul, nella *Corinna* di Madame de Staël e poi via via nella poesia di Lamartine, in quella molto ventilata dei romantici inglesi, come strumento prodigioso che emana una musica suonata direttamente dalla natura stessa, come simbolo di un'idea di poesia che sgorga spontanea, a intermittenza, senza nessuna mediazione o atto di volontà.

Nella versione di Tournier, l'arpa eolia diventa uno strumento "elementare", che suona una musica funebre e pura:

> Robinson le vit plusieurs jours durant tendre entre les deux traverses, à l'aide de chevilles, les douze boyaux qui pouvaient garnir les cornes et le front d'Andoar. Avec un sens inné de la musique, il les accordait, non à la tierce ou à la quinte comme les cordes d'un instrument ordinaire, mais tantôt à l'unisson, tantôt à l'octave afin qu'elles puissent retentir toutes ensemble

sans discordance. Car il ne s'agissait pas d'une lyre ou d'un cithare dont il aurait lui-même pincé, mais d'un instrument *élémentaire*, d'une harpe éolienne, dont le vent serait le seul exécutant. [...] La harpe éolienne trouva place dans les branches d'un cyprès mort qui dressait sa maigre silhouette au milieu du chaos, en un endroit exposé à toute la rose des vents. A peine installée d'ailleurs, elle émit un son flûté, grêle et plaintif, bien que le temps fût tout à fait calme. Vendredi s'absorba longtemps dans l'audition de cette musique funèbre et pure.

[...] Une tourmente s'était levée.

[...] Robinson cru entendre un concert céleste où se mêlaient des flûtes et des violons. Ce n'était pas une mélodie dont les notes successives entraînent le coeur dans leur ronde et lui impriment l'élan qui est en elle. C'était une note unique – mais riche d'harmoniques infinis – qui refermait sur l'âme une emprise définitive, un accord formé de composantes innombrables dont la puissance soutenue avait quelques chose de fatal et d'implacable qui fascinait.

[...] Et il y avait surtout ce brame puissant et mélodieux, musique véritablement *élémentaire*, inhumaine, qui était à la fois la voix ténébreuse de la terre, l'harmonie des sphères célestes et la plainte rauque du grand bouc sacrifié.

[...] La terre, l'arbre et le vent célébraient à l'unisson l'apothéose nocturne d'Andoar. (pp. 207-208)

Se si tiene conto della forte polemica, che ha percorso tanta letteratura della modernità, contro le sdolcinature, i languori, le ingenue immagini della natura tipiche di tanto romanticismo, forse quest'improvvisa ricomparsa dello strumento caro a Lamartine nell'isola settecentesca dei Robinson e Venerdì di Tournier, dove fa aleggiare una musica primigenia e funebre a un tempo, forse più profonda e significativa di tutte le musiche umane, segnala anche un ritorno e una rivisitazione, che possiamo forse considerare postmoderni, della grande mitologia romantica.

Il tema dei mondi possibili

C'è un'immagine molto significativa nel libro di Tournier. Quando Robinson si vede davanti i componenti della piccola società umana sbarcata dalla nave *Whitebird*, è come se lui li osservasse con il cannocchiale che gli è rimasto dopo il disastro, avendolo rovesciato. Da una parte c'è, per lui, la corposità, il peso esistenziale, la permanenza ontologica dell'isola di Speranza, dall'altra ci sono quegli uomini, ciascuno racchiuso dentro un mondo fenomenologico, un mondo *possibile* (la parola è in corsivo nel testo), ciascuno con una tendenza a ridurre il mondo a piccole mappe, astrazioni, razionalizzazioni, fenomeni del presente, pure ipotesi su cui commisurare l'ingordigia e l'avidità che li governa:

Robinson savait qu'il avait été semblable à eux, mû par les mêmes ressorts – la cupidité, l'orgueil, la violence –, qu'il était encore des leurs par toute une part de lui-même. Mais en même temps il les voyait avec la détachement intéressé d'un entomologiste penché sur une communauté d'insectes, des abeilles ou des fourmis, ou ces rassemblements suspects de cloportes qu'on surprend en soulevant une pierre.

Chacun des ces hommes était un monde *possible,* assez cohérent, avec ses valeurs, ses foyers d'attraction et de répulsion, son centre de gravité. Pour différents qu'ils fussent les uns des autres, ces *possibles* avaient actuellement en commun une petite image de Speranza – combien sommaire et superficielle! – autour de laquelle ils s'organisaient, et dans un coin de laquelle se trouvaient un naufragé nommé Robinson et son serviteur métis. Mais pour centrale que fût cette image, elle était chez chacun marquée du signe du provisoire, de l'éphémère, condamnée à retourner à bref délai dans le néant d'où l'avait tirée le déroutage accidentel du *Whitebird*. Et chacun de ces mondes possibles proclamait naïvement sa réalité. C'était cela autrui: un possible qui s'acharne à passer pour réel. (pp. 238-239)

Lo sdoppiamento ottico dell'immagine (Robinson che guarda i suoi simili, esseri umani come lui, come da un microscopio; loro che guardano Robinson con interesse fugace e lo trascrivono su una mappa mentale, lo fotografano nel ricordo, lo rimpiccioliscono e trasformano in un puro segno di richiamo) ha un forte effetto di straniamento, ma anche di ricerca delle domande ultime, ontologiche. Quegli uomini, con un procedimento che sembra anticipare quelli attribuiti alla cultura postmoderna, procedono o per semplice comunicazione di gesti e parole, o per apprendimento riassuntivo, superficiale, privo di contestualità e profondità, astraente. Un'esperienza ricca e sconvolgente come quella di Robinson non viene colta, raccontata, interpretata; viene solo trascritta in un segno provvisorio, che ha dell'effimero.

Quegli uomini collocano incontri ed esperienze sulla loro mappa mentale, li trascrivono e codificano secondo le categorie della loro enciclopedia culturale, ampia di presenze e riferimenti, esile di spessore. Portano via, da quelle esperienze, solo delle possibilità o virtualità. Le portano con sé in un mondo, quello della loro nave, che sembra lontanissimo da quello che Conrad ha attribuito alle comunità di marinai che si formavano sulle navi battenti bandiera britannica da lui conosciute e rette da rigide regole e codici di forte valore etico elaborati da quelle piccola società autonome in miniatura. Robinson, cresciuto anche lui in uno di quei mondi possibili, ha avuto su Speranza delle esperienze di grande densità, non più riducibili a quella dimensione. Al suo bisogno di completezza quegli uomini contrappongono soltanto l'esperienza della relatività:

Ce qui le rebutait principalement, ce n'était point tant la brutalité, la haine et la rapacité que ces hommes civilisés et hautement honorables étalaient avec une naïve tranquillité. Il restait toujours facile d'imaginer – et sans doute serait-ce possible de trouver – d'autres hommes à la place de ceux-ci qui fussent, eux, doux, bienveillants et généreux. Pour Robinson le mal était bien plus profond. Il le dénonçait par-devers lui-même dans l'irrémédiable *relativité* des fins qu'il les voyait tous poursuivre fiévreusement. Car ce qu'ils avaient tous en but, c'était telle acquisition, telle richesse, telle satisfaction, mais pourquoi cette acquisition, cette richesse, cette satisfaction? Certes aucun n'aurait su le dire. Et Robinson imaginait sans cesse le dialogue qui finirait bien par l'opposer à l'un de ces hommes, le commandant par exemple. "Pourquoi vis-tu?" lui demanderait-il. Hunter ne saurait évidemment que répondre, et son seul recours serait alors de retourner la question au Solitaire. Alors Robinson lui montrerait la terre de Speranza de sa main gauche, tandis que sa main droite s'élèverait vers le soleil. (pp. 243-244)

Un romanzo di formazione, un conte philosophique *o un romanzo allegorico?*

Già il Robinson di Defoe era un romanzo di genere misto, un po' cronaca immaginaria di una vita avventurosa, un po' romanzo picaresco, un po' romanzo settecentesco di viaggio e di esplorazione, un po' un primo, embrionale romanzo di formazione (elemento fondativo, quindi, dell'immaginario della modernità).

Il *Vendredi* di Tournier è ancora per certi aspetti attaccato a quei modi e a quelle problematiche. Esso inserisce su quelle modalità narrative il gusto dell'enciclopedia naturale, quello del romanzo antropologico, quello del romanzo psicologico (o psicanalitico). Ci aggiunge anche, per un gusto suo personale che tornerà negli altri suoi libri, non pochi elementi fiabeschi, di un fiabesco che sconfina con l'allucinatorio e lo psicanalitico, ma che si compiace anche di mescolare a elementi di turbamento e quasi di perversione tonalità sognanti, romanzesche, infantili.

E non basta: in un testo che appare a prima vista così semplice e limpido, ricorrono anche altre modalità, che ci spingono a pensare alla presenza anche dei modi tipici del *conte philosophique* e del romanzo allegorico. All'allegoria rinviano non soltanto la frequente presentazione dell'isola sotto forma di paesaggio moralizzato, ma anche l'esemplarità significativa di molte delle vicende, le frequenti considerazioni filosofiche del protagonista, e soprattutto la presenza di elementi di cultura mitico-filosofica come le cosmologie astrali, le mitologie antiche, le antropologie primitive e le allegorie figurate, come quelle che apparivano sulle carte dei Tarocchi, a cominciare dalla carta dell'Eremita, o del Solitario, che sta alla base di una delle ultime immagini del libro: quella di Robinson, il Solitario, che indica con la mano sinistra l'isola di Speranza e con la destra il sole.

Ma il momento in cui la decifrazione dei messaggi misteriosi e intricati delle carte dei Tarocchi domina il romanzo e ne determina la modalità allegorica è l'introduzione, nella quale Robinson, mentre fuori infuria la tempesta, sta controvoglia a colloquio con il capitano Van Deyssel. La scena ha un colore cupo, un po' brueghéliano. Il capitano Van Deyssel è un personaggio di forte spessore, grasso, materialista, godereccio, borghese e fiammingo, fornito di un'intelligenza acuta e penetrante, di un epicureismo satirico che lo imparenta con filoni della filosofia classico-rinascimentale, con filosofi moderni come Bachelard, con personaggi della tradizione letteraria, da Ellery Queen a Maigret.

Le carte dei tarocchi non parlano, vanno fatte parlare da chi le legge. Qui abbiamo un lettore-interprete d'eccezione, il quale invece di interpretare la vita attorno a sé e avvertire i pericolo verso cui corre la sua nave (anzi fallendo totalmente in questo) interpreta con grande lucidità il destino del giovane Robinson e ne predice in modo cifrato tutti gli sviluppi (anticipando così, sia pure con messaggi non immediatamente leggibili, tutta la trama del libro).

La situazione narrativa risulta in questo modo rovesciata rispetto a quella del romanzo di Defoe. Il Robinson di Defoe si avvia a percorrere le sue avventure straordinarie e imprevedibili, di cui sappiamo soltanto che alla fine si sono concluse felicemente, altrimenti non sarebbe lì a raccontarcele. Ben presto, comunque, ci accorgiamo che è nelle mani della Provvidenza, la quale interviene in modo efficace e meraviglioso ad aiutarlo e con la sua mano invisibile sorregge il suo destino e porta la sua avventura a buon fine, per dimostrare a tutti che gli imprenditori capaci e virtuosi meritano un premio.

Il Robinson di Tournier parte con un destino già determinato, racchiuso nei messaggi misteriosi delle carte. Si tratterà mano a mano, per noi lettori, di constatare la verità segreta di quei messaggi e la loro corrispondenza con gli avvenimenti: dall'imminente naufragio all'ultimo arrivo, nel segno di Giove, di un fanciullo d'oro, dentro la città solare, che prenderà a suo tempo il giusto nome di Giovedì.

Naturalmente il capitano mette le mani avanti e con un'abile spiegazione della chiave narrativa del romanzo rivela la funzione dei tarocchi:

Telle est justement la sagesse du Tarot qu'il ne nous éclaire jamais sur notre avenir en termes clairs. Imaginez-vous les désordres qu'engendrerait une prévision lucide de l'avenir? Non, tout au plus nous permet-il de *pressentir* notre avenir. Le petit discours que je vous ai tenu est en quelque sorte chiffré, et la grille se trouve être votre avenir lui-même. Chaque événement futur de votre vie vous révélera en se produisant la vérité de telle ou telle de mes prédictions. (p. 13)

Il lettore è messo in guardia. Deve gareggiare con il personaggio, tener pronto nella memoria il quadro di queste allegorie che gli serviranno a cogliere il significato profondo dei singoli avvenimenti, costruire lui stesso un sistema gerarchico delle allegorie, nel quale, per dare significato a tutta la storia, dovrà avere un posto dominante e centrale la figura del Leone, simbolo dell'erotismo solare sublime e supremo, diffuso e circolare, a cui Robinson, e con lui tutta una cultura della modernità, dovranno portare in sacrificio il loro empirismo e il loro puritanesimo.

Suzanne Branciforte

IN A DIFFERENT VOICE: WOMEN WRITING WORLD WAR II

Few would dispute that women participated in the struggle against fascism in Italy; accounts of women's roles have been transmitted to us in various narrative modes. From the careful documentation of historians like Anna Bravo, Anna Maria Bruzzone, Rachele Farina and others, we have learned of the important contribution women made to the Resistance, and have a better understanding of where women were and what they were doing during the war.[1] Anna Bravo and Daniele Jalla's *La vita offesa: Storia e memoria dei Lager nazisti nei racconti di duecento sopravvissuti* treats another aspect of political activity for women antifascists: deportation and imprisonment.[2] However, as Victoria De Grazia has accurately pointed out, "When the time came to celebrate the victories of the Resistance, the contribution of women was by and large 'silenced'" (p. 278).

The canonical literature describing the war years in Italy has strangely neglected the female voice. The texts written by men which talk about antifascist sentiment, the partisan struggle, and wartime experiences are well-known: from Carlo Levi's *Cristo si è fermato a Eboli* (1945), to Vittorini's *Uomini e no* (1945), from Primo Levi's *Se questo è un uomo* (1947) to Calvino's *Il sentiero dei nidi di ragno* (1947), what have come to be recognized as the canonical texts of the war and of neorealism ignore the contribution of women. Moreover, those texts by women who told of their wartime experiences, filtering them into fictional narratives, have slipped into undeserved obscurity. The important literary contributions of writers Renata Viganò and Liana Millu – women partisans, communists and antifascists – privilege the female lens. And it is precisely this lens, and the experience on which it focuses its attention, that has been overlooked.

---

[1] Before the surge in women's studies started in the 1970s, the lacuna was apparent. As Bruzzone and Farina point out in the introduction to their ground-breaking study *La Resistenza taciuta* (1976): "... ci colpì il ruolo ancora una volta subalterno riservato alle donne e la sostanziale assenza, nei discorsi come negli scritti, di una seria analisi di quella che fu la reale partecipazione femminile alla Guerra di liberazione in Italia" (p. 7).

[2] The oral histories collected by these historians (Milano, Franco Angeli, 1986) provide invaluable insights as well as valuable contextual information. On this subject, I would also point to Vera Laska's, *Women in the Resistance and in the Holocaust: The Voices of Eyewitnesses*, Westport, Connecticut, Greenwood Press, 1983.

Two collections of short stories – Viganò's *Matrimonio in brigata* and Millu's *Il fumo di Birkenau* – lend themselves to comparison and reveal interesting parallels. While Renata Viganò's short stories focus on the partisan war and Liana Millu's on women's experience in a Nazi lager, considered together their works yield fascinating insights on how women experienced the Second World War. Viganò and Millu are representative of that generation of writers who dedicated their lives, their works, their voices to that primary driving force behind 20th-century narrative, and the world-changing experience which they had shared: namely, World War II.[3]

Renata Viganò is best known for her novel *L'Agnese va a morire*.[4] Despite the widespread, positive reception of *L'Agnese,* the novel and its author remain largely ignored. Viganò's place in Italian literary history as recorded by *La Nuova Enciclopedia della Letteratura Garzanti* earns her seven paltry lines and the *Dizionario Critico della Letteratura Italiana* (U.T.E.T.) ignores her completely; Liana Millu is entirely overlooked by both works. More worrisome is the almost complete lack of critical attention to these authors' works. As Andrea Battistini has pointed out with regards to Viganò's *L'Agnese*, there is

qualche menzione, sporadica e convenzionale, nei manuali di letteratura contemporanea, alcune pagine nelle storie della narrativa della Resistenza, ma nessuna analisi specifica e dettagliata. Le cause di questa parziale indifferenza sono più d'una, sia sul crinale ideologico, sia su quello letterario (p. 3).[5]

Known for her partisan activities in her native Emilia Romagna, Renata Viganò clearly focuses her attention on that particular struggle. Liana Millu, a Tuscan and a Jew, survived the experience of a concentration camp and wrote about that phenomenon. While the male versions of those experiences are familiar to all, the female point of view and women's experience of the war has been ignored, if not 'silenced'. Moreover, when the women's story has been told and acknowledged, it has often been the view from the home, and not from the front. Morante's *La Storia* and Moravia's *La Ciociara* are fine examples of how female protagonists may experience war and its myriad horrors while retaining traditional female roles. Without detracting from these works, it is imperative that the other voices be heard: the voices of violence, of struggle, of danger and of hardship as experienced by women who actively participated in the war.

---

[3] It is clear that the experience of World War II continues to generate narrative, even as the century draws to a close, as evidenced in recent prize-winning novels and films such as *The English Patient, Schindler's List.*

[4] Published in 1949 and winner of the Premio Viareggio in that year, *L'Agnese va a morire* was adapted to the cinema by Giuliano Montaldo in 1976.

[5] Among the 'menzioni sporadiche' are Silvia Spellanzon's brief review (1961). See Bibliography.

Frank Rosengarten includes *L'Agnese va a morire* among "seven works (that) stand out as representative of the main problems and themes that have most deeply concerned Italian anti-Fascist writers" (p. 218). Charles Klopp actually dedicates an entire article to the novel, stating that the novel "stands out" due to "... its uncompromising moral fervor... and to its purely artistic excellence..." (p. 36).

As Carol Gilligan has pointed out, it is worrisome "how accustomed we have become to seeing life through men's eyes" (p. 6). Like Gilligan, my concern is narratological: how have the stories that have been told shaped our collective view of history? As a female reader, I am aware of the difference on both ends, the telling and the listening; I am interested "in the interaction of experience and thought, in different voices and the dialogues to which they give rise, in the way we listen... in the stories we tell..." (p. 2).

What happened to *L'Agnese va a morire*? When it came out in 1949 it was recognized as a part of that first wave of neorealist prose that included Vittorini's *Uomini e no* (1945), Calvino's *Il sentiero dei nidi di ragno* (1947). Yet the other texts seem to have garnered all the critical attention. On its appearance in 1949, *L'Agnese* was defined as "il miglior libro che la nostra narrativa ci abbia dato sulla guerra di liberazione..." (F. Calamandrei in Battistini, p. 14). Emilio Castellani considered Calvino's first novel and Vigano's *L'Agnese* together in a review in *Il movimento di liberazione in Italia*, published in November 1949. Of Vigano's work he says,

... ci troviamo dinanzi a un vero 'romanzo partigiano': forse il più schietto esempio del genere apparso finora, almeno a nostra conoscenza, in Italia. Niente fiabe qui, niente profumo di gioventù come nel *Sentiero dei nidi di ragno*; e tanto meno problematiche intellettuali e sia pur nobili 'evasioni' o 'sfoghi' come, mettiamo, in *Uomini e no*... (p. 51)

Italo Calvino actually praised Vigano's Resistance novel when it appeared, calling it a "'cronaca-romanzo' dall'esauriente documentazione" (Battistini, 32, n. 46, Calvino in *L'Unità*, XXVI, 4 agosto 1949).[6] It was not enough to secure the text a position among the canonical texts of the post-war period. Giovanni Falaschi in his critically important *La Resistenza armata nella narrativa italiana* (1976) called it "il romanzo ufficiale della Resistenza" (p. 76). *L'Agnese va a morire* has reached a broad audience; it has been translated into fourteen languages. But English speakers are not among those able to appreciate Vigano's tale of the war as lived by a simple *partigiana*. That this work, and indeed all of Vigano's works are inaccessible to the English-speaking world is a great tragedy and one which should be remedied.[7]

The work of Liana Millu has received critical acclaim in translation; surprisingly, one might say she has fared better than her Bolognese counterpart.[8] *Il fumo di Bir-*

---

[6] An important article by I. CALVINO, "La letteratura italiana sulla resistenza" that appeared in *Il movimento di liberazione in Italia* (July 1949) does not mention Vigano's work, clearly because Vigano's novel came out later that summer.

[7] Clearly, it is the responsibility of Italianists working in the English-speaking world to bring the literature we study into the lives of those around us. The lack of good available translations of Italian books into English has been documented by the American Academy in Rome. The results were presented in 1982 in *The Italian Book and American Publishing*.

[8] It is somewhat ironic and unfair that Vigano's works have suffered such an ignoble fate in English. The ad-

kenau (1947) was translated in 1991 as *Smoke Over Birkenau* by the novelist and short story writer Lynn Sharon Schwartz, who won a PEN Renato Poggioli translation award.[9] This collection of stories, published by The Jewish Publication Society, benefits from the intensive and exhaustive effort by Jewish groups to preserve Holocaust history. However, as has been pointed out by Joan Ringelheim, "until quite recently there has been no feminist perspective in Holocaust scholarship" (p. 374). Ringelheim's work has pursued a feminist line of inquiry, asking "Were women's experiences during the Holocaust different from men's in some respects? Were there differences in work, relationships, roles and in maintenance possibilities or capabilities – that is, in what a person did or tried to do simply to deep going, to make it from day to day?" (p. 375). Millu's fiction answers these questions, in part, as it filters her lived experience into a narrative form.

A glance at Viganò's titles alone already indicates her 'different voice': *Arriva la cicogna, Matrimonio in brigata, L'Agnese va a morire*.[10] Not only has she marked time, those milestones of the human existence – birth, matrimony, and death – but she has given a distinctly feminine slant to it. This is the first and perhaps most obvious difference one might note in comparing Viganò's works to those of her male counterparts; the stork's arrival and a wedding in the brigade are not titles one might expect from a male author. Even the novel clearly indicates the female perspective with the protagonist's name – l'Agnese. In contrast, the distinctly anthropocentric ring to Vittorini's and Levi's titles (*Uomini e no, Se questo è un uomo*) is unmistakable, reinforcing the stereotype that war and all it entails is a man's business.

The collection *Matrimonio in brigata*, which takes its title from the first story, was published posthumously in 1976 and includes some stories from the earlier collection. It consists of nineteen stories, actually seventeen fictional short stories and two autobiographical accounts which are deliberately marked as such. Clearly, all of Viganò's stories are autobiographical, based on her real life participation. One even comes to identify certain characters who reappear in different stories, or certain incidents which are referred to in more than one story. Read alongside her non-fiction work, *Donne della Resistenza*, in which the unmasked accounts of women's lives are reported, one is provided with ample, fertile ground for compari-

ditional perspective these works by women provide would benefit scholars in numerous fields. Women's studies courses, courses which focus on oral history and microhistory, Italian literature courses in translation, and history courses on World War II could profit from the accessibility of Viganò's and Millu's works.

[9] See VICTORIA DE GRAZIA's brief review in *The New York Times Book Review*, June 21, 1992, in which De Grazia says Millu's prose "recalls the neorealist Italian cinema of the postwar era; ...".

[10] RENATA VIGANÒ, born in 1900 in Bologna, came out with two very early books of poetry, *Ginestra in fiore* (1913) and *Piccola fiamma* (1916). After *L'Agnese*, she published a collection of short stories, *Arriva la cicogna* (1954) and another novel *Una storia di ragazze* (1962). A microhistorical work, *Donne della Resistenza* (1955), is a biographical compendium of women who dedicated their lives to the partisan struggle in Emilia-Romagna.

son. It becomes possible to piece together bits of history, and in turn, to truly appreciate the rhetorical skill of the author in her fictional renderings of painful memories.

What becomes apparent in an analytical look at the composition of this work is that, clearly, the focus is on the women's experience. Although Viganò employs a first person narrator only once in the fictionalized accounts, it is a female narrator. For the other stories, she prefers an omniscient viewpoint. Of the seventeen fictional stories, six have a female protagonist, and only two have no female characters at all. Seven of the stories place some kind of emphasis on the mother-child relationship. The family and close emotional relationships among family members are touchingly and intimately portrayed, revealing Viganò's distinct point of view. Six stories have as a central theme a relationship with a mother, a wife or a sister. Although Viganò is obviously concerned with depicting family ties, and the complexities of these relationships set within the context of the war and the Resistance, she is most concerned with portraying the actions of the brave women who actively contributed to and participated in the struggle. In eleven stories the deeds of *female* partisans are recounted. Quantifying Renata Viganò's stories in this schematic way reveals their themes. It is revealing, for the difference in her voice becomes apparent. In Carol Gilligan's words:

> Sensitivity to the needs of others and the assumption of responsibility for taking care lead women to attend to voices other than their own and to include in their judgment other points of view... Thus women not only define themselves in a context of human relationship but also judge themselves in terms of their ability to care (pp. 16-17).

The same almost selfless attention to 'attend to voices other than (one's) own' and to perceive oneself 'in terms of (one's) ability to care' is also quite present in the stories of Liana Millu. *Il fumo di Birkenau*, first published in 1947 and reprinted in 1986, is comprised of only six short stories, but each of these is much longer and more developed than Viganò's seventeen stories. Where Renata Viganò's watercolors are sketched with brief strokes forming a compact, vivid image, Millu's oils paint deep and complex portraits with all the elements of a fully balanced narrative. Set in Birkenau, the all-female sister camp to Auschwitz where Millu was incarcerated during the last two years of the war, these six stories emblematically represent the female prisoners' experiences.

Due to the setting, all of the stories have female protagonists; indeed, the characters are almost exclusively female. The tone is pessimistic: in five of the six stories the protagonists meet death at the end. In all the stories some enormous sacrifice of self takes place, usually in order to benefit someone else. This theme is common to the stories of Renata Viganò, where death is again omnipresent, although with the difference that often it is some unjust death (the murder of a loved one at the hands of the Fascists or the Nazis) which prompts an individual to act, to join the local partisan group or brigade. There is, therefore, a dark optimism among Viganò's messages.

It is nigh on impossible to find that shred of hope or flicker of optimism in Millu's narratives. The suspension of all morality in the camps, the unfathomable human instinct for survival, the 'truths' about human nature which reveal themselves when put to that excruciating test, contribute to the reader's sense of helplessness, incomprehension, frustration.

The poetry that Viganò achieves in style, evocatively capturing the sights and sounds of an intensely lived moment, Millu achieves in juxtaposition of content. In Renata Viganò's "Il ritratto di Garibaldi," it is the death of a young husband, beautifully sketched in the opening paragraph, which occasions his wife's and family's participation in the partisan struggle.

> Mario salì in bicicletta e salutò un compagno sul ponte. Si oscurava piano il tramonto di maggio, splendevano nelle case rade nei campi i vetri delle finestre. La guerra pareva non ci fosse in quell'ora verde e dorata della valle, con le nebbie pallide che cominciavano a salire dalle paludi. Mario fermò i pedali, andò giù rapido in discesa frusciando sui copertoni frusti. La strada si era fatta grigia e deserta, lui guardava il colore dell'asfalto, lo riconosceva per averlo percorso tante volte, come il pavimento della sua stanza... Così distratto, all'improvviso, vide a destra il muro di casa, frenò, mise un piede a terra.
>
> E proprio in quel punto lo colse un lampo e un rumore, e il pensiero gli si spense. ...
> ... Gli altri "neri" se ne andarono dietro un ordine secco: "Raus".
>
> L'ultimo diede un calcio alla bicicletta che serpeggiò ribaltandosi nel fosso. Era già quasi buio e fresco nella sera: dall'interno della casa venivano lamenti e pianti sottili. Le voci degli armati risuonarono invece forte di lontano su passo di marcia imitando parole tedesche. Parlavano in italiano come i tedeschi, facevano come i tedeschi, ma erano, purtroppo, fascisti italiani.

This brief passage illustrates Viganò's economy of language and her ability to depict a moment in all its emotional complexity. Millu employs a very different technique, as she meticulously constructs plot.

In Millu's story, "Alta tensione," as the title's play on words indicates, the author carefully and slowly builds the tension. Millu was among Italian prisoners, which lends the tale a homely air:

> Avevo lavorato tanti mesi sperduta in "Comandi" completamente stranieri, sempre circondata da maggioranze ostili, sempre chiamata 'macaroni,' e così mi sentivo felice di ritrovarmi un po' con la mia gente a parlare anch'io alla svelta, senza bisogno di interpreti o di tortuosi giri di frasi (p. 77).

It is through talking, communication, sharing of their common and uncommon plights, that Liana learns of the prisoner Bruna's particular quest: to see, to save for, to in some way provide for and protect her son Pinin.

Pinin is a prisoner at nearby Auschwitz and the women's factory jobs take them by the camp. Bruna catches the occasional glimpse of him; she cleverly manipulates her resources in order to pass him extra food through the fence that divides them. When Pinin is no longer among the boys seen through the fence, the group of women share in her grief as sisters. But they are separate from it, too: "Bruna camminava vicino a noi, ma né io né le altre ragazze la guardavamo... non per farle del bene l'avevamo lasciata sola, ma perchè il contatto con la sua angoscia ci riusciva pesante e sgradito" (pp. 90-91). The gradual decline of Bruna into insanity is documented by Millu, as she so acutely observes and describes human suffering around her in the camp. There is a sense of loss of control as Bruna spirals downward in her grief, culminating in the final, chilling scene:

Piovigginava: terra e cielo incupivano nella nebbia... vidi Bruna correre verso la rete ad alta tensione. Dall'altra parte il figlio stava a guardarla.
Vieni dalla tua mamma! – gridava Bruna con le braccia tese. – Vieni dalla tua mamma, Pinin! Corri!
Il ragazzo ebbe un attimo di esitazione. Ma la madre seguitò a chiamarlo, e allora si precipitò verso la rete invocando: "Mamma! mamma!" Raggiunse i fili, e nell'istante in cui le piccole braccia si saldavano a quelle della madre, ci fu uno scoppiettio di fiamme violette, un ronzio si propagò sui fili violentemente urtati, in fine si sparse intorno un acre odor di bruciato (pp. 95-96).

As the rhythms of the camp resume, marching over and ignoring human life and suffering, Liana Millu lingers one final time, the final image an emblem: "Prima di allontanarmi mi voltai: Bruna e Pinin erano ancora là strettamente abbracciati e la testa della madre posava su quella del figlio come volesse proteggerne il sonno" (p. 96).

Primo Levi, who wrote an introduction to Millu's collection, points out that "La loro condizione [delle donne] era assai peggiore di quella degli uomini, e ciò per vari motivi: la minore resistenza fisica di fronte a lavori più pesanti e umilianti di quelli inflitti agli uomini; il tormento degli affetti familiari; la presenza ossessiva dei crematori, le cui ciminiere, [erano] situate nel bel mezzo del campo femminile..." (p. 7). He calls Millu "un occhio che penetra, una coscienza mirabilmente vigile che registra e trascrive, in un linguaggio sempre dignitoso e misurato, questi eventi che pure sono al di fuori di ogni misura umana" (p. 7). Of course, a comparison of Levi's work to that of his female counterpart also beckons. Levi appreciates Millu's style, which imbues the world with "un'aura di tristezza lirica..." (p. 8).

The first story of *Il fumo di Birkenau*, "Lili Marlene," is the only one where the title blatantly reveals the female focal point. It is the story of a young, beautiful Hungarian girl who is sent to the ovens by a jealous Kapo, caught in a risky and ultimately deadly love triangle. As women live almost exclusively among women here in Birkenau, Millu explores the complexity of female relationships as they are permutated by imbalances of power among prisoners.

The women whom Millu describes are mothers, wives, lovers, sisters and they struggle to carefully preserve these roles or at least the memory of them. Millu maintains her outstanding ability to nurture and to care, fight to remain human, to preserve her female qualities. The extraordinary nature of this feat becomes apparent as we see other women harden: mothers who have watched their children torn from them and sent to the crematorium; wives who learn of their husbands' deaths through the remarkable concentration camp underground news network; siblings who have seen a sister prostitute herself to the enemy for an extra piece of bread or a coveted carrot. Millu's concerns are interpersonal relationships, the family, the ability to love. Even an occasional Kapo will fall in love with a male prisoner from a neighboring camp. In what are not trivial touches, the women prisoners attempt to preserve dignity by attention to clothes, make-up and hair, and even soap and perfume as obtained through what in camp terminology is called 'organizing.'

These passages, equally beautiful and terrible for their description of the minute, in their detailing of human suffering, in their attention to the human dimension and concentration on the individual, are representative of these authors' styles, and put into relief their concerns and their approach. The works of Viganò and Millu depict a world of interpersonal relationships, emotions, the minutiae of everyday life as the individual attempts to survive with dignity in the face of adversity, maintaining some human element of concern for others. But has this focus, this approach to writing and to life, 'weakened' these authors' works in the eyes of critics? As Carol Gilligan has written citing an earlier study: "... concern with relationships appears as a weakness of women rather than as a human strength" (Miller, 1976, p. 17). But it is precisely this concern which characterizes the female narrative. And so the stories of the war are told 'in a different voice.'

Calvino was sensitive to that difference and to the multiplicity of voices rising from the experiences of the war. In his famous 1964 introduction to *Il sentiero*, he talks about the different voices that defined neorealism: "Il 'neorealismo' non fu una scuola... Fu un insieme di voci, in gran parte periferiche, una molteplice scoperta delle diverse Italie, anche – o specialmente – delle Italie fino allora più inedite per la letteratura" (p. 9). Indeed, Viganò's and Millu's voices were from the margins, describing an experience previously unknown to literature. If during the past half century the sound of their voices has been lost, it is not because they were lacking in strength, but because of our definition of strength, and of war, history and what constitutes the 'canon'.[11] It is now up to us to recuperate the lost voices of women who told of their wartime experiences, in voices distinctively female, because these voices very much need to be heard and more importantly listened to.

---

[11] For a fuller discussion of this, see Marotti's *Italian Women Writers from the Renaissance to the Present*, in particular the articles in Part I which discuss canon formation. Also, Marotti's article "Filial Discourses" discusses how "Italian women's autobiography displays noncanonical forms" and characteristics that are "yet another sign of the marginalization of women's writings..." (p. 65).

BIBLIOGRAPHY

A. BATTISTINI, *Pugillaria: Le parole in guerra: lingua e ideologia dell'Agnese va a morire*, Bologna, Italo Bovolenta Editore, 1982.

L. BONAPARTE, *Giuliano Montaldo e L'Agnese va a morire*, Milano, Ghisoni Editore, 1976.

A. Bravo and D. Jalla, eds., *La vita offesa: Storia e memoria dei Lager nazisti nei racconti di duecento sopravvissuti*, Milano, Franco Angeli, 1986.

A. M. Bruzzone and R. Farina, eds., *La Resistenza taciuta*, Milano, La Pietra, 1976.

I. CALVINO, *Il sentiero dei nidi di ragno*, Milano, Garzanti, 1987 (1947).

– "Il Movimento di liberazione in Italia", in *La Letteratura italiana sulla Resistenza*, vol. 1 (1949), pp. 40-46.

E. CASTELLANI, Reviews of Calvino's *Il sentiero dei nidi di ragno* and Viganò's *L'Agnese va a morire* in *Il movimento di liberazione in Italia*, Vol. 1, no. 3, (November 1949), pp. 50-53.

V. DE GRAZIA, *How Fascism Ruled Women: Italy 1922-1945*, Berkeley and Los Angeles, University of California Press, 1992.

– Review of *Smoke Over Birkenau* in *The New York Times Book Review*, June 21, 1992.

G. FALASCHI, *La Resistenza armata nella narrativa italiana*, Torino, Einaudi, 1976.

– *Realtà e retorica: La letteratura del neorealismo italiano*, Messina-Firenze, Casa editrice G. D'Anna, 1977.

C. GILLIGAN, *In a Different Voice: Psychological Theory and Women's Development*, Cambridge, MA, Harvard University Press, 1982.

C. D. KLOPP, "Nature and Human Nature in Renata Viganò's *L'Agnese va a morire*", in *Italian Quarterly*, vol. 19, no. 73-74 (1975), pp. 35-52.

Il Dizionario Critico della Letteratura Italiana, V. Branca ed., 3 voll., Torino, U.T.E.T., 1974.

La Nuova Enciclopedia della Letteratura Garzanti, Garzanti Editore, 1985.

M. Marotti ed., *Italian Women Writers from the Renaissance to the Present*, University Park, PA, Pennsylvania University Press, 1996.

M. MAROTTI, "Filial Discourses: Feminism and Femininity in Italian Women's Autobiography", in *Feminine Feminists: Cultural Practices in Italy*, Giovanna Miceli Jeffries ed., Minneapolis, University of Minnesota Press, 1994.

L. MILLU, *Il fumo di Birkenau*, Firenze, La Giuntina, 1986 (1947).

– *Smoke over Birkenau*, Lynne Sharon Schwartz trans., New York, The Jewish Publication Society, 1991.

J. RINGELHEIM, "Voices of Reflection", in *Different Voices: Women and the Holocaust*, Carol Rittner and John K. Roth eds., New York, Paragon House, 1993.

F. ROSENGARTEN, "The Italian Resistance Novel (1945-1962)", in *From Verismo to Experimentalism: Essays on the Modern Italian Novel*, Sergio Pacifici ed., Bloomington, Indiana University Press, 1969.

S. SPELLANZON, "Renata Viganò Poeta Popolare," in *Letterature Moderne*, XI, n. 6 (1961), Bologna, Cappelli Editore.

R. VIGANÒ, *L'Agnese va a morire*, Torino, Einaudi, 1945.
– *Donne della Resistenza*, Bologna, S.T.E.B., 1955.
– *Matrimonio in brigata*, Milano, Vangelista, 1976.
E. VITTORINI, *Uomini e no*, Mondadori, 1965, (Bompiani, 1945).

Luigi Burzio – Elvira G. Di Fabio

CORRISPONDENZE ACCENTUALI

1. *Premessa*

Il presente lavoro è una versione riveduta di Burzio e Di Fabio (1994). La decisione degli autori di riproporlo è basata sul suo particolare rilievo sia per alcuni sviluppi teorici recenti, sia per l'obiettivo del volume che è rendere omaggio a Dante Della Terza.

Nei pochi anni trascorsi dalla pubblicazione della prima versione, la teoria linguistica generativa nel campo della morfo-fonologia ha subito una evoluzione profonda dovuta all'ascesa virtualmente incontestata della *Optimality Theory* di Prince e Smolensky (1993) (v. Burzio, 1995b). La *Optimality Theory* propone una organizzazione del lessico "in parallelo", in cui le regolarità morfo-fonologiche rifletto-no condizioni che si applicano simultaneamente ed in blocco ad una unica rappresentazione di superficie. Tali condizioni sono violabili in caso esse entrino in conflitto l'una con l'altra, ed i conflitti vengono risolti a vantaggio della condizione che ha rango più elevato su una data scala gerarchica. Questo quadro si contrappone a quello più tradizionale, in cui il calcolo della struttura morfo-fonologica veniva affidato ad una organizzazione in serie, basato su regole di riscrittura che trasformavano man mano la struttura applicandosi l'una dopo l'altra. Il rilievo particolare del presente lavoro è quello di aver anticipato, con Burzio (1991, 1992, 1993, 1994a, b), Di Fabio (1990) su cui esso è basato, i temi principali della *Optimality Theory* e l'ipotesi dell'organizzazione del lessico in parallelo.

Nel riproporlo, ambedue gli autori intendono allo stesso tempo riconoscere il generoso aiuto ricevuto da Dante Della Terza e la solidarietà scientifica che egli sempre concesse agli studi di linguistica romanza condotti nel Department of Romance Languages and Literatures della Harvard University.

1. *Introduzione*

I "morfemi" sono, per definizione, unità che compaiono in parole diverse con struttura sonora e semantica relativamente costante. In questo lavoro, sosterremo che l'accentuazione, un aspetto della struttura sonora, rimane anch'essa relativamente costante per ciascun morfema. Tenteremo di dimostrare che due fenomeni tradizionalmente non connessi l'uno con l'altro sono in effetti manifestazioni di un unico principio di "Corrispondenza accentuale". Uno di questi è il mantenimento dell'accento nel processo di suffissazione in inglese, come in *propagánda => propagándist*. L'altro è la soppressione di certi morfemi in italiano in contesti che ne richiederebbero altrimenti la riaccentazione, come illustrato in (1).

(1) a. fin   -ísc   -o
      fin   -iámo

    b.   vol   -é   -re
        vol   -ró [vorró]

In (1), sia l'infisso *-isc-* che la vocale tematica *e* vengono realizzati soltanto quando possono essere accentuati. Se l'accento viene a cadere altrove, qui sul suffisso, essi sono soppressi.

2. *Condizioni accentuali e Conservazione dell'accento*

Per mettere meglio in risalto le questioni teoriche in gioco, considereremo prima l'inglese, che manifesta i due fenomeni di corrispondenza accentuale in (2a) e (2b).

(2) a. *Corrispondenza accentuale debole*
      medícinal => medìcinálity

   b. *Corrispondenza accentuale forte*
      propagánda => propagándist

In (2a), l'accento primario della parola base *medícinal* (rappresentato dall'accento acuto) viene mantenuto "debolmente" come accento secondario (rappresentato dall'accento grave) nella parola derivata *medìcinálity*, e questo effetto si verifica soltanto in condizioni ristrette. In particolare si verifica se e solo se il raggruppamento accentuale, o "piede" risultante è bisillabico, cioè (σσ), in cui σ sta per sillaba, oppure trisillabico con una sillaba breve ("B") in posizione media, cioè (σBσ), come illustrato ai punti (3a, b) qui sotto, dove le sillabe "accentualmente corrispondenti" sono date in grassetto. In tutti gli altri casi, in particolare se il piede risultante è trisillabico ma con sillaba mediana lunga (H per "heavy"), cioè (σHσ) o monosillabico, cioè (σ), il mantenimento dell'accento non si verifica, come è mostrato ai punti (3c,d), dove gli asterischi indicano agrammaticalità.[1]

(3) a. <u>(σσ)</u>: medícinal => me(dìci)nálity
di(vìsi)bílity, fa(mìli)árity, su(pèri)órity, re(lìgi)ósity, an(tàgo)nístic, na(pòle)ónic, phe(nòme)nólogy, he(rèdi)tárian, ...

b. <u>(σBσ)</u>: persónify => per(sònifi)cátion
syl(làbifi)cátion, as(sìmila)bílity, as(sòcia)tívity,...

c.[2] *<u>(σHσ)</u>: òphthalmólogy => *(óphthalmo)lógic
oph(thàlmo)lógic

*(láryngo)lógic,...

d. *<u>(σ)</u>: infórm => *in(fòr)mátion
(ìnfor)mátion

*ca(tàs)tróphic, *in(tèr)nálity, *uni(vèr)sálity, *a(dàp)tátion, *con(sùl)tátion, *ce(mèn)tátion, *e(xìs)téntial, *propa(gàn)dístic,...

Diversamente dal caso (2a), nel caso (2b) l'accento primario è conservato come tale nella parola derivata, fenomeno che si verifica regolarmente con certi suffissi, come quelli esemplificati in (4) qui sotto.

(4) a. *-able*: accéptable, affórdable, oppósable, refúndable, respéctable, sustáinable, abólishable, álterable, ánswerable, inhábitable, intérpretable, périshable

b. *-ist/ -ism*: pharmacólogist, perféctionist, genéticist, romànticist, extrémist, húmorist, térrorist, américanist, cápitalist, módernist, mónarchist, absentéism, alármism, deféatism, extrémism, féderalism, líberalism, rádicalism, fávoritism

c. *-ant/ -ent/ -ance/ -ence*: consúltant, detérminant, expéctant, inhábitant, resúltant, complíance, delíverance, inhéritance, resístance, séverance, absórbent, an-

---

[1] Usiamo il simbolo H per sillaba lunga / "heavy" e B per sillaba breve / "light", evitando L che può suscitare confusione suggerendo sia "lunga" che "light". Una sillaba breve (B) è una sillaba che termina con una vocale semplice e breve, mentre una sillaba lunga (H) termina o con una vocale lunga / dittongata, come la penultima sillaba [ray] in ho.ri.zon, o con una consonante, come la penultima sillaba [pen] in ap.pen.dix.

[2] È irrilevante che l'accento che è preservato in questi casi sia secondario già nella parola base. Analogamente è pure irrilevante che l'accento preservato nei casi in (i) sia primario nella parola composta.

(i) a. cómpensàte => *(cómpensa)tòry
com(pénsa)tòry
*(cónfisca)tòry, *(éxculpa)tòry, ...
b. ínfant => *(ínfanti)cìde
in(fánti)cìde
*(ródenti)cìde, ...

Il motivo è che la distinzione tra accento primario e secondario è data da un principio molto semplice esposto più avanti ed indipendente dalle questioni discusse nel testo. La distinzione del testo tra corrispondenza accentuale debole e forte è da vedersi piuttosto in termini di produttività. La prima si verifica solo quando la parola base ha caratteristiche particolari nel senso illustrato appunto in (3), mentre la seconda si verifica sempre, con certi suffissi.

tecédent, consístent, convérgent, depéndent, reminíscent, subsístent, transcéndent

d. -ize: anthropomórphize, européanize, itálicize, románticize, compúterize, gélatinize, monópolize, revolútionize, cápitalize, munícipalize, famíliarize, pópularize, américanize

Nell'ambito dell'approccio generativo tradizionale degli anni tra il '60 e il '90, che considera l'accento come risultato di regole fonologiche derivazionali, non esisterebbe nessuna relazione precisa tra i due fenomeni dei punti (2a, b). Infatti, il primo veniva comunemente attribuito all'ipotesi che le regole fonologiche si applicassero in modo "ciclico", cioè prima alla struttura più interna, dando ad esempio [napóleon]-ic, e poi alla struttura più complessa, mantenendo però nel passaggio i risultati della prima applicazione per quanto possibile, da cui napòleónic, anziché l'altrimenti atteso *nàpoleónic parallelamente al non derivato wìnnepessaúkee (con accento secondario sulla prima sillaba). D'altro canto il secondo fenomeno, in (2b), veniva attribuito alla abilità di certi suffissi di evadere completamente gli effetti dell'apparato accentuale, o perché inseriti troppo "tardi" nella derivazione – il "level 2" della Lexical Phonology di Kiparsky (1982a, b) – o perché contrassegnati diacriticamente come "non-cyclic", come nel quadro di Halle e Vergnaud (1987), Halle e Kenstowicz (1991), e come tali non soggetti all'apparato accentuale che è (per lo più) ciclico. Da questo punto di vista, i fenomeni in (2a, b) e la loro coesistenza in inglese, hanno un carattere altamente fortuito, nel senso che varie altre ipotesi, elencate in (5) ed ugualente formulabili data l'architettura del sistema, debbono essere escluse per stipulazione.

(5) *Ipotesi formulabili ma non attestate*
    a. L'assegnazione di accento è post-ciclica anziché ciclica.

    b. L'assegnazione di accento in un certo ciclo cancella sempre l'accento assegnato nei cicli precedenti, anziché cancellarlo solo in casi come quelli in (3b, c)!

    c. Il mantenimento dell'accento avviene in condizioni diverse da quelle illustrate dai casi in (3a, b).

    d. I suffissi dei casi (3) anziché quelli dei casi (4) sono di "level 2" o "non-cyclic".

Vedremo più avanti che il quadro di Burzio (1994a) supera queste difficoltà. Tale quadro avanza una ipotesi radicalmente diversa da quella tradizionale, secondo la quale l'accento non è inserito da regole derivazionali, ma fa invece parte della rappresentazione lessicale. La regolarità che esiste nella posizione dell'accento in termini di conteggio di sillabe (in inglese, come in italiano, dalla fine di parola), è attribuito ad un inventario fisso di gruppi accentuali o "piedi" che svolge funzione di verifica dell'accento, vagliando cosí la buona formazione della rappresentazione. L'analisi proposta in Burzio (1991-1994a, b) differisce inoltre dalla tradizione immediatamente precedente ispirata ad Hayes (1982, 1985) nel supporre che il campo di variazione nei piedi accentuali possibili in lingue come il latino, l'italiano e l'inglese fra le altre, non sia tra il piede monosyllabico (H) ed il bisillabico (σB), ma piuttosto tra il piede bisillabico (Hσ) e il trisillabico (σBσ), differenza risultante dal fatto che la sillaba finale "estrametrica" postulata da Hayes, come in a(méri)<ca>, fa qui semplicemente parte del piede finale, come in a(mérica), i piedi nelle lingue in questione aventi ritmo trocaico, cioè con accento sul margine sinistro. Nell'analisi dell'inglese di Burzio esiste nondimeno una nozione di estrametricità di sillabe finali, ma essa non è generale come nel quadro di Hayes, ma è invece limitata ad una classe specifica di sillabe speciali definite "deboli" (D), il cui nucleo è appunto debole rispetto alle sue proprietà acustiche / fonetiche, ed è a volte foneticamente nullo. Il funzionamento di tale analisi che, come si è detto comprende: a) i due piedi (Hσ) / (σBσ) e, b) estrametricità di sillabe deboli finali (che è opzionale), è illustrato in (6) (dove il segno ':' sta ad indicare una vocale lunga / dittongata). Si vedano i lavori citati per ulteriori dettagli.[3]

(6) *a. D inclusa: ... D)*   *b. D estrametrica: ...)D*
per(vér t)   (pér ver)t ø
an(tí pa thy)   (éf fi ca)cy
ob(jéc ti)ve   (ád jec)tive
ad(vén tu)re   (á per)ture, (tém pe ra)ture
a(pós tle)   (vé ge ta)ble
de(cém ber)   (chá rac)ter

c. Con sillaba finale non D
a(mérica), ari(zó:na), a(génda)

Come vedremo più sotto, in questa prospettiva in cui l'accento è presente lessicalmente e soltanto "verificato" dall'apparato fonologico, che comprende la definizione di quali piedi sono possibili e di quali sillabe possono essere estrametriche, i due fenomeni in (2a, b) vengono spiegati unitariamente dal principio postulato in (7).

(7) *Corrispondenza accentuale*
    I morfemi mantengono proprietà accentuali fisse.

Sembra improbabile che tale principio rifletta proprietà specifiche al sistema ac-

---

[3] Si noti che mentre appurare lo statuto acustico/ fonetico speciale delle sillabe deboli è di per se importante, la questione è indipendente dagli obiettivi del testo. La ragione è che, a parte le sillabe con nucleo nullo ø, la cui esistenza è interna alla nostra analisi, le altre sillabe deboli hanno comportamento accentuale anomalo come dato di fatto, richiedendo quindi una analisi particolare da qualsiasi punto di vista. Per quando riguarda i nuclei nulli ø, la loro esistenza è motivata indipendentemente dall'analisi testo, da considerazioni di struttura sillabica. È ben noto che in inglese le sillabe finali sembrano poter accogliere una consonante in più rispetto alla struttura massima CVC, dando quindi CVCC, come in per.verT. Il nucleo nullo ø fa luce su questo fatto altrimenti oscuro consentendo la sillabificazione per.ver.tø, in cui la consonante altrimenti inattesa fa parte di una sillaba con nucleo nullo ma strutturalmente normale.

centuale. Più plausibilmente, esso riflette proprietà intrinsiche all'organizzazione del lessico, l'abilità di parole diverse di condividere le sottostrutture chiamate appunto "morfemi". Da questo punto di vista, il principio in (7) non fa dunque altro che affermare che la struttura accentuale ha lo stesso statuto della struttura segmentale o sillabica, che viene appunto mantenuta nella formazione di parole.[4]

Il principio in (7) è evidentemente non inviolabile, ma piuttosto subordinato alle condizioni generali sulle strutture accentuali, specificamente la definizione di quali piedi sono possibili e di quali sillabe possono rimanere estrametriche in fine di parola. Mettendo queste ultime da parte per il momento, la previsione che ne segue è che la preservazione di accento sia possibile se e solo se i piedi risultanti sono tra quelli possibili, esattamente come si era già visto al punto (3). È questo uso di condizioni violabili che fa di questa analisi (presente nei nostri lavori citati a partire dal 1990) un precursore della *Optimality Theory* di cui si è detto nella Premessa.

Il fatto che l'accento primario diventi secondario nelle parole derivate in (3) è anch'esso prevedibile da condizioni generali. L'accento primario in inglese si manifesta *sull'ultimo piede debole* dove la definizione di piede "debole" è: *piede bisillabico contenente una sillaba debole*, cioè (σD). Esempi di piedi deboli (sempre finali, visto che le sillabe D sono solo finali), sono dati in (8).

(8) *Piedi finali «deboli» (σD)*
    artícu(là:te), cóntro (vèr sy), ínno (và: ti)ve,
    árchi (tèc tu)re, táber (nà cle), álli (gà: tor)

Si noti che questo fenomeno identifica esattamente la stessa classe di sillabe D che quello illustrato in (6d). Esse sono: sillabe con nucleo nullo ø; sillabe con nucleo *y* (foneticamente [i] rilassata); le sillabe corrispondenti alle sequenze ortografiche *ive*, *ure*; e le sillabe con nuclei consonantici *L, R*, come [bL], [kL], [tR].

Il fenomeno della corrispondenza accentuale forte di (2b) è da questo punto di vista anch'esso ridotto al principio in (7), applicantesi qui in circostanze diverse. Si può dimostrare che suffissi come *-able*, *-ist*, *-ize*, ed in generale tutti quelli che sono accentualmente "neutri", hanno la capacità di integrare la loro struttura accentuale con quella di ognuna base con cui si combinano, senza richiedere nessun muta-

---

[4] Questa semplice uniformità concettuale tra accento e altre strutture è inesprimibile nel quadro dell'approccio generativo tradizionale, che postula l'assegnazione dell'accento tramite regole a partire da una rappresentazione iniziale (*underlying representation*) che è priva di accento. Allo stesso tempo tale quadro tratta l'allomorfia (occorrenze in parole diverse di uno stesso morfema) attribuendo una rappresentazione iniziale unica a ciascun morfema. Ne segue che la struttura accentuale (che non fa parte della rappresentazione iniziale) non possa far parte delle proprietà costanti dei morfemi, contrariamente a (7), ma debba invece riflettere soltanto proprietà del contesto in cui il morfema è inserito (ed il conteggio di sillabe ad esso relativo). Il principio in (7), nell'implicare un rifiuto di questo apparato che non può rendere conto dei fatti in questione, suggerisce una riconcettualizzazione radicale della teoria del lessico, in cui le relazioni morfologiche tra parole sono stabilite direttamente a livello di superficie (*surface structure*) dove le strutture accentuali sono propriamente rappresentate, riconcettualizzazione che rende la nozione di rappresentazione iniziale (*underlying representation*) superflua. Per un resoconto più esplicito, si veda Burzio (1995a, 1996, 1997)

mento di quest'ultima. Questa abilità risulta dipendere dalla presenza di una sillaba finale debole, che come si è visto in (6) può venire conteggiata o meno, consentendo quindi anche le strutture in (9a, b) che soddisfano la corrispondenza accentuale di (7) rispetto a ciascuna parola base (*inhábit, propagánda, anthropomórphy, américan, romántic*).

(9) a. in(hábita)ble, propa(gándis)t ø, anthropo(mórphi:)ze

b. a(mérica)(nìst ø), ro(mánti)(cì:ze)

Nei casi in (9a), il suffisso entra nel conteggio con una sola sillaba, lasciando la sillaba finale D estrametrica. D'altra parte, in (9d), il suffisso è scandito come piede che risulta "debole" data la definizione in (8), portando quindi solo accento secondario e consentendo il mantenimento dell'accento primario sulla base. Questa analisi, diversamente da quelle che l'hanno preceduta, rende immediatamente conto del fatto che lingue che non hanno sillabe finali D, come l'italiano, non manifestano mai il fenomeno di corrispondenza accentuale forte di (2b), (9), cioè la neutralità accentuale di molti suffissi (v. *propagánda propagandísta*, non *propagándista*, ecc.). In contrasto, la corrispondenza accentuale "debole" del punto (2a), che non dipende dall'esistenza di sillabe D, si trova anche in italiano con modalità relativamente simili. Si veda Vogel e Scalise (1982) su questo punto.

La domanda che si pone a questo punto è naturalmente che cosa distingua i suffissi accentualmente "neutrali" dei casi in (2b) e (9) da quelli dei casi (2a), (3), che danno solo la corrispondenza accentuale debole e distribuzionalmente limitata nel senso di (3). La risposta è che tale differenza è prevedibile da una combinatoria di struttura accentuale della base (ad esempio i verbi differiscono dai nomi nel conteggiare una sillaba finale D con nucleo nullo: *per(vértø), (pérver)tø*) e struttura sillabica del suffisso. Tale combinatoria consente a certi suffissi ma non ad altri di integrarsi sistematicamente nella struttura accentuale della base. Si veda qui Burzio (1991), o (1994a, 8.4).[5]

Da questo punto di vista esistono quindi solo condizioni generali sulla struttura accentuale, con alcuni gradi di variabilità quale la duplicità di sillabe finali D, ed il principio di corrispondenza accentuale (7), soddisfatto entro tali limiti di variabilità. Il carattere esplicativo di questa analisi è dimostrato dal fatto che esclude in

---

[5] Si noti però che esiste un'altra suddivisione di suffissi, oltre a quella data dalla neutralità accentuale. Questa è tra i suffissi che inducono modifiche segmentali nella base, come in *criti[k] => criti[s]-ism, sat[ay]re => sat[i]r-ist*, e quelli che non ne inducono, come in *provo[k] => provo[k]-ing, cr[ay]me => cr[ay]me-les*. In inglese, queste due classi corrispondono con buona approssimazione ai suffissi rispettivamente di etimologia latina e germanica. Questa seconda distinzione si correla a sua volta (ed in modo esatto) con altre, quali la possibilità, esclusa con i suffissi germanici, di avere basi non-indipendenti (*bound stems*) come in *electr-ic*, dove *electr* non esiste indipendentemente, e con la posizione interna dei suffissi latini rispetto a quella esterna dei suffissi germanici, come in *natur-al-ness*, ma non *faith-less-ity*. La neutralità accentuale non fa invece parte di questo gruppo di proprietà, visto che essa suddivide i suffissi latini, altrimenti omogenei (vedi qui Burzio, 1994a, 10.4).

linea di principio piuttosto che per stipulazione, varie ipotesi non attestate quali quelle citate al punto (5).

3. *Condizioni accentuali e soppressione di morfemi*

L'italiano, lingua che non dispone di sillabe finali D, presenta altri fenomeni che si riducono alla corrispondenza accentuale (7), esaminati dettagliatamente in Di Fabio (1990) (v. anche Burzio, 1996). Uno di questi è la distribuzione del morfema *-isc-*, inserito tra la radice e la desinenza di molti verbi della terza coniugazione nel modo illustrato in (10).

(10) a. fin-ísc-o

    b. fin-ísc-i

    c. fin-ísc-e

    d. fin -iámo

    e. fin -íte

    f. fin-ísc-ono

La mancanza di *isc* nella prima e seconda persona del plurale è esplicabile come corrispondenza accentuale, visto che quando appare, il morfema *isc* ha sempre la rappresentazione data in (11), che include l'accento:

(11)   ísc

Nei casi in cui *isc* è mancante, la desinenza verbale è accentata (fatto appurabile indipendentemente). Questo esclude la possibilità che *isc* sia esso stesso accentato dato il fatto ben noto che le sillabe accentate non si trovano mai adiacenti l'una all'altra, fatto che segue immediatamente nell'analisi presente che esclude i piedi monosillabici. In tali casi, *isc* sarebbe quindi costretto a rimanere inaccentato, violando la corrispondenza accentuale rispetto a (11). La sua soppressione evita dunque questa violazione.

Lo stesso resoconto può estendersi all'uso della forma suppletiva *and* per il verbo *andare* illustrato in (12), in cui la radice *vad* compare soltanto come in (13), cioè con l'accento.

(12) a. vád-o

    b. vád-i   [=> vai]

    c. vád-a   [=> va]

    d. and-iámo

    e. and-áte

    f. vád-ono   [=> vanno]

(13) vád

Così come *isc*, *vad* scompare quando non potrebbe portare l'accento, cosa che violerebbe la corrispondenza accentuale rispetto a (13). In tali condizioni, *vad* lascia il posto alla forma suppletiva *and*, che soddisfa la corrispondenza accentuale (7) in quanto compare sempre e soltanto inaccentata.

Continuando a prendere l'accento come parte della rappresentazione lessicale, le due sottoconiugazioni in *-ére* ed *-ere* avranno rappresentazioni accentualmente diverse come (14a, b), cosa che ci consentirà di rendere conto della differenza illustrata in (15a, b).

(14) a. pérd-e-re
    scrívere, méttere, léggere, rispóndere, préndere, chiédere, chiédere, conóscere, crédere, créscere, divídere, náscere, sórgere, spégnere, spéndere, spíngere, uccídere, piángere, scégliere...

    b. vol-é-re
    dovére, potére, volére, godére, tenére, valére, rimanére, cadére, parére, vedére, sapére, piacére, tacére...

(15) a. pérd-e-r-ó => perderó
    scriveró, metteró, leggeró, risponderó, prenderó, chicderó, chiúderó, conosceró, crederó, cresceró, divideró, nasceró, sorgeró, spegneró, spenderó, spingeró, uccideró, piangeró, sceglieró

    b. vol-é-r-ó => volró [=>vorró]
    dovró, potró, godró, terró, varró, rimarró, cadró, parró, vedró, sapró

Il contrasto tra (15a) e (15b) è superficialmente sorprendente in quanto illustra un fenomeno di sincope che interessa la vocale accentata *é*, risparmiando la sua controparte non accentata *e*. Questo è esattamente l'opposto di quanto accade comunemente, essendo le vocali non accentate il contesto tipico della sincope. Nondimeno, il contrasto segue dalla Corrispondenza accentuale (7), in quanto la vocale soppressa è precisamente quella che, mentre è normalmente accentata, non potrebbe mantenere l'accento in questo caso, a causa della sua adiacenza alla desinenza accentata del futuro.

Un altro caso di sincope rintracciabile alla Corrispondenza accentuale (7) è illustrato in (16a), che contrasta con la mancanza di sincope in (16b).

(16) a. pérd-ú-to   =>   pérso / perdúto
   scritto, messo, letto, risposto, preso, chiesto, chiuso, diviso, nato, sorto, spento, speso, spinto, ucciso, pianto, scelto...

   b. vol-ú-to   =>   volúto
   dovúto, potúto, godúto, tenúto, cadúto, vedúto, sapúto, piaciúto, taciúto...

La asimmetria in (16) è ancora una volta riducibile alla Corrispondenza accentuale, in quanto la soppressione della *u* participiale, che è sempre accentata, è ciò che consente alla radice *pérd*, ecc., di mantenere l'accento che essa ha nella forma dell'infinito. Nessuna ragione analoga esiste in (16b), in cui la radice è priva di accento nell'infinito, da cui l'assenza di sincope nel participio. La sincope nei participi di verbi in *-ere* (senza accento) non è però sistematica, vedi *perdúto* che coesiste con *perso*, e *vendúto, ricevúto, cedúto, ripetúto, premúto*, ed altri. Tale participi non sincopati si possono attribuire al fatto che la sincope in effetti viola la corrispondenza a livello segmentale, dando al morfema participiale una realizzazione diversa da quella prevalente che è *-ut-*. Corrispondenza accentuale e segmentale sono quindi in concorrenza l'una con l'altra, soddisfatte come sono rispettivamente da sincope e mancanza di sincope. La variazione osservata suggerisce che esse abbiano forza (il rango gerarchico della *Optimality Theory*) equivalente. Per un trattamento più esauriente, si veda Burzio (1996). La relazione tra sincope del participio e accento sulla radice, che la Corrispondenza accentuale coglie, rimane in ogni caso chiara vista la quasi totale assenza di sincope nei participi dei verbi in *-ére* (il caso *valére* / *valso* essendo molto raro. V. Di Fabio, 1990).

L'approccio alle due sottoconiugazioni in *-ere* di cui sopra risulta utile per la caratterizzazione di altre proprietà distribuzionali dell'infisso *-isc-* nella coniugazione in *-ire*. Tale infisso ha l'effetto di suddividere la coniugazione in *-ire* in due sottoconiugazioni, illustrate in (17a, b).

(17) a. part-í-re / párt-o
   dormire, coprire, morire, sentire, venire, aprire, servire, vestire, seguire, salire, fuggire, soffrire, offrire, cucire, pentire...

   b. fin-í-re / fin-ísc-o
   capire, obbedire, agire, patire, punire, tradire, imbellire, impazzire, fallire, favorire, alleggerire, fiorire, stupidire, unire, bianchire, ingiallire, impiccolire, incuriosire (quasi 85% dei verbi in *ire*)...

I verbi in (17a), rappresentanti la minoranza, non utilizzano *-isc-*, contrariamente alla maggioranza, rappresentata in (17b). Questa differenza, che non appare riflettere alcun criterio preciso, almeno dal punto di vista sincronico, si può nondimeno esprimere nei termini della discussione precedente, supponendo che il comportamento idiosincratico della minoranza in (17a) consista di corrispondenza accentuale con una forma astratta della radice quale quella in (18a), portante l'accento, mentre la corrispondenza in gioco nella maggioranza in (17b) sia con la radice dell'infinito, che non è accentata, come in (18b).

(18) a. párt-
    dórm-, cópr-, mór-, sént-, vén-, ápr-, sérv-, vést-, ségu-, sál-, fúgg-, sóffr-, óffr-, pént-...

    b. fin-
    cap-, obbed-, ag-, pat-, pun-, trad-, imbell-, impazz-, fall-, favor-, allegger-, fior-, un-, bianch-, ingiall-, impiccol-, incurios-...

In questo senso le due sottoconiugazioni in *-ire*, rispettivamente con radici accentate e non, diventerebbero così analoghe alle due in *-ere*. Questo approccio consente di ridurre l'assenza di *-isc-* con i verbi in (17a) alle stesse ragioni formali che lo escludono in *fin-iámo*, *fin-íte*, ecc., cioè la corrispondenza accentuale. L'accento di *-ísc-* non potrà coesistere con quello di *párt-* di (18a) data la loro adiacenza. Questo solleva naturalmente la questione di come possano altri morfemi accentati, come la desinenza dell'infinito *-íre*, comparire nello stesso contesto, dando luogo alla differenza in (19).

(19) a. *párt -ísc-o*   =>   **partísco*

    b. *párt-íte*   =>   *partíte*

Si noti qui che la questione che si pone in ogni caso ed indipendentemente dalla proposta in (18a), dato ad esempio *pérd-ere* / *perd-iámo*, in cui la Corrispondenza accentuale è violata rispetto alla radice. La soluzione sta ancora una volta nel fatto che la Corripondenza accentuale, come altre condizioni fonologiche del presente quadro teorico, è violabile, ed è sempre violata quando questo soddisfa condizioni di rango gerarchico più elevato. Ciò che rende la desinenza infinitiva in (19b) non cancellabile diversamente dall'infisso *-isc-* è evidentemente il suo ruolo semantico nel rendere *part-ire* interpretabile come infinito. Analogamente, le desinenze di persona e numero *-iamo*, *-ite*, pure non cancellabili, svolgono un ruolo semantico preciso, mentre nessun ruolo semantico paragonabile sembra essere svolto da *-isc-*. Si noti che morfemi che sono semanticamente essenziali e che sarebbero quindi non cancellabili lo diventano quando esistono forme suppletive che li possono sostituire, cosí come nel caso di *vád-*, sostituibile da *and-*, e plausibilmente anche nel caso dell'affisso participiale *-út-* sostituibile dalle forme sincopate *-s-* e *-t-*, come in *per-s-o* e *vin-t-o*. La gamma di risposte ad una potenziale violazione di Corrispondenza accentuale è quindi quella riassunta qui di seguito.

(20) *Violazione di corrispondenza accentuale:*
a. Evitata, tramite forma suppletiva.   *vád*:   *and*-iámo
                                         út: per-*s*-o

b. Evitata, tramite cancellazione. *-isc*: fin-Ø-íte, párt-Ø-o

é:	vol-Ø-ró
ú:	pérd-Ø-tó

c. Incorsa, tramite riaccentazione.

pérd:	perd-éte, *perd-ú-to*
párt:	part-íte, *part-í-to*

La possibilità in (20a) è naturalmente limitata ai casi in cui la forma suppletiva esiste nel lessico. D'altro canto, tale esistenza non è interamente indipendente, ma è parzialmente interpretabile come necessità creata dalla Corrispondenza accentuale stessa. La possibilità in (20b) è limitata come si è detto ai morfemi che sono semanticamente eliminabili (essendo la *e* dell'infinito plausibilmente anch'essa superflua nell'interpretazione del futuro). La eliminazione di un morfema semanticamente essenziale costituirà d'altra parte una violazione più grave che non la violazione della Corrispondenza accentuale stessa come si è detto, da cui la possibilità (20c).

Tornando alla proposta in (18a) su come analizzare i verbi in *-ire* che non usano *-isc-* notiamo che in non pochi dialetti regionali, come il piemontese, il cremonese ed il siciliano, tali verbi sono stati smistati alla coniugazione in *-ere*, rendendo cosí la coniugazione in *-ire* totalmente regolare rispetto alla selezione di *-isc-* (Di Fabio, 1990). Questo fatto sarebbe di per sé di ordinaria amministrazione, dato il carattere idiosincratico della suddivisione tra le due classi in *-ire*. Ciò che è superficialmente sorprendente è però il fatto, illustrato in (21) più sotto per il piemontese, che in ciascuno di questi dialetti un verbo di tipo *partíre* sia diventato di tipo *pártere* anziché *partére*, che sembrerebbe superficialmente più simile. L'enigma è immediatamente svelato dalla proposta in (18a). Nello smistamento ad un'altra coniugazione, tali verbi mantengono semplicemente il loro accento sulla radice, come in *párt- párt-ere*, non *part-ére*.

(21) a. italiano: *partíre* (*ire* senza *-isc-*)
dormíre, sentíre, servíre, veníre, vestíre...

b. piemontese: *párte* (<= *pártere*) (smistamento a *-ere*)
déurme, sénte, sérve, véne, véste...

La presenza di accento sulla radice dei verbi in *-ire* che non usano *-isc-* è confermato ulteriormente dal fatto che i loro participi sono spesso soggetti a sincope, contrariamente a quello dei verbi in *-ire* che usano *-isc-*, come è mostrato dalla coppia minima *apparire / sparire* in (22) qui sotto. Dal punto di vista dell'analisi in (18a), la sincope del participio in (22a) seguirà dai fattori ormai noti che danno anche la soppressione di *-isc-*, ed il contrasto tra le due sottoconiugazioni in *-ire* in (22) relativamente alla sincope del participio diventerà parallelo al contrasto in (16) tra le due coniugazioni in *-ere*.

(22) a. appár-íre   => appar-íre

       appár-ísc-o   => appár-ø-o   [=> appáio]

       appár-í-to   => appár-ø-to   [=> appárso]

   b. spar-íre   => spar-íre

       spar-ísc-o   => spar-ísc-o

       spar-í-to   => spar-í-to

4. *Conclusione*

Si è voluto mostrare che certi fenomeni di soppressione di morfemi e di uso di forme suppletive che si verificano in italiano seguono dallo stesso principio che controlla fenomeni superficialmente molto diversi in inglese quali il mantenimento dell'accento di una parola base sotto suffissazione. Il principio in questione è un principio di Corrispondenza accentuale, che richiede che i morfemi (sia radici che suffissi) mantengano proprietà accentuali fisse. Tale principio può essere soddisfatto direttamente solo quando le condizioni generali sull'accentuazione (gamma di piedi accentuali possibili) lo permettono. In caso contrario, esistono tre strategie possibili: sostituzione del morfema violatore con una forma suppletiva ove questa esista; eliminazione completa del morfema ove non ne risulti una violazione di integrità semantica grave; riaccentazione con violazione del principio di Corrispondenza accentuale come ultima risorsa.

Ciò che rende possibile la unificazione è il fatto che la corrispondenza accentuale è una condizione che si applica fra rappresentazioni di superficie che sono abbinate da criteri morfologici. Nessuna unificazione del genere può avvenire nell'ambito di un approccio all'accentazione come quello tradizionale basato sulle regole di riscrittura. Se le strutture accentuali fossero costruite derivazionalmente partendo dalla struttura sillabica come in tale approccio, soltanto parole che hanno strutture sillabiche simili dovrebbero avere strutture accentuali simili. La parola *napòleónic* dovrebbe cosí avere la scansione di *àbracadábra* (accento sulla prima sillaba) piuttosto che quella di *napóleon*, e *cápitalist* dovrebbe essere simile and *antágonist*, anziché a *cápital*. Inoltre, la soppressione di morfemi in italiano non troverebbe nessuna spiegazione e sarebbe in effetti del tutto inesprimibile. Mentre il calcolo dell'accento a partire dalla struttura sillabica richiede ovviamente la presenza di sillabe, si è visto che la presenza di alcune sillabe dipende dalla struttura accentuale. La relazione tra struttura sillabica e struttura accentuale è quindi bi-direzionale. Tale relazione è realizzabile in una architettura in parallelo in cui tutte le condizioni si applicano simultaneamente, ma è paradossale per un architettura in serie in cui ogni relazione ha necessariamente un carattere sequenziale.

BIBLIOGRAFIA

L. Burzio, (1991b) "On The Metrical Unity of Latinate Affixes", in *Proceeding of the Eighth Eastern States Conference on Linguistics*, a cura di German Westphal e altri, Department of Linguistics, Ohio State University. Ristampato in *Rivista di Grammatica Generativa* 16, 1-27. Versione riveduta in H. Campos, and P. M. Kempchinsky (1995) *Evolution and Revolution in Linguistic Theory: Essays in Honor of Carlos Otero*, Georgetown University Press.

L. Burzio, (1992) "Principles in Phonology", in *Proceedings of the XVII Meeting on Generative Grammar*, a cura di E. Fava (Trieste, February 22-24, 1991), pp. 97-119, Rosenberg and Sellier, Torino.

L. Burzio, (1993) "English Stress, Vowel Length and Modularity", *Journal of Linguistics*, 29.2, pp. 359-418.

L. Burzio, (1994a) *Principles of English Stress*, Cambridge University Press.

L. Burzio, (1994b) "Metrical Consistency," in *Language Computations*, a cura di E. S. Ristad, American Mathematical Society, Providence RI.

L. Burzio, (1995a) "Surface Constraints versus Underlying Representation", ms., Johns Hopkins University, to appear in: *Current Trends in Phonology: Models and Methods*, J. Durand & B. Laks (eds.), CNRS, Paris X, and University of Salford, University of Salford Publications.

L. Burzio, (1995b) "The Rise of Optimality Theory," *GLOT International* 1.6, 3-7 University of Leiden.

L. Burzio, (1996) "Multiple Correspondence", ms., Johns Hopkins University.

L. Burzio, (1997) "Cycles, Non-Derived-Environment Blocking, and Correspondence", ms., Johns Hopkins University.

L. Burzio, and E. Di Fabio (1994), "Accentual Stability", in *Issues and Theory in Romance Linguistics*, a cura di M. Mazzola, (LSRL XXIII), Georgetown University Press, Washington, D.C.

N. Chomsky and M. Halle, (1968) *The Sound Pattern of English*, Harper and Row, New York.

E. Di Fabio, (1990) *The Morphology of the Verbal Infix /-isk-/ in Italian and in Romance*, Doctoral Dissertation, Harvard University.

G. Griva, (1980) *Grammatica della lingua piemontese*, Andrea Viglongo & Co., Torino.

M. Halle and M. Kenstowicz, (1991) "The Free Element Condition and Cyclic versus Noncyclic Stress", *Linguistic Inquiry* 22.3, pp. 457-501.

M. Halle and J. R. Vergnaud, (1987a) *An Essay on Stress*, MIT Press.

B. Hayes, (1982) "Extrametricality and English Stress," *Linguistic Inquiry* 13, pp. 227-276.

B. Hayes,(1985) "A Metrical Theory of Stress Rules," *Garland Publishing*, New York.

M. Kenstowicz, (1994) *Phonology in Generative Grammar*, Cambridge, Massachusetts, Blackwell.

P. Kiparsky, (1979) "Metrical Structure Assignment is Cyclic," *Linguistic Inquiry* 10, pp. 421-442.

P. KIPARSKY, (1982a) "Lexical Phonology and Morphology," in *Linguistics in the Morning Calm*, a cura di I. S. Yange, Seoul.

P. KIPARSKY, (1982b) "From cyclic phonology to lexical phonology," in *The Structure of Phonological Representations*, a cura di van der Hulst, H. and N. Smith (1982), (Part I), pp. 131-175. Dordrecht, Foris.

A. PRINCE and P. SMOLENSKY, (1993) *Optimality Theory: Constraint Interaction in Generative Grammar*, ms., Rutgers University, New Brunswick and University of Colorado, Boulder. To appear, MIT Press.

A. LEONE, (1980) *La Morfologia del verbo nelle parlate della Sicilia sud-orientale*, Centro di Studi filogici e linguistici siciliani, Palermo. (Biblioteca del Centro di studi filologici e linguistici siciliani, n.s. 4).

G. ROSSINI, (1975) *Capitoli di morfologia e sintassi del dialetto cremonese*, La Nuova Italia, Firenze. (Pubblicazioni dell'Istituto di glottologia dell'università di Milano. Sezione a cura dell'Istituto di glottologia; 2).

G. SANGA, (1987) *Lingua e dialetti di Bergamo e delle valli*, Lubrina, Bergamo (Biblioteca di lingue e culture locali; 5).

I. VOGEL and S. SCALISE, (1982) "Secondary Stress in Italian," *Lingua* 58, 213-242.

A. ZAMBONI, (1983a) "La morfologia verbale latina in +sc+ e la sua evoluzione romanza: appunti per una nuova esplicativa," *Quaderni patavini di linguistica*, 3, 87-138.

A. ZAMBONI, (1983b) "Note aggiuntive alla questione dei verbi in -isco," *Studi di grammatica italiana*, XII, pp. 231-237.

Alfredo Stussi

CONTRIBUTO ALLA CONOSCENZA
DEL PADOVANO TRECENTESCO*

Proseguo nel trar fuori dall'Archivio di Stato di Padova documenti del volgare antico (cfr. Stussi 1995), in vista d'una raccolta complessiva che o prima o poi varrà la pena di allestire. Si tratta ora della busta 258 della sezione notarile, comprendente 13 fascicoli cartacei di varia consistenza dove si leggono rare date che vanno dal 1356 (c. 392^v) al 1405 (c. 227^r). I primi cinque fascicoli, dove prevalgono descrizioni di proprietà immobiliari, con date comprese tra il 1363 (c. 21^r) e il 1373 (c. 213^r), spettano al notaio Pietro Saraceno (cui appartiene anche il contenuto delle buste 256 e 257). In particolare nel quarto (cc. 141-158, con date 1370 a c. 147^r, 1365 a c. 150^v, 1368 a c. 153^v, 1371 a c. 154^r, 1368 a c. 155^r) le attuali cc. 157 e 158 sono carte singole senza corrispondente nella prima metà del fascicolo, cui sono fissate con un listello incollato nel senso dell'altezza. Questo ancoraggio, di cui nella medesima busta esistono numerosi altri esempi, avvenne durante il riordino dell'archivio notarile, alla fine del Seicento, quando ai registri della stessa busta fu apposta una cartulazione progressiva che riguarda indistintamente anche gli allegati, come nel nostro caso. La c. 157, senza filigrana, di cm 30 × 22, non interessa perché contiene soltanto, sul recto, uno scarno elenco in latino di acquisti terrieri. La c. 158, di cm 24,5 × 21, anch'essa senza filigrana, presenta su un lato un promemoria in volgare che più avanti sarà riprodotto e sull'altro note (attraversate da due righe verticali: di cancellatura?), relative soprattutto a decime, che trascrivo sciogliendo direttamente tutte le abbreviazioni: *soldi xxxj picoli ij dai ligati* / *soldi x pro decima Pape* / *soldi x pro decima* / *soldi x pro decima* /*soldi x pro decima* e un po' più a sinistra *soldi xj pro expensis*. Tutto ciò è scritto al centro del riquadro prodotto dall'intersezione delle tracce di due piegature orizzontali e di altrettante verticali, a modo di lettera, perché in tale forma verosimilmente il promemoria fu consegnato al notaio. Certo non fu lui a scriverlo, come è evidente da un sia pur rapido confronto delle scritture (per altro coeve), ma è probabile che sia stato lui a collocarlo dove ora si trova, cioè insieme a

---

* Lavoro eseguito nell'àmbito del programma di ricerca *Vocabolario storico dei dialetti veneti* (cofinanziamento MURST) con sede centrale Padova. Ringrazio Sante Bortolami per utili e frequenti consultazioni nel corso delle mie indagini presso l'archivio padovano.

strumenti del periodo 1368-1371, coi quali doveva intrattenere un rapporto indiretto che per ciò stesso oggi ci sfugge (e niente di utile in tal senso vien fuori neanche dagli altri fascicoli della busta). Tuttavia, siccome di norma è verificabile che le carte sciolte furono scrupolosamente fissate senza alterarne l'originaria collocazione, c'è motivo di ritenere che ciò possa essere avvenuto anche nel nostro caso e che dunque il promemoria risalga al primo-secondo decennio dopo la metà del Trecento.

Il promemoria è scritto in modo talvolta frettoloso e poco accurato, come mostra la cattiva esecuzione della prima *e* di *Segnore* 4-5 molto simile a una *o*; inoltre la riga 8 inizia con una lettera non identificabile cancellata e qui stesso la *v* di *xxv* sembra risultare da correzione di precedente *i*; altri errori corretti si hanno nel caso di *el cho(n)tà* 7, riscritto di seguito aggiungendo la erre mancante, e di *el Segore* 11 con una *n* aggiunta nello spazio soprastante tra *g* e *o* (per altro, *g* per *gn* sarebbe stata grafia non priva di valida documentazione nell'Italia settentrionale e nel Veneto in particolare: cfr. Salvioni 1892, p. 383 e nota 4, Belloni-Pozza 1987, p. 12). È rimasto invece un *l'ata* 5 per *l'atra* che nella successiva edizione è riprodotto con *r* integrata in corsivo. Nessun intervento editoriale è stato effettuato su *ciricha* 7 per *circha* non potendosi del tutto escludere l'eventualità che la seconda *i* sia non una parziale diplografia, ma la rappresentazione d'un vero e proprio suono anaptittico (qualcosa di analogo segnala Avalle 1992, p. CLXX); infine, dopo *circha viij* 4 manca evidentemente *cha(n)pi*.

Quanto agli usi grafici, merita d'esser notato che l'affricata palatale sorda davanti ad *a* è rappresentata sempre con *c* in *peca* 1, 4, 7, 9, 11 tanto da render probabile che *te(r)co* 10 sia da intendere come equivalente a *te(r)cio* piuttosto che come *te(r)-ço* con omissione di cediglia. In parallelo l'occlusiva velare sorda davanti ad *a* e *o* è rappresentata col digramma *ch* in *circha* 1, 4, 9, 11, *ciricha* 7, *cha(n)pi* 1, 11, *cha(n)po* 6, *cho(n)trà* 1, 7, 11, *cho(n)trata* 4, *chatare* 10, *chativo* 12, cioè sempre, tranne *ca(n)pi* 9 e *co(n)trà* 9; quanto alla sonora, si ha soltanto *Meiàsega* 11.

Il testo viene riprodotto secondo criteri tradizionali, sciogliendo tra parentesi tonde le abbreviazioni, ma lasciando intatte *It.* per *Item* e *lbr.* per *libre*; in corsivo viene integrata, come si è già detto, una *r* omessa per manifesto errore, mentre il punto in alto segnala legittima mancanza di *-n* per assimilazione e scempiamento in fonetica di frase.

It. una peca de prò circha vj cha(n)pi e· la cho(n)trà de Rialto, da una de le pa(r)te el Segnore / da l'atra pa(r)te mes(er) l'abè da San Daniele, da l'atra pa(r)te mes(er) l'abè da Praia, / i qual prè s'afita lbr. xx. /

It. una peca de tera araura circha viij in cho(n)trata Rialti, da una de le pa(r)te el
5   Se//gnore, da l'atra pa(r)te el monestero da Praia, da l'a*tr*a pa(r)te el monestero, / le qual tere re(n)de qua(r)tiri v el cha(n)po de forme(n)to. /

It. una peca de prò ciricha vij el cho(n)tà el cho(n)trà de Sirun, da tute pa(r)te el Segnore, / i qual prè s'afita lbr. xxv. /

It. una peca de tera araura circha xxxvj ca(n)pi e· la co(n)trà de Sirun, da tute pa(r)te
10   el Segnore, // le qual tere se po chatare la pa(r)te la mitè de i grosule, el te(r)co de minù. /

Padova, Archivio di Stato, sez. not. b. 258, c.158ʳ.

It. una peca de spini circa xij cha(n)pi el cho(n)trà de Meiàsega, da tute pa(r)te el
Segnore. / De queste siei è chativo re(n)deo.

Si tratta d'una descrizione di proprietà immobiliari consistenti in appezzamen-
ti (*peca*) a prato, da arare o *de spini* 11, di cui sono fornite le misure in 'campi' e
indicati i confini con proprietà del Signore di Padova (*el Segnore* 1, 4-5, 7, 9, 11,
verosimilmente Francesco il Vecchio da Carrara, Signore di Padova dal 1350 al
1388) e degli abati dei monasteri benedettini di San Daniele in Monte (*l'abè da
San Daniele* 3, non identificabile; cfr. sul monastero Barcaro 1986) e di Santa
Maria di Praglia (*l'abè da Praia* 3, *el monestero da Praia* 7: Bonifacio da Carrara,
cfr. Penco 1985, pp. 12-13).

Quest'ultimi tuttora validi riferimenti toponomastici indicano che le terre descritte si trovano a sud-est di Abano Terme. Meno ovvia è l'identificazione di
due corsi d'acqua: al primo, nominato in *la cho(n)trà de Rialto* 1, *cho(n)trata Rialti*
4, corrisponde oggi uno scolo Rialto che scende da nord a sud tra l'abbazia di Praglia e San Daniele in Monte, piegando poi a est verso Battaglia Terme (cfr. Istituto
geografico militare, Carta d'Italia 1:25000 F° 50 II S. O. Abano Terme); negli Statuti carraresi del 1362 si legge che «incipit in confinio Credule, Montismerli et
Pratalee, et protenditur per confinia Montis rubei, Montagnonis usque ad flumen»
(Gloria 1855, p. 163 e cfr. anche Gloria 1880-1881, pp. 606-607, nota 2). Del
secondo idronimo, *Sirun* 7 e 9, non ho trovato moderna sopravvivenza (a parte
un Sirón a Barbarano vicentino citato da Olivieri 1961a, p. 115, nota 3), ma
non c'è dubbio che si tratti del Canale Bisatto ('anguilla' in dialetto), derivato
dal Bacchiglione, che bagna Este. Decisiva in tal senso è la testimonianza di Alessi
1776, da cui risulta innanzi tutto che «ora è ridotto il Sirone alla qualità d'un angusto fosso, che unendosi alla Liona [nel Vicentino, dalla omonima valle], vi perde
il nome» (p. 268); più dettagliatamente, «il fiume, che da più secoli passa per Este,
si chiamava una volta il Sirone; nome che è rimasto ad un fiumicello del Vicentino,
che imbocca nel nostro; e da cui il nostro ebbe la sua prima origine, e la sua prima
denominazione. Ricevuta poi in sé una porzion dell'acqua del Bacchiglione, colla
Riviera dedotta da Longare: in progresso di tempo si cominciò a chiamar Bacchiglione anch'esso; e poi da alcuni Bisatto, per la sua tortuosità; come con ambedue
questi nomi tuttora si chiama. Questo scorreva in Este tra la Terra e 'l Castello: e
avviandosi verso Monselice, non proseguiva per quel canale, che ora lo conduce
alla Rivella e alla Battaglia: ma giunto a Monselice torceva a man dritta, circuiva
in parte quel monte e drizzavasi verso Pernumia; dove scorreva forse per quell'al-
veo, per cui ora scorre l'acqua, che vien da Bagnarolo [= Ponte Bagnarolo a Galzi-
gnano]: e ricevendo il fiumicello di Lispia [= Lispida, una collinetta vicino a Gal-
zignano], correva a Carrara a congiungersi col Rialto, che scende dalla parte di Re-
volone [= Rovolon], Mont'Ortone e Toreglia» (p. 533). Il fatto che il Sirone, come
scrive l'Alessi, «correva a Carrara» ci riporta dunque, rispetto a Este, più a nord,
fino alla congiunzione col Rialto, e quindi a una zona un po' più occidentale,

ma alla stessa altezza dei già ricordati San Daniele e Praglia (cfr. anche la carta idrografica della zona ricostruita da Gloria 1877). Quanto al nome *Sirun*, piuttosto che a uno dei derivati di SERIOLA, indicanti fossati o simili (REW 7851, ma cfr. ora Soranzo 1996 con esauriente bibliografia), Olivieri 1961b, pp. 502 e 507 pensa alla base, forse preindoeuropea, presente, tra l'altro, anche nel nome del fiume lombardo Serio. Nessun preciso corrispondente moderno si riesce a fornire per *Meiàsega* 11, certo derivato da (AE)MILIA > *Meia* (cfr. poco a nord di Padova *Meianìga*) più un suffisso di appartenenza -ATICA > -*àsega* con sibilante sonora, lo stesso di *Albignàsego*, poco a sud di Padova, toponimo studiato da Pellegrini 1987, pp. 351-359, confermando sostanzialmente l'intuizione di Olivieri 1961a «che da -*àdego* si sia passati ad -*àzego* per la falsa opinione che si trattasse di un *d* da *z*», e cioè che si abbia a che fare col riflesso di antica interdentale.

Dal punto di vista della pertinenza al padovano antico, già alla prima riga si incontra un tipico indicatore nel singolare *prò* 1 e 7 'prato' con riduzione ad *ò* del dittongo secondario -*ào* da -ATUM, seguito dal non meno significativo plurale *prè* 3 e 8 che insieme ad *abè* 2 e *mitè* 10 esemplifica il parallelo passaggio ad *è* di -*ai* e -*ae* da -ATI e -ATEM; e sempre in tema di gruppi vocalici secondari sono del pari pertinenti gli esiti -*ù* di -*ùo* da -UTUM in *minù* 10 nonché -*à* di -*àa* da -ATAM in *cho(n)trà* 1, 7, 11 e *co(n)trà* 9 (cfr. in generale Ineichen 1957, pp. 77-82) con costante dileguo delle occlusive dentali sorde intervocaliche, come anche in *araura* 4 e 9 'arativa' (cfr. Stussi 1995, p. 77), *Praia* 2, 5 < PRATALIA, *re(n)deo* 12.

Coerenti col tipo padovano sono inoltre la riduzione del dittongo in *qua(r)tiri* 6 (Ineichen 1957, p. 70); l'ulteriore chiusura di *o* chiusa tonica per influsso di iod in *araura* 4 e 9 (cfr. *coverturo* 'coperta' in Folena-Mellini 1962, p. 125) e, per influsso della nasale seguente, in *Sirun* (Ineichen 1957, p. 97); l'evoluzione di LJ a iod in *Praia* 2, 5 e *Meiàsega* 11; la caduta di -*e* solo dopo nasale e non dopo erre e quindi *chatare* 10, laddove ovviamente *mes(er)* 2 è forma troncata in fonetica di frase; l'uso della preposizione *da* con valore di specificazione/appartenenza in *l'abè da San Daniele* 2, *l'abè da Praia* 2, *el monestero da Praia* 5 (cfr. Folena-Mellini 1962, p. 125, Ineichen 1962-1966, II, p. 404). D'ordinaria amministrazione sono la tendenza ad avere in protonia la vocale palatale di timbro più aperto in *Segnore* 1, 4-5, 7, 9, 11, *mes(er)* 2, *monestero* 5, oltre a *de* ed *el* passim; le forme verbali di terza plurale uguale alla terza singolare come *s'afita* 3 e 8, *re(n)de* 6, *se po chatare* 10; lo scempiamento consonantico rappresentato graficamente senza eccezioni di sorta.

Meritano infine attenzione, anche se non specifici dal punto di vista geolinguistico, alcuni esempi di assimilazione e di dissimilazione consonantica in fonetica di frase, a cominciare dal ben noto tipo *un altro* / *l'atro* qui presente solo nella forma dissimilata *l'atra* 2, *l'atra* 5; altrettanto usuale è l'assimilazione tra -*n* ed *l-* con scempiamento in *e· la cho(n)trà* 1, *e· la co(n)trà* 9. Più raro è invece il caso di *el cho(n)tà el cho(n)trà* 7 e di *el cho(n)trà* 11 dove *el* sarà falsa ricostruzione per *en* a partire da un'opposizione *en* / *el* neutralizzata in *e* (ma si noti qui anche il contesto propizio alla dissimilazione offerto delle nasali contigue), fenomeno di cui offre esempi nei due sensi Avalle 1992, pp. CXX-CXXI.

Dal punto di vista lessicale, a quanto già osservato si aggiunga *cho(n)trà* 1 ecc. 'zona', spazio senza rilevanza giuridica, eventualmente con insediamenti sparsi senza consistenza di villaggio; *una peca de spini* 11 cioè un appezzamento lasciato alla crescita di 'rovi', per cui cfr. AIS III 608 (in alcuni punti a nord di Padova, e sempre maschile come confermato da AIS III 563), nonché Penzig 1924, I, p. 368 s. v. *prunus spinosa* e Pajello 1896, p. 271 (*spinaro* 'arbusto o insieme di arbusti provvisti di spine' a Cinto Euganeo è segnalato da Selmin 1982, p. 188); *siei* 12 'siepi' (formate appunto dai rovi suddetti), rappresentante, com'è tipico del Veneto centro-meridionale, il tipo SAEPES (la cui distribuzione complementare a CAESA ben risulta da AIS VII 1422; cfr. anche Pellegrini 1985) con dittongo da vocale aperta italoromanza e ladina centrale e dileguo (rispetto al più diffuso *sieve*, nonché *Sieve* oronimo euganeo, cfr. Pellegrini 1990, p. 200) di *-v-* < -P- documentato per il padovano antico (Ineichen 1957, p. 96) e più a nord (per es. *sié* in Tagliavini 1934, p. 286 e un plurale *siei* punto di partenza per *siech* in Bartolomeo Cavassico secondo Pellegrini 1977, pp. 195-196); la misura di superficie, come usava nel Padovano, è *cha(n)po* 6, *cha(n)pi* 1 e 11, *ca(n)pi* 9 (cfr. Stussi 1995, p. 77); la misura del frumento è *qua(r)tiri* 6 'quartieri', cioè la quarta parte dello staio (Gloria 1862, I, p. 151) e, quanto ai cereali, oltre all'indicazione particolare del *forme(n)to* 6 (forma metatetica ben nota anche al padovano antico, cfr. Ineichen 1957, p. 100), si distinguono cereali grossi (tra i quali si contavano anche legumi) e minuti (miglio, panico, meliga) designati rispettivamente come *i grosule* e *minù* 10, per cui soccorre Sella 1944, p. 278 che registra *grossile*, *grossule*, *grossumen* con esempi da testi mediolatini padovani e vicentini (per es.: «de blava ... starium unum grosulis et unum de minuto»). Alla distinzione in grossi e minuti, legata almeno in parte alla diversa dimensione dei chicchi, corrisponde, come ha mostrato Montanari 1975, l'opposizione tra semina invernale dei primi e semina primaverile dei secondi; si può anche precisare che metà dei *grossulia* e un terzo dei *minuta* rappresentavano un canone standard e che gli statuti veneti quattrocenteschi definiscono *grossulia* innanzi tutto il frumento e poi segale, orzo, spelta, avena, fava e legumi, esclusi i fagioli (De Sandre Gasparini 1979, pp. 54-55 e 59). Quanto infine al *chativo re(n)deo* 12 della *peca de spini* si tratterà genericamente di 'cattiva rendita', non di 'cattive decime', secondo un particolare significato di *redditum* pur presente nel latino medievale, ma in area diversa dalla nostra (Petracco Sicardi 1970, pp. 383-385).

BIBLIOGRAFIA

AIS: K. JABERG-J. JUD, *Sprach- und Sachatlas Italiens und der Südschweiz*, Zofingen, Ringier & Co., 1929.

I. ALESSI, *Ricerche istorico-critiche delle antichità di Este dalla sua origine fino all'anno MCCXIII dell'era cristiana*, Padova, Stamperia Penada, 1776.

d'A. S. Avalle (a cura di), *Concordanze della lingua poetica italiana delle origini (CLPIO)*, Milano-Napoli, Ricciardi, 1992.

F. A. BARCARO, *San Daniele in Monte ed Abano dal Mille ad oggi*, Padova, Edizioni Erredicì, 1986.

G. BELLONI-M. POZZA, *Sei testi veneti antichi*, Roma, Jouvence, 1987.

G. DE SANDRE GASPARINI, *Contadini, chiesa, confraternita in un paese veneto di bonifica. Villa del Bosco nel Quattrocento*, Padova, Istituto per la storia ecclesiastica padovana, 1979.

G. Folena-G. L. Mellini (a cura di), *Bibbia istoriata padovana della fine del Trecento. Pentateuco - Giosuè - Ruth*, Venezia, Neri Pozza, 1962.

A. GLORIA, *Della agricoltura nel padovano leggi e cenni storici*, Padova, Tipografia Sicca, 1855 (= «Scritti raccolti e pubblicati dalla Società d'incoraggiamento per la Provincia di Padova», II/1).

A. GLORIA, *Il territorio padovano illustrato*, Padova, Prosperini, 1862, 2 voll. [anast. Bologna, Atesa Ed., 1973].

A. GLORIA, *Studj intorno al corso de' fiumi principali del territorio padovano dal secolo I. a tutto il secolo XI.*, «Rivista periodica dei lavori della R. Accademia di scienze, lettere ed arti in Padova», XXVII, 1877, pp. 115-246.

A. GLORIA, *L'agro patavino dai tempi romani alla pace di Costanza (25 giugno 1183)*, «Atti del reale Istituto veneto di scienze, lettere ed arti», s. V, t. VII, 1880-1881, pp. 555-638.

G. INEICHEN, *Die paduanische Mundart am Ende des 14. Jahrhunderts auf Grund des Erbario Carrarese*, «Zeitschrift für romanische Philologie», LXXIII, 1957, pp. 38-123.

G. INEICHEN, *El libro agregà de Serapiom*, Venezia-Roma, Istituto per la collaborazione culturale, 2 voll., 1962-1966.

M. MONTANARI, *Cereali e legumi nell'alto medioevo. Italia del nord, secoli IX-X*, «Rivista storica italiana», LXXXVII, 1975, pp. 439-492.

D. OLIVIERI, *Toponomastica veneta*, Venezia-Roma, Istituto per la collaborazione culturale, 1961 (= 1961a).

D. OLIVIERI, *Dizionario di toponomastica lombarda*, Milano, Ceschina, 1961 (= 1961b).

L. PAJELLO, *Dizionario vicentino-italiano e italiano-vicentino*, Vicenza, Brunello e Pastorio, 1896.

G. B. PELLEGRINI, *Studi di dialettologia e filologia veneta*, Pisa, Pacini, 1977.

G. B. PELLEGRINI, *La 'siepe' nei dialetti friulani ed alpini orientali*, «Le Globe», CXXV (1985), pp. 207-218 (= *Les Alpes dans le temps et dans l'espace. Mélanges offerts au Professeur Paul Guichonnet*).

G. B. PELLEGRINI, *Ricerche di toponomastica veneta*, Padova, Clesp, 1987.

G. B. PELLEGRINI, *Toponomastica italiana*, Milano, Hoepli, 1990.

G. PENCO, *Cenni storici*, in C. CARPANESE-F. TROLESE, *L'Abbazia di Santa Maria di Praglia*, Milano, Silvana Editoriale, 1985.

O. PENZIG, *Flora popolare italiana*, Genova, a cura dell'Autore, 2 voll., 1924 (rist. anast. Bologna, Edizioni Agricole, 1972).

G. PETRACCO SICARDI, *Osservazioni sulla lingua dei contratti agrari altomedievali*, «Bollettino del Centro di studi filologici e linguistici siciliani», XI, 1970, pp. 372-408.

REW = W. MEYER-LÜBKE, *Romanisches etymologisches Wörterbuch*, Heidelberg, Winter, 1935³.

C. SALVIONI, *Annotazioni sistematiche alla Antica Parafrasi lombarda del 'Neminem laedi nisi a se ipso' di S. Giovanni Grisostomo (Archivio VII 1-120) e alle Antiche scritture lombarde (Archivio IX 3-22)*, «Archivio glottologico italiano», XII, 1892, pp. 375-440.

P. SELLA, *Glossario latino italiano. Stato della Chiesa - Veneto Abruzzi*, Città del Vaticano, Biblioteca Apostolica Vaticana, 1944.

F. SELMIN, *Il bosco e la vite in dialetto*, in M. Cortelazzo (a cura di), *Guida ai dialetti veneti IV*, Padova, Cleup, 1982, pp. 185-194.

D. SORANZO, *I corsi d'acqua chiamati "Seriola" e "Candelara"*, "Archivio per l'Alto Adige", XC, 1996, pp. 125-138; anche «Padova e il suo territorio», XI/63, 1996, pp. 37-40.

A. STUSSI, *Padova 1388*, «L'Italia dialettale», LVIII, 1995, pp. 69-83.

C. TAGLIAVINI, *Il dialetto del Livinallongo. Saggio lessicale*, Bolzano, Istituto di studi per l'Alto Adige, 1934.

Maria Bendinelli Predelli

THE *FIER BAISER* MOTIF BETWEEN LITERATURE AND FOLKLORE

In his *Studies on "Libeaus Desconus"* William Schofield stated that "The idea of the *fier baiser* is one of the most widely spread in the domain of folk-lore, and in some places is in full force to the present day."[1] In fact, he drew up a list of 34 occurrences of the motif, listing together literary and folkloric, medieval and modern sources, which include romances, novellas, theatre, geography books, chronicles, ballads and folktales and cover practically the whole range of European languages and countries. That Medieval romances bear structural and material resemblance with folktales is well known, but the nature of this relationship appears rather confuse even in some of the best critical literature. The purpose of this article is to review the occurrences of the *fier baiser* motif in Medieval and early Renaissance texts, in the hope of contributing to shed some light on the difficult question of the relations between Medieval literature and folklore.

We shall start by analysing the 'literary' texts, as the realm of folklore has been dealt with by the Aarne-Thompson *Index* which subdivides motif D735 "Disenchantment by a kiss" in a number of sub-types. Excluding the folksongs and folktales collected in the 19th century, our corpus is composed of the following main texts, listed in an approximate chronological order: 1) the German poem *Lanzelet* by Ulrich von Zatzikhoven (early XIII century); 2) the French courtly poem *Bel Inconnu* by Renaud de Beaujeu (early XIII century); 3) the purported *Book of travels* by Jean de Mandeville (XIV century); 4) the Middle English romance *Lybeaus Desconus* (XIV-XV); 5) the Italian *cantare Carduino* (XIV-XV) 6) the Italian *cantare Ponzela Gaia* (XV century); 7) the *Peregrinatio ad Terram Sanctam* by Italian notary Nicola de Martoni (1394-95); 8) Cristoforo Buondelmonti's *Liber insularum Archipelagi* (1420); 9) a chronicle by Neapolitan courtier Angelo de Tummulillis, titled *Notabilia temporum* (1464); 10) the Catalan novel *Tirant lo Blanc* by Joanot de Martorell (1468);[2] 11) Matteo Boiardo's *Orlando Innamorato* (between1476 and 1494); 12) Jeanne Flore's *Comptes amoureux* (1510); 13) an Italian baroque

---

[1] W. H. Schofield, p. 199.
[2] The final portion of the book, where the 'motif' is found may not be by Joanot.

novel by the title *Il principe Sferamundi* (1610); 14) C. Gozzi's play *La donna serpente* (1762).

To ascertain the derivation of some of these occurrences by others will significantly reduce the types to be taken into consideration. In fact, a parallel reading of the texts shows that: Jeanne Flore's *Comptes amoureux* and C. Gozzi's *La donna serpente* are clearly derived from Boiardo's *Orlando Innamorato*; the *Tirant lo Blanc* episode transcribes almost literally Mandeville's version; in turn, the catalan novel is the source of the *Principe Sferamundi*'s adventure. In all of these cases, the means of transmission is certainly a written text. All these testimonies may, therefore, be discarded as non relevant to our present discussion.

We may now proceed to regroup the remaining versions into basic types.

a) The *Bel Inconnu* poem has two close parallels in the Middle English romance *Lybeaus Desconus* and in the Italian *cantare Carduino*, transmitted both by 15th century mss. and probably to be ascribed to the turn of the 14th. Since the relations between these three poems are still not clearly defined, I shall refer to this tradition as to the Fair Unknown story: in spite of presenting itself in three distinct versions, the Fair Unknown story is, in fact, clearly identifiable in the context of the other occurrences of the motif, and represents one of the main variants of it. The *Orlando Innamorato* version was in all likelyhood inspired by a Fair Unknown story; it is problematic to state whether Boiardo had read his source or heard it told by an Italian *canterino*, but in any case the version he elaborated upon is that which is best represented by the French poem *Le bel inconnu*.[3]

b) The Mandeville's version too has parallels in later travel books, which all situate the legend in the island of Lango (Cos): the Latin account of a travel to the Holy Land by the Italian notary Nicolas De Martoni (1394-95) and Cristoforo Buondelmonti's Geography book *Liber insularum Archipelagi* (1420).[4] Again the resemblances between these versions are so important that we may refer to this tradition as to the 'travel book' variant of the motif.

c) The version found in an episode of the German poem *Lanzelet*[5] remains isolated, although it is closer to the travel book tradition than to the Fair Unknown one.[6]

---

[3] In *Orlando Innamorato* (Book II, canto 26) it is the hero, Brandimarte, that must kiss the serpent's mouth as in both *Carduino* and *Lanzelet*, whereas in Renaud de Beaujeu's *Le bel inconnu* the 'wivre' itself kisses the knight. However, the fact that the *fier baiser* adventure takes place in an enchanted castle, the hesitations of Brandimarte before the serpent, his instinctual reaction of defending himself with the sword and the repeated attemps to overcome his own fear all link the *Orlando Innamorato* episode to the versions of the Fair Unknown story.

[4] The legend is faithfully repeated in later geography books, such as F. FABER, *Evagatorium* (ca. 1484), T. PORCACCHI, *L'isole più famose del mondo* (1572), M. BOSCHINI, *L'Arcipelago* (1658), O. DOPPER, *Description exacte des îles de l'Archipel* (1703).

[5] The author of *Lanzelet*, Ulrich von Zatzikhoven, introduces his book as translation of a French (Anglo-Norman) book brought to Germany in 1194.

[6] In 1918, G. Huet had already remarked that among the various versions of the motif, the one that occurred in Mandeville's *Travels* bore the closest resemblances with the versions of early Medieval romances.

d) We should mention that a fourth variant of the serpent-maiden motif appears in the 15th century cantare *Ponzela Gaia*, in its reelaboration *L'innamoramento di Galvano* by Matteo Fossa[7] and in the 16th century poem *Innamoramento di Lancillotto e di Ginevra* by Nicolò degli Agostini (continued by Marco Guazzo),[8] as one of the adventures of Gawain. The association with Gawain leads me to believe that this version too owes to the tradition of the *Bel Inconnu* poem, where the hero is revealed to be Gawain's son; perhaps this tradition was conflated with aspects of the other variants.[9] The redeeming kiss has however disappeared from these 15th and 16th century versions,[10] and the motif of the damsel's transformation does not appear as relevant as in the other types. We are confronted here with a late and confuse reminiscence of a motif which in earlier romances had been much more significant.

Between the end of the 12th and the end of the 14th century, therefore, there were three basic variants of the motif: the *Lanzelet* episode, the Fair Unknown story, and the belief related by Mandeville about the island of Cos. Let us now examine and characterize these variants a little more carefully.

The *Lanzelet* version of the *fier baiser* is the culminating episode in Ulrich's poem: even if the episode occurs some 1500 lines before the end of the poem, all that is left to the hero and his wife after the *fier baiser* episode is to reap the benefits of their demonstrated excellence. One may read in the position of the episode whatever meaning may seem appropriate (Lanzelet as perfect knight not only in deeds of valour but also in matters of courtly love?);[11] it is indisputable, in any case, that the episode finishes up the portrait of the hero whom the book explicitly intends to celebrate as the paragon of every knightly virtue:

> Hie mite was ez bewæret,
> dô diu magt alsô genas,
> daz bî Lanzeletes zîten was
> dehein rîter alsô guot.
> Er behabet ân allen widermuot
> den prîs vor sînen gesellen.
> (vv. 7972-7977)

---

[7] *Libro novo dello Innamoramento de Galvano* (Mediolani, per Petrum Martirem et fratres eius de Mâtegatiis, XVI in.); *Libro de Galvano* (Venetiis, Melch. Sessa, 1508).

[8] Venice, Giuseppe Antonelli, 1839, 4 vols. The episode is found in canto V, octave 84 ff. Cfr. *Ponzela Gaia*, XLV-XLVII and G. VARANINI, *A proposito della Pulzella Gaia in Eubea*, "Lettere italiane", XXVI, 1974, pp. 231-233. In the second publication a misprint shows the latter poem as belonging to the 14th instead of the 16th century.

[9] Gawain finds the monster in the wilderness, like Lanzelet (but where else are serpents found but in the wilderness?); one may wonder whether the name of the Ponzela Gaia's enemy, Dina, is reminiscent of the name of the goddess Diana who, according to Mandeville, was the one who threw the spell on Yppocrate's daughter.

[10] In the *Innamoramento di Lancillotto e di Ginevra* the serpent is once again delivered by the knight's kiss. The author may, however, have found the motif in Boiardo's *Orlando Innamorato*, of which Nicolò degli Agostini wrote one of the continuations.

[11] ... dô begundens gâhen/ zuo dem küenen Lanzelete, / der sô frümeclîchen tete / daz er getorste bestân / daz dinc daz nie mê wart getân (... they hastened to the bold Lanzelet, who had acted so gallantly in daring to face what had never been faced before), vv. 7942-7946.

Hereby was it proved, when the maid was thus restored to happiness, that in Lanzelet's time there was no knight so good. He received without any opposition the supreme honor before all his friends.

It is, however, only an episode in the long list of adventures that characterize Lanzelet's life.

In the Fair Unknown story the spell and the tension towards the disenchantment is the pivot of the entire story. The whole sequence, from beginning to end, is the consistent development of the basic motif: a princess has been transformed into a serpent by an evil magician; only an extraordinarily good knight would be able to free the princess from the spell; the reward would be the hand and the kingdom of the princess. Consequently, the story tells of the arrival at Arthur's court of an unknown and seemingly simple knight who obtains from the king the gift of the first available adventure, and of the arrival of a damsel who has come to Arthur's court to look for an extraordinarily good knight. The sequel of adventures that take place during the trip between Arthur's court and the hero's destination are necessary for the unknown knight to demonstrate his valour and gain the trust of his disdainful guide. Of course the knight succeeds in freeing the princess from the magician(s) and from the spell, and becomes her spouse.[12]

In both these variants the misfortune of the damsel transformed into a dragon, or serpent, comes to an end: she finds the excellent knight who succeeds in freeing her. We are in the realm of narrative and the motif is embodied in an episode, or in a story. When we turn to the travel book variant, the main difference is that the motif takes the form of an open ended situation:

> Mais quant il vendra un si hardy qui l'ose aler baisier, il ne mourra mie; ainçois revendra la damoiselle en sa droite fourme, et sera sire du pays.[13]

This is in fact more conform to the nature of a legend or a traditional belief, and the writers insist on the oral nature of their tale:

> Et dist on que en celle ylle de Angho est encore la fille Ypocras, en guise d'un grant dragon [...] si comme on le dist; car je ne l'ay mie veu.[14]
> de qua quodam mirabile michi fuit narratum et certificatum michi per dictum dominum fratrem Dominicum, dum fui cum eo in civitate Rodi, quod filia Ypocrate...[15]
> Dicitur etiam et affirmatur quod filia Hippocratis...[16]

---

[12] This is in essence the plot of the story that must have been Renaud de Beaujeu's source and is basically reflected in the French and Italian poems. The studies which tend to show the unity of the *Bel Inconnu* may be right in terms of aesthetic analysis and poetic meaning, but in terms of content, it seems indisputable to me that Renaud de Beaujeu has fused in his poems disparate materials, one of which must have been the Fair Unknown story.

[13] *Mandeville's Travels*, vol II, p. 241.

[14] *Mandeville's Travels*, vol II, p. 240.

[15] *Relation du Pélerinage à Jérusalem de Nicolas de Martoni notaire italien (1394-1395)*, p. 644.

[16] C. BUONDELMONTI, *Liber insularum Archipelagi*, p. 103, quoted by G. Huet, p. 53.

The question then arises: is it plausible that the romantic versions have their origin in an orally transmitted tale about a damsel transformed into a dragon and awaiting for the best knight to kiss her deformed mouth? This theory was maintained by G. Paris[17] and G. Huet, and also more recently the *fier baiser* motif was given as one of the examples that demonstrate the "enracinement folklorique du roman arthurien," to quote a very interesting article by J. Ch. Payen who, insisting on the intention of the knighthood to distance itself from clerical supremacy, points to "leur souci, plus fréquent qu'on ne le croit, de se prévaloir de traditions diverses dont l'ancienneté garantit la valeur d'*auctoritas*." Such "traditions diverses" were often found, according to Payen, in the realm of folklore:

Folklorique, l'énigme mortelle posé par un géant (je pense à la première partie du *Tristan en prose*). Folklorique, l'intervention de la bête blanche, souvent victime d'un enchantement. Folklorique, le fier baiser consenti à un monstre qui se transforme en princesse, et qui signifie le mariage avec la souveraineté [...] épisodes, qui constituent pour l'auditoire autant de repères familiers. La façon dont ils sont traités implique toute une oralité latente, toute une familiarité avec des contes qui circulent beaucoup plus largement que dans l'aire restreinte du château.[18]

Even if Payen claims that he does not envisage a "culture populaire au sens étroit," i.e. "une culture plébéienne ou rurale, propre au couches les plus modestes de la populations," but rather a culture "qui se rattache à un terroir et procède d'une inspiration régionale ou nationale," he points quite explicitly to a culture of peasants. His enthusiasm for this "ensemble obscur et diffus qui appartient authentiquement au folklore" induces him to maintain that there must have been circulation between the culture of the aristocrats and that of the lower classes:

La culture aristocratique, si fermée soit-elle, communique avec une culture paysanne qui lui est tout proche. Le seigneur ne s'est pas superbement isolé de ses vilains. Il connaît les conteurs qui les fascinent et les invite peut-être, quelquefois, à le distraire à son tour. [...] Il fallait un relatif courage, aux poètes romans pour aller puiser leurs trésors dans le monde, pour eux marginal, du moins sur le plan culturel, des vilains et de la rusticité.[19]

R. S. Loomis, on the other hand, maintained instead that the Fair Unknown story ultimately derives from a Celtic tradition, documented in a number of old

[17] Cfr. G. Paris, *Guinglain ou Le Bel Inconnu, par Renaud de Beaujeu*, "Romania" XV, 1886, and *Histoire littéraire de France*, vol. XXX, pp. 171-199.
[18] J. Ch. Payen, pp. 432-433.
[19] J. Ch. Payen, p. 433, 435. This statement echoes a passage from K. H. Jackson's, *The International Popular Tale and Early Welsh Tradition* (Cardiff, University of Wales Press, 1961, pp. 3-4): "before the Renaissance the stories genuinely popular and current among the upper classes had a great deal in common with those popular with the unlettered peasantry, and their plots were very often the same... Hence there was a constant give and take between the two, a constant process whereby literary men adopted stories from folk sources and folktale tellers made use of materials which they acquired in various ways from literary sources".

Irish tales. One of these tells of a young son of a king who, in order to provide water to his men, accepted to kiss a "monstruous hag". She not only was changed into a wonderful young woman, but revealed to be the "Sovereignty of Ireland" itself, so that the young man was designed as the heir to the throne. Beyond the story, the motif was held to be the reflection of a naturalistic myth signifying the sun "embracing the bleak, wintry land of Ireland and transforming her by his caresses into a vision of flowery loveliness, clad in a mantle of green".[20] What is relevant to our purposes is that, in Loomis' perspective and in most of the Anglosaxon school, the French romantic stories presupposes not peasant folklore, but rather the narrative tradition of the Celtic poets and storytellers.[21]

I would like to scrutinize more closely these two positions as far as the *fier baiser* motif is concerned. As for the Celtic myth hypothesis, it is certainly true that the motif was not an invention of Renaud de Beaujeu, in that he must have followed an earlier Fair Unknown story. I also believe, with a number of modern Anglosaxon scholars, that the tales of arthurian romances were more likely to originate in the activity of professional storytellers rather than in peasants' folklore. That the *fier baiser* motif was present in the Celtic narrative lore cannot, however, be proven. The concordances between our motif and that of the Sovereignty of Ireland are, in my view, very loose: the narrative structure of the Irish stories centered on the Sovereignty of Ireland motif is quite different from that of the Fair Unknown story;[22] that the liberated damsel would marry his rescuer and associate him in the reign of her kingdom are features so widespread in world narrative that they represent no cogent concordance; most of all, an old hag is not a terrifying dragon, or serpent. I do not find, therefore, Loomis' hypothesis a convincing one.

The Greek folklore hypothesis was best argued in an article by G. Huet, who gave an accurate critical analysis of the Mandeville's account, putting the question whether the rumor related by Mandeville could be held as an authentic folkloric motif. He supplied very good reasons not to believe the authenticity of Mandeville's account as an oral tale:

on peut affirmer que [...] Mandeville n'a pas été lui-même à Cos et, par conséquent, n'a pu y recueillir notre récit. On se rappelle en effet qu'il distingue, au début, entre "l'ille de Cohos" et celle de "Langho" ou "Angho". Or, Lango est tout simplement le nom médiéval

---

[20] R. SH. LOOMIS, *The Fier Baiser*, p. 111.

[21] In examining the various occurrences of the motif in German folktales, Emma Frank concluded that it ultimately derives from the literary versions of the Middle Ages. Cfr. E. FRANK, *Der Schlagenküss. Die Geschichte eines Erlösungs-motivs in deutscher Volksdichtung*, "Form und Geist" IX, 1928.

[22] In an earlier version of the Fair Unknown story, the culminating feat was probably the freeing of the princess from an unwanted suitor, who put the heads of his slain adversaries on a row of pickets around the castle. Such pattern is better reflected in Malory's *Book of Sir Gareth* and Hue de Rotelande's *Ipomedon*. If this is true, the dragon-maiden motif should be held as a substitution for the culminating feat of the earlier version. Bibliography about the Fair Unknown story can be found in my *Alle origini del 'Bel Gherardino'*, Firenze, Olschki, 1990, pp. 225-226.

de Cos. Un voyageur qui eût été lui-même sur les lieux n'eût jamais commis une confusion aussi ridicule. La narration contient encore un autre détail, qui peut en tout cas nous faire douter qu'elle soit la transcription absolument fidèle d'une légende qui avait cours à Cos parmi le peuple: la transformation de la jeune fille en dragon y est attribuée à Diane. Or, le nom d'Artémis, l'équivalent grec de Diane, est aujourd'hui inconnu du peuple en Grèce propre.

Furthermore,

La version que Mandeville aurait suivie ne peut être bien ancienne [...]: on se rappelle qu'il y est question d'un "chevalier de l'Hospital du chastel de Rodes". On sait que les chevaliers de l'Hôpital ne s'établirent à Rhodes qu'en 1310.

Huet was also very aware that Mandeville "pille sans vergogne dans les récits des autres": "plus on l'a étudié de près, plus son crédit a baissé", so much so that he was described as an "habile géographe de chambre." [23] He concluded however his discussion of the question by cautiously reaffirming the authenticity of the tale as a folkloric legend, although he admitted that the legend might have been "primitivement indépendente d'Hippocrate et rattaché après coup à son nom". Huet's reasons to believe in the authenticity of the legend were 1) the existence of a number of other legends about Hippocrates, witnessed by the *Conte del Graal* and a Catalan version of the *Seven Sages*, which appear to be of Byzantine origin; 2) the existence of a second historical source, Cristoforo Buondelmonti's *Liber insularum Archipelagi* (1420), which relates the legend of Hippocrates' daughter in terms that show his independence from the Mandeville's version. Had Huet known Martoni's account of his pilgrimage to the Holy Land with his version of the legend, he would have had no doubts about the nature of the legend as an authentic popular belief, since Martoni stresses that he received the legend from an oral source. The Italian notary's account of his travel to the Holy Land is not subject to the caution of Mandeville's narrative and he seems to relate faithfully the events of his trip. From his Latin account,

viene fuori il ritratto vivacissimo d'un uomo... ricco di umanità e animato da uno spirito di curiosa e attenta osservazione... Nonostante le difficoltà e i disagi del viaggio e la situazione

[23] The latest Mandeville's scholar, Christiane Deluz, is much more appreciative of the French geographer's merits. She believes that Mandeville did in fact travel in the Mediterranean, and that he collected the dragon-maiden legend "sur les lieux". She does not, however, discuss Huet's arguments, and P. Hamelius' statement that "all but a few pages have been proven to be stolen from some older book" (P. HAMELIUS, *Mandeville's Travels translated from the French of Jean d'Outremeuse*, II, Introduction and Notes, EETS, London, Oxford University Press, 1923 [reprint 1961], p. 19) is, in essence, confirmed by Deluz's scrutiny of Mandeville's sources. Among these the most important were Vincent of Beauvais' and Brunetto Latini's encyclopedias (*Speculum Naturale, Speculum Historiale* and *Livre dou Tresor*), William of Boldensele's pilgrimage to the Holy Land, Friar Odoric de Pordenone's travels to Palestine and the Far East, William of Tripoli's *De statu Saracenorum*, the historical works of Jacques de Vitry, Albert d'Aix, Hayton, and the romances in vernacular, especially those about Alexander the Great. As Ms Deluz states, "Les sources sont ici... comparables à celles d'encyclopédies ou d'*Images de Monde*" (p. 59).

473

pericolosa, il Martoni cedette a un suo interesse strettamente culturale nel voler visitare con cura i monumenti della città affidandosi a guide locali ("Rogavi quosdam de dicta civitate ut me conducerent ad videndum ipsa hedificia et res antiquas"), dalle quali raccolse notizie e tradizioni leggendarie che poi trascrisse fedelmente nella sua relazione. [24]

It must be stressed that the three travel book versions are fairly different from each other, so that no direct connections can be established. [25] When we consider together the testimonies of Mandeville (ca. 1366-1370), [26] Martoni (1395) and Buondelmonti (1420), therefore, we can hardly doubt that from the middle of the 14th century on, a legend about a dragon-maiden awaiting for a most valorous knight to kiss her on her mouth was attached to the island of Cos and was kept alive not only through written but also oral transmission. It is worth noting, however, that this legend appears to be attached to the order of the Hospitallers in Rhodes no less than to the island of Cos. Both Mandeville and Martoni mention the unfortunate attempt of a knight of the military order of Saint John. [27] Martoni heard of the legend not in Cos but in Rhodes, from a member of that order and about a member of that order. Surely the Hospitallers had brought with them the mainland traditions and literature, and it is well known that legendary beliefs attached to certain places in Greek territories in the Middel Ages had their origin in, precisely, romanesque literature of ultimately Anglo-Norman or French origin. Already Huet pointed out that

cette légende [Hippocrates' daughter] n'est pas le seul conte de ce genre qui se trouve dans le livre du pseudo-voyageur: on y lit de même la légende du "château de l'Épervier". Or, l'authenticité de cette histoire, soi-disant arménienne, paraît fort sujette à caution, quand on remarque, avec M. Warner, que "le nom de *Castrum de Espervier* se lit déjà chez Gervais de Tilbury, rattaché à une toute autre légende, qui ressemble à celle de Mélusine." [28]

Silvia Poli di Spilimbergo noted in Martoni's account another local legend which identified a certain old castle in an island of the Gulf of Euboea as the "castrum Fate Morgane, domine Laci, matris Pozelle Gage; in quo castro dicitur fuisse captivum dominum Calvanum." [29] His informants were "certos nobiles de dicta civitate [Negroponte], confratres cujsdam [*sic*] hospitalis noviter editi in dicta ci-

---

[24] S. POLI DI SPILIMBERGO, *Un ricordo della Pulzella Gaia in Eubea*, "Lettere Italiane", XXV, 1973, pp. 356-357. Ms Poli refers to the article of M. PASTORE STOCCHI, *Note su alcuni itinerari in Terrasanta dei secoli XIV-XV*, "Rivista di storia e letteratura religiosa", II, 1967, pp. 197-199.

[25] The translation of Mandeville's *Travels* "in antico toscano" edited by Zambrini belongs to the second half of the 15th century.

[26] C. Deluz tends to anticipate Mandeville's actual trip to 1342.

[27] The order of the Knights of Saint John in Jerusalem, grew out of a hospital founded in Jerusalem about 1048, whence the vocable of Hospitallers.

[28] P. 51. Cfr. also R. S. LOOMIS, *Arthurian Tradition and Chrétien de Troyes*, New York, Columbia University Press, 1949, pp. 92-95.

[29] Quoted from S. POLI DI SPILIMBERGO, p. 358.

vitate" (Hospitallers, once again?]. Quite apart from the lateness of the reference to the Hospitallers, who moved to Rhodes only in 1310, it is inherent to the *fier baiser* motif that the rescuer be a knight, and an excellent one. This character is so pertinent to Medieval feudal mores and ideals reflected in Medieval romanesque literature that the hypothesis of the legend as a truly local and ancient motif becomes less and less convincing. One is induced at this point to agree with Loomis' surmise that "the tale of Hippocrates' daughter represents an episode from Arthurian romance, transplanted and localized in the Mediterranean."[30] The resemblance between the ruins of the "gaste cité" of the Fair Unknown story and the ruins of Hippocrates' palace[31] might have been just the contact point that originated the association of Cos with the dragon-maiden legend.

It appears, in conclusion, that even if at the end of the 14th century and at the beginning of the 15th the legend collected by Martoni and Buondelmonti, was in fact a legend orally transmitted, it is quite unlikely both 1) that this legend be a local and folkloric belief going back to classical antiquity; and 2) that the Cos legend be at the origin of the romantic versions of the motif. Furthermore, the fact that Martoni collected in 1394 the legend from the Hospitallers in Rhodes does not exclude, *per se*, the possibility that Mandeville found his legend in some written text, and that the legend collected by Martoni was the result rather than the cause of the statements found in Mandeville's travel book.

To these general warnings about the credibility of the origins of the *fier baiser* motif in Greek folklore, I should like to add some remarks about the *Lanzelet* episode which, even if they will not openly reveal its origin, may perhaps hint at a partial solution. Once the episode of the dragon-maiden is concluded, the omniscient author of *Lanzelet* addresses his public directly to supply further information about the enchanted damsel:

> Durch der liute niugerne
> so entouc mir niht zenberne,
> ich sage iu daz ze mære,
> wer diu vrowe wære,
> diu von dem wurme ein wîp wart. (vv.7983-7987)
> [...]
> siu hiez diu schne Elidîa,
> von Thîle eines küneges kint.
> daz wizzent wol die wîse sint
> und die die welt hânt erkant,
> daz Thîle ist ein einlant,

---

[30] R. SH. LOOMIS, *The Fier Baiser*, p. 112.

[31] Domus que fuerunt Ypocrate sunt extra terram modo per duos jactus lapidis cum manu... domus ipse hostendunt magnum fuisse hedificium, sicut unum castrum, cum multis magnis et diversis hedificiis, nun vero sunt dirructe et in ipsarum aliquibus partibus includuntur animalia illorum de terra Langonis. *Relation du Pélerinage*, p. 644.

> ein breit insele in dem mer.
> dâ ist von wunder manic her,
> diu nieman kunde geahten.
> Ein wochen vor Wîhnahten
> sint sô kurz dâ die tage
> nâch Rômære buoche sage,
> dâ manic wunder an stât,
> daz ein loufer kûme gât
> vor naht ein halbe mîle.
> Die tage sint ouch ze Thîle
> ze sumer langer danne hie.
> Ir envrieschent vremder mære nie
> dan uns dannen sint geseit.
> Swelch wîp sich an ir hübscheit
> verwurke und des gedenke,
> daz si den beschrenke,
> der ir dienet umb ir minne,
> daz kumet ir ze ungewinne.
> (vv. 7990-8012)

On account of people's curiosity I must not fail to inform you who the lady was who changed from dragon into woman. [...] She was called Elidia [Clidra] the Fair, daughter of a king of Thyle. The wise know well, and those who are acquainted with the world, that Thyle is an island, a broad island in the sea. There they have a great lore of marvels which no one could reckon. A week before Christmas the days are so short, according to the authority of the Roman books, which contain many marvels, that a runner scarcely goes a half a mile before nightfall. Moreover, the days in Thyle are longer in summer than here. You never heard stranger tales than are told us of that place. Whatever woman there should sin against courtly etiquette and think to deceive a man who is serving her for her love will come to misfortune...

In this passage the author clearly tries to (mockingly) corroborate the credibility of the incredible episode he just told with even more marvels of the land of Thyle. It is also clear that, to do so, he borrows his discourse from a source that sounds a lot like a geography, or travel book, or more precisely like one of those works which, like the *Letter of Alexander to Aristotle*, disguised their account of *mirabilia mundi* as if it were the account of real or literary travels.[32] Interestingly enough, such a travel book discourse also penetrates the episode of the dragon-maiden: when Lanzelet first speaks to the dragon-maiden, he says: "ich gesach nie tier sô grimme/ noch als engeslîch getân/ aldes ich ervarn hân/ in wazzer oder an lande" ("Never in all my travels on water or on land saw I a beast so grim nor so fright-

---

[32] Loomis pointed out as "characteristic of Anglo-Norman Britain [...] the fascination of *mirabilia*, natural wonders," documented for example by Giraldus Cambrensis' *Itinerarium Cambriae* (c. 1191), which can be recognized in the descriptions of "the Shrieking Marsh, the Growing Lookout, and the Hill of the Marvelous Ball in *Lanzelet*" (Introduction to the translation of *Lanzelet*, New York, Columbia University Press, 1951, pp. 7-8).

fully shaped");[33] to which the dragon itself replays: "Got hât liut unde lant/ von manegem wunder gemaht,/ mit sîner tougen bedaht" ("God has made many people and lands of many strange kinds, conceived by his miraculous power").[34] Such propositions reflect an attitude which is similar to that, for example, of the prologue to the *Letter of Prester John* found in the ms. Yale, University Library, 395, a versified version composed around 1190:

> Curteis est Deus ki tut cria,
> Qui tut governe et tuit fet a.
> Tuit vait a sun commandement:
> Ciel e terre e ewe e vent.
> Quanque ad fet, ki garde em prent,
> Miracle est tut veraiment.
> [...]
> Mult i a ke nus savum
> E plus asez ke n'entendum,
> Mes assez ad de cele gent
> Que ne creient ke seit nïent
> Fors sul tant cum il unt veü
> E par eus meismes entendu.
> Mes plus i a, ke bien enquiert;
> Cum plus irra, plus ciert en iert:
> [...]
> Ne sevent cil de l'Occident
> Les grant miracles de l'Orient
> Dunt ci poez alkes aprendre,
> Si vus volez a moi entendre.
>   (vv. 1-6, 38-44, 47-50).[35]

What is more, the information about the length of days in summer and winter echoes precisely an information which classical and Medieval geography books constantly repeat about the island of Thule (identified usually with Iceland).[36] Plinius the Elder, for example (followed by Isidorus, Priscianus, Julius Solinus, Bede, the Icelandic historian Are, the author of the *Imago mundi* (ca. 1100)[37] and his

---

[33] Vv. 7898-7901.

[34] Vv. 7906-7908.

[35] Martin Gosman, *La lettre du Prêtre Jean. Édition des versions en ancien français et en ancien occitan*, Groningen, Bouma's Boekhuis, 1982.

[36] The German text explicitly refers to "the authority of Roman books", and the way the shortness of the day is indicated ("that a runner scarcely goes half a mile before nightfall") seems in fact to evoke a classical antiquity context. The winter solstice is, however, replaced by the christian festivity of Christmas, which shows a Medieval reelaboration of the astronomical datum. For a discussion about the geographical identification ot Thyle cfr. W. Richter 1934, pp. 70-71.

[37] Erroneously attributed to Honorius Augustodunenses, it may be the work of an English monk, in view of the unusually precise knowledge he possessed of the islands to the North and West of Europe. Cfr. P. Duhem, *Le Système du monde. Histoire des doctrines cosmologiques de Platon à Copernic*, Paris, 1913-1917, III, pp. 24 ff.

Anglo-Norman remaker)[38] makes reference to the solstice of summer when, as he says, there are no nights, and the solstice of winter when there are no days:

> Ultima omnium quae memorantur Thyle, in qua solstitio nullas esse noctes indicavimus, cancri signum sole transeunte, nullosque contra per brumam dies (Book 4).

Dicuil's *Liber de mensura orbis terrae*, written in 825 and the first book to report information on Iceland based on experience, is more precise and corrects the opinion commonly held:

> non solum in aestivo solstitio, sed in diebus circa illud in vespertina hora occidens sol abscondit se quasi trans parvulum tumulum [...] in medio illius minimi temporis medium noctis fit in medio orbis terrae, et sic puto e contrario hiemali solstitio et in paucis diebus circa illud auroram in minimo spacio in Thile apparere, quando meridies fit in medio orbis terrae et idcirco mentientes falluntur, qui [...] a vernali aequinoctio usque ad autunnale continuum diem sine nocte atque ab autunnale versa vice usque ad vernale aequinoctium assiduam quidem noctem, dum illi navigantes in naturali tempore magni frigoris eam intrabant ac manentes in ipsa dies noctesque semper praeter solstitii tempus alternatim habebant.[39]

It is possible therefore to think that the *Lanzelet* episode may have originated from a text which spoke of a serpent-woman as one of the marvels of the world, the same unknown text which may ultimately be responsible for Mandeville's account. Did this text already speak of the disenchantment by a kiss, or was this a conflation with the Sovereignty of Ireland tradition? Did this text associate the legend with Thule or with some other island? How much of what we read today in the *Lanzelet* belong to the Anglo-Norman source and how much is Ulrich's interpolation? All these questions are bound to remain without answer. We can only assume that the episode of the disenchantment by a kiss of a serpent-woman was already in Ulrich's source, if we keep in mind that the association of woman and serpent is well documented in Anglo-Norman *milieux* at the turn of the 12th century. Apart from the Fair Unknown story,[40] one of Walter Map's *nugae* (1181-1193) relates that the supernatural wife of Henno is changed every Sunday into a dragon.[41] In addition, Geoffroi of Auxerre's sermons *Super Apocalypsim*, composed between 1187 and 1194, tells the story of a nobleman who married an unknown woman met in a forest, the latter being nothing but a "serpentis... in specie mulieris". The woman

---

[38] *La petite philosophie, an Anglo-Norman poem of the 13th century*, William Hilliard Trethewey editor, New York, Johnson Reprint, 1967.

[39] Pp. 42-44.

[40] Cfr. W. H. SCHOFIELD, 175-179.

[41] Videt eam igitur summo mane die dominica, egresso ad ecclesiam Hennone, balneum ingressam et de pulcherrima muliere draconem fieri... WALTER MAP, *De nugis curialium*, IV, 9.

"prouvait un plaisir extraordinaire à se baigner et passait le plus clair de son temps à cette occupation. Et elle refusait de se laisser voir nue, même par l'une de ses servantes: quant tout était prêt, elle les renvoyait, restait seule dans la chambre et fermait la porte de l'intérieur." [...] Une servante profite d'une fente dans la paroi pour surprendre le secret de sa maîtresse: elle assiste à la métamorphose de la fée et voit "non pas une femme mais un serpent qui déroule ses anneaux dans l'eau du bain."[42]

A few years later Gervase of Tilbury, who lived in London for some time and composed his *Otia imperialia* between 1209 and 1213, stated: "De serpentibus tradunt vulgares, quod sunt quaedam foeminae, quae mutantur in serpentes". The statement is only apparently condescending towards "vulgares," since Gervase himself relates a story very similar to that of Geoffroi of Auxerre, about Raymond de Château Rousset (*Otia imperialia*, I, 15).

The association of the supernatural women evoked by Walter Map, Geoffroi of Auxerre, Gervase of Tilbury with water is a recurring feature of such stories. In the same way in *Lanzelet*'s episode, "Zehant vlôch der wurm hin dan / da ein schne wazzer ran, / und badet sînen rûhen lîp. / Er wart daz schnest wîp, / die ieman ie dâ vor gesach" (At once the dragon flew away to where a beautiful brook ran and bathed its rough bodying, whereat it became the loveliest woman than anyone had ever seen).[43] There are therefore good reasons to believe that the dragon-maiden motif took shape in the Anglo-Norman literary milieux, open to the fascination of books, or stories, dealing with *mirabilia mundi*.

It is interesting to note that in the latest of the travel book versions which we have considered, that of Buondelmonti, a *strenuus vir* succeeds in liberating the island from the *serpens maximus* which devoured the flocks and terrorized the inhabitants: it seems that by its own nature the legend called for a conclusion and that even without the influence of the romantic versions the oral tale had to be quickly modified and became a 'story.' Another instance of the open-ended situation of the oral legend being brought to the conclusion of a happy mating between the enchanted damsel and her rescuer is to be found in the chronicle of Angelo de Tummulillis da Sant'Elia, a notary of the Neapolitan kingdom at the time of the last Angevin queens and of king Ferdinando of Aragon. He personally witnessed most of the facts he relates in his *Memorabilia temporum*, an account of the most notable things happening in his times and covering the period from ca. 1390 to ca. 1477. The *fier baiser* episode is reported as if it had happened in the year 1464. Angelo's version of the *fier baiser* motif was quoted by Mauda Bregoli Russo as proof of the presence in Italy of the Anglo-Norman source (Ms Bregoli Russo supposes a musical lay) of *Lanzelet*.[44] Although the theory that the

---

[42] *Super Apocalypsim*, XV, edited by Castaldelli, Roma, 1970. Quoted from L. HARF-LANCNER, *Les fées au Moyen Âge*, Génève, Slatkine, 1984, p. 150.

[43] Vv. 7935-7939.

[44] M. BREGOLI RUSSO, *Un riscontro francese nell'"Orlando Innamorato" del Boiardo*, "Studi e problemi di critica testuale", XXIII, 1981, pp. 97-105.

sources of the German *Lanzelet* were musical lays and that these may still be in circulation in 15th century Italy is highly improbable, there is no doubt that Angelo's
story is a late echo of the same old romantic motif. The detail that the beast itself
speaks to the hero, "dicens ne aufugeret, quia bonum ei contingeret si timore postposito auderet ipsum osculari; quia ex tali osculo ipse serpens deberet converti in spetiosam mulierem" is singularly close to the *Lanzelet* version: to Lanzelet manifesting
his desire to "keep away from 'it',"

> "Neinâ, helt, daz verbir
> sprach der grôze serpant:
> [...]
> Wan lebet nu ritter dehein,
> der mich kuste an mînen munt!
> sô wurde ich schne und sâ gesunt.
> Ich enmohts ab nieman nie erbiten,
> si envlühen gar mit unsiten,
> alle die mich ie gesâhen.
> Doch möhter gerne gâhen,
> ein ritter, daz er kuste mich:
> dâ mite bezzert er sich
> [...]
> lse mich. Ezn ist niht mîn spot,
> wan ich will dich manen mêre
> durch allen vrowen êre.
> (vv. 7904-7905; 7926-7928; 7910-7918)

"No, no, hero, do not so!" spoke the great serpent [...] Would that there now lived a
knight who would kiss me on the mouth. Then should I instantly be restored and beautiful. But I have never been able to persuade anyone. All who ever saw me fled disgracefully.
Yet if a knight were willing to kiss me, without delay he would thus better himself [...]
Release me! It is no jest on my part, for I will entreat you further by the honor of all ladies...

In contrast, Mandeville and Martoni and (albeit confusely) Buondelmonti's versions have Hippocrates' daughter speak to the potential rescuer in her human
shape. The cave, the treasure and the promise to marry the rescuer, however,
do not appear in the *Lanzelet* version, but are all present in Martoni's account.
The pastoral setting is already in Buondelmonti's account. There has obviously
been a conflation and fusion of versions, as in orally transmitted stories.

An interesting thing I would like to point out is that while Angelo purports to
relate the rumor of a certain event, and even transcribes a letter that witnesses to
that event, his account of the story is, in fact, different from what the document
shows. In other words Angelo's understanding of the event was influenced by the
Cos legend, which he already knew from some other source. I reproduce below the
texts of Martoni and of Angelo de Tummulillis, which are probably less widely

known to scholars of the *fier baiser* motif than the romantic or Mandeville's versions.

De filia Ypocrate conversa in serpentem et quid accidit cuidam frerio qui promisit ipsam osculari. – Est in domibus ipsis quedam magna et profunda clicta fabricata, de qua quodam mirabile michi fuit narratum et certificatum michi per dictum dominum fratrem Dominicum, dum fui cum eo in civitate Rodi, quod filia Ypocrate reducta fuit in serpentem, que manet in dicta clicta et multotiens exit de dicta clicta et hostendit hominibus in formam pulcerime mulieris et querit semper ut oscularetur a quodam viro, ipsa existente in forma serpentis, propter quod ipsa promittit multa et magna thesaura et divitias multas volenti ipsam in forma serpentis osculari, et ipsum accipere in virum. Quadam die hiis temporibus non longe preteritis quidam frerius Sancti Johannis stabat in terra Langonis, quia est una consuetudo quod omnes frerii Sancti Johannis qui vadunt ad civitatem Rodi debent morari per annum unum in terra Langonis ad serviendum ibi pro defensione illius insule Langonis que est prope Turchiam, vel quod ibi serviant per substitutum, qui frerius, sciens et audiens de dicto serpente qui exiebat de dicta clicta, aliquando ibat illuc causa videndi illum in forma mulieris. Qui quadam die exivit dictus serpens in formam pulcerime mulieris; que mulier dixit ei, si volebat eam osculari in formam serpentis, quod sibi dabat multa thesaura et magnas divitias. Qui frerius promisit sibi. Mulier dixit sibi: "Vide, quia volo hostendere tibi quomodo ego me tibi demonstrabo. Cogita si eris tanti cordis, venias cras et oscularis me in ore, et si non, dicas michi." Qui dixit ei ut se hostenderet sibi in qua forma erat ventura. Que mulier sic fecit et hostendit se sibi in forma turpissimi ac magni et orribilis serpentis, et postea reducta in forma mulieris, petiit a dicto frerio de sua intentione. Qui sibi respondit quod paratus erat facere et promisit illuc accedere mane sequenti. Adveniente mane dictus frerius paravit se et illuc accessit eques et invenit dictam mulierem in forma magni et orribilis serpentis; timidus valde, descendit de equo ut iret ad osculandum illum. Serpens hostendit se magis terribilem et turpem, et frerius perterritus timore magno equitavit et aufugit, et serpens sequtus fuit ipsum cum magno rumore usque ad castrum, ita quod vis potuit evadere quod non occideretur a serpente. Dictus frerius tribus diebus vixit et ex magno timore mortuus fuit. Dicunt illi de Langone quod sepe sepius dictus serpens videtur ante dictam clictam. Insula Langonis girat milearia CL et est multum fertilis victualium (*Relation du Pélerinage*, pp. 644-645).

Set inter audite fabulam et non fabulam hiis preteritis diebus undique in nostris partibus divulgatam, adparentibus etiam licteris infrascriptis; quia in ipso anno .M.CCCC.LXIIII. de mense ianuarii .XIIII. indictione in partibus Romanis et in pertinentiis mangnifice civitatis Cesene, dum quidam pauper homo nomine Johannes Salvalalgly mercenarius cuiusdam divitis ipsius civitatis uno dierum in quodam nemore pasceret porcos suos secus quemdam montem, apparuit belua in modum mangni et mirabilis serpentis, cui pre timore exterrito dictus serpens allocutus est, dicens ne aufugeret, quia bonum ei contingeret si timore postposito auderet ipsum osculari; quia ex tali osculo ipse serpens deberet converti in spetiosam mulierem, quam si dictus Iohannes voluisset accipere in consortem et coniugem, spondebat ipsum facere beatum et opulentiorem pre ceteris habendum huius seculi. quo Johanne respondente non posse hoc legitime fieri, eo quod haberet aliam uxorem, ipse serpens replicavit: "vera dicis"; et predixit sibi omnia que de ea futura erant, dicens: "tua uxor est pregnans et in nocte proxime nativitatis domini nostri Jehsu Christi, intellige de preterita, debet parturire et procreare duos infantulos mares, et ipsa mater debet mori in ipso partu cum uno ex dictis filiis". ex quibus verbis dictus Johannes securus osculatum est eum; qui statim conversus in mulierem, ut predixerat, duxit ipsum Johannem in speluncam suam, ubi invenit inextimabilem thesaurum, et celebrato concubito cum ea, promisit illi thesaurum ipsum, et proinde docuit quid facturum esset. de quibus omnibus potuit lictera directa per quemdam venerabilem et religiosum virum fratrem de Cesena ad quemdam amicum suum in Perusio, cuius tenor talis est: "Per farve parte delle cose da cqua, mirabili et incredibili ad chy no lle vede, ve adviso como, secuta la morte della molglie de Salvalalglyo, allo termene che da lluy continuo era dicto, nel dì della Nativitate et alle .xx. hore quando li apareo la fata soa et dixe che andasse alla sua cupa la nocte sequente, che era quella de Sancto Stefano, et che il serpe dormia; et dixe che a llui tolzesse quella catenella de oro che havea allo collo et portassela seco, cha nolli porria nocere alcuna cosa, et admaczasse lu serpente, ca lu thesauro serrìa allo sou commando. unde lu dicto Salvalalglyo tolze la dicta catenella et menò seco secte balistreri con secte balestre, li quali disserraro le dicte balestre per forma che lo serpente morì collo ayuto de Salvalalglyo, che li moczò la testa. morto che fo lu serpente fo tanto il venino, che tucti li balestreri morerono de facto, et Salvalalglyo è deventato nella faccia palido como se fosse opilato, cavando della cupa predicta grandissimo thesoro, del quale le monete ne scrivo cqua de socto como so facte. have anche cavata una coracza che non c'è spingarda che li noccya, inseme con una targa d'aczaro all'antica, como se depingono quelli delli paladini, de oro, dove so scolpiti tre chyovi spontati con lictere intorno, quale descriverò de socto, in greco et in latino..." (*Notabilia temporum*, pp. 124-125).

As it can be easily verified, the letter in Italian speaks of a peasant who was helped by a fairy to kill a serpent and thus collect an inestimable treasure; Angelo's account speaks very clearly of a dragon who *is* a woman and reproduces the main traits of the legend as found in the travel books. He further adds the detail of the hero's wife and her death, which he probably takes from the historical event (or rumor of), since it appears in the Italian letter: "secuta la morte della moglie del Salvalaglyo, etc."[45] The Neapolitan chronicle is therefore a very interesting example of how, even when writers purport to relate contemporary events – or rather the account of them – and rumors perceived as popular ("fabulam et non fabulam hiis preteritis diebus undique in nostris partibus divulgatam") they superimpose their own understanding of the facts, to the point of modifying the immediate account of the historical events according to preexisting structures and tales. In this case, the preexisting tale might have been 'folklore' itself, i.e. a legend transmitted through oral means, as Martoni's account would make us believe, but certainly reinforced and spread through written texts such as the travel books. A folklore legend modified by another folklore legend?

---

[45] It may also be worth noting that the *Tirant lo Blanc*'s version owes not only to Mandeville's text, but also to the version of the legend as it must have been current in Italy in the 15th century. As in Buondelmonti, the land is devastated, the setting is rural and pastoral (not a wild forest as in *Lanzelet*) and once the knight Espercius has succeeded in kissing the monster, she takes him to her bedroom in the cave and "celebrat concubitum cum eo" as the hero of Angelo's account. Although we know that the section of *Tirant* where the episode of Espercius is found was probably not written by Joanot Martorell himself, it must be pointed out that Joanot had visited Italy precisely in the same years as Angelo was writing his chronicle.

The episode points to the complexity of the study of Medieval folklore, in the absence of any authentic record of it, and of a precise definition of what is to be considered folklore, or *culture populaire*: a definition which should furthermore take into account the differences in class distribution and social organization according to the different times and places. Even if we must, of course, admit the oral circulation of tales and legends, such as that about Hippocrate's daughter, there is no doubt that distant transmission and persistence of such tales owe to the authority of written texts.

As for the occurrence of the same motifs in Medieval romances and in folktales collected centuries later, the explanation must be found, in my view, elsewhere than in the collusion of *culture aristocratique* and *culture paysanne, seigneur* and *vilains*. Research on romantic narrative shows that it is normally possible to trace the features of any *roman* (be it at the level of structure or content) to earlier works; this chain of transmission is of course broken when the written texts presuppose an activity of oral storytelling not documented in writing, such as that of Celtic *conteurs*. Not surprisingly 'folkloric' motifs such as fairy lovers, fight with dragon, *fier baiser*, wild hunt etc. appear already in the earliest extant French romances of Breton subject. One should however wonder whether the motifs which we quickly label as folkloric, i. e. associated with the lower classes, were perceived in exactly the same way by the aristocratic audiences of the castle. Such motifs were quite likely part of the traditional lore transmitted by the storytellers of prefeudal societies to the continental *fabulatores* and from these to the courtly writers of romances.[46] This early storytelling too presupposes, however, an aristocratic audience as recent studies on the *Mabinogi* and the other Welsh tales point out. To account for the spreading of the same tales and motifs among commoners, we must think of the occasions in which lords and servants, knights and peasants would be convened together in the same place and listen to the same stories. In feudal and pre-feudal societies storytelling was often part of a feast, and the feast was represented by the gathering of as many people as possible: in such occasions hospitality was often extended to a larger community, including the poor and the peasants; some of them may have been called upon to provide the additional service needed to host the visitors. The setting was therefore provided for the non-aristocrats to listen to the tales of the professionals storytellers. Furthermore, it is well known that *jongleurs* performed not only at court but more often in front of commoners. Since in oral cultures tales are easily remembered, it is easy to explain why traditional tales were spread and further transmitted even among the peasantry. Ultimately, the storytellers' activity may also account for the spreading of certain motifs in tales repeated by everyone (not necessarily the peasants), with

---

[46] Cfr. C. BULLOCK-DAVIES, *Professional Interpreters and the Matter of Britain*, Cardiff, University of Wales Press, 1966.

no intention of composing literary works, such as those related by Gervase of Tilbury, for example. Occasionally, some of these oral tales may have provided ideas and motifs to *conteurs'* stories. Professional storytellers cannot, however, be equated with the peasantry. In spite of the contempt shown by aristocratic narrators such as Chrétien (and, later, Boccaccio), the storytellers had their own type of professional skills and knowledge of their lore. Furthermore, written texts had an important role in the *conteurs* learning and transmitting their stories.

We must therefore understand the relationship between literature and folklore, particularly in the case of narrative lore, as a complex process which takes into account the means of transmission (oral and written; literary genres and their audiences), the specifically medieval settings for transmitting traditional lore, and the span of time necessary for traditional tales to become folklore. This process has its key figure in the professional storyteller: he has access to books; he performs his job sometimes in front of aristocratic audiences, often also in front of commoners. It is not surprising that his tales, or parts of them, quickly become folktales and acquire a life of their own as genuine folklore.

FREQUENTLY QUOTED WORKS

C. Buondelmonti, *Liber insularum Archipelagi*, G.R.L. De Sinner ed., Leipzig-Berlin, Reimer, 1824.

C. Deluz, *Le livre de Mandeville. Une 'géographie' au XIVe siècle*, Louvain-la-Neuve, Institut d'études médiévales, 1988.

A. De Tummulillis da Sant'Elia, *Notabilia temporum*, C. Corvisieri ed., Livorno, Vigo, 1890, pp. 124-126.

Dicuili, *Liber de mensura orbis terrae*, G. Parthey ed., Berolini [Berlin], A. Effert & L. Lindtner, 1870.

L. Harf-Lancner, *Les fées au Moyen Age*, Génève, Slatkine, 1984.

G. Huet, *La légende de la fille d'Hippocrate à Cos*, "Bibliothèque de l'école des chartes", LXXIX, 1918, pp. 45-59.

É. Le Grand, *Relation du pélerinage à Jérusalem de Nicolas de Martoni notaire italien (1394-95)*, "Revue de l'Orient latin", III, 1898, pp. 566-669.

R. S. Loomis, *The 'Fier Baiser' in Mandeville's Travels, Arthurian romance, and Irish saga*, "Studi medievali", New series, XVII, 1951, pp. 104-113.

Mandeville's Travels., M. Letts ed., London, Hakluyt Society, 1953 (2nd Series, voll. 101-102).

J. Ch. Payen, *L'enracinement folklorique du roman arthurien*, "Travaux de linguistique et de littérature", XVI, 1978, pp. 427-437.

S. Poli di Spilimbergo, *Un ricordo della Pulzella Gaia in Eubea*, "Lettere Italiane", XXV, 1973, pp. 356-360.

Ponzela Gaia. Cantare dialettale del secolo XV, G.Varanini ed., Bologna, Commissione per i testi di lingua, 1957.

W. Richter, *Der Lanzelet des Ulrich von Zatzikhoven*, Frankfurt am Main, Moritz Diesterweg, 1934 (Deutsche Forschungen).

W. H. Schofield, *Studies on 'Libeaus Desconus'*, Boston, Modern Language Departments of Harvard University, 1895 (Studies and Notes in Philology and Literature, vol. IV).

U. von Zatzikhoven, *Lanzelet*, translated from the Middle High German by K. G. T. Webster, provided with additional notes and an Introduction by R. S. Loomis, New York, Columbia University Press, 1951.

U. von Zatzikhoven, *Lanzelet*, F. Norman ed., Berlin, De Gruyter, 1965.

MADISON U. SOWELL

"THE JINGLING SOUND OF LIKE ENDINGS": GENESIS AND EVOLUTION OF THE *GREMBO-NEMBO-LEMBO* RHYME

No Italian humanist ever proved more instrumental than Francesco Petrarca in promoting enthusiasm for classical letters, whose authors by and large seem to have avoided any consistent use of rhyme.[1] At the same time, few Italian poets have been more enamored of "matching sounds at the end of words" than the composer of the *Rime sparse*, who included many rhyming tours de force among his collected sonnets, *sestine*, and *canzoni*.[2] It should not come as a surprise, therefore, that exactly three centuries after the death of Petrarca, John Milton, in a prefatory note to the second edition of *Paradise Lost* (1674), defended the choice of "*English* Heroic Verse without Rime" (Milton's italics) for his own epic by appealing *not* to Petrarca but directly to the ancient examples of Homer and Virgil.

In the process of pillorying "the troublesome and modern [i.e., seventeenth-century] bondage of Riming", Milton boldly asserted, without providing documentation, that

Not without cause... some... *Italian*... Poets of prime note have rejected Rime both in longer and shorter Works... as a thing of itself, to all judicious ears, trivial and of no true musical delight; which consists only in apt Numbers, fit quantity of Syllables, and the sense variously drawn out from one Verse into another, not in the jingling sound of like endings, a fault avoided by the learned Ancients both in Poetry and all good Oratory.[3]

---

[1] From 1975-79, I enjoyed the privilege of studying with Dante Della Terza at Harvard University. My time as a graduate student coincided with the first four years of the New England Inter-University Seminar in Italian Studies, founded on the initiative of Professor Della Terza in cooperation with Franco Fido, Maria Picchio Simonelli, and Giuseppe Velli. The seminar was taught by luminaries from both sides of the Atlantic, from Cesare Segre to Maristella Lorch. Those halcyon years also provided me with golden opportunities to study with and attend lectures by some of this century's greatest historians, literary scholars, and poets, including Felix Gilbert, Harry Levin, and Robert Fitzgerald, to name only three. But it was my mentor's lectures and writings – particularly D. DELLA TERZA's, *Forma e memoria: Saggi e ricerche sulla tradizione letteraria italiana da Dante a Vico* (Roma, Bulzoni, 1979) – that sparked my thinking about Petrarchan echoes in Italian literature and led me to dedicate this particular essay to him.

[2] My initial definition of rhyme comes from NORTHRUP FRYE, SHERIDAN BAKER, and GEORGE PERKINS, *The Harper Handbook to Literature*, New York, Harper & Row, 1985, p. 396. A prime example of Petrarca's rhyming prowess is Poem 29 of the *Rime sparse* ("Verdi panni sanguigni oscuri o persi"), in which verses rhyme only from stanza to stanza (including internal rhymes in the fourth and sixth verses of each stanza).

[3] As reprinted in JOHN MILTON, *Complete Poems and Major Prose*, ed. Merritt Y. Hughes, Indianapolis, Bobbs-Merrill, 1975, p. 210.

The English poet's acrimonious attack on rhyme (or rime, an older spelling), while presaging the twentieth century's preference for unrhymed verse, ignored or trivialized a venerable and centuries-old tradition in Italian poetry that even in Milton's day had already stretched from Dante's *terza rima* to Marino's nearly forty-one thousand lines of *ottave* in the *Adone*. Although the Italian tradition of employing rhymes in verse has continued, notwithstanding Milton's scorn, past the Renaissance and up to Montale's adoption of rhymes and highly inventive sound patterns in his non-aulic poetry, very few contemporary critics have attempted to trace the genesis and evolution of any particular rhyme. While critical essays on the history and meaning of particular rhymes may appear anomalous in an era emphasizing literary theory, such essays actually complement studies in the theory and "anxiety of influence".

What follows is an examination of the origin of one of Petrarca's rhymes (-*embo*) in his justly famous *canzone* 126 ("Chiare fresche et dolci acque") and a suggestion that the richness of the rhyme under consideration arises from the poet's subtle manipulation of Virgilian and Dantean sources. Second, I trace the evolutionary high points of this same rhyme through various poets and varying contexts down to the present century.

1. *The Origin of the* grembo-nembo-lembo *rhyme*

Etymological dictionaries reveal that the three words most commonly associated with the -*embo* rhyme – *grembo* (lap or womb), *nembo* (rain cloud), and *lembo* (hem or edge) – have their origins in Indo-European roots with similarly symbolic meanings: gwelbh-, meaning womb (in Greek *delphus*, womb); nem-, which can refer to a sacred grove (in Latin *nemus*, grove); lem-, which carries with it either the notion of breaking in pieces or nocturnal spirits (cf. Latin *Lemures*, ghosts).[4] The archetypal and religious symbolism traceable even to the root meanings of *grembo*, *nembo*, and *lembo*, however, can be easily overlooked because of either the catchiness of this particular rhyme or even the way we define rhyme.

Most handbooks define rhyme or *rima* quite simply: "Close similarity or identity of *sound* between accented syllables occupying corresponding positions in two or more lines of verse" or "perfetta identità di *suono* dell'uscita del verso a partire dall'ultima vocale tonica" (emphasis mine, both here and later).[5] Such definitions, with their predictably exclusive emphasis on sound rather than also on sense or

---

[4] See, for example, *The American Heritage Dictionary of Indo-European Roots*, rev. and ed. Calvert Watkins, Boston, Houghton Mifflin, 1985.

[5] For the English definition, C. HUGH HOLMAN, *A Handbook to Literature*, 4 ed., Indianapolis, Bobbs-Mer-

symbolism connected to sounds, occasionally (and understandably) direct our minds away from the richness of linguistic texture which rhymes may possess. Admittedly, poets may employ rhyme merely as a decoration or simply as a device of versification. When poets of any era consistently compose ornamental, facile, or shallow rhymes, we are quick to refer to such poets as rhymers or rhymesters, *rimatori* in Italian. Our use of such disparaging words – all of which emphasize the element of rhyme or *rima* in the poetaster's compositions – should not obscure the fact that a skilled poet can and often does use rhyme to sustain a complex idea or to capture a profound thought. That a rhyme employed by a careful poet invariably points to more meaning than readily meets the ear is a basic premiss behind this essay.

By definition, the repetition of rhyme at regular intervals constitutes an integral part of a stanza's form. In the case of the *Divine Comedy*, Dante considered rhyme so quintessential to his Christian philosophy that he repeated it in a tripartite fashion throughout the tercets that form each canto. He thus invented *terza rima* to mirror his theological argument and to assist his didactic purposes. Because of Dante's desire to create a medieval encyclopedia of knowledge and a richly allegorical poem, the rhyme word for him, in the opinion of Alfonso De Savio, "could not be a mere ornament as is often the case with Dante's predecessors and contemporaries."[6]

Quite aware of Dante's successful invention and use of *terza rima*, Petrarca adopted it as his own rhyme scheme in the *Trionfi*. Perhaps because of such overt imitation, Francesco De Sanctis, in his celebrated *Saggio critico sul Petrarca*, avowed that Petrarca

Non aveva né originalità, né profondità: cioè a dire, non aveva né la forza di trovar nuove idee e nuovi rapporti, e stamparvi su il proprio suggello, né la forza di squarciare la superficie..., cogliere il sostanziale. Aveva invece le qualità scimie di quelle, che imitano gli stessi procedimenti meccanici, con tanto più di ostentazione con quanto meno di forza.[7]

Notwithstanding this distinguished critic's unfavorable view of Petrarca's innate intellect, I should nevertheless like to examine a unique and particularly revelatory rhyme in the *Canzoniere*. In so doing I shall also touch upon an intriguing question, one which is implicit in De Sanctis's harsh evaluation of Petrarca: how significantly could and did Petrarca modify his sources?

In the history of Italian poetry few rhymes have enjoyed so rich and varied a history as that of *lembo-nembo-grembo*. Although the -*embo* rhyme occurs prior to Petrarca's *canzone* 126 – in Dante's *Purgatorio* 7.67-72, in the form of *grem-*

---

rill, 1980, p. 381. For the Italian, W. TH. ELWERT, *Versificazione italiana dalle origini ai giorni nostri*, Firenze, Le Monnier, 1976, 83.

[6] ALFONSO DE SAVIO, *The Rhyme Words in the 'Divina Commedia'*, Paris, Honoré Champion, 1929, p. 1.

[7] FRANCESCO DE SANCTIS, *Saggio critico sul Petrarca*, a cura di Niccolò Galla, Torino, Einaudi, 1983, p. 37.

bo-schembo-lembo – and contemporary with Petrarca's usage – in Niccolò di Mino Cicerchia's *La risurrezione* (Cantare 2, ottava 154), as the variant *limbo-schimbo-grimbo* – it was clearly the Humanist poet's invention of the neologism *nembo*, from the ablative of the Latin *nimbus*, and seminal use of it with *lembo* and *grembo* in "Chiare fresche et dolci acque" that immortalized this particular rhyme.

The Accademia della Crusca's concordance to the *Canzoniere* reveals that the word *grembo* appears three times in the *Rime sparse*, though only twice in rhyme position; *lembo* appears twice, both times as a rhyme; *nembo*, on the other hand, constitutes an example of *hapax legomenon* – that is, a word used only once in the *Canzoniere* and apparently unique to that corpus until copied by fifteenth-century Petrarchists.[8] Salvatore Battaglia's *Grande dizionario*, the Italian equivalent of the Oxford English Dictionary, sustains this observation, listing Petrarca's *nembo* as the first recorded use of the word.[9] Certainly this word is found neither in Dante's *Commedia* nor in Boccaccio's *Decameron*, as attested by concordances to both authors.[10] Although these facts are fairly easy to ascertain, I have discovered no other scholar or commentator who has highlighted or identified *nembo*'s uniqueness or who has commented on why Petrarca invented this obvious Latinism and substituted it, in the *-embo* rhyme in *canzone* 126, for the Dantean choice of *schembo*.[11] And yet there has been no end to poets making use of Petrarca's felicitous and catchy rhyme (as we shall see in the second part of this essay), thus calling repeated attention to it. But the question remains: what spawned the *lembo-nembo-grembo* rhyme? And what are the reasons for its creation?

As mentioned earlier, in the seventh canto of the *Purgatorio* the *-embo* rhyme occurs probably for the first time in Italian letters. It appears, at least in part, in the words of Sordello to Virgil and Dante, when the Provençal poet indicates the location of the Valley of the Princes – that is, the *grembo*, lap, secure place, or, more mythically and less materialistically, dark womb where the preoccupied princes ponder, meditate, rest, and wait for the night to pass (vss. 67-69):

"Colà, disse quell'ombra [Sordello], n'anderemo

---

[8] See *Concordanza del 'Canzoniere' di Francesco Petrarca*, Firenze, Accademia della Crusca, 1971, 2 voll.

[9] See SALVATORE BATTAGLIA, *Grande dizionario della lingua italiana*, Torino, UTET, 1961-, which documents numerous subsequent appearances of *nembo* after Petrarca.

[10] See *Concordanza della 'Commedia' di Dante Alighieri*, a cura di Luciano Lovera con la collaborazione di Rosanna Bettarini e Anna Mazzarello, Torino, Einaudi, 1975, 3 voll., and *Concordanze del 'Decameron'*, a cura di Alfredo Barbina, Firenze, G. Barbèra, 1969, 2 voll.

[11] Natalino Sapegno's magisterial commentary on "Chiare fresche e dolci acque" offers only these words on *nembo*: "nuvola di fiori, mossi e agitati da Amore". See FRANCESCO PETRARCA, *Dalle Rime e dai Trionfi e dalle Opere minori latine: Pagine scelte e commentate*, a cura di Natalino Sapegno, Firenze, La Nuova Italia, 1972[2], p. 89. Giuseppe Mazzotta, who approaches *canzone* 126 with an avowedly philological hand, simply but astutely remarks that *nembo* "translates the Latin *nimbus* by which poets and painters conceal and at the same time reveal Divinity". In *The Worlds of Petrarch*, Durham, Duke University Press, 1993, p. 178.

> dove la costa face di sé *grembo*,
> e là il novo giorno attenderemo".

The rhyme continues in Dante's narrative description of the valley. "There was", he says, "a slanting path [un sentiero *schembo*], between steep and level, which brought us to the side of that hollow, there where its edge [il *lembo*] more than half dies away."[12] This passage marks the only time *schembo* or, in some mss. *sghembo*, appears in the *Commedia*. The two other words appear elsewhere in the *Comedy* – *grembo* in *Inferno* 12.119 and 20.74, *Purgatorio* 5.75 and 8.37, and *Paradiso* 8.9 and 11.115 and *lembo* in *Inferno* 15.24 and *Purgatorio* 27.30 – but never in rhyme position.

Not unlike a classical drama, Petrarca's *canzone* "Chiare fresche e dolci acque" is divided into five main parts and an *envoi* or epilogue. Each of the five stanzas contains the 13 verses of either eleven or seven syllables (*endecasillabi* or *settenari*) typical of the *canzone* form. However, it is the fourth stanza which interests us. As if in a vision, Petrarca's *persona* describes the glorification of Laura: a rain of flowers falls on her bosom or lap ("suo grembo") even as she is covered by a loving cloud ("amoroso nembo"); some of the flowers, our visionary notes, fall on her skirt or hem ("sul lembo"). That stanza, describing Laura sitting by the banks of a river (presumably the Sorgue) and covered by a cloud of flowers, reads in its entirety as follows:

> Da' be' rami scendea
> (dolce ne la memoria)
> una pioggia di fior sovra 'l suo *grembo*,
>   et ella si sedea
> umile in tanta gloria,
> coverta già de l'amoroso *nembo*;
>   qual fior cadea sul *lembo*,
> qual su le treccie bionde
> ch'oro forbito et perle
> eran quel dì a vederle,
> qual si posava in terra et qual su l'onde,
> qual con un vago errore
> girando parea dir: "Qui regna Amore."[13]

Although Nancy Vickers in a 1981 issue of *Modern Language Notes* insightfully discusses Dantean echoes in the fourth stanza of "Chiare fresche et dolci acque", she does not identify the -*embo* rhyme as a Danteism.[14] She concentrates instead

---

[12] All quotations from Dante, as well as the English translations, come from DANTE ALIGHIERI, *The Divine Comedy*, trans. with commentary by C. S. Singleton, Princeton, Princeton University Press, 1970-75.

[13] *Petrarch's Lyric Poems: The 'Rime sparse' and Other Lyrics*, trans. and ed. Robert M. Durling, Cambridge, Harvard University Press, 1976. All quotations from Petrarca comes from this edition.

[14] See NANCY VICKERS, "Re-membering Dante: Petrarch's 'Chiare, fresche et dolci acque'", *Modern Language Notes* 96 (1981), pp. 1-11.

on parallels between Laura's cloud of flowers and Beatrice's "nuvola di fiori" in *Purgatorio* 30. I view the -*embo* rhyme as possibly an additional allusion to Dante for two main reasons. First, Dante established an immediate and available precedent for using -*embo* in rhyme in the celebrated Valley of Princes episode in *Purgatorio* 7, a canto redolent with Edenic imagery and one that foreshadows the pastoral imagery of the Terrestrial Paradise discussed by Vickers. Even though Petrarca claims never to have read Dante seriously, scholars in the four decades since Aldo Bernardo's influential 1955 article on "Petrarch's Attitude Toward Dante" have shown that Dantean influence in Petrarca's lyrics is practically ubiquitous and too often overlooked.[15] Second, the continued narrative description in *Purgatorio* 7 contains elements very much present in Petrarca's *canzone*. More specifically, in both the description of the *locus amoenus* enjoyed by the princes and in the portrayal of the natural beauty surrounding Laura, flowers and the color of gold figure prominently in the narratives. While classical analogues may account in part for such idealistic portrayals of nature in both poets, the fact remains that in each case we are dealing with literary and/or historical figures whose humility is emphasized even though they are highly favored in and by an idyllic setting. The princes reveled in earthly glory and the tribute of men; they now humbly sit and sing their praises to the Virgin. Laura, though she reigned not as a literal queen on the earth, also enjoys an enviable position. For in Petrarca's fantasy of her apotheosis she too sits and is "Humile in tanta gloria".

I do not wish, however, to carry the parallels between the two scenes to an extreme, only to indicate that Petrarca, in including the -*embo* rhyme in *canzone* 126, subtly imitates and carefully modifies a Dantesque rhyme; he is drawing our attention, again in a nuanced fashion, to another idyllic nature setting with religious overtones and mythic implications. This supports my contention that this whole *canzone* should be read much less materialistically and much more mythically.[16] It also points to the type of skillful transformation inherent in much of Petrarca's handling of sources. But what are we to make of the change in rhyme words from the Dantean to the Petrarchan text? Dante chose to rhyme *grembo* and *lembo* with *schembo*. Petrarca prefers instead to create a Latinism (*nembo*) and to substitute it for *schembo*. Certainly *nembo* is more poetically pleasing to

---

[15] See ALDO S. BERNARDO, "Petrarch's Attitude Toward Dante", *PMLA* 70 (1955), 488-517, and such studies as MARCO SANTAGATA, "Presenze di Dante 'comico' nel 'Canzoniere' del Petrarca", *Giornale storico della letteratura italiana* 146, pp. 163-211, and PAOLO TROVATO, *Dante in Petrarca: Per un inventario dei dantismi nei 'Rerum vulgarium fragmenta'*, Firenze, Olschki, 1979.

[16] For an example of the "materialistic" reading of *canzone* 126, see FRANCESCO PETRARCA, *Rime sparse*, a cura di Giovanni Ponte, Milano, Mursia, 1979, p. 177, where "dolci acque" is glossed in this highly precise and geographical manner: "del Sorga (più probabilmente presso Thor o Châteauneuf de Gadagne, a metà strada fra Avignone e Valchiusa, dove il corso del fiume è meno rapido, e sono meno gelide le sue acque". I prefer not to emphasize that the clear, fresh, and dulcet waters by which Laura sits constitute the Sorgue River and that the ground upon which she sits is at a certain spot in Southern France. Much more interesting is the juxtaposition of water, ground, and heaven to an earthly figure whose lap (but also womb, *grembo*) and whose dress (but also marginally, *lembo*) are underscored by a rhyme.

the ear than either *schembo* or *sghembo* (we are not sure which form Petrarca would have known in Dante, as neither word ever appears in the Petrarchan corpus). Even more remarkable, however, is the vast difference between *schembo* and *nembo* from the point of view of archetypal imagery. While the word *schembo* refers primarily and simply to something that is slanting or oblique, *nembo*, which I translate as "raincloud", has far richer connotations. It can refer not only to a violent storm cloud but also, in iconography and the classical literary tradition, to the presence of divinity. One of Battaglia's definitions of *nembo* reads: "Nella tradizione iconografica e letteraria di origine classica, nuvola che spesso precede, vela, sostiene o circonda divinità, angeli, santi, creature celesti, che accompagna o preannuncia eventi miracolosi, oppure che rappresenta la divinità stessa".

Was Petrarca aware of such possible, supernatural implications when he chose to represent Laura sitting beneath a cloud? The answer is an emphatic yes. Because the cloud pours forth flowers rather than rain, we are obviously not to view it as a typical storm cloud; rather it represents the holy honor and divine glory which the humble Laura merits. Certainly both the Old and New Testaments provided the poet with powerful examples connecting clouds, deity, and the honoring of mortals. To cite only two instances – there is God's appearance in a cloud to Moses on Mount Sinai (Exodus 24:15-18) and the presence of a cloud covering the Mount of Transfiguration (Matthew 17:5). In both cases, Jerome's Vulgate employs *nubes* for cloud.

But is there an immediate source for the creation of a new word in the vernacular? The Italian *nembo*, although it appears only once in Petrarca's vernacular works, does not necessarily lack for a parallel in his total poetic corpus. The Latin *nimbo* appears in a key passage in Book 5 of Petrarca's epic *Africa*. It even occurs at the end of a verse so as to draw attention to itself (v. 180): "Et clavum et remos et vela fluentia *nimbo*". Perhaps more significantly, it is found in a section detailing Massinissa's tragic falling in love with Sophonisba. Although the word is there used in a strictly meteorological simile in which the love-stricken Massinissa is compared to a tempest-tossed sailor, it pointedly recalls an earlier episode from Book 4 of Virgil's *Aeneid*, which contains the parallel and equally tragic tale of Dido and Aeneas. In Virgil's account the goddess Juno decides to send down a dark raincloud (or *nimbum*) to drive Dido and Aeneas into a cave where they will marry. Note the association of the cloud with divinity, even though the meteorological is stressed more than the divine. Dido is described as wearing "a Sidonian robe" (the Latin *limbo*, significantly, is used at the end of *Aeneid* 4.137, only 17 lines after *nimbum* closes another verse); and, like Laura, "her tresses are knotted into gold, golden is the buckle to clasp her purple cloak."[17] This calls to mind, even more

---

[17] All quotations from and English translations of Virgil come from the Loeb Classical Library edition and translation: Virgil, *Eclogues, Georgics, Aeneid*, trans. H. R. Fairclough, Cambridge, Harvard University Press, 1986, 2 vols.

forcefully, the concluding two tercets of Petrarca's sonnet 185, "Questa fenice de l'aurata piuma", which reads:

> Purpurea vesta d'un ceruleo lembo
>   Sparso di rose i belli homeri vela:
>   Novo habito, et bellezza unica et sola.
> Fama ne l'odorato et ricco grembo
>   D'arabi monti lei ripone et cela,
>   Che per lo nostro ciel si altera vola.

This is the only other time that *lembo* appears in the *Canzoniere*. Because it directly refers to the purple robe or *limbo* of *Aeneid* 4.137, I believe we may also trace the rhyming *nembo* of *canzone* 126 through the *Africa* to the *Aeneid*. The tranquility, therefore, seemingly symbolized by the flower-giving cloud or "amoroso nembo" in "Chiare fresche et dolci acque", will in reality be shortlived, at least for the poem's *persona*. Just as love can both delight and destroy, so can a cloud prove mercurial and changeable. For the same *nembo* that can represent deity and God's goodness can also be an instrument of punishment to him who exalts the creature above the creator.

Petrarca's substitution, therefore, of *nembo* for the Dantean *sghembo* assuredly carries with it more tension and ambiguity than have been previously noted. For the connection of such famous and tragically unhappy pairs as Dido and Aeneas, and Sophonisba and Massinissa, to Laura and Petrarca hardly portends continuous joy for the last couple. The stanza may conclude with an exaltation of Love's reign – "Qui regna Amore" – but we know from the juxtaposition of at least two other Petrarchan poems – the sonnets "Benedetto sia 'l giorno e 'l mese et l'anno" (61) and "Padre del Ciel, dopo i perduti giorni" (62) – that the exaltation of love often leads, and only too soon, to dejection and despair. Just as the fair cloud may turn into a *nimbus* or thundercloud and just as Petrarca's perception of Laura as *figura Christi* may at times change so that she becomes a *figura Daphnae*, so the archetypal elements inherent in *grembo*, *nembo*, and *lembo* may one day lead us to see Laura not so much as a historical or quasi-historical figure sitting along the banks of the Sorgue but as a poetic representation of an Earthly (or Earth) Goddess who carries within herself not only the gift of life but also the possibility of death within her sometimes dark womb.

2. *Grembo-nembo-lembo* after Petrarca

The richness and ambiguity present in Petrarca's choice of *grembo*, *nembo*, and *lembo* have been variously picked up or played upon by subsequent users of the *-embo* rhyme. In this section I treat how subsequent Petrarchan imitators,

494

both *bona fide* Petrarchists and much more distant admirers (or critics) of the poet, have approached a particular image cluster that appears only once in Petrarca's vernacular corpus. I must underscore, however, that there has been no end to poets making use of Petrarca's felicitous rhyme. Italian poets of some note who have subsequently adopted the *-embo* rhyme in their poetic compositions include Poliziano, Pulci, Boiardo, Gaspare Visconti, Firenzuola, F. M. Molza, Luigi Alamanni, Lodovico Martelli, I. P. Mutio, Tasso, Federico della Valle, Marino, Bernando Morando, Bartolommeo Corsini, Francesco de Lemene, Alfieri, Parini, Pindemonte, Leopardi, Tommaseo, Mamiani, D'Annunzio, and, last but not least, Montale.[18]

Some of the fifteenth- and sixteenth-century authors cited are Petrarchists. But the phenomenon of Petrarchism cannot account for all the uses of this particular rhyme. Several poets, including Montale in the first poem of *Ossi di seppia*, drew on the pregnant imagery inherent in Petrarca's rhyme and used it for their own unique purposes in poetry ranging from epic to lyrical and from devotional to existential. I shall focus on but a few examples to illustrate the range of uses which the *-embo* rhyme has served over the centuries.

In the Quattrocento it was Poliziano in his *Stanze per la giostra di Giuliano de' Medici* who first made significant use of the *-embo* rhyme (three times in all) to evoke Petrarca. When Giuliano and his lady first glimpse each other in the poem, her action is described in distinctly Petrarchan terms (1.47):

> Ell'era assisa sopra la verdura
> allegra, e ghirlandetta avea contesta

---

[18] The references for those authors whom I do not have the space to treat follow hereafter. One should assume that the complete *grembo-nembo-lembo* rhyme (though not necessarily in that order) is employed unless otherwise noted: MATTEO MARIA BOIARDO, *Orlando innamorato*, a cura di Aldo Scaglione, Torino, UTET, 1966, Libro II, Canto 27, Ottava 54, rhyming *lembo* with *grembo*; FRANCESCO MARIA MOLZA, *Delle poesie volgari e latine*, Bergamo, Lancellotti, 1747, in stanza 29 of the poem "La ninfa Tiberina" vol. 1, p. 178; LUIGI ALAMANNI, *Gyrone il cortese*, Parigi, Rinaldo & Claudio Calderio, 1548, Libro V, Ottava 1; LODOVICO MARTELLI, *Opere*, Firenze, Bernardo Di Giunta, 1548, in the poem that begins "Deh perché n'hai lasciati, ò gentil'alma" (p. 56ʳ), rhyming *nembo* and *grembo*; IUSTINO POLITIANO MUTIO, *Rime diverse*, Vinegia, Gabriel Iolito de Ferrari, 1551, in "Dhe se pietosa sete", rhyming *nembo* and *grembo* (p. 23ʳ); FEDERICO DELLA VALLE, *Tutte le opere*, a cura di Pietro Cazzani, Verona, Mondadori, 1955, in the tragicomedy *Adelonda di Frigia*, rhyming *lembo* and *nembo* (Act 3, Scene 1), which the commentator cites as "un ricordo preciso della canzone petrarchesca [126]"; GIAMBATTISTA MARINO, *Adone*, a cura di Marzio Pieri, Bari, Laterza, 1975, Canto 5, Ottava 126, rhyming *lembo* and *grembo*; BERNARDO MORANDO's "La visitazione" in *Opere scelte di Giovan Battista Marino e dei Marinisti*, a cura di Giovanni Getto, Torino, UTET, 1962, Volume II: *I Marinisti*, pp. 233-34, rhyming *lembo* and *grembo*, with *nembo* found within a preceding verse; BARTOLOMMEO CORSINI, *Il Torracchione desolato: Poema eroicomico*, a cura di Giuseppe Baccini, Firenze, Baccini, 1887, Canto 9, Ottava 67; FRANCESCO DE LEMENE, *Il Narciso: Favola boschereccia* in *Teatro pastorale drammatico del secolo XVII*, Venezia, Antonio Zatta, 1788, in Act 3, Scene 12, *grembo* and *nembo*; GIUSEPPE PARINI, *Tutte le opere*, a cura di Guido Mazzoni, Firenze, Barbèra, 1925, in the ode "Per il Cardinal Angelo Maria Durini", *grembo* and *nembo*; IPPOLITO PINDEMONTE, *Le più belle pagine... scelte da G. B. Angioletti*, Milano, Treves, 1933, in the poem "La sera"; NICCOLÒ TOMMASEO, *Memorie poetiche*, Bari, Laterza, 1964, in his poetic commentary on the Bible (p. 73); TERENZIO MAMIANI, *Poesie*, Firenze, Le Monnier, 1857, in the poem "La scampagnata", rhyming *grembo* and *lembo* (p. 183); and GABRIELE D'ANNUNZIO, *Versi d'amore e di gloria*, Milano, Mondadori, 1959, in *Primo vere*'s "Vespro d'agosto", rhyming *sghembo* and *lembo* (vol. 1, p. 91).

> di quanti fior creassi mai natura,
> de' quai tutta dipinta era sua vesta.
> E come prima al gioven puose cura,
> alquanto paurosa alzò la testa;
> poi colla bianca man ripreso il *lembo*,
> levossi in piè con di fior pieno un *grembo*.[19]

While this first use of *-embo* occurs in a rhymed couplet and only makes use of the two rhyme words which Dante and Petrarca share, the next two occasions of the rhyme – in 1.79 and 1.122 – include all three of Petrarca's choices – *lembo*, *grembo*, and *nembo* – and in equally obvious Petrarchan-inspired pastoral love settings. In fact, 1.79 employs the phrases "amoroso nembo" and "purpureo lembo" to highlight the poet's homage to Petrarca. Dante's less poetic *schembo* is clearly eschewed in every case.

At about the same time Luigi Pulci was writing the *Morgante* and making use of Petrarca's choices in a rather different way in his generally light-hearted epic. In *Morgante* 26.39 we find Orlando's concluding words to his troops at Roncisvalle before the battle begins, his vision of their apotheosis after death in the battle field:

> Io veggo un nuvoletto in aire, un *nembo*,
> che certo vien per voi di paradiso,
> e già di Miccael si scuopre un *lembo*,
> tal ch'io non posso contemplarlo fiso;
> parmi vedervi giubilare in *grembo*
> di quello Amor che tutto applaude in riso,
> come que' padri già in Ciel felici siamo.[20]

In Pulci's octave the *nembo* is certainly associated with an otherwordly Paradise, but the *lembo* belongs to the Angel Michael's robe (rather than any woman's); and while the *grembo* is connected to Amor (personified as a male with a capital "A"), it is cross-gendered and a masculine Love "che tutto applaude in riso", underscoring the comic Pulci's trademark concept of laughter as leveler.

In both these cases we have poets working with the octave, which allows at most three rhyme words with *-embo*. But what of the sonnet form so popular in the fifteenth century? Is there no example of four rhyme words with *-embo*? There is, and it comes from the pen of Gaspare Visconti (1461 to 1499). A member of the court of Gian Galeazzo Sforza and his wife Beatrice d'Este, Visconti also served Ludovico il Moro, Gian Galeazzo's uncle and successor. In a poem entitled "Per uno che haveva persa la gratia de la amorosa" we find *grembo*, *nembo*, and *lembo* rhymed with the Dantean *schembo* in the first two quatrains:

[19] ANGELO POLIZIANO, *Poesie italiane*, a cura di Saverio Orlando, Milano, Rizzoli, 1976.
[20] LUIGI PULCI, *Morgante*, a cura di Davide Puccini, Milano, Garzanti, 1989, 2 voll.

> Già fu, hor non son più: serò annchor forse
> Come soleva de fortuna in *grembo*
> E ben che irata me guati hora a *schembo*
> Non può sua rota mai per ferma porse
> Più volte in un momento ella già scorse
> Letitia, a chi piovea di pianto un *nembo*
> E a chi tenne coperto sotto il *lembo*
> La felice umbra, in doglia acerba torse.[21]

The very title indicates, of course, a theme known to both Petrarca and Dante, that of the lover who has lost the favor of his beloved. Although I believe the spirit of this poem is decidedly more Petrarchan than Dantean, one might wonder, at this point, what other choices does a poet have than the four -*embo* words offered to us by Dante and Petrarca.

The answer to this query is found in a sixteenth-century work by Agnolo Firenzuola. In a poem entitled "In lode delle campane" we find a *terza rima* address to contemporary poets which even discusses the poet's right to incorporate the rhymes of other poets:

> Poeti, non m'attaccate un sonaglio,
> con dir che spesso una rima medesima
> ripiglio, e 'n la grammatica m'abbaglio;
> ch'io vel vo' dir, per non tenervi a cresima,
> che 'n lodar le campane, o salde, o fesse,
> Io non mi curo guastar la quaresima:
> Ed anche quando ben disposto avesse
> ad osservar le regole del *Bembo*,
> sare' forza al battaglio m'arrendesse;
> e quante volte mel cacciasse in *grembo*,
> tante fare' a suo mo', cotal m'aggrada
> sentir dar quei suoi tocchi per *isghembo*.[22]

Here Firenzuola openly speaks of the Petrarchising rules of Cardinal Pietro Bembo and then rhymes, with no little irony, the name of Bembo with *grembo* (à la Petrarca) and *isghembo* (à la Dante).[23]

During the Counter-Reformation and with Torquato Tasso we have one of the most evocative uses of the -*embo* rhyme. In the *Gerusalemme liberata* it is used as a

---

[21] GASPARE VISCONTI, *Rime*, a cura di Alessandro Cutolo, Bologna, Palmaverde, 1952.

[22] AGNOLO FIRENZUOLA, *Opere*, Milano, Classici Italiani, 1802, 4:221.

[23] See also VINCENZO MARTELLI's "In lode delle menzogne" in *Il secondo libro dell'Opere burlesche... del Martelli... e d'altri autori*, Usecht al Reno, Jacopo Broedelet, 1771, p. 65, which spoofingly concludes: "Io vi ho già visto intorno a farvi onore / Delle vostre Menzogne in l'aria un *nembo*, / Girando parer dir, qui regna Amore: / E voi raccorvi questa schiera in *grembo*, / E comporne un poema in lingua nostra, / Che nol regoleria 'l Trissino, o 'l *Bembo*".

frame for the episode of the Christian warrior Rinaldo and the pagan temptress Armida. In canto 15, octave 9, we read of the magic ship touching the shores of Armida's isle:

> A pena ha tocco la mirabil nave
> de la marina allor turbata il *lembo,*
> che spariscon le nubi e cessa il grave
> Noto, che minacciava oscuro *nembo*:
> spiana i monti de l'onde aura soave,
> e solo increspa il bel ceruleo *grembo*:
> e d'un dolce seren diffuso rìde
> il ciel, che sé più chiaro unqua non vide.

In a subtle manner the Petrarchan *lembo-nembo-grembo* rhyme proleptically prepares the reader for the *locus amoenus* about to be encountered in Armida's enchanted garden. Perhaps it even foreshadows Rinaldo's rejection of Armida's affection which will take place in the pastoral setting. The words *grembo* and *nembo* occur another time in a rhymed couplet after the repentant Rinaldo returns to the Christian camp and goes to the Mount of Olives to pray for forgiveness. In canto 18, octave 15, we read:

> Così pregava, e gli sorgeva a fronte,
> fatta già d'auro, la vermiglia aurora
> che l'elmo e l'arme e intorno a lui del monte
> le verdi cime illuminando indora;
> e ventillar nel petto e ne la fronte
> sentìa gli spirti di piacevol ora,
> che sovra il capo suo scotea dal *grembo*
> de la bell'alba un rugiadoso *nembo.*

Here the *grembo* is neither Dido's nor Maria's, but rather that of the dawn of a new day, the symbol of hope, life, and the resurrection. The raincloud, similarly, represents not a threat to life but the cleansing waters of baptism so desperately needed by Rinaldo to rededicate himself to the Christian cause.

Tasso comes, of course, at the beginning of the Baroque era, a literary period which also found use for Petrarca's rhyme. Marino, for example, sought to improve it in the seventeenth century by using it in the plural in the *Adone* (6.107), where we find *lembi, grembi,* and *nembi.* In the following century Alfieri, for pre-Risorgimento purposes, found the rhyme quite appropriate for the concluding verses of the fifth ode of *L'America libera*:

> Pace era quella, che d'Atene in *grembo*
> Con libertade ogni bell'arte univa;
> Dove a un tempo si udiva
> Di varie e dotte opinïoni un *nembo.* –

Ma, in questa età, che è *lembo*
D'ogni bell'opra estremo,
Qual fia tema di canto? a chi secura
Volgo mia voce, mentr'io piango e tremo? -
"Ahi, null'altro che Forza, al mondo dura!"[24]

The ending to this political ode strikes one as more reminiscent of the Valley-of-the-Princes episode than of any Petrarchan pastoral idyll. By the time we arrive at the Risorgimento period much of Italy's previous poetry is being mined for its political implications which, if not explicit, may be inferred by any resolutely political poet. But one of the greatest Italian Romantic poets, Giacomo Leopardi, interestingly enough, uses the complete *lembo-nembo-grembo* rhyme only once and in a minor canto. The rhyme appears in "Spento il diurno raggio in occidente", in a largely meteorological description, emphasizing an a-political reading of the *-embo* rhyme:

E la nube, crescendo, in giù calava
ver la marina sì, che l'un suo *lembo*
toccava i monti, e l'altro il mar toccava.
Già tutto a cieca oscuritade in *grembo*,
s'incominciava udir fremer la pioggia,
e il suon cresceva all'appressar del *nembo*.[25]

While space permits only a glance at one final poet who uses the *-embo* rhyme in our own century, I trust that this survey has, if nothing else, served to raise academic consciousness as to the varied purposes a rhyme may serve. A skilled poet can, and often does, use rhyme to sustain a memorable image or to express a moving thought. By means of resonances to other poems, a distinctive rhyme may point to more meaning than initially meets the ear.

To conclude, we turn to Montale. The first poem of "In limine" in the collection *Ossi di seppia* is "Godi se il vento ch'entra nel pomario". Because the poems in this section deal with the concept of liminality, *lembo* – which denotes both a border and a margin – is a key word. Montale's rhyme scheme, however, allows for only one other word to rhyme with it; he chooses, significantly I believe, *grembo* over *nembo*. For the modern poet prefers, to the darkness of a thundercloud, the archetypal somberness of the "eternal womb". And so we read, in vss. 6-9:

Il frullo che tu senti non è un volo,
ma il commuoversi dell'eterno *grembo*;
vedi che si trasforma questo *lembo*
di terra solitario in un crogiuolo.[26]

---

[24] VITTORIO ALFIERI, *Rime*, a cura di Francesco Maggini, Firenze, Le Monnier, 1933.
[25] GIACOMO LEOPARDI, *Opere*, a cura di Giovanni Getto, Milano, Mursia, 1967.
[26] EUGENIO MONTALE, *Tutte le poesie*, Milano, Mondadori, 1977, 13. Montale also rhymes *grembo* and *lembo*

Although the divine presence, as symbolized by the cloud or *nembo*, is lacking from this poem, it is *nembo*'s absence that makes the meaning of the *-embo* rhyme all the more telling. In *nembo*'s place is the crucible – the *crogiuolo* – an image of purifying fire to replace that of fructifying rain. Nevertheless the agonizing situation of Montale's *persona* is not unlike that of Petrarca's. For both there is disappointment; for both there is an understanding of poetry, recollected memory.

in his poem "Crisalide". In another poem, "Nel parco di Caserta" he ends a line with *sghembo*, but it is not in rhyme. Finally, in "Il ritorno: Bocca di Magra" he terminates another non-rhyming line with *lembo*.

CESARE SEGRE

CRITICA STILISTICA E STORIA DEL LINGUAGGIO
NEL CARTEGGIO SPITZER-SCHIAFFINI

La straordinaria fortuna di Spitzer in Italia richiederebbe un lungo discorso.[1]
Qui mi accontento di indicarne in Benedetto Croce il primo e più autorevole fautore in ambito critico, insieme con Mario Fubini e Alfredo Schiaffini; mentre nel
campo filologico-linguistico bisogna assegnare posti di particolare rilievo a Gianfranco Contini e Benvenuto Terracini.

Per Benedetto Croce basterà rinviare alle principali recensioni a lavori di Spitzer[2] o
ai molti accenni a Spitzer nel carteggio Croce-Vossler;[3] ma vanno soprattutto ricordate la dedica a Spitzer dei *Nuovi saggi sul Goethe* (Bari, Laterza, 1934) e la splendida
e coraggiosa lettera del 1938 al rettore Hammer (Università di Stoccolma), esprimendo «orrore per le odierne atroci persecuzioni degli Ebrei in Germania e in Austria» e stima per Spitzer costretto all'esilio.[4] Di Fubini basta ricordare il vigoroso
intervento teorico sulla stilistica,[5] mentre su Schiaffini mi soffermerò subito dopo.
Quanto al diverso spirito (ma al simile entusiasmo) con cui Spitzer poteva esser letto
all'inizio degli anni '30 da un giovane filologo, si trova una bella pagina di Contini,[6]

---

[1] Si veda anzitutto H. HATZFELD, *Recent Italian Stylistic Theory and Stylistic Criticism*, in *Studia philologica et litteraria in honorem L. Spitzer*, Bern, Francke, 1958, pp. 227-43.

[2] Si veda per es. «Il Baretti», III, 1926, 8, poi in *Conversazioni critiche*, III, Bari, Laterza, 1932, pp. 101-5; «La Critica», XXXII, 1934, 58-61, poi in *Conversazioni critiche*, V, Bari, Laterza, 1939, pp. 129-34; «Quaderni de 'La critica'», IV, 1948, 12, poi in *Terze pagine sparse*, Bari, Laterza, 1955, II, pp. 130-33.

[3] *Carteggio Croce-Vossler (1899-1949)*, con Prefazione e a cura di V. De Caprariis, Bari, Laterza, 1951; per es. pp. 333 e 345.

[4] La lettera, del 5 agosto 1938, fu pubblicata in vari giornali stranieri (non tedeschi, s'intende), ed è riportata nelle *Pagine sparse*, II, Napoli, R. Ricciardi, 1943, pp. 410-11.

[5] M. FUBINI, *Legittimità e limiti di una critica stilistica*, in «Rassegna d'Italia», 1946, poi in ID., *Critica e poesia*, Bari, Laterza, 1956, pp. 95-121; vedi pure, dello stesso, *Ragioni storiche e ragioni teoriche della critica stilistica*, «Giornale storico della letteratura italiana», 133, 1956, 489-509

[6] G. CONTINI, *Giustificazione*, in L. SPITZER, *Saggi di critica stilistica*, con un prologo e un epilogo di G. Contini, Firenze, Sansoni, 1985, pp. 7-12, alle pp. 8-9. Contini, confrontando la scelta che progettava (vedi oltre) con quella di Schiaffini di cui trattiamo, osserva in una lettera del 27-XII-1950 a Einaudi: «Il piano [della scelta Schiaffini] è completamente diverso (Croce sceglie scritterelli teorici, con minori applicazioni saggistiche prese fra le più innocue), ma è evidente che Croce intende annettersi Spitzer, mentre io vorrei presentare uno Spitzer certo per nulla anticrociano, ma recisamente postcrociano» (G. CONTINI, *Lettere all'editore (1945-54)*, a cura di P. Di Stefano, Torino, Einaudi, 1990, p. 29).

che poi nelle lezioni friburghesi dei primi anni '40 faceva di Spitzer uno dei punti di forza dell'insegnamento stilistico; mentre negli stessi anni Benvenuto Terracini, che sarebbe poi stato l'esponente più attivo e originale della stilistica in Italia,[7] ricorreva spesso a Spitzer nel suo insegnamento argentino allargatosi ad argomenti letterari dopo inizi rigorosamente dialettologici e linguistici.[8]

Spitzer diventa comunque autore di ampia notorietà italiana con l'uscita del volume *Critica stilistica e storia del linguaggio. Saggi* raccolti a cura e con presentazione di Alfredo Schiaffini, Bari, Laterza, 1954. Il numero delle recensioni, gli echi giornalistici e accademici, anche le polemiche ideologiche, mostrano che la novità fu colta in pieno. Il fatto più notevole è che da allora Spitzer si fece, in certo senso, italiano, intensificando i soggiorni nella penisola – luogo prediletto Forte dei Marmi –, scrivendo di testi italiani in italiano e su riviste italiane, discutendo con studiosi italiani, in particolare Giacomo Devoto, a proposito dell'interpretazione del Verga.[9]

Parlare del volume *Critica stilistica e storia del linguaggio* (d'ora in avanti *CSSL*) mi riesce particolarmente produttivo perché ho sotto mano quasi tutto il relativo carteggio, conservato ordinatamente dal curatore, lo storico della lingua e critico Alfredo Schiaffini: egli non si limitò alle lettere di Spitzer, ma tenne in ordine il resto della corrispondenza, i documenti dell'editore, persino, in qualche caso, la bozza delle proprie risposte.[10] Le prime tracce di preparazione del volume risalgono al 1950, quando deve già essere stata contattata la prima traduttrice, Lore Terracini (lettera del 9.2.1951).[11] L'idea del volume dev'essere stata di Benedetto Croce, come risulta dall'intensa opera di coordinamento della figlia Alda Croce (moltissime le sue lettere). Non stupisce se la curatela fu assegnata ad Alfredo Schiaffini, vicino a Croce e affine a Spitzer per l'ambito d'interessi, tra critica, filologia e linguistica.[12]

Sulla genesi di *CSSL* è fondamentale quanto dice Schiaffini in una lettera a

---

[7] Cito solo la grande trattazione complessiva *Analisi stilistica (Teoria, storia, problemi)*, Milano, Feltrinelli, 1966.

[8] Vedi per esempio l'ampio uso fatto di spunti spitzeriani nei *Conflictos de lenguas y de cultura*, Buenos Aires, Imán, 1951, poi in italiano, Neri Pozza, Venezia, 1957. Ma Spitzer è già un punto di riferimento in articoli del 1935 e 1938: si vedano scritti di quegli anni in B. Terracini, *Linguistica al bivio*, Napoli, Guida, 1981, pp. 175-231 e Id., *I segni, la storia*, Napoli, Guida, 1976, pp. 45-55.

[9] G. Devoto, *I "piani del racconto" in due capitoli dei «Malavoglia»*, «Bollettino del Centro di Studi filologici e linguistici siciliani», 2, 1954, 5-13, poi in Id., *Nuovi studi di stilistica*, Firenze 1962, pp. 202-14; L. Spitzer, *L'originalità della narrazione nei Malavoglia*, «Belfagor», 11, 1956, 37-53, poi in Id., *Romanische Literaturstudien 1936-1956*, Tübingen, Niemeyer, 1959, pp. 624-44, anticipato in parte in *Le due stilistiche*, «Lo Spettatore italiano», sett. 1955.

[10] Ringrazio vivamente Silvia De Laude, nipote di Schiaffini, e la famiglia per avermi messo a disposizione i documenti.

[11] Tradusse i capitoli *Linguistica e storia letteraria*, *Il "récit de Théramène"*, *Semantica storica* e *Storia della parola "razza"*.

[12] L'attenzione anche teorica di Schiaffini per la stilistica di Spitzer risulta non solo dalla magnifica presentazione a *CSSL*, pp. 1-26, ma anche dal contributo *La stilistica letteraria*, in *Momenti di storia della lingua italiana*, Roma, Editrice Studium,1953[2], pp.165-86.

Franco Laterza del 2.3.1953, che citerò ancora. Egli scrive: «Il piano è stato preparato in casa Croce (la signora Alda Croce doveva pubblicare il volume) ed è stato approvato da Spitzer: al quale lo mandai io, prima di cercare le traduttrici. Lo feci vedere anche a Contini e Santoli».

Poco dopo l'avvio dei lavori Maria Luisa Spaziani (lettera del 25.5.1951) rende noto che sta preparando, su «accordi da *lei* presi con l'autore stesso», un volume contenente, di Spitzer, un saggio teorico e gli articoli su Proust e Claudel. Però la Spaziani dice pure di essere stata invitata a inserire le proprie traduzioni in «un'antologia spitzeriana raccolta da Gianfranco Contini». Le stesse notizie raccoglieva Alda Croce, citando, da una lettera di Spitzer, queste frasi: «Il prof. Contini a Friburgo aveva l'intenzione parecchi anni fa di pubblicare una serie di miei saggi presso l'editore Bompiani. [13] Ma l'affare sembra essersi inciampato in difficoltà. Sarebbe forse meglio di informarsi presso il Contini». Spitzer dava pure notizia del volume che doveva esser preparato dalla Spaziani.

Qui mancano alcuni passaggi, ma si capisce chiaramente: 1) che la Spaziani fu arruolata nell'impresa di Schiaffini, dove infatti appare fra le traduttrici; [14] 2) che la precoce iniziativa di Contini, già languente, fu momentaneamente sospesa: solo nel 1959 uscì, da lui promossa, la raccolta einaudiana di saggi francesi; [15] e si deve aspettare il 1985 per incontrare una raccolta spitzeriana curata da lui. [16]

Ai primi traduttori di *CSSL* furono ancora aggiunti Luisa Vertova [17] e Donato Barbone. [18] Episodio curioso e simpatico: dato che il compenso per i traduttori era piuttosto modesto, Schiaffini lo fece raddoppiare rinunciando a quello che gli era destinato per l'introduzione e la curatela (lettera di Franco Laterza del 28.11.1951). I lavori devono essere proseguiti con relativa velocità, perché Franco Laterza dà ricevuta del dattiloscritto del volume l'11.2.1953.

Qui però ha luogo un piccolo colpo di scena: due settimane dopo (26.2.1953), Franco Laterza contesta la scelta dei capitoli, considera necessaria l'eliminazione di quelli sul termine *l'avant-guerre* [19] («incompleto nella documentazione italiana»), su

[13] Per questo basta vedere quanto scrive G. Contini nelle già citate *Lettere all'editore*, p. 28: «Fino dal '45 o '46 sono impegnato da Bompiani per un'antologia di scritti di Spitzer, scelti dai *Beiträge*, dalle *Stilstudien* e dalle *Romanische Stil- und Literaturstudien*. Spitzer, veramente, voleva anche un altro volume, scelto dall'ultima [e per noi meno «arrazzante»] fase della sua attività; oppure, se un tomo solo, questo secondo. Si era rimasti più o meno d'accordo che si sarebbe fatto il primo, con promessa, opzione o non so che altro quanto al secondo. Ma *Portico* non è più andato innanzi, e Bompiani ha rinviato di fatto la cosa *sine die*, pur tenendo in piedi l'idea».

[14] Tradusse i capitoli *Stilistica e linguistica* e *L'arte della «transizione» in La Fontaine*.

[15] L. SPITZER, *Marcel Proust e altri saggi di letteratura francese moderna*. Con un saggio introduttivo di P. Citati, Torino, Einaudi, 1959. Il saggio *Sullo stile di Proust* proviene certamente dal volume peparato dalla Spaziani, dato che è tradotto da lei. Che l'indice di questa scelta ricalchi sostanzialmente quello di Contini risulta da una lettera di quest'ultimo nelle *Lettere all'editore* cit., pp. 28-29, e da quanto riferisce nelle note P. Di Stefano.

[16] *Saggi di critica stilistica*, cit.

[17] Tradusse *L'interpretazione linguistica delle opere letterarie*.

[18] Tradusse L'"*explication de texte*" applicata a Voltaire.

[19] In «Zeitschrift für französische Sprache und Literatur», 54, 1930, pp. 207-18.

Rabelais[20] (perché «ampiamente riassunto a cartella 243 ss. [pp. 125-32 di *CSSL*] donde non si può eliminare»), su Malherbe,[21] su Vigny[22] («è poco *esemplare* per un volume di critica stilistica che si può dire inauguri certi studi») e su Proust,[23] propone invece l'inserzione di altri capitoli: quelli su Voltaire e sulla parola *razza*. Una lettera di Schiaffini a Franco Laterza difende le scelte operate, anche appellandosi all'approvazione di Spitzer. Ma l'ebbe vinta Laterza, forse strappando l'accordo a Spitzer, cui deve aver sottoposto i suoi dubbi (è lecito inferirlo dal fatto che Schiaffini gl'indica l'indirizzo di Spitzer): lo conferma l'indice definitivo del volume, che corrisponde esattamente alla sua volontà, mentre quello originario si deduce appunto dalla lettera di Franco Laterza. Questo contrasto rallenta evidentemente la pubblicazione del volume, che appare solo nell'ottobre 1954.

Nascevano intanto altre iniziative di raccolte spitzeriane. Oltre alle due già ricordate (quella della Spaziani, rientrata, e quella di Contini, rinviata; uscirà poi quella di Citati), si apprende da una lettera dell'ispanista torinese Giovanni Maria Bertini (27.2.1952) che i «Quaderni ibero-americani» da lui diretti intendevano pubblicare saggi spagnoli del critico austriaco: Bertini scriveva per evitare collisioni. Il risultato fu un grosso volume, uscito però dieci anni dopo.[24]

Schiaffini era in relazione con Spitzer da lungo tempo. Nella sua corrispondenza trovo cartoline postali di Spitzer del 10.10.1929 (da Marburgo), del 13.2.1931 e 19.3.1931 (da Colonia), ecc. Sono brevi messaggi, in tedesco, relativi a scambi di estratti. Per quanto riguarda *CSSL*, la prima lettera, qui riportata, fa intendere che i contatti iniziali devono essere stati tenuti da altri, con ogni probabilità da Alda Croce.

16.2.1951.[25]

Carissimo amico,

Sono lietissimo di saper la "Presentazione" della traduzione della mia raccolta nelle Sue mani, così esperte.

---

[20] Quella che è «ampiamente riassunta» ecc. è la tesi di abilitazione L. SPITZER, *Die Wortbildung als stilistisches Mittel bei Rabelais*, Halle, Niemeyer, 1910, in realtà inadatta a un volume come *CSSL*, per le dimensioni e l'aspetto, in molte pagine, di spoglio. Difatti il capitolo destinato al volume, ed eliminato per volontà di Laterza, è, come risulta da un appunto di Schiaffini, *Zur Auffassung Rabelais'*, in L. Spitzer, *Romanische Stil- und Literaturstudien*, Marburg a.L., Elwert, 1931, voll. 2, nel II, pp. 109-34.

[21] *Ehrenrettung von Malherbes "Consolation à Monsieur Du Pérrier"*, in L. SPITZER, *Stilstudien*. II. *Stilsprachen*, München, Max Hueber, 1928, pp. 18-29.

[22] *Vigny's "Le cor"*, «Germanisch-Romanische Monatsschrift», 16, 1928, 399-414, poi in L. SPITZER, *Romanische Stil- und Literaturstudien*, cit., II, pp. 244-63.

[23] *Zum Stil Marcel Proust's*, in L. SPITZER, *Stilstudien*, II, *Stilsprachen*, München, Max Hueber, 1928, pp. 365-497; poi tradotto in italiano in *Marcel Proust*, ecc., cit., pp. 245-352.

[24] L. SPITZER, *Cinque saggi di ispanistica*. Presentazione e contributo bibliografico a cura di G. M. Bertini, Torino, Giappichelli, 1962.

[25] Su carta intestata: *The Johns Hopkins University / Baltimore-18, Maryland*.

L'articolo di Hythier[26] piace anche a me, per il tono di simpatia sincera e di 'bonhomie taquinante'. Naturalmente, non credo che sia tanto personale il mio metodo come lui lo dice.

C'è qualcosa sui miei studj nel volume di Wellek e Warren, *Theory of Literature*[27] – però soltanto sui primi tempi della mia attività. Rifiuterò parecchi di questi giudizi nella nuova[28] rivista inglese di linguistica fra qualche mese.

Cercherò di trovare l'articolo su *Inferno* XIII[29] e, trovatolo, glielo[30] manderò immediatamente.

Mi creda il Suo dev.[mo]

Leo Spitzer

La lettera successiva si riferisce già a informazioni utili per la stesura della presentazione di *CSSL*.

24.5.1952[31]

Carissimo amico e collega,

Le ho già mandato il *Hopkins Magazine* (con uno schizzo autobiografico e fotografia).[32] L'articolo di Salinas si trova nel mio volume «Essays in Historical Semantics»[33] che Lei deve avere. Una caratteristica carta apparve in *Vox romanica* (critica degli *Essays* dal Jud).[34] Così speriamo che il Suo (mio) volume progredisca bene!

Tante grazie dal Suo dev.[mo]

Leo Spitzer

Intanto Schiaffini aveva pubblicato lo studio su *La stilistica letteraria*.[35] Spitzer, nel ringraziarlo, discute la filiazione Croce-Vossler-Spitzer, accolta da Schiaffini. La lettera che segue è già stata riportata in buona parte nella *Presentazione* di Schiaffini a *CSSL* (pp. 5-6); ritengo comunque utile trascriverla integralmente, anche per do-

[26] J. HYTIER, *La méthode de M. Leo Spitzer*, «Romanic Review», XLI, 1950, 42-59.

[27] R. WELLEK e A. WARREN, *Theory of Literature*, New York, Harcourt, Brace and Co., 1949; trad. it., *Teoria della letteratura e metodologia dello studio letterario*, Bologna, Il mulino, 1956: vedi le pp. 246-48.

[28] Prima: *in una*, cancellato.

[29] *Speech and language in Inferno XIII*, «Italica», XIX, 1942, 82-104.

[30] Prima solo *lo*.

[31] Su carta con la medesima intestazione.

[32] Si tratta di «The Johns Hopkins Magazine» dell'aprile 1952, p. 19 sgg.

[33] P. SALINAS, *Esquicio de Leo Spitzer*, premesso, senza numerazione delle quattro pagine, al *Foreword* a L. Spitzer, *Essays in Historical Semantics*, New York, Russel & Russel, 1948; 1968[2].

[34] In «Vox Romanica», 11, 1950, 245-48; altre recensioni di Jud a lavori di Spitzer: «Vox Romanica», 6, 1941, 1/2, 373-4; 9, 1947, 351-52.

[35] In *Momenti di storia della lingua italiana* cit., pp. 165-86, poi in A. SCHIAFFINI, *Italiano antico e moderno*, Milano-Napoli, R. Ricciardi, 1975, pp. 241-60.

cumentare con completezza l'italiano di Spitzer (già esemplificato dalle precedenti missive), con i suoi lievi arcaismi nella morfologia e nell'uso dei pronomi enclitici, i latinismi grafici, i pochi francesismi e germanismi sintattici. Le varianti di stesura, da me riportate in nota, mostrano l'eccezionale scioltezza con cui Spitzer usa la nostra lingua.

Baltimora, 9 giugno 1953.[36]

Carissimo amico e collega:

Sono commosso dalla Sua presentazione dei miei lavori nel Suo articolo «La stilistica letteraria» – commosso perchè veder la propria opera, così esitante e contraddittoria, nella cornice oggettiva[37] mi fa intenerirmi sugli anni passati e anche mi dà un profondo senso di riconoscenza per chi ci legga con tanta attenzione. Insomma, uno non si sente solo nel mondo – grazie per questo!

È curioso quanta sia la logica della filiazione Croce-Vossler-Spitzer. Logica storica, questa, innegabile. Eppure, potrebbe Lei credere che la filiazione non fu questa in un certo senso, almeno per quanto io possa rendermene conto? Nel 1911, quando scrivevo sui neologismi di Rabelais,[38] non sapevo niente di Vossler e ancora meno di Croce: quando io era[39] allievo di Meyer-Lübke, Vossler era l'autore di certi lavori sui trovatori e sul dolce stil nuovo, ma non si citava "Positivismo e idealismo" (nota marginale: p. 167 non *Erschöpfung*, ma *Schöpfung*)[40] e pensar in questi termini sarebbe stato eresia. Non conosco[41] i miei genitori spirituali *veri*, che abbiano influito su di me nel rintracciare la 'radice' dei neologismi nella psiche di Rabelais. Naturalmente, più tardi ho conosciuto e usato categorie derivanti dal Vossler e dal Croce (ed infatti la distinzione tra *Stilsprachen* e *Sprachstile* è vossleriana),[42] ma mi sono staccato dai due maestri in un certo punto: non ammetto l'origine *estetica* di tutte le evoluzioni generali della lingua, e credo che ci sia del buono nella definizione dello Schleiermacher ('logica+musica', purchè si estenda il concetto di musica). Non ho mai potuto pensare che le categorie della grammatica non fossero[43] di ordine *logico* (e in questo m'incoraggiano i lavori della signorina Hatcher[44] che Lei conosce). È soltanto il mio gusto o talento personale che mi guida[45] verso i fenomeni

---

[36] In carta senza intestazione.

[37] Forse su *obiettiva*.

[38] L. SPITZER, *Die Wortbildung*, ecc., cit.; poi ampliata, e con titolo leggermente mutato: *Die Wortbildung als stilistisches Mittel exemplifiziert an Rabelais. Nebst einem Anhang über die Wortbildung bei Balzac in seinen "Contes drolatiques"*, Halle, Niemeyer, 1910 (Beihefte zur «Zeitschrift für romanische Philologie», 19).

[39] Prima *fui*, cancellato.

[40] Spitzer segnala un colto errore di Schiaffini, *art. cit.*, p. 167. Il titolo dell'opera di Vossler è *Positivismus und Idealismus in der Sprachwissenschaft*, Heidelberg, Winter, 1904; traduzione italiana a cura di T. Gnoli, Bari, Laterza, 1909.

[41] Su *so*, cancellato.

[42] La distinzione è consacrata nel titolo dei due volumi che compongono le *Stilstudien*, cit.

[43] Prima *siano*, cancellato.

[44] Probabilmente si tratta dell'articolo *"Voir" as a Modern Novelistic Device* di Anna G. Hatcher, «Philological Quarterly», 23, 1944, 354-74, citato da Spitzer nel capitolo su *Il "récit de Théramène"*, in *CSSL*, pp. 227-92, a p. 285.

[45] Prima *attrae*, cancellato.

estetici (in scrittori o nella lingua comune).[46] Il Croce era molto generoso verso di me: è generosissimo il suo pensiero della pianticella piantata da lui "cresciuta per opera di agri-cultori...",[47] generoso perchè non era l'indole sua, del gran filosofo che era, di immerger-si[48] nei dettagli e di estrarne un'essenza. Lui la intuiva da sè!... Ma, naturalmente, sono d'accordo col Croce quando polemizza con quelli che dividono "il significato dal signi-ficante,[49] la forma dal contenuto, l'intuizione dall'espressione"[50] ed ho espresso idee si-mili nell'articolo sui metodi 'esistenziali' di Georges Poulet (le ho spedito questo artico-lo?).[51]

Mi lasci ancora una volta ringraziarLe *ex imo cordis* e stringerLe la mano,
il Suo devotissimo

Leo Spitzer

La risposta di Schiaffini, come risulta da una prima stesura conservata nella cor-rispondenza, senza data, suona così:

Roma 19.VI.'53

Caro Amico,

grazie della Sua lettera, alta e amabile.

Il mio storicismo e la mia strenua logicità mi hanno condotto indubbiamente a costrin-gere la Sua figura dentro una cornice troppo regolare e, insomma, angusta.

Ma sarà mia cura di scrutare più a fondo, per vedere meglio la realtà.

Mi aiuti anche Lei, fornendomi dati utili: per esempio, lo scritto, a cui si richiama e che io non conosco, sulla critica 'esistenzialista'.

Mi creda, con la più devota amicizia,

Suo
A.S.

Finalmente giunge a Spitzer, insieme con la lettera di Schiaffini, il volume *CSSL* appena uscito. Riporto qui la lettera di ringraziamento di Spitzer:

---

[46] Prima *commune*, con la seconda *m* cancellata.
[47] In una recensione a due scritti di Spitzer, su *Wortkunst und Sprachwissenschaft*, ne «Il Baretti», III, 1926, n. 8, poi in B. CROCE, *Conversazioni critiche*, III, Bari, Laterza, 1932, pp. 101-105.
[48] Prima *indole sua di immergersi*.
[49] Su *significato*, ripetuto mnemonicamente.
[50] B. CROCE, *La critica stilistica*, in ID., *Indagini su Hegel e schiarimenti filosofici*, Bari, Laterza, 1952, pp. 248-51.
[51] L. SPITZER, *A propos de la Vie de Marianne (Lettre à M. Georges Poulet)*, «Romanic Review» XLIV, 1953, 102-26, poi in ID., *Romanische Literaturstudien 1936-1956*, cit., pp. 248-76.

27.11.1954[52]

Carissimo amico Schiaffini,

Che dirLe della Sua lettera e del volume che mi vedo davanti? Sono intimamente commosso da tutt'e due come[53] manifestazioni dell'amicizia più profonda.

Lei stesso, caro amico, conoscerà[54] abbastanza l'effetto sul suo 'io' interiore degli onori che ci[55] vengono nella seconda metà della nostra vita: dall'una parte c'è qualche cosa in noi che dice tranquillamente 'ebbene, qualche cosa[56] non era del tutto immeritato', ma subito dopo viene un'altra voce che dice: '*proprio questo* non era meritato'. E questa voce non è quella di una falsa modestia (come neppure la prima voce era quella di una arroganza che falsifica le gerarchie), ma c'è la coscienza che in questa vita merito e successo non sono mai proporzionali – e perchè lo sarebbero proprio nel mio caso? D'altra parte, ho sempre pensato che il mio talento (se talento c'è) era un talento *normale*, infatti quello che si poteva aspettare da un allievo del ginnasio di Vienna che abbia poi studiato sotto il Meyer-Lübke, il Meillet e lo Gilliéron. È vero anche che nel corso della mia vita ho dovuto costatare che il livello 'ginnasio-Meyer-Lübke' ecc. era abbastanza alto quando si[57] comparava con altri livelli. Eppure ritengo che la mia opera era 'data dalle circostanze'.[58]

Per spiegarmi, dunque, come accada che onori così 'impensati' come questo bellissimo volume (e l'altro onore,[59] impensabile, di cui Lei indica una possibilità) si realizzano, non c'è altro ricorso[60] che quello all'*amor intellectualis*, quella scintilla che si infiamma qui e non altrove. Era quella scintilla che ardeva nel Croce e che lui trasmetteva a Lei, ai traduttori, all'editore. C'è probabilmente nel mondo un *bisogno di amare altrui*, e chiunque diventa l'oggetto di tale amore deve umilmente ringraziare la Providenza.

L'amore con cui questo volume è stato concepito e realizzato si vede su ogni pagina della Sua introduzione e anche nelle traduzioni, secondo ciò che ho potuto esaminare, tutte eccellenti. Ciò che mi piace oltre misura è che la ricchissima bibliografia[61] dia un carattere *filologico* al testo di un filologo, testo che non regge da sé, ma soltanto grazie a scritti paralleli di altri critici o filologi. L'altro tratto importante è quello dell'evoluzione che è illustrata dai[62] miei studj stilistici: non appaiono come un blocco monolitico o massiccio, ma come tappe non definitive.

Le sono riconoscentissimo per quella Sua cortesia di inserire la mia lettera auto-critica a p. 5 della Sua introduzione.[63]

---

[52] Su carta intestata come la prima.

[53] Prima *le*, cancellato.

[54] L'ultima sillaba è aggiunta.

[55] Aggiunto in un secondo tempo.

[56] *qualche cosa* è stato aggiunto.

[57] Prima *lo si*.

[58] Tutta la frase dev'essere stata aggiunta dopo.

[59] Si tratta probabilmente del Premio Feltrinelli internazionale per Filologia e critica letteraria, che fu conferito a Spitzer dall'Accademia Nazionale dei Lincei l'anno successivo, sempre ad opera di Schiaffini. Poco prima della morte Spitzer fu anche eletto socio straniero dei Lincei; nomina non ratificata per l'intervenuto decesso.

[60] Prima, *altra p*; poi è stato scritto *ricorso*, correggendo *altro*.

[61] Prima *le numerose bibliografie*.

[62] Prima *dell'evoluzione dei*.

[63] Si tratta della lettera precedentemente riportata.

Rileggendo[64] la mia lettera, vedo che ho considerato il volume soltanto come agisce su di mè – ma il volume è uno di saggi «raccolto[65] a cura e con presentazione» di Alfredo Schiaffini. E vuol dire tanta 'cura', tanto lavoro, non soltanto di presentazione, di *arrangement*, ma di creazione, cioè della creazione d'un ritratto in cui il pittore (A. Sch.) si è ritirato discretamente dietro la persona ritrattata. E come non ringraziarLa di nuovo di questo amor intellectualis del pittore?

Le stringo la mano affettuosamente!

Il Suo vecchio amico

Leo Spitzer.

Scriverò al Laterza uno di questi giorni. Si incaricherà Lei di trasmettere i miei ringraziamenti ai quattro traduttori e alla signora Alda Croce?

Ha ricevuto il mio studio sul sonetto *de l'Idée* di Du Bellay?[66] L'avevo mandato al vecchio indirizzo (Via Tracia)![67]

Intanto erano uscite numerose recensioni a *CSSL*,[68] inviate prontamente da Schiaffini a Spitzer, che in questa lettera le commenta, oltre a dar notizia di sue nuove pubblicazioni italiane.

il 22 aprile 1955[69]

Carissimo amico:

Grazie mille per l'invio delle quattro recensioni e pel Suo gesto amichevole come sempre. Come può capire, mi ha interessato il più la polemica onesta e cortese di Cesare Cases:[70] chi è e dov'è? Vorrei ringraziarlo in una lettera particolare. Naturalmente ha ragione dicendo che un critico è sempre chiuso in sè, «scopre il proprio ombelico» – ma crede lui che non lo sappia io stesso? Ho dimostrato un *modo di fare* mio, che deve essere il fare anche dell'epoca e del ceto che sono miei. E quando insiste sulle contraddizioni nel mio fare, ha anche ragione: ma come evitare contraddizioni in una lunga vita? – vedo che un economista celebre è stato l'oggetto, nello[71] stesso fascicolo,[72] di uno studio sui suoi

---

[64] Con questa frase incomincia il secondo foglio della lettera, scritta sulla stessa carta del primo foglio.

[65] Forse Spitzer voleva scrivere *raccolti*.

[66] L. SPITZER, *The Poetic Treatment of a Platonic Christian Theme*, «Comparative Literature», VI, 1954, 193-217.

[67] L'esclamativo è su un precedente interrogativo, erroneo.

[68] Se ne trova l'elenco nella nuova edizione di *CSSL*, con titolo cambiato: *Critica stilistica e semantica storica*, Bari, Laterza, 1966 (Universale Laterza), p. 252.

[69] Sulla solita carta intestata. Accanto, a penna: «fino al 15 maggio: 24 Lindon Lane, Princeton, N.J., USA».

[70] C. CASES, *I limiti della critica stilistica e i problemi della critica letteraria*, «Società» 11, 1955, 1, 46-63; 2, 266-91, poi, col titolo *Leo Spitzer e la critica stilistica*, in ID., *Il testimone secondario. Saggi e interventi sulla cultura del Novecento*, Torino, Einaudi, 1985, pp. 215-53.

[71] Prima *nella*.

[72] Spitzer allude all'articolo di L. OCCHIONERO, *Errori di gioventù e palinodia di un economista: Erich Roll e la "Storia del pensiero economico"*, «Società» 11, 1955,1, 181-87.

«errori di gioventù e palinodia». Ma ciò che mi fa piacere nel Cases è la sua familiarità coi miei scritti: lui può davvero dimostrare le mie deficenze perchè li conosce tutti. Scriverò anche al Puppo, tanto gentile.

Lei saprà che il Contini mi ha domandato la permissione di far tradurre il mio primo «Racine» per *Paragone*[73] e il Simone ha ricevuto un articolo mio sul *Canto delle Creature* per *Convivium*.[74] Di più Einaudi vuole fare una riedizione aggiornata dei *Meisterwerke der rom. Sprachwissenschaft*,[75] e il Bertini prepara un altro volumetto di studi stilistici tradotti.[76] Tutte queste testimonianze mi commuovono, ma anche mi dànno un sentimento di irrealtà: è come se diventassi un 'fenomeno storico' davanti a me stesso – può capire come questo 'auto-storicismo' mi fa paura? Suppongo che un Croce era più grande anche nel senso che calmamente si considerava un fenomeno storico (e lo era davvero, mentre che io, poveretto...). Ma, naturalmente, ci[77] fa bene anche il sapere che non si è soli: è veramente, tutto questo, una ricompensa[78] che non meritavo.

A Lei, carissimo amico, i[79] più caldi ringraziamenti! Almeno vedo con piacere che tutte le recensioni esaltano la *sua* opera di presentazione!

Tante cose dal Suo
L. Spitzer

Le mando tre studi linguistici recenti

Lo scambio epistolare continua abbastanza fitto, legato non solo agli inviti a Roma, Università e Accademia dei Lincei, e agli incontri al mare (Forte dei Marmi, Portofino, ecc.), ma anche a nuove recensioni a *CSSL* o a progetti di altre raccolte: quella di saggi spagnoli di Bertini, una di saggi italiani proposta da Raffaele Mattioli all'editore Vigevani, e non giunta ad esecuzione. Una corrispondenza affettuosa e fervida, che occorrerà pubblicare anch'essa.

---

[73] Non apparso, a quanto mi risulta.

[74] L. SPITZER, *Nuove considerazioni sul Cantico di Frate Sole*, «Convivium», 23, 1955, 257-70, seguite da *Postilla*, «Convivium», 24, 1956, 234-5 e da *Altre considerazioni sul Cantico di Frate Sole*, «Convivium», 25, 1957, 84-7. Poi ristampati in *Romanische Literaturstudien*, cit., pp. 464-87.

[75] Della bellissima antologia della linguistica, pubblicata da Spitzer nel 1929-30 (*Meisterwerke der romanischen Sprachwissenschaft*, München, Max Hueber, 1929-1930, 2 volumi), Einaudi progettò in quegli anni la traduzione, poi bloccata da una serie di difficoltà. Dalle lettere di Contini (*Lettere all'editore*, cit., pp. 72, 79, 84, 87) risulta che il progetto era molto avanzato, anzi Spitzer aveva già scelto (p. 88) i brani da sostituire o aggiungere per aggiornare la scelta, tenendo conto in particolare della corrente strutturalistica.

[76] *Cinque saggi di ispanistica*, cit.

[77] Aggiunto in un secondo tempo.

[78] Prima *compensazione*.

[79] Prima *tutti i*.

TABULA GRATULATORIA

James Ackerman, Harvard University

Sarah Adler, Scripps College

Stefania Amodeo, University of Maryland

Hugh Amory, Harvard University

Mario Aste, University of Massachusetts at Lowell

Ronnie Banerjee, Five Colleges

Laura Benedetti, Harvard University

Paul Bénichou, Harvard University

Manuela Bertone, Université de Chambéry

Donald and Georgia Bianchi, Northridge, California

Vincenzo Binetti, University of Chicago

Giuseppe Bisaccia, Norwood, Massachusetts

Luigi Blasucci, Scuola Normale Superiore di Pisa

Lina Bolzoni, Università di Pisa

Glen Bowersock, Princeton University

Suzanne Branciforte, College of the Holy Cross

Giuliana Bruno, Harvard University

Ilaria Caputi, Arlington, Virgina

L. Rino Caputo, Università Tor Vergata di Roma

Gunilla Carlson, Uppsala, Svezia

Mario Casalini, Fiesole

Ernesto Caserta, Duke University

Teodolinda Barolini Caverly, Columbia University

Giovanni Cecchetti, University of California, Los Angeles

Remo Ceserani, Università di Bologna

Paolo and Judy Cherchi, University of Chicago

James Chiampi, University of California, Irvine

Marguerite Mills Chiarenza, University of British Columbia

Giovannella Cingano-Giavazzi, Milano

Wendell Clausen, Harvard University

Joaquim Francisco Coelho, Harvard University

Gustavo Costa, University of California, Berkeley

Natalia Costa, University of San Francisco

Antonio D'Andrea, McGill University

Giovanni Da Pozzo, Università di Padova

Nancy Dersofie, Bryn Mawr College

Maria Luisa Arena Doglio, Università di Torino

Robert S. Dombroski, Graduate School, University Center, CUNY

Douglas and Grazia Dunn, New York, New York

Mei-Mei A. Ellerman, Wellesley, Massachusetts

Brad Epps, Harvard University

Edoardo Esposito, Università di Milano

Marianne Faithfull, Maynooth County Kildair, Irlanda

Donald Fanger, Harvard University

Giulio Ferroni, Università La Sapienza di Roma

Franco Fido, Harvard University

Gonaria Floris, Università di Cagliari

Luigi Fontanella, SUNY at Stony Brook

Pier Massimo Forni, The Johns Hopkins University

John Freccero, New York University

Giovanni Germano, Italian Consulate General, Boston, Massachusetts

C.A.S.I.T., Boston, Massachusetts

Teresa Gilman, Cambridge, Massachusetts

Thomas M. Greene, New Haven, Connecticut

Claudio Guillen, Harvard University

Philip Haerle, Feldmeilen, Svizzera

Alan Heimert, Winchester, Massachusetts

Margherita Heyer-Caput, Università di Berna

Patrice Higonnet, Harvard University

Amilcare Iannucci, University of Toronto

Christopher Jones, Harvard University

Charles Klopp, Ohio State University

P. O. Kristeller, Columbia University

Angeliki Laiou, Washington D.C.
Rena A. Lamparska, Boston College
Denah Lida, Cambridge, Massachusetts
Charles Maier, Harvard University
Donna Mancusi-Ungaro, Ann Arbor, Michigan
Juan Marichal and Solita Salinas, Harvard University
Francisco Márquez, Harvard University
Cecilia Mattii, Boston College
Angelo Mazzocco, Mount Holyoke College
Elizabeth Mazzocco, University of Massachusetts at Amherst
Laura Minervini, Università di Napoli
Kristen Olsen Murtaugh, Delray, Florida
Lisa Muto, Wellesley, Massachusetts
Per Nykrog, Harvard University
Anthony Oldcorn, Brown University
Nuccio Ordine, Università della Calabria
Deborah Parker, University of Virginia
Lino Pertile, Harvard University
Anita Piemonti, Università di Pisa
Maria Predelli, McGill University
Piero Pucci, Cornell University
Luciano Rebay, Columbia University

Wilga Rivers, Harvard University
Tonia Caterina Riviello, Santa Clara University
Sergio Romagnoli, Università di Firenze
Neil Rudenstine, Harvard University
Charles Russell, University of Maryland at College Park
Eduard and Patricia Sekler, Harvard University
John Sherman, Harvard University
Michael Shinagel, Harvard University
Rosalie and Alan Soons, Amherst, Massachusetts
Madison Sowell, Brigham Young University
Pamela D. Stewart, McGill University
Roger Stoddard, Harvard University
Susan Suleiman, Harvard University
Pasquale G. Tatò, Cambridge, Massachusetts
Francesca Trentin Baratto, Università di Venezia
Paolo Valesio, Yale University
Rebecca West, University of Chicago
Cristina Zecca, New York, New York
Jan Ziolkowski, Harvard University

Finito di stampare
nel mese di maggio 1998
dalla TIBERGRAPH s.r.l.
Città di Castello (PG)